*The*

# DICTION

*of*

# FILM
# QUOTATIONS

# The
# DICTIONARY
## of
# FILM
# QUOTATIONS

*6,000 Provocative Movie Quotes
from 1,000 Movies*

## MELINDA COREY
## &
## GEORGE OCHOA

CROWN TRADE PAPERBACKS
NEW YORK

Published by Crown Trade Paperbacks, 201 East 50th Street, New York, New York 10022. Member of the Crown Publishing Group.

Random House, Inc. New York, Toronto, London, Sydney, Auckland

CROWN TRADE PAPERBACKS and colophon are trademarks of Crown Publishers, Inc.

Manufactured in the United of America

Book Design by Deborah Kerner

Library of Congress Cataloging-in-Publication Data
Corey, Melinda.
   The dictionary of film quotations / Melinda Corey and George Ochoa.—1st ed.
   1. Motion pictures—Quotations, maxims, etc.   I. Ochoa, George.   II. Title.
PN1994.9.C67   1995
791.43′75—dc20                                                    94-44227
                                                                   CIP

ISBN 0-517-88067-9

10   9   8   7   6   5   4   3   2   1

First Edition

To our parents,
who took us to our first movies,
and to Martha,
whom we will take to hers

—M.C. and G.O.

# ACKNOWLEDGMENTS

This book would not have been possible without the people who helped to see it to completion. For his tireless hours of research and unstinting interest in movies, we thank Roy Groenewold. For additional research, we thank Kerry Benson, Rick Starr, and Alice Barmore. For help with keyboarding, we thank Tom Brown and Matthew Rettenmund. For their late-night suggestions and answers to queries, we thank the members of CompuServe's Showbiz forum. Finally, for their support, we thank our editor Brandt Aymar and our agent Jane Jordan Browne.

# INTRODUCTION

The *Dictionary of Film Quotations* is a collection of 6,000 quotes from over 1,000 films. It contains many of the most noteworthy quips, retorts, speeches, declarations, and social commentary spoken over the past century of filmmaking. It offers the lines that define a star—"What a dump!"; "Made it ma, top of the world!"; "The calla lillies are in bloom again"; "Hasta la vista, baby." It offers lines that define a film—"The list is life"; "The stuff that dreams are made of"; "I've a feeling we're not in Kansas anymore." It offers lines that have become part of the American lexicon—"Go ahead, make my day"; "Here's looking at you, kid"; "I'm gonna make him an offer he can't refuse."

Given the hundreds of films made each year, 1,000 films can be only a representative sampling. We have chosen the most acclaimed, popular, and characteristic films of the day. Nearly all Academy Award–winning films are included, even those whose notoriety has diminished with time, like *Cimarron*. The century's box-office blockbusters are represented, from *Gone With the Wind* to *The Sound of Music* to *Jurassic Park*. Cult favorites, in all their variety, are mined, including *The Rocky Horror Picture Show, The Red Shoes,* and *Reservoir Dogs.*

The majority of quotes in *The Dictionary of Film Quotations* derive from English-language sound films. Some major silent films (such as *Potemkin* and *The Gold Rush*) are included, as is a sampling of foreign films (*Grand Illusion* and *Babette's Feast,* for example), but their number is limited. Memorable quotes seem to be the ones that can reverberate in the mind through a speaker's voice; title cards and subtitles leave less of a lasting impression.

Although we aimed for inclusiveness and balance in our choics, the book unavoidably reflects our idiosyncratic preferences. Horror films, from James Whale to David Cronenberg are well represented, as is science fiction, from the famous (*2001: A Space Odyssey*) to the infamous (*Plan 9 From Outer Space*). We also more than sampled the canons of John Ford, Howard Hawks, and Frank Capra, largely to record memories of the voices of Cary Grant, James Stewart, and John Wayne.

In addition, we strove to represent the witty quipsters of movies, the character actors who, though never achieving traditional stardom, consistently provided both social commentary and comic relief. Among the actors whose lines we found especially delightful are William Demarest, Oscar Levant, Tony Randall, Ruth Hussey, Eric Blore, Divine, any bit player in a Barry Levinson Baltimore movie, and above all, Thelma Ritter. Whether as a masseuse for Jimmy Stewart or a housekeeper for Doris Day, she offered the funniest and most acidic views of the human condition.

While the actors make the quotes in *The Dictionary of Film Quotations* come alive, it is the screenwriters who made the quotes possible. This book is a salute to them. In this spirit, we owe a special debt of gratitude to director/screenwriter Billy Wilder. Over the course of viewing hundreds of movies, we found him to be the single most prolific source of quotable lines in film. They are unmistakable—pithy, topical, and humane.

The films in this book span eighty years of filmmaking, beginning with *The Birth of a Nation* (1915) and ending with *Forrest Gump* (1994). To represent as many movies as possible, we limited the number of quotes per film to about fifteen. In a few cases, such as *Gone With the Wind* and *The Godfather, Part II* we increased the number to nineteen. Such discipline was not always easy: the first review of *Lawrence of Arabia* yielded ninety-five quotes.

With rare exception, the quotes in *The Dictionary of Film Quotations* were gleaned through original research. We watched hundreds of movies to choose quotes and re-watched many parts of them to verify what we had chosen. It took multiple listenings of *The Fugitive* to determine how many times Tommy Lee Jones utters "My" before he says, "what a mess" and even more to tally how often Robert De Niro chants to himself

"I'm the boss" before the credits roll in *Raging Bull*. Complicated voices, like fast-talkers Cary Grant and Rosalind Russell in *His Girl Friday*, low-talkers like Marlon Brando, Warren Beatty, and Christian Slater, and high-pitched talkers like Miriam Hopkins and Carole Lombard provided different challenges. Some loquacious speakers, like Orson Welles in *The Magnificent Ambersons*, were quoted less than the quality of their words might have warranted. We just gave up.

Viewing films was necessary, because it was the only way to assure accuracy. Published screenplays often do not accurately represent the dialogue spoken on screen. Only if repeated viewings yielded indecipherable transcriptions, did we turn to screenplays for assistance. For example, in Alfred Hitchcock's *The Lady Vanishes*, when free spirit Margaret Lockwood contemplates her impending marriage in a high British voice, we could transcribe the quote only as, "I've eaten caviar at Cannes, sausages at the docks. I've played baccarat at Biarritz, and danced with the Rue Rodri." Sausages at the docks? Danced with the Rue Rodri? The screenplay revealed the correct translation: "I've eaten caviar at Cannes, sausage rolls at the dogs. I've played baccarat at Biarritz, and darts with the rural dean."

Close listening to movies also showed us that some well-known lines are actually paraphrased or nonexistent. In the 1949 crime drama *White Heat*, inmate James Cagney is told of his mother's death and is believed to mumble, "Ma's dead," before he breaks down. However, in the film, he prefaces his fit of grief only with the question, "Dead?" A more suprising discovery was that *Shane*, contrary to popular belief, does not end with the words, "Shane. Shane. Come back." Rather, as Alan Ladd rides off, Brandon de Wilde calls two final words that sound to us like either "Bye, Shane" or "Thank you." After numerous replayings by several researchers, we committed ourselves to "Bye, Shane."

Beginning with *Abandon Ship!* and ending with *Zorba the Greek,* the quotes in *The Dictionary of Film Quotations* are arranged alphabetically by film. Within each film, quotes are generally listed in the order in which they are spoken. We determined that this organization allows for the greatest flexibility as a reference and browsing book, in addition to most accurately reflecting the way in which people recall film dialogue.

In most cases, lines are quoted whole. However, in the interest of succinctness, long speeches (such as the last lines of *Fort Apache*) or lengthy exchanges (such as the rump-slapping episode in *Adam's Rib*) are sometimes abridged, with any gaps in the dialogue indicated by ellipses.

Credit information is given for each film, including year, studio, country (if other than the United States), director (noted as D), and screenwriter (noted as S). If the screenplay is adapted from another source, such as a story, play, or novel, the source is noted under "Fr" (for "from").

Individual quotes are attributed to the actor speaking the line, with the character name given in parentheses the first time the actor is named. On occasion, the actor playing the role or the name of the character was not identifiable, in which case enough description is given to make clear who is speaking.

In many cases, the first ("Rosebud") or last ("Well, nobody's perfect") lines of a film are among its most memorable and significant ones; sometimes they are all that is remembered. For ease in searching for them, we have flagged them with the tags "FIRST LINE" or "LAST LINE."

To assist in searching for the quotes of a favorite actor or on a particular topic, indexes by speaker and subject are provided. Whether "Frankly, my dear, I don't give a damn" is queried through *Gone With the Wind,* Clark Gable, or parting lines, it can be located. The subject index is especially useful when you want to look up Hollywood's collected wisdom on such topics as vampires (four citations), baseball (ten), and sex (forty-six).

For us, movie voices have long lived in our minds. They pop up regularly to comfort ("L'amour!"), put things in perspective ("Everybody in Casablanca has problems. Yours may work out"), even advise on dinner ("some fava beans and a nice chianti"). We expect that to some degree the same will be true for readers of *The Dictionary of Film Quotations.* Helping to nurture such a happy obsession has been our intent in this book.

# The
# DICTIONARY
## of
# FILM
# QUOTATIONS

**ABANDON SHIP!** *(UK: Columbia, 1956). D: Richard Sale. S: Richard Sale.*

**LAST LINE**

*1.* "If you had been a member of the jury, how would you have voted? Guilty or innocent?"

*Narrator, leaving to the audience the case of Tyrone Power (Capt. Alexander Holmes), convicted of murder for sacrificing weak lifeboat survivors*

**ABBOTT AND COSTELLO MEET FRANKENSTEIN** *(Universal, 1948). D: Charles Barton. S: Robert Lees, Frederic I. Rinaldo, John Grant. Fr: Mary Shelley (characters, Frankenstein).*

*1.* LON CHANEY, JR. *(Lawrence Talbot):* "Years ago, I was bitten by a werewolf. Ever since, when the full moon rises, I turn into a wolf myself."

LOU COSTELLO *(Wilbur Grey):* "Oh, pal, that's all right. I'm sort of a wolf myself."

**LAST LINE**

*2.* "Allow me to introduce myself. I'm the Invisible Man."

*Vincent Price (the Invisible Man) to Costello and Bud Abbott (Chick Young), after they have escaped from the other monsters and Abbott wants to know whose voice he is hearing*

**ABSENCE OF MALICE** *(Columbia, 1981). D: Sydney Pollack. S: Kurt Luedtke.*

*1.* "As a matter of law, the truth of your story is irrelevant. We have no knowledge the story is false, therefore, we're absent malice."

*John Harkins (Davidek), the newspaper's lawyer, to Sally Field (Meg Carter), a reporter*

*2.* "A wonderful thing—a subpoena."

*Wilford Brimley (James Wells), when Don Hood (Quinn) starts talking at the threat of a subpoena*

**ABSENT-MINDED PROFESSOR, THE** *(Buena Vista, 1961). D: Robert Stevenson. S: Bill Walsh. Fr: Samuel W. Taylor (story).*

*1.* "We've got to give it a name, Charlie. Let's see. Flying rubber. Flubber? All right. Substance X, we dub thee: Flubber."

*Fred MacMurray (Ned Brainard) to his dog Charlie, when he names his new gravity-defying substance*

*2.* "What am I supposed to do? There's nothing in the rule book that says one team can't jump higher than the other!"

*Alan Carney (Referee) to Gordon Jones (Basketball Coach), on the opposing team's use of flubber*

*3.* "Corners beautifully, doesn't it?"

*MacMurray to Nancy Olson (Betsy Carlisle), when he uses flubber to drive on the side of a building*

**ACCIDENTAL TOURIST, THE** *(Warner Bros., 1988). D: Lawrence Kasdan. S: Frank Galati, Lawrence Kasdan. Fr: Anne Tyler (novel).*

*1.* "A business traveler should bring only what fits in a carry-on bag. Checking your luggage is asking for trouble."

*William Hurt (Macon Leary), a writer of tour and travel books, in narration*

**2.** "There's something so muffled about the way you experience things. It's as if you were trying to slip through life unchanged."

*Kathleen Turner (Sarah Leary), Hurt's wife, to Hurt*

**3.** "While armchair travelers dream of going places, traveling armchairs dream of staying put."

*Bill Pullman (Julian), Hurt's publisher*

**4.** "I really don't care for movies. They make everything seem so close up."

*Hurt to Geena Davis (Muriel Pritchett)*

**5.** "I'm beginning to think that maybe it's not just how much you love someone. Maybe what matters is who you are when you're with them."

*Hurt to Turner*

**ACCUSED, THE** *(Paramount, 1988). D: Jonathan Kaplan. S: Tom Topor.*

**1.** "I heard someone screaming and it was me."

*Jodie Foster (Sarah Tobias), recalling her rape*

LAST LINE
**2.** "I don't know, I'd like to go home and I'd like to play with my dog."

*Foster, when asked what she plans to do after the trial convicting her assailants*

**ACE IN THE HOLE** *(Paramount, 1951). D: Billy Wilder. S: Billy Wilder, Lesser Samuels, Walter Newman.*

**1.** "I met a lot of hard-boiled eggs in my life, but you—you're twenty minutes!"

*Jan Sterling (Lorraine) to Kirk Douglas (Charles Tatum)*

**2.** "I don't go to church. Kneeling bags my nylons."

*Sterling to Douglas*

**ACROSS THE PACIFIC** *(Warner Bros., 1942). D: John Huston. S: Richard Macaulay. Fr: Robert Carson (serial, "Aloha Means Goodbye").*

**1.** "Any of your friends in Tokyo have trouble committing hara-kiri, those boys will be glad to help them out."

*Secret agent Humphrey Bogart (Richard Lomas Leland), talking tough about the Japanese*

**ACTION IN THE NORTH ATLANTIC** *(Warner Bros.–First National, 1943). D: Lloyd Bacon. S: John Howard Lawson. Fr: Guy Gilpatric (novel).*

**1.** "If a torpedo ever connected with this ship, we'd go up like a match lighted to cellophane. You ain't got a chance. Boom! And you're in the hero department, just like that. And the next thing you know, you're picking the Milky Way out of your ears."

*Dane Clark (Johnny Pulaski) to Alan Hale (Boats O'Hara) and Sam Levene (Chips Abrams)*

**2.** "I got faith in God, President Roosevelt, and the Brooklyn Dodgers, in the order of their importance."

*Levene to Clark, on how he deals with the uncertainty of war*

**3.** "So you want a safe job, huh? Go ask the Czechs, and the Poles, and the Greeks. They were figuring on safe jobs. They're lined up in front of guns digging each other's graves."

*Levene, responding to Clark's explanation of why he doesn't want to rejoin the Merchant Marines*

**4.** "You know, people got a funny idea that being brave is not being scared. I don't know. I always figured that if you weren't scared, there was nothing to be brave about. Trick is: how much scaring can you take?"

*Humphrey Bogart (Joe Rossi) to Dick Hogan (Cadet Robert Parker)*

**5.** "You know what I'm doing when this is over? I'm putting into port. I'm getting off the ship. I'm putting an oar on my shoulder, and I'm starting inland. And the first time a guy says to me, 'What's that on your shoulder?' that's where I'm settling for the rest of my life."

*Hale to Levene, when they are trying to evade a Nazi submarine*

**6.** "Any one of us could be lying here tomorrow, and somebody reads a book over us, and get tossed in the sea, but that ain't what's important. A lot more people are going to die before this is over. And it's up to the ones that come through to make sure that they didn't die for nothing."

*Bogart*

**ADAM'S RIB** *(MGM, 1949). D: George Cukor. S: Ruth Gordon, Garson Kanin.*

**1.** "All I'm trying to say is that there's lots of things that a man can do and in society's eyes it's all hunky-dory. A woman does the same thing—the same thing, mind you—and she's an outcast."

*Defense attorney Katharine Hepburn (Amanda Bonner) to her husband, prosecutor Spencer Tracy (Adam Bonner)*

**2.** HEPBURN, interviewing a woman accused of shooting her husband: "And after you shot him—how did you feel then?"

JUDY HOLLIDAY *(Doris Attinger)*: "Hungry."

**3.** "A girl named Doris Attinger shot her husband. I'm going to defend her."

*Hepburn to her father, in a statement overheard by Tracy, who is arguing the other side, and who loses control of a tray of glasses over the news*

**4.** "Bonner Epics present 'THE MORTGAGE THE MERRIER' *A Too Real Epic*"

*Credits to Tracy and Hepburn's home movie*

**5.** "Oh, what are you gonna do, object before I ask the question?"

*Tracy to Hepburn in courtroom*

**6.** HEPBURN, expressing outrage at Tracy for slapping her on the backside: "You meant that, didn't you? You really meant that. . . . Yes, you did, I know your type. I know a slap from a slug. . . . I'm not so sure I care to expose myself to typical instinctive masculine brutality. . . . And it felt not only as though you meant it but as though you felt you had a right to. I can tell."

TRACY: "What've you got back there, radar equipment?"

**7.** "What is marriage? Tell me that. . . . It's a contract. It's the law. Are you going to outsmart that the way you've outsmarted all other laws? That's clever. That's very clever. You've outsmarted yourself and you've outsmarted me and you've outsmarted everything."

*Tracy to Hepburn*

**8.** "I'm old-fashioned. I like two sexes."

*Tracy to Hepburn*

**9.** "Ladies and jutlemen of the gerry—"

*Tracy, rattled by Hepburn, garbling his closing argument*

**10.** TRACY, sheepishly repeating for the record his courtroom use of a pet name for Hepburn: " 'Sit down, Pinkie.' "

MARVIN KAPLAN (*Court Stenographer*): "Pinkie?"

TRACY: "Yes."

KAPLAN: "What's that, a name?"

**11.** "Lawyers should never marry other lawyers. This is called inbreeding, from which comes idiot children and more lawyers."

*David Wayne (Kip Lurie) to Hepburn*

**12.** "Licorice. Mmm. If there's anything I'm a sucker for, it's licorice."

*Tracy to Hepburn, after he eats a licorice gun he's been pointing at Hepburn and Wayne*

**LAST LINES:**

**13.** TRACY, on the little difference between men and women that Hepburn has grudgingly acknowledged: *"Vive la difference."*

HEPBURN: "Which means?"

TRACY: "Which means, 'Hooray for that little difference.' "

**ADDAMS FAMILY, THE** (Orion/Paramount, 1991). D: Barry Sonnenfeld. S: Caroline Thompson, Larry Wilson. Fr: Charles Addams (characters).

**1.** "Look at her. I would die for her. I would kill for her. Either way, what bliss."

*Raul Julia (Gomez Addams), soliloquizing on Anjelica Huston (Morticia Addams)*

**2.** JULIA: "Unhappy, darling?

HUSTON: "Oh, yes, yes, completely."

**3.** "Tish! That's French."

*Julia to Huston*

**4.** "Don't torture yourself, Gomez. That's my job."

*Huston to Julia*

**5.** "Thing, you're a handful."

*Huston to Thing, the disembodied "hand" servant*

**6.** CHRISTINA RICCI (*Wednesday*): "May I have the salt?"

HUSTON: "What do we say?"

RICCI: "Now."

**7.** "Showtime!"

*Julia to Christopher Lloyd (Uncle Fester), when he brings out the home movies*

**8.** "Look, children—a new chapter—Scabs!"

*Lloyd to Ricci and Jimmy Workman (Pugsley), referring to the book* Wounds, Scars, and Gouges

**9.** "How can I compete? You're twice the woman I am."

*Huston to Siamese twins Maureen Sue Levin and Darlene Levin (Flora and Fauna Amor)*

**ADVENTURES OF BARON MUNCHAUSEN, THE** (UK/Germany: Columbia/TriStar, 1989). D: Terry Gilliam. S: Charles McKeown, Terry Gilliam. Fr: Rudolph Erich Raspe (stories).

**1.** "I'm afraid, sir, you have rather a weak grasp of reality."

*Jonathan Pryce (Horatio Jackson), understating the case to the tale-spinning John Neville (Baron Munchausen)*

**2.** "No, let me go! I've got tides to regulate! Comets to direct! I don't have time for flatulence and orgasms!"

*Robin Williams's (King of the Moon's) disembodied head as it is recaptured by his body*

## ADVENTURES OF DON JUAN, THE *(Warner Bros., 1949). D: Vincent Sherman. S: George Oppenheimer, Harry Kurnitz. Fr: Herbert Dalmas (story).*

**LAST LINE**

**1.** "My dear friend, there's a little bit of Don Juan in every man, but since I am Don Juan, there must be more of it in me."

*Errol Flynn (Don Juan), on his role in life*

## ADVENTURES OF ROBIN HOOD, THE *(Warner Bros.–First National, 1938). D: Michael Curtiz. S: Norman Reilly Raine, Seton I. Miller. Fr: legends.*

**1.** "By my faith, but you're a bold rascal."

*Claude Rains (Prince John) to Errol Flynn (Robin Hood)*

**2.** "What a pity your manners don't match your looks, Your Highness."

*Flynn sparring with Olivia de Havilland (Maid Marian)*

**3.** DE HAVILLAND: "Why, you speak treason."
FLYNN: "Fluently."

**4.** "I'll organize a revolt, exact a death for a death, and I'll never rest until every Saxon in this shire can stand up free men and strike a blow for Richard and England."

*Flynn, explaining his plans to Rains*

**5.** "I'll have him dangling in a week."

*Basil Rathbone (Sir Guy of Gisbourne), explaining his plans for what to do with Flynn*

**6.** "I wanted to see what you were made of, and I did."

*Flynn to Alan Hale (Little John), after being dunked following their battle atop a log across a stream*

**7.** "One of us? He looks like three of us."

*Patric Knowles (Will Scarlet) on the hefty Eugene Pallette (Friar Tuck)*

**8.** "Welcome to Sherwood, my lady!"

*Flynn's dashing treetop welcome to de Havilland, after his merry men have captured her and her caravan in his Sherwood Forest domain*

**9.** "Hanging would be a small price to pay for the company of such a charming lady.

*Flynn, wooing de Havilland*

**10.** "To the tables, everybody, and stuff yourselves!"

*Member of Robin's band, calling his comrades to a forest banquet*

**11.** "I'm afraid of nothing, least of all you."

*de Havilland, expressing her disdain for Flynn*

**12.** "You're very charming, Lady Marian, but not exactly clever."

*Rathbone, seeing through de Havilland's protestations of innocence regarding her association with Robin Hood*

**13.** "Sire!"

*Flynn, kneeling in awe before his acknowledged and long-missing sovereign Ian Hunter (King Richard the Lion-Hearted)*

**LAST LINE**

**14.** "May I obey all your commands with equal pleasure, Sire!"

*Flynn, accepting Hunter's order to marry de Havilland*

**AFFAIR TO REMEMBER, AN** *(20th Century–Fox, 1957). D: Leo McCarey. S: Delmer Daves, Leo McCarey. Fr: Leo McCarey, Mildred Cram (story).*

**1.** "This ship is going much too fast."

*Cary Grant (Nickie Ferrante), beginning a shipboard romance with Deborah Kerr (Terry McKay)*

**2.** "He's always attracted by the art he isn't practicing, the place he hasn't been, the girl he hasn't met."

*Grant's grandmother, Cathleen Nesbitt, describing Grant to Kerr*

**3.** "I told you, that's what beauty does to me."

*Kerr, after kissing Grant, on how beauty makes her cry*

**4.** "Being a woman I'm naturally more cautious, and I can think more clearly when you're not around."

*Kerr to Grant, asking him to leave her cabin*

**5.** KERR: "What makes life so difficult?"
GRANT: "People?"

**6.** "Oh, darling. Don't . . . don't worry, darling. If . . . if you can paint, I can walk. Anything can happen."

*Kerr, reuniting with Grant, after being crippled in an accident*

**AFRICAN QUEEN, THE** *(UA, 1951). D: John Huston. S: James Agee, John Huston. Fr: C. S. Forester (novel).*

**1.** "There ain't nobody in Africa except yours truly who can get up a good head of steam on the old *African Queen*."

*Humphrey Bogart (Charlie Allnut)*

**2.** "The only reason I ain't done it up to now is that I kind of like kicking it. She's all I've got."

*Bogart, explaining why he doesn't fix the boiler instead of kicking it to keep it from blowing up*

**3.** "I never dreamed that any mere physical experience could be so stimulating."

*Katharine Hepburn (Rose Sayer), on running the rapids*

**4.** "Now that I've had a taste of it, I don't wonder you love boating, Mr. Allnut."

*Hepburn to Bogart*

**5.** "Lady, you got ten absurd ideas for my one."

*Bogart to Hepburn*

**6.** "I asked you on board 'cause I was sorry for you on account of your losing your brother and all. That's what you get for feeling sorry for someone. Well, I ain't sorry no more, you crazy, psalm-singing, skinny old maid!"

*Bogart, drunk and losing his temper*

**7.** "A man alone, he gets to living like a hog."

*Bogart*

**8.** "Nature, Mr. Allnut, is what we are put in this world to rise above."

*Hepburn to Bogart*

**9.** "Head up, chin out, hair blowing in the wind. The living picture of the hero-eyne."

*Bogart's impression of Hepburn*

**10.** "If there's anything in the world I hate it's leeches. Filthy little devils."

*Bogart*

**11.** "She ought to look her best, representing as she does the Royal Navy."

*Bogart, on cleaning up the African Queen before blowing up the German warship Louisa*

**12.** "Oh, Charlie, we're having our first quarrel."

*Hepburn to Bogart, after arguing about who should blow up the Louisa*

**13.** "It'll be you at the tiller and me at the engine, just like it was from the start."

*Bogart to Hepburn, on deciding to blow up the ship together*

**14.** "I shall hang you twice, I think."

*Peter Bull (Captain of the Louisa), exasperated with Bogart*

**15.** "Nevertheless."

*Hepburn's response when Bull says their journey down the river was impossible*

**16.** "By the authority vested in me by Kaiser Wilhelm II, I pronounce you man and wife. Proceed with the execution."

*Bull, going through with his agreement to marry Bogart and Hepburn prior to their hanging*

**17.** "Pretty good for an old married man."

*Bogart to Hepburn, after their plan to blow up the Louisa works*

**AGE OF INNOCENCE, THE** *(Columbia, 1993). D: Martin Scorsese. S: Jay Cocks, Martin Scorsese. Fr: Edith Wharton (novel).*

**1.** "It was widely known in New York, but never acknowledged, that Americans want to get away from amusement even more quickly than they want to get to it."

*Joanne Woodward (Narrator), on society people leaving the opera in a hurry*

**2.** "This was a world balanced so precariously that its harmony could be shattered by a whisper."

*Woodward*

**3.** MICHELLE PFEIFFER (*Countess Ellen Olenska*), on her attempts to divorce her husband and cast off the shadow of scandal that pursued her in Europe: "Now I want to cast off all my old life to become a complete American and try to be like everybody else."

DANIEL DAY-LEWIS (*Newland Archer*): "I don't think you'll ever quite be like everybody else."

**4.** "Our legislation favors divorce but our social customs don't."

*Day-Lewis to Pfeiffer, on her plans for divorce*

**5.** "He was a prisoner in the center of an armed camp and the key to his release had been returned the day before, by mail, unopened."

*Woodward, on Day-Lewis's condition as he struggles unsuccessfully to see Pfeiffer*

**6.** "I'm afraid you can't, dear. Not unless you take me with you."

*Winona Ryder (May Welland) to husband Day-Lewis, on his plan to take a long trip abroad*

**7.** "It was the room in which most of the real things of his life had happened."

*Woodward on Day-Lewis's den*

**8.** "Lovely—I don't know. She was different."

*Day-Lewis, reminiscing about Pfeiffer years later with his son Robert Sean Leonard (Ted Archer)*

**9.** "She had become the complete vision of all that he had missed."

*Woodward, on Day-Lewis's feelings toward Pfeiffer*

**10.** "She said she knew we were safe with you and we always would be because once when she asked you to, you gave up the thing that you wanted most."

> Leonard to Day-Lewis, on what Ryder told her children before she died

**11.** "It seemed to take an iron band from his heart to know that after all someone had guessed and pitied, and that it should have been his wife moved him inexpressibly."

> Woodward, on Day-Lewis's reaction on learning that Ryder was aware of his feelings for Pfeiffer

**Last Line**

**12.** "Just say I'm old-fashioned. That should be enough. Go on, go on."

> Day-Lewis to Leonard, on what to tell Pfeiffer about why he wouldn't go up to see her

**AGONY AND THE ECSTASY, THE** (20th Century–Fox, 1965). D: Carol Reed. S: Philip Dunne. Fr: Irving Stone (novel).

**1.** "You dare to dicker with your pontiff?"

> Rex Harrison (Pope Julius II) to Charlton Heston (Michelangelo)

**AIRPLANE!** (Paramount, 1980). D: Jim Abrahams, David Zucker, Jerry Zucker. S: Jim Abrahams, David Zucker, Jerry Zucker.

**1.** NO SMOKING/EL NO A YOU SMOKO FASTEN SEATBELTS/PUTANA DA SEATBELTZ

> Bilingual sign in airplane

**2.** KAREEM ABDUL-JABBAR (Murdock, a co-pilot): "We have clearance, Clarence."
PETER GRAVES (Captain Oveur, the pilot): "Roger, Roger. What's our vector, Victor?"

**3.** "You ever seen a grown man naked?"

> Graves, coming on to little boy Rossie Harris (Joey)

**4.** "Joey, have you ever been in—in a Turkish prison?"

> Graves, coming on again to Harris

**5.** "By the way, is there anyone on board who knows how to fly a plane?"

> Flight attendant Julie Hagerty (Elaine), making an in-flight announcement

**6.** ROBERT HAYS (Ted Striker): "Surely you can't be serious."
LESLIE NIELSEN (Dr. Rumack): "I am serious, and don't call me Shirley."

**7.** "Oh, stewardess, I speak jive."

> White lady Barbara Billingsley, offering to interpret the speech of two black people

**8.** "Looks like I picked the wrong week to quit amphetamines."

> Air traffic controller Lloyd Bridges (McCroskey), who has also said he picked the wrong week to quit smoking and drinking

**9.** "Ted, that was probably the lousiest landing in the history of this airport, but some of us here, particularly me, would like to buy you a drink and shake your hand."

> Air traffic controller Robert Stack (Kramer), on radio to Hays after he brings the plane down safely

**AIRPORT** (Universal, 1970). D: George Seaton. S: George Seaton. Fr: Arthur Hailey (novel).

**1.** "The only thing we've got left in common is the same mattress."

> Burt Lancaster (Mel Bakersfield) to Jean Seberg (Tanya Livingston), referring to his wife

**2.** "I'm thinking of those pilots upstairs waiting to land, flying blind in that muck and circling in holding patterns, and praying to God that some tired, overworked, underpaid controller in the tower doesn't have another plane on the same course."

*Lancaster, arguing for a bigger, more modern airport*

**3.** "You might fly these things, but I take them apart and put them back together again."

*George Kennedy (Patroni) to a pilot*

**4.** "The guy sitting next to me was about 170 pounds. He went through that little space like a hunk of hamburger going down a disposal."

*Kennedy*

**5.** "Grab him! He's got a bomb!"

*Unknown actor on the plane, referring to Van Heflin (D. O. Guerrero)*

**6.** "Roger, Lincoln. You just freed the slaves again."

*Dean Martin (Vernon Demerest), when Lincoln Airport clears runway two-nine*

**ALADDIN** *(Buena Vista, 1992). D: John Musker, Ron Clements. S: Ron Clements, John Musker, Ted Elliot, Terry Rossio. Fr: Arabian Nights.*

**1.** "You've heard of the golden rule? He who has the gold, makes the rules."

*Jonathan Freeman (Jafar), the Sultan's wisest advisor, to Scott Weinger (Aladdin)*

**2.** "Ten thousand years will give you such a crick in the neck."

*Robin Williams (The Genie), when he comes out of the lamp for the first time*

**3.** "Hang on to your turban, kid. We're going to make you a star."

*Williams, when Weinger wishes to be made a prince*

**4.** "I'm getting kind of fond of you, kid. Not that I want to pick out curtains or anything."

*Williams, after saving Weinger's life*

**5.** "I'm history! No, I'm not, I'm mythology! I don't care what I am. I'm free!"

*Williams, when he leaves*

**LAST LINE**
**6.** "Made you look!"

*Williams, as he picks up the last frame of the movie off the screen and winks at the audience*

**ALAMO, THE** *(UA, 1960). D: John Wayne. S: James Edward Grant.*

**1.** "Republic. I like the sound of the word."

*John Wayne (Col. David Crockett) on Texas becoming an independent republic*

**ALFIE** *(UK: Paramount, 1966). D: Lewis Gilbert. S: Bill Naughton. Fr: Bill Naughton (play).*

**1.** "My understanding of women goes only as far as the pleasures."

*Michael Caine (Alfie)*

**ALGIERS** *(UA, 1938). D: John Cromwell. S: John Howard Lawson, James M. Cain. Fr: Roger D'Ashelbe (novel, Pepe Le Moko).*

**LAST LINES**
**1.** JOSEPH CALLEIA *(Slimane)*: "I'm sorry, Pepe. He thought you were going to escape."

CHARLES BOYER (*Pepe Le Moko, dying*): "And so I have, my friend."

**ALICE** (*Orion, 1990*). D: Woody Allen. S: Woody Allen.

*1.* "If you want we can go talk for a few minutes about a kindergarten that would give him the best chances of eventually getting into an Ivy League college."

*Teacher offering to discuss the future of Mia Farrow's (Alice's) little boy*

*2.* "Considering you're dead, you look great."

*Farrow to the ghost of her dead boyfriend Alec Baldwin (Ed)*

*3.* "Thou shalt not commit adultery. That's not my line, I read it."

*Baldwin to Farrow*

*4.* "There's nothing sexier than a lapsed Catholic."

*Joe Mantegna (Joe) to Farrow*

*5.* "Jeez, nothing shocks New York cab drivers."

*Mantegna, as he and Farrow, both invisible, step out of a cab*

*6.* "Love is most complex emotion. Human beings unpredictable. No logic to emotion. Where there is no logic there is no rational thought. Where there is no rational thought, there can be much romance, but much suffering."

*Keye Luke (Dr. Yang) to Farrow*

**ALICE DOESN'T LIVE HERE ANYMORE** (*Warner Bros., 1974*). D: Martin Scorsese. S: Robert Getchell.

*1.* DIANE LADD (*Flo*): "What is it you want?"
ELLEN BURSTYN (*Alice Hyatt*): "If I knew that, I wouldn't be sitting here crying in the toilet."

**ALICE IN WONDERLAND** (*RKO, 1951*). D: Clyde Geronimi. S: Winston Hibler, Bill Peet, Joe Rinaldi, Bill Cottrell, Joe Grant, et al. Fr: Lewis Carroll (stories).

*1.* "What could a rabbit possibly be late for?"

*Kathryn Beaumont (Alice)*

*2.* "Curiouser and curiouser."

*Beaumont*

*3.* "How could one possibly pay attention to a book with no pictures in it?"

*Beaumont*

*4.* "Don't just do something, stand there!"

*Bill Thompson (The White Rabbit)*

*5.* "You may have noticed that I'm not all there myself."

*Sterling Holloway (The Cheshire Cat), as he disappears*

*6.* "It would be so nice if something made sense for a change."

*Beaumont*

*7.* "Off with their heads!"

*Verna Felton's (The Queen of Hearts's) reaction to just about everything*

**ALIENS** (*20th Century–Fox, 1986*). D: James Cameron. S: James Cameron. Fr: James Cameron, David Giler, Walter Hill (story), Dan O'Bannon, Ronald Shusett (characters).

**1.** "You're going out there to destroy them, right? Not to study, not to bring back, but to wipe them out?"

*Sigourney Weaver (Ripley), discussing the aliens with Paul Reiser (Burke)*

**2.** "Is this gonna be a stand-up fight, sir, or another bug hunt?"

*Bill Paxton (Private Hudson) to William Hope (Lieutenant Gorman), asking what kind of enemy the Marines will encounter*

**3.** "I say we take off, nuke the site from orbit. It's the only way to be sure."

*Michael Biehn (Corporal Hicks), taking Weaver's advice about what to do about the aliens*

**4.** "Get away from her, you bitch."

*Weaver, warning the alien queen to get away from Carrie Henn (Newt)*

**Last Lines**
**5.** WEAVER: "Sleep tight."
HENN: "Affirmative."

*Going into suspended animation for the flight home, after the aliens are destroyed*

**ALL ABOUT EVE** (20th Century–Fox, 1950). D: Joseph L. Mankiewicz. S: Joseph L. Mankiewicz. Fr: Mary Orr (story, "The Wisdom of Eve").

**1.** "And no brighter light has ever dazzled the eyes than Eve Harrington. Eve. But more of Eve later, all about Eve, in fact."

*George Sanders (Addison De Witt), in voice-over*

**2.** "Margo Channing is a star of the theater. She made her first stage appearance at the age of four in *A Midsummer Night's Dream*. She played the fairy and entered

quite unexpectedly, stark naked. She has been a star ever since. Margo is a great star, a true star. She never was nor ever will be anything else."

*Sanders, in voice-over about Bette Davis (Margo Channing)*

**3.** "Autograph fiends, they're not people. Those are little beasts that run around in packs like coyotes."

*Davis to Celeste Holm (Karen Richards)*

**4.** "I'd like anything Miss Channing played in."

*Anne Baxter (Eve Harrington) to Davis, Holm, and Hugh Marlowe (Lloyd Richards)*

**5.** "I haven't got a union. I'm slave labor."

*Thelma Ritter (Birdie) to her boss Davis*

**6.** "Fasten your seat belts, it's going to be a bumpy night."

*Davis to party group*

**7.** "Miss Caswell is an actress. A graduate of the Copacabana School of Dramatic Arts."

*Sanders to Davis about his date, Marilyn Monroe (Miss Caswell)*

**8.** "Why do they always look like unhappy rabbits?"

*Monroe to Sanders, about producers*

**9.** "Everybody has a heart, except some people."

*Davis to Gary Merrill (Bill Sampson)*

**10.** "Bill's thirty-two. He looks thirty-two. He looked it five years ago. He'll look it twenty years from now. I hate men."

*Davis to Marlowe*

**11.** "So little, did you say? Why, if there's nothing else, there's applause. I've listened backstage to people applaud. It's like, like waves of love coming over the footlights and wrapping you up."

*Baxter to Holm, on why she adores acting*

**12.** "Funny business, a woman's career. The things you drop on your way up the ladder so you can move faster. You forget you'll need them again when you get back to being a woman."

*Davis to Holm*

**13.** "Something simple. A fur coat over a nightgown."

*Davis to Holm, on what she'll wear to her wedding*

**14.** "The mark of a true killer. Sleep tight, rest easy, and come out fighting."

*Sanders to Baxter, on her sense of calm at her theatrical debut*

**15.** "Nice speech, Eve, but I wouldn't worry too much about your heart. You can always put that award where your heart ought to be."

*Davis to Baxter*

**16.** "Well, lots of actresses come from Brooklyn. Barbara Stanwyck and Susan Hayward. Of course, they're just movie stars."

*Barbara Bates (Phoebe) to her idol Baxter*

**ALL OF ME** *(Universal, 1984). D: Carl Reiner. S: Phil Alden Robinson, Henry Olek. Fr: Ed Davis (novel, Me Too).*

**1.** "I've never ridden my horses. I've never been to the ballet. I've never danced. But Cutwaters aren't quitters. So I've decided that if my wealth cannot help me in this life, then by God, it's going to buy me a new one."

*Lily Tomlin (Edwina Cutwater) to Steve Martin (Roger Cobb), her lawyer*

**2.** "Just because my grandfather didn't rape the environment and exploit the workers, doesn't make me a peasant! And it's not that he didn't want to rape the environment and exploit the workers, I'm sure he did! It's just that as a barber, he didn't have that much opportunity!"

*Martin to Tomlin*

**3.** "I can't even die right."

*Tomlin to Martin, when she discovers her soul has entered Martin's body*

**4.** "I'm not exactly having one of my best days, either. I died five minutes ago."

*Tomlin to Martin*

**5.** MARTIN: "Your problem is you don't understand that life is to be lived. It's meant to be experienced and savored."

TOMLIN: "Oh, I know that, you big dope. Why do you think I've gone to so much trouble and expense to buy myself another chance?"

**6.** "I'm going to dance, Roger. I'm going to twirl and whirl and spin. I'm going to cha-cha-cha and merengue and I'm going to dip deeply."

*Tomlin to Martin*

**7.** "I spent my life in a sickbed. What's your excuse?"

*Tomlin to Martin*

**8.** "What's so important about s—? That's like saying, 'What's so important about laughing or Duke Ellington or the World Series?'"

Martin to Tomlin when Martin wants to have sex with Victoria Tennant (Terry Hoskins) but Tomlin refuses to cooperate

**9.** MARTIN: "Unlike you, most of us only get to go around once in life, and I'm not going to spend the rest of mine sitting behind a desk."
   TOMLIN: "Ooh, I love it when you talk like a beer commercial."

**LAST LINE**
**10.** "Try it with your own feet."
   *Martin to Tomlin, who is now inhabiting Tennant's body and who is just learning to dance*

## ALL QUIET ON THE WESTERN FRONT
*(Universal, 1930). D: Lewis Milestone. S: Del Andrews, Maxwell Anderson, George Abbott, Lewis Milestone (uncredited). Fr: Erich Maria Remarque (novel).*

**1.** "You'll have to forgive me, comrade."
   *Lew Ayres (Paul Baumer) to the Frenchman (Raymond Griffith) he has killed*

**2.** "When it comes to dying for your country, it's better not to die at all."
   *Ayres*

## ALL THAT HEAVEN ALLOWS *(Universal, 1955). D: Douglas Sirk. S: Peggy Fenwick. Fr: Edna and Harry Lee (story).*

**1.** "As Freud says, when you reach a certain age, sex becomes incongruous."
   *Gloria Talbot (Kay Scott) to Jane Wyman (Cary Scott), on middle-aged romance*

**2.** "Of course, there's nothing like red for attracting attention, is there? I suppose that's why so few widows wear it."
   *Jacqueline De Witt (Mona Fish) to widow Wyman, commenting on her red dress*

**3.** "If you're impatient, you have no business growing trees."
   *Rock Hudson (Ron Kirby) to Wyman, about whether tree farming ever makes him impatient*

**4.** "You can't sit around here with nothing to do. You should at least get a television set."
   *Agnes Moorehead (Sara Warren) to Wyman*

**5.** "Oh, I don't think Ron's ever read it. He just lives it."
   *Virginia Grey (Alida Anderson) to Wyman, about whether Hudson has ever read* Walden

**6.** "You can't be serious. Your gardener?"
   *Moorehead to Wyman, about her attraction to Hudson*

**7.** "Mother, this is no time for martinis."
   *William Reynolds (Ned Scott) to Wyman, about her involvement with Hudson*

**8.** "So that's Cary's nature boy."
   *Male guest to another at social set party introducing Hudson*

**9.** "Oh, my dear, he's fascinating. And that tan, I suppose from working outdoors. 'Course I'm sure he's handy indoors, too."
   *De Witt to Wyman about Hudson*

**10.** "All you have to do is turn the dial and you have all the company you want. Right there on the screen. Drama, comedy, life's parade at your fingertips."
   *TV salesman to Wyman*

## ALL THAT JAZZ *(Columbia/20th Century–Fox, 1979). D: Bob Fosse. S: Robert Alan Arthur, Bob Fosse.*

**1.** "Do you suppose Stanley Kubrick ever gets depressed?"

*Roy Scheider (Joe Gideon)*

**2.** "I don't get married again because I can't find anyone I dislike enough to inflict that kind on torture on."

*Scheider*

**3.** "You could be the first show on Broadway to make a profit without really opening."

*Wallace Shawn, referring to Scheider's death benefits*

**4.** "What's the matter? Don't you like musical comedy?"

*Scheider to God at a rehearsal, as his health rapidly deteriorates*

**ALL THE KING'S MEN** (Columbia, 1949). D: Robert Rossen. S: Robert Rossen. Fr: Robert Penn Warren (novel).

**1.** "Jack, there's something on everybody. Man is conceived in sin and born in corruption."

*Broderick Crawford (Willie Stark) to John Ireland (Jack Burden)*

**2.** "Your brother is an old-fashioned man. He believes in his sister's honor. Me? I'm a modern man. The twentieth-century type. I run."

*Ireland to Joanne Dru (Anne Stanton)*

**3.** "Willie couldn't steal a vote from Abe Lincoln in the cradle of the Confederacy."

*Ireland to Mercedes McCambridge (Sadie Burke), on Crawford's vote-getting ability*

**4.** "Make them cry. Make them laugh. Make them mad, even mad at you. Stir them up and they'll love it, and come back for more, but, for heaven's sake, don't try to improve their minds."

*Ireland to Crawford, on voters*

**5.** "You throw money around like it was money."

*Ireland to Crawford*

**6.** "Out of bad. That's what good comes out of. Because you can't make it out of anything else. You didn't know that, did you?"

*Crawford*

**7.** "It is the right of the people that they shall not be deprived of hope."

*Crawford, in a speech*

**8.** "A man builds for his son. That's all he builds for."

*Crawford, when his son John Derek (Tom Stark) gets in an accident while driving drunk*

**9.** "Dirt's a funny thing. It rubs off on everybody."

*Crawford*

**10.** "Now, listen to me, you hicks. Yeah, you're hicks too, and they fooled you a thousand times, just like they fooled me. But this time, I'm going to fool somebody. I'm going to stay in this race. I'm on my own and I'm out for blood."

*Crawford, in a speech*

**LAST LINE**
**11.** "It could have been the whole world—Willie Stark. The whole world—Willie Stark. Why did he do it to me—Willie Stark? Why?"

*Crawford*

**ALL THE PRESIDENT'S MEN** (Warner Bros., 1976). D: Alan J. Pakula. S: William

Goldman. Fr: Carl Bernstein, Bob Wood-ward (book).

**1.** "There's a cartoon on his wall. The caption reads, 'When you got them by the balls, their hearts and minds will follow.' "

*Jack Warden (Harry Rosenfeld) to Robert Redford (Bob Woodward), referring to Charles Colson*

**2.** "They volunteered he was innocent when nobody asked if he was guilty."

*Redford, on Watergate conspirator Howard Hunt*

**3.** "I don't mind what you did. I mind the way you did it."

*Redford to Dustin Hoffman (Carl Bernstein), when Hoffman rewrites his story*

**4.** "Follow the money."

*Hal Holbrook (Deep Throat) to Redford, advising him on how to break open the Watergate story*

**5.** "You're both paranoid. She's afraid of John Mitchell and you're afraid of Walter Cronkite."

*Redford to Hoffman, referring to Jane Alexander, a bookkeeper*

**6.** "Goddamn it! When is somebody going to go on the record in this story?"

*Jason Robards (Ben Bradlee)*

**7.** "I can't do my reporting for my reporters, which means I have to trust them, and I hate trusting anybody."

*Robards to Redford and Hoffman*

**8.** "I knew we had enemies, but I didn't know we were this popular."

*Warden*

**9.** "Nothing's riding on this except the First Amendment of the Constitution, freedom of the press, and maybe the future of the country."

*Robards to Redford and Hoffman*

**10.** "In a conspiracy like this, you build from the outer edges, and you go step by step. If you shoot too high and miss, everybody feels more secure."

*Holbrook to Redford*

**AMADEUS** (Orion, 1984). D: Milos Forman. S: Peter Shaffer. Fr: Peter Shaffer (play).

**1.** "Did I do it?"

*F. Murray Abraham (Antonio Salieri), on whether he murdered Tom Hulce (Wolfgang Amadeus Mozart)*

**LAST LINE**
**2.** "Mediocrities everywhere, I absolve you. I absolve you. I absolve you. I absolve you all."

*Abraham*

**AMERICAN GRAFFITI** (Universal, 1973). D: George Lucas. S: George Lucas, Gloria Katz, Willard Huyck.

**1.** "You just can't stay seventeen forever."

*Ron Howard (Steve Bolander) to Richard Dreyfuss (Curt Henderson), on Dreyfuss's ambivalence about leaving town for college*

**2.** "I love you."

*Suzanne Somers (Girl in White Thunderbird), mouthing come-on to Dreyfuss from her car*

**3.** "If I had a boyfriend, he'd pound you."

*Mackenzie Phillips (Carol) to Paul LeMat (John Milner)*

**4.** "Hey, did anybody ever tell you you look just like Connie Stevens?"

*Charles Martin Smith (Terry Fields) to Candy Clark (Debbie), as he tries to pick her up*

**5.** "You know, I always thought I looked like Sandra Dee."

*Clark to Smith*

**6.** "I just love it when guys peel out."

*Clark to Smith*

**7.** "Lemme have a Three Musketeers and a ballpoint pen, one of those combs there, a pint of Old Harper, a couple of flashlight batteries, and some beef jerky."

*Smith to liquor store clerk, in an attempt to buy liquor without I.D.*

**8.** "You know what I want out of life. It's just not in this town."

*Howard to Cindy Williams (Laurie), about the town he never leaves*

**9.** "You picked me up and we got some hard stuff, went saw a hold-up, then we went to the canal and you got your car stolen and then I got to watch you get sick, then got into a really bitchin' fight. I really had a good time."

*Clark to Smith, at the end of their evening*

**10.** "If the Wolfman was here, he'd say get your ass in gear. The Wolfman comes in here occasionally bringing tapes, you know, and to check up on me and what not, and the places he talks about that he's been and the things he's seen. There's a great big beautiful world out there and here I sit sucking popsicles."

*Wolfman Jack (Himself) to Dreyfuss*

**11.** "Just follow this street straight out of town."

*Williams to Harrison Ford (Falfa), on how to reach Paradise Road, site of race between him and LeMat*

**12.** "Oh, Steven, please don't leave me."

*Williams to Howard, as they embrace following the car wreck*

**13.** "The man had me, he was beatin' me."

*LeMat to Smith, on the likely outcome of the race had there been no accident*

**14.** "Okay, Toad, we'll take 'em all."

*LeMat to Smith, an unlikely pair*

**15.** "John Milner was killed by a drunk driver in December 1964. Terry Fields was reported missing in action near An Loc in December 1965. Steve Bolander is an insurance agent in Modesto, California. Curt Henderson is a writer living in Canada."

*The fates of the four main characters, as flashed on the screen*

**AMERICAN IN PARIS, AN** *(MGM, 1951). D: Vincente Minnelli. S: Alan Jay Lerner.*

**1.** "For a painter, the mecca of the world for study, for inspiration, and for living is here on this star called Paris. Just look at it. No wonder so many artists have come here and called it home. Brother, if you can't paint in Paris, you'd better give up and marry the boss's daughter."

*Gene Kelly (Jerry Mulligan)*

**2.** "Back home everyone said I didn't have any talent. They might be saying the same thing over here, but it sounds better in French."

*Kelly, giving another view of why he came to Paris to paint*

**3.** "It's not a pretty face, I grant you, but underneath its flabby exterior is an enormous lack of character."

Oscar Levant (Adam Cook)

**4.** "That's quite a dress you almost have on."

Kelly to Nina Foch (Milo Roberts)

**ANASTASIA** (UK: 20th Century–Fox, 1956). D: Anatole Litvak. S: Arthur Laurents. Fr: Marcelle Maurette (play), Guy Bolton (adaptation).

**1.** "I don't know who I am anymore. I don't know what I remember and what I've been told I remember. What is real? Am I?"

Ingrid Bergman (Anastasia) to Yul Brynner (Bounine)

**ANATOMY OF A MURDER** (Columbia, 1959). D: Otto Preminger. S: Wendell Mayes.

**1.** "Don't let him pay you off in purple hearts. Those professional soldiers never have a dime. I ought to know. I was married to one."

Eve Arden (Maida) to lawyer James Stewart (Paul Biegler), on soldier and accused murderer Ben Gazzara (Frederick Manion)

**2.** "Well, don't knock it. That's the American dream. Those boys made the grade."

Stewart to Gazzara, on the Ten Most Wanted list

**3.** "The unwritten law is a myth, Lieutenant. There is no such thing as the unwritten law, and anyone who commits murder on the theory that it does exist has bought himself room and board in the state penitentiary, maybe for life."

Stewart to Gazzara

**4.** "Maybe you're too pure, Paul. Too pure for the natural impurities of the law."

Arthur O'Connell (Parnell McCarthy) to Stewart

**5.** "There's only one thing more devious than a Philadelphia lawyer, and that's an Irish lawyer."

Stewart to the Irish O'Connell

**6.** "I don't usually complain about an attractive jiggle, but you save that jiggle for your husband to look at if and when I get him out of jail."

Stewart to Gazzara's wife, Lee Remick (Laura Manion)

**7.** "The cat's out of the bag. It's fair game for me to chase it."

Stewart, during the trial

**8.** "The prosecution would like to separate the motive from the act. Well, that's like trying to take the core from an apple without breaking the skin."

Stewart

**9.** "Twelve people go off into a room. Twelve different minds, twelve different hearts, twelve different walks of life. Twelve sets of eyes, ears, shapes, and sizes, and these twelve people are asked to judge another human being as different from them as they are from each other. And in their judgment, they must become of one mind. Unanimous. I swear, the miracle is of man's disorganized soul that they can do it, and in most instances, do it right well. God bless juries."

O'Connell

**10.** "You know, I used to think the world looked better through a glass of whiskey. It doesn't."

O'Connell

**11.** "So sorry, but I had to leave suddenly. I was seized by an irresistible impulse."

*O'Connell to Stewart, reading the farewell note of Gazzara, who has disappeared without paying his lawyer after being acquitted on an "irresistible impulse" defense*

**. . . AND JUSTICE FOR ALL** (Columbia, 1979). D: Norman Jewison. S: Valerie Curtin, Barry Levinson.

**1.** "Gentlemen, need I remind you you are in a court of law?"

*Jack Warden (Judge Rayford), after shooting his gun at the ceiling to get attention*

**2.** "There's law and there's order. And that's order."

*Warden to Al Pacino (Arthur Kirkland), referring to his gun*

**3.** "I can't appeal! He's dead!"

*Pacino to Larry Bryggman (Warren Fresnell), when Bryggman, having allowed Pacino's client to go to jail, tells Pacino he can appeal*

**4.** "The idea of 'punishment to fit the crime' doesn't work. We need unjust punishment. Hang somebody for armed robbery! Try it! We got nothing to lose!"

*John Forsythe (Judge Fleming), the man Pacino is defending against rape charges*

**5.** "You're out of order! You're out of order! The whole trial is out of order!"

*Pacino to Warden, after being told he is out of order*

**AND THEN THERE WERE NONE** (20th Century–Fox, 1945). D: René Clair. S: Dudley Nichols. Fr: Agatha Christie (story, "Ten Little Indians").

**1.** "Very stupid to kill the only servant in the house. Now we don't even know where to find the marmalade."

*Judith Anderson (Emily Brent) on the murder of Richard Haydn (Rogers)*

**ANDROMEDA STRAIN, THE** (Universal, 1971). D: Robert Wise. S: Nelson Gidding. Fr: Michael Crichton (novel).

**1.** "Hell of a way to run a hospital."

*George Mitchell (Jackson), confused elderly patient, on the strange happenings at the biological laboratory where the Andromeda Strain, a deadly extraterrestrial microbe, has gotten loose*

**2.** "There are now five minutes to self-destruct."

*Female announcer, counting down the minutes until the center explodes in a nuclear blast*

**3.** "Self-destruct has been canceled."

*Announcer calling off the explosion*

**4.** "Eight seconds to spare. Hardly even exciting."

*Kate Reid (Dr. Ruth Leavitt) on how much time was left before James Olson (Dr. Mark Hall) succeeded in canceling the explosion*

**LAST LINE**
**5.** "Precisely, Senator. What do we do?"

*Arthur Hill (Dr. Jeremy Stone) to senator, when asked what to do if another biological crisis occurs*

**ANDY HARDY MEETS DEBUTANTE** (MGM, 1940). D: George B. Seitz. S: Annalee Whitmore, Thomas Seller.

**LAST LINE**
**1.** "Gosh, how one's women do mount up."

*Mickey Rooney (Andy Hardy)*

**ANDY WARHOL'S DRACULA** *(France/ Italy: CFDC, 1974). D: Paul Morrissey. S: Paul Morrissey.*

***1.*** "Right now, he's a disgusting person with money. After the revolution, he'll be a disgusting person with no money."

*Joe Dallesandro (Nicholas), on Count Dracula*

***2.*** "Count Dracula may not seem like the ideal husband, though he's of a very good family."

*Maxine McKendry, a mother convincing her daughters that Dracula is quite a catch*

**ANGELS WITH DIRTY FACES** *(Warner Bros., 1938). D: Michael Curtiz. S: John Wexley, Warren Duff. Fr: Rowland Brown (story).*

***1.*** "What do you hear? What do you say?"

*Gangster James Cagney's (Rocky Sullivan) trademark greeting to priest Pat O'Brien (Jerry Connolly)*

***2.*** "That's funny. I got an idea on top of a bus one time. Got me six years."

*Cagney, on hearing that O'Brien decided to become a priest when riding on top of a bus past the cathedral*

***3.*** "Yeah, sure. I'll help you with the collection."

*Cagney to O'Brien, on whether he will attend Mass on Sunday*

***4.*** "Never bother anybody in their own neighborhood."

*Cagney's advice to Billy Halop (Soapy) and the other Dead End Kids*

***5.*** "Nice day for murder."

*Cagney to George Bancroft (Mac Keefer)*

***6.*** "Before I finished reading about you being arrested, there were headlines saying you were out."

*O'Brien, on Cagney's deftness in escaping the law*

***7.*** "You been reading a lot of stuff about 'Crime don't pay.' Don't be a sucker. That's for yaps and small-timers on shoestrings. Not for people like us. You belong in the big- shot class. Both of us do."

*Cagney to Ann Sheridan (Laury Martin)*

***8.*** "Sure, I want to get it started, but I don't want to build it on rotten foundations."

*O'Brien to Cagney, on building a youth center with stolen money*

***9.*** "What earthly good is it for me to teach that honesty is the best policy, when all around they see that dishonesty is the better policy? That the hoodlum and the gangster is looked up to with the same respect as the successful businessman or the popular hero?"

*O'Brien to Cagney*

***10.*** "In order to be afraid, I think you've got to have a heart. I don't think I got one. I got it cut out of me a long time ago."

*Cagney to O'Brien, just before going to the electric chair*

***11.*** ROCKY DIES YELLOW
KILLER COWARD AT END

*Newspaper headline announcing Cagney's behavior at his execution; Cagney pretended to be afraid at O'Brien's request, to provide an unglamorous model for the neighborhood kids*

**LAST LINE**

***12.*** "It's true, boys. Every word of it. He died like they said. All right, fellows, let's go and say a prayer for a boy who couldn't run as fast as I could."

*O'Brien to Halop and the other kids, on Cagney's death*

**ANIMAL CRACKERS** *(Paramount, 1930). D: Victor Heerman. S: Morris Ryskind. Fr: Morris Ryskind, George S. Kaufman (play).*

**1.** "Why, you're one of the most beautiful women I've ever seen, and that's not saying much for you."

*Groucho Marx (Capt. Jeffrey T. Spalding) to Margaret Dumont (Mrs. Rittenhouse)*

**2.** "One morning I shot an elephant in my pajamas. How he got in my pajamas I don't know."

*Marx*

**ANNA CHRISTIE** *(MGM, 1930). D: Clarence Brown. S: Frances Marion. Fr: Eugene O'Neill (play).*

**1.** "Gimme a whiskey, ginger ale on the side. And don't be stingy, baby."

*Greta Garbo's (Blanche Sweet) first line on screen*

**LAST LINE**
**2.** "Fog, fog all time. You can't tell where you was going. Only that old devil sea, she knows."

*George F. Marion (Chris Christopherson)*

**ANNIE HALL** *(UA, 1977). D: Woody Allen. S: Woody Allen, Marshall Brickman.*

**1.** "You're here in Brooklyn. Brooklyn is not expanding."

*Joan Newman (Alvy Singer's mother) to her son Jonathan Munk (young Alvy Singer), who is depressed because the universe is expanding*

**2.** "I used to be a heroin addict, now I'm a methadone addict."

*One of Woody Allen's (adult Alvy Singer's) grade school classmates, projecting what he will be doing many years from now*

**3.** "You know, I was having lunch with some guys from NBC, so I said, 'Did you eat yet or what?' and Tom Christie said, 'No, jew?' "

*Allen to friend Tony Roberts (Rob), citing evidence of anti-semitism*

**4.** "I don't want to live in a city where the only cultural advantage is that you can make a right turn on a red light."

*Allen, on living in Los Angeles*

**5.** "I heard what you were saying. You know nothing of my work. You mean my whole fallacy is wrong. How you ever got to teach a course in anything is totally amazing."

*Marshall McLuhan, conveniently emerging from behind a lobby display to contradict the theories of a pompous bore on a movie line who is annoying Allen*

**6.** "Well, la-di-da."

*Diane Keaton's (Annie Hall's) favorite refrain*

**7.** "I'm gonna give him one more year and then I'm going to Lourdes."

*Allen, on his psychoanalyst of many years*

**8.** "That was the most fun I've ever had without laughing."

*Allen, on having sex with Keaton for the first time*

**9.** "Life is divided up into the horrible and the miserable."

*Allen, on the two categories of life experience*

**10.** "Love is, is too weak a word for the way I feel—I lurve you, you know, I loave you, I luff you."

*Allen, expressing his feelings for Keaton*

**11.** "Just don't take any course where they make you read *Beowulf*."

*Allen, discussing adult education classes with Keaton*

**12.** "I looked within the soul of the boy sitting next to me."

*Allen, on how he flunked for cheating on his metaphysics exam*

**13.** "Hey, don't knock masturbation. It's sex with someone I love."

*Allen*

**14.** "I'm one of the few males who suffers from that."

*Allen, on penis envy*

**15.** "Darling, I've been killing spiders since I was thirty."

*Allen, expressing confidence about being able to kill the spider in Keaton's bathroom*

**16.** "They don't throw their garbage away. They make it into television shows."

*Allen, on Los Angeles*

**17.** "A relationship, I think, is, is like a shark, you know, it has to constantly move forward or it dies, and I think what we got on our hands is a dead shark."

*Allen to Keaton*

**18.** "You only gave me books with the word 'death' in the title."

*Keaton to Allen*

**LAST LINE**

**19.** "Well, I guess that's pretty much now how I feel about relationships. You know, they're totally irrational and crazy and absurd and—but, uh, I guess we keep goin' through it because most of us need the eggs."

*Allen*

**ANOTHER PART OF THE FOREST** *(Universal-International, 1948). D: Michael Gordon. S: Vladimir Pozner. Fr: Lillian Hellman (play).*

**1.** "Try to remember that, though ignorance becomes a Southern gentleman, cowardice does not."

*Fredric March (Marcus Hubbard) to his son Dan Duryea (Oscar Hubbard)*

**APARTMENT, THE** *(UA, 1960). D: Billy Wilder. S: Billy Wilder, I. A. L. Diamond.*

**1.** "My name is C. C. Baxter: C for Calvin, C for Clifford."

*Jack Lemmon (C. C. Baxter), introducing himself in voice-over*

**2.** "You see, I have this little problem with my apartment."

*Lemmon, in voice-over*

**3.** "Never close at Buddy Boy's."

*Lemmon, after being coerced once again to surrender his apartment to office philanderers*

**4.** "Premium-wise and billing-wise we are eighteen percent ahead, October-wise."

*David Lewis (Mr. Kirkeby) into dictaphone, demonstrating common business jargon*

**5.** FRED MACMURRAY (*J. D. Sheldrake*), referring obliquely to his affair with SHIRLEY MACLAINE (*Fran Kubelik*): "You see a girl a couple of times a week and sooner or later she thinks you'll divorce your wife. Not fair, is it?"

LEMMON: "No, especially to your wife."

**6.** "Just because I wear a uniform doesn't mean I'm a Girl Scout."

*MacLaine to Lemmon*

**7.** LEMMON: "The mirror. It's broken."
MACLAINE: "Yes, I like it that way. Makes me look the way I feel."

**8.** "When you're in love with a married man, you shouldn't wear mascara."

*MacLaine to Lemmon, after crying over Mac-Murray*

**9.** "Why do people have to love people anyway?"

*MacLaine to Lemmon*

**10.** MACLAINE: "Why can't I ever fall in love with someone nice like you?"
        LEMMON: "Well, that's the way it crumbles, cookie-wise."

**LAST LINES**
**11.** LEMMON: "You hear what I said, Miss Kubelik? I absolutely adore you."
        MACLAINE: "Shut up and deal."

**APOCALYPSE NOW** *(Zoetrope Studios, 1979). D: Francis Ford Coppola. S: John Milius, Francis Ford Coppola. Fr: Joseph Conrad (novel,* Heart of Darkness*).*

**1.** "Everyone gets everything he wants. I wanted a mission, and for my sins they gave me one."

*Martin Sheen (Capt. Benjamin Willard), in narration*

**2.** "Terminate with extreme prejudice."

*Jerry Ziesmer (Civilian), spelling out the order for Sheen to kill Marlon Brando (Colonel Kurtz)*

**3.** "Charging a man with murder in this place was like handing out speeding tickets at the Indy 500."

*Sheen, on Vietnam*

**4.** "He was one of those guys that had that weird light around him. You just knew he wasn't gonna get so much as a scratch here."

*Sheen, on Robert Duvall (Lieutenant Colonel Kilgore)*

**5.** "I love the smell of napalm in the morning. . . . Smells like—victory."

*Duvall*

**6.** "Never get out of the boat. Absolutely goddamn right. Unless you were going all the way."

*Sheen, narrating the story of his river journey to find Brando*

**7.** SHEEN: "Who's the commanding officer here?
MACHINE-GUNNER: "Ain't you?"

**8.** "The heads. You're lookin' at the heads. Eh, uh—sometimes he goes too far, you know, and he's the first one to admit it."

*Dennis Hopper (Photojournalist), on the decapitated heads cluttering Brando's compound*

**9.** BRANDO: "Are my methods unsound."
SHEEN: "I don't see any method at all, sir."

**10.** "He broke from them, and then he broke from himself. I'd never seen a man so broken up and ripped apart."

*Sheen on Brando*

**11.** "We left the camp after we had inoculated some children, and this old man came running after us and he was crying, he couldn't see. We went back there, and they had come and hacked off every inoculated arm. There they were in a pile, a pile of little arms."

*Brando, remembering an incident from his days with Special Forces*

**12.** "Because it's judgment that defeats us."

*Brando, on why he wants men who can kill without judgment*

**13.** "Even the jungle wanted him dead, and that's who he really took his orders from anyway."

*Sheen, on Brando*

LAST LINE
**14.** "The horror. The horror."

*Brando's dying words, repeated in voice-over at the end*

**ARISTOCATS, THE** *(Buena Vista, 1971). D: Wolfgang Reitherman. S: Larry Clemmons, Vance Gerry, Ken Anderson, Frank Thomas, Eric Cleworth, et al.*

**1.** "Ladies don't start fights, but they finish them."

*Liz English (Marie), a kitten*

**AROUND THE WORLD IN 80 DAYS** *(UA, 1956). D: Michael Anderson. S: S. J. Perelman, John Farrow (uncredited), James Poe (uncredited). Fr: Jules Verne (novel).*

**1.** "An Englishman never jokes about a wager."

*Impeccable English gentleman David Niven (Phileas Fogg), taking on a bet to go around the world in eighty days*

**2.** "In Yokohama I must not sneeze at geisha girls."

*Fogg's valet Cantinflas (Passepartout), remembering a rule of travel*

**3.** "It's not often one needs an elephant in a hurry."

*Niven, explaining why he paid so much for an elephant*

**4.** "Bulldog tenacity, Mr. Fix, that's the spirit that built an empire."

*British official to Robert Newton (Inspector Fix), on board an imperial ship to Hong Kong*

**5.** "Mr. Fogg, why must you be so . . . so British?"

*Shirley MacLaine (Indian Princess Aouda) to Niven, who has rescued her from being ceremonially burned alive on her late husband's funeral pyre*

**6.** "Would you care to join me on the veranda? I understand they serve an outstanding melon squash."

*Niven, being British to MacLaine*

**7.** "This is a very primitive country. We're going to need some protection."

*Niven, who has traveled throughout India and the Far East, on arriving in the United States*

**8.** "Oh, these American trains. Quite impossible."

*Niven, encountering yet another delay on his trip through the United States*

**9.** "Mr. Fix, now that you have successfully thwarted me and placed in my path the only obstacle for which I was unable to make provision, I feel that I can tell you: I have never really enjoyed your company very much, and furthermore, you play an abominable game of whist."

*Niven to police inspector Newton, who has pursued him around the world on erroneous charges and arrested him just long enough for the globe-trotting bet to appear lost*

**10.** "Because that could spell the end of the British Empire.

*Niven, on why no woman has ever set foot in the Reform Club; MacLaine does so*

**ARSENIC AND OLD LACE** *(Warner Bros., 1944). D: Frank Capra. S: Julius J. Epstein, Philip G. Epstein. Fr: Joseph Kesselring (play).*

**1.** "He thinks he's Teddy Roosevelt. So what? There's a lot of worse guys he could think he was."

*Edward McNamara (Brophy) to Jack Carson (O'Hara), on John Alexander (Teddy Brewster)*

**2.** PRISCILLA LANE (*Elaine Harper*): "But, Mortimer, you're going to love me for my mind, too?"
CARY GRANT (*Mortimer Brewster*): "One thing at a time."

**3.** "For a gallon of elderberry wine, I take one teaspoonful of arsenic, then I add a half a teaspoon of strychnine, and then just a pinch of cyanide."

*Jean Adair (Martha Brewster) to Grant, on her recipe for murdering old men*

**4.** "He said I looked a lot like Boris Karloff."

*Raymond Massey (Jonathan Brewster) to Peter Lorre (Dr. Einstein), on why he killed Mr. Spinalzo*

**5.** "I get wonderful ideas, but I can't spell them."

*Carson to Grant, on his playwriting aspirations*

**6.** "Insanity runs in my family. It practically gallops."

*Grant to Lane*

**7.** "When Johnny's in that mood, he's a madman! He's a maniac! And then things happen, horrible things."

*Lorre to Grant, on Massey*

**8.** "Did you ever see anybody in a play act like they got any intelligence?"

*Grant to Lorre*

**LAST LINE**
**9.** "I'm not a cabdriver. I'm a coffeepot!"

*Garry Owen (Taxi Driver)*

**ARTHUR** *(Warner Bros., 1981). D: Steve Gordon. S: Steve Gordon.*

**1.** "I race cars, I play tennis, I fondle women, but I have weekends off, and I am my own boss."

*Alcoholic multimillionaire Dudley Moore (Arthur Bach) to prostitute Marjorie Barnes, on what he does for a living*

**2.** "I wish I had a dime for every dime I have."

*Moore to Barnes*

**3.** MOORE: "I'm going to take a bath."
JOHN GIELGUD (*Hobson*), the butler: "I'll alert the media."

**4.** "Fish must get awfully tired of seafood."

*Moore, making an observation to Gielgud*

**5.** "There are so many girls, and so few princes."

*Liza Minnelli (Linda Marolla) to her father Barney Martin (Ralph Marolla), on why girls marry badly*

**6.** MOORE: "I've never taken care of any-one. Everyone's always taken care of me. But if you got sick, or anything, I'd take care of you."

MINNELLI: "Then I'll get sick."

**7.** STEPHEN ELLIOTT (*Burt Johnson*), Moore's prospective father-in-law: "I don't drink because drinking affects your decision-making."

MOORE: "You may be right. I can't decide."

**8.** "Where's the rest of this moose?"

*Moore to Elliott, on the moose head mounted on the wall*

**9.** "Everyone who drinks is not a poet. Some of us drink because we're not poets."

*Moore to fiancée Jill Eikenberry (Susan Johnson)*

**10.** MOORE: "You know the worst part of being me?"

GIELGUD: "I should imagine your breath."

**11.** "You're a man who has everything, haven't you? But that's not enough. You feel unloved, Arthur. Welcome to the world. Everyone is unloved. Now, stop feeling sorry for yourself and, incidentally, I love you."

*Gielgud to Moore*

**12.** "I can't tell you what a lousy wedding that was, Bitterman."

*Moore to his chauffeur Ted Ross (Bitterman), after refusing to marry Eikenberry and getting beat up by her father, Elliott*

**13.** "Oh, I turned her down. . . . Well, she invited us for dinner and I said we're having our tunafish sandwich so I turned her down. I took the money—I mean, I'm not crazy."

*Moore to Minnelli, on his grandmother Geraldine Fitzgerald's (Martha Bach's) offer to bequeath him the family fortune*

**ASPHALT JUNGLE, THE** (MGM, 1950). D: John Huston. S: Ben Maddow, John Huston. Fr: W. R. Burnett (novel).

**1.** "Crime is a left-handed form of human endeavor."

*Sam Jaffe (Riedenschneider)*

**AT THE CIRCUS** (MGM, 1939). D: Edward Buzzell. S: Edward Buzzell.

**1.** "I'll bet your father spent the first year of your life throwing rocks at the stork."

*Groucho Marx (J. Cheever Loophole) to Chico Marx*

**2.** "We were young, gay, reckless! The night I drank champagne from your slipper—two quarts. It would have held more, but you were wearing innersoles."

*Groucho, romancing his old flame Margaret Dumont*

**ATLANTIC CITY** (Paramount, 1981). D: Louis Malle. S: John Guare.

**1.** "I worked for the people who worked for the people."

*Burt Lancaster (Lou) to Robert Joy (Dave), on indirectly knowing such famous mobsters as Al Capone and Lucky Luciano*

**2.** "Atlantic City had *floy floy* coming out of its ears in those days."

*Lancaster to Joy, referring to the song "The Flatfoot Floogy with the Floy Floy"*

**3.** "Yes, it used to be beautiful—what with the rackets, whoring, guns."

> *Lancaster to Joy, reminiscing about the good old days*

**4.** "The Atlantic Ocean was something then. Yes, you should have seen the Atlantic Ocean in those days."

> *Lancaster to Joy*

## ATTACK OF THE 50-FOOT WOMAN
*(Allied Artists, 1958). D: Nathan Hertz. S: Mark Hanna.*

**1.** "You just hide out and let her blow up like a balloon."

> *Yvette Vickers (Honey Parker) to her lover William Hudson (Harry Archer), advising him to hide, while his wife Allison Hayes (Nancy Archer) keeps growing due to a dose of extraterrestrial rays*

**2.** "She's loose!"

> *Eileen Stevens (nurse), panicking when the giant Hayes breaks free*

**3.** "I know where my husband is! He's with that woman! I'll find him!"

> *Hayes, now at full fifty-foot height and on the rampage against her philandering husband*

**4.** "I can't shoot a lady!"

> *Deputy unable to shoot the fifty-foot woman*

**LAST LINE**
**5.** "She finally got Harry all to herself."

> *Roy Gordon (Dr. Cushing), on Hayes, who managed to kill her husband, Hudson, before being killed by the police*

## AUNTIE MAME *(Warner Bros., 1958). D: Morton DaCosta. S: Betty Comden, Adolph* Green. Fr: Patrick Dennis *(novel)*, Jerome Lawrence, Robert E. Lee *(play)*.

**1.** "But, darling, I'm your Auntie Mame!"

> *Rosalind Russell (Mame Dennis) to Jan Handzlik (Patrick Dennis as a child)*

**2.** "Karl Marx—is he one of the Marx brothers?"

> *Handzlik to Russell*

**3.** "She's not English, darling. She's from Pittsburgh."

> *Russell to Handzlik, about Coral Browne (Vera Charles)*

**4.** "Such talented fingers, but oh, what he did to my bust."

> *Russell to Handzlik, about the artist who created an objet d'art in her apartment*

**5.** "Auntie Mame says olives take up too much room in such a little glass."

> *Handzlik to Fred Clark (Mr. Babcock), about cocktail glasses*

**6.** "Life is a banquet, and most poor suckers are starving to death!"

> *Russell to Peggy Cass (Agnes Gooch)*

**LAST LINE**
**7.** "Oh, what times we're going to have! What vistas we're going to explore together! We'll spend a day at an ancient Hindu temple. The head monk there is a very good friend of Auntie Mame's, and perhaps he'll let you ring the temple bells that bring the monks to prayer. And there on the highest tower, on a clear day, you can see the Taj Mahal and beyond that the beautiful . . ."

> *Russell to her great-nephew*

**AVALON** *(TriStar, 1990). D: Barry Levinson. S: Barry Levinson.*

**FIRST LINE**

*1.* "I came to America in 1914 . . . by way of Philadelphia . . . That's where I got off the boat, and then I came to Baltimore. It was the most beautiful place you've ever seen in your life."

> *Armin Mueller-Stahl (Sam Krichinsky), in narration; remembered in the film's last line by Tom Wood (Michael as an adult)*

**AWAKENINGS** *(Columbia, 1990). D: Penny Marshall. S: Steve Zailian. Fr: Oliver Sacks (book).*

*1.* JULIE KAVNER *(Eleanor Costello)*: "There's something else that reaches them, Doctor."
ROBIN WILLIAMS *(Dr. Malcolm Sayer)*: "What?"
KAVNER: "Human contact."

*2.* "What I believe, what I know, is that these people are alive inside."

> *Williams to John Heard (Dr. Kaufman), the head of the hospital*

*3.* "Go to sleep. When you wake up in the morning, it'll be the next morning. I promise."

> *Kavner to Williams*

*4.* "What a wonderful place the Bronx has become!"

> *Robert De Niro (Leonard Lowe) to Williams, when he is taken outside for the first time*

*5.* "My name is Leonard Lowe. It has been explained to me that I have been away for quite some time. I'm back."

> *De Niro, in a film shown to patrons of the hospital*

*6.* "You didn't wake a thing. You woke a person."

> *De Niro to the board, when he asks to go for a walk by himself*

*7.* "That summer was extraordinary. It was a season of rebirth and innocence, a miracle. . . . But now we have to adjust to the realities of miracles. . . . The reality is, we don't know what went wrong any more than we know what went right. What we do know is as the chemical window closed, another awakening took place: that the human spirit is more powerful than any drug."

> *Williams to the board*

**LAST LINE**

*8.* "Let's begin."

> *Williams, in a reprise of an earlier scene when he uses a ouija board to get De Niro to spell his name*

**AWFUL TRUTH, THE** *(Columbia, 1937). D: Leo McCarey. S: Vina Delmar. Fr: Arthur Richman (play).*

*1.* "The road to Reno is paved with suspicions, and the first thing you know they all end up in a divorce court."

> *Cary Grant (Jerry Warriner) to group of friends*

*2.* "Yes, that's right, I have a Continental mind. Will you have an eggnog?"

> *Grant to Alexander D'Arcy (Armand Duvalle)*

*3.* "American women aren't accustomed to chivalry."

> *Irene Dunne (Lucy Warriner) to D'Arcy*

*4.* "How can I believe you? The car broke down. People stopped believing that one before cars started breaking down."

> *Grant to Dunne, on her alibi*

**5.** RALPH BELLAMY (*Daniel Leeson*): "I'm in oil, you know."

CECIL CUNNINGHAM (*Aunt Patsy*): "Marinated in it, so to speak."

**6.** "Back on my ranch I got a little red rooster and a little brown hen, and they fight all the time, too, but every once in a while they make up again and they're right friendly."

*Bellamy to Dunne and Cunningham, on marital discord*

**7.** "I guess it was easier for her to change her name than for her whole family to change theirs."

*Dunne to Grant, on the dreadful singing act of Joyce Compton (Toots Binswanger/Dixie Belle Lee)*

**8.** "Our divorce was one of those tragedies that you read about in the papers. A trusting woman and a worthless man."

*Grant to Esther Dale (Mrs. Leeson), Bellamy's mother*

**9.** "I only made one bad investment."

*Dunne to Grant, on whether she needs money to make up for bad investments*

**10.** "To you, my little prairie flower:
I'm thinkin' of you every hour.
Though now you're just a friend to me,
I wonder what the end will be.
Oh, you would make my life divine
If you would change your name to mine."

*Bellamy, professing love to Dunne as Grant stands behind door*

**11.** "Every time I open the door, somebody walks in."

*Cunningham, as she admits D'Arcy*

**12.** "Well, I guess a man's best friend is his mother."

*Bellamy to Dunne*

**13.** "We call him Jerry the nipper."

*Dunne, in disguised identity of Lola, about Grant and his drinking habits*

**14.** "Things are the way you think I made them. I didn't make them that way at all. Things are just the same as they always were, only you're the same as you were, too, so I guess things will never be the same again."

*Grant to Dunne, on the road to reconciliation*

**BABE RUTH STORY, THE** (*Monogram/Allied Artists, 1948*). D: Roy Del Ruth. S: Bob Considine, George Callahan. Fr: Bob Considine (book).

**LAST LINE**

**1.** "His name will live as long as there is a ball, a bat, and a boy."

*Knox Manning (Narrator), on William Bendix (Babe Ruth)*

**BABES ON BROADWAY** (*MGM, 1941*). D: Busby Berkeley. S: Fred Finklehoffe, Elaine Ryan. Fr: Burton Lane (story).

**FIRST LINE**

**1.** "Broadway—they call it the Great White Way. But it shines with a radiance no electrical company can inspire. It comes from the likes of you. One word of advice—take what you can get. Grab the chances as they come along. Act in hallways, sing in doorways, and if you have to, dance in cellars."

*Alexander Woollcott (Himself), giving advice to would-be Broadway stars*

**2.** "You know, I have a feeling that—that you're going to be that unknown quantity in my life."

*Mickey Rooney (Tommy Williams) to Judy Garland (Penny Morris)*

**3.** "Please! Wait! Don't send my brother to the chair. Don't let him burn. Please, please, Warden, please."

*Toddler actress Margaret O'Brien, in her screen debut, auditioning hyperdramatically for skeptical producer James Gleason (Thornton Reed)*

**4.** "Hunky-dory. That's American for okay."

*Young English refugee, broadcasting to her mother by shortwave radio*

**5.** "Oh, no, you're gonna talk me out of my love scene."

*Rooney to Garland*

**6.** "Isn't it wonderful what you can find these days in drugstores?"

*Rooney to Garland, on the place where they met*

**7.** "Honey, every theater's a haunted house. Ghosts with greasepaint. Ghosts that sing and dance and laugh and cry. Gosh, think of all the shows there've been in this theater. Flops, successes, bad shows, great shows. Oh, you can't tell me that that ever dies."

*Rooney to Garland, on the abandoned theater in which they are standing*

**BABETTE'S FEAST** *(Denmark: Orion Classics, 1987). D: Gabriel Axel. S: Gabriel Axel. Fr: Isak Dinesen (story).*

**FIRST LINE**

**1.** "In this remote spot there once lived two sisters who were both past the first flush of youth."

*Ghita Norby (Narrator), on Bodil Kjer (Old Filippa) and Birgitte Federspiel (Old Martina)*

**2.** "Babette's presence in the house of the two sisters can only be explained through the hidden regions of the heart."

*Norby, on Stephane Audran (Babette Hersant)*

**3.** "Babette knows how to cook."

*Jean-Philippe Lafont (Achille Papin), understating the facts in his letter to Kjer*

**4.** "I am not too happy about this French dinner, either."

*Federspiel to Kjer, on the dinner Audran plans to cook for their austere Scandinavian religious community*

**5.** "You must prove to me that the choice I made was the right one."

*Jarl Kulle (Old Lorenz Lowenhielm) to the image of his younger self in a chair, on giving up his love for Federspiel to pursue a military career*

**6.** "It must be some kind of lemonade."

*Old woman, tasting champagne for the first time at Audran's feast*

**7.** "A love affair that made no distinction between bodily appetite and spiritual appetite."

*Norby, on what Audran's dinner has become*

**8.** "I have been with you every day of my life."

*Kulle to his lost love, Federspiel*

**9.** KJER: "The stars have moved closer."
FEDERSPIEL: "Perhaps they move closer every night."

**10.** "An artist is never poor."

*Audran, on spending all her money to prepare the feast*

**LAST LINE**

*11.* "In Paradise you will be the great artist God meant you to be. Ah, how you will delight the angels!"

*Kjer to Audran*

## BACHELOR AND THE BOBBY-SOXER, THE *(RKO, 1947). D: Irving Reis. S: Sidney Sheldon.*

*1.* "Susan's growing pains are rapidly becoming a major disease."

*Myrna Loy (Margaret) to Rudy Vallee (Tommy), about her sister Shirley Temple (Susan)*

*2.* RAY COLLINS (*Beemesh*): "I'm the court psychiatrist."

CARY GRANT (*Dick*): "Come back in an hour. I'll be crazy by then."

*3.* VEDA ANN BORG (*Agnes Prescott*), talking about Grant: "Now, there's a guy who never goes out of a girl's mind. He just stays there like a heavy meal."

DON BEDDOE (*Tony*): "What am I like?"

BORG: "Orange juice."

**LAST LINES**

*4.* LOY: "You remind me of a man."

GRANT: "What man?"

LOY: "The man with the power."

GRANT: "What power?"

LOY: "The power of Hoodoo."

GRANT: "Who do?"

LOY: "You do."

GRANT: "Do what?"

LOY: "Remind me of a man."

GRANT: "What man?"

LOY: "The man with the power."

GRANT: "What power?"

LOY: "Give up?"

GRANT: "Give up. Let's go."

## BACK TO BATAAN *(RKO, 1945). D: Edward Dmytryk. S: Ben Barzman, Richard Landau. Fr: Aeneas MacKenzie, William Gordon (story).*

*1.* "What're you guys celebrating down there, New Year's?"

*John Wayne (Colonel Madden) to comrades in battle, using too much ammunition*

*2.* "But remember, we are kindly but not indulgent. We shall not hesitate to spank the unruly ones."

*Japanese overlord, warning Filipino Fely Franquelli (Dalisay Delgado) on the new order of things in the Japanese-occupied Philippines*

*3.* "Kill more Japs and get more guns."

*Wayne, leader of a Filipino resistance force, outlining his arms-acquisition strategy*

*4.* "The place matters not/Cypress or laurel or lily white/Scaffold or open plain/Combat or martyrdom's plight."

*Epitaph for Vladimir Sokoloff (Buenaventura J. Bello), a Filipino school principal hung by the Japanese for refusing to lower an American flag, quoted from a Filipino national hero*

*5.* "This kind of a war, you've gotta believe in what you're fighting for."

*Wayne, on guerrilla war*

*6.* "Okay, Andres, we're crazy. We and seventeen million Filipinos."

*Wayne to reluctant Filipino patriot Anthony Quinn (Andres Bonifacio), who doubts whether the resistance can succeed*

*7.* "The Japanese have offered us what they call independence. Let this be our answer."

*Franquelli, a double-agent who has spied for the Allies while broadcasting propaganda for the Japanese, openly broadcasting her defiance during a battle*

**8.** "DUCKY" LOUIE (*Maximo*), a patriotic Filipino boy dying after being assaulted by the Japanese: "I'm sorry I didn't say good-bye. I'm sorry I didn't learn to spell 'liberty.'"

BEULAH BONDI (*Bertha Barnes*), his teacher: "Dear God! Whoever learned it so well."

**9.** "Trickery, commander, sheer trickery."

*Wayne, on how the Filipino freedom fighters will accomplish their mission*

**10.** "Hey! You're three minutes late!"

*Wayne to American forces relieving him and his outnumbered troops, who have managed to hold the line*

**BACK TO SCHOOL** (*Orion, 1986*). D: Alan Metter. S: Steven Kampmann, Will Porter, Peter Torokvei, Harold Ramis. Fr: Rodney Dangerfield, Greg Fields, Dennis Snee (story).

**1.** "Bring a pitcher of beer every seven minutes till somebody passes out, and then bring one every ten minutes."

*Rodney Dangerfield (Thornton Melon) to waitress*

**BACK TO THE FUTURE** (*Amblin-Universal, 1985*). D: Robert Zemeckis. S: Robert Zemeckis, Bob Gale.

**1.** "Wait a minute, Doc—are you telling me you built a time machine out of a Delorean?"

*Michael J. Fox (Marty McFly) to time-machine-inventor Christopher Lloyd (Dr. Emmett Brown)*

**2.** "Well, that is your name, isn't it? Calvin Klein? It's written all over your underwear."

*Lea Thompson (Lorraine Baines), 1950s teenager and Fox's future mother, to the time-traveling Fox*

**3.** "Better get used to these bars, kid."

*Fox to his future jailbird uncle, Joey, encountered as a baby in a crib*

**4.** "Ronald Reagan? The actor? Then who's vice-president—Jerry Lewis?"

*Lloyd to Fox, unable to believe that Reagan will one day be president*

**5.** "Next Saturday night we're sending you back to the future!"

*Lloyd to Fox*

**6.** "Jesus! Didn't that guy ever have hair?"

*Fox, on encountering a perennially bald teacher, James Tolkan (Mr. Strickland)*

**7.** "I'm George—George McFly. I'm your density—I mean, your destiny."

*Crispin Glover (George McFly) trying to woo his future wife Thompson*

**8.** "Chuck! Chuck! It's Marvin—your cousin, Marvin Berry. You know that new sound you're looking for? Well, listen to this."

*Musician Harry Waters, Jr. (Marvin Berry), on the phone with his cousin Chuck Berry, expressing excitement as Fox performs the future Chuck Berry hit "Johnny B. Goode"*

**9.** "Well, I figured—what the hell."

*Lloyd, on why he decided not to worry about destroying the future by reading a note given to him by Fox*

LAST LINE

**10.** "Roads? Where we're going we don't need—roads."

*Lloyd to Fox and his girlfriend Claudia Wells (Jennifer), as they embark on a trip to the future*

**BAD DAY AT BLACK ROCK** (*MGM, 1955*). D: John Sturges. S: Millard Kaufman. Fr: Howard Breslin (story).

**1.** SPENCER TRACY (*John J. Macreedy*): "Oh, I'll only be here twenty-four hours."

CONDUCTOR: "In a place like this, it could be a lifetime."

**2.** "You look like you need a hand."

*Lee Marvin (Hector David) to one-armed Tracy*

**3.** "This guy's like a carrier of small pox. Since he's arrived, this town has a fever, an infection, and it's spreading."

*Robert Ryan (Reno Smith) to rest of the town, referring to Tracy*

**4.** "I don't care anything about Black Rock. Only it just seems to me that there aren't many towns like this in America. But one town like it is enough, and because I think something kind of bad happened here, Miss Wirth, something I can't quite seem to find a handle to."

*Tracy to Anne Francis (Liz Wirth)*

**5.** "I believe a man is as big as what'll make him mad."

*Ryan to Tracy, referring to the fact that despite the hard time they have given Tracy, he has yet to get angry*

**6.** "Somebody's always looking for something in this part of the West. To the historian, it's the old West. To the book writer, it's the wild West. To the businessman, it's the undeveloped West. They say we're all poor and backward, and I guess we are. We don't even have enough blood. But to us, this place is our West, and I wish they'd leave us alone."

*Ryan to Tracy*

**7.** "I'm consumed with apathy."

*Walter Brennan (Doc Velie) to Tracy*

**8.** TRACY: "What have you got?"
COOK: "Chili and beans."

TRACY: "Anything else?"
COOK: "Chili without beans."

**9.** "You're not only wrong, you're wrong at the top of your voice."

*Tracy to Ernest Borgnine (Coley Trimble)*

**10.** "Four years ago, something terrible happened here. We did nothing about it. Nothing! The whole town fell into a sort of settled melancholy, and all the people in it closed their eyes, and held their tongues, and failed the test with a whimper. And something terrible's going to happen again. And, in a way, we're lucky because we've been given a second chance."

*Brennan to Dean Jagger (Tim Horn), trying to prevent Tracy's murder*

**11.** "Strange how a man will cling to the Earth, when he feels he isn't going to see it again."

*Tracy to Brennan*

**BAD NEWS BEARS, THE** (Paramount, 1976). D: Michael Ritchie. S: Bill Lancaster.

**1.** "All right, boys. Let's get back to basics. This is a baseball. The object of the game is to keep the baseball within the confines of the playing field."

*Walter Matthau (Coach Buttermaker), when one of the boys throws the ball through his windshield*

**2.** "We got a game with the Athletics, next Wednesday, and that means only one thing! Bad news for the Athletics."

*Matthau to his team*

**3.** MATTHAU: "Who do you think you are, Catfish Hunter?"

TATUM O'NEAL (*Manda Whurlizer*): "Who's he?"

**4.** "Are you crazy? An intentional walk with the bases empty? This is baseball, not backgammon!

*Matthau*

**LAST LINE**

**5.** "Just wait till next year!"

*Quinn Smith (Lupus) to Vic Morrow (Roy Turner) and the Yankee team*

**BADLANDS** (Warner Bros., 1974). D: Edward H. Griffith. S: Terrence Malick.

**1.** "I wasn't popular at school on account of having no personality and not being pretty."

*Sissy Spacek (Holly) to Martin Sheen (Kit)*

**BALL OF FIRE** (UA, 1941). D: Edward H. Griffith. S: Charles Brackett, Billy Wilder. Fr: Thomas Monroe, Billy Wilder (story, "From A to Z").

**1.** "You see, the word 'puss' means *face*, as for instance 'sourpuss.' . . . 'Sugarpuss' implies a certain sweetness in her appearance."

*Gary Cooper (Professor Bertram Potts), explaining the peculiar name of showgirl Barbara Stanwyck (Sugarpuss O'Shea) to his scholarly colleagues*

**2.** "Well, I got thinking it over, and pooh, I said to myself, who am I to give science the brush?"

*Stanwyck to Cooper, on why she agreed to participate in his study of slang*

**3.** "Or when a guy comes to see a girl and says, 'Let's turn off the lights, it hurts my eyes'—brother, that's corn."

*Stanwyck, defining "corn" for Cooper*

**4.** "Professor Gurkakoff has been trying to reconstruct it by compound fractions."

Richard Haydn (Professor Oddly), on his colleague Oscar Homolka's (Professor Gurkakoff's) efforts to reconstruct the conga taught them by Stanwyck

**5.** "That is the kind of woman that makes whole civilizations topple."

*Housekeeper Kathleen Howard (Miss Bragg), on Stanwyck*

**6.** "No mistake, I shall regret the absence of your keen mind. Unfortunately it is inseparable from an extremely disturbing body."

*Cooper to Stanwyck*

**7.** "I'm gonna show you what yum-yum is. Here's yum. Here's the other yum. And here's yum-yum."

*Stanwyck, kissing Cooper*

**8.** "People like that just—Well, you see, dust piles up on their hearts, and it took you to blow it away."

*Cooper to Stanwyck, about himself*

**9.** "We feel that you are marrying all of us, a little."

*One of Cooper's colleagues to Stanwyck, on her marrying Cooper*

**10.** "Being a botanist, I find an astonishing parallel between a woman's heart and the windflower or *Anemone nemorosa*."

*Haydn, revealing his knowledge of women*

**11.** "Why, the very idea that I should have to spend my honeymoon watching her paint in watercolors just because she's like somebody from the buttercup family—I-I'm a man in love."

*Cooper, disagreeing with Haydn's suggestion that sex should not be part of a honeymoon*

**12.** "You've given us all a fine course in the theory and practice of being a sucker."

*Cooper to Stanwyck, when he feels betrayed by her*

**13.** "Yes, I love him. I love those hick shirts he wears with the boiled cuffs and the way he always has his vest buttoned wrong. Looks like a giraffe and I love him. I love him because he's the kind of guy that gets drunk on a glass of buttermilk, and I love the way he blushes right up over his ears. I love him because he doesn't know how to kiss—the jerk! I love him, Joe. That's what I'm trying to tell you."

*Stanwyck to Dana Andrews (Joe Lilac), about Cooper*

**14.** "I feel like yodeling."

*Cooper, on learning that Stanwyck loves him*

**15.** "I think it is known as an upstick."

*Haydn, trying to say "stickup"*

**BAMBI** (RKO, 1942). D: David Hand. S: Perce Pearce, Larry Morey. Fr: Felix Salten (story).

**1.** "A new prince is born!"

*Peter Behn (Thumper), on the birth of Bobby Stewart (Bambi)*

**2.** "I'm thumpin', that's why they call me Thumper."

*Behn*

**3.** "He can call me a flower if he wants to. I don't mind."

*Stan Alexander (Flower)*

**4.** "Eating flowers is a special treat,
It makes long ears and great big feet,
But it sure is awful stuff to eat.
I made that last part up myself."

*Behn to Stewart, when asked to repeat what his father said about eating the blossoms and leaving the greens*

**5.** STEWART: "What happened, Mother? Why did we all run?"
BAMBI'S MOTHER: "Man was in the forest."

**6.** "Mother! Mother, where are you? Mother!"

*Stewart, when his mother is killed by a hunter*

**BANANAS** (UA, 1971). D: Woody Allen. S: Woody Allen, Mickey Rose.

**1.** "I was in the Black Studies program. By now, I could've been black."

*Product-tester Woody Allen (Fielding Mellish), on the career he could have had if he'd stayed in college*

**2.** "I may be bombing an office building, but I'll find out."

*Radical activist Louise Lasser (Nancy) to Allen, discussing her plans for Saturday*

**3.** "Well, freedom is wonderful. On the other hand, if you're dead, it's a tremendous drawback to your sex life."

*Allen, on choosing between freedom and death*

**4.** "What's the Spanish word for straitjacket?"

*Allen, on hearing the insane new president of San Marcos give a speech*

**5.** "You've gotta be smart to be a president. Let me be vice president, that's a real idiot's job."

*Allen, on being asked to become president of San Marcos*

**6.** AIDE TO PRESIDENT ALLEN: "What is the chief export of San Marcos?"
ALLEN: "Dysentery."

**LAST LINE**

**7.** "Now, on behalf of Nancy and Fielding Mellish and all of the others who have made this possible, this is Howard Cosell thanking you for joining us and wishing you a most pleasant good night."

*Howard Cosell (Himself), having provided live coverage of Allen's and Lasser's wedding night*

## BAND WAGON, THE (MGM, 1953). D: Vincente Minnelli. S: Betty Comden, Adolph Green.

**1.** "Well, he was good twelve to fifteen years ago, but the columnists out there say he's through."

*Train passenger, about Fred Astaire (Tony Hunter)*

**2.** "I can stand anything but pain."

*Oscar Levant (Lester Marton), after having his foot stepped on on Forty-Second Street, New York City*

**3.** "This story's a modern version of Faust."

*Jack Buchanan (Jeffrey Cordova), on Levant and Nanette Fabray's (Lily Marton's) idea for a musical comedy about a children's book illustrator*

**4.** BUCHANAN: "Just like Faust, this man is tempted by the devil. And his compromise, his sellout, must end in eternal damnation."
LEVANT: "That'll leave them laughing."

**5.** " 'Did you ever try spreading ideals on a cracker?' "

*Astaire to Cyd Charisse (Gaby Berard), reading a line from Buchanan's ill-fated Faust musical*

**6.** "I can stand anything but failure."

*Levant, when the Faust version of* The Band Wagon *flops*

**7.** " 'She was bad. She was dangerous. I wouldn't trust her any farther than I could throw her. But she was my kind of woman.' "

*Astaire, at the end of the number "The Girl Hunt"*

**8.** "The show's going to run a long time. As far as I'm concerned, it's going to run forever."

*Charisse to Astaire, after the successful premiere of the revised* The Band Wagon

**LAST LINE**

**9.** "Tony, may we say something?"

*Fabray, Buchanan, and Levant before breaking into the song "That's Entertainment"*

## BANG THE DRUM SLOWLY (Paramount, 1973). D: John Hancock. S: Mark Harris. Fr: Mark Harris (novel).

**FIRST LINE**

**1.** "You're drivin' along with a man who's been told he's dyin', and yet everything keeps goin' on."

*Michael Moriarty (Henry Wiggen), in voice-over about Robert De Niro (Bruce Pierson)*

**2.** "All right, I will agree to the clause."

*Vincent Gardenia (Dutch Schnell) to Moriarty, on the clause in his contract that keeps De Niro on the team*

**3.** "You gotta get hip like them guys, man. That's part of . . . you know, the whole image of a baseball player. He has to look good. Why don't you like, you know, read some kind of fashion magazines, something like* Esquire?*"

*Fellow ballplayer to the unhip De Niro*

**4.** "How can he be so sick and play so well?"

*Patrick McVey (Pierson's Father) to Moriarty*

**5.** "Hey, Arthur, don't forget to send me a scorecard from the Series."

*De Niro to Moriarty, as his illness prevents him from going to the World Series*

**6.** "He wasn't a bad fellow, no worse than most and probably no better than some, and not a bad ball player neither when they gave him the chance, when they laid off him long enough. From here on in I rag nobody."

*Moriarty, in voice-over*

**BANK DICK, THE** *(Universal, 1940). D: Eddie Cline. S: Mahatma Kane Jeeves, (pseudonym for W. C. Fields).*

**1.** "I never smoked a cigarette until I was nine."

*W. C. Fields (Egbert Sousé)*

**BAREFOOT CONTESSA, THE** *(UA, 1954). D: Joseph L. Mankiewicz. S: Joseph L. Mankiewicz.*

**1.** "Just this once, Kirk, why don't you empty your own ashtrays?"

*Edmond O'Brien (Oscar Muldoon) to Warren Stevens (Kirk Edwards)*

**BAREFOOT IN THE PARK** *(Paramount, 1967). D: Gene Saks. S: Neil Simon. Fr: Neil Simon (play).*

**1.** "So long, Gramercy 5-9971. Have a nice marriage. And may you soon have many extensions."

*Herb Edelman (Harry Pepper), after installing a telephone for the newlyweds*

**2.** "I remember when you were a little girl. You said you wanted to live on the moon. I thought you were joking."

*Mildred Natwick (Mrs. Banks) to daughter Jane Fonda (Corie Bratter), after climbing the several flights to Fonda's apartment*

**3.** "Once a month, I try to make pretty, young girls nervous, just to keep my ego from going out."

*Charles Boyer (Victor Velasco) to Fonda*

**4.** "You know what you are, Paul? You're a watcher. You're a watcher. There are watchers in this world and there are doers. And the watchers sit around watching the doers do. Well, tonight, you watched and I did."

*Fonda to Redford*

**5.** FONDA: "You have absolutely no sense of the ridiculous. Like last Thursday night, you wouldn't walk barefoot with me in Washington Square Park. Why not?"
REDFORD: "Simple answer. It was seventeen degrees."
FONDA: "Exactly. It's very logical. It's very sensible, but it's no fun."

**6.** "Oh, good, they made up."
*Natwick, on the young couple*

**BARKLEYS OF BROADWAY, THE** *(MGM, 1949). D: Charles Walters. S: Betty Comden, Adolph Green.*

**1.** "I find that girl completely resistible."
*Oscar Levant (Ezra Miller)*

**BARTON FINK** *(20th Century–Fox, 1991). D: Joel Coen. S: Ethan Coen, Joel Coen.*

**1.** "We all want it to have that Barton Fink feeling. I mean, I guess we all have that Barton Fink feeling, but since you're Barton Fink, I'm assuming you have it in spades."

*Michael Lerner (Lipnick), the studio head, to John Turturro (Barton Fink), a playwright and would-be screenwriter*

**2.** "I create for a living. I'm a creator. This is my uniform. This is how I serve the common man."

*Turturro, pointing to his head*

**3.** "We're only interested in one thing. Can you tell a story, Bart? Can you make us laugh? Can you make us cry? Can you make us want to break out in joyous song? Is that more than one thing? Okay."

*Lerner to Turturro*

**4.** "The life of the mind. There's no road map for that territory. Exploring it can be painful. I have a pain most people don't know anything about."

*Turturro to John Goodman (Charlie Meadows), a traveling insurance salesman*

**5.** "Maybe I only had one idea in me. My play. Maybe, once that was done, I was done being a writer."

*Turturro to Goodman, on his writer's block*

**BATMAN** *(Warner Bros., 1989). D: Tim Burton. S: Sam Hamm, Warren Skaaren. Fr: Bob Kane, DC Comics (characters).*

**1.** MICHAEL KEATON (*Batman/Bruce Wayne*), dangling mugger over roof's edge: "I'm not going to kill you. I want you to do me a favor. I want you to tell all your friends about me."
MUGGER: "What are you?"
KEATON: "I'm Batman."

**2.** "Lieutenant, is there a six-foot bat in Gotham City? And if so, is he on the police payroll? And if so, what's he pulling down—after taxes?"

*Reporter Robert Wuhl (Alexander Knox) to police lieutenant*

**3.** JACK PALANCE (*Boss Carl Grissom*): "Jack—listen. Maybe we can cut a deal."
JACK NICHOLSON (*Joker/Jack Napier*): "Jack? Jack is dead, my friend. You can call me—Joker. And as you can see, I'm a lot happier."

**4.** "Eh, what a day."
*Nicholson, after killing Palance*

**5.** "Wait'll they get a load of me."
*Nicholson, after reading a newspaper headline calling Keaton a "winged freak"*

**6.** "Can somebody tell me what kind of a world we live in where a man dressed up as a bat gets all of my press?"

*Nicholson, after watching TV news about Keaton*

**7.** "Where does he get those wonderful toys?"

*Nicholson, impressed by another display of Keaton's gadgetry*

**8.** KIM BASINGER (*Vicki Vale*): "I mean, let's face it. You're not exactly normal, are you?"
KEATON: "It's not exactly a normal world, is it?"

**9.** "Did you ever dance with the devil in the pale moonlight?"

*Nicholson to Keaton, just before trying to kill him; also said in variant form by Nicholson as a younger man to Keaton as a boy, and later by Keaton to Nicholson*

**10.** "Please inform the citizens of Gotham that Gotham City's earned a rest from crime. But if the forces of evil should rise again to cast a shadow on the heart of the city, call me."

*Keaton's letter to the city, read by Billy Dee Williams (Harvey Dent)*

**LAST LINES**

**11.** MICHAEL GOUGH (*Alfred*) the butler: "Mr. Wayne told me to tell you that he might be a little late."

BASINGER: "I'm not a bit surprised."

**BATMAN RETURNS** (*Warner Bros., 1992*). D: Tim Burton. S: Daniel Waters, Sam Hamm. Fr: Daniel Waters, Sam Hamm (story), Bob Kane, DC Comics (characters).

**1.** "I don't know about you, Miss Kitty, but I feel—so much yummier."

*Michelle Pfeiffer (Catwoman/Selina Kyle), after becoming Catwoman*

**2.** "I'm Catwoman. Hear me roar."

*Pfeiffer*

**3.** "One can never have too much power. If my life has a meaning, that's the meaning."

*Christopher Walken (Max Shreck)*

**4.** "Meow."

*Pfeiffer to Michael Keaton (Batman/Bruce Wayne) and Danny DeVito (Penguin/Oswald Cobblepot)*

**5.** "Life's a bitch. Now so am I."

*Pfeiffer to Keaton*

**6.** "He knocked me off a building just when I was starting to feel good about myself."

*Pfeiffer, complaining about Keaton*

**7.** KEATON (*as Wayne*): "You have kind of a . . . kind of a dark side, don't you?"

PFEIFFER (*as Kyle*): "No darker than yours, Bruce."

**8.** "It's the so-called normal guys who always let you down. Sickos never scare me. At least they're committed."

*Pfeiffer (as Kyle) to Keaton (as Wayne)*

**9.** "Oh, please. I wouldn't touch you to scratch you."

*Pfeiffer, resisting DeVito's advances*

**10.** "Oh, my God. Does this mean we have to start fighting?"

*Pfeiffer (as Selina) to Keaton (as Wayne), when they each find out the other's secret identity*

**11.** "They wouldn't put me on a pedestal, so I'm layin' 'em on a slab."

*DeVito, on his plot to destroy Gotham City with missiles launched by penguins*

**LAST LINE**

**12.** "Merry Christmas, Alfred. Goodwill toward men—and women."

*Keaton (as Wayne) to Michael Gough (Alfred) the butler, thinking of Pfeiffer*

**BATTLEGROUND** (*MGM, 1949*). D: William A. Wellman. S: Robert Pirosh.

**LAST LINE**

**1.** "One, two, three, four, one, two, three, four . . . "

*Marching soldiers*

**BEASTMASTER, THE** (*MGM/UA, 1982*). D: Don Coscarelli. S: Don Coscarelli, Paul Pepperman.

**LAST LINE**

*1.* "You trained Tal well, and he will make a fine king."

*Marc Singer (Dar), on Josh Milrad (Tal)*

**BEAT THE DEVIL** (UA, 1954). D: John Huston. S: John Huston, Truman Capote. Fr: James Helvick (novel).

*1.* "Harry, we must beware of those men. They're desperate characters. . . . Not one of them looked at my legs."

*Jennifer Jones (Gwendolyn Chelm) to Edward Underdown (Harry Chelm)*

**BEAUTY AND THE BEAST** (Buena Vista, 1991). D: Kirk Wise, Gary Trousdale. S: Linda Woolverton. Fr: Kelly Asbury, Brenda Chapman, Tom Ellery, Kevin Harkey, Robert Lence, Burny Mattinson, et al. (story).

*1.* "So, you've come to stare at the beast, have you?"

*Robby Benson (The Beast)*

*2.* "As I always say, if it isn't baroque, don't fix it."

*David Ogden Stiers (Cogsworth)*

*3.* "There's the usual things: flowers, choco-lates, promises you don't intend to keep."

*Stiers, advising Benson on how to court Paige O'Hara (Belle)*

*4.* "The girl has lost her father and her free-dom all in one day."

*Angela Lansbury (Mrs. Potts)*

*5.* "You fall in love with her. She falls in love with you. And poof, the spell is broken. We'll be human again by midnight!"

*Jerry Ohrbach (Lumière) to Benson*

*6.* BENSON: "You'll come out or I'll break down the door!"

OHRBACH: "Master, I could be wrong, but that may not be the best way to win the girl's affection."

*7.* BENSON, after he gets wounded rescuing Belle from the wolves: "If you hadn't run away, this wouldn't have happened."

O'HARA: "If you hadn't frightened me, I wouldn't have run away."

**LAST LINE**

*8.* "Do I still have to sleep in the cupboard?"

*Bradley Michael Pierce (Chip), the teacup trans-formed into a child*

**BECKY SHARP** (RKO, 1935). D: Rouben Mamoulian. S: Francis Edward Faragoh. Fr: Langdon Mitchell (play), William M. Thack-eray (novel, Vanity Fair).

*1.* "Oh, no, Laura, no tears. We orphans must learn that the luxury of emotions is for our betters."

*Miriam Hopkins (Becky Sharp) to friend, on not shedding tears for leaving school*

*2.* "Life owes me many things, and I intend to get them."

*Hopkins, to Alan Mowbray (Rawdon Crawley)*

*3.* "I'm not very good at giving answers; I so seldom listen to the questions."

*Hopkins on giving answers to a suitor*

*4.* "I am flattered that a midnight visit from the wolf should prove so exciting to a lamb of your coolness and self-possession."

*Cedric Hardwicke (Marquis of Steyne) to mar-ried woman Hopkins*

**5.** "Returning husbands can hardly be called intruders."

*Hopkins to Hardwicke, on her husband Mowbray*

**6.** "Why bother? Why squabble about something that you don't own and I don't want?"

*Hardwicke to Mowbray, on fighting over his wife Hopkins*

**7.** "Oh, they'll laugh at me. Oh, how they'll laugh."

*Hopkins, after Mowbray leaves her, facing the most bitter pill*

**8.** "Well, you can forget about it if you drink enough brandy."

*Hopkins, on the past*

**BEDTIME FOR BONZO** *(Universal, 1951). D: Frederick De Cordova. S: Val Burton, Lou Breslow. Fr: Raphael David Blau, Ted Berkman (story).*

**1.** "Even a monkey, brought up in the right surroundings, can learn the meaning of decency and honesty."

*Ronald Reagan (Professor Peter Boyd) to Diana Lynn (Jane), as he tries to prove that individuals are shaped by their environments*

**2.** "Who expects a psychologist to think? Especially when you're so busy thinking what you think other people are thinking."

*Walter Slezak (Professor Hans Neumann) to Reagan*

**LAST LINE**
**3.** "By golly, I'm the richest man in six counties."

*Reagan to Lynn and Bonzo*

**BEETLEJUICE** *(Warner Bros., 1988). D: Tim Burton. S: Michael McDowell, Warren Skaaren. Fr: Michael McDowell, Larry Wilson (story).*

**LAST LINE**
**1.** "Oh, hey, wait a, hey, stop it, hey, you're messing up my hair. Come on, whoa, whoa, stop it. Whoa. Hey, this might be a good look for me."

*Michael Keaton (Betelgeuse), getting his head shrunk in the waiting room of the hereafter*

**BEING THERE** *(UA, 1979). D: Hal Ashby. S: Jerzy Kosinski. Fr: Jerzy Kosinski (novel).*

**1.** "This is just like television, only you can see much further."

*Peter Sellers (Chauncey Gardener), a former recluse, to Shirley MacLaine (Eve Rand), on looking out a car window*

**2.** "An old habit that goes along with power. Keep them waiting."

*Melvyn Douglas (Benjamin Rand) to Sellers, referring to keeping Jack Warden (President Bobby) waiting*

**3.** "On television, Mr. President, you look much smaller."

*Sellers to Warden*

**4.** "As long as the roots are not severed, all is well, and all will be well in the garden."

*Sellers to Warden, who mistakes Sellers's gardening wisdom for economic genius*

**5.** "All you got to be is white in America to get whatever you want."

*Ruth Attaway (Louise), remarking on the position Sellers has reached despite his idiocy*

**6.** "You have the gift of being natural. That's a great talent, my boy."

*Douglas to Sellers*

**7.** "I like to watch TV."

*Sellers to Laurie Jefferson (a TV reporter)*

**8.** "I've seen this before. It happens to old people."

*Sellers, when Douglas dies*

**LAST LINE**
**9.** "Life is a state of mind."

*Warden, eulogizing Douglas*

**BELL, BOOK, AND CANDLE** (Columbia, 1958). D: Richard Quine. S: Daniel Taradash. Fr: John Van Druten (play).

**1.** "What would you say if I told you I was a witch?"

*Elsa Lanchester (Queenie) to Kim Novak (Gillian Holrody), imagining a mortal's reaction to her confession*

**2.** "Don't you ever wish that you weren't what we are?"

*Novak to Lanchester*

**3.** "I'm not drunk. I may be intoxicated, but I'm not drunk."

*James Stewart (Shepard Henderson) to Janice Rule (Merle Kittridge)*

**4.** "Ring the bell. Close the book. Quench the candle. That's how they used to exorcise them—put them out of business—in medieval times, of course."

*Ernie Kovacs (Sidney Redlitch) to Stewart, referring to witches*

**5.** "There's always a rational explanation, if you want it."

*Novak to Stewart, on how mortals explain away magic*

**6.** "It never pays to get mixed up with human beings."

*Jack Lemmon (Mickey Holrody) to Lanchester*

**LAST LINES**
**7.** STEWART: "Who's to say what magic is? Oh, Gill, don't you want to stop crying now?"
    NOVAK: "I don't think I can. I'm only human."

**BELLS ARE RINGING** (MGM, 1960). D: Vincente Minnelli. S: Betty Comden, Adolph Green. Fr: Betty Comden, Adolph Green, Jule Styne (musical play).

**LAST LINE**
**1.** "And so, ladies and gentlemen, you, too, like this satisfied customer, can solve all your problems by subscribing to an answering service."

*Narrator, on Dean Martin (Jeffrey Moss), who is satisfied by answering-service operator Judy Holliday (Ella Peterson)*

**BELLS OF ST. MARY'S, THE** (RKO, 1945). D: Leo McCarey. S: Dudley Nichols. Fr: Leo McCarey (story).

**1.** "Did anyone ever tell you that you have a dishonest face—for a priest, I mean?"

*Ingrid Bergman (Sister Benedict) to Bing Crosby (Father Chuck O'Malley)*

**2.** CROSBY: "If you ever need anything, no matter what it is or wherever you happen to be—"
    BERGMAN: "Yes, I know. I just dial O for O'Malley."

**BEN-HUR** (MGM, 1959). D: William Wyler. S: Karl Tunberg. Fr: Lew Wallace (novel).

**1.** "Rome is an affront to God. Rome is strangling my people and my country and the whole earth."

Charlton Heston (Judah Ben-Hur) to his Roman friend Stephen Boyd (Messala)

**2.** "Your eyes are full of hate, Forty-One. That's good. Hate keeps a man alive."

Roman officer Jack Hawkins (Quintus Arrius) to galley slave Heston, known by his number, Forty-One

**3.** "We keep you alive to serve this ship. Row well and live."

Heston, having rescued Hawkins from the wreckage of his ship, repeating back Hawkins's advice to the galley slaves

**4.** "In his eagerness to save you, your God has also saved the Roman fleet."

Hawkins to Heston

**LAST LINE**
**5.** "And I felt His voice take the sword out of my hand."

Heston, on Claude Heater (The Christ)

**BEST MAN, THE** (UA, 1964). D: Franklin J. Schaffner. S: Gore Vidal. Fr: Gore Vidal (play).

**1.** "He has every characteristic of a dog except loyalty."

Henry Fonda (William Russell), about Cliff Robertson (Joe Cantwell)

**BEST YEARS OF OUR LIVES, THE** (RKO, 1946). D: William Wyler. S: Robert E. Sherwood. Fr: MacKinlay Kantor (novella, Glory for Me).

**1.** "I hope Wilma is a swell girl."

Returning World War II veteran Fredric March (Al Stephenson) to fellow veteran Dana Andrews (Fred Derry), referring to the girlfriend of Harold Russell (Homer Parrish), left handless in the war

**2.** "Some of them look brand new, from the factory to the scrap heap. That's all they're good for now."

Andrews, on seeing no-longer-needed warplanes at the airfield

**3.** "They couldn't train him to put his arms around his girl, or stroke her hair."

March, on the training Russell got in the use of his prosthetic hooks

**4.** "Feels as if I were going in to hit a beach."

March, outside the door of his home, anxious about entering

**5.** "I look terrible."

Myrna Loy's (Millie Stephenson's) first words after her husband March surprises her with his return

**6.** "I tried to stop them, to keep them just as they were when you left, but they got away from me."

Loy to March, about how much the children grew while he was away

**7.** "It isn't easy for those Air Force glamour boys when they get grounded. Now, when you've been in the infantry, any change is bound to be an improvement."

March to Loy, about Andrews's postwar problems

**8.** "Last year it was kill Japs and this year it's make money."

March, on how quickly he is expected to readjust to civilian life

**9.** "Whenever I get wise to myself, I guess. Whenever I wake up and realize I'm not an officer and a gentleman anymore, I'm just another soda jerk out of a job."

*Andrews, discussing his future with unsympathetic wife Virginia Mayo (Virginia Derry)*

**10.** "I haven't called you a heel—yet."

*March, arguing with Andrews about the latter's interest in March's daughter, Teresa Wright (Peggy)*

**11.** "We fought the wrong people, that's all. Just read the facts, my friend. Find out for yourself why you had to lose your hands, and then go out and do something about it."

*Ray Teal (Mr. Mollett), a fascist at the drugstore counter questioning why Russell lost his hands in the war*

**12.** "Don't say it, chum. The customer's always right, so I'm fired. But this customer wasn't right."

*Soda jerk Andrews to his boss at the drugstore, after punching Teal*

**13.** "This is when I know I'm helpless. My hands are down there on the bed. I can't put them on again without calling to somebody for help. Can't smoke a cigarette or read a book. If that door should blow shut, I can't open it to get out of this room. I'm as dependent as a baby that doesn't know how to get anything except to cry for it."

*Russell to his girlfriend Cathy O'Donnell (Wilma Cameron)*

**14.** "I gave up the best years of my life, and what have you done? You flopped!"

*Mayo, berating Andrews for his failure to hold a job after the war*

**15.** "I used to work in one of those."

*Andrews, looking at a bomber*

LAST LINE

**16.** "You know what it'll be, don't you, Peggy? It may take us years to get anywhere. We'll have no money, no decent place to live. We'll have to work, get kicked around . . ."

*Andrews to Wright, just before they kiss*

**BEVERLY HILLS COP** *(Paramount, 1984). D: Martin Brest. S: Daniel Petrie, Jr. Fr: Daniel Petrie, Jr., Danilo Bach (story).*

**1.** "I was going to call the article 'Michael Jackson Is Sitting on Top of the World,' but now I think I might as well just call it 'Michael Jackson Can Sit on Top of the World Just as Long as He Doesn't Sit in the Beverly Palm Hotel Because There Is No Niggers Allowed in There.'"

*Detroit cop Eddie Murphy (Axel Foley), bluffing his way into a posh Beverly Hills hotel by claiming to be a reporter doing a story on Michael Jackson*

**2.** "This is the cleanest and nicest police car I've ever been in in my life. This thing's nicer than my apartment."

*Murphy to policemen who have arrested him*

**3.** "These aren't just regular cops, okay, they're supercops, and the only things missing on these guys are capes."

*Murphy, covering for John Ashton (Sergeant Taggart) and Judge Reinhold (Detective Billy Rosewood)*

**4.** "Could you put this in a good spot, 'cause all this stuff happened the last time I parked here."

*Murphy, giving his beat-up car to parking valet*

**5.** "Tell Victor that Ramon—the fellow he met about a week ago—tell him that Ramon went to the clinic today and I found out that

I have—um, herpes simplex ten, and I think Victor should go check himself out with his physician to make sure everything is fine before things start falling off on the man."

*Murphy, making up a story to get into a private club to see Steven Berkoff (Victor Maitland)*

**6.** "I got a hunch, okay. That's a technique by which many crimes outside of Beverly Hills get solved."

*Murphy to Reinhold*

**7.** "You want it with a laimon twist?"

*Art gallery employee Bronson Pinchot (Serge), offering drink to Reinhold with his unplaceable foreign accent*

**8.** "It's Billy, he's doin' somethin' dumb again."

*Ashton, on his partner, Reinhold*

**9.** "You do that again, I'll shoot you myself."

*Ashton to Reinhold, when he almost gets them killed*

**10.** STEPHEN ELLIOTT (*Chief Hubbard*): "What's this man doing here?"
    MURPHY: "Bleeding, sir."

**11.** "You were lying your head off."

*Murphy, admiringly, to Ronny Cox (Lieutenant Bogomil)*

**LAST LINE**
**12.** "I know the perfect place, you guys will love it. Trust me."

*Murphy to Reinhold and Ashton*

**BEYOND THE FOREST** (*Warner Bros., 1949*). D: King Vidor. S: Lenore Coffee. Fr: Stuart Engstrand (novel).

**1.** "What a dump!"

*Bette Davis (Rosa Moline)*

**BIG** (*20th Century–Fox, 1988*). D: Penny Marshall. S: Gary Ross, Anne Spielberg.

**1.** "I wish I were big."

*David Moscow (Young Josh Baskin), making a wish to a mystical carnival machine that results in him growing up overnight into Tom Hanks*

**2.** "Okay, but I get to be on top."

*Hanks, allowing Elizabeth Perkins (Susan Lawrence) to sleep over, as long as Hanks can sleep in the top bunk*

**BIG BROADCAST OF 1938, THE** (*Paramount, 1938*). D: Mitchell Leisen. S: Walter DeLeon, Francis Martin, Ken Englund. Fr: Frederick H. Brennan (story), Howard Lindsay, Russel Crouse (adaptation).

**1.** "I can lick my weight in wildflowers."

*W. C. Fields (T. Frothingwell Bellows/S. B. Bellows)*

**2.** "Never mind what I tell you to do—do what I tell you."

*Fields*

**BIG CHILL, THE** (*Columbia, 1983*). D: Lawrence Kasdan. S: Lawrence Kasdan, Barbara Benedek.

**1.** "Amazing tradition. They throw a great party for you on the one day they know you can't come."

*Jeff Goldblum (Michael) to William Hurt (Nick), at the funeral luncheon of their friend Alex*

**2.** TOM BERENGER (*Sam*): "Who would have thought we'd both make so much bread? Two revolutionaries."
    KEVIN KLINE (*Harold*): "Yeah. Good thing it's not important to us."

**3.** "I just didn't think they'd be so guilty."

*Mary Kay Place (Meg) to group, on her clients as a public defender*

**4.** "There is no other music, not in my house."

*Kline to group, on 1960s pop music*

**5.** "Where I work, we have only one editorial rule. We can't write anything longer than the average person can read during the average crap."

*Goldblum to the group, on the editorial policy of* People *magazine*

**6.** "Don't knock rationalization. Where would we be without it? I don't know anybody who can get through the day without two or three juicy rationalizations. They're more important than sex. . . . Have you ever gone a week without a rationalization?"

*Goldblum to Berenger*

**7.** "You've given me a massive headache."

*Berenger to Place, when she asks him to father her child*

**8.** "This is a big decision. I'll get back to you in the third quarter."

*Place to Goldblum, on his offer to father her child*

**9.** "I don't like talking about my past as much as you guys do."

*Meg Tilly (Chloe) to Hurt*

**10.** "I don't know why anyone does anything. I don't know why I chose these socks this morning."

*Hurt to group, speculating about the reasons behind Alex's suicide*

**11.** "I haven't met that many happy people in my life. How do they act?"

*Tilly to group, on whether her lover Alex was happy*

**12.** "A long time ago we knew each other for a short period. . . . It was easy back then. No one had a cushier berth than we did. It's not surprising our friendship could survive that. It's only out there in the real world that it gets tough."

*Hurt to group*

**13.** "This bed has always been lucky for Sarah and me."

*Kline to Place, on the bed in which he is to father Place's child*

**14.** "I feel like I got a great break on a used car."

*Place, about to sleep with Kline*

**15.** "Did you have to be in such a good mood?"

*Glenn Close (Sarah) to Kline, on the morning after he and Place have slept together*

**LAST LINE**
**16.** "That won't be necessary. You see, Sarah, Harold, we took a secret vote. We're not leaving. We're never leaving."

*Goldblum to Close and Kline*

**BIG SLEEP, THE** *(Warner Bros., 1946). D: Howard Hawks. S: William Faulkner, Jules Furthman, Leigh Brackett. Fr: Raymond Chandler (novel).*

**1.** "You're not very tall, are you?"

*Girlish vamp Martha Vickers's (Carmen Sternwood's) first words to private eye Humphrey Bogart (Philip Marlowe)*

**2.** "Nice state of affairs when a man has to indulge his vices by proxy."

*Charles Waldron (General Sternwood), sick, aging millionaire forbidden to drink liquor, to Bogart, whom he has invited to have a drink*

**3.** "Then she tried to sit in my lap while I was standing up."

*Bogart to Charles D. Brown (Norris), the butler, on Vickers's antics*

**4.** "They're alike only in having the same corrupt blood. Vivian is spoiled, exacting, smart, and ruthless. Carmen is still a little child who likes to pull the wings off flies. I assume they have all the usual vices, besides those they've invented for themselves."

*Waldron, on his daughters Lauren Bacall (Vivian) and Vickers (Carmen)*

**5.** BROWN: "Are you attempting to tell me my duties, sir?"
BOGART: "No, just having fun trying to guess what they are."

**6.** "So you're a private detective. I didn't know they existed, except in books—or else they were greasy little men snooping around hotel corridors."

*Bacall, taunting Bogart*

**7.** "I don't mind if you don't like my manners. I don't like them myself. They're pretty bad. I grieve over them long winter evenings."

*Bogart*

**8.** "So you do get up. I was beginning to think perhaps you worked in bed, like Marcel Proust."

*Bacall to Bogart, after waiting a long time for him outside his office*

**9.** "My, my, my, such a lot of guns around town and so few brains."

*Bogart*

**10.** BOGART, comparing Bacall to a horse: "You've got a touch of class, but, uh . . . I don't know how—how far you can go."
BACALL: "A lot depends on who's in the saddle."

**11.** "Somebody's always giving me guns."

*Bogart, disarming yet another thug*

**12.** "I like that. I'd like more."

*Bacall, when Bogart kisses her*

**13.** "You want me to count three or something, like a movie?"

*Hired killer Bob Steele (Canino), as he threatens the doomed Elisha Cook, Jr. (Jones); repeated by Bogart later to Steele's boss John Ridgely (Eddie Mars)*

**14.** "Too many people told me to stop."

*Humphrey Bogart, explaining why he stayed on the Sternwood case*

**15.** "Look, Angel, I'm tired. My jaw hurts and my ribs ache. I killed a man back there, and I had to stand by while a harmless little guy was killed."

*Bogart to Bacall*

**LAST LINES**
**16.** BOGART: "What's wrong with you?"
BACALL: "Nothing you can't fix."

**BIG STORE, THE** *(MGM, 1941). D: Charles Reisner. S: Sid Kuller, Hal Firnberg, Ray Golden. Fr: Nat Perrin (story).*

**1.** MARGARET DUMONT *(Martha)* to her beau GROUCHO MARX *(Wolf J. Flywheel)*: "Oh, where did you ever learn to write such beautiful poetry?"
GROUCHO: "I worked five years for Burma Shave."

**2.** MARX: "Martha dear, there are many bonds that will hold us together through eternity."

DUMONT: "Really, Wolf? What are they?"

MARX: "Your government bonds, your savings bonds, your liberty bonds . . . "

**BILLY BUDD** (UK: UA, 1962). D: Peter Ustinov. S: Peter Ustinov, Robert Rossen. Fr: Herman Melville (novel).

**1.** "God bless Captain Vere!"

*Terence Stamp (Billy Budd) to Peter Ustinov (Edward Fairfax Vere)*

**BILOXI BLUES** (Universal, 1988). D: Mike Nichols. S: Neil Simon. Fr: Neil Simon (play).

**LAST LINE**

**1.** "I liked it for the most selfish reason of all, because I was young. We all were, me and Epstein and Wykowski, Selridge, Carney, Hennesey, and even Sergeant Toomey. I didn't really like most of those guys then, but today I love every damn one of them. Life is weird, you know."

*Matthew Broderick (Eugene), thinking back on why he liked the Army*

**BIRDMAN OF ALCATRAZ** (UA, 1962). D: John Frankenheimer. S: Guy Trosper. Fr: Thomas E. Gaddis (book).

**1.** "That's the island of Alcatraz. There's a man leaving there today after seventy years imprisonment. He spent most of his life behind bars, including forty-three years in solitary confinement. He has never used a telephone, or driven an automobile. The last time he broke bread with another human being was in 1916, the year Kaiser Wilhelm ordered the sinking of the *Lusitania* in World War I."

*Edmond O'Brien (Tom Gaddis), in narration*

**2.** "You ain't got much, Stroud, but you keep subtracting from it."

*Prison guard Graham Denton (Kramer) to Burt Lancaster (Robert Stroud), the "Birdman of Alcatraz"*

**3.** "Look around you, Stroud. This is going to be your home for as long as you live."

*Karl Malden (Warden Shoemaker) to Lancaster*

**4.** "Well, I guess they won't mind. Canaries are always behind bars anyway."

*Neville Brand (Bull Ransom), when Lancaster tells him canaries are going to be born inside Alacatraz*

**5.** "Go out there and bite the stars for me. Find yourself a fat mama and make a family. You hear?"

*Lancaster to a bird he is trying to set free*

**6.** "One thing I've learned is not to abuse time."

*Lancaster to Betty Field (Stella Johnson)*

**7.** "You're always bringing me new words, like love and faith."

*Lancaster to Field*

**8.** "What's wrong with dying? 'Cause life is too precious a gift. That's why. Because the first duty of life is to live."

*Lancaster*

**BIRTH OF A NATION, THE** (Epoch Producing Co., 1915). D: D. W. Griffith. S: D. W. Griffith, Frank E. Woods. Fr: Thomas Dixon, Jr. (novel/play, The Clansman), Thomas Dixon, Jr. (novel, The Leopard's Spots).

**1.** "The bringing of the African to America planted the first seed of disunion."

*Title*

**2.** "I shall deal with them as though they had never been away."

*Joseph Henaberry (Abraham Lincoln), on the defeated South*

**3.** "Sic semper tyrannis!"

*Raoul Walsh (John Wilkes Booth), on assassinating Henaberry*

**4.** "Our best friend is gone. What is to become of us now?"

*Southern aristocrat Spottiswood Aitken (Dr. Cameron), on the death of Henaberry*

**5.** "This is an historical presentation of the Civil War and Reconstruction Period, and is not meant to reflect on any race or people of today."

*Title after intermission, disclaiming responsibility*

**6.** "The white men were roused by a mere instinct of self-preservation . . . until at last there had sprung into existence a great Ku Klux Klan, a veritable empire of the South, to protect the Southern country."

*Woodrow Wilson, from "History of the American People," according to title*

**7.** "We shall wish the white South under the heel of the black South."

*Radical Republican Ralph Lewis (Austin Stoneman) to mulatto George Siegmann (Silas Lynch)*

**8.** "I want to marry a white woman."

*Mulatto Siegmann to Lewis, expressing the film's cardinal sin*

**LAST LINE**
**9.** "Liberty and union, one and inseparable, *now and forever!*"

*End title*

**BIRTH OF THE BLUES, THE** *(Paramount, 1941). D: Victor Schertzinger. S: Harry Tugend, Walter DeLeon. Fr: Harry Tugend (story).*

**LAST LINE**
**1.** "That ain't mine. That's gonna be everybody's blue music."

*Bing Crosby (Jeff Lambert)*

**BLACK SUNDAY** *(Paramount, 1977). D: John Frankenheimer. S: Ernest Lehman, Ivan Moffat, Kenneth Ross. Fr: Thomas Harris (novel).*

**1.** "People of America. This situation is unbearable for us. From now on, you will share our suffering. The choice is yours."

*Marthe Keller (Dalia Iyad), a terrorist, making threats*

**2.** "If peace, if real peace, ever comes to Israel, you won't know how to live anymore. They'll have to put you down like an old war dog."

*Robert Shaw (David Kabakov), an Israeli soldier, to Steven Keats (Morshevsky)*

**3.** "For thirty years, I have been killing and murdering. What have I achieved? Same world. Same wars. Same enemies. Same friends. And same victims."

*Shaw to Keats*

**4.** "Doubt has entered in. That's no good."

*Shaw to Keats*

**5.** "My mother once said, 'Anybody who has a nervous breakdown, has got something wrong with them.' "

*Shaw to Keats*

**6.** "Colonel, we have fought many battles on opposite sides. We've had some victories. We've had some defeats. If this happens, for both of us, it is a defeat."

*Shaw to Walter Gotell (Colonel Riaf), referring to Black September's plan to destroy the Super Bowl*

**BLADE RUNNER** *(Warner Bros./Ladd Co., 1982). D: Ridley Scott. S: Hampton Fancher, David Peoples. Fr: Philip K. Dick (novel, Do Androids Dream of Electric Sheep?).*

**1.** "Wake up. Time to die."

*Android Brion James (Leon) to Harrison Ford (Deckard)*

**2.** "I don't know why he saved my life. Maybe in those last moments, he loved life more than he ever had before. Not just his life—anybody's life. My life.'"

*Ford, in narration, on why dying android Rutger Hauer (Roy Batty) spared him*

**LAST LINE**

**3.** "Tyrell had told me Rachael was special, no termination date. I didn't know how long we'd have together. Who does?"

*Ford (Deckard), in narration, on android Sean Young (Rachael)*

**BLAZING SADDLES** *(Warner Bros., 1974). D: Mel Brooks. S: Mel Brooks, Norman Steinberg, Andrew Bergman, Richard Pryor, Alan Uger. Fr: Andrew Bergman (story).*

**1.** "What in the wide, wide world of sports is a-going on here?"

*Railroad overseer Slim Pickens (Taggart), finding his henchmen dancing while black railroad workers look on amused*

**2.** "That's all right, shhh, it's all right, Taggart. Just a man and a horse being hung out there."

*Scheming villain Harvey Korman (Hedley Lamarr), comforting his underling Pickens, who is frightened by the sound of a gallows*

**3.** KORMAN, correcting the pronunciation of his name for the umpteenth time: "It's not Hedy, it's Hedley. Hedley Lamarr."

MEL BROOKS *(Governor Lepetomane)*: "What the hell are you worried about? This is 1874. You'll be able to sue her."

**4.** "Excuse me while I whip this out."

*Black sheriff Cleavon Little (Bart), startling the people of Rock Ridge with a multiple-entendre as he pulls out a speech accepting his position as sheriff*

**5.** "Hold it. The next man makes a move, the nigger gets it."

*Little, holding a lynch mob at bay by threatening to shoot himself*

**6.** "Oh, baby, you are so talented, and they are so dumb."

*Little, marveling at his own skill in rescuing himself from the mob*

**7.** "Yeah, but I shoot with this hand."

*Gene Wilder (The Waco Kid), an alcoholic former gunfighter, showing how much his left hand shakes, despite the steadiness of his right hand*

**8.** "You've got to remember that these are just simple farmers. They're people of the land. The common clay of the New West. You know—morons."

*Wilder, comforting Little after his efforts to win over the townspeople have met with insult*

**9.** "No, no, don't do that. Don't do that. If you shoot him, you'll just make him mad."

*Wilder, warning Little not to pack a gun when he goes to face the gargantuan killer Alex Karras (Mongo)*

**10.** "Hello, handsome, is that a ten-gallon hat or are you just enjoying the show?"

*Sultry Teutonic singer Madeline Kahn (Lili Von Shtupp), toying with a cowboy during her stage act*

**11.** "Wilkommen, bienvenu, welcome, c'mon in."

*Kahn's Cabaret-inspired way of answering the door*

**12.** "Ooh, a wed wose. How womantic."

*Kahn, lispingly accepting a rose from Little*

**13.** "Tell me, schwartzie, is it twue what they say about the way you people are gifted? (*Opens zipper.*) Oh, it's twue. It's twue, it's twue, it's twue . . . "

*Kahn, investigating Little's physical endowments in the dark*

**14.** KAHN, at breakfast after their night of passion, handing Little another huge sausage: "Would you care for another schnitzengruben?"

LITTLE: "No, thank you. Fifteen is my limit."

**15.** "Mongo only pawn in game of life."

*Karras, waxing philosophical on himself*

**16.** "Badges? We don't need no stinking badges!"

*Mexican bandit to Korman, quoting The Treasure of the Sierra Madre on being issued a badge for the villainous assault on Rock Ridge*

**17.** "Now, you'll only be risking your lives, whilst I will be risking an almost certain Academy Award nomination for Best Supporting Actor!"

*Korman, delivering a pep talk to his mob of cutthroats*

**18.** "How did he do such fantastic stunts with such little feet?"

*Korman, dying in front of a movie theater while studying the cement footprints of Douglas Fairbanks*

**19.** "Keep the faith, brothers!"

*Little, saying good-bye to the people of Rock Ridge*

**BLOCK-HEADS** (MGM, 1938). D: John G. Blystone. S: Charles Rogers, Felix Adler, James Parrott, Harry Langdon, Arnold Belgard.

**1.** "If I hadn't have seen you, I never would have known you!"

*Stan Laurel (Himself) to Oliver Hardy (Himself)*

**2.** "Remember how dumb I used to be? Well, I'm better now."

*Laurel to Hardy*

**3.** LAUREL: "How long did you say it would take us to get up there?"

HARDY: "Oh, just a jiffy."

LAUREL: "How far's a jiffy?"

HARDY: "About three shakes of a dead lamb's tail."

LAUREL: "Didn't think it was so far. Surprising the distance."

**4.** JAMES FINLAYSON (*Mr. Finn*): "I'm talking to you, you big, overstuffed pollywog!"

HARDY: "You smile when you call me that!"

**5.** LAUREL: "Everybody thought I was dead. Didn't they?"

PATSY MORAN: "How did you find out you weren't?"

LAUREL: "Well, I figured that . . . Well, I saw my picture in the paper. Didn't I?"

**6.** "Anytime I want something done right, I'll always have to do it myself!"

*Hardy, lighting the oven with a match, just before blowing himself up*

**BLONDIE** *(Columbia, 1938). D: Frank R. Strayer. S: Richard Flournoy. Fr: Chic Young (comic strip).*

**LAST LINE**

**1.** "Sometimes I think it's harder to raise a husband than a baby."

*Penny Singleton (Blondie), on Arthur Lake (Dagwood)*

**BLONDIE BRINGS UP BABY** *(Columbia, 1939). D: Frank R. Strayer. S: Gladys Lehman, Richard Flournoy. Fr: Robert Chapin, Karen de Wolf, Richard Flournoy (story), Chic Young (comic strip).*

**LAST LINE**

**1.** "Blondie!"

*Arthur Lake (Dagwood), making his perennial cry for wife Penny Singleton (Blondie)*

**BLOOD ON THE SUN** *(UA, 1945). D: Frank Lloyd. S: Lester Cole. Fr: Garrett Fort (story).*

**LAST LINE**

**1.** "Sure, forgive your enemies, but first get even."

*James Cagney (Nick Condon)*

**BLOW OUT** *(Filmways, 1981). D: Brian DePalma. S: Brian DePalma.*

**LAST LINE**

**1.** "It's a good scream. It's a good scream."

*John Travolta (Jack)*

**BLUE ANGEL, THE** *(Germany: Paramount, 1930). D: Josef von Sternberg. S: Robert Liebmann, Karl Vollmoller, Carl Zuckmayer. Fr: Heinrich Mann (novel, Professor Unrat).*

**1.** "They call me Lola."

*Marlene Dietrich (Lola Frohlich) to Emil Jannings (Professor Immanuel Rath)*

**BLUE VELVET** *(De Laurentiis Entertainment Group, 1986). D: David Lynch. S: David Lynch.*

**1.** "There are opportunities in life for gaining knowledge and experience. Sometimes, it's necessary to take a risk."

*Kyle MacLachlan (Jeffrey Beaumont) to Laura Dern (Sandy Williams), enlisting her help in solving a mystery*

**2.** "I like to sing 'Blue Velvet.'"

*Isabella Rossellini (Dorothy Vallens)*

**3.** "Do it for Van Gogh."

*Dennis Hopper (Frank Booth) to Rossellini*

**LAST LINE**

**4.** "It's a strange world. Isn't it?"

*Dern to MacLachlan*

**BLUES BROTHERS, THE** *(Universal, 1980). D: John Landis. S: John Landis, Dan Aykroyd.*

**1.** "They're not gonna catch us. We're on a mission from God."

*Dan Aykroyd (Elwood) to John Belushi (Jake)*

**2.** WOMAN AT BOARDINGHOUSE: "Are you the police?"

AYKROYD: "No, ma'am. We're musicians."

**3.** "I hate Illinois Nazis."

*Belushi, on watching neo-Nazis march in Illinois*

**4.** "Oh, bad. Thursday night they serve a wicked pepper steak."

*Belushi, on the prison conditions at Joliet*

**BOB AND CAROL AND TED AND ALICE** (Columbia, 1969). D: Paul Mazursky. S: Paul Mazursky, Larry Tucker.

**1.** "First we'll have an orgy, then we'll go see Tony Bennett."

*Elliott Gould (Ted)*

**BODY DOUBLE** (Columbia, 1984). D: Brian DePalma. S: Brian DePalma, Robert J. Avrech. Fr: Brian DePalma (story).

**1.** "We need more comedians in our business."

*Melanie Griffith (Holly), referring to porno movies*

**BODY HEAT** (Warner Bros., 1981). D: Lawrence Kasdan. S: Lawrence Kasdan.

**1.** "You're not too smart, are you? I like that in a man."

*Kathleen Turner (Matty Walker) to William Hurt (Ned Racine)*

**BODYGUARD, THE** (Warner Bros., 1992). D: Mick Jackson. S: Lawrence Kasdan. Fr: Lawrence Kasdan (story).

**1.** "Disapproval is a luxury I can't afford."

*Bodyguard Kevin Costner (Frank Farmer), on whether he disapproves of his client, pop star Whitney Houston (Rachel Marron)*

**2.** "I'm here to keep you alive, not help you shop."

*Costner to Houston, in a boutique*

**3.** "Don't worry, I'll protect you."

*Houston, turning the tables on Costner, when he's startled by the noise of glass breaking while they dance*

**BONNIE AND CLYDE** (Warner Bros.–Seven Arts, 1967). D: Arthur Penn. S: David Newman, Robert Benton.

**1.** "We rob banks."

*Warren Beatty (Clyde Barrow)*

**BORDERTOWN** (Warner Bros., 1935). D: Archie Mayo. S: Laird Doyle, Wallace Smith. Fr: Carroll Graham (novel), Robert Lord (adaptation).

**1.** "The only fun I get is feeding the goldfish, and they only eat once a day."

*Bette Davis (Marie Roark)*

**BORN FREE** (UK: Columbia, 1965). D: James Hill. S: Gerald L. C. Copley. Fr: Joy Adamson (book).

**LAST LINE**
**1.** "We saw her many times again, born free and living free. But to us, she was always the same, our friend Elsa."

*Virginia McKenna (Joy Adamson), on the lion Elsa, whom she and her husband rescued and restored to the wild*

**BORN ON THE FOURTH OF JULY** (Universal, 1989). D: Oliver Stone. S: Oliver Stone, Ron Kovic. Fr: Ron Kovic (autobiography).

LAST LINE

**1.** "Welcome home, Ronnie!"

*Audience member, greeting disabled Vietnam veteran and antiwar spokesperson Tom Cruise (Ron Kovic)*

**BORN YESTERDAY** (Columbia, 1950). D: George Cukor. S: Albert Mannheimer. Fr: Garson Kanin (play).

**1.** "You're just not couth!"

*Judy Holliday (Billie Dawn) to Broderick Crawford (Harry Brock)*

**2.** "Look, when I say I want a whole floor, I don't want one wing and I don't want two wings. I want the whole bird."

*Crawford to a hotel official*

**BOY AND HIS DOG, A** (LQJaf, 1975). D: L. Q. Jones. S: L. Q. Jones. Fr: Harlan Ellison (novella, A Boy and His Dog).

**1.** "Breeding is an ugly thing."

*Tim McIntire (Voice of Blood the dog)*

**2.** "You're starting to sound like a goddamn poodle!"

*Don Johnson (Vic) to McIntire, when McIntire refuses to find him females until he is fed*

**3.** "I locate females. I don't guarantee their behavior."

*McIntire to Johnson, when Johnson complains that a female won't cooperate and give him sexual pleasure*

**BOYS FROM BRAZIL, THE** (20th Century–Fox, 1978). D: Franklin J. Schaffner. S: Heywood Gould. Fr: Ira Levin (novel).

**1.** "It may be a blinding revelation to you that there are Nazis in Paraguay, but I assure you, it is no news to me. And if you stay there much longer, there will still be Nazis in Paraguay, but there will be one less Jewish boy in the world."

*Laurence Olivier (Ezra Lieberman), a Nazi hunter, to Steve Guttenberg (Barry Kohler)*

**2.** "Without help. Without money. Without time. What else is new?"

*Olivier to Lilli Palmer (Esther Lieberman), on how he manages to keep fighting Nazis*

**3.** OLIVIER, referring to GREGORY PECK (*Dr. Josef Mengele*), who is trying to clone little Hitlers: "A sadist with an M.D. and a Ph. D."

BRUNO GANZ (*Professor Bruckner*): "Well, some people would say that's a perfect definition of a scientist."

**4.** "Not Mozart, Doctor. Not Picasso. Not a genius who would enrich the world, but a lonely little boy with a domineering father, a customs officer who was fifty-two when he was born, and an affectionate, doting mother who was twenty-nine. The father died at sixty-five, when the boy was nearly fourteen. Adolph Hitler."

*Olivier to Ganz, referring to Peck's cloning plans*

**5.** "He was thrilled by the idea. The right Hitler for the right future. A Hitler tailor-made for the 1980s, '90s, 2000s."

*Peck to Olivier, on Hitler's reaction to the idea of a clone of himself*

**6.** "Have you ever felt superior to those around you, like a prince among peasants?"

*Peck to Jeremy Black (Bobby Wheelock), a little Hitler*

**BOYS TOWN** *(MGM, 1938). D: Norman Taurog. S: John Meehan, Dore Schary. Fr: Dore Schary, Eleanore Griffin (story).*

**1.** "In a pinch I can be tougher than you are, and I guess maybe this is the pinch."

*Spencer Tracy (Father Flanagan) to Mickey Rooney (Whitey Marsh)*

**LAST LINE**
**2.** "There is no bad boy."

*Tracy*

**BRAM STOKER'S DRACULA** *(Columbia, 1992). D: Francis Ford Coppola. S: James V. Hart. Fr: Bram Stoker (novel, Dracula).*

**1.** "Welcome to my home. Enter freely of your own will and leave some of the happiness you bring."

*Gary Oldman (Dracula), greeting Keanu Reeves (Jonathan Harker)*

**2.** "You will, I trust, excuse me if I do not join you. But I have already dined and I never drink—wine."

*Oldman, serving Reeves, reprising a phrase from the 1931 Dracula*

**3.** "Would you care for an hors d'oeuvre, Dr. Seward, or a canapé?"

*Madman Tom Waits (Renfield), offering a dish of bugs to Richard E. Grant (Dr. Seward)*

**4.** "Do not put your faith in such trinkets of deceit. We are in Transylvania, and Transylvania is not England. Our ways are not your ways, and you shall see many strange things."

*Oldman to Reeves, on the crucifix worn by the latter*

**5.** "I have crossed oceans of time to find you."

*Oldman to Winona Ryder (Mina Murray), whom he takes to be the reincarnation of his lost love Elisabeta*

**6.** "In fact, civilization and syphilization have advanced together."

*Anthony Hopkins (Professor Abraham Van Helsing) to his students*

**7.** "Tell me, Prince. Tell me of your home."

*Ryder to Oldman*

**8.** "It is the cause. It is the cause, my soul. It is Dracula, the undead. The foe I have pursued all my life."

*Hopkins, on identifying Oldman for what he is*

**9.** "No, no, no, not exactly. I just want to cut off her head and take out her heart."

*Hopkins to Grant, on whether he wants to do an autopsy on Sadie Frost (Lucy Westenra), made a vampire by Oldman*

**10.** "She lives beyond the grace of God, a wanderer in the outer darkness. She is Vampyr, Nosferatu."

*Hopkins, on Frost's fate*

**11.** "I am the monster that greedy men would kill. I am Dracula."

*Oldman to Ryder*

**12.** "We've all become God's madmen. All of us."

*Hopkins to his comrades in the fight against Oldman*

**LAST LINE**
**13.** "Give me peace."

*Oldman to Ryder, before she drives the stake into his heart*

**BRAZIL** (UK: Universal, 1985). D: Terry Gilliam. S: Terry Gilliam, Tom Stoppard, Charles McKeown.

**1.** "The wrong man was delivered to me as the right man. I accepted him on good faith as the right man. Was I wrong?"

*Michael Palin (Spoor), on killing an innocent man*

**2.** "We're all in it together, kid."

*Robert De Niro (Richard Tuttle), a repairman, to Jonathan Pryce (Sam Lowry)*

**3.** "Care for a little necrophilia?"

*Kim Greist (Jill Layton), Pryce's dream girl, appearing to him in a dream after she has been killed*

**4.** BARBARA HICKS (*Mrs. Terrain*): "Can you do something about these terrorists?"
PRYCE: "It's my lunch hour. Besides, it's not my department."

**BREAKER MORANT** (Australia: New World, 1979). D: Bruce Beresford. S: Bruce Beresford, Jonathan Hardy, David Stevens. Fr: Kenneth Ross (play).

**1.** "I was just wondering how much more serious things could be."

*Bryan Brown (Lt. Peter Hancock), threatened with a charge of contempt when he's already been served with a charge of murder*

**2.** "We were out in the veldt fighting the Boer the way he fought us. I'll tell you what rule we applied, sir. We applied rule 303. We caught them and we shot them under rule 303."

*Edward Woodward (Lt. Harry Morant) to the court*

**3.** "A slice off a cut loaf is never missed."

*Brown, on sleeping with a married woman*

**4.** "Every life ends in a dreadful execution, George. Yours will be much quicker and less painful than most."

*Woodward to Lewis Fitzgerald (Lt. George Witton)*

**5.** "No prisoners. The gentlemen's war is over."

*Terence Donovan (Capt. Simon Hurst) to Woodward, giving him the order to kill all prisoners (shown in flashback during the trial)*

**6.** "It's a new kind of war, George. It's a new war for a new century. I suppose this is the first time the enemy hasn't been in uniform. They're farmers. They're people from small towns. And they shoot at us from houses and from paddocks. Some of them are women. Some of them are children. And some of them are missionaries, George."

*Woodward to Fitzgerald, on why he ordered Fitzgerald to kill a missionary*

**7.** "You can't always choose, George, which side you're going to fight on. Can you? And these days, it's so easy to be on the wrong side."

*Woodward to Fitzgerald*

**8.** "Shoot straight, you bastards! Don't make a mess of it!"

*Woodward to his firing squad*

**BREAKFAST AT TIFFANY'S** (Paramount, 1961). D: Blake Edwards. S: George Axelrod. Fr: Truman Capote (novella).

**1.** "Miss Go-Lightly, I protest!"

*Mickey Rooney (Mr. Yunioshi) to Audrey Hepburn (Holly Golightly), complaining about her awakening him; repeated throughout the film*

**2.** "You know those days when you get the mean reds. . . . No, the blues are because you're getting fat or maybe it's been raining too long, that's all. The mean reds are horrible. Suddenly you're afraid and you don't know what you're afraid of. . . . Well, when I get it, the only thing that does any good is to jump into a cab and go to Tiffany's."

*Hepburn to George Peppard (Paul Varjak)*

**3.** "I mean, a girl just can't go to Sing-Sing with a green face."

*Hepburn to Peppard*

**4.** "I mean, any gentleman with the slightest chic will give a girl a fifty-dollar bill for the powder room."

*Hepburn to Peppard*

**5.** "How do I look?"

*Hepburn to Peppard, after a frenzied transformation for her trip to Sing-Sing*

**6.** "You're wrong, ha. But on the other hand you're right. Because she's a real phony. You know why? Because she honestly believes all this phony junk that she believes in."

*Martin Balsam (O. J. Berman) to Peppard, about Hepburn*

**7.** "Timber!"

*Hepburn to party group, as Dorothy Whitney (Mag Wildwood) keels over*

**8.** "It's a mistake you always made, Doc, trying to love a wild thing. . . . You mustn't give your heart to a wild thing."

*Hepburn to Buddy Ebsen (Doc Golightly)*

**9.** "Of course, personally, I think it's a bit tacky to wear diamonds before I'm forty."

*Hepburn to Peppard, appraising the jewels at Tiffany's*

**10.** "Well, frankly, madam, within that price range the variety of merchandise is rather limited."

*John McGiver (Tiffany's Clerk) to Hepburn, on merchandise under ten dollars*

**11.** "Do they still really have prizes in Cracker Jack boxes? . . . That's nice to know. Gives one a feeling of solidarity, almost of continuity with the past, that sort of thing."

*McGiver to Hepburn and Peppard, on their Cracker Jacks box ring to be engraved*

**12.** "I just meet Mr. Shaughnessy at Hamburger Heaven and give him the weather report."

*Hepburn to reporters, on her involvement with the mob*

**13.** "A girl can't read that sort of thing with . . . without her lipstick."

*Hepburn to Peppard, about farewell letter from Vilallonga (José da Silva Perriera)*

**14.** "There are certain shades of limelight that can wreck a girl's complexion."

*Hepburn to Peppard*

**15.** PEPPARD: "I love you. You belong to me."
   HEPBURN: "No, people don't belong to people."
   PEPPARD: "Of course they do."

**LAST LINE**
**16.** "Cat, cat!"

*Hepburn to Putney (Cat), upon finding him*

**BREAKFAST CLUB, THE** *(Universal, 1985).*
*D: John Hughes. S: John Hughes.*

*1.* "I wanna be just like you. I figure all I needs a lobotomy and some tights."

*Judd Nelson (John Bender) to high school wrestler Emilio Estevez (Andrew Clark)*

**BREAKING AWAY** *(20th Century–Fox, 1979). D: Peter Yates. S: Steve Tesich.*

*1.* "They're gonna keep calling us cutters. To them it's just a dirty word."

*Dennis Quaid (Mike), on what the college kids call them*

**LAST LINE**
*2.* "Bonjour, Papa."

*Dennis Christopher (Dave) to father Paul Dooley (Mr. Stohler)*

**BREATHLESS** *(France: Imperia, 1959). D: Jean-Luc Godard. S: Jean-Luc Godard. Fr: Francois Truffaut (idea).*

*1.* "Killers kill, squealers squeal."

*Jean-Paul Belmondo (Michel Poiccard/Laszlo Kovacs) to Jean Seberg (Patricia Franchini)*

**BRIDE OF FRANKENSTEIN, THE** *(Universal, 1935). D: James Whale. S: William Hurlbut, John L. Balderston. Fr: Mary Shelley (novel).*

*1.* "Tell him that Dr. Pretorius is here on a secret matter of grave importance and must see him alone tonight."

*Ernest Thesiger (Dr. Pretorius), announcing himself to Una O'Connor (Minnie), servant of Colin Clive (Henry Frankenstein)*

*2.* "Do you like gin? It's my only weakness."

*Thesiger to Clive; he later claims cigars are also his only weakness*

*3.* "To a new world of gods and monsters!"

*Thesiger to fellow monster-maker Clive*

*4.* "Sometimes I have wondered whether life wouldn't be much more amusing if we were all devils and no nonsense about angels and being good."

*Thesiger to Clive*

*5.* "Monster indeed. Tush, tush."

*E. E. Clive (Burgomaster), expressing skepticism about Boris Karloff (the Monster)*

*6.* "Alone bad. Friend good. Friend good!"

*Karloff to blind hermit O. P. Heggie*

*7.* "Fire no good!"

*Karloff to Heggie*

*8.* "I'll wait here for a bit. I rather like this place."

*Thesiger, inside a tomb*

*9.* "This is no life for murderers."

*Dwight Frye (Karl), sneaking out of cemetery after a night of grave robbing*

*10.* KARLOFF, asking what Thesiger is doing in the cemetery: "You make man like me?"
THESIGER: "No. Woman. Friend for you."

*11.* "Made me from dead. I love dead. Hate living."

*Karloff, expressing his understanding that Clive is his creator*

*12.* "The bride of Frankenstein!"

*Thesiger, on beholding Elsa Lanchester (The Bride) in full monstrous splendor*

*13.* "Friend? Friend?"

*Karloff, hopefully reaching out to Lanchester*

*14.* "She hate me—like others."

*Karloff, rejected by Lanchester*

**15.** "Yes, go—you live. Go. You stay. We belong dead."

*Karloff preparing to pull lever to blow up the laboratory, sparing Clive and his wife Valerie Hobson (Elizabeth) while destroying Thesiger, Lanchester, and himself*

**BRIDE WALKS OUT, THE** (RKO, 1936). D: Leigh Jason. S: P. J. Wolfson, Philip G. Epstein. Fr: Howard Emmett Rogers (story).

**1.** "Ah, I don't know. It was raining, and we were in Pittsburgh."

*Helen Broderick (Mattie Dodson), explaining why she got married*

**BRIDGE ON THE RIVER KWAI, THE** (UK: Columbia, 1957). D: David Lean. S: Pierre Boulle, Michael Wilson (uncredited), Carl Foreman (uncredited). Fr: Pierre Boulle (novel).

**1.** "Be happy in your work."

*Japanese officer Sessue Hayakawa's (Colonel Saito's) motto for the inmates of his prisoner-of-war camp*

**2.** "I must say he seems quite a reasonable type."

*Alec Guinness (Colonel Nicholson), erroneously, on Hayakawa*

**3.** WILLIAM HOLDEN (*Shears*), on the prison camp: "Here there is no civilization."
GUINNESS: "Then we have the opportunity to introduce it."

**4.** "As for me I'm just a slave. A living slave."

*Holden, responding to Guinness's view that prisoners of war should feel they are soldiers and not slaves*

**5.** "He is mad, your colonel. Quite mad."

*Hayakawa to Army doctor James Donald (Major Clipton), on Guinness, who refuses to allow his officers to work at manual labor in the prison camp*

**6.** "That man's the worst commanding officer I've ever come across. Actually I think he's mad."

*Guinness, imprisoned in a heat box for disobedience, to Donald, on Hayakawa*

**7.** "English prisoners! Let us ask the question: Why does the bridge not progress? You know why: because your officers are lazy!"

*Hayakawa, railing to the prisoners building the Japanese bridge, about the British officers whom Guinness has forbidden to work*

**8.** "All work and no play make Jack a dull boy."

*Hayakawa, generously, in his view, giving time off to the prisoners*

**9.** "It's essential for an officer to have that respect, I'm sure you agree. If he loses it, he ceases to command. And what happens then? Demoralization and chaos. A pretty poor commander I would be if I allowed that to happen to my men."

*Guinness to Hayakawa*

**10.** "I hate the British. You are defeated but you have no shame. You are stubborn but you have no pride. You endure but you have no courage. I hate the British!"

*Hayakawa, in a rage at Guinness's obstinacy*

**11.** "He's done it!"

*Amazed shout from a captive British officer, when Hayakawa decides to release Guinness without requiring his officers to do manual labor*

**12.** "Six hundred years. That would be quite something."

> *Guinness, on how long his bridge might last*

**13.** "I haven't the foggiest."

> *Guinness's frequent response to questions*

**14.** "You're a fine doctor, Clipton, but you've a lot to learn about the Army."

> *Guinness to Donald, who is mystified by Guinness's determination to do a good job on the bridge*

**15.** THIS BRIDGE WAS DESIGNED AND CONSTRUCTED BY SOLDIERS OF THE BRITISH ARMY, FEB–MAY 1943, LT. COL. L. NICHOLSON, D.S.O., COMMANDING

> *Sign on completed bridge, indicating Guinness's pride in the prisoners' achievement*

**16.** "But there are times when suddenly you realize you're nearer the end than the beginning. . . . I don't know whether that kind of thinking's very healthy, but I must admit I've had some thoughts on those lines from time to time."

> *Guinness to Hayakawa, contemplating life, death, and futility while standing on the bridge*

**17.** "What have I done?"

> *Guinness, realizing he's betrayed the Allied plan to blow up the bridge*

**LAST LINE**
**18.** "Madness. Madness."

> *Donald, surveying the corpse-littered scene of the destroyed bridge*

**BRIGHTON BEACH MEMOIRS** (Universal, 1986). D: Gene Saks. S: Neil Simon. Fr: Neil Simon (play).

**LAST LINE**
**1.** "October the second, 1937, an historic moment in the life of Eugene Morris Jerome. I have just seen the golden palace of the Himalayas. Puberty is over. Onwards and upwards."

> *Jonathan Silverman (Eugene), on his initiation into sexual matters*

**BRINGING UP BABY** (RKO, 1938). D: Howard Hawks. S: Dudley Nichols, Hagar Wilde, Robert McGowan (uncredited), Gertrude Purcell (uncredited). Fr: Hagar Wilde (story).

**1.** "*This* will be our child."

> *Virginia Walker (Alice Swallow) to her fiancé and fellow paleontologist Cary Grant (David Huxley), pointing to their brontosaurus skeleton and intimating that there will be no sex in their marriage*

**2.** "I'll be with you in a minute, Mr. Peabody!"

> *Grant, helplessly calling out to golf partner George Irving (Peabody) as Katharine Hepburn (Susan Vance) drives Grant's car away with Grant perched on the running board*

**3.** "Everything's going to be all right."

> *Hepburn's frequent unkept promise to Grant*

**4.** "I said, 'Good morning, David,' and I said, 'Do you want a leopard?'"

> *Hepburn, repeating herself on the phone to Grant*

**5.** "Because I just went gay all of a sudden!"

> *Grant, explaining to May Robson (Aunt Elizabeth) why he's wearing a woman's negligee*

**6.** "If he gets some clothes, he'll go away. And he's the only man I've ever loved!"

*Hepburn, explaining to Robson why she does-n't want Grant to find clothes to replace the ones she took away from him*

**7.** "You're so good-looking without your glasses."

*Hepburn, distracted when Grant asks her to concentrate*

**8.** "David and Susan need that bone. It's a nasty old bone. It's hundreds of years old. That's David's bone."

*Hepburn, trying to reason with her dog Asta (George), who has buried the intercostal clavi-cle, Grant's priceless fossil bone*

**9.** "I've heard many a loon, and if there ever was a loon, that is a loon."

*Charles Ruggles (Major Applegate), mistaking the sound of a leopard for a loon*

**10.** "Yes, but, I don't like to say so, sir, at this moment, sir, but everybody knows you're crazy."

*Ruggles to Grant, on Grant's assertion that Nissa (Baby) is a tame leopard*

**11.** "Born on the side of a hill. I was born on the side of a hill."

*Hepburn, playing games after breaking off her heel*

**12.** "There is a leopard on your roof and it's my leopard and I have to get it. And to get it I have to sing."

*Hepburn to Fritz Feld (Dr. Digby), explaining why she is singing at his roof*

**13.** "Vaunce, kiddie, Vaunce. That's my society moniker. But the mob all calls me 'Swingin'-Door Susie.'"

*Hepburn, making up a gangster story to gratify her jailer, constable Walter Catlett (Slocum)*

**14.** "You're just a butterfly."

*Walker, telling her fiancé Grant what she thinks of him*

**15.** "I've just discovered that was the best day I ever had in my whole life!"

*Grant, surprising Hepburn*

**LAST LINE**
**16.** "Oh, dear. Oh, my. Hmmm."

*Grant, surrendering to Hepburn in an embrace after his dinosaur is destroyed*

**BROADCAST NEWS** (20th Century–Fox, 1987). D: James L. Brooks. S: James L. Brooks.

**1.** "You'll never make more than $19,000 a year. Ha, ha, ha!"

*Dwayne Markee (Young Aaron), taunting his high school tormentors*

**2.** "Hey, If anything happens to me, you tell every woman I've ever gone out with I was talking about her at the end. That way they'll have to reevaluate me."

*TV reporter Albert Brooks (Aaron Altman) to producer Holly Hunter (Jane Craig)*

**3.** News director PETER HACKES (Paul Moore): "It must be nice to always believe you know better, to always think you're the smartest person in the room."
HUNTER: "No, it's awful."

**4.** "What a feeling having you inside my head!"

*Anchor William Hurt (Tom Grunick) to Hunter, after she uses an earphone to guide him through a broadcast*

**5.** "This is more than Nixon ever sweated."

*Stagehand watching Brooks sweat profusely as he tries to anchor the news*

**6.** "You just can't stop editing me, huh?"

*Hurt to Hunter, who is coaching him on how to woo her*

**7.** "I know you care about him. I've never seen you like this with anybody, so don't get me wrong when I tell you that Tom, while being a very nice guy, is the devil."

*Brooks telling Hunter about his objections to Hurt*

**8.** "Except for socially, you're my role model."

*Joan Cusack (Blair Litton) saying good-bye to Hunter*

**BROADWAY DANNY ROSE** *(Orion, 1984). D: Woody Allen. S: Woody Allen.*

**1.** "Before you go out on stage, you got to look in the mirror, and you got to say your three S's: star, smile, strong."

*Theatrical manager Woody Allen (Danny Rose) to Bob and Etta Rollins, balloon folders*

**2.** "Take my Aunt Rose, not a beautiful woman at all. She looked like something you'd buy in a live bait store. But why? She had wisdom. And she used to say, 'You can't ride two horses with one behind.'"

*Allen to client Nick Apollo Forte (Lou Canova), on adultery*

**3.** "What do you mean, you don't want to pay? A cat ate his bird. That comes under the act-of-God clause."

*Allen to a theater manager, defending a bird act with no bird*

**4.** "I promise you. He's cheating with you. He's got integrity. He cheats with one person at a time only. That's his style."

*Allen defending Forte to Forte's mistress Mia Farrow (Tina Vitale)*

**5.** "My father, may he rest in peace, said, 'In business, friendly, but not familiar.'"

*Allen to Farrow*

**6.** "I'm never going to be Cary Grant. I don't care what anybody says."

*Allen to Farrow*

**7.** "It's very important to be guilty. I'm guilty all the time, and I never did anything."

*Allen to Farrow*

**8.** "I need a Valium the size of a hockey puck."

*Allen to Farrow*

**9.** "You know what my philosophy of life is? That it's important to have some laughs, no question about it, but you got to suffer a little, too, because otherwise you miss the whole point of life."

*Allen to Farrow*

**10.** "The man has an axe. There's two of us. There'll be four of us in no time."

*Allen to Farrow*

**BRONCO BILLY** *(Warner Bros./Columbia, 1980). D: Clint Eastwood. S: Dennis Hackin.*

**Last Line**
**1.** "And so, as our friends south of the border say, adios, amigos."

*Clint Eastwood (Bronco Billy)*

**BROTHERS KARAMAZOV, THE** *(MGM, 1958). D: Richard Brooks. S: Richard Brooks. Fr: Julius J. Epstein, Philip G. Epstein (adaptation), Fyodor Dostoyevsky (novel).*

**1.** "You save your soul by eating a fish every day. You think God can be bribed with a stinking fish?"

*Lee J. Cobb (Fyodor Karamazov), the father to Yul Brynner (Dmitri Karamazov)*

**2.** "If there is a God, He's responsible for my ideas, and for what I do. If there is no God, then I am my own master and capable of anything without fear of God's punishment."

*Albert Salmi (Smerdyakov) to Cobb*

**3.** CLAIRE BLOOM (*Katya*): "But you said it was only passion."
MARIA SCHELL (*Grushenka*): "Only? Dearest lady, you must try it sometime. You'll never call it only."

**4.** "If I were God, I'd forgive everyone."
*Schell to Brynner*

**5.** "The only hell is being unable to love."
*Brynner to Schell*

**BUCCANEER, THE** (*Paramount, 1958*). D: Anthony Quinn. S: Jesse L. Lasky, Jr., Bernice Mosk. Fr: Harold Lamb (screenplay), Edwin Justus Mayer, C. Gardner Sullivan, Jeanie Macpherson (adaptation), Lyle Saxon (book, *Lafitte the Pirate*).

**1.** "When you steal on the sea, you're a buccaneer. When you steal on the land, you're a thief."

*Charles Boyer (Dominique You)*

**2.** "Loving you is costing me a lot of money."

*Yul Brynner (Jean Lafitte), famous pirate, to Inger Stevens (Annette Claiborne), when he will not attack an American ship because of her*

**3.** "You just don't know what it means to belong to a country."

*Stevens to Brynner*

**4.** "This, Mr. Pyke, is to remind myself of all the lies they tell about land. Motherland. Fatherland. Homeland. When all they mean is the dirt they bury you in when you've spilled your blood defending it. I say we belong to the sea."

*Boyer to George Matthews (Pyke), when asked why he wears a sack of French dirt around his neck*

**5.** "There's nothing special about a house. It's just a hull in dry dock. You dream all your life of owning one, and when you get it, it's on the wrong street."

*Brynner*

**6.** "The side I'm on will be the winning side."

*Brynner, when asked if he wants to be on the winning side of the War of 1812*

**7.** BRYNNER: "The combination of Claiborne, Jackson, and Lafitte. We could conquer the world."
E. G. MARSHALL (*Governor Claiborne*): "I'm not so ambitious, Lafitte. All I want to do is save the United States."

**8.** "Let me make this very clear, gentlemen. Before I surrender this city, I will burn it to the ground."

*Charlton Heston (Gen. Andrew Jackson), referring to Lorne Greene's (Mercier's) panicked call to surrender New Orleans to the advancing British army*

**LAST LINES**
**9.** BOYER: "When a man loses everything else, he still has the sea. This deck is the only country we have."

CLAIRE BLOOM (*Bonnie Brown*): "This is all the country I want."

**BUCK PRIVATES** (*Universal, 1941*). D: Arthur Lubin. S: Arthur T. Horman, John Grant.

**1.** BUD ABBOTT (*Slicker Smith*): "Suppose you're forty and you're in love with a little girl who's ten years old."
LOU COSTELLO (*Herbie Brown*): "This one's gonna be a pip. Now I'm goin' around with a ten-year-old girl. You got a good idea where I'm gonna wind up."

> The beginning of Abbott and Costello's "You're Forty, She's Ten" routine, which reaches the seemingly inevitable conclusion that the little girl will one day be older than the middle-aged man

**BUGSY** (*TriStar, 1991*). D: Barry Levinson. S: James Toback. Fr: Dean Jennings (book, We Only Kill Eath Other: The Life and Bad Time of Bugsy Siegel).

**1.** "Twenty dwarves took turns doing handstands on the carpet."

> Gangster Warren Beatty (*Benjamin "Bugsy" Siegel*), practicing his elocution while driving

**2.** "Ben has only one problem. . . . He doesn't respect money."

> Ben Kingsley (*Meyer Lansky*) to fellow gangster, on Beatty

**3.** "If you want a simple yes or no, you're gonna have to finish the question."

> Annette Bening (*Virginia Hill*), flirting with Beatty as he attempts to ask to light her cigarette

**4.** "It's only dirty paper."

> Beatty to Joe Mantegna (*George Raft*), on money

**BULL DURHAM** (*Orion, 1988*). D: Ron Shelton. S: Ron Shelton.

**1.** "There's never been a ball player slept with me who didn't have the best year of his career."

> Susan Sarandon (*Annie Savoy*) in voice-over

**2.** "I've tried 'em all—I really have—and the only church that truly feeds the soul, day in, day out, is the church of baseball."

> Sarandon, in voice-over

**3.** "I'm the player to be named later."

> Kevin Costner (*Crash Davis*) to Robert Wuhl (*Larry Hockett*) and Trey Wilson (*Joe "Skip" Riggins*)

**4.** "I'm Crash Davis. I'm your new catcher, and you just got lesson number one: Don't think, it will only hurt the ball club."

> Costner to Tim Robbins (*Ebby Calvin "Nuke" LaLoosh*)

**5.** "These are the ground rules. I hook up with one guy a season. It usually takes me a couple weeks to pick the guy—kind of my own spring training, and, well, you two are the most promising prospects of the season so far, so I just thought we should try to get to know each other."

> Sarandon to Costner and Robbins

**6.** "Well, I believe in the soul, the dawn, the evening, the small of a woman's back, the hangin' curveball, high fiber, good scotch, that the novels of Susan Sontag are self-indulgent, overrated crap. . . . I believe in the sweet spot, soft-core pornography, opening your presents Christmas morning rather than Christmas Eve, and I believe in long, slow, deep, soft, wet kisses that last three days."

> Costner to Sarandon

**7.** "Oh my."

*Sarandon to Costner, after he relates his philosophy to her*

**8.** SARANDON, to Robbins, who is tied up in bed: "You heard about Walt Whitman?" ROBBINS: "Who's he play for?"

**9.** "It's my job to give him life's wisdom and help him get on to the major leagues."

*Sarandon to Costner, about Robbins*

**10.** "She may get woolly.
Young girls they do get woolly, because of all the stress.
Yes, when they get woolly, try a little tenderness."

*Robbins, mangling song lyrics on the bus*

**11.** "Okay, well, this is the damndest season I've ever seen. I mean, the Durham Bulls can't lose and I can't get laid."

*Sarandon to Costner*

**12.** "Well, Nuke's scared 'cause his eyelids are jammed and his old man's here. We need a live roos—Is it a live rooster? We need a live rooster to take the curse off Jose's glove, and nobody seems to know what to get Millie or Jimmy for their wedding present. Is that about right? . . . We're dealing with a lot of shit."

*Costner to Wuhl*

**13.** "I have been known on occasion to howl at the moon."

*Costner to Robbins*

**LAST LINE**
**14.** "Walt Whitman once said, 'I see great things in baseball. It's our game. The American game. It will repair our losses and be a blessing to us.' You could look it up."

*Sarandon, in voice-over*

**BUTCH CASSIDY AND THE SUNDANCE KID** *(20th Century–Fox, 1969). D: George Roy Hill. S: William Goldman.*

**1.** "Small price to pay for beauty."

*Outlaw Paul Newman (Butch Cassidy), on the closing of a beautiful old bank because of frequent robberies*

**2.** "You just keep thinkin', Butch. That's what you're good at."

*Robert Redford's (Sundance Kid's) frequent refrain to Cassidy*

**3.** "Boy, I got vision and the rest of the world wears bifocals."

*Newman to Redford*

**4.** "Listen, I don't mean to be a sore loser, but when it's done, if I'm dead, kill him."

*Newman to Redford, on Ted Cassidy (Harvey Logan), who has challenged him to a knife fight*

**5.** "Rules? In a knife fight?"

*Cassidy to Newman, just before being kicked in the groin*

**6.** "Who *are* those guys?"

*Newman and Redford, at different times, about the posse that keeps following them*

**7.** "I never met a soul more affable than you, Butch, or faster than the kid, but you're still nothin' but two-bit outlaws on the dodge. It's over. Don't you get that? Your times is over and you're gonna die bloody, and all you can do is choose where."

*Jeff Corey (Sheriff Bledsoe) to Newman and Redford*

**8.** "Kid, the next time I say let's go someplace like Bolivia, let's go someplace like Bolivia."

*Newman to Redford*

**9.** "Why, you crazy—the fall'll probably kill you!"

*Newman, on learning that Redford is afraid of jumping into the river far below because he can't swim*

**10.** "I'm twenty-six and I'm single and a schoolteacher, and that's the bottom of the pit, and the only excitement I've known is here with me now. So I'll go with you, and I won't whine, and I'll sew your socks, and I'll stitch you when you're wounded, and I'll do anything you ask of me, except one thing: I won't watch you die. I'll miss that scene if you don't mind."

*Katharine Ross (Etta Place) to Newman and Redford, on going with them to Bolivia*

**11.** "The future's all yours, you lousy bicycle."

*Newman, throwing away his bicycle*

**12.** "He'll feel a lot better after we've robbed a couple of banks."

*Newman about Redford, on his unhappiness with Bolivia*

**13.** "Esto es un robo."

*Newman, announcing a bank robbery in Spanish*

**14.** "I'm better when I move."

*Redford, on his shooting style*

**15.** "Don't you get sick of being right all the time?"

*Redford to Newman, when Redford is proven wrong once again*

**16.** NEWMAN: "Is that what you call giving cover?"

 REDFORD: "Is that what you call running?"

*The outlaws during a shoot-out, where Redford provides cover for Newman*

LAST LINE
**17.** "For a moment there I thought we were in trouble."

*Newman to Redford, as they emerge from hiding for their last shoot-out*

**BUTTERFIELD 8** (MGM, 1960). D: Daniel Mann. S: Charles Schnee, John Michael Hayes. Fr: John O'Hara (novel).

**1.** "Well, I started at Amherst and I worked my way through the alphabet to Yale. I'm stuck there."

*Elizabeth Taylor (Gloria Wandrous), discussing her promiscuity with Laurence Harvey (Weston Liggett)*

**2.** "Mama, face it. I was the slut of all time."

*Taylor to Mildred Dunnock (Mrs. Wandrous)*

**BYE BYE BIRDIE** (Columbia, 1963). D: George Sidney. S: Irving Brecher. Fr: Michael Stewart, Charles Strouse, Lee Adams (musical play).

**1.** "Next time I have a daughter, I hope it's a boy."

*Paul Lynde (Mr. McAfee) to Dick Van Dyke (Albert Peterson), on daughter Ann-Margret's (Kim McAfee's) teenage antics*

**2.** MARY LAROCHE (Mrs. McAfee): "What does your husband do?"

 MAUREEN STAPLETON (Mama Peterson): "I don't know, he's dead."

**3.** "The Russians. First they take over Czechoslovakia, now they take my four minutes."

*Van Dyke, upset that the four-minute spot with Jesse Pearson (Conrad Birdie) singing his song on "The Ed Sullivan Show" will be cut to thirty seconds because of a Russian balle*

**CABARET** (Allied Artists, 1972). D: Bob Fosse. S: Jay Presson Allen. Fr: Joe Masteroff, John Kander, Fred Ebb (musical play), John Van Druten (play, I Am a Camera), Christopher Isherwood (Berlin Stories).

LAST LINE
1. "Where are your troubles now? Forgotten. I told you so. We have no troubles here. Here life is beautiful. The girls are beautiful. Even the orchestra is beautiful."

Joel Grey (Master of Ceremonies), on the cabaret

**CABIN IN THE COTTON** (Warner Bros.–First National, 1932). D: Michael Curtiz. S: Paul Green. Fr: Harry Harrison Kroll (novel).

1. "I'd love to kiss you, but I just washed my hair."

Bette Davis (Madge)

**CABINET OF DR. CALIGARI, THE** (Germany: Decla-Bioscop/Goldwyn, 1919). D: Robert Wiene. S: Robert Bloch.

1. "A TALE of the modern re-appearance of an 11th Century Myth involving the strange and mysterious influence of a mountebank monk over a somnambulist."

Opening title

2. "Spirits surround us on every side—they have driven me from hearth and home, from wife and child."

Old man to Friedrich Feher (Francis), his companion on a park bench

3. "Wake up, Cesare! I, Caligari, your master, command you!"

Mountebank Werner Krauss (Dr. Caligari) to Conrad Veidt (Cesare), a somnambulist under his hypnotic control

4. "There is something frightful in our midst!"

Feher to police, after two mysterious murders have occurred

5. "You fools, this man is plotting our doom! We die at dawn! He is Caligari!"

Feher, now insane, warning other asylum inmates of the danger he perceives from Krauss

LAST LINE
6. "At last I recognize his mania. He believes me to be the mystical Caligari. Astonishing! But I think I know how to cure him now."

Krauss, the head of the asylum, whom the audience has previously believed to be Caligari, expressing his understanding of Feher's madness

**CACTUS FLOWER** (Columbia, 1969). D: Gene Saks. S: I. A. L. Diamond. Fr: Abe Burrows (play), Barillet and Gredy (play).

1. "In this job, you don't meet anything but married men. I suppose all the single ones have good teeth."

Ingrid Bergman (Stephanie Dickinson), a dental receptionist to Walter Matthau (Julian Winston), a bachelor dentist

2. "You look different when you're all dressed up. In the office, you sort of look like a large Band-Aid."

Jack Weston (Harvey Greenfield) to Bergman, when he's pretending to be her boyfriend

3. "Toni, you're a kook, but a nice kook."

Rick Lenz (Igor Sullivan) to Goldie Hawn (Toni Simmons), Matthau's mistress

**4.** "Doctor, you once compared me to my cactus plant. Well, every so often that prickly little thing puts out a flower."

*Bergman to Matthau*

**CAHILL—U.S. MARSHAL** (Warner Bros., 1973). D: Andrew V. McLaglen. S: Harry Julian Fink, Rita Fink. Fr: Barney Slater (story).

**1.** "'Cause even grown men need understanding."

*John Wayne (Marshal J. D. Cahill), showing a gentle side to his son Gary Grimes (Danny)*

**CAINE MUTINY, THE** (Columbia, 1954). D: Edward Dmytryk. S: Stanley Roberts. Fr: Herman Wouk (play/novel).

**1.** "Ah, but the strawberries! That's . . . that's where I had them. They laughed and made jokes, but I proved beyond a shadow of a doubt, and with geometric logic, that a duplicate key to the wardroom icebox did exist."

*Humphrey Bogart (Captain Queeg)*

**CAMELOT** (Warner Bros.–Seven Arts, 1967). D: Joshua Logan. S: Alan Jay Lerner. Fr: Alan Jay Lerner, Frederick Loewe (musical play), T. H. White (book, The Once and Future King).

**1.** "You will run behind the lines and hide until it is over, and then you will return home to England alive to grow up and grow old. Do you understand? You will remember what I the king tell you, and do, do as I command."

*Richard Harris (King Arthur), commanding a boy, Garry Marsh (Tom), to survive to tell the tale of Camelot*

**LAST LINE**

**2.** "One of what we all are, Pelly. Less than a drop in the great blue motion of the sunlit sea. But it seems that some of the drops sparkle, Pelly. Some of them do sparkle! Run, boy! Run, boy! Run! Oh, run, my boy."

*Harris, telling Lionel Jeffries (King Pellinore) who Marsh is, and calling to Marsh, moments before the battle that will bring an end to Camelot*

**CAMILLE** (Fox, 1936). D: J. Gordon Edwards. S: Zoe Akins, Frances Marion, James Hilton. Fr: Alexandre Dumas, fils (novel, play, La Dame aux Camelias).

**1.** "It's a great mistake for any woman to have a heart bigger than her purse."

*Laura Hope Crews (Prudence) to Greta Garbo (Marguerite Gauthier)*

**2.** "I'm afraid of nothing except being bored."

*Garbo to Robert Taylor (Armand Duvall), who is desperately in love with her*

**3.** "I learned not to believe a man when he says he's leaving town."

*Garbo to Henry Daniell (Baron de Varville) her husband, when he returns unexpectedly*

**4.** "How can you change one's entire life and build a new one in one moment of love? And yet, that's what you make me want to close my eyes and do."

*Garbo to Taylor*

**5.** "Why can't anything be perfect?"
*Garbo to Crews*

**6.** "Wine used to go to my head, and make me gay. And now it goes to my legs, and makes me old."

*Crews*

**7.** "What you probably feel is the melancholy of happiness. That mood that comes over all of us when we realize that even love can't remain at flood tide forever."

*Lionel Barrymore (General Duval) to Garbo*

**8.** "Try to realize that everything you're ashamed of in your own past would only taint the future."

*Barrymore to Garbo, on Taylor*

**9.** "We don't make our own hearts."

*Garbo to Taylor, when she rejects him*

**10.** "It's my heart. It's not used to being happy."

*Garbo to Taylor, on her deathbed*

**11.** "Perhaps it's better if I live in your heart, where the world can't see me."

*Garbo to Taylor, as she dies*

**CAPE FEAR** (Universal-International, 1962). D: J. Lee Thompson. S: James R. Webb. Fr: John D. MacDonald (novel, The Executioners).

**1.** "Didn't remember me right off, did you? Well, I guess I've changed a little. Where I've been, if you don't change, they're real disappointed."

*Robert Mitchum (Max Cady), to Gregory Peck (Sam Bowden)*

**2.** "You can't put a man in jail for what he *might* do. And thank heaven for that."

*Martin Balsam (Chief Dutton) to Peck*

**3.** "Either we have too many laws or not enough."

*Balsam to Peck*

**4.** "Max Cady, what I like about you is you're rock bottom. I wouldn't expect you to

understand this, but it's a great comfort for a girl to know she could not possibly sink any lower."

*Barrie Chase (Diane) to Mitchum*

**5.** "I like to put values on things, like the value of eight years, the value of a family. Interesting calculations. Wouldn't you say, Counselor?"

*Mitchum to Peck, when discussing retribution*

**6.** "Go ahead. Go ahead. I just don't give a damn."

*Mitchum to Peck, as Peck has him cornered at gunpoint.*

**Last Line**
**7.** "You're strong, Cady. You're going to live a long life. In a cage. That's where you belong and that's where you're going. And this time for life. Bang your head against the walls. Count the years, the months, the hours. Until the day you rot."

*Peck to Mitchum*

**CAPTAINS COURAGEOUS** (MGM, 1937). D: Victor Fleming. S: John Lee Mahin, Marc Connelly, Dale Van Every. Fr: Rudyard Kipling (novel).

**1.** "People give presents after someone's been nice to them, don't they? So what's dishonest with giving presents before someone's nice to you?"

*Freddie Bartholomew (Harvey Cheyne), defending a bribe*

**2.** "Say, sometimes a song so big and sweet inside, I . . . I just can't get him out, and then I look up at stars, and maybe cry, it feels so good."

*Spencer Tracy (Manuel) to Bartholomew*

**3.** "I no bet on sure thing. I bet on myself. Just as good."

*Tracy to Bartholomew, when he bets John Carradine (Long Jack) on who can bring in the most fish*

**4.** "That fish, he have meeting down below. He tell other fish there something not so funny going on."

*Tracy to Bartholomew*

**5.** "I got maybe five, six girls in Gloucester. I tell each one I like her best. You got to tell big lies to girls to make them happy."

*Tracy to Bartholomew*

**6.** "Manuel, he be watching you. You be best fisherman ever lived."

*Tracy to Bartholomew, just before Tracy sinks and drowns*

**7.** "That's where the poor, and old, and crippled of us sit on a sunny porch and try to outlie each other."

*Lionel Barrymore (Disko), referring to the Fisherman's Home*

**CAROUSEL** *(20th Century–Fox, 1956). D: Henry King. S: Phoebe Ephron, Henry Ephron. Fr: Richard Rodgers, Oscar Hammerstein II (musical play), Benjamin F. Glazer (adaptation), Ferenc Molnar (play, Liliom).*

**LAST LINE**

**1.** "I loved you, Julie. Know that. I loved you."

*The ghost of Gordon MacRae (Billy) to Shirley Jones (Julie)*

**CARRIE** *(UA, 1976). D: Brian De Palma. S: Lawrence D. Cohen. Fr: Stephen King (novel).*

**1.** "Please see that I'm not like you, Mama. I'm funny. I mean all the kids think I'm funny. I don't want to be funny. I want to be normal. I want to start to try to be a whole person before it's too late for me."

*Sissy Spacek (Carrie White) to Piper Laurie (Margaret White), her mother, when she's invited to the prom*

**2.** "If I concentrate hard enough, I can move things."

*Spacek to Laurie*

**3.** "They're all going to laugh at you."

*Laurie to Spacek*

**CASABLANCA** *(Warner Bros., 1942). D: Michael Curtiz. S: Julius J. Epstein, Phillip G. Epstein, Howard Koch. Fr: Murray Burnett, Joan Alison (play, Everbody Goes to Rick's).*

**1.** "Everybody comes to Rick's."

*Claude Rains (Capt. Louis Renault), on Humphrey Bogart's (Rick Blaine's) saloon*

**2.** BOGART: "I came to Casablanca for the waters."

RAINS: "The waters? What waters? We're in the desert."

BOGART: "I was misinformed."

**3.** "I stick my neck out for nobody."

*Bogart*

**4.** "Your business is politics. Mine is running a saloon."

*Bogart to Conrad Veidt (Major Strasser), Rains, and others at their table*

**5.** "Well, mademoiselle, he is the kind of man that—well, if I were a woman, and I were not around, I should be in love with Rick."

Rains, describing Bogart to Ingrid Bergman (Ilsa Lund)

**6.** "Play it, Sam. Play 'As Time Goes By.'"
Bergman to Dooley Wilson (Sam)

**7.** "I remember every detail. The Germans wore gray, you wore blue."

Bogart, reminiscing with Bergman

**8.** "Of all the gin joints in all the towns in all the world, she walks into mine."

Bogart, despairing about Bergman

**9.** "You played it for her, you can play it for me. . . . If she can stand it, I can. Play it."

Bogart to Wilson

**10.** "Here's looking at you, kid."
Bogart's trademark line to Bergman, repeated several times

**11.** "Was that cannon fire or is it my heart pounding?"
Bergman to Bogart, in a flashback to the day the Germans marched into Paris

**12.** "Yes, well, everybody in Casablanca has problems. Yours may work out."
Bogart to Bulgarian woman asking for his advice

**13.** "I'm shocked, shocked to find that gambling is going on in here!"
Rains, closing Rick's saloon just before being handed his winnings

**14.** "If that plane leaves the ground and you're not with him, you'll regret it. Maybe not today, and maybe not tomorrow, but soon and for the rest of your life."
Bogart to Bergman, at airport, urging her to leave Casablanca with her husband, Paul Henreid (Victor Laszlo)

**15.** "We'll always have Paris."
Bogart to Bergman

**16.** "Ilsa, I'm no good at being noble, but it doesn't take much to see that the problems of three little people don't amount to a hill of beans in this crazy world."
Bogart to Bergman

**17.** "Welcome back to the fight. This time I know our side will win."
Henreid to Bogart

**18.** "Major Strasser has been shot. Round up the usual suspects."
Rains to his men, indicating that he will not arrest Bogart for killing Veidt

**LAST LINE**
**19.** "Louis, I think this is the beginning of a beautiful friendship."
Bogart to Rains, walking off into the fog

**CASANOVA'S BIG NIGHT** (Paramount, 1954). D: Norman Z. McLeod. S: Hal Kanter, Edmund Hartmann. Fr: Aubrey Wisberg (story).

**LAST LINE**
**1.** "What's the matter with this theater, don't they sell popcorn?"
Bob Hope (Pippo Popolino), surprised that theater audience members are not holding up their popcorn to call for an ending in which he escapes execution

**CASINO ROYALE** (Columbia, 1967). D: John Huston, Ken Hughes, Robert Parrish, Joe McGrath, Val Guest. S: Wolf Mankowitz, John Law, Michael Sayers. Fr: Ian Fleming (novel).

**1.** "In my day, spying was an alternative to war. And the spy was a member of a select and immaculate priesthood, vocationally devoted, sublimely disinterested."

*David Niven (James Bond) to John Huston (M)*

**2.** "I have a very low threshhold of death."

*Woody Allen (Jimmy Bond) to his firing squad*

**3.** "So, that's your plan, huh? A world full of beautiful women, and all men shorter than yourself."

*Niven to Allen*

**4.** "Think of it. A world free of poverty, and pestilence, and war. A world where all men are created equal. Where a man, no matter how short, can score with a top broad. Where each man, regardless of race, creed, color, gets free dental work, and a chance of subscription buying of all the good things in life."

*Allen to Daliah Lavi (The Detainer)*

**CAT AND THE CANARY, THE** *(Paramount, 1939). D: Elliott Nugent. S: Walter De Leon, Lynn Starling. Fr: John Willard (play).*

**1.** NYDIA WESTMAN (*Cicily*): "Don't big empty houses scare you?"
BOB HOPE (*Wallie Campbell*): "Not me, I used to be in vaudeville."

**CAT ON A HOT TIN ROOF** *(MGM, 1958). D: Richard Brooks. S: Richard Brooks, James Poe. Fr: Tennessee Williams (play).*

**1.** "I'm not living with you. We occupy the same cage, that's all."

*Elizabeth Taylor (Maggie) to Paul Newman (Brick)*

**2.** "Big Daddy! Now what makes him so big? His big heart? His big belly? Or his big money?"

*Paul Newman, on his father Burl Ives (Big Daddy)*

**3.** "If I was married to you three years, you'd have the living proof. You'd have three kids already and the fourth in the oven."

*Ives to his childless daughter-in-law Taylor*

**CAT PEOPLE** *(RKO, 1942). D: Jacques Tourneur. S: Dewitt Bodeen.*

**1.** "Even as fog continues to lie in the valleys, so does ancient sin cling to the low places, the depressions in the world consciousness."

*From The Anatomy of Atavism by Dr. Louis Judd, as quoted in the opening title*

**2.** "These things are very simple for psychiatrists."

*Psychiatrist Tom Conway (Louis Judd), showing his ignorance about Simone Simon's (Irene Dubrovna) shape-changing illness, which periodically turns her into a deadly panther*

**3.** "What does one tell a husband? One tells him nothing."

*Conway, giving his professional views on marriage*

**4.** "There are some things a woman doesn't want other women to understand."

*Simon, angered on discovering that her husband Kent Smith (Oliver Reed) told another woman about their marital problems*

**CATCH-22** *(Paramount, 1970). D: Mike Nichols. S: Buck Henry. Fr: Joseph Heller (novel).*

**1.** "Anyone who wants to get out of combat isn't really crazy, so I can't ground him."

Jack Gilford (Doc Daneeka), explaining "Catch-22" to Alan Arkin (Yossarian)

**CATERED AFFAIR, THE** (MGM, 1956). D: Richard Brooks. S: Gore Vidal. Fr: Paddy Chayefsky (teleplay).

**1.** "You're going to have a big wedding whether you like it or not. And if you don't like it, you don't have to come."

Bette Davis (Agnes Hurley), a poor mother who wants to give her daughter a lavish wedding, to Debbie Reynolds (Jane Hurley), the bride

**2.** "I want you to have this one fine thing with all the trimmings. Something to remember when . . . well, when the bad days come and you're all wore out and growing old like me."

Davis to Reynolds

**3.** "I belong to a long line of bachelors. That is to say, my uncles were all bachelors."

Barry Fitzgerald (Uncle Jack Conlon)

**4.** "And then one day, you'll find out a lot of time's gone by. And you'll wake up knowing this is the way it's always going to be. Just like this. Day after day. Year after year. Just the same. And that's why being married is such a big thing."

Davis to Reynolds

**CHALK GARDEN, THE** (UK: Universal-International, 1964). D: Ronald Neame. S: John Michael Hayes. Fr: Edith Bagnold (play).

**1.** "At our last meeting, I died. It alters the appearance."

Deborah Kerr (Miss Madrigal) to Felix Aylmer (Judge McWhirrey), the judge who once sentenced her to death

**2.** " 'Hurry,' Maitland, is the curse of civilization."

Edith Evans (Mrs. St. Maugham), responding to butler John Mills's (Maitland's) impatience

**CHAMPION** (UA, 1949). D: Mark Robson. S: Carl Foreman. Fr: Ring Lardner (story).

**1.** "I suppose you know you have a wonderful body. I'd like to do it in clay."

Lola Albright (Mrs. Harris) to boxer Kirk Douglas (Midge Kelly)

**2.** "It's like any other business, only here the blood shows."

Douglas, on boxing

**3.** "This is the only sport in the world where two guys get paid for doing something they'd be arrested for if they got drunk and did it for nothing."

Paul Stewart (Tommy Haley), discussing boxing with Douglas

**4.** "We're not hitchhiking anymore. We're riding."

Douglas's dying words

**LAST LINE**
**5.** "He was a champion. He went out like a champion. He was a credit to the fight game to the very end."

Arthur Kennedy (Connie Kelly), on his late brother Douglas

**CHARADE** (Universal, 1963). D: Stanley Donen. S: Peter Stone. Fr: Marc Behm, Peter Stone (story, "The Unsuspecting Wife").

**1.** "I don't bite, you know—unless it's called for."

*Audrey Hepburn (Regina Lambert), flirting with Cary Grant (Peter Joshua)*

**2.** HEPBURN: "Do you know what's wrong with you?"
GRANT: "No, what?"
HEPBURN: "Nothing."

**CHARIOTS OF FIRE** *(UK: 20th Century–Fox, 1981). D: Hugh Hudson. S: Colin Welland.*

**1.** "I believe that God made me for a purpose. For China. But he also made me fast. And when I run, I feel his pleasure."

*Ian Charleson (Eric Liddell) on being a runner and a missionary in China*

**CHILDREN OF A LESSER GOD** *(Paramount, 1986). D: Randa Haines. S: Hesper Anderson, Mark Medoff. Fr: Mark Medoff (play).*

**1.** "Maybe I don't like to hear myself talk."

*William Hurt (James Leeds), a teacher of the deaf, to Marlee Matlin (Sarah Norman), trying to get her to make a sound*

**2.** "I can't enjoy it. I can't because you can't."

*Hurt to Matlin, on listening to Bach*

**3.** "What do you hear? I mean is it just silence? No one has ever gotten in here to find out. Will you ever let me in?"

*Hurt to Matlin*

**4.** "This sign, 'to connect,' simple, but it means so much more when I do this. Now it means to be joined in a relationship, separate, but one. That's what I want."

*Hurt, interpreting Matlin's sign language*

LAST LINE
**5.** "Do you think that we could find a place where we can meet, not in silence and not in sound?"

*Hurt to Matlin*

**CHILDREN'S HOUR, THE** *(UA, 1962). D: William Wyler. S: John Michael Hayes. Fr: Lillian Hellman (play, adaptation).*

**1.** "Well, I suppose we'll have to feed the duchess. Even vultures have to eat."

*Shirley MacLaine (Martha Dobie) on her Aunt Miriam Hopkins (Lily Mortar)*

**CHINATOWN** *(Paramount, 1974). D: Roman Polanski. S: Robert Towne.*

**1.** "I don't get tough with anyone, Mr. Gittes. My lawyer does."

*Faye Dunaway (Evelyn Mulwray) to private detective Jack Nicholson (J. J. Gittes)*

**2.** "You're a very nosy fellow, kitty-cat, huh?"

*Thug Roman Polanski to Nicholson, before cutting his nostril*

**3.** "Politicians, ugly buildings, and whores all get respectable if they last long enough."

*Corrupt tycoon John Huston (Noah Cross)*

**4.** "He passed away two weeks ago and he bought the land a week ago. . . . That's unusual."

*Nicholson*

**5.** "She's my sister and my daughter!"

*Dunaway, confessing the truth to Nicholson*

**6.** "See, Mr. Gittes, most people never have to face the fact that at the right time and the right place they are capable of anything."

*Huston to Nicholson*

**7.** "It's not worth it, Mr. Gittes. It's really not worth it."

*Huston advising Nicholson to do what he says, rather than get shot*

**8.** "As little as possible."

*Nicholson, summarizing what police in China-town are told to do*

**9.** "Forget it, Jake, it's Chinatown."

*Operative Bruce Glover (Duffy) to his boss Nicholson*

**CHOCOLATE WAR, THE** *(Management Co. Entertainment, 1988). D: Keith Gordon. S: Keith Gordon. Fr: Robert Cormier (novel).*

**1.** "Going to school every day on the bus, and coming home every day on the bus. It's sort of . . . It's sort of like you're middle-aged at fifteen."

*Jenny Wright (Lisa) to Ilan Mitchell-Smith (Jerry)*

**2.** "There's more to life than a lousy chocolate sale."

*Wally Ward (Archie)*

**CHRISTMAS IN JULY** *(Paramount, 1940). D: Preston Sturges. S: Preston Sturges.*

**1.** "If you can't sleep at night, it isn't the coffee—it's the bunk."

*Dick Powell's (Jimmy MacDonald's) prize-winning coffee slogan*

**CIMARRON** *(RKO, 1931). D: Wesley Ruggles. S: Howard Estabrook. Fr: Edna Ferber (novel).*

**1.** "Creation. That took six days. This was done in one. History made in an hour. Why, it's like a miracle out of the Old Testament."

*Richard Dix (Yancey Cravat), referring to the Oklahoma Land Rush*

**2.** "*The Oklahoma Wigwam* prints all the news all the time, knowing no law except the law of God and the government of the United States."

*Dix to Irene Dunne (Sabra Cravat), referring to his new newspaper*

**3.** "I never figured we'd end up on the opposite sides of the fence, kid."

*Dix to old childhood friend William Collier, Jr. (The Kid), after shooting him*

**4.** "They will always talk about Yancey. He's going to be part of the history of the great Southwest. It's men like him that build the world. The rest of them, like me, we just come along and live in it."

*George E. Stone (Sol Levy) to Dunne, when she hasn't heard a word from Dix in five years, after he takes off to participate in the Cherokee Land Rush*

**CINDERELLA** *(Disney/RKO, 1950). D: Wilfred Jackson, Hamilton Luske, Clyde Geronimi. S: William Peet, Ted Sears, Homer Brightman, Kenneth Anderson, Erdman Penner, et al. Fr: Charles Perrault (original story).*

**1.** "Love? Hah! Just a boy meeting a girl under the right conditions. So, we're arranging the conditions."

*Luis Van Rooten (King and Grand Duke), regarding staging a ball to find a bride for his son*

**2.** "Oh, well, what's a royal ball? After all, I suppose it would be frightfully dull, and boring, and completely . . . completely wonderful."

*Ilene Woods (Cinderella), when she has no dress to wear and can't go*

**3.** "We have to hurry because even miracles take a little time."

*Verna Felton (Fairy Godmother), preparing Cinderella for the ball*

**4.** "You'll try this on every maid in the kingdom, and if the shoe fits, bring her in."

*Van Rooten, advising the Duke to use the glass slipper to search for the woman whom William Phipps (Prince Charming) wants to marry*

**5.** "But, you see, I have the other slipper."

*Woods, after one of the glass slippers is shattered, revealing to the Duke that she's the woman he's been looking for*

**CITIZEN KANE** *(RKO, 1941). D: Orson Welles. S: Herman J. Mankiewicz, Orson Welles.*

**FIRST LINE**

**1.** "Rosebud."

*Orson Welles's (Charles Foster Kane's) dying word*

**2.** "I am, have been, and will be only one thing—an American."

*Welles to group of suited men, recorded for newsreel*

**3.** "As it must to all men, death came to Charles Foster Kane."

*"News on the March" newsreel announcer*

**4.** "I think it would be fun to run a newspaper."

*George Coulouris (Walter Parks Thatcher), reading letter from Welles*

**5.** "I don't know how to run a newspaper, Mr. Thatcher. I just try everything I can think of."

*Welles to Coulouris*

**6.** "Dear Wheeler, you provide the prose poems. I'll provide the war."

*Welles to Everett Sloane (Mr. Bernstein), dictating an answer to a telegram from a correspondent in Cuba*

**7.** "You know, Mr. Thatcher, at the rate of a million dollars a year, I'll have to close this place in sixty years."

*Welles to Coulouris*

**8.** "A white dress she had on. She was carrying a white parasol. I only saw her for one second. She didn't see me at all, but I'll bet a month hasn't gone by since that I haven't thought of that girl."

*Sloane to William Alland (Thompson), reporter, on the nature of memory and a girl he glimpsed on a ferry in 1896*

**9.** "Mr. Carter, if the headline is big enough, it makes the news big enough."

*Welles to Erskine Sanford (Herbert Carter)*

**10.** "Maybe that was something he lost. Mr. Kane was a man who lost almost everything he had."

*Sloane to Alland, speculating on the meaning of Rosebud*

**11.** "Just old age. It's the only disease, Mr. Thompson, that you don't look forward to being cured of."

*Sloane to Alland*

**12.** "I was his oldest friend, and as far as I was concerned he behaved like a swine.

Not that Charlie was ever brutal; he just did brutal things. Maybe I wasn't his friend, but if I wasn't, he never had one."

*Joseph Cotten (Jedediah Leland) to Alland*

**13.** "He married for love. Love—that's why he did everything. That's why he went into politics. It seems we weren't enough. He wanted all the voters to love him, too. That's all he really wanted out of life was love. That's Charlie's story—how he lost it. You see, he just didn't have any to give."

*Cotten to Alland*

**14.** "I run a couple of newspapers. What do you do?"

*Welles to Dorothy Comingore (Susan Alexander)*

**15.** "A toast, Jedediah, to love on my terms. Those are the only terms anybody ever knows, his own."

*Welles to Cotten*

**16.** COTTEN: "Hello, Charlie. I didn't know we were speaking."
WELLES: "Sure we're speaking, Jedediah. You're fired."

**17.** "Everything was his idea, except my leaving him."

*Comingore to Alland*

**18.** "I don't think any word can explain a man's life. No, I guess Rosebud is just a piece in a jigsaw puzzle, a missing piece."

*Alland*

LAST LINE
**19.** "Throw that junk in."

*Paul Stewart (Raymond) to workers, as Rosebud is thrown into the flames.*

**CITY FOR CONQUEST** *(Warner Bros.–First National, 1940). D: Anatole Litvak. S: John Wexley. Fr: Aben Kandel (novel).*

**1.** "Yes, my brother made music with his fists so that I might make a gentler music—the symphony that you have heard tonight."

*Arthur Kennedy (Eddie Kenny), thanking his brother James Cagney (Danny Kenny) as he addresses an audience*

**CITY SLICKERS** *(Columbia, 1991). D: Ron Underwood. S: Lowell Ganz, Babaloo Mandel. Fr: Billy Crystal (story).*

**1.** "Don't sew up anything that's supposed to remain open."

*Billy Crystal (Mitch Robbins) to his doctor, after being chased by a bull*

**2.** "Ed, have you noticed the older you get, the younger your girlfriends get? Soon, you'll be dating sperm."

*Crystal to Bruno Kirby (Ed Furillo)*

**3.** "Did you ever reach a point in your life, where you say to yourself, 'This is the best I'm ever going to look, the best I'm ever going to feel, the best I'm ever going to do,' and it ain't that great?"

*Crystal*

**4.** "The seventies, you and your wife retire to Ft. Lauderdale. You start eating dinner at two o'clock in the afternoon. You have lunch around ten. Breakfast, the night before. Spend most of your time wandering around malls looking for the ultimate soft yogurt, and muttering, 'How come the kids don't call? How come the kids don't call?'"

*Crystal, to a schoolroom on career day*

**5.** "They got me by the balls. She's got one. He's got the other."

*Daniel Stern (Phil Berquist), referring to his wife and father-in-law*

**6.** "At this age, where you are, you are."

*Stern to Crystal*

**7.** "Go and find your smile."

*Patricia Wettig (Barbara Robbins), Crystal's wife*

**8.** "When I was alive, I would have found her attractive."

*Stern to Crystal, referring to Helen Slater (Bonnie Rayeburn)*

**9.** "You came out here city slickers. You're going to go home cowboys."

*Noble Willingham (Clay Stone)*

**10.** "Women need a reason to have sex. Men just need a place."

*Crystal to Kirby*

**11.** "I crap bigger than you."

*Jack Palance (Curly) to Crystal*

**12.** CRYSTAL: "Hi, Curly, kill anyone today?"
PALANCE: "Day ain't over yet."

**13.** PALANCE, holding up a finger to signify the secret of life: "One thing. Just one thing. You stick to that and everything else don't mean shit."
CRYSTAL: "That's great, but what's the one thing?"
PALANCE: "That's what you've got to figure out."

**14.** "Lord, we give you Curly. Try not to piss him off."

*Tracey Walter (Cookie), giving Palance's eulogy*

**CLASH OF THE TITANS** *(UK: CIC, 1981). D: Desmond Davis. S: Beverley Cross.*

**LAST LINE**
**1.** "Even if we, the gods, are abandoned or forgotten, the stars will never fade, never. They will burn till the end of time."

*Laurence Olivier (Zeus)*

**CLEAR AND PRESENT DANGER** *(Paramount, 1994). D: Phillip Noyce. S: Donald Stewart, Steven Zaillian, John Milius. Fr: Tom Clancy (novel).*

**1.** "Not black and white: right or wrong."

*Spy Harrison Ford (Jack Ryan), on being told he sees things in black and white*

**CLEOPATRA** *(20th Century–Fox, 1963). D: Joseph L. Mankiewicz. S: Joseph L. Mankiewicz, Ranald MacDougall, Sidney Buchman. Fr: Plutarch (works), Appian (works), Suetonius (works), Carlo Mario Franzero (novel, The Life and Times of Cleopatra).*

**1.** "There has never been such a silence . . . "

*Elizabeth Taylor (Cleopatra), on Richard Burton's (Marc Antony's) death*

**CLOCKWORK ORANGE, A** *(UK: Warner Bros., 1972). D: Stanley Kubrick. S: Stanley Kubrick. Fr: Anthony Burgess (novel).*

**FIRST LINE**
**1.** "There was me, that is Alex, and my three droogs, that is Pete, Georgy, and Dim, and we sat in the Korova Milkbar trying to make up our rassoodocks what to do with the evening. The Korova Milkbar sold Milkplus, Milkplus Vellocet, or Synthemesc or

Drencrom, which is what we were drinking. This would sharpen you up and make you ready for a bit of the old ultraviolence."

*Malcolm McDowell (Alex), narrating*

**2.** "Oh, it's no world for an old man any longer."

*Paul Farrell, an old tramp about to be beaten by McDowell and his droogs*

**3.** "They were getting ready to perform a little of the old in-out in-out on a weepy young devotchka they had there."

*McDowell, narrating how he came across a rival gang attempting to rape a woman*

**4.** "Viddy well, little brother, viddy well."

*McDowell, telling writer Patrick Magee (Mr. Alexander) to watch as he prepares to rape his wife Adrienne Corri (Mrs. Alexander)*

**5.** "It was a bit from the Glorious Ninth by Ludwig Van."

*McDowell, hearing a woman in the Milkbar sing part of Beethoven's Ninth Symphony*

**6.** "Welly, welly, welly, welly, welly, welly, well."

*McDowell, making conversation with his droogs*

**7.** "You're becoming healthy, that's all. By this time tomorrow you'll be healthier still."

*Madge Ryan (Dr. Branom), on the torments of the Ludovico treatment intended to cure McDowell of his criminal tendencies*

**8.** "Can't be helped. Here's the punishment element perhaps. Governor ought to be pleased."

*Carl Duering (Dr. Brodsky), on inadvertently teaching Alex to have a horror of Beethoven's Ninth Symphony*

**9.** "These are subtleties. We're not concerned with motives, with the higher ethics. We are concerned only with cutting down crime."

*Anthony Sharp (Minister of the Interior), on the moral objections of prison chaplain Godfrey Quigley to the scientific rehabilitation of McDowell*

**10.** "As an unmuddied lake, Fred. As clear as an azure sky of deepest summer. You can rely on me, Fred."

*McDowell to Sharp, on whether he is clear about the terms of their collaboration, repeating a line said earlier to parole officer Aubrey Morris (P. R. Deltoid)*

**LAST LINE**
**11.** "I was cured, all right."

*McDowell, on being restored to his old violent self*


**CLOSE ENCOUNTERS OF THE THIRD KIND** (Columbia, 1977). D: Steven Spielberg. S: Steven Spielberg.

*1.* "This means something. This is important."

*Richard Dreyfuss (Roy Neary) to his family, when he makes a model of the Devil's Tower in mashed potatoes*

**2.** "I just want to know that it's really happening."

*Dreyfuss to Francois Truffaut (Claude Lacombe), referring to the alien visitation*

**3.** "Monsieur, I envy you."

*Truffaut to Dreyfuss, who is going away with the alien ship*

**4.** "Bye."

*Cary Guffey (Berry Guiler), the little boy who was temporarily abducted by the aliens, saying good-bye to the departing spaceship*

**COCOANUTS, THE** (Paramount, 1929). D: Joseph Santley, Robert Florey. S: Morris Ryskind. Fr: George S. Kaufman, Irving Berlin (play).

**1.** "Three years ago I came to Florida without a nickel in my pocket. And now I've got a nickel in my pocket."

*Groucho Marx (Mr. Hammer), hotel manager*

**2.** CHICO MARX (*Hotel Guest*): "We want a room, but no bath."
GROUCHO: "Oh, I see. You're just here for the winter."

**3.** "Your eyes—they shine like the pants of a blue serge suit."

*Groucho, making love to Margaret Dumont (Mrs. Potter)*

**4.** "I'll meet you tonight under the moon. Oh, I can see you now, you and the moon. You wear a necktie so I'll know you."

*Groucho to Dumont*

**5.** "Say, the next time I see you, remind me not to talk to you, will you?"

*Groucho to Chico*

**6.** "Why a duck?"

*Chico, getting travel directions from Groucho and misunderstanding what Groucho means by a "viaduct"*

**7.** "Believe me, you have to get up early if you want to get out of bed."

*Groucho*

**COCOON** (20th Century–Fox, 1985). D: Ron Howard. S: Tom Benedek.

**1.** HUME CRONYN (*Joe Finley*): "Doctors don't know everything."

WILFORD BRIMLEY (*Ben Luckett*): "Well, there is a school of thought that says they don't know nothing."

**2.** "I feel tremendous! I'm ready to take on the world."

*Don Ameche (Art Selwyn), feeling the effects of the cocoon*

**3.** "Every ten or eleven thousand years or so, I make a terrible mistake."

*Brian Dennehy (Walter), letting the old men use the pool*

**4.** "I hope you're not going to take your skin off, 'cause I really like skin on a woman."

*Steve Guttenberg (Jack Bonner), to Tawnee Welch (Kitty)*

**5.** "If this is foreplay, I'm a dead man."

*Guttenberg, at Welch's extraterrestrial display of affection*

**6.** "We'll never get sick. We won't get any older, and we'll never die."

*Brimley, to his grandson, explaining what it'll be like where he's going*

**7.** "Men should be explorers, no matter how old they are."

*Ameche*

**8.** "I don't want to live forever if you're not going to be with me."

*Hume Cronyn (Joe Finley) to Jessica Tandy (Alma Finley)*

**COLD FEET** (Avenue, 1989). D: Robert Dornhelm. S: Tom McGuane, Jim Harrison.

**LAST LINE**
**1.** "Laura wakes in the middle of the night and starts laughing for no reason. There's

nothing like a woman's laughter to tell you you've done the right thing."

*Bill Pullman (Buck)*

**COLOR OF MONEY, THE** *(Buena Vista, 1986). D: Martin Scorsese. S: Richard Price. Fr: Walter Tevis (novel).*

**1.** "I never kid about money."

*Pool hustler Paul Newman (Eddie Felson)*

**2.** "If you got an area of excellence . . . if you're good at something . . . you're the best at something, anything, then rich can be arranged."

*Newman to Tom Cruise (Vincent Lauria)*

**3.** "You are a natural character. You're an incredible flake. But that's a gift. See, guys spend half their lives trying to invent something like that."

*Newman to Cruise*

**4.** "You couldn't find big time if you had a road map."

*Newman to Cruise*

**5.** "You got to be a student of human moves. See, all the greats that I know of, to a man, were students of human moves."

*Newman to Cruise, on pool hustling*

**6.** "He's got to learn how to be himself, but on purpose."

*Newman to Mary Elizabeth Mastrantonio (Carmen), on Cruise*

**7.** "Sometimes, if you lose, you win."

*Newman to Cruise, on hustling*

**8.** "It ain't about pool. It ain't about sex. It ain't about love. It's about money. I mean the best is the guy with the most. That's the whole show. The best is the guy with the most in all walks of life."

*Newman to Cruise*

**9.** "You never ease off on somebody like that, not when there's money involved. That's the problem with mercy, kid. Just be a professional."

*Newman to Cruise*

**10.** "We got a racehorse, here. A thoroughbred. You make him feel good. I teach him how to run."

*Newman to Mastrantonio, on Cruise*

**11.** "I can always go back to whiskey. It's been very good to me."

*Newman to Cruise*

**12.** "Money won is twice as sweet as money earned."

*Newman to Cruise*

**13.** "You got to have two things to win. You got to have brains, and you got to have balls. Now, you've got too much of one, and not enough of the other."

*Newman to Cruise*

**LAST LINES**
**14.** CRUISE: "What makes you so sure?"
     NEWMAN: "Hey, I'm back."

**COLOR PURPLE, THE** *(Warner Bros., 1985). D: Steven Spielberg. S: Menno Meyjes. Fr: Alice Walker (novel).*

**1.** "I don't know how to fight. All I know how to do is stay alive."

*Desreta Jackson (Young Celie) to Young Nettie*

**2.** "Young women no good these days. Got their legs open for every Tom, Dick, and Harpo."

*Danny Glover (Albert Johnson)*

**3.** "This life be over soon. Heaven lasts always."

*Whoopi Goldberg (Celie)*

**4.** "You sure is ugly!"

*Margaret Avery (Shug Avery) to Goldberg*

**5.** "He beat me for not being you."

*Goldberg to Avery, referring to Glover*

**6.** "I don't know y'all no more."

*Oprah Winfrey (Sophia) to her family, when she sees them for the first time after a long while*

**7.** "It's time for me to get away from you. And end your creation. And your dead body be just the welcome mat I need."

*Goldberg to Glover*

**8.** "I'm poor, black. I may even be ugly, but, dear God, I'm here. I'm here!"

*Goldberg to Glover*

**9.** "I think it pisses God off if you walk by the color purple in a field, and don't notice it."

*Avery to Goldberg*

**COME BACK, LITTLE SHEBA** (Paramount, 1952). D: Daniel Mann. S: Ketti Frings. Fr: William Inge (play).

**1.** BURT LANCASTER (*Doc Delaney*): "Please don't ever leave me."

SHIRLEY BOOTH (*Lola Delaney*): "I'd never leave you, Daddy. You're all I got, Doc. You're all I'll ever have."

**2.** "I don't think Little Sheba is ever coming back. I ain't gonna call her no more."

*Booth to Lancaster, about her beloved pet dog*

**LAST LINE**
**3.** "It's good to be home."

*Lancaster to Booth*

**COMING HOME** (UA, 1978). D: Hal Ashby. S: Waldo Salt, Robert C. Jones. Fr: Nancy Dowd (story).

**1.** "This isn't 'Have a gimp over for dinner' night, is it?"

*Disabled Vietnam veteran Jon Voight (Luke Martin) to Jane Fonda (Sally Hyde)*

**LAST LINE**
**2.** "And I'm just telling you there's a choice to be made here."

*Voight, addressing high school students on the Vietnam War*

**COMING TO AMERICA** (Paramount, 1988). D: John Landis. S: David Sheffield, Barry W. Blaustein. Fr: Eddie Murphy (story).

**1.** "The land is so big. The choices so infinite. Where shall we go? Los Angeles or New York?"

*Arsenio Hall (Semi), servant to Eddie Murphy (Prince Akeem), a foreign prince who has come to America to find his bride*

**2.** HALL: "Where in New York can one find a woman with grace, elegance, taste, and culture? A woman suitable for a king?"
MURPHY: "Queens."

**3.** "What does 'dumb fuck' mean?"

*Murphy to Hall, inquiring after a local calls him same*

**COMPANY OF WOLVES, THE** (UK: Palace/Cannon, 1984). D: Neil Jordan. S: Angela Carter, Neil Jordan. Fr: Angela Carter (story collection).

**1.** "Never stray from the path, never eat a windfall apple, and never trust a man whose eyebrows meet."

*Angela Lansbury (Granny), giving folk advice to Sarah Patterson (Rosaleen)*

**2.** "The worst kind of wolves are hairy on the inside, and when they bite you, they drag you with them to Hell."

*Lansbury to Patterson*

**3.** "I don't come from Hell. I come from the forest."

*Micha Bergese (huntsman and werewolf) to Lansbury*

**4.** "I love the company of wolves."

*Bergese*

**5.** "They say the prince of darkness is a gentleman."

*Patterson to Bergese*

**6.** "Jesus, what big teeth you have!"

*Patterson, on kissing Bergese*

**7.** "She went into the world below, and that's all I'll tell you, because that's all I know."

*Patterson to Bergese, finishing a story about a wounded werewolf girl*

**COMPETITION, THE** (Columbia, 1980). D: Joel Oliansky. S: Joel Oliansky. Fr: Joel Oliansky, William Sackheim (story).

**LAST LINE**
**1.** "You've got about a century to wait before evolution produces the man you have in mind. So in the meantime, get out there and dance with what there is."

*Lee Remick (Greta Vandemann)*

**CONTINENTAL DIVIDE** (Universal, 1981). D: Michael Apted. S: Lawrence Kasdan.

**1.** "It's so quiet up here, you can hear a mouse get a hard-on."

*John Belushi, a Chicago reporter (Ernie Souchak), who is sent to the Rockies to cover the story of a woman who studies eagles*

**COOL HAND LUKE** (Warner Bros., 1967). D: Stuart Rosenberg. S: Donn Pearce, Frank R. Pierson. Fr: Donn Pearce (novel).

**1.** "What we've got here is a failure to communicate."

*Strother Martin (Captain) to Paul Newman (Luke)*

**LAST LINE**
**2.** "Old Luke, he was some boy. Cool Hand Luke, hell, he's a natural-born world-shaker."

*George Kennedy (Dragline), on Newman*

**COP AND A HALF** (Universal, 1993). D: Henry Winkler. S: Lawrence Konner, Mark Rosenthal, Arne Olsen.

**1.** "I'm your worst nightmare. An eight-year-old with a badge."

*Norman D. Golden II (Devon Butler) to Burt Reynolds (Nick McKenna), in a line alluding to 48HRS.*

**COUNTRY GIRL, THE** (Paramount, 1954). D: George Seaton. S: George Seaton. Fr: Clifford Odets (play).

**1.** "May you smoke? What's that supposed to be—homage to a lady?"

*Grace Kelly (Georgie Elgin), deflating William Holden's (Bernie Dodd's) attempt at politeness*

**COURT JESTER, THE** (Paramount, 1956). D: Norman Panama. S: Norman Panama, Melvin Frank.

**1.** "Oh, I see . . . the pellet with the poison's in the flagon with the dragon; the vessel with the pestle has the brew that is true."

*Danny Kaye (Hawkins) to Robert Middleton (Sir Griswold)*

**COVER GIRL** (Columbia, 1944). D: Charles Vidor. S: Virginia Van Upp, Marion Parsonnet, Paul Gangelin. Fr: Erwin Gelsey (story).

**1.** "Your grapes are so sour I can smell 'em from here."

*Chorus girl to Leslie Brooks (Maurine Martin)*

**2.** "Brooklyn, James."

*Broadway producer Lee Bowman (Noel Wheaton), ordering his chauffeur to take Rita Hayworth (Rusty Parker/Maribelle Hicks) home to where her heart is*

**3.** "I can't risk getting struck dead, can I?"

*Bowman, letting Hayworth go at the altar so she can go back to Gene Kelly (Danny McGuire)*

**CRIMES AND MISDEMEANORS** (Orion, 1989). D: Woody Allen. S: Woody Allen.

**1.** "It's like thousands of straight lines just looking for a punch line."

*Comedy maven Alan Alda (Lester), on New York City*

**2.** "God is a luxury I can't afford."

*Martin Landau (Judah Rosenthal), adulterer and murderer*

**3.** "The eyes of God see all."

*Landau's father, in a childhood flashback Landau has upon seeing the dead Anjelica Huston (Dolores Paley)*

**4.** "April 20. I remember the date exactly 'cause it was Hitler's birthday."

*Woody Allen (Cliff Stern) to his wife, on the date she stopped sleeping with him*

**5.** "It's worse than dog eat dog. It's dog doesn't return other dog's phone calls."

*Allen, on show business*

**6.** "Where I grew up in Brooklyn nobody killed themselves. They were too unhappy."

*Allen to Mia Farrow (Halley Reed)*

**7.** "One sin leads to a deeper sin."

*Landau to brother and professional criminal Jerry Orbach (Jack Rosenthal)*

**8.** "If it bends, it's funny. If it breaks, it isn't."

*Alda's views on comedy, later dubbed onto a horse in an Allen documentary skewering Alda's pomposity*

**9.** "What is the guy so upset about? He's not the first person to be compared to Mussolini."

*Allen to Farrow, wondering why Alda was so upset about the documentary on him*

**10.** "I'm so self-conscious. Every single thing on me is rented."

*Allen, in a tuxedo at a formal party at Carnegie Hall*

**11.** "It's probably just as well. I plagiarized most of it from James Joyce. You probably wondered about all the references to Dublin."

*Allen to Farrow, as she returns his love letter to him*

**LAST LINE**

**12.** "Human happiness does not seem to have been included in the design of creation. It is only we, with our capacity to love, that give meaning to the indifferent universe. And yet most human beings seem to have the ability to keep trying and even to find joy from simple things, like their family, their work, and from the hope that future generations might understand more."

*Martin Bergmann (Professor Louis Levy)*

**CRIMES OF PASSION** *(New World, 1984). D: Ken Russell. S: Barry Sandler.*

**1.** "The last reverend who tried to save me lived to regret it. I chased him all round the church until I caught him by the organ."

*Prostitute Kathleen Turner (Joanna Crane/ China Blue) to bogus minister Anthony Perkins (Reverend Peter Shyane)*

**2.** "This is the fantasy business, Reverend. You can have any truth you want."

*Turner, when her customer Perkins asks her to be her true self*

**3.** "Whores and metaphors don't mix."

*Perkins to Turner*

**4.** "B movies have always been my inspiration."

*Turner to Perkins*

**5.** "I'm a hooker. You're a trick. Why ruin a perfect relationship?"

*Turner to Perkins*

**CRIMSON PIRATE, THE** *(UK: Warner Bros., 1952). D: Robert Siodmak. S: Roland Kibbee.*

**1.** "Remember, in a pirate ship, in pirate waters, in a pirate world, ask no questions. Believe only what you see. No, believe half of what you see."

*Burt Lancaster (Vallo) to the audience*

**2.** LANCASTER: "Why did you bolt your cabin door last night?"
EVA BARTOK *(Consuelo):* "If you knew it was bolted you must have tried it. If you tried it, you know why it was bolted."

**3.** "All my life I've watched injustice and dishonesty fly the flag of decency. I don't trust it."

*Lancaster to Bartok*

**4.** "Yellow was never a pirate's color."

*Lancaster, referring to cowardice*

**"CROCODILE" DUNDEE** *(Australia: Paramount, 1986). D: Peter Faiman. S: Paul Hogan, Ken Shadie, John Cornell. Fr: Paul Hogan (story).*

**1.** "G'day."

*Paul Hogan's (Michael J. "Crocodile" Dundee's) habitual greeting*

**2.** "That's not a knife. *That's* a knife."

*Hogan, showing a mugger what a real knife looks like*

**CROSS CREEK** *(Universal, 1983). D: Martin Ritt. S: Dalene Young. Fr: Marjorie Kinnan Rawlings (book).*

**LAST LINE**

**1.** "Cross Creek belongs to the wind and the

rain, to the sun and seasons, to the cosmic secrecy of seed, and beyond all to time."

*Mary Steenburgen (Marjorie Kinnan Rawlings)*

**CROSSING DELANCEY** *(Warner Bros., 1988). D: Joan Micklin Silver. S: Susan Sandler. Fr: Susan Sandler (play).*

**1.** "I am a happy person."

*Amy Irving (Isabelle "Izzy" Grossman) to Reizl Bozyk (Bubbie Kantor), on her unsettled, unmarried state*

**2.** "A joke and a pickle for only a nickel."

*Peter Riegert's (Sam Posner's) Lower East Side pickle stand sign*

**3.** "I don't know what to do with you. You're a nice guy."

*Irving to Riegert*

**CRYING GAME, THE** *(UK: Miramax, 1992). D: Neil Jordan. S: Neil Jordan.*

**1.** JAYE DAVIDSON (*Dil*), referring to Stephen Rea's (*Fergus's*) prison sentence: "I'm counting the days—2,234 left."
REA (*Fergus*): "Thirty-five."

**2.** "Fergus, Fergus, my love, light of my life."

*Davidson to Rea*

**LAST LINE**
**3.** "I can't help it. It's in my nature."

*Rea, reporting what the scorpion said to the frog, according to story told him earlier by Forest Whitaker (Jody), applied now to why Rea is doing time for Davidson*

**CURSE OF THE DEMON** *(Columbia, 1958). D: Jacques Tourneur. S: Charles Bennett, Hal*

E. Chester. Fr: Montague R. James (story, "Casting the Runes").

**LAST LINE**
**1.** "You're right. Maybe it's better not to know."

*Dana Andrews (John Holden) to Peggy Cummins (Joanna Harrington), about the death of Niall MacGinnis (Dr. Karswell) at the hands of a demon*

**CYRANO DE BERGERAC** *(UA, 1950). D: Michael Gordon. S: Carl Foreman. Fr: Edmond Rostand (play).*

**1.** "When it bleeds—the Red Sea!"

*Jose Ferrer (Cyrano), on his nose*

**DAISY KENYON** *(20th Century–Fox, 1947). D: Otto Preminger. S: David Hertz. Fr: Elizabeth Janeway (novel).*

**1.** "When you hear the tone, Daisy Kenyon will have been stood up for the first time in her life."

*Joan Crawford (Daisy Kenyon) to telephone operator, when she's been stood up by suitor Henry Fonda (Peter Lapham)*

**2.** "I love you, too, I guess."

*Crawford, somewhat uncertainly, to lover Dana Andrews (Dan O'Mara), who is married to another woman*

**3.** "I can't wander all my life. I've got to be going somewhere, even if it's to the movies."

*Crawford to Andrews, opting to go to the movies instead of continuing to talk to him*

**4.** CRAWFORD: "You're using me, sort of."
FONDA: "Yes, aren't you using me?"

**DAMN YANKEES** *(Warner Bros., 1958). D: George Abbott, Stanley Donen. S: George Abbott. Fr: George Abbott (play), Douglas Wallop (novel,* The Year the Yankees Lost the Pennant*).*

LAST LINE

**1.** "Listen to me, you wife-loving louse. You belong to me. You sold me your soul. You can't run out on me like this. Ya thief. Ya crook. You robbed me, that's what you did. You robbed me. You robbed me."

*Ray Walston (Applegate, the Devil) to Robert Shafer (Joe Boyd), who has eluded his grasp*

**DANCE, FOOLS, DANCE** *(MGM, 1931). D: Harry Beaumont. S: Aurania Rouverol, Richard Schayer. Fr: Aurania Rouverol (story).*

**1.** "Wealthy bachelors don't grow on every rosebush."

*William Blakewell (Rodney Jordan)*

**2.** "Nothing left but my reputation."

*Joan Crawford (Bonnie Jordan), after losing everything in the stock market crash*

**3.** "They'd cut the Lord's prayer down to a one-line squib."

*Cliff Edwards (Bert Scranton), remarking on editors*

**DANCES WITH WOLVES** *(Orion, 1990). D: Kevin Costner. S: Michael Blake. Fr: Michael Blake (novel).*

**1.** "In trying to produce my own death, I was elevated to the status of a living hero."

*Kevin Costner (Lt. Dunbar), in narration*

**2.** COSTNER: "I've always wanted to see the frontier."
PLACEMENT OFFICER: "You want to see the frontier?"
COSTNER: "Yes, sir. Before it's gone."

**3.** "Only a white man would make a fire for everyone to see."

*Wes Studi (Pawnee), seeing smoke from Robert Pastorelli's (Timmons's) fire*

**4.** "Most of our progress has been built on the basis of failure, rather than success."

*Costner, in narration, referring to going out to meet the Indians*

**5.** "A dance is always a good idea."

*Indian chief, on Graham Greene's (Kicking Bird's) idea for a dance*

**6.** "Voices that had been joyous all morning were now as silent as the dead buffalo left to rot in this valley, killed only for their tongues and the price of their hides."

*Costner, in narration*

**7.** "This is a good trade."

*Costner, referring to trading his uniform jacket for Indian garb*

**8.** "It seems every day ends with a miracle here. And whatever God may be, I thank God for this day."

*Costner, in narration*

**9.** "I tell him that the white people will most likely pass through this country and nothing more. But I am speaking in half-truths. One day, there will be too many, but I cannot bring myself to tell him that."

*Costner, in narration*

**10.** "I'd never been in a battle like this one. There was no dark political objective. This was not a fight for territory, or riches, or to make men free. It had been fought to preserve the food stores that would see us through the winter, to protect the lives of women and children, and loved ones only a few feet away."

*Costner, in narration*

**11.** "I'd never really known who John Dunbar was. Perhaps the name itself had no meaning, but as I heard my Sioux name being called over and over, I knew for the first time who I really was."

*Costner, in narration*

**12.** "I was just thinking that of all the trails in this life, there is one that matters most. It is the trail of a true human being. I think you are on this trail, and it is good to see."

*Greene to Costner, when Costner marries Mary McDonnell (Stands with a Fist) and tries to have a child*

**DANGEROUS LIAISONS** *(Warner Bros., 1988). D: Stephen Frears. S: Christopher Hampton. Fr: Christopher Hampton (play), Choderlos de Laclos (novel,* Les Liaisons Dangereuses*).*

**1.** "To seduce a woman famous for strict morals, religious fervor, and the happiness of her marriage—what could possibly be more prestigious?"

*John Malkovich (Vicomte de Valmont) to Glenn Close (Marquise de Merteuil), on his motivation for seducing Michelle Pfeiffer (Madame de Tourvel)*

**2.** MALKOVICH: "I often wonder how you managed to invent yourself."
CLOSE: "Well, I had no choice, did I? I'm a woman. . . . And I've succeeded because I've always known I was born to dominate your sex and avenge my own."

**3.** "And in the end I distilled everything to one wonderfully simple principle: win or die."

*Close to Malkovich*

**4.** "So I promise—no more refusals, no more regrets."

*Pfeiffer, surrendering to Malkovich's advances*

**5.** "She was astonishing. So much so that I ended by falling on my knees and pledging her eternal love. And do you know that at that time and for several hours afterward I actually meant it."

*Malkovich to Close, on his liaison with Pfeiffer*

**6.** "It's beyond my control."

*Malkovich to Pfeiffer, explaining why he must end their relationship*

**DARK CORNER, THE** *(20th Century–Fox, 1946). D: Henry Hathaway. S: Jay Dratler, Bernard Schoenfeld. Fr: Leo Rosten (short story).*

**1.** "How I detest the dawn! The grass always looks like it's been left out all night."

*Clifton Webb (Hardy Cathcart)*

**DARK MIRROR, THE** *(Universal-International, 1946). D: Robert Siodmak. S: Nunnally Johnson. Fr: Vladimir Pozner (novel).*

**1.** "There ought to be a state law against selling gloves to murderers."

*Thomas Mitchell (Detective Stevenson), when no fingerprints are found*

**2.** "I don't mind ordinary music. It's the wonderful stuff that bores me."

*Mitchell*

**DARK VICTORY** (First National–Warner Bros., 1939). D: Edmund Goulding. S: Casey Robinson. Fr: George Emerson Brewer, Jr., Bertram Bloch (play).

**1.** "Nothing can hurt us now. What we have can't be destroyed. That's our victory—our victory over the dark. It is a victory because we're not afraid."

*Bette Davis (Judith Traherne)*

**DARLING** (UK: Anglo-Amalgamated, 1965). D: John Schlesinger. S: Frederic Raphael. Fr: Frederic Raphael, John Schlesinger, Joseph Janni (story).

**1.** "Your idea of fidelity is not having more than one man in bed at the same time."

*Dirk Bogarde (Robert Gold) to Julie Christie (Diana Scott)*

**DAVID COPPERFIELD** (MGM, 1935). D: George Cukor. S: Howard Estabrook, Hugh Walpole. Fr: Charles Dickens (novel).

**1.** "Poor Father. How lonely and dark it must be for him at night, while we're at home by the fire."

*Freddie Bartholomew (David Copperfield, the younger), at his father's grave*

**2.** "You'll find us rough, sir, but you'll find us ready."

*Lionel Barrymore (Dan Peggotty) to Bartholomew, when Bartholomew comes to visit the Peggotty house*

**3.** BASIL RATHBONE (*Mr. Murdstone*): "When I have an obstinate horse I'm about to deal with, what do you think I do?"

BARTHOLOMEW: "I don't know."

RATHBONE: "I beat him. I make him wince and smart. I say to myself, 'I'll conquer that fellow,' and if it were to cost him all the blood he had, I'd do it."

*Rathbone to Bartholomew, just before Rathbone beats him*

**4.** "Young friend, I counsel you. Annual income twenty pounds, annual expenditure nineteen pounds, result: happiness. Annual income twenty pounds, annual expenditure twenty-one pounds, result: misery."

*Perennial debtor W. C. Fields (Micawber) to Bartholomew, when Bartholomew leaves*

**5.** "You must make us proud, David. Never be mean in anything. Never be false. Never be cruel. Avoid these three vices and I can always be hopeful of you."

*Edna May Oliver (Betsey Trotwood), when Bartholomew goes away to school*

**6.** "The old sun must be amused by the constant spectacle of romantic lovers."

*Hugh Williams (Steerforth), to Frank Lawton (David Copperfield, as a man), at sunset*

**DAY AT THE RACES, A** (MGM, 1937). D: Sam Wood. S: Robert Pirosh, George Seaton, George Oppenheimer. Fr: Robert Pirosh, George Seaton (story).

**1.** ALLAN JONES (*Gil*) to GROUCHO MARX (*Dr. Hackenbush*): "Are you a man or a mouse?"

GROUCHO: "You put a piece of cheese down here and you'll find out."

**2.** GROUCHO, on his medical training: "Oh, well, to begin with I took four years at Vassar."

MARGARET DUMONT (*Mrs. Upjohn*): "Vassar? But that's a girls' college."

GROUCHO: "I found that out the third year. I'd've been there yet, but I went out for the swimming team."

**3.** "It's the old story. Boy meets girl—Romeo and Juliet—Minneapolis and St. Paul!"

*Groucho, romancing Dumont*

**4.** "Get your ice cream. Tootsie-fruitsie ice cream."

*Constant cry of ice-cream vendor and racetrack con artist Chico Marx (Tony)*

**5.** "And don't point that beard at me—it might go off!"

*Groucho to the pointy-bearded Sig Rumann (Dr. Steinberg)*

**6.** CHICO, pretending to be a hotel detective interrupting Groucho's hot date: "Have you got a woman in here?"

GROUCHO: "If I haven't, I've wasted thirty minutes of valuable time."

**7.** ESTHER MUIR (*Flo*) to Groucho: "Oh, hold me closer! Closer! Closer!"

GROUCHO: "If I hold you any closer I'll be in back of you!"

**DAY OF THE TRIFFIDS, THE** (*UK: Allied Artists, 1963*). D: Steve Sekely. S: Philip Yordan. Fr: John Wyndham (novel).

**1.** "Keep behind me. There's no sense in being killed by a plant."

*Marine biologist Kieron Moore (Tom Goodwin) to his wife Janette Scott (Karen Goodwin)*

**2.** "Once you taste this coffee of mine, you'll know nothing worse can happen."

*Howard Keel (Bill Masen), getting coffee ready in the midst of apocalypse*

**DAY THE EARTH STOOD STILL, THE** (*20th Century–Fox, 1951*). D: Robert Wise. S: Edmund H. North. Fr: Harry Bates (story).

**1.** "Gort. Klaatu baraada nikto."

*Patricia Neal (Helen Benson), conveying a mysterious alien instruction to the robot Gort (Lock Martin)*

**2.** "Your choice is simple: join us and live in peace, or pursue your present course and face obliteration. We shall be waiting for your answer. The decision rests with you."

*Alien visitor Michael Rennie (Klaatu), delivering an ultimatum to a crowd of international dignitaries representing the people of the Earth*

**DAYS OF HEAVEN** (*Paramount, 1978*). D: Terence Malick. S: Terrence Malick.

LAST LINE
**1.** "This girl, she didn't know where she was going or what she was going to do. She didn't have no money on her. Maybe she'd meet up with a character. I was hoping things would work out for her. She was a good friend of mine."

*Linda Manz (Linda), narrating, about her friend*

**DAYS OF WINE AND ROSES** (*Warner Bros., 1962*). D: Blake Edwards. S: J. P. Miller. Fr: J. P. Miller (teleplay).

**1.** "C'mon, look at us. See? A couple of bums."

*Jack Lemmon (Joe Clay), showing Lee Remick (Kirsten Arnesen) their image in a mirror*

**2.** "This is the way I look when I'm sober. It's enough to make a person drink, wouldn't you say?"

*Remick to Lemmon*

**DEAD AGAIN** (Paramount, 1991). D: Kenneth Branagh. S: Scott Frank.

**1.** "You take what you learn from this life and you use it in the next. That's karma."

Robin Williams (Dr. Cozy Carlisle), explaining reincarnation to Kenneth Branagh (Mike Church) and Emma Thompson (Grace), in the throes of a mystery involving their former lives

**2.** "If fate works at all, it works because people think that this time it isn't going to happen."

Derek Jacobi (Franklyn Madson) to Thompson

**3.** "Well, I for one am very interested to see what's going to happen next."

Jacobi to Thompson and Branagh, wondering which of them will kill which first

**LAST LINE**
**4.** "It's okay. It's okay. The door just closed."

Branagh to Thompson, now that the door to their past lives has closed

**DEAD END** (Samuel Goldwyn/UA, 1937). D: William Wyler. S: Lillian Hellman. Fr: Sidney Kingsley (play).

**1.** HUMPHREY BOGART (Baby Face Martin): "Why didn't you starve first?"
CLAIRE TREVOR (Francey): "Why didn't you?"

Former neighborhood friends commenting on each other's professions, as gangster and prostitute, respectively

**2.** "Enemies of society, it says in the paper. Why not? What have they got to be friendly about?"

Joel McCrea (Dave), on kids raised in the slums

**3.** "You'd think if they didn't have to work they'd sit quiet and have a nice beer."

Doorman Ward Bond, on a fancy and noisy party upstairs

**4.** "Not enough left for a good postmortem."

Intern Don Barry, on Bogart's bullet-riddled corpse

**5.** "I live on this block and I work on this block and I got a right to see what's going on."

Neighborhood woman Esther Howard to cop telling her to move along from the scene of Bogart's death

**6.** "I pity the guy who snitched."

Bernard Punsley (Milty), putting fear into Leo Gorcey's (Spit's) heart, after Gorcey has informed on a companion

**DEAD POETS SOCIETY** (Buena Vista, 1989). D: Peter Weir. S: Tom Schulman.

**1.** "Seize the day!"

English teacher Robin Williams (John Keating), giving advice to his class

**2.** "Did they wait till it was too late to make from their lives even one iota of what they were capable? Because you see, gentlemen, these boys are now fertilizing daffodils."

Williams, showing the class pictures of previous alumni

**3.** "How can you describe poetry like 'American Bandstand'? I like Byron. I give him a forty-two, but I can't dance to it."

Williams

**4.** "This is a battle, a war, and the casualties could be your hearts and souls."

Williams

**5.** "My class, you will learn to think for yourselves again. You will learn to savor words and language. No matter what anybody tells you, words and ideas can change the world."

*Williams*

**6.** "That the powerful play goes on and you may contribute a verse. What will your verse be?"

*Williams*

**7.** "We were romantics. We didn't just read poetry. We let it drip from our tongues like honey. Spirits soared. Women swooned, and gods were created, gentlemen. Not a bad way to spend an evening, eh?"

*Williams*

**8.** "Boys, you must strive to find your own voice because the longer you wait to begin, the less likely you are to find it at all."

*Williams*

**DEAD ZONE, THE** (Paramount, 1983). D: David Cronenberg. S: Jeffrey Boam. Fr: Stephen King (novel).

**1.** "I saw his face."

*Christopher Walken (Johnny Smith), reliving the scene of a murder and identifying the Castle Rock Killer*

**2.** "The missiles are flying! Hallelujah!"

*Martin Sheen (Greg Stillson), in Walken's vision of Sheen as President, firing nuclear weapons.*

**3.** HERBERT LOM (*Dr. Sam Welzak*): "Not only can you see the future, you can . . . ."
WALKEN: "I can change it."

**DEADLINE U.S.A.** (20th Century–Fox, 1952). D: Richard Brooks. S: Richard Brooks.

**1.** "There's only one kind of martyr, friend—dead ones."

*Thug, warning Humphrey Bogart (Ed Hutcheson)*

**2.** "That's the press, baby, the press, and there's nothing you can do about it, nothing."

*Bogart, on a free press*

**DEATH BECOMES HER** (Universal, 1992). D: Robert Zemeckis. S: Martin Donovan, David Koepp.

**1.** "We are creatures of the spring, you and I."

*Youth-serum priestess Isabella Rossellini (Lisle Von Rhumans) to youth-seeker Meryl Streep (Madeline Ashton)*

**2.** "Now a warning?"

*Streep, after drinking Rossellini's youth serum and learning that a warning is attached*

**3.** "I'm gonna get a second opinion."

*Sydney Pollack (Doctor), after determining that Streep is a walking corpse*

**4.** "She was a home wrecker, she was a man-eater, and she was a bad actress."

*Goldie Hawn (Helen Sharp) on Streep*

**5.** "That was totally uncalled for."

*Walking corpse Hawn, after being killed by Streep*

**DEATH OF A SALESMAN** (Columbia, 1952). D: Laslo Benedek. S: Stanley Roberts. Fr: Arthur Miller (play).

**1.** "A Salesman's gotta dream, boy. It comes with the territory."

> *Royal Beal (Ben) to Fredric March (Willy Loman)*

**DEER HUNTER, THE** *(Warner Bros., 1978).* D: Michael Cimino. S: Deric Washburn. Fr: Michael Cimino, Deric Washburn, Louis Garfinkle, Quinn K. Redeker (story).

**1.** "You have to think about one shot. One shot is what it's all about. The deer has to be taken with one shot."

> *Robert De Niro (Michael) to Christopher Walken (Nick), on hunting*

**2.** DE NIRO, asking about Vietnam: "What's it like over there? Can you tell us anything?" PAUL D'AMATO (*Green Beret*): "Fuck it."

**3.** "Every time he comes up here, he's got no knife, he's got no jacket, he's got no pants, he's got no boots. All he's got is that stupid gun he carries around like John Wayne."

> *De Niro, on John Cazale (Stan) on the hunting trip*

**4.** "I feel a lot of distance, and I feel far away."

> *De Niro to Meryl Streep (Linda), on returning home from Vietnam*

**5.** "Is this what you want? I love you, man."

> *De Niro to Walken, playing Russian roulette for money in Saigon, just before he shoots a blank*

**6.** WALKEN: "One shot."
DE NIRO: "One shot."

> *Still playing Russian roulette, just before Walken kills himself*

**LAST LINE**
**7.** "Here's to Nick."

> *De Niro, toasting Walken at his funeral*

**DESERT BLOOM** *(Columbia, 1985).* D: Eugene Corr. S: Eugene Corr. Fr: Linda Remy (story).

**LAST LINE**
**1.** "Good morning, survivors, this is radio Keno, Las Vegas. Well, the A-bomb went off and we're all still here, folks. It's forty-seven degrees and six A.M."

> *Voice on the radio*

**DESERT TRAIL** *(Monarch, 1935).* D: Cullin Lewis. S: Lindsley Parsons.

**1.** "It's talk that always gets you into trouble with a woman."

> *Eddy Chandler (Kansas Charlie) to his partner John Wayne (John Scott)*

**2.** "So long, Moses, and I hope you get out of the wilderness."

> *Wayne, bidding farewell to Chandler*

**DESIGNING WOMAN** *(MGM, 1957).* D: Vincente Minnelli. S: George Wells. Fr: Helen Rose (suggestion).

**1.** "How is it that you cannot stand the sight of blood on anyone except me?"

> *Gregory Peck (Mike Hagen) to Lauren Bacall (Marilla Hagen)*

**DESK SET** *(20th Century–Fox, 1957).* D: Walter Lang. S: Phoebe Ephron, Henry Ephron. Fr: William Marchant (play).

**1.** "Available? You're like an old coat that's hanging in his closet. Every time he reaches in, there you are. Don't be there once."

> *Joan Blondell (Peg Costello), advising Katharine Hepburn (Bunny Watson) about how to handle Gig Young (Mike Cutler)*

**DESPERATE JOURNEY** (Warner Bros., 1942). D: Raoul Walsh. S: Arthur T. Horman. Fr: Arthur T. Horman (story, "Forced Landing").

**LAST LINE**

**1.** "Now for Australia and a crack at those Japs!"

Errol Flynn (Flight Lt. Terence Forbes)

**DESTINATION MOON** (Eagle-Lion, 1950). D: Irving Pichel. S: Rip van Ronkel, Robert A. Heinlein, James O'Hanlon. Fr: Robert A. Heinlein (novel, Rocketship Galileo).

**1.** "Well, what do you say, Jim? Do we go to lunch or do we go to the moon?"

Tom Powers (General Thayer), proposing the world's first lunar mission to John Archer (Jim Barnes)

**2.** "The race is on and we'd better win, because there is absolutely no way to stop an attack from outer space. The first country that can use the moon for the launching of missiles will control the Earth. That, gentlemen, is the most important military fact of this century."

Powers, invoking Cold War fear to urge businessmen and scientists to support the lunar mission

**3.** "It'll never budge."

Brooklynite technician Dick Wesson (Joe Sweeney), looking over the rocket designed to travel to the moon

**4.** WESSON, in space, looking through porthole at the distant Earth: "Do you see Brooklyn?"
ARCHER: "Sure, there's Brooklyn."
WESSON: "I wonder who's pitching."

**5.** "By the grace of God, and in the name of the United States of America, I take possession of this planet on behalf of and for the benefit of all mankind."

Warner Anderson (Charles Cargraves) lays claim to the moon

**DESTINATION TOKYO** (Warner Bros., 1943). D: Delmer Daves. S: Albert Maltz, Delmer Daves. Fr: Steve Fisher (story).

**LAST LINE**

**1.** "To the gallant officers and men of the silent service, to our submarines now on war patrol in hostile waters, good luck and good hunting."

Lou Marcelle (Narrator)

**DETECTIVE STORY** (Paramount, 1951). D: William Wyler. S: Philip Yordan, Robert Wyler. Fr: Sidney Kingsley (play).

**1.** "What do you got in place of a conscience? Don't answer. I know: a lawyer."

Kirk Douglas (Jim McLeod) to criminal George Macready (Karl Schneider)

**DETOUR** (Producers Releasing Corp., 1945). D: Edgar G. Ulmer. S: Martin Goldsmith.

**LAST LINE**

**1.** "But one thing I don't have to wonder about; I know. Someday a car will stop to pick me up that I never thumbed. Yes, fate or some mysterious force can put the finger on you or me for no good reason at all."

Hitchhiker Tom Neal (Al Roberts)

**DEVIL AND DANIEL WEBSTER, THE** (RKO, 1941). D: William Dieterle. S: Dan Totheroh. Fr: Stephen Vincent Benet (story).

**FIRST LINE**

**1.** "You're only wasting your time writing speeches like that. Why worry about the people and their problems? Think of your own."

*Walter Huston (Scratch the Devil) to Edward Arnold (Daniel Webster)*

**2.** "That's enough to make a man sell his soul to the Devil! And I would for about two cents!"

*James Craig (Jabez Stone), as two pennies appear in his hand*

**3.** "Do you deny that you called me? I've known people in other states who went back on their word, but I . . . I didn''t expect it in New Hampshire."

*Huston to Craig*

**4.** "A soul is nothing. Can you see it, smell it, touch it? No. This soul, your soul, is nothing against seven years of good luck. You'll have money, and all that money can buy."

*Huston to Craig*

**5.** "A firm signature. One that will last till doomsday."

*Huston to Craig, when Craig sells his soul*

**6.** "Well, thank God, you can always depend on New Hampshire for weather. We've got enough for the whole United States."

*Jane Darwell (Ma Stone) to Craig*

**7.** "A man can always change things. That's what makes him different from the barnyard critters."

*Darwell to Craig*

**8.** "Who has a better right? When the first wrong was done to the first Indian, I was there. When the first slave was put off from the Congo, I stood on the deck. Am I not still

spoken of in every church in New England? It's true the North claims me for a Southerner, and the South for a Northerner, but I'm neither. Tell the truth, Mr. Webster, though I don't like to boast of it, my name's older in the country than yours."

*Huston to Arnold*

**9.** "Gentlemen of the jury, I ask you to give Jabez Stone another chance to walk upon this earth, among the trees, the growing corn, and the smell of grasses in the spring."

*Arnold's defense of Craig to the jury of the damned*

**10.** "Gentlemen of the jury. Don't let this country go to the Devil! Free Jabez Stone! God bless this United States and the men who made her free!"

*Arnold's defense for Craig to the jury of the damned*

**DIAL M FOR MURDER** (Warner Bros., 1954). D: Alfred Hitchcock. S: Frederick Knott. Fr: Frederick Knott (play).

**1.** "I can see this is going to be a rough evening. All of us saying nice things to each other."

*Bob Cummings (Mark Halliday) to Grace Kelly (Margo Wendice), anticipating an evening with Kelly's husband, Ray Milland (Tony Wendice). Cummings and Kelly are lovers.*

**2.** "That's the trouble with these latchkeys. They're all alike."

*John Williams's (Chief Inspector Hubbard's) complaint to Milland, which becomes the "key" to the whole solution*

**3.** "They talk about flat-footed policemen. May the saints protect us from the gifted amateur."

*Williams to Cummings*

**DIARY OF ANNE FRANK, THE** (20th Century–Fox, 1959). D: George Stevens. S: Frances Goodrich, Albert Hackett. Fr: Frances Goodrich, Albert Hackett (play, Anne Frank: Diary of a Young Girl), Anne Frank (memoir).

LAST LINE

**1.** "In spite of everything, I still believe that people are really good at heart."

*Millie Perkins (Anne Frank)*

**DICK TRACY** (Touchstone, 1990). D: Warren Beatty. S: Jim Cash, Jack Epps, Jr. Fr: Chester Gould (characters).

**1.** "I'm on my way."

*Warren Beatty (Dick Tracy), into his two-way wrist radio*

**2.** "Tess, there's about as much chance of me getting behind a desk as there is of me getting a new girlfriend."

*Beatty to Glenne Headly (Tess Trueheart)*

**3.** AL PACINO (*Big Boy Caprice*): "Around me, if a woman doesn't wear mink, she don't wear nothing."
MADONNA (*Breathless Mahoney*): "Well, I look good both ways."

**4.** BEATTY: "You know it's legal for me to take you down to the station, and sweat it out of you under the lights."
MADONNA: "I sweat a lot better in the dark."

**5.** "I know how you feel. You don't know if you want to hit me or kiss me. I get a lot of that."

*Madonna to Beatty*

**6.** "You mind if I call you Dick?"

*Pacino to Beatty*

**7.** "What's the matter? You bums forgot how to kill people? Doesn't your work mean anything to you anymore? Have you no sense of pride in what you do? No sense of duty? No sense of destiny? I'm looking for generals! What do I got? Foot soldiers!"

*Pacino, exhorting his henchmen to kill Beatty*

LAST LINE

**8.** "You know something, Tracy, I kind of like that dame."

*Charlie Korsmo (Kid) to Beatty, about Headly*

**DINER** (MGM/UA, 1982). D: Barry Levinson. S: Barry Levinson.

**1.** "You know what word I'm not comfortable with? Nuance. It's not a real word. Like ges-gesture's a good word. At least you know where you stand with gesture, but nuance. I don't know, maybe I'm wrong."

*Kevin Bacon (Fenwick)*

**2.** "You can't compare Mathis to Sinatra. There's no way, no way. They're in totally different leagues."

*Steve Guttenberg (Eddie), arguing with friends at the diner*

**3.** "Eddie's giving Elise a football quiz. If she fails, the wedding is off."

*Mickey Rourke (Boogie) to Timothy Daly (Billy), about Guttenberg's wedding preparations*

**4.** "I saw 'Bonanza' over at my in-laws, and it was not for me. The Ponderosa looked fake. Hardly recognized Little Joe."

*"Bonanza" opponent to Daniel Stern (Shrevie)*

**5.** "An accident? Your thing just got into a box of popcorn?"

*Irate date to Rourke, who has tried a surreptitious pass at her at the movies*

**6.** "I'll tell you a big part of the problem, though, when you get married. You know, when you're dating, everything is talking about sex, right? Where can we do it? You know, why can't we do it? . . . . But then when you get married—it's crazy. I don't know. I mean you get it whenever you want it. You wake up in the morning and she's there, and you come home from work and she's there. And so all that sex-planning talk is over."

*Stern*

**7.** "So, you know, I can come down here and we can bullshit the whole night away, but I cannot hold a five-minute conversation with Beth."

*Stern, comparing his male friends at the diner with wife Ellen Barkin (Beth)*

**8.** "Well, we always got the diner."

*Guttenberg to Stern*

**9.** DALY, trying to explain the movie *The Seventh Seal*: "That's Death walking on the beach."

GUTTENBERG: "I've been to Atlantic City a hundred times and never saw Death walk on a beach."

**10.** "Look, put the sheep down. We'll pick up the three wise men and we'll get out of here."

*Stern to Bacon, on raiding a nativity scene*

**11.** "It's the Colts marching song. Very tasteful, very tasteful."

*Paul Reiser (Modell), answering his mother's question about the song being played at Guttenberg's wedding*

**12.** "We all know that most marriages depend on a firm grasp of football trivia."

*Reiser, in wedding toast, on Guttenberg's unusual prenuptial test of his bride*

**13.** "People do not come from swamps, they come from Europe."

*Reiser, in voice-over during end credits, arguing about evolution*

**14.** "Now we're older and we're cooler and we're still hanging out here."

*Stern, in voice-over during end credits*

**DINNER AT EIGHT** (MGM, 1933). D: George Cukor. S: Frances Marion, Herman J. Mankiewicz, Donald Ogden Stewart.

**1.** "Carlotta has no age."

*Lionel Barrymore (Oliver Jordan), on the autumnal Marie Dressler (Carlotta Vance)*

**2.** "I'll have my double chins in private."

*Former actress Dressler, declining to return to the stage*

**3.** "Ladies must live."

*Dressler to Barrymore, on her need for money*

**4.** "I didn't do so badly for a girl from Quincy, Illinois."

*Dressler to Barrymore*

**5.** "Look at those pouches under your eyes. Look at those creases. You sag like an old woman."

*Lee Tracy (Max Kane) to aging actor Barrymore*

**6.** "Ask that common little woman to the house with that noisy, vulgar man? He smells Oklahoma!"

*Billie Burke (Mrs. Oliver Jordan) to Barrymore, about Jean Harlow (Kitty Packard) and Wallace Beery (Dan Packard)*

**7.** "I've told you a million times not to talk to me when I'm doing my lashes."

*Harlow*

**8.** "I'm going to be a lady if it kills me."
*Harlow*

**9.** "That's the unfortunate thing about death. It's so terribly final."
*Dressler to Madge Evans (Paula Jordan)*

**10.** "If there's one thing I know, it's men. I ought to. It's been my life's work."
*Dressler to Evans*

**11.** JEAN HARLOW: "I was reading a book the other day. . . . Do you know that the guy said that machinery is going to take the place of every profession."
MARIE DRESSLER: "Oh, my dear, that's something you need never worry about."

**DIRTY DOZEN, THE** (UK: MGM, 1967). D: Robert Aldrich. S: Lukas Heller, Nunnally Johnson. Fr: E. M. Nathanson (novel).

**1.** "Well, Major, what'd you think of the hanging?"
*Ernest Borgnine (General Warden) to Lee Marvin (Major Reisman), on a military execution*

**2.** "Y'know, if you're gonna act tough, you should be learning how to take care of yourself. You really should."
*Marvin to convict John Cassavetes (Victor Franko), who he has beaten up*

**3.** "Don't sweet-talk me, Whitey."
*Black convict Jim Brown (Robert Jefferson) to Marvin*

**4.** "You've all volunteered for a mission which gives you just three ways to go. Either you can foul up in training and be shipped back here for immediate execution of sentence, or you can foul up in combat, in which case I will personally blow your brains out, or you can do as you're told, in which case you might just get by."
*Marvin, presenting the Army's bargain to the twelve condemned men*

**5.** "Along with these other results, it gives you just about the most twisted, antisocial bunch of psychopathic deformities I have ever run into."
*Army psychologist Ralph Meeker (Capt. Stuart Kinder), analyzing the twelve men for Marvin*

**6.** "You've got one religious maniac, one malignant dwarf, two near idiots, and the rest I don't even want to think about."
*Meeker to Marvin*

**7.** "So you wanna stink, huh?. . . . Well, that's okay with me because I don't have to smell you."
*Marvin to the men, when they refuse to shave or wash in cold water*

**8.** "So now if you . . . you dirty dozen have no objections, we will get our equipment and we will start in right now."
*Richard Jaeckel (Sergeant Bowren), giving a moniker to the twelve unwashed men*

**9.** "You're still the dirtiest soldiers in this man's army and you're gettin' filthier every day."
*Marvin to the dirty dozen, after the completion of their training*

**10.** PROSTITUTE, encountering the dirty dozen for the first time: "Blimey, they're filthy."
JAECKEL: "They may be, lady, but they sure do mean well."

**11.** "You guys foul up on this one, none of us will ever play the violin again."
*Marvin to the men*

**12.** "Just act mean and grunt, huh?"

*Marvin, telling Charles Bronson (Joseph Wladislaw) how to pretend to be a German*

**13.** "Well, free the French and kill the Germans."

*Marvin, on what to do with captured servants at the German château*

**14.** "Boy-oh-boy-oh-boy. Killing generals could get to be a habit with me."

*Bronson to Marvin, in the last line of dialogue, after enduring glib congratulations from the generals*

**LAST LINE**

**15.** "They lost their lives in the line of duty."

*Narrator, after reading off the names of dead members of the dirty dozen*

**DIRTY HARRY** *(Warner Bros., 1971). D: Don Siegel. S: Harry Julian Fink, Rita M. Fink, Dean Riesner. Fr: Harry Julian Fink, Rita M. Fink (unpublished story).*

**1.** "The city of San Francisco does not pay criminals not to commit crimes. Instead we pay the police department."

*John Vernon (Mayor) to Harry Guardino (Bressler)*

**2.** "When an adult male is chasing a female with intent to commit rape, I shoot the bastard. That's my policy."

*Clint Eastwood (Harry Callahan) to Vernon*

**3.** "When a naked man is chasing a woman through an alley with a butcher knife and a hard-on, I figure he isn't out collecting for the Red Cross."

*Eastwood to Vernon*

**4.** "I know what you're thinking. Did he fire six shots or only five? Well, to tell you the truth, in all this excitement, I've kind of lost track myself. But being as this is a 44 Magnum, the most powerful handgun in the world, and would blow your head clean off, you've got to ask yourself one question: Do I feel lucky? Well, do ya punk?"

*Eastwood to bank robber, repeated later almost verbatim to Andy Robinson (Scorpio Killer)*

**5.** "Hey . . . I gots to know."

*Bank robber to Eastwood, on number of bullets remaining in gun*

**6.** "For $29.50, let it hurt."

*Eastwood to doctor who wants to cut Eastwood's trousers to treat wound*

**7.** "That'll be the day."

*Eastwood to Guardino*

**8.** "Now you know why they call me Dirty Harry. Every dirty job that comes along."

*Eastwood to Reni Santoni (Chico), after Eastwood coaxes a would-be suicide victim from a high window ledge*

**9.** "You owe it to yourself to live a little, Harry."

*Eastwood to himself, on viewing a naked woman through his binoculars*

**10.** "My, that's a big one."

*Robinson to Eastwood, on seeing his gun*

**11.** "I have rights. I want a lawyer."

*Robinson to Eastwood, after Eastwood shoots him in the leg and asks the location of the buried girl*

**12.** "'Cause he likes it."

*Eastwood to district attorney, on why Robinson will kill again*

**13.** "'Cause he looks too damn good, that's how."

*Eastwood to John Larch (Chief), on how anyone could tell that Eastwood had not beaten Robinson*

**14.** "Inspector 2211 San Francisco Police"

*Eastwood's badge number, revealed before badge is thrown into the water*

**DIVA** (France: GEF CCFC, 1982). D: Jean-Jacques Beineix. S: Jean-Jacques Beineix, Jean Van Hamme. Fr: Delacorta (novel).

**1.** "It suits you so badly, that it suits you very well."

*Wilhelmenia Wiggins Fernandez (Cynthia), remarking on the name "Jules"*

**2.** "Music. It comes and goes. Don't try to keep it."

*Fernandez, on why she doesn't record her music*

**DO THE RIGHT THING** (Universal, 1989). D: Spike Lee. S: Spike Lee.

**FIRST LINE**

**1.** "Wake up! Wake up, wake up, wake up, up you wake, up you wake, up you wake, up you wake! This is Mr. Señor Love Daddy, your voice of choice, the world's only twelve-hour-strongman on the air, here on We Love Radio, 108 FM, the last on your dial but first in your hearts and that's the truth, Ruth."

*Radio disk jockey Sam Jackson (Mr. Señor Love Daddy), beginning a new day*

**2.** "I hate this freakin' place. I detest it like a sickness."

*John Turturro (Pino) to his father and boss Danny Aiello (Sal), on working at the family pizzeria in Bedford-Stuyvesant*

**3.** "All right, all right, but you're askin' a lot to make a man change his beer, you're askin' a lot, Doctor."

*Ossie Davis (Da Mayor) to Korean deli owners who don't carry Miller High-Life, his favorite beer*

**4.** "Hey, hey, Sal, how come you ain't got no brothers up on the wall here?"

*Giancarlo Esposito (Buggin Out), asking Aiello why there are no black people on his Wall of Fame*

**5.** "Mook, stay black."

*Esposito to Spike Lee (Mookie)*

**6.** DAVIS: "Always do the right thing."
LEE: "That's it?"
DAVIS: "That's it."
LEE: "I got it, I'm gone."

**7.** "Who told you to step on my sneakers? Who told you to walk on my side of the block? Who told you to be in my neighborhood?"

*Esposito to white neighbor John Savage (Clifton)*

**8.** "Let me tell you the story of right hand, left hand. It's a tale of good and evil. Hate—it was with this hand that Cain iced his brother. Love—these five fingers, they go straight to the soul of man: the right hand, the hand of love."

*Bill Nunn (Radio Raheem) alluding to Night of the Hunter as he tells Lee about his two sets of brass knuckles, the left one saying hate, the right one love*

**9.** "I mean, for chrissakes, Pino, they grew up on my food. On my food."

*Aiello, telling Turturro why he keeps his pizzeria in the same neighborhood*

**10.** "What you ought to do is boycott that goddamned barber that fucked up your head."

*Robin Wright (Sweet Dick Willie), commenting on Esposito's unusual haircut*

**11.** "Mookie, the last time I trusted you, we ended up with a son."

*Rosie Perez (Tina) to Lee*

**12.** "I just killed your fucking radio."

*Aiello to Nunn, on destroying his radio with a baseball bat*

**13.** "You see this fuckin' place? I built this fuckin' place with my bare fuckin' hands! Every light socket, every piece of tile. Me, with these fuckin' hands!"

*Aiello to Lee, on the burnt-out wreckage of his pizzeria, after the riot following Nunn's death*

**14.** "Make that money, get paid."

*Lee to Aiello, on what he plans to do with himself*

**LAST LINE**
**15.** "This is Mr. Señor Love Daddy coming at you from what's last on your dial but first in your hearts, and that's the quintessential truth, Ruth. The next record goes out to Radio Raheem. We love you, brother."

*Jackson, on the air*

**DR. JEKYLL AND MR. HYDE** *(Paramount, 1932). D: Rouben Mamoulian. S: Samuel Hoffenstein, Percy Heath. Fr: Robert Louis Stevenson (novel, The Strange Case of Dr. Jekyll and Mr. Hyde).*

**1.** "Free—free at last!"

*Fredric March (Dr. Henry Jekyll) as Hyde, emerging out of Jekyll*

**DR. JEKYLL AND MR. HYDE** *(MGM, 1941). D: Victor Fleming. S: John Lee Mahin. Fr: Robert Louis Stevenson (novel, The Strange Case of Dr. Jekyll and Mr. Hyde).*

**1.** "Good and evil are so close they are chained together in the soul."

*Spencer Tracy (Dr. Henry Jekyll)*

**DR. NO** *(UK: UA, 1962). D: Terence Young. S: Richard Malbaum, Johanna Harwood, Berkley Mather. Fr: Ian Fleming (novel).*

**1.** "Bond. James Bond."

*Sean Connery, introducing himself onscreen for the first time as James Bond, to fellow gambler Eunice Gayson (Sylvia Trench)*

**2.** CONNERY to LOIS MAXWELL (*Miss Moneypenny*): "Moneypenny? What gives?"
MAXWELL: "Me—given an ounce of encouragement."

**3.** BERNARD LEE (*M*): "When do you sleep, 007?"
CONNERY: "Never on the crown's time, sir."

**4.** "If you carry a double-oh number, it means you're licensed to kill, not get killed."

*Lee, chastising Connery for carrying a light beretta instead of a heavier weapon*

**5.** "That's a Smith and Wesson, and you've had your six."

*Connery to Anthony Dawson (Professor Dent), who has tried to shoot Connery with an empty gun, just before Connery shoots him*

**6.** "I can assure you my intentions are strictly honorable."

*Connery, unconvincingly, to Ursula Andress (Honey), who has appeared on the beach in a white bikini*

**7.** JOSEPH WISEMAN (*Dr. No*), on seeing Connery grab a bottle as a weapon: "That's a Dom Perignon '55. It would be a pity to break it."

CONNERY: "I prefer the '53 myself."

**8.** "SPECTRE. Special Executive for Counterintelligence, Terrorism, Revenge, Extortion. The four great cornerstones of power, headed by the greatest brains in the world."

*Wiseman, describing the organization that employs him*

**9.** "Unfortunately I misjudged you. You are just a stupid policeman whose luck has run out."

*Wiseman sizing up Connery*

**10.** "I never fail, Mr. Bond."

*Wiseman, wrongly, to Connery*

**DR. STRANGELOVE OR: HOW I LEARNED TO STOP WORRYING AND LOVE THE BOMB** (Columbia, 1964). *D: Stanley Kubrick. S: Stanley Kubrick, Terry Southern, Peter George. Fr: Peter George (novel,* Red Alert*).*

**1.** PEACE IS OUR PROFESSION

*Motto in Air Force base from which comes the order to start a nuclear war*

**2.** "Well, boys, I reckon this is it—nuclear combat toe to toe with the Russkies."

*Bomber commander Slim Pickens (Major Kong), informing his crew of their mission*

**3.** "I just thought I might mosey over to the war room for a few minutes, see what's doing over there."

*George C. Scott (Gen. Buck Turgidson), acting nonchalant with his mistress about the nuclear crisis*

**4.** "I can no longer sit back and allow Communist infiltration, Communist indoctrination, Communist subversion, and the international Communist conspiracy to sap and impurify all of our precious bodily fluids."

*Sterling Hayden (Gen. Jack D. Ripper), explaining his reasons for starting a nuclear war*

**5.** "I'm not saying we wouldn't get our hair mussed, but I do say no more than ten to twenty million people killed, tops—depending on the breaks."

*Scott, reassuring Peter Sellers (President Merkin Muffley) about how America would fare in a nuclear war*

**6.** "He'll see everything. He'll see the big board!"

*Scott, worried about security if Peter Bull (Russian Ambassador de Sadesky) gets into the war room*

**7.** "Gentlemen, you can't fight in here, this is the war room!"

*President Sellers intervening in dispute between Scott and Bull*

**8.** "Gee, I wish we had one of them Doomsday Machine things."

*Scott, envying the apocalyptic nuclear weapon devised by the Soviets*

**9.** "It was to be announced at the party congress on Monday. As you know, the premier loves surprises."

*Bull, on the Doomsday Machine, a weapon that can destroy the whole world*

**10.** "Well, boys, we've got three engines out, we got more holes in us than a horse trader's mule, radio's gone and we're leaking fuel, and if we was flying any lower, why, we'd need sleigh bells on this thing."

*Pickens to his bomber crew, reviewing their situation as they approach their target in Russia*

**11.** KEENAN WYNN (*Colonel Bat Guano*), agreeing to shoot a Coke machine for change: "Okay, I'm gonna get your money for you, but if you don't get the President of the United States on that phone, you know what's gonna happen to you?"

SELLERS (*Group Captain Lionel Mandrake*): "What?"

WYNN: "You're gonna have to answer to the Coca-Cola Company."

**12.** "Dimitri, there's no point in you getting hysterical at a time like this."

President Sellers on the phone, trying to calm down the Soviet premier

**13.** "I hasten to add that since each man will be required to do prodigious service along these lines, the women will have to be selected for their sexual characteristics, which will have to be of a highly stimulating nature."

Sellers (Dr. Strangelove), eagerly envisioning the world after the nuclear war, when a handful of men, including those present in the war room, will have to repopulate the country

**14.** "Mr. President, we must not allow a mine-shaft gap!"

Scott, insisting that the United States must prevail over the Soviet Union in the number of mine shafts it has for survivors of the nuclear war

LAST LINE
**15.** "Mein Führer! I can walk!"

Sellers (Dr. Strangelove), miraculously cured of his disability as the world ends

**DOCTOR X** (*Warner Bros.–First National, 1932*). D: Michael Curtiz. S: Robert Tasker, Earl Baldwin. Fr: Howard W. Comstock, Allen C. Miller (play).

**1.** "We are all a little strange *up here*."

George Rosener (Otto), a decidedly strange butler, pointing knowingly to his head

**2.** "Synthetic flesh! Synthetic flesh!"

Preston Foster (Dr. Wells) to himself, as he transforms himself into a monster by donning a synthetic hand and face

**DOCTOR ZHIVAGO** (*MGM, 1965*). D: David Lean. S: Robert Bolt. Fr: Boris Pasternak (novel).

**1.** "There are two kinds of men, and only two. And that young man is one kind. He is high-minded. He is pure. He is the kind of man that the world pretends to look up to, and, in fact, despises. . . . There is another kind. Not high-minded. Not pure, but alive."

Rod Steiger (Victor Komarovsky) to Julie Christie (Lara), just before he rapes her

**2.** "I told myself it was beneath my dignity to arrest a man for pilfering firewood, but nothing warranted by the party is beneath the dignity of any man."

Alec Guinness (Yevgraf), in narration

**3.** "Cutting out the tumors of injustice. That's a deep operation. Someone must keep life alive while you do it, by living."

Omar Sharif (Yuri) to Guinness

**4.** "I hate everything you say, but not enough to kill you for it."

Sharif to Tom Courtenay (Pasha)

**DODGE CITY** (*Warner Bros.–First National, 1939*). D: Michael Curtiz. S: Robert Buckner.

**1.** "Gentlemen, that's the symbol of America's future—progress. Iron men and iron horses. You can't beat them."

Henry O'Neill (Colonel Dodge)

**2.** "There's no law west of Chicago, and west of Dodge City, no God."

> *Henry Travers (Dr. Irving), quoting New York newspapers*

**3.** "I'll wager two minutes after you were born, you were telling the doctor what to do."

> *Olivia de Havilland (Abbie Irving) to Errol Flynn (Wade Hatton)*

**4.** "We better get you to a bathtub before somebody shoots you for a buffalo."

> *Flynn to Alan Hale (Rusty Hart), upon his arrival in Dodge City*

**5.** "I never heard of him. What part of Texas he from?"

> *Hale, referring to William Shakespeare*

**6.** HALE: "I'm just going to mosey around and take in the sights."
FLYNN: "Well, look out you don't become one of them."

**7.** "Somebody's going to pay for this, and it ain't going to be with money."

> *Bruce Cabot (Jeff Surrett), after the bar is destroyed in a brawl*

**8.** "You're the sort who doesn't really get into trouble until they start nailing the lid down on your coffin."

> *Flynn to Hale*

**9.** "The only real native of Kansas is the buffalo. He's got a very hard head, a very uncertain temper, and a very lonely future. Apart from that, there's hardly any comparison between you."

> *Flynn to de Havilland*

**10.** "Getting married has ruined a lot of good men."

> *Guinn "Big Boy" Williams (Tex Baird), when Flynn and de Havilland get married*

**11.** "Colonel Dodge, when do we start for Virginia City?"

> *de Havilland to Flynn*

**DOG DAY AFTERNOON** (Warner Bros., 1975). D: Sidney Lumet. S: Frank Pierson. Fr: P. F. Kluge, Thomas Moore (article).

**1.** "To my darling wife, Leon, whom I love more than any man has loved another man in all eternity, I leave $2,700 borrowed from a $10,000 life insurance policy to be used for your sex change operation."

> *Bank robber Al Pacino (Sonny), dictating his will to bank hostage Penny Allen (Sylvia)*

**2.** "Attica! Attica!"

> *Pacino leading a chant to rally the crowd against the police*

**DON'T BOTHER TO KNOCK** (20th Century–Fox, 1952). D: Roy Ward Baker. S: Daniel Taradash. Fr: Charlotte Armstrong (novel).

**1.** "I can't figure you out. You're silk on one side and sandpaper on the other."

> *Richard Widmark (Jed Towers) to Marilyn Monroe (Nell Forbes)*

**DOUBLE INDEMNITY** (Paramount, 1944). D: Billy Wilder. S: Raymond Chandler, Billy Wilder. Fr: James M. Cain (novel).

**1.** "I killed him for money and for a woman. And I didn't get the money and I didn't get the woman. Pretty, isn't it?"

> *Insurance agent Fred MacMurray (Walter Neff), confessing his murder of Tom Powers (Mr. Dietrichson) to claims adjustor Edward G. Robinson (Barton Keyes) over a dictaphone*

**2.** "That's a honey of an anklet you're wearing, Mrs. Dietrichson."

*MacMurray to Barbara Stanwyck (Phyllis Dietrichson)*

**3.** "It was a hot afternoon, and I can still remember the smell of honeysuckle all along that street. How could I have known that murder can sometimes smell like honeysuckle?"

*MacMurray, on leaving Stanwyck's house for the first time*

**4.** "Every month hundreds of claims come to this desk. Some of them are phonies. And I know which ones. How do I know? Because my little man tells me. . . . The little man in here. Every time one of these phonies comes along, it ties knots in my stomach."

*Robinson*

**5.** "I knew I had hold of a red-hot poker, and the time to drop it was before it burned my hand off."

*MacMurray, on keeping out of Stanwyck's scheme to murder her husband*

**6.** "I fought it, only I guess I didn't fight it hard enough."

*MacMurray*

**7.** "This has got to be perfect, do you understand? Straight down the line."

*MacMurray to Stanwyck, on getting involved in the murder scheme*

**8.** "Listen, baby, there's a clause in every accident policy on a thing called double indemnity."

*MacMurray to Stanwyck, explaining his plan*

**9.** "A claims man is a doctor and a bloodhound and a cop and a judge and a jury and a father confessor all in one."

*Robinson, on his profession*

**10.** "Guess I was wrong. You're not smarter, Walter. You're just a little taller."

*Robinson to MacMurray*

**11.** "I couldn't hear my own footsteps. It was the walk of a dead man."

*MacMurray, on how he felt after the murder*

**12.** "They've committed a murder, and it's not like taking a trolley ride together where they can get off at different stops. They're stuck with each other and they've got to ride all the way to the end of the line, and it's a one-way trip and the last stop is the cemetery."

*Robinson, on what happens when two people commit murder*

**13.** "Good-bye, baby."

*MacMurray to Stanwyck, just before he shoots her*

**14.** MACMURRAY (on his confession): "Kind of a crazy story with a crazy twist to it—one you didn't quite figure out."

ROBINSON: "Well, you can't figure them all, Walter."

**LAST LINES**

**15.** MACMURRAY: "You know why you couldn't figure this one, Keyes? I'll tell you. The guy you were looking for was too close. He was right across the desk from you."

ROBINSON: "Closer than that, Walter."

MACMURRAY: "I love you, too."

**DRACULA** *(Universal, 1931). D: Tod Browning. S: Garrett Fort. Fr: Hamilton Deane, John Balderston (play), Bram Stoker (novel).*

**1.** "I am Dracula."

*Bela Lugosi (Count Dracula), introducing himself to Dwight Frye (Renfield)*

**2.** "Listen to them. Children of the night. What music they make."

*Lugosi, expressing his appreciation for the howling of wolves*

**3.** "I never drink—wine."

*Lugosi*

**4.** "There are far worse things facing man than death."

*Lugosi*

**5.** "Flies! Flies! Poor puny things. Who wants to eat flies?. . . . Not when I can get nice fat spiders."

*The insane Frye, discussing his culinary preferences*

**6.** "For one who has not lived even a single lifetime, you are a wise man, Van Helsing."

*Lugosi, giving grudging praise to his adversary Edward Van Sloan (Van Helsing)*

**7.** "They're all crazy. They're all crazy except you and me. Sometimes I have me doubts about you."

*Asylum keeper Charles Gerrard (Martin) to maid Joan Standing*

**DRESSED TO KILL** *(Universal, 1946). D: Roy William Neill. S: Leonard Lee, Frank Gruber. Fr: Arthur Conan Doyle (story).*

LAST LINE
**1.** "Oh, thank you, Inspector. I don't think I could have done it entirely without Mr. Holmes's help, you know."

*Nigel Bruce (Dr. Watson), graciously sharing credit with Basil Rathbone (Sherlock Holmes)*

**DRESSER, THE** *(UK: Columbia, 1983). D: Peter Yates. S: Ronald Harwood. Fr: Ronald Harwood (play).*

**1.** "We all have our little sorrows, Ducky. You're not the only one. The littler you are, the larger the sorrow."

*Tom Courtenay (Norman) to Zena Walker (Her Ladyship), expressing his own sorrow over Albert Finney's (Sir's) death*

**DRIVING MISS DAISY** *(Warner Bros., 1989). D: Bruce Beresford. S: Alfred Uhry. Fr: Alfred Uhry (play).*

**1.** "Mama, cars don't behave. They are behaved upon."

*Dan Aykroyd (Boolie Werthan) to Jessica Tandy (Daisy Werthan), after she blames her car for an accident*

**2.** "She's all there. Too much there is the problem."

*Aykroyd to Morgan Freeman (Hoke Colburn), explaining why he's being hired to drive Tandy*

**3.** "I'm just trying to drive you to the store."

*Freeman to Tandy, as he is driving slowly alongside her and she walks*

**4.** "I just love the smell of a new car. Don't you, Miss Daisy?"

*Freeman to Tandy*

**5.** "It only took me six days. Same time it took the Lord to make the world."

*Freeman to Aykroyd, referring to how long it took Tandy to let him drive*

**6.** "If I had a nose like Florine, I wouldn't go around saying Merry Christmas to anybody."

*Tandy to Freeman, on Aykroyd's wife Patti Lupone (Florine Werthan)*

**7.** TANDY: "It's seven-sixteen."
AYKROYD: "You ought to have a job on the radio announcing the time."

**8.** "Yes'm. I got the air conditioner checked. I don't know what for. Don't never allow me to turn it on."

*Freeman to Tandy*

**9.** "An old nigger and an old Jew woman taking off down the road together. That is one sorry sight."

*Ray McKinnon (Trooper #1)*

**10.** "How do you think I feel having to sit up here and ask you, 'Can I go make water?' like I'm some child?. . . . Well, I ain't no child, Miss Daisy. And I ain't just some back of the neck you look at while you going wherever you got to go. I'm a man, I'm near about seventy years old, and I know when my bladder's full."

*Freeman to Tandy*

**11.** "You're my best friend."

*Tandy to Freeman*

**DRUGSTORE COWBOY** *(Avenue, 1989). D: Gus Van Sant, Jr. S: Gus Van Sant, Jr., Daniel Yost. Fr: James Fogle (novel).*

**FIRST LINE**

**1.** "I was once a shameless, full-time dope fiend."

*Matt Dillon (Bob), in narration*

**DUCK SOUP** *(Paramount, 1933). D: Leo McCarey. S: Bert Kalmar, Harry Ruby, Arthur Sheekman, Nat Perrin.*

**1.** MARGARET DUMONT *(Mrs. Teasdale)*, on Groucho's being elected president of Freedonia: "As chairwoman of the reception committee, I welcome you with open arms."

GROUCHO *(Rufus T. Firefly)*: "Is that so? How late do you stay open?"

**2.** "I hear they're going to tear you down and put up an office building where you're standing."

*Groucho to Dumont*

**3.** DUMONT, gushingly: "Oh, your Excellency!"

GROUCHO: "You're not so bad yourself."

**4.** "I could dance with you till the cows come home. On second thought, I'd rather dance with the cows till you came home."

*Groucho to Latin temptress Raquel Torres (Vera Marcal)*

**5.** "Why, a four-year-old child could understand this report. Run out and get me a four-year-old child. I can't make head nor tail out of it."

*Groucho to his secretary Zeppo Marx (Bob Rolland)*

**6.** EDWIN MAXWELL *(Minister of War)*: "Sir, you try my patience!"

GROUCHO: "I don't mind if I do. You must come over and try mine sometime."

**7.** "I've got a good mind to join a club and beat you over the head with it."

*Groucho to foreign spy and general pest Chico Marx (Chicolini)*

**8.** "This is the fifth trip I've made today, and I haven't been anywhere yet."

*Groucho, after getting left behind in the sidecar yet again while his motorcycle driver Harpo (Pinkie) rides off*

**9.** "I still like 'upstart' the best."

*Groucho, deciding which insulting name most annoys him*

**10.** JOIN THE ARMY AND SEE THE NAVY

*Freedonian recruiting sign, carried by Harpo*

**11.** "Victory is ours!"

*Dumont's last words before bursting into song and being pelted by the Marx Brothers*

**DUEL IN THE SUN** *(Selznick Releasing Org., 1946). D: King Vidor. S: Oliver H. P. Garrett, David O. Selznick. Fr: Niven Busch (novel).*

**1.** "Pearl, you're curved in the flesh of temptation. Resistance is going to be a darn sight harder for you than for females protected by the shape of sows."

*Walter Huston ("The Sinkiller") to Jennifer Jones (Pearl Chavez)*

**DUMBO** *(RKO, 1941). D: Ben Sharpsteen. S: Joe Grant, Dick Huemer. Fr: Helen Aberson, Harold Pearl (book).*

**1.** "Him with those ears that only a mother could love."

*Verna Felton (Elephant), reacting to the rudeness of Dumbo's mother*

**2.** "Lots of people with big ears are famous."

*Ed Brophy (Timothy Q. Mouse), trying to cheer Dumbo up*

**3.** "Dumbo, your ears! They're perfect wings! The very things that have been holding you down are going to carry you up, and up, and up."

*Brophy, realizing Dumbo can fly*

**4.** "Let us take the solemn vow. From now on, he is no longer an elephant."

*Felton, when Dumbo is made into a clown*

**E.T. THE EXTRA-TERRESTRIAL** *(Universal, 1982). D: Steven Spielberg. S: Melissa Mathison.*

**1.** "I'm keeping him."

*Henry Thomas (Elliott) to Drew Barrymore (Gertie) and Robert McNaughton (Mike), on finding the lost extraterrestrial known as E.T.*

**2.** "E.T. phone home."

*E.T., wanting to contact his home planet*

**3.** "E.T., I love you."

*Thomas to E.T.*

**4.** "Well, why can't he just beam up?"

*K. C. Martel (Greg), on hearing that E.T. is an extraterrestrial who has to be taken to his spaceship*

**5.** "Ouch."

*E.T., pointing to his heart when it is time to leave Thomas*

**6.** "I'll be right here."

*E.T. to Thomas, touching his head before leaving Earth, reiterating Thomas's earlier line to E.T.*

**EACH DAWN I DIE** *(Warner Bros., 1939). D: William Keighley. S: Norman Reilly Raine, Warren Duff, Charles Perry. Fr: Jerome Odlum (novel).*

**1.** "New bunch of fish, huh?"

*Prison guard Stanley Ridges (Mueller), looking over new prisoners, including James Cagney (Frank Ross), who has been framed for manslaughter*

**2.** "From now on, the rules are off! I'm gonna talk when I please and do what I like. I'm gonna be as mean and dirty and hard to handle as the worst con in the joint, and I'll skull-drag any rat or screw that gets in my way, do you hear? Now, let me out of here, do you hear—you muddle-headed copper!"

*Cagney, fed up with his treatment in prison*

**3.** "You're a blind, stupid, selfish, contemptible, tinhorn crook."

*Cagney's girlfriend Jane Bryan (Joyce Conover), telling off George Raft (Hood Stacey), the hoodlum who double-crossed Cagney*

**4.** "And now I'm a convict. I act like a convict, smell like a convict. I think and hate like a convict. But I'll get out, I'll get out, if I have to kill every screw in the joint!"

*Cagney*

**5.** "I'd have plenty to say if I could think of anything scummy enough to call you."

*Cagney to his parole board, which has refused his request for parole*

**6.** "We're crashing out! Who's coming with us?"

*Ed Pawley (Dale), a convict who leads a prison breakout*

**7.** "Listen, you dirty rats in there!"

*Pawley, saying a line that will become better associated with Cagney*

**8.** "If you know any prayers, don't say 'em now, they won't do you any good."

*Raft to Pawley, as the prison rioters are cornered by law-enforcement officials*

**9.** "Funny, just an hour ago I had 199 years, and now I ain't got no time at all."

*Raft, facing certain death as the prison riot is crushed*

**10.** "Okay, canary, start singing."

*Raft, forcing a confession from the convict who framed Cagney*

**11.** "To Ross—I found a square guy. 14520."

*Farewell note to Cagney, on mug shot of Raft, who has given his life to get Cagney out of prison; the number is Raft's prisoner number*

**EARTH GIRLS ARE EASY** *(Vestron, 1989). D: Julien Temple. S: Julie Brown, Charlie Coffey, Terrence E. McNally.*

**1.** "You're an alien and I'm from the Valley."

*Valley girl Geena Davis (Valerie Dale) to extraterrestrial Jeff Goldblum (Mac), on why their relationship would not work*

**EAST OF EDEN** *(Warner Bros., 1955). D: Elia Kazan. S: Paul Osborn. Fr: John Steinbeck (novel).*

**1.** "I don't have to explain anything to anybody."

*James Dean (Cal Trask) to Julie Harris (Abra)*

**EASY RIDER** *(Columbia, 1969). D: Dennis Hopper. S: Peter Fonda, Dennis Hopper, Terry Southern.*

**1.** "Well, they got this here, see, scissor-happy 'Beautify America' thing going on around here. They're trying to make everybody look like Yul Brynner."

*Alcoholic lawyer Jack Nicholson (George Hanson) to Peter Fonda (Wyatt) and Dennis Hopper (Billy), on his town's distaste for longhaired men*

**2.** "Nic-nic-nic-f-f-f—Indians!"

*Nicholson's favorite phrase after taking a drink; he also says it as "Nic-nic-nic-nic-fire!"*

**EATING RAOUL** (20th Century–Fox, 1982). D: Paul Bartel. S: Paul Bartel, Richard Blackburn.

*1.* "It's amazing what you can do with a cheap piece of meat if you know how to treat it."

*Paul Bartel (Paul Bland) about the dish of human meat he is serving*

**EDISON, THE MAN** (MGM, 1940). D: Clarence Brown. S: Talbot Jennings, Bradbury Foote. Fr: Dore Schary, Hugo Butler (story).

LAST LINE
*1.* "What man's mind can conceive, man's character can control. Man must learn that, and then we needn't be afraid of tomorrow. And man will go forward toward more light."

*Spencer Tracy (Thomas Alva Edison)*

**EDUCATING RITA** (UK: Columbia, 1983). D: Lewis Gilbert. S: Willy Russell. Fr: Willy Russell (play).

*1.* "Of course, I'm drunk. You don't really expect me to teach this when I'm sober."

*Michael Caine (Dr. Frank Bryant)*

*2.* "Howard's End? Sounds filthy, doesn't it?"

*Julie Walters (Rita) to Caine*

*3.* "Needs you? Most of the time he can hardly see you!"

*Michael Williams (Brian), telling Walters about Caine*

*4.* "Must only be used for poetry, by strictest order—Rita."

*Caine, reading the inscription on a pen, a gift from Walters*

**EGG AND I, THE** (Universal, 1947). D: Chester Erskine. S: Chester Erskine, Fred Finkelhoffe. Fr: Betty MacDonald (novel).

*1.* "I bet you think an egg is something you casually order for breakfast when you can't think of anything else. Well, so did I, once, but that was before the egg and I."

*Claudette Colbert (Betty MacDonald) to the audience*

*2.* "You and I, my friend, are not going to get along at all."

*Colbert to the stove*

*3.* "We're your neighbors just down the road a spell. Kettle's the name. Folks call me 'Pa.'"

*Percy Kilbride (Pa Kettle) to Colbert*

*4.* "Much obliged for everything."

*Kilbride, saying grace*

*5.* "When I think of the years I spent learning how to be irresistible to my husband. . . . All you have to do is cackle."

*Colbert to Fred MacMurray (Bob MacDonald), when MacMurray says he likes a woman who knows chickens*

*6.* "I can't make Pa change and be neat, so I'll have to change and be dirty. Been peace in this house ever since."

*Marjorie Main (Ma Kettle) to Colbert*

*7.* "What do you think I am, a cannibal?"

*Colbert to MacMurray, when their pig is served as sandwiches*

LAST LINE
*8.* "You see what I mean? I could write a book."

*Colbert to the audience*

**EIGHT MEN OUT** *(Orion, 1988). D: John Sayles. S: John Sayles. Fr: Eliot Asinof (book).*

**LAST LINE**

*1.* "He was one of the guys that threw the series back in nineteen. One of them bums from Chicago, kid. One of the Black Sox."

*Spectator at baseball game*

**ELECTRIC HORSEMAN, THE** *(Columbia/ Universal, 1979). D: Sydney Pollack. S: Robert Garland. Fr: Robert Garland, Paul Gaer (screenplay), Shelly Burton (story).*

*1.* "You're just walking around to save funeral expenses."

*Valerie Perrine (Charlotta) to Robert Redford (Sonny Steele)*

**ELEPHANT MAN, THE** *(UK: EMI/Paramount, 1980). D: David Lynch. S: Christopher DeVore, Eric Bergren, David Lynch. Fr: Ashley Montagu (book, The Elephant Man: A Study in Human Dignity), Sir Frederick Treves (book, The Elephant Man and Other Reminiscences).*

*1.* "I am not an animal!"

*John Hurt (John Merrick)*

**ELMER GANTRY** *(UA, 1960). D: Richard Brooks. S: Richard Brooks. Fr: Sinclair Lewis (novel).*

*1.* "And what is love? Love is the mornin' and the evenin' star."

*Burt Lancaster (Elmer Gantry)*

**EMPIRE STRIKES BACK, THE** *(20th Century–Fox, 1980). D: Irvin Kershner. S: Leigh Brackett, Lawrence Kasdan. Fr: George Lucas (story).*

*1.* "Would it help if I got out and pushed?"

*Carrie Fisher (Princess Leia) to Harrison Ford (Han Solo), annoyed at his inability to get his spaceship off the ground*

*2.* "Never tell me the odds."

*Ford to droid Anthony Daniels (C3PO), when Daniels calculates the slim chances for successfully navigating an asteroid field*

*3.* "You do have your moments. Not many of them, but you do have them."

*Fisher, softening toward Ford*

*4.* FISHER, to Ford, just before he is forced to go into carbon freeze: "I love you."
FORD: "I know."

*5.* "I'm standing here in pieces, and you're having delusions of grandeur."

*Daniels, dismantled once again, to his fellow droid Kenny Baker (R2D2)*

**ESCAPE ME NEVER** *(Warner Bros., 1947). D: Peter Godfrey. S: Thomas Williamson. Fr: Margaret Kennedy (novel, The Fool of the Family, and play, Escape Me Never).*

**LAST LINE**

*1.* "But I don't want a better man, Sebastian. I just want you."

*Ida Lupino (Gemma Smith) to Errol Flynn (Sebastian Dubrok)*

**EVERY WHICH WAY BUT LOOSE** *(Warner Bros./Columbia, 1978). D: James Fargo. S: Jeremy Joe Kronsberg.*

*1.* "Left turn, Clyde."

*Clint Eastwood (Philo Beddoe), directing his orangutan's driving*

**EVERYTHING YOU ALWAYS WANTED TO KNOW ABOUT SEX (BUT WERE AFRAID TO ASK)** *(UA, 1972). D: Woody Allen. S: Woody Allen. Fr: David Reuben (book).*

LAST LINE

*1.* "Fatigue reading four and a half. Looks good! We're going for seconds. Attention, gonads, we're going for a record."

> *In-body operator Tony Randall, overseeing a sexual act from inside*

**EXCALIBUR** *(Orion/Warner Bros., 1981). D: John Boorman. S: Rospo Pallenberg, John Boorman. Fr: Thomas Malory (romance, Le Mort D'Arthur).*

*1.* "The future has taken root in the present. It is done."

> *Nicol Williamson (Merlin), when Arthur is conceived*

*2.* "I remember my first joust. It looks far worse than it feels."

> *Clive Swift (Sir Ector)*

*3.* "I once stood exposed to the dragon's breath so that a man could lie one night with a woman. It took me nine months to recover. And all for this lunacy called love. This mad distemper that strikes down both beggar and king. Never again!"

> *Williamson to Nigel Terry (King Arthur)*

*4.* "Remember, there's always something cleverer than yourself."

> *Williamson to Terry, when trying to catch a fish*

*5.* "What is the secret of the Grail? Who does it serve?"

> *Terry to himself, in a curious mood, with a sense of wonder*

**EXORCIST, THE** *(Warner Bros., 1973). D: William Friedkin. S: William Peter Blatty.*

*1.* "There seems to be an alien pubic hair in my gin."

> *Film director Jack MacGowran (Burke Dennings), drunk at a party*

*2.* "You're gonna die up there."

> *Linda Blair (Regan MacNeil) to an astronaut at the party*

*3.* "Mrs. MacNeil, the problem with your daughter is not her bed, it's her brain."

> *Doctor to Ellen Burstyn (Chris MacNeil), on her daughter, whose bed has been mysteriously shaking*

*4.* "Keep away! The sow is mine!"

> *Mercedes McCambridge (Voice of demon), possessing Blair*

*5.* "You're telling me that I should take my daughter to a witch doctor, is that it?"

> *Burstyn, on hearing the doctors' suggestion that she consult an exorcist*

*6.* "What an excellent day for an exorcism."

> *McCambridge to priest Jason Miller (Father Karras)*

*7.* "Nowonmai."

> *McCambridge, saying "I am no one" backward*

*8.* "Merrin! Merrin!"

> *McCambridge, calling for the demon's adversary, exorcist Max von Sydow (Father Merrin)*

*9.* "help me"

> *Raised letters mysteriously appearing on Blair's abdomen*

*10.* "Especially important is the warning to avoid conversations with the demon. We may ask what is relevant, but anything beyond that is dangerous. He's a liar, the demon is a liar. He will lie to confuse us, but he will also mix lies with the truth to attack us."

*von Sydow, instructing Miller as they prepare for the exorcism*

**11.** "Your mother suck cocks in hell."

*McCambridge, taunting Miller*

**12.** "The power of Christ compels you!"

*Priests to demon, during the exorcism*

**EYEWITNESS** *(20th Century–Fox, 1981). D: Peter Yates. S: Steve Tesich.*

**1.** "I'll tell you right now, it's gonna be wonderful."

*William Hurt (Darryl Deever), promising good sex to Sigourney Weaver (Tony Sokolow)*

**2.** HURT, in bed with the wealthy Weaver: "The rich always marry the rich, why is that?"
WEAVER: "That's the only people they know."

**FACE IN THE CROWD, A** *(Warner Bros., 1957). D: Elia Kazan. S: Budd Schulberg. Fr: Budd Schulberg (short story, "The Arkansas Traveler").*

**1.** "I'm Mr. Me, Myself, and I."

*Conman Andy Griffith (Lonesome Rhodes), charming radio talk-show host Patricia Neal (Marcia Jeffries)*

**2.** "A guitar beats a woman every time."

*Griffith, explaining to his public why guitars are more trustworthy than women*

**3.** "They was pretty strict. Didn't allow us to touch hard liquor till we was ten or eleven."

*Griffith, about his "folks back home," giving Neal a thumbnail biography for his devoted fans*

**4.** "All them millions of people believing in me. Doing what I tell them to. It scares me."

*Griffith to Neal*

**5.** "A hometown boy, not only making good, but making everybody."

*Walter Matthau (Mel Miller), on Griffith*

**6.** "He lives on a diet of nitroglycerine."

*Matthau, referring to the head of the television network that airs Griffith's show*

**7.** "Just let the vermouth blow a kiss at the gin."

*Neal, ordering a martini with the same instructions previously given by Matthau*

**8.** "He's got the courage of his ignorance."

*Matthau, on Griffith's continuing belief in the faith of his flock even after he has unwittingly betrayed himself*

**FALL OF THE ROMAN EMPIRE, THE** *(Paramount, 1964). D: Anthony Mann. S: Ben Barzman, Basilio Franchina, Philip Yordan.*

**LAST LINE**
**1.** "A great civilization is not conquered from without until it has destroyed itself from within."

*Narrator*

**FALLING DOWN** *(Warner Bros., 1993). D: Joel Schumacher. S: Ebbe Roe Smith.*

**1.** "I'm the bad guy?"

*Gun-toting maniac Michael Douglas (D-Fens), incredulously*

**FAME** (MGM/UA, 1980). D: Alan Parker. S: Christopher Gore.

**1.** "I know there's nothing wrong with me. That's what's wrong with me. Everybody else here is colorful, or eccentric, or charismatic, and I'm perfectly normal."

*Maureen Teefy (Doris)*

**2.** "How bright our spirits go shooting into space depends on how much we contributed to the earthly brilliance of this world, and I mean to be a major contributor."

*Irene Cara (Coco)*

**3.** "Marlon Brando slurred his words, you know. Montgomery Clift slurred his words. James Dean slurred his words. They were the greatest actors in the world, and nobody could understand a word they said."

*Barry Miller (Ralph), when told that he's been slurring his words*

**FAR COUNTRY, THE** (Universal-International, 1954). D: Anthony Mann. S: Borden Chase.

LAST LINE
**1.** "I know, we eat, we sleep, we rest, and soon we be all better again."

*James Stewart (Jeff)*

**FAREWELL TO ARMS, A** (Paramount, 1932). D: Frank Borzage. S: Benjamin Glazer, Oliver H. P. Garrett. Fr: Ernest Hemingway (novel).

**1.** "I was blown up eating cheese."

*Gary Cooper (Lt. Frederick Henry) to Adolphe Menjou (Rinaldi), explaining why he's not a hero*

**2.** "I'm afraid of the rain because sometimes I see me dead in it. . . . And sometimes, I see you dead in it."

*Helen Hayes (Catherine Barkley) to Cooper*

**3.** "I will come back to Catherine. I'll always come back."

*Cooper to Hayes, when he leaves for the war*

**4.** "Sacred subjects are not good for soldiers. Why don't you be like me, all fire and smoke, with nothing inside?"

*Menjou to Cooper*

**5.** "What does this war mean to me anymore? What does anything mean but finding her?"

*Cooper to Jack LaRue (The Priest), when Hayes has been transferred*

**6.** "Peace. Peace."

*Cooper, when Hayes dies*

**FATAL ATTRACTION** (Paramount, 1987). D: Adrian Lyne. S: James Dearden.

**1.** "If looks could kill . . . "

*Friend of Michael Douglas (Dan Gallagher), on receiving a look from Glenn Close (Alex Forrest) at a party*

**2.** "Have you ever done it in an elevator?"

*Close to Douglas, just before they do it*

**3.** "What happened? I woke up, you weren't here. I hate that."

*Close, calling Douglas the day after their liaison*

**4.** "Well, bring the dog. I love animals. I'm a great cook."

*Close, on the phone to Douglas, foreshadowing her later boiling of a pet rabbit*

**5.** "I'm not gonna be ignored, Dan."

*Close to Douglas*

**FATHER OF THE BRIDE** *(MGM, 1950). D: Vincente Minnelli. S: Frances Goodrich, Albert Hackett. Fr: Edward Streeter (novel).*

**LAST LINE**

**1.** "Nothing's really changed, has it? You know what they say: My son's my son till he gets him a wife, but my daughter's my daughter all of her life. All of our life."

*Spencer Tracy (Stanley T. Banks), after his daughter's wedding*

**FATHER'S LITTLE DIVIDEND** *(MGM, 1951). D: Vincente Minnelli. S: Frances Goodrich, Albert Hackett. Fr: Edward Streeter (characters).*

**LAST LINE**

**1.** "Stanley Banks, my grandchild. My first grandchild."

*Spencer Tracy (Stanley Banks)*

**FEMALE ON THE BEACH, THE** *(Universal, 1955). D: Joseph Pevney. S: Robert Hill, Richard Alan Simmons. Fr: Robert Hill (play, The Besieged Heart).*

**1.** "I wouldn't have you if you were hung with diamonds—upside down!"

*Joan Crawford (Lynn Markham) to Jeff Chandler (Drummond Hall)*

**2.** "I know it's considered noble to accept apologies, but I'm afraid I'm not the noble type."

*Crawford to Jan Sterling (Amy Rawlinson)*

**FERRIS BUELLER'S DAY OFF** *(Paramount, 1986). D: John Hughes. S: John Hughes.*

**1.** "This is my ninth sick day this semester. It's getting pretty tough coming up with new illnesses. If I go for ten, I'm probably gonna have to barf up a lung."

*Matthew Broderick (Ferris Bueller)*

**2.** "Life moves pretty fast. If you don't stop and look around once in a while, you could miss it."

*Broderick*

**FEW GOOD MEN, A** *(Columbia, 1992). D: Rob Reiner. S: Aaron Sorkin. Fr: Aaron Sorkin (play).*

**1.** DEMI MOORE (*Lt. Comdr. JoAnne Galloway*): "The Marines in Guantanamo are fanatical."
    KEVIN POLLAK (*Lt. Sam Weinberg*): "About what?"
    MOORE: "About being Marines."

**2.** "You don't even know me. Ordinarily, it takes someone hours to discover I'm not fit to handle a defense."

*Tom Cruise (Lt. Daniel Kaffee), defense attorney for two Marines who are charged with murder*

**3.** "Walk softly and carry an armored tank division."

*Jack Nicholson (Col. Nathan Jessep)*

**4.** "You want to investigate me, roll the dice and take your chances. I eat breakfast three hundred yards from four thousand Cubans who are trained to kill me, so don't think for one second that you can come down here, flash a badge, and make me nervous."

*Nicholson to Moore*

**5.** "I don't want money and I don't want medals. What I do want is for you to stand there in that faggotty white uniform and with your Harvard mouth extend me some fucking courtesy. You got to ask me nicely."

*Nicholson to Cruise*

**6.** "It doesn't matter what I believe. It only matters what I can prove."

*Cruise to Moore*

**7.** "You know nothing about the law. You're a used-car salesman, Daniel. You're an ambulance chaser with a rank. You're nothing. Live with that."

*Moore to Cruise*

**8.** "So, this is what a courtroom looks like."

*Cruise*

**9.** "My father always said a jury trial is not just about the law. It's about assigning blame."

*Cruise*

**10.** POLLAK: "Why do you like them so much?"

MOORE: " 'Cause they stand on a wall, and they say, 'Nothing's going to hurt you tonight. Not on my watch.' "

**11.** "We follow orders or people die. It's that simple. Are we clear?"

*Nicholson to Cruise*

**12.** "You can't handle the truth! Son, we live in a world that has walls, and those walls have to be guarded by men with guns. Who's going to do it? You?"

*Nicholson to Cruise*

**13.** "I have neither the time nor the inclination to explain myself to a man who rises and sleeps under a blanket of the very freedom that I provide, and then questions the manner in which I provide it. I would rather you just said, 'Thank you,' and went on your way. Otherwise, I suggest you pick up a weapon and stand a post. Either way, I don't give a damn what you think you are entitled to."

*Nicholson to Cruise*

**FIELD OF DREAMS** (Universal, 1989). D: Phil Alden Robinson. S: Phil Alden Robinson. Fr: W. P. Kinsella (novel, Shoeless Joe).

**1.** "If you build it, he will come."

*Ray Liotta ("Shoeless" Joe Jackson) to Kevin Costner (Ray Kinsella)*

**2.** "I think it means that if I build a baseball field out there, that 'Shoeless' Joe Jackson will get to come back and play again."

*Costner to his wife Amy Madigan (Annie Kinsella)*

**3.** "I never forgave him for getting old."

*Costner to Madigan, on his father*

**4.** LIOTTA: "Is this Heaven?"
COSTNER: "No, it's Iowa"

**5.** "I just loved this game. I'd have played for food money. It was the game. The sounds. The smells."

*Liotta to Costner*

**6.** JAMES EARL JONES (*Terence Mann*): "Oh, my God!"

COSTNER: "What?"
JONES: "You're from the sixties!"

**7.** "I spent all my misery years ago. I have no more pain left for anything. I gave at the office."

*Jones to Costner*

**8.** "I never got to bat in the major leagues. I would have liked to have that chance, just once. To stare down a big league pitcher. To stare him down and, just as he goes into his windup, make him think you know something he doesn't. That's what I wish for."

*Burt Lancaster ("Moonlight" Archie Graham) to Costner*

**9.** COSTNER: "It would kill some men to get that close to their dream and not touch it. They'd consider it a tragedy."
LANCASTER: "Son, if I'd only gotten to be a doctor for five minutes, now, that would have been a tragedy."

**10.** JONES, when he sees the field: "Unbelievable!"
COSTNER: "It's more than that. It's perfect."

**11.** "It'll be as if they'd dipped themselves in magic waters. The memories will be so thick, they'll have to brush them away from their faces."

*Jones to Costner*

**12.** "Oh, people will come, Ray. People will most definitely come."

*Jones to Costner*

**13.** COSTNER: "Hey, Dad! You want to have a catch?"
DWIER BROWN (*John Kinsella*): "I'd like that."

**FIRE DOWN BELOW** *(Columbia, 1957). D: Robert Parrish. S: Irwin Shaw. Fr: Max Catto (novel).*

**1.** "Armies have marched over me."
*Rita Hayworth (Irena)*

**FIRST BLOOD** *(Orion, 1982). D: Ted Kotcheff. S: Michael Kozoll, William Sackheim, Q. Moonblood. Fr: David Morrell (novel).*

**1.** "If you want some friendly advice, get a haircut and take a bath. You wouldn't get hassled so much."

*Brian Dennehy (Sheriff Teasle) to Sylvester Stallone (Rambo), as Dennehy gives Stallone an unwelcome ride out of town*

**2.** DENNEHY: "What do you hunt with a knife?"
STALLONE: "The enemy."

**3.** "Don't push it, or I'll give you a war you won't believe."

*Stallone to Dennehy, after Stallone has killed all of Dennehy's deputies and has a knife to his throat*

**4.** "God didn't make Rambo. I made him."
*Richard Crenna (Troutman)*

**5.** "In Vietnam, his job was to dispose of the enemy personnel, to kill, period. Win by attrition. Well, Rambo was the best."

*Crenna to Dennehy*

**6.** "They drew first blood, not me."
*Stallone to Crenna*

**FISH CALLED WANDA, A** *(MGM/UA, 1988). D: Charles Crichton. S: John Cleese. Fr: John Cleese, Charles Crichton (story).*

**1.** "Hello, Wanda."

*Michael Palin (Ken) to his favorite fish, during opening credit sequence*

**2.** "Oh, that's quite a stutter you've got there, Ken."

*Kevin Kline (Otto), making a typically insensitive remark about Palin's speech impediment*

**3.** "What was the middle thing?"

*Kline's frequent way of asking for clarification of what he fails to understand*

**4.** KLINE, in lotus position in car: "It's a Buddhist meditation technique. Focuses your aggression. The monks used to do it before they went into battle."

JAMIE LEE CURTIS (*Wanda Gerschwitz*): "What kind of Buddhism is this, Otto?"

**5.** "Don't call me stupid."

*Kline's characteristic warning, repeated in several variations to different people*

**6.** "Oh, you English are so superior, aren't you? Well, would you like to know where you'd be without us, the old U.S. of A., to protect you? I'll tell you. The smallest fucking province in the Russian Empire!"

*Ultra-American Kline, venting his anger against the very British Maria Aitken (Wendy Leach)*

**7.** "Wanda, do you have any idea what it's like being English? Being so correct all the time, being so stifled by this dread of doing the wrong thing?. . . . You see, Wanda, we're all terrified of embarrassment. That's why we're so . . . dead."

*John Cleese (Archie Leach) to Curtis*

**8.** "Apologize."

*Kline to Cleese, in a request later enforced by hanging him upside down from a window*

**9.** "Now let me correct you on a couple of things, okay? Aristotle was not Belgian. The central message of Buddhism is not every man for himself. . . . And the London Underground is not a political movement."

*Curtis, disabusing Kline of some of his pet notions*

**10.** "The English contribution to world cuisine. The chip."

*Kline, holding up a chip*

**11.** "I'll make a deal with you. I'll put one up."

*Kline, failing to take seriously Cleese's order to put his hands up*

**12.** "Winners like . . . North Vietnam?"

*Cleese, on Kline's charge that the British differ from Americans in not liking winners*

**LAST LINE**
**13.** "Asshole!"

*Kline, as he is thrown from the exterior of a plane taking off; also his favorite line when he crashes into other people's cars*

**FISHER KING, THE** *(TriStar, 1991). D: Terry Gilliam. S: Richard LaGravenese.*

**1.** "They don't feel love. They only negotiate love moments. They're evil, Edwin. They're repulsed by imperfection. Horrified by the banal. Everything that America stands for. Everything that you and I fight for. They must be stopped before it's too late. It's us or them."

*Radio talk show host Jeff Bridges (Jack Lucas), on yuppies; Bridges's remarks lead a listener to kill yuppies in a bar*

**2.** "There are two kinds of people in the world. People who are destined for greatness like Walt Disney and Hitler. And then there's the rest of us."

*Bridges to himself*

**3.** "You know, boys. There are three things in this world that you need. Respect for all kinds of life, a nice bowel movement on a regular basis, and a navy blazer. Oh! One more thing. Never take your eye off the ball."

*Insane homeless person Robin Williams (Perry a.k.a. Henry Sagan) to punks Jayce Bartok and Dan Futterman*

**4.** "I'm the janitor of God."

*Williams to Bridges*

**5.** "I think men were made in the Devil's image, and women were created out of God, 'cause, after all, women can have babies, which is kind of like creating. And which also accounts for the fact that women are so attracted to men, 'cause, let's face it, the Devil is a hell of a lot more interesting."

*Mercedes Ruehl (Anne) to Bridges*

**6.** "I love this guy!!"

*Williams to New York, when Bridges shows that he cares*

**7.** BRIDGES: "You are out of your fucking mind!"
WILLIAMS: *"Bingo!!"*

**8.** "I just hope, when they put me away, they find a place right next to his."

*Bridges to himself*

**FIVE EASY PIECES** *(Columbia, 1970). D: Bob Rafelson. S: Adrien Joyce, (pseudonym for Carol Eastman). Fr: Joyce Rafelson, Bob Rafelson (story).*

**1.** "I'll go out with you, or I'll stay in with you, or I'll do anything that you like for me to do, if you tell me that you love me."

*Karen Black (Rayette Dupeau) to Jack Nicholson (Robert Dupeau)*

**2.** "Now all you have to do is hold the chicken, bring me the toast, give me a check for the chicken salad sandwich, and you haven't broken any rules."

*Nicholson to waitress who refuses to serve him plain toast because it isn't on the menu*

**3.** "If you wouldn't open your mouth, everything would be just fine."

*Nicholson to Black*

**4.** "I'm sorry it didn't work out."

*Nicholson to his father, William Challee (Nicholas Dupeau), on their relationship, after Challee suffers a stroke*

**FLASHDANCE** *(Paramount, 1983). D: Adrian Lyne. S: Tom Hedley, Joe Esterhas. Fr: Tom Hedley (story).*

**1.** "When you give up your dreams, you die."

*Michael Nouri (Nick Hurley) urging welder Jennifer Beals (Alex Owens) not to give up her hopes of being a great dancer*

**FLETCH** *(Universal, 1985). D: Michael Ritchie. S: Andrew Bergman. Fr: Gregory Mcdonald (novel).*

**1.** "You know, if you shoot me you'll lose a lot of these humanitarian awards."

*Chevy Chase (Fletch), warning a villain*

**FLINTSTONES, THE** *(Universal, 1994). D: Brian Levant. S: Brian Levant. Fr: TV series.*

1. "Yabba-dabba-doo!"

   *John Goodman's (Fred Flintstone's) first words onscreen*

2. GEORGE LUCAS—TAR WARS

   *Film playing at the prehistoric drive-in*

3. "Fred's no Albert Einstone."

   *Rosie O'Donnell (Betty Rubble), on Goodman*

4. "Charge it!"

   *O'Donnell and Elizabeth Perkins (Wilma Flintstone), preparing to go on a shopping spree*

5. NO DINOSAURS WERE HARMED IN THE MAKING OF THIS MOTION PICTURE

   *End title*

**FLY, THE** (20th Century–Fox, 1986). D: David Cronenberg. S: Charles Edward Pogue, David Cronenberg. Fr: George Langelaan (story).

1. "Designer phone booths. Very cute."

   *Geena Davis (Veronice Quaife), looking at scientist Jeff Goldblum's (Seth Brundle's) experimental telepods for the first time*

2. "You get it, all right; you just can't handle it."

   *Goldblum to Davis, on her inability to believe that her stocking has just been teleported*

3. "I must not know enough about the flesh myself."

   *Goldblum, on why his telepod can't handle living things, only inanimate objects*

4. "I just want to eat you up. That's why old ladies pinch babies. It's the flesh. It just makes you crazy."

   *Davis to Goldblum, in bed, giving him a clue as to how he can teach his telepod to work with living things—the flesh*

5. "No. Be afraid. Be very afraid."

   *Davis to Joy Boushel (Tawny), Goldblum's date for the evening, after Goldblum tells her not to be afraid of being teleported*

6. "It mated us, me and the fly. We hadn't even been properly introduced."

   *Goldblum, on how the telepod's computer fused him and a fly at the molecular-genetic level*

7. "Help me. Please help me."

   *Goldblum to Davis, echoing a line from the original version of The Fly, when a fly with the head of a scientist was caught in a spiderweb*

8. "I'm becoming . . . Brundlefly. Don't you think that's worth a Nobel Prize or two?"

   *Goldblum to Davis, as he mutates into a fly-human creature*

9. "Have you ever heard of insect politics? Neither have I. Insects don't have politics. They're very brutal. No compassion. No compromise. We can't trust the insect."

   *Goldblum, on what he is becoming*

10. "I'm saying I'll hurt you if you stay."

    *Goldblum, urging Davis to leave*

**FLYING DOWN TO RIO** (RKO, 1933). D: Thornton Freeland. S: Cyril Hume, H. W. Hanemann, Erwin Gelsey. Fr: Anne Caldwell (play), Lou Brock (original story).

1. "I'll bet he's broken both legs running after two women at the same time."

   *Ginger Rogers (Honey Hale), on ladies' man Gene Raymond (Roger Bond)*

**FLYING LEATHERNECKS** (RKO, 1951). D: Nicholas Ray. S: James Edward Grant. Fr: Kenneth Gamet (story).

**LAST LINE**

*1.* "For the future record, all orders are right away."

> *Robert Ryan (Capt. Carl Griffin)*

**FOLLOW THE FLEET** *(RKO, 1936). D: Mark Sandrich. S: Dwight Taylor, Allan Scott. Fr: Hubert Osborne (play, Shore Leave).*

*1.* "Oh, I see. Women aren't even admitted to Paradise without a man."

> *Harriet Hilliard (Connie Martin) to clerk at the Paradise dance hall who refuses to admit her without an escort*

*2.* "You know, it isn't that gentlemen really prefer blondes, it's just that we look dumber."

> *The blond Ginger Rogers (Sherry Martin), urging her brunette, bookish sister Hilliard to make herself over to look less intelligent*

*3.* "Gosh, you're glad to see me."

> *Fred Astaire (Bake Baker), making a typically self-centered remark to his erstwhile love interest Rogers*

*4.* HILLIARD, dreaming about the Navy man she has met: "Hey, Sherry, how much does a chief petty officer get?"
> ROGERS: "Whatever he told you, just cut it in half."

*5.* "I don't often try to apologize, 'cause I seldom make any mistakes."

> *Astaire, not quite apologizing to Rogers*

**FOOTLIGHT PARADE** *(Warner Bros.–Vitaphone, 1933). D: Lloyd Bacon. S: Manuel Seff, James Seymour.*

*1.* "As long as they've got sidewalks, you've got a job."

> *Joan Blondell (Nan Prescott) to Claire Dodd (Vivian Rich)*

**FOR THE BOYS** *(20th Century–Fox, 1991). D: Mark Rydell. S: Marshall Brickman, Neal Jimenez, Lindy Laub. Fr: Neal Jimenez, Lindy Laub (story).*

*1.* "The thing you want to avoid is outlasting everybody."

> *Bette Midler (Dixie Leonard)*

*2.* "I see the years have not mellowed you."

> *James Caan (Eddie Sparks), on being reunited with old stage partner Midler*

*3.* CAAN: "I think I'm getting excited."
MIDLER: "Let me know when you're sure."

**FOR WHOM THE BELL TOLLS** *(Paramount, 1943). D: Sam Wood. S: Dudley Nichols. Fr: Ernest Hemingway (novel).*

*1.* "I don't know how to kiss, or I would kiss you. Where do the noses go?"

> *Ingrid Bergman (Maria) to Gary Cooper (Robert Jordan)*

*2.* "A man fights for what he believes in, Fernando."

> *Cooper*

**FORBIDDEN PLANET** *(MGM, 1956). D: Fred M. Wilcox. S: Cyril Hume. Fr: Irving Block, Allen Adler (story).*

*1.* "I rarely use it myself, sir. It promotes rust."

> *Robby the Robot, on oxygen*

**2.** "Mister, I've been from here to there in this galaxy, and I just want you to know, you're the most understanding soul I ever met up with."

> *Alcohol-craving Earl Holliman (Cookie) to Robby the Robot, when the latter offers to make him sixty gallons of bourbon*

**3.** "It's an old custom. All the really high civilizations go in for it. . . . It stimulates the whole system. As a matter of fact, you can't be in tip-top health without it."

> *Jack Kelly (Lieutenant Farman), explaining kissing to Anne Francis (Altaira), isolated all her life from men*

**4.** "It's all right, sir. A commanding officer doesn't need brains, just a good loud voice."

> *Walter Pidgeon (Morbius) to Leslie Nielsen (Commander Adams), when Nielsen performs poorly on the intelligence meter designed by the lost alien Krell civilization*

**5.** "Monsters, John. Monsters from the Id."

> *Warren Stevens (Lt. "Doc" Ostrow), on the monsters from the unconscious that destroyed the Krell civilization*

**6.** "My poor Krell! After a million years of shining sanity, they could hardly have understood what power was destroying them."

> *Pidgeon, mourning the fall of the Krell at the hands of the monsters from the Id*

**7.** "Guilty! Guilty! My evil self is at that door—and I have no power to stop it!"

> *Pidgeon, panicking as the Monster from the Id closes in on him, his daughter Francis, and Nielsen*

**FOREIGN AFFAIR, A** *(Paramount, 1948). D: Billy Wilder. S: Charles Brackett, Billy Wilder, Richard Breen, Robert Harari. Fr: David Shaw (story).*

**1.** "Really, Colonel Plummer, you should have your brakes relined."

> *Jean Arthur (Phoebe Frost), reprimanding Millard Mitchell (Col. Rufus J. Plummer)*

**FORREST GUMP** *(Paramount, 1994). D: Robert Zemeckis. S: Eric Roth. Fr: Winston Groom (novel).*

**1.** "Hello. My name's Forrest. Forrest Gump. Do you want a chocolate?"

> *Tom Hanks (Forrest Gump) to listener at bus stop*

**2.** "My mama always said, life was like a box of chocolates. You never know what you're gonna get."

> *Hanks to listener*

**3.** "Mama says stupid is as stupid does."

> *Michael Connor Humphreys (Young Forrest Gump); repeated later by Hanks*

**4.** "I believe he said he has to go pee."

> *John F. Kennedy, on Hanks at a White House reception*

**5.** "My name's Forrest Gump. People call me Forrest Gump."

> *Hanks*

**6.** "Sorry I had a fight in the middle of your Black Panther party."

> *Hanks leaving a meeting of Black Panthers*

**7.** ROBIN WRIGHT (*Jenny*): "Why are you so good to me?"
> HANKS: "You're my girl."
> WRIGHT: "I'll always be your girl."

**8.** "He never actually said so, but I think he made his peace with God."

*Hanks, on amputee Gary Sinise (Lt. Dan Taylor)*

**9.** "Mama always had a way of explaining things so I could understand."

*Hanks, on his mother Sally Field*

**10.** "And that's all I have to say about that."

*Hanks's habitual phrase about death*

**11.** "Now mama said there's only so much fortune a man really needs and the rest is just for showing off."

*Hanks*

**12.** "Sometimes I guess there just aren't enough rocks."

*Hanks, on Wright throwing rocks at the house of her father, who abused her as a child*

**13.** "I just felt like running."

*Hanks, on why he started running across the country*

**14.** HANKS, avoiding stepping on dog feces as he inadvertently develops a new slogan: "It happens."

BUMPER STICKER ENTREPRENEUR: "What, shit?"

HANKS: "Sometimes."

**15.** "Have a nice day."

*Hanks, coming up with another slogan when he throws a T-shirt with a smiling face at another entrepreneur*

**16.** "I'm pretty tired. Think I'll go home now."

*Hanks to his followers, when he decides to stop after three years of running*

**17.** "But I think maybe it's both. Maybe both is happening at the same time."

*Hanks, on whether lives are ruled by destiny or chance*

**FORT APACHE** *(Argosy Pictures–RKO Radio, 1948). D: John Ford. S: Frank S. Nugent. Fr: James Warner Bellah (story, "Massacre").*

**1.** "I am not a general, Captain. A man is what he is paid for. I am paid in the rank of lieutenant colonel."

*Henry Fonda (Lt. Col. Owen Thursday) to John Wayne (Capt. Kirby York), when he calls Fonda a general*

**2.** "The uniform, gentlemen, is not a subject for individual, whimsical expression. We're not cowboys at this post or freighters with a load of buffalo."

*Fonda to officers at Fort Apache*

**3.** "Understand me, gentlemen, I am not a martinet."

*Fonda to officers at Fort Apache*

**4.** "What does a woman do in the Army?"

*Shirley Temple (Philadelphia Thursday) to Anna Lee (Emily Collingswood)*

**5.** VICTOR MCLAGLEN *(Sgt. Festus Mulcahy)*, on finding whiskey in a box that was said to contain Bibles: "Bibles, sir."

FONDA: "Sergeant, pour me some scripture."

**6.** "Well, boys, we've a man's work ahead of us this day."

*McLaglen to soldiers taking up cups when told to destroy a stash of whiskey*

**7.** FONDA, on how Wayne was used to trick Cochise into returning to the United States:

"Your word to a breechclouted savage, an illiterate uncivilized murderer and treaty breaker? There's no question of honor, sir, between an American officer and Cochise."

WAYNE: "There is to me, sir."

**8.** WAYNE, on viewing the Apaches: "They outnumber us four to one. Do we talk or fight?"

FONDA: "You seem easily impressed by numbers, Captain."

**9.** "Get to Fort Grant. Tell 'em where we are. Tell 'em we may still be alive if they hurry. Move! And marry that girl."

*Wayne to John Agar (Lt. Col. Michael "Mickey" O'Rourke); the girl referred to is Temple*

**10.** "No questions."

*Wayne, as Fonda rides off to his demise against the Apaches*

**11.** "He must have been a great man and a great soldier."

*Reporter to Wayne, about Fonda, after the general's death*

**12.** "You're wrong there because they haven't died. They're living, right out there, Collingwood and all the rest. They'll keep on living as long as the regiment lives. The pay is thirteen dollars a month, their diet beans and ham, maybe horse meat before this campaign is over. Fight over cards or rotgut whiskey, but share the last drop in their canteens. The faces may change, and names, but they're the regiment, the regular army."

*Wayne to reporter who doubts regular soldiers will be remembered*

**FORTUNE COOKIE, THE** (UA, 1966). D: Billy Wilder. S: Billy Wilder, I. A. L. Diamond.

**1.** "Too bad it didn't happen further down the street—in front of the May Company. From *them* you can collect. Couldn't you have dragged yourself another twenty feet?"

*Walter Matthau (Willie Gingrich) to accident victim Howard McNear*

**48HRS.** (Paramount, 1983). D: Walter Hill. S: Roger Spottiswoode, Walter Hill, Larry Gross, Steven E. de Souza.

**1.** "I'm your worst nightmare, a nigger with a badge."

*Furloughed convict Eddie Murphy (Reggie Hammond), flashing police credentials at a bar full of tough whites*

**42ND STREET** (Warner Bros., 1933). D: Lloyd Bacon. S: James Seymour, Rian James. Fr: Bradford Ropes (novel).

**1.** "That gal sticks to him like dandruff to a blue suit."

*Harry Akst (Jerry), on Una Merkel (Lorraine Fleming)*

**2.** "Turn slowly—let me see the legs, please."

*Warner Baxter (Julian Marsh), choosing chorus girls for his show*

**3.** "And the technical name for that, my darling, is the great American runaround!"

*Ginger Rogers (Ann) to Ruby Keeler (Peggy Sawyer), after Bebe Daniels (Dorothy Brock) gives the brush-off to Guy Kibbee (Abner Dillon)*

**4.** "We're going to open on schedule time, and I *mean* schedule time. You're going to work and sweat and work some more—you're going to work days and you're going to work nights—and you're going to work between times when I think you need it—

you're going to dance until your feet fall off—and you aren't able to stand up. But six weeks from now—we're going to have a *show!*"

*Baxter, rallying the troupe*

**5.** "After three weeks of this, a leg ain't nothin' to me but somethin' to walk with."

*Kibbee, weary*

**6.** "Happy? I remember that word—from my crossword puzzle days."

*George Brent (Pat Denning)*

**7.** "Just because there's a depression on, some folks think a landlady's got to stand for anything."

*Keeler's landlady, annoyed at finding Keeler with Brent*

**8.** "You're supposed to be a dancer. All you need is a couple of license plates and you'd look like a T Model Ford!"

*Baxter, calling Dick Powell (Billy Lawler) on the carpet*

**9.** "You don't make much money, but you get a lot of exercise."

*George E. Stone (Andy Lee), summing up show business*

**10.** "I don't want anybody in here for the next five hours. I'll either have a live leading woman—or a dead chorus girl."

*Baxter, preparing to whip Ruby Keeler into shape as Daniels's replacement*

**11.** "Go out there and be so swell you'll make me hate you!"

*Daniels, giving understudy Keeler her blessing*

**12.** "And, Sawyer, you're going out a youngster, but you've *got* to come back a star!"

*Baxter to Keeler*

**13.** "Just another show!"

*Baxter, relaxing after the audience files out*

**FOUR FEATHERS, THE** (UK: UA, 1939). D: Zoltan Korda. S: R. C. Sherriff, Lajos Biro, Arthur Wimperis. Fr: A. E. W. Mason (novel).

**1.** "To be a soldier and a coward is to be an imposter, a menace to the men whose lives are in your hands."

*John Clements (Harry Faversham), a soldier branded as a coward*

**2.** "In England, the white feather is the mark of a coward."

*Clements*

**3.** "You've always got some confoundedly cold-blooded reason for doing nothing."

*Ralph Richardson (John Durrance) to Frederick Culley (Dr. Sutton)*

**FRANKENSTEIN** (Universal, 1931). D: James Whale. S: Garrett Fort, Francis Edwards Faragoh, Robert Florey (uncredited). Fr: Mary Shelley (novel), Peggy Webling (play).

**1.** "Quite a good scene, isn't it? One man crazy—and three very sane spectators."

*Colin Clive (Henry Frankenstein), comparing himself to the frightened witnesses of his attempt to create life*

**2.** "It's alive! It's alive!"

*Clive, on bringing Boris Karloff (the Monster) to life*

**3.** JOHN BOLES (*Victor Moritz*): "Henry—in the name of God."

CLIVE: "Oh—in the name of God. Now I know what it feels like to be God."

**4.** "Have you never wanted to look beyond the clouds and the stars or to know what causes the trees to bud? And what changes darkness into light? But if you talk like that, people call you crazy."

*Clive*

**5.** "I made him with these hands, and with these hands I will destroy him."

*Clive*

**6.** "Burn the mill! Burn it down! Burn the mill!"

*Villagers, as they set fire to the windmill where Karloff is trapped*

**7.** FREDERICK KERR (*Baron Frankenstein*), raising a toast: "As I said before, I say again: Here's . . . here's to a son to the House of Frankenstein."

MAIDS: "Indeed, sir. We hope so, sir."

## FRANKENSTEIN MEETS THE WOLF MAN

(*Universal, 1942*). D: Roy William Neill. S: Curt Siodmak.

**1.** "He is not insane. He simply wants to die."

*Gypsy Maria Ouspenskaya (Maleva), defending the sanity of tormented Lon Chaney, Jr. (Wolf Man/Lawrence Talbot)*

## FRENCH CONNECTION, THE (20th Century–Fox, 1971). D: William Friedkin. S: Ernest Tidyman. Fr: Robin Moore (book).

**1.** "You ever been to Poughkeepsie? Huh? Have you ever been to Poughkeepsie?"

*Undercover cop Gene Hackman (Popeye Doyle), grilling a suspect*

**2.** "All right, Popeye's here!"

*Hackman, announcing a drug bust*

**3.** "It's like a goddamn desert full of junkies out there."

*Roy Scheider (Buddy Russo), on the situation in the streets as junkies await a big drug shipment from France*

**4.** "He's a good cop, basically a good cop. He's got good hunches every once in a while."

*Randy Jurgensen (Police sergeant), on Hackman*

**5.** "Blast off—one eight oh. Two hundred—*Good Housekeeping* Seal of Approval. Two ten—U.S. government certified. Two twenty—lunar trajectory, junk of the month club, sirloin steak. Two thirty—Grade A poison. Absolute dynamite. Eighty-nine percent pure junk. Best I've ever seen. If the rest is like this, you'll be dealing on this load for two years."

*Pat McDermott (Chemist), looking at rising thermometer as he tests the quality of the heroin*

**6.** "What about you, Sal? Are you everything they say you are?"

*Drug kingpin Harold Gary (Weinstock) to minor dealer Tony LoBianco (Sal Boca)*

**7.** "This is Doyle. I'm sittin' on Frog One."

*Hackman, on the phone with FBI colleagues, while tailing French criminal Fernando Rey (Alain Charnier) in the subway*

**LAST LINE**
**8.** "The son of a bitch is here. I saw him. I'm gonna get him."

*Hackman, still hunting for Rey, whose trail has gone cold*

## FRENCH LIEUTENANT'S WOMAN, THE
(UK: UA, 1981). D: Karel Reisz. S: Harold Pinter. Fr: John Fowles (novel).

LAST LINE

**1.** "Sarah!"

> Jeremy Irons (Charles/Mike), calling futilely for Meryl Streep (Sarah/Anna)

## FRIED GREEN TOMATOES (Universal, 1991). D: Jon Avnet. S: Fannie Flagg, Carol Sobieski. Fr: Fannie Flagg (novel, Fried Green Tomatoes at the Whistle Stop Cafe).

**1.** "Face it, girls, I'm older and I have more insurance."

> Kathy Bates (Evelyn Couch) to two obnoxious young women whose car she has just wrecked

**2.** "How many of those hormones you takin', honey?"

> Jessica Tandy (Ninny Threadgoode) to Bates, on hearing about the accident

**3.** "What I can't understand is how you can hit someone six times by accident."

> Gailard Sartain (Ed Couch) to his wife Bates, after hearing about the collision

## FRIENDLY PERSUASION (Allied Artists, 1956). D: William Wyler. S: Michael Wilson (uncredited). Fr: Jessamyn West (novel, The Friendly Persuasion).

**1.** "If thee talked as much to the Almighty as thee does to that horse, thee might stand more squarely in the light."

> Dorothy McGuire (Eliza Birdwell) to Gary Cooper (Jess Birdwell)

## FROM HERE TO ETERNITY (Columbia, 1953). D: Fred Zinnemann. S: Daniel Taradash. Fr: James Jones (novel).

**1.** "Looks to me as if you're trying to acquire a reputation as a lone wolf, Prewitt. You should know that in the Army it's not the individual that counts."

> Philip Ober (Capt. Dana Holmes) to Montgomery Clift (Pvt. Robert E. Lee Prewitt), who is refusing to join the captain's boxing team

**2.** "He ain't like the others. He'll make it tough on you, but he'll draw himself a line he thinks fair and he won't come over it. You don't see many top kicks like him no more."

> Jack Warden (Corporal Buckley) to Clift, about Burt Lancaster (Sgt. Milton Warden)

**3.** "Well, on the other hand, I've got a bathing suit under my dress."

> Deborah Kerr (Karen Holmes) to Lancaster

**4.** "Only my friends call me wop."

> Frank Sinatra (Pvt. Angelo Maggio), objecting to Ernest Borgnine's (Sgt. "Fatso" Judson's) use of an ethnic slur

**5.** "I never knew it could be like this."

> Kerr, rolling in the surf with Lancaster

**6.** "Okay, Fatso, if it's killing you want, come on."

> Lancaster, wielding a broken bottle as he breaks up a barroom fight between Borgnine and Sinatra

**7.** "I'm gonna escape from this dump. Gimbels basement couldn't hold me, neither can no lousy stockade."

> Sinatra to guard, while walking to prison

**8.** "Hello, tough monkey."

*Stockade sergeant Borgnine, greeting Sinatra upon his arrival at the stockade*

**9.** LANCASTER: "I've never been so miserable in my life as I have since I met you."

KERR: "Neither have I."

LANCASTER: "I wouldn't trade a minute of it."

KERR: "Neither would I."

**10.** "He's a good man."

*Clift's opinion of Lancaster and, later, Sinatra*

**11.** "Watch out for Fatso."

*Sinatra, dying after vicious beatings from Borgnine, to Clift*

**12.** "You just don't want to marry me. You're already married—to the Army."

*Kerr to Lancaster*

**13.** "Who do they think they're fighting? They're pickin' trouble with the best army in the world."

*Clift, on the Japanese attacking Pearl Harbor*

**14.** "What do I want to go back to the Army for? I'm a soldier."

*Clift's reason to his love Donna Reed (Alma Lorene) for going back to base to join in the defense against the Japanese*

**15.** "He was always a hardhead, sir. But he was a good soldier. He loved the Army more than any soldier I ever knew."

*Lancaster, on Clift's death*

**16.** "You just couldn't play it smart, could you. All you had to do was box, but no, not you, you hardhead. Funny thing is there ain't gonna be any boxing championships this year."

*Lancaster to the dead Clift*

**17.** "There's a legend. If they float in toward shore you'll come back someday. If they float out to sea, you won't."

*Kerr to Reed, throwing leis into the water as they leave Hawaii after the Japanese attack*

**LAST LINE**

**18.** "Robert E. Lee Prewitt. Isn't that a silly old name."

*Reed to Kerr, as their ship leaves Hawaii*

**FROM RUSSIA WITH LOVE** (UK: UA, 1963). D: Terence Young. S: Richard Maibaum, Johanna Harwood. Fr: Ian Fleming (novel).

**1.** "Well, I've just been reviewing an old case."

*Sean Connery (James Bond) to Lois Maxwell (Miss Moneypenny), on his delay in reporting to the head office, due to an afternoon tryst*

**2.** "From Russia with Love"

*Connery's handwritten note on a picture of double agent Daniela Bianchi (Tania), which he is giving to Maxwell*

**3.** "Red wine with fish. Well, that should've told me something."

*Connery, on assassin Robert Shaw's (Red Grant's) bad table etiquette*

**4.** SHAW, threatening Connery: "The first one won't kill you. Nor the second. Not even the third. Not till you crawl over here and kiss my foot."

CONNERY, staying cool: "How 'bout a cigarette?"

**5.** "She's had her kicks."

*Connery, on the death of Lotte Lenya (Rosa Klebb), a SPECTRE operative with a poisoned stiletto in the toe of her shoe*

**FRONT PAGE, THE** *(UA, 1931). D: Lewis Milestone. S: Bartlett Cormack, Ben Hecht (uncredited), Charles Lederer (uncredited). Fr: Ben Hecht, Charles MacArthur (play).*

LAST LINE

**1.** "The son of a bitch stole my watch."

*Newspaper editor Adolphe Menjou (Walter Burns), calling for the arrest of reporter Pat O'Brien (Hildy Johnson), with the word "bitch" strategically blotted out on the sound track*

**FRONT, THE** *(Columbia, 1976). D: Martin Ritt. S: Walter Bernstein.*

LAST LINE

**1.** "Fellows, I don't recognize the right of this committee to ask me these kind of questions. And furthermore, you can all go fuck yourselves."

*Woody Allen (Howard Prince) to investigative committee*

**FUGITIVE, THE** *(Warner Bros., 1993). D: Andrew Davis. S: Jeb Stuart, David Twohy. Fr: David Twohy (story), TV series.*

**1.** "My, my, my, my, my. What a mess."

*Tommy Lee Jones (Deputy Samuel Gerard), surveying scene of train and bus wreckage*

**2.** "You know, we're always fascinated when we find leg irons with no legs in 'em."

*Jones, finding the cast-off leg irons of escaped prisoner Harrison Ford (Dr. Richard Kimble)*

**3.** "Listen up, ladies and gentlemen. Our fugitive has been on the run for ninety minutes. Average foot speed over uneven ground, barring injury, is four miles an hour. That gives us a radius of six miles. What I want out of each and every one of you is a hard target search of every gas station, residence, warehouse, farmhouse, henhouse, outhouse, and doghouse in that area. Checkpoints go up at fifteen miles. Your fugitive's name is Dr. Richard Kimble. Go get 'im."

*Jones to his people*

**4.** "Well, think me up a cup of coffee and a chocolate doughnut with some of those little sprinkles on top, will you, as long as you're thinkin'."

*Jones to subordinate Tom Wood (Newman), on Wood's claim to be busy thinking*

**5.** FORD, holding Jones at gunpoint: "I didn't kill my wife."
JONES: "I don't care."

**6.** "I don't bargain."

*Jones, on why he risked Wood's life rather than bargain with a fugitive*

**7.** "So he showed up not dead yet. Let that be a lesson to you, boys and girls: Don't ever argue with the big dog. Big dog is always right."

*Jones to his people, on finding Ford alive*

**8.** "Give it up. It's time to stop running."
*Jones, asking Ford to surrender*

LAST LINES
**9.** FORD, when Jones releases him from his handcuffs: "Thought you didn't care."
JONES: "I don't. Don't tell anybody, okay?"

**FULL METAL JACKET** *(Warner Bros., 1987). D: Stanley Kubrick. S: Stanley Kubrick, Michael Herr, Gustav Hasford. Fr: Gustav Hasford (novel,* The Short-Timers*).*

FIRST LINE

1. "I am Gunnery Sergeant Hartman, your senior drill instructor. From now on, you will speak only when spoken to, and the first and last words out of your filthy sewers will be 'Sir!' Do you maggots understand this?"

*Lee Ermey (Gunnery Sergeant Hartman) to new Marine recruits*

2. "Is that you, John Wayne? Is this me?"

*Matthew Modine (Private Joker), under his breath*

3. "Private Joker is silly and he's ignorant, but he's got guts, and guts is enough."

*Ermey, on Modine*

4. "Those individuals showed what one motivated Marine and his rifle can do! And before you ladies leave my island, you will be able to do the same thing!"

*Ermey, on Kennedy assassin Lee Harvey Oswald and mass-murderer Charles Whitman, both former Marines and expert marksmen*

5. "Didn't Mommy and Daddy show you enough attention when you were a child?"

*Lee Ermey to the crazed Vincent D'Onofrio (Private Pyle), just before D'Onofrio shoots him*

6. "We have a new directive from M.A.F. on this. In the future, in place of 'search and destroy,' substitute the phrase 'sweep and clear.'"

*John Terry (Lieutenant Lockhart), at editorial meeting of Marine newspaper*

7. "I think I was trying to suggest something about the duality of man, sir."

*Modine, on why he wears both a peace button and a helmet on which are the words "BORN TO KILL"*

8. "You talk the talk. Do you walk the walk?"

*Hardened soldier Adam Baldwin (Animal Mother), facing down Modine*

9. "Hard core, man. Fucking hard core."

*Marine onlooker, after Modine shoots a wounded Vietnamese sniper (Ngoc Le)*

LAST LINE

10. "I'm so happy that I am alive, in one piece and short. I'm in a world of shit, yes. But I am alive. And I am not afraid."

*Modine, in voice-over, as the Marines march past a burning city*

**FUNNY FACE** *(Paramount, 1957). D: Stanley Donen. S: Leonard Gershe. Fr: Leonard Gershe (musical play,* Wedding Day*).*

1. "Now hear this!"

*Kay Thompson (Maggie Prescott), addressing her staff at the fashion magazine* Quality

2. "Of course—one of those sinister places in Greenwich Village."

*Thompson to Astaire, on a site for a fashion shoot—a bookstore in Greenwich Village*

3. "It's chichi and an unrealistic approach to self-impressions as well as economics."

*Audrey Hepburn (Jo Stockton) to Astaire, on fashion magazines*

4. "She's got to be more than all right. She's got to have bizazz."

*Thompson, on the new* Quality *woman*

5. "That thing from the bookshop?"

*Thompson, on Hepburn as the potential* Quality *woman*

**6.** "I think her face is perfectly funny."

*Thompson, on Hepburn*

**7.** "The bones are good. . . . Girls, the eyebrows up, a light powder; I want a little rouge right here. She needs a marvelous mouth. The hair—the hair is awful. It must come off."

*Thompson to staff, about Hepburn and her original plans to remake her*

**8.** "I have no illusions about my looks. I think my face is funny."

*Hepburn to Astaire*

**9.** "When I get through with you, you'll look like . . . what do you call beautiful? A tree—you'll look like a tree."

*Astaire to Hepburn*

**10.** "Well, I'm so tired, it's an effort for me to say I'm so tired."

*Astaire to Thompson and Hepburn, on arriving in Paris*

**11.** HEPBURN: "It's all part of empathicalism. We don't have to communicate with words. They understand me through the way I feel and the tone of my voice."
ASTAIRE: "Sort of like a dog."

**12.** "I don't want to stop. I like it. Take the picture, take the picture."

*Hepburn to Astaire, on their fashion shoot*

**13.** "He's about as interested in your intellect as I am."

*Astaire to Hepburn, on Professor Michael Auclaire's (Emile Flostre's) intentions*

**14.** "Professor Flostre, I came here to talk with a philosopher. You're talking like a man."

*Hepburn to Auclair*

**FUNNY GIRL** *(Columbia, 1968). D: William Wyler. S: Isobel Lennart. Fr: Jule Styne, Bob Merrill, Isobel Lennart (musical).*

**FIRST LINE**

**1.** "Hello, gorgeous."

*Barbra Streisand (Fanny Brice) to mirror at theater*

**2.** "I'm a bagel on a plateful of onion rolls."

*Streisand to Frank Faylen (Keeney)*

**3.** "One night there's going to be a knock on the door and it will be Flo Ziegfeld."

*Streisand to dancers, just before Omar Sharif (Nick Arnstein) first knocks on the door*

**4.** "But it was my joke. They laughed with me, not at me."

*Streisand to Walter Pidgeon (Florenz Ziegfeld), on why she turned her bridal character into a pregnant bride*

**5.** "Live . . . and on the side I gamble."

*Sharif to Streisand, on his profession*

**6.** "What with the Follies and an indecent proposal, it's been quite a night."

*Streisand to Sharif*

**7.** "You always ask me out whenever you run into me. I've never met anyone so polite."

*Streisand to Sharif*

**8.** "A blue marble egg . . . It's one of my favorite things, so I thought you might like to have it."

*Sharif to Streisand, recalled later as something he gave to her that she could not have gotten for herself*

**9.** "Oh, boy, if I can't tell when you're ordering roast beef and potatoes, how will I know when you're making advances?"

*Streisand to Sharif, after he orders a fancy dinner*

**10.** "The ruffled shirt."

*Kay Medford (Rose Brice) to group of friends, describing Sharif*

**11.** "Don't tell me—"

*Streisand to group advising her not to chase after Sharif, before bursting into the song "Don't Rain on My Parade"*

**12.** "I wanna be a Sadie."

*Streisand to Sharif, on her desire to become a married lady*

**13.** "So long, funny girl."

*Sharif to Streisand, as he leaves her*

**FUNNY THING HAPPENED ON THE WAY TO THE FORUM, A** *(UK: UA, 1966). D: Richard Lester. S: Melvin Frank, Michael Pertwee. Fr: Burt Shevelove, Larry Gelbart (musical play).*

**1.** "Also in this house dwells Pseudolus, slave to his son. Pseudolus is probably my favorite character in the piece, a role of enormous variety and nuance, and played by an actor of such versatility, such magnificent. . . . Let me put it this way. I play the part."

*Zero Mostel (Pseudolus), in his prologue to the story*

**2.** "A lesson to remember: Never fall in love during a total eclipse."

*Unhappy husband Michael Hordern (Senex)*

**3.** "Was One a good year?"

*Mostel, inquiring about a bottle of wine*

**4.** ANNETTE ANDREW (*Philia*), a courtesan who is not in love with her owner, Hordern: "Though you may have my body, you shall never have my heart."

HORDERN: "Oh, you can't have everything."

**5.** "Stand aside, everyone. I take large steps."

*Self-infatuated general Leon Greene (Miles Gloriosus)*

**6.** "Arrange food, drink, entertainment, and a sit-down orgy for forty."

*Greene, ordering hospitality for his troops*

**7.** PHIL SILVERS (*Lycus*), describing his nemesis to a listener: "The lyingest, cheatingest, sloppiest slave in all Rome."

LISTENER: "Oh. Pseudolus."

**8.** "A new god but a very hard worker."

*Silvers, a procurer of courtesans, on the patron god of procurers, panderers, and go-betweens*

**9.** "Just lie still and think dead thoughts."

*Mostel to his accomplice Jack Gilford (Hysterius), who is in drag pretending to be the dead Andrew*

**10.** "Yes, poor girl. To have died so young without ever having experienced me."

*Greene, when he thinks his destined mate, Andrew, is dead*

**11.** "It's against Roman law to take one's own life. The penalty is death."

*Soldier to heartbroken lover Michael Crawford (Hero), who is bent on suicide*

LAST LINE

**12.** "Son, if you're as happy as your mother and I have been, my heart bleeds for you."

*Hordern to his son Crawford*

**GALLIPOLI** (Australia: Paramount, 1981). D: Peter Weir. S: David Williamson. Fr: Peter Weir (story).

**1.** MARK LEE (*Archy*): "There's always water, if you know how to find it."

MEL GIBSON (*Frank Dunne*): "How do you find it?"

LEE: "Cockatoos. Sunset, they'll lead you straight to it."

GIBSON: "Oh, that's lovely. We put our lives in the hands of a mother parrot."

**2.** "The thing I can't stand about you, mate, is that you're always so bloody cheerful."

*Gibson to Lee, when they are being fired upon and Lee is whistling and making breakfast*

**3.** "No Turk in his right mind is going to waste a bullet on you."

*Lee to Gibson, the night before going over the top*

**4.** "I know you still haven't forgiven me for running off, but I'm sure in my own mind that I was right, and so would you, if you were here with me now. We're getting ready to make an all-out assault on Johnny Turk, and we know we're going to give a good account of ourselves and our country. Everyone is terribly excited. There's a feeling that we're all involved in an adventure that's somehow larger than life."

*Lee, writing a letter home*

LAST LINE

**5.** "What are your legs? Springs. Steel springs. What are they going to do? They're going to hold me down the track. How fast can you run? As fast as a leopard. How fast are you going to run? As fast as a leopard. Then let's see you do it."

*Lee, repeating to himself how his father trained him to run, just before he goes over the top*

**GANDHI** (UK: Columbia, 1982). D: Richard Attenborough. S: John Briley.

**1.** "If you are a minority of one, the truth is the truth."

*Indian civil resistance leader Ben Kingsley (Mohandas Gandhi) to American journalist Martin Sheen (Walker)*

**2.** "They may torture my body, break my bones, even kill me. Then they will have my dead body—not my obedience."

*Kingsley on fighting discriminatory laws*

**3.** "These are my clothes now."

*Kingsley, to Ian Charleson (Reverend Charlie Andrews), on his wearing only a white loincloth in solidarity with the poor of India*

**4.** "They're calling you Mahatma—great soul."

*Roshan Seth (Pandit Nehru) to Kingsley*

**5.** "We think it is time you recognized that you are masters in someone else's home."

*Kingsley to representatives of British rule in India*

**6.** BRITISH GENERAL: "You don't think we're just going to walk out of India."

KINGSLEY: "Yes. In the end you will walk out, because 100,000 Englishmen simply cannot control 350 million Indians if those Indians refuse to cooperate."

**7.** "An eye for an eye only ends up making the whole world blind."

*Kingsley, on violence and retribution*

**8.** "It is impossible for me to ignore that you are in a different category from any person I have ever tried or am likely to try."

*Trevor Howard (Judge Broomfield) to defendant Kingsley*

**9.** "Mr. Gandhi will find it takes a great deal more than a pinch of salt to bring down the British Empire."

*British viceroy John Gielgud (Lord Irwin), on Kingsley's proposed salt march*

**10.** "They are not in control, we are. That is the strength of civil resistance."

*Kingsley, on taking the initiative against the opponent*

**11.** "Thank him for his letter. Put him in jail. . . . And, Fields . . . keep that salt works open."

*Gielgud, giving orders in response to Kingsley's threat to lead a raid on the Dharasana Salt Works*

**12.** "Whatever moral ascendancy the West held was lost here today. India is free, for she has taken all that steel and cruelty can give and she has neither cringed nor retreated."

*Sheen, on telephone, reporting on the beating of resisters during the salt works action*

**13.** "I know a way out of hell. Find a child, a child whose mother and father have been killed, a little boy about this high, and raise him as your own. Only be sure that he is a Muslim and that you raise him as one."

*Kingsley to Hindu rioter stricken with guilt for killing a Muslim child in retaliation for the murder of his own son by Muslims*

**14.** "I may be blinded by my love for him, but I believe when we most needed it he offered the world a way out of madness. But he doesn't see it. Neither does the world."

*Devoted follower Geraldine James (Mirabell), on Kingsley*

**LAST LINE**

**15.** "When I despair, I remember that all through history the way of truth and love has always won. There have been tyrants and murderers and for a time they can seem invincible, but in the end they always fall. Think of it. Always."

*Kingsley, in voice-over as his ashes are spread on the water*

**GASLIGHT** (MGM, 1944). D: George Cukor. S: John Van Druten, Walter Reisch, John L. Balderston. Fr: Patrick Hamilton (play, *Angel Street*).

**1.** "Happiness is better than art."

*Emil Rameau (Maestro Guardi) to Ingrid Bergman (Paula Alquist), when she chooses to marry and give up a singing career*

**2.** "I haven't been afraid since I've known you."

*Bergman to Charles Boyer (Gregory Anton)*

**3.** "The whole place seems to smell of death."

*Bergman to Boyer*

**4.** "Jewels are wonderful things. They have a life of their own."

> Boyer, remarking on the history of the crown jewels in the Tower of London

**5.** "Suddenly, I'm beginning not to trust my memory at all."

> Bergman to Boyer

**6.** "I hope I find you better in the morning."
> Boyer to Bergman

**7.** "Do you know anything about anything you do?"

> Boyer to Bergman

**8.** "Because I'm mad, I'm rejoicing in my heart, without a shred of pity, without a shred of regret, watching you go with glory in my heart!"

> Bergman to Boyer, upon his arrest

**9.** "In the morning, when the sun rises, sometimes it's hard to believe there ever was a night."

> Joseph Cotten (Brian Cameron) to Bergman

**GAY DIVORCEE, THE** (RKO, 1934). D: Mark Sandrich. S: George Marion, Jr., Dorothy Yost, Edward Kaufman. Fr: Dwight Taylor, Cole Porter (musical play, The Gay Divorce), Kenneth Webb, Samuel Hoffenstein (adaptation).

**1.** "Oh, it's no crime to be married. It just shows a weakness on the part of men that women take advantage of."

> Edward Everett Horton (Egbert Fitzgerald)

**2.** "Chance is the fool's name for fate."

> Fred Astaire (Guy Holden) to Horton, in a phrase later garbled by professional divorce correspondent Erik Rhodes (Rodolfo Tonetti)

LAST LINE
**3.** "Scusi! Scusi! I'm also very good at parties!"

> Rhodes

**GENTLEMAN'S AGREEMENT** (Paramount, 1946). D: George Pearson. S: Moss Hart. Fr: Laura Z. Hobson (novel).

**1.** "Tell me, why is it that every man who seems attractive these days is either married or barred on a technicality?"

> Celeste Holm (Anne)

**GENTLEMEN PREFER BLONDES** (20th Century–Fox, 1953). D: Howard Hawks. S: Charles Lederer. Fr: Anita Loos, Joseph Fields (play).

**1.** "You know, I think you're the only girl in the world who can stand on a stage with a spotlight in her eye and still see a diamond inside a man's pocket."

> Jane Russell (Dorothy) to Marilyn Monroe (Lorelei), on her powers of vision

**2.** TOMMY NOONAN (Gus Esmond), contemplating the diamond he has just given her: "Is it the right size?"
> MONROE: "Well, it can never be too big."

**3.** "Looks like it ought to have a highball around it."

> Russell to Monroe, on the diamond from Noonan

**4.** "Is this the way to Europe, France?"
> Monroe to ship clerk

**5.** "No, money is rather a hobby of Lorelei's."

*Russell to Elliot Reid (Malone), a private detective investigating Monroe*

**6.** "I just love finding new places to wear diamonds."

*Monroe, on discovering the correct placement of a tiara*

**7.** "I'm old enough to appreciate a good-looking girl when I see one."

*George Winslow (Henry Spofford III) to Russell, on his tender age*

**8.** "Thank you ever so."

*Monroe to Charles Coburn (Sir Francis Beekman), on his request for a dance, and repeated at various times throughout the film*

**9.** "All right, I'll help you. I'll help you for two reasons. . . . The first reason is I'm too young to be sent to jail. The second reason is you've got a lot of animal magnetism."

*Winslow to Monroe, on why he will help her to escape the porthole window in which she is stuck*

**10.** "If we can't empty his pockets between us we're not worthy of the name 'woman.'"

*Russell to Monroe, on their search for incriminating photographs Reid may be carrying*

**11.** "I always say a kiss on the hand might feel very good but a diamond tiara lasts forever."

*Monroe to Coburn, on his suggested payment to her for keeping him out of trouble*

**12.** "Oh, you just feel that way because he's poor."

*Monroe to Russell, on Reid, the man she loves*

**13.** "I really do love Gus. There's not another millionaire in the world with such a gentle disposition. He never wins an argu-

ment, always does anything I ask. He's got the money to do it with. How can I help loving a man like that?"

*Monroe to Russell, on the nature of her love for Noonan*

**14.** "Let's see, that'll take an hour and forty-five minutes."

*Monroe to Russell, on how long it will take to raise the $15,000 needed to replace a diamond tiara*

**15.** "Don't you know that a man being rich is like a girl being pretty? You might not marry a girl just because she's pretty, but my goodness, doesn't it help? And if you had a daughter, wouldn't you rather she didn't marry a poor man? . . . You'd want her to have the most wonderful things in the world and to be very happy. Well, why is it wrong for me to want those things?"

*Monroe to Taylor Holmes (Gus Esmond, Sr.)*

**LAST LINE**
**16.** "Remember, honey, on your wedding day it's all right to say yes."

*Russell to Monroe, as they walk down the aisle in a double wedding*

**GEORGY GIRL** (UK: Columbia, 1966). D: Silvio Narizzano. S: Margaret Forster, Peter Nichols. Fr: Margaret Forster (novel).

**1.** "God always has another custard pie up His sleeve."

*Lynn Redgrave (Georgy)*

**GHOST** (Paramount, 1990). D: Jerry Zucker. S: Bruce Joel Rubin.

**1.** "I know you don't think I'm gonna give this four million dollars to a bunch of nuns."

Whoopi Goldberg (Oda Mae Brown) to ghost Patrick Swayze (Sam Wheat), when he demands that she donate a very large, illegally obtained check to charity

**2.** "Don't you see, I'm not a fake, not about this."

Goldberg trying to persuade Demi Moore (Molly Jensen) that Goldberg really is in contact with Swayze, Moore's dead lover

**3.** "Sam, I can hear you."

Moore, making contact with Swayze

**4.** "Sam—they're waitin' for you, Sam."

Goldberg, summoning Swayze to leave Moore and go on to the afterlife

**GHOST AND MRS. MUIR, THE** (20th Century–Fox, 1947). D: Joseph L. Mankiewicz. S: Philip Dunne. Fr: R.,A. Dick (novel).

**1.** "It is easy to understand why the most beautiful poems about England in the spring were written by poets living in Italy at the time."

George Sanders (Miles Fairley) to Gene Tierney (Lucy)

**GHOST BREAKERS, THE** (Paramount, 1940). D: George Marshall. S: Walter De Leon. Fr: Paul Dickey, Charles Goddard (play).

**1.** RICHARD CARLSON (Geoff Montgomery): ". . . A zombie has no will of his own. You see them sometimes walking around blindly, with dead eyes, following orders, not knowing what they do, not caring."

BOB HOPE (Larry Lawrence): "You mean like Democrats?"

**GHOSTBUSTERS** (Columbia, 1984). D: Ivan Reitman. S: Dan Aykroyd, Harold Ramis.

**1.** "Back off, man, I'm a scientist."

Bill Murray (Dr. Peter Venkman)

**2.** "Hello, I'm Peter. Where are you from—originally?"

Murray, approaching a ghost in the New York Public Library

**3.** "Okay, so, she's a dog."

Murray, on seeing his girlfriend transformed into a devil dog

**4.** "Let's show this prehistoric bitch how we do things downtown."

Murray, getting mad at the demon Gozer

**5.** ERNIE HUDSON (Winston Zeddemore): "We have the tools, we have the talent."

MURRAY: "It's Miller time!"

**6.** "There's something you don't see every day."

Murray, on viewing the giant Marshmallow Man

**7.** RICK MORANIS (Louis Tully): "Who are you?"

DAN AYKROYD (Dr. Raymond Stantz): "We're the Ghostbusters."

MORANIS: "Who does your taxes?"

**LAST LINE**
**8.** "I love this town!"

Hudson

**GHOSTBUSTERS II** (Columbia, 1989). D: Ivan Reitman. S: Harold Ramis, Dan Aykroyd.

**1.** "But I don't blame them, 'cause one time I turned into a dog and they helped me."

Attorney Rick Moranis (Louis Tully), defending the Ghostbusters by referring to a plot element in the earlier movie

**2.** "Ghostbusters. Yes, we're back."

Annie Potts (Janine Melnitz), answering the phone at the revived Ghostbusters office

**GIANT** (Warner Bros., 1956). D: George Stevens. S: Fred Guiol, Ivan Moffat. Fr: Edna Ferber (novel).

**1.** "Come on, darling. Why don't you kick off your spurs?"

Elizabeth Taylor (Leslie Lynnton), inviting Rock Hudson (Jordan Benedict) to bed

**LAST LINE**
**2.** "You want to know something, Leslie? If I live to be ninety, I'm never going to figure you out."

Hudson to Taylor

**GIDGET** (Columbia, 1959). D: Paul Wendkos. S: Gabrielle Upton. Fr: Frederick Kohner (novel).

**LAST LINE**
**1.** "Honest to goodness, it's the absolute ultimate."

Sandra Dee (Gidget)

**GIGI** (MGM, 1958). D: Vincente Minnelli. S: Alan Jay Lerner. Fr: Anita Loos (play), Colette (novel).

**1.** "It doesn't matter who gives them as long as you never wear anything second-rate. Wait for the first-class jewels, Gigi. Hold onto your ideals."

Isabel Jeans (Aunt Alicia) to Leslie Caron (Gigi)

**2.** "One has to be as rich as you, Gaston, to be bored at Monte Carlo."

Hermione Gingold (Mme. Alvarez) to Louis Jourdan (Gaston Lachaille)

**LAST LINE**
**3.** "Thank heaven."

Gingold, alluding to the musical's most famous song, "Thank Heaven for Little Girls"

**GILDA** (Columbia, 1946). D: Charles Vidor. S: Marion Parsonnet. Fr: E. A. Ellington (original story), Joe Eisinger (adaptation).

**FIRST LINE**
**1.** "To me a dollar was a dollar in any language."

Glenn Ford (Johnny Farrell), narrating his opening tale of how he won cheating at dice with a bunch of crapshooters in Buenos Aires

**2.** "It is a most faithful and obedient friend. It is silent when I wish it to be silent; it talks when I wish it to talk."

Casino owner George Macready (Ballin Mundson) to Glenn Ford, on the blade enclosed in his cane

**3.** "As usual I made my own luck, and I knew just when to stop letting it ride."

Ford, narrating the story of his rise as an employee in Macready's casino

**4.** "Get this, Mr. Mundson. I was born last night when you met me in that alley. That way I'm no past and all future, see? And I like it that way."

Ford to Macready, who rescued him from a thug in an alley the night before

**5.** MACREADY, checking before bringing Ford into the bedroom of his wife Rita Hayworth: "Gilda, are you decent?"

HAYWORTH, looking alluring: "Me? Sure, I'm decent."

**6.** "Oh, I'm sorry. Johnny is such a hard name to remember, and so easy to forget."

*Hayworth, on Ford, an old flame*

**7.** "I can never get a zipper to close. Maybe that stands for something, what do you think?"

*Hayworth*

**8.** "The young man would love it, too, but he can't afford it."

*Hayworth, on why Ford doesn't ask her to dance*

**9.** "Pardon me, but your husband is showing."

*Ford to Hayworth, dancing with another man as her husband approaches*

**10.** FORD, to Hayworth, on her constant flirting: "Doesn't it bother you at all that you're married?"

HAYWORTH: "What I want to know is, does it bother you?"

**11.** "You're a child, Gilda. A beautiful greedy child. And it amuses me to feed you beautiful things because you eat with such a good appetite."

*Macready to Hayworth*

**12.** "If I'd been a ranch, they would've named me the Bar Nothing."

*Hayworth to a male escort*

**13.** "Well? Here's the laundry waiting to be picked up."

*Hayworth to Ford, who has said he will take her to and pick her up from her dates with men, just as he would take and pick up Macready's laundry*

**14.** "Statistics show that there are more women in the world than anything else— except insects."

*Ford to Macready*

**15.** "You wouldn't think one woman could marry two insane men in one lifetime, now, would you?"

*Hayworth to Ford, who has succeeded Macready as her husband*

**GLASS KEY, THE** (Paramount, 1942). D: Stuart Heisler. S: Jonathan Latimer. Fr: Dashiell Hammett (novel).

**1.** "I just met the swellest dame. . . . She smacked me in the kisser."

*Political boss Brian Donlevy (Paul Madvig) revealing the type of woman he likes*

**GLASS MENAGERIE, THE** (Warner Bros., 1950). D: Irving Rapper. S: Tennessee Williams, Peter Berneis. Fr: Tennessee Williams (play).

**LAST LINE**
**1.** "And that is how I remember them, my mother and my sister. Good-bye."

*Arthur Kennedy (Tom Wingfield)*

**GLENGARRY GLEN ROSS** (New Line, 1992). D: James Foley. S: David Mamet. Fr: David Mamet (play).

**1.** "First prize is a Cadillac Eldorado. Second prize is a set of steak knives. Third prize is you're fired."

*Alec Baldwin (Blake), announcing a competition to real estate salesmen*

**2.** "You drove a Hyundai to get her tonight, I drove an $80,000 BMW, that's my name."

*Baldwin, telling Ed Harris (Dave Moss) his name*

**3.** "Only one thing counts in this life: Get them to sign on the line which is dotted."

*Baldwin*

**4.** "You owe me the car. See, 'cause this is how we keep score, ba-bing."

*Al Pacino (Ricky Roma), claiming first prize*

**5.** "You know your business, I know mine. Your business is being an asshole."

*Pacino to office manager Kevin Spacey (John Williamson)*

**6.** "You never open your mouth until you know what the shot is."

*Pacino, telling Spacey the first rule of salesmanship*

**7.** "It is not a world of men. It is not a world of men, Machine. It's a world of clock-watchers, bureaucrats."

*Pacino to Jack Lemmon (Shelley "The Machine" Levine)*

**GLENN MILLER STORY, THE** (Universal-International, 1953). D: Anthony Mann. S: Valentine Davies, Oscar Brodney.

LAST LINE
**1.** "As some of you might know, Major Miller is not with us today. But in his absence we shall do this program exactly as he had planned it. . . . This tune should be a familiar one. Especially to the members of Major Miller's family across the ocean who are listening."

*Charles Drake (Don Haynes), on James Stewart (Glenn Miller), who is missing and presumed dead*

**GLORIA** (Columbia, 1980). D: John Cassavetes. S: John Cassavettes.

**1.** "Frank, what are you going to do? Shoot a six-year-old kid on the street?"

*Gena Rowlands (Gloria Swenson) to the mafia hit man threatening the orphan she is sheltering*

**2.** "We're not interested in accidents."

*Rowlands, to a cabdriver asking questions about the car crash she just caused*

**3.** "All dead people's together anyway. It doesn't make any difference."

*Rowlands, responding to John Adames's (Philip Dawn's) objection that his parents are not buried in this particular cemetery*

**4.** "It's nothing for me to blow someone's brains out, believe me. Just hope it's someone I know."

*Rowlands to Adames, preparing him for the worst*

**GLORY** (TriStar, 1989). D: Edward Zwick. S: Kevin Jarre. Fr: Lincoln Kirstein (book, Lay This Laurel), Peter Burchard (book, One Gallant Rush), Robert Gould Shaw (letters).

**1.** "A colored soldier can stop a bullet as good as a white."

*African-American Civil War soldier Denzel Washington (Trip)*

**GO TELL THE SPARTANS** (Avco Embassy, 1978). D: Ted Post. S: Wendell Mayes. Fr: Daniel Ford (novel, Incident at Muc Wa).

**1.** "Abraham Lincoln. How would you like to go through life with a moniker like that? No wonder the poor bastard looks like he's caved in."

*Burt Lancaster (Maj. Asa Barker), when reviewing his troops*

**2.** "My command is spread thinner than the hairs on a baby's ass."

*Lancaster*

**3.** "The VC doesn't do anything accidentally."

*Lancaster*

**4.** "Stranger, when you find us lying here, go tell the Spartans we obeyed their orders."

*Craig Wasson (Cpl. Stephen Courcey), reading the inscription over a cemetery*

**5.** "In the whole history of the United States, they have never asked for the return of anything. Be it guns, money, boats, or howitzer shells. If they did, it would screw up the bookkeeping."

*Lancaster, when his offer of howitzer shells to the South Vietnamese is turned down because the United States might want them back*

**6.** "Too bad we couldn't've shown you a better war."

*Lancaster to Wasson, who volunteered for this mission*

**GO WEST** (MGM, 1940). D: Edward Buzzell. S: Irving Brecher.

**1.** "Oh, those are shoes? I thought that was fungus with buttons."

*Groucho Marx (S. Quentin Quale), commenting on the quality of Harpo Marx's (Rusty's) ragged shoes*

**2.** "Any resemblance between these two characters and living persons is purely coincidental."

*Groucho on Chico Marx (Panello) and Harpo*

**3.** "Let's go somewhere where we can be alone. Ah, there doesn't seem to be anyone on this couch."

*Groucho, romancing an old flame*

**GODDESS, THE** (Columbia, 1958). D: John Cromwell. S: Paddy Chayevsky.

**1.** "She's got what I call, er—it's a quality of availability. . . . It makes every man in the audience think he can make her if he only knew her."

*Bert Freed (Lester Brackman), discussing movie actress Kim Stanley (Emily Ann Faulkner) with her husband Lloyd Bridges (Dutch Seymour)*

**GODFATHER, THE** (Paramount, 1972). D: Francis Ford Coppola. S: Mario Puzo, Francis Ford Coppola, Robert Towne (uncredited). Fr: Mario Puzo (novel).

**FIRST LINE**

**1.** "I believe in America."

*Undertaker Salvatore Corsitto (Bonasera) beginning his plea to Marlon Brando (Don Vito Corleone) for vengeance against the men who assaulted his daughter*

**2.** "Someday, and that day may never come, I'll call upon you to do a service. Until that day, accept this justice as a gift on my daughter's wedding day."

*Brando to Corsitto, promising to grant the undertaker's request*

**3.** "I'm gonna make him an offer he can't refuse."

*Brando to Al Martino (Johnny Fontane), about movie producer John Marley (Woltz); repeated by Al Pacino (Michael Corleone) to his brother John Cazale (Fredo), about rival gangster Alex Rocco (Moe Greene)*

**4.** "Now, if there's nothing else, I'd like to go to my daughter's wedding."

*Brando*

**5.** "I don't like violence, Tom. I'm a businessman. Blood is a big expense."

*Al Lettieri (Sollozzo) to Robert Duvall (Tom Hagen), after having Brando shot*

**6.** "He's still alive! They hit him with five shots and he's still alive!"

*Lettieri to Duvall, on Brando surviving the hit*

**7.** "It's a Sicilian message. It means Luca Brasi sleeps with the fishes."

*Abe Vigoda (Tessio), explaining the meaning of a package of fish to James Caan (Sonny Corleone)*

**8.** "Leave the gun. Take the cannolis."

*Richard Castellano (Clemenza) to henchman, after John Martino (Paulie) is shot*

**9.** "You know, you gotta stop them at the beginning. Like they shoulda stopped Hitler at Munich. They shoulda never let him get away with that."

*Castellano to Pacino, about rival gangsters*

**10.** "I'm a superstitious man. And if some unlucky accident should befall my son, if my son is struck by a bolt of lightning, I will blame some of the people here."

*Brando, issuing a warning to the heads of the other crime families*

**11.** "Fredo, you're my older brother and I love you. But don't ever take sides with anyone against the family again. Ever."

*Pacino, warning Cazale*

**12.** "I never . . . I never wanted this for you. I worked my whole life—I don't apologize—to take care of my family. And I refused to be a fool dancing on a string held by all those . . . big shots. I don't apologize; that's my life. But I thought that . . . when it was your time that . . . that you would be the one to hold the strings."

*Brando to Pacino*

**13.** "Tell Mike it was only business."

*Vigoda to Duvall, before being killed for betraying Pacino*

**14.** "Don't ask me about my business, Kay."

*Pacino to his wife Diane Keaton (Kay Corleone)*

**LAST LINE**
**15.** "Don Corleone."

*Visitor, paying homage to Pacino as the new head of the crime family*

**GODFATHER PART II, THE** (Paramount, 1974). D: Francis Ford Coppola. S: Francis Ford Coppola, Mario Puzo. Fr: Mario Puzo (novel, The Godfather).

**1.** "You're my brother, Fredo. You don't have to apologize to me."

*Al Pacino (Michael Corleone) to John Cazale (Fredo)*

**2.** "Your father did business with Hyman Roth, your father respected Hyman Roth, but your father never trusted Hyman Roth, or his Sicilian messenger boy Johnny Ola."

*Michael V. Gazzo (Frank Pentangeli) to Pacino, on elder gangster Lee Strasberg (Hyman Roth) and his henchman Dominic Chianese (Johnny Ola)*

**3.** "Keep your friends close, but your enemies closer."

*Pacino, recalling a bit of his father's advice*

**4.** "Michael Corleone says hello."

*Danny Aiello, assassin, attempting to garrot Gazzo, apparently on Pacino's order*

**5.** PACINO, on watching Castroite rebels fight Cuban soldiers: "The soldiers are paid to fight. The rebels aren't."
STRASBERG: "What does that tell you?"
PACINO: "They can win."

**6.** "Michael, we're bigger than U.S. Steel."

*Strasberg to Pacino, on sealing their deal in Cuba*

**7.** "Hyman Roth will never see the new year."

*Pacino, announcing his intention to execute his partner Strasberg, whom he believes tried to murder him*

**8.** "And I said to myself, this is the business we've chosen. I didn't ask who gave the order, because it had nothing to do with business."

*Strasberg, on Pacino's order to execute mobster Alex Rocco (Moe Greene) in* The Godfather *(1972)*

**9.** "I know it was you, Fredo. You broke my heart. You broke my heart."

*Pacino kissing his brother Cazale at the stroke of midnight on New Year's Eve, after discovering that Cazale conspired to have Pacino killed*

**10.** "I'll make an offer he don't refuse."

*Robert De Niro (Vito Corleone), reprising the menacing line made famous in* The Godfather, *this time about Gaston Moschin (Fanutti)*

**11.** "Right, yeah, a buffer. The family had a lot of buffers."

*Joe Spinell (Willie Cicci) testifying at Senate hearings about the layers of the chain of command that keep the head of the family, Pacino, free of direct involvement in murder*

**12.** "He was being strong—strong for his family. But by being strong for his family, could he . . . lose it?"

*Pacino, in Italian with English subtitles, to his mother (Morgana King), asking questions about his father, founder of the Corleone crime family*

**13.** "Fredo, you're nothing to me now. You're not a brother. You're not a friend. I don't want to know you or what you do. I don't want to see you at the hotels. I don't want you near my house. When you see our mother, I want to know a day in advance so I won't be there."

*Pacino, banishing Cazale*

**14.** "I don't want anything to happen to him while my mother's alive."

*Pacino to henchman Richard Bright (Al Neri), postponing his revenge against Cazale for the sake of their mother*

**15.** "I didn't want your son, Michael. I wouldn't bring another one of your sons into this world."

*Diane Keaton (Kay) to her husband Pacino, explaining why she aborted their unborn son*

**16.** "Tom, you know, you surprise me. If anything in this life is certain, if history has taught us anything, it's that you can kill anyone."

*Pacino to Robert Duvall (Tom Hagen), on hearing that Strasberg is impossible to kill*

**17.** "I don't feel that I have to wipe everybody out, Tom. Just my enemies. That's all."

*Pacino to Duvall, on his need for revenge against Strasberg*

**GODFATHER PART III, THE** (Paramount, 1990). D: Francis Ford Coppola. S: Mario

*Puzo, Francis Ford Coppola. Fr: Mario Puzo (characters).*

**1.** "You know, Michael, now that you're so respectable I think you're more dangerous than you ever were. In fact, I preferred you when you were just a common Mafia hood."

*Diane Keaton (Kay) to Al Pacino (Michael Corleone)*

**2.** "That's your big thing, isn't it, Michael? Reason, backed up by murder?"

*Keaton to Pacino*

**3.** "I don't hate you. I dread you."

*Keaton to Pacino*

**4.** "We always can use a good judge."

*Pacino, on using his influence to help an acquaintance become a judge*

**5.** "Mr. Corleone, all bastards are liars. Shakespeare wrote poems about it."

*Joe Mantegna (Joey Zasa) to Pacino, about his nemesis Andy Garcia (Vincent), illegitimate son of Pacino's late brother Sonny*

**6.** "It seems in today's world the power to absolve debt is greater than the power of forgiveness."

*Donal Donnelly (Archbishop), on making a deal to obtain Pacino's help in resolving a shortfall in the Vatican accounts*

**7.** "Never hate your enemies; it affects your judgment."

*Pacino, giving advice to Garcia, whom he is grooming as a successor*

**8.** "Just when I thought I was out, they pull me back in."

*Pacino, on being dragged back into gangland affairs after years of trying to gain respectability*

**9.** "It was not what I wanted!"

*Pacino, on Garcia's killing of Mantegna*

**10.** "Your enemies always get strong on what you leave behind."

*Sicilian gangster's advice, given in Italian with English subtitles*

**11.** "You understand guns. Finance is a gun. Politics is knowing when to pull the trigger."

*Enzo Robutti (Don Lucchesi) to Garcia*

**12.** "I betrayed my wife. . . . I betrayed myself. I killed men and I ordered men to be killed. . . . I killed—I ordered the death of my brother. He injured me. I killed my mother's son. I killed my father's son."

*Pacino, confessing his sins to Raf Vallone (Cardinal Lamberto), who will become Pope John Paul I*

**13.** "You were so loved, Don Tommasino. Why was I so feared and you so loved?"

*Pacino, over the open casket of his mentor Vittorio Duse (Don Tommasino)*

**14.** GARCIA, inviting Pacino to accept him as his successor: "I'm your son. Command me in all things."

PACINO: "Give up my daughter. That's the price you pay for the life you choose."

**15.** "Nephew, from this moment on, call yourself Vincent Corleone."

*Pacino, accepting Garcia as his successor*

**16.** "Power wears out those who don't have it."

*Message from the Corleone family, spoken to Robutti by his assassin*

**17.** "Dad, why are you doing this to me?"

*Sofia Coppola (Mary) to her father Pacino, on his breaking up her romance with Garcia, moments before she is fatally shot by an assassin intending to kill Pacino*

**GODS MUST BE CRAZY, THE** *(South Africa: Mimosa/CAT, 1984). D: Jamie Uys. S: Jamie Uys.*

**LAST LINE**

**1.** "Xi was beginning to think he would never find the end of the Earth. And one day, suddenly, there it was."

*Paddy O'Byrne (Narrator) on N!xau (Xi)*

**GOING MY WAY** *(Paramount, 1944). D: Leo McCarey. S: Frank Butler, Frank Cavett. Fr: Leo McCarey (story).*

**1.** "You even throw like an atheist."

*Bing Crosby (Father Chuck O'Malley) to irate neighbor and atheist Porter Hall (Mr. Belknap), who has clumsily thrown away a baseball that had been hurled through his window*

**2.** "All churches have mortgages. It isn't respectable for a church not to have one."

*Crosby to Gene Lockhart (Ted Haines, Sr.), who holds the mortgage on Crosby's church*

**3.** "Y'know, at one time I had quite a decision to make: whether to write the nation's songs or go my way."

*Crosby, on how he decided to give up a career in music to become a priest*

**4.** "After all, it wouldn't be a church without a mortgage."

*Lockhart, agreeing to give the rebuilt church a new mortgage*

**GOLD DIGGERS OF 1933** *(Warner Bros., 1933). D: Mervyn LeRoy. S: Erwin Gelsey,* James Seymour, David Boehm, Ben Markson. Fr: Avery Hopwood (play, Gold Diggers of Broadway).

**1.** "Let's get up and look for work. I hate starving in bed."

*Ruby Keeler (Polly Parker) to her roommates, all unemployed chorus girls*

**2.** "That's it, that's what this show's about—the Depression. Men marching, marching in the rain, donuts and crullers, men marching, job, jobs, and in the background, Carol, spirit of the Depression—a blues song, no, not a blues song, but a wailing, a wailing, and this gorgeous woman singing this song that'll tear their hearts out. The big parade, the big parade of tears. That's it, that's it, work on it, work on it."

*Ned Sparks (Barney Hopkins), inspired by Dick Powell's (Brad Roberts's) piano playing*

**3.** "Faith, hope, and charity. You have faith, Barney hopes, and we all need charity."

*Aline MacMahon (Trixie Lorraine) to fellow chorus girl Keeler*

**4.** "I remember in my early youth I trod the primrose path on the Great White Way. There I learned the bitter truth that all women of the theater were chiselers, parasites—as we called them, gold diggers."

*Guy Kibbee (Faneuil H. Peabody), respectable Boston lawyer, warning younger men of the evils of show business women*

**5.** "Fanny is Faneuil H. Peabody, the kind of man I've been looking for—lots of money and no resistance."

*MacMahon, setting her sights on Kibbee*

**6.** "Let's go on playing this game. Gee, it's for prizes."

MacMahon, gloating over the gifts she's getting from Kibbee

**7.** "Oh, you're as light as a heifer—uh, feather."

*MacMahon to the portly Kibbee*

**8.** "Can you imagine me getting sentimental, the most hard-boiled dame on the Dirty White Way?"

*MacMahon, starting to fall for Kibbee*

**9.** "Carol, that's my name, cheap and vulgar Carol. Daughter of a Brooklyn saloon keeper and a woman who took in washing. Carol, torch singer at Coney Island. Cheap and vulgar."

*Joan Blondell (Carol King), feeling low*

**GOLD RUSH, THE** *(UA, 1925). D: Charles Chaplin. S: Charles Chaplin.*

**1.** "Three days from anywhere, A Lone Prospector."

*Title introducing Charlie Chaplin (The Lone Prospector)*

**2.** "Thanksgiving Dinner."

*Title describing the shoe Chaplin is cooking for himself and fellow miner Mack Swain (Big Jim McKay), both stranded by snow*

**3.** "I thought you was a chicken."

*Swain to Chaplin, after a vivid hallucination brought on by hunger*

**4.** "Chicken or no chicken, his friend looks appetizing."

*Title on Swain's feelings for Chaplin*

**GOLDEN BOY** *(Columbia, 1939). D: Rouben Mamoulian. S: Lewis Meltzer,* Daniel Taradash, Sara Y. Mason, Victor Heerman. Fr: Clifford Odets (play).

**1.** "I'm a dame from Newark and I know a dozen ways."

*Barbara Stanwyck (Lorna Moon), on how she can convince sometime boxer William Holden (Joe Bonaparte) to fight*

**2.** "You take a chance the day you're born. Why stop now?"

*Stanwyck*

**LAST LINE**
**3.** "Papa, I've come home."

*Holden to father Lee J. Cobb (Mr. Bonaparte)*

**GOLDFINGER** *(UK: UA, 1964). D: Guy Hamilton. S: Richard Maibaum, Paul Dehn. Fr: Ian Fleming (novel).*

**1.** "Now hear this, Goldfinger, your luck has just changed."

*Sean Connery (James Bond), speaking into the earphone of Gert Frobe (Goldfinger) while Frobe tries to cheat in a poker game*

**2.** "The only gold I know is the kind you wear—you know, on the third finger of your left hand?"

*Lois Maxwell (Miss Moneypenny), flirting with Connery*

**3.** "I never joke about my work, 007."

*Master of espionage wizardry Desmond Llewellyn (Q), annoyed as always by Connery's amused attitude toward Llewellyn's gadgets*

**4.** "Discipline, 007. Discipline."

*Connery, stopping himself from chasing a woman while on duty*

**5.** "This is gold, Mr. Bond. All my life I've been in love with its color, its brilliance, its divine heaviness."

*Frobe to Connery*

**6.** "Choose your next witticism carefully, Mr. Bond. It may be your last."

*Frobe, menacing Connery*

**7.** CONNERY, strapped to a table with a laser beam coming his way: "Do you expect me to talk?"
FROBE: "No, Mr. Bond, I expect you to die."

**8.** HONOR BLACKMAN (*Pussy Galore*), introducing herself: "My name is Pussy Galore."
CONNERY: "I must be dreaming."

**9.** "Just a drink—a martini, shaken, not stirred."

*Connery, ordering his usual beverage*

**10.** "You're a woman of many parts, Pussy."

*Connery, complimenting Blackman*

**11.** "We must have a few first falls together sometime."

*Connery to Blackman, on her skill at judo*

**12.** "As you said, he had a pressing engagement."

*Connery, on a dead man entombed in a crushed car*

**13.** "Oh, he blew a fuse."

*Connery, on the electrocution of Frobe's lethal hat–wielding henchman Harold Sakata (Oddjob)*

**14.** "Playing his golden harp."

*Connery, on the fate of Frobe, sucked out through an airplane window*

**GONE WITH THE WIND** (*MGM, 1939*). *D: Victor Fleming. S: Sidney Howard, Jo Swerling (uncredited), Charles MacArthur (uncredited), Ben Hecht (uncredited), John Lee Mahin (uncredited), and others uncredited Fr: Margaret Mitchell (novel).*

**1.** "Fiddle-dee-dee. War, war, war. This war talk's spoiling all the fun at every party this spring."

*Vivien Leigh's (Scarlett O'Hara's) first line, spoken to suitors Fred Crane and George Reeves (Brent and Stuart Tarleton)*

**2.** "Why, land's the only thing in the world worth working for, worth fighting for, worth dying for, because it's the only thing that lasts."

*Thomas Mitchell (Gerald O'Hara) to his daughter Leigh, on the family plantation, Tara*

**3.** "I seem to be spoiling everybody's brandy and cigars and dreams of victory."

*Clark Gable (Rhett Butler), on his pessimistic view of the South's prospects in the imminent Civil War*

**4.** LEIGH: "Sir, you are no gentleman."
GABLE: "And you, miss, are no lady."
*The couple at their first meeting*

**5.** "I believe in Rhett Butler. He's the only cause I know. The rest doesn't mean much to me."

*Gable to Leigh*

**6.** "You should be kissed, and often, and by someone who knows how."

*Gable to Leigh*

**7.** "I don't know nothin' 'bout birthin' babies!"

*Butterfly McQueen (Prissy) to Leigh, on assisting in the birth of Olivia de Havilland's (Melanie Hamilton's) baby*

**8.** "You helpless? Heaven help the Yankees if they capture you."

*Gable to Leigh, disputing her claim that she will be helpless if he leaves*

**9.** "In spite of you and me and the whole silly world going to pieces around us, I love you, because we're alike, bad lots both of us, selfish and shrewd, but able to look things in the eyes and call them by their right names."

*Gable to Leigh*

**10.** "As God is my witness, as God is my witness, they're not going to lick me! I'm going to live through this, and when it's all over, I'll never be hungry again—no, nor any of my folks! If I have to lie, steal, cheat, or kill—as God is my witness, I'll never be hungry again!"

*Leigh, alone in the field after the war is over*

**11.** "Well, I guess I've done murder. I won't think about that now. I'll think about it tomorrow."

*Leigh, after killing an intruder*

**12.** "Yes, there is something. Something you love better than me, though you may not know it. Tara."

*Leslie Howard (Ashley Wilkes) to Leigh, on what she has to live for without him*

**13.** "Tell me, Scarlett, do you never shrink from marrying men you don't love?"

*Gable to Leigh*

**14.** "Don't worry about me. I can shoot straight, if I don't have to shoot too far."

*Leigh to Gable, on traveling alone through dangerous country*

**15.** "Don't drink alone, Scarlett. People always find out, and it ruins the reputation."

*Gable to Leigh*

**16.** "You've turned me out while you chased Ashley Wilkes, while you dreamed of Ashley Wilkes. This is one night you're not turning me out."

*Gable to Leigh, now his wife, before carrying her up the stairs*

**17.** "Never in any crisis of your life have I known you to have a handkerchief."

*Gable, reacting to another of Leigh's fits of crying*

**18.** "Frankly, my dear, I don't give a damn."

*Gable, as he parts from Leigh, on where she will go or what she will do without him*

**LAST LINE**
**19.** "Tara! Home! I'll go home, and I'll think of some way to get him back. After all, tomorrow is another day."

*Leigh, by herself, on what she will do*

**GOOD EARTH, THE** (MGM, 1937). D: Sidney Franklin. S: Talbot Jennings, Tess Schlesinger, Claudine West, Frances Marion (uncredited). Fr: Pearl S. Buck (novel).

**LAST LINE**
**1.** "O-lan, you are the earth."
*Paul Muni (Wang Lung)*

**GOOD MORNING, VIETNAM** (Buena Vista, 1987). D: Barry Levinson. S: Mitch Markowitz.

**1.** "Goo-ood morning, Vietnam!"
*Robin Williams's (Adrian Kronauer's) radio wake-up call*

**LAST LINE**
**2.** "Oh, these are special. They're ruby slippers, Adrian. Put these on and say there's no

place like home, there's no place like home, and you can be there. Ha, ha, ha, I hope, I hope we all could."

*Williams, saying farewell to his listeners before leaving Vietnam*

## GOODBYE GIRL, THE (MGM/Warner Bros., 1977). D: Herbert Ross. S: Neil Simon.

**LAST LINE**

*1.* "Never mind that, you're rusting my guitar."

*Richard Dreyfuss (Elliott Garfield) to Marsha Mason (Paula McFadden)*

## GOODBYE, MR. CHIPS (UK: MGM, 1939). D: Sam Wood. S: W. C. Sheriff, Claudine West, Eric Maschwitz, Sidney Franklin. Fr: James Hilton (novella).

*1.* "Oh, but I have. Thousands of them. And all boys!"

*Teacher Robert Donat (Charles Chipping), on his deathbed, in response to regrets that he had no children*

**LAST LINE**

*2.* "Goodbye, Mr. Chips. Goodbye."

*Terry Kilburn (Peter Colley III) to Donat*

## GOODFELLAS (Warner Bros., 1990). D: Martin Scorsese. S: Nicholas Pileggi, Martin Scorsese. Fr: Nicholas Pileggi (book, Wiseguy).

*1.* "As far back as I can remember I always wanted to be a gangster."

*Ray Liotta (Henry Hill), narrating*

*2.* "Never rat on your friends and always keep your mouth shut."

*Robert De Niro (James Conway) to Christopher Serrone (Young Henry Hill), on the two greatest rules*

*3.* "Whenever we needed money, we'd rob the airport. To us it was better than Citibank."

*Liotta, narrating*

*4.* "You got some nerve standing me up. Nobody does that to me. Who the hell do you think you are? Frankie Valli or some kind of big shot?"

*Lorraine Bracco (Karen) to future husband Liotta*

*5.* BRACCO: "What do you do?"
LIOTTA: "I'm in construction."
BRACCO: "You don't feel like you're in construction."
LIOTTA: "Well, I'm a union delegate."

*6.* "I know there are women like my best friends who would have gotten out of there the minute their boyfriend gave them a gun to hide. But I didn't. I gotta admit the truth. It turned me on."

*Bracco, narrating, after being handed a gun by Liotta*

*7.* "There must have been two dozen Peters and Pauls at the wedding, plus they were all married to girls named Marie."

*Bracco, narrating, on meeting Liotta's gangster friends at their wedding*

*8.* "Nobody goes to jail unless they want to. Unless they make themselves get caught. They don't have things organized."

*Liotta to Bracco, reassuring her that he will not get caught*

*9.* JOE PESCI (*Tommy De Vito*): "I need this knife. I'm gonna take this. It's okay?"
CATHERINE SCORSESE, *his mother*: "Okay."

PESCI: "I just need it for a little while."

SCORSESE: "Bring it back, though, you know."

*Pesci, at dinner with his mother, obtaining a knife for cutting up a body*

**10.** SCORSESE: "Why don't you get yourself a nice girl?"

PESCI: "I get a nice one almost every night, Ma."

**11.** "She'll kill him but she won't divorce him."

*De Niro to Paul Sorvino (Pauly Cicero), about Bracco and Liotta*

**12.** "You know, we always called each other goodfellas. Like you'd say to somebody, 'You're gonna like this guy, he's all right, he's a goodfella, he's one of us.' You understand? We were goodfellas, wiseguys."

*Liotta, in narration*

**13.** "If you're part of a crew, nobody tells you that they're going to kill you. . . . Your murderers come with smiles. They come as your friend."

*Liotta, in narration, describing Pesci's murder by fellow gangsters*

**14.** "My birth certificate and my arrest sheet. That's all you'd ever have to know I was alive."

*Liotta, on having his identity changed when he becomes a mob informer*

**15.** "Today everything is different. There's no action. I have to wait around like everyone else. Can't even get decent food. Right after I got here I ordered some spaghetti with marinara sauce and I got egg noodles and catsup. I'm an average nobody. Get to live the rest of my life like a schnook."

*Liotta, on his life after becoming an informer*

**GRADUATE, THE** *(Embassy, 1967). D: Mike Nichols. S: Calder Willingham, Buck Henry. Fr: Charles Webb (novel).*

**1.** "I just want to say one word to you—just one word. . . . Plastics."

*Walter Brooke (Mr. Maguire), giving advice to Dustin Hoffman (Benjamin Braddock)*

**2.** "Mrs. Robinson, you're trying to seduce me."

*Hoffman to Anne Bancroft (Mrs. Robinson)*

**3.** "Are you here for an affair, sir?"

*Hotel clerk Buck Henry to Hoffman*

**4.** "I think you're the most attractive of all my parents' friends."

*Hoffman, complimenting Bancroft*

**5.** "Mrs. Robinson, do you think we could say a few words to each other first this time?"

*Hoffman, asking for a time-out before sex*

**6.** HOFFMAN: "In a car you did it?"

BANCROFT: "Well, I don't think we were the first."

*The two on the conception of Elaine Robinson (Katharine Ross)*

**7.** WILLIAM DANIELS (*Mr. Braddock*), on Hoffman's plans to marry Ross: "Ben, this whole idea sounds pretty half-baked."

HOFFMAN: "No, it's not; it's completely baked."

**8.** "Well, how 'bout this for a coincidence?"

*Hoffman to Ross, after chasing her onto a bus*

**9.** "He said he thought we'd make a pretty good team."

*Ross to Hoffman, explaining how her preppie boyfriend proposed*

**10.** "I think we have everything quite under control now, Benjamin. Would you like a quick drink before you go?"

*Bancroft, after calling the police to come arrest Hoffman for breaking in*

**11.** "Elaine!"

*Hoffman to bride-to-be Ross, from the back of the church*

**GRAND HOTEL** (MGM, 1932). D: Edmund Goulding. S: William A. Drake. Fr: Vicki Baum (novel, Menschen im Hotel), William A. Drake (play).

**1.** "That's my creed, Kringelein. A short life and a gay one."

*John Barrymore (Baron Felix von Geigern), a man desperate for money, to Lionel Barrymore (Otto Kringelein), a man with a fatal disease*

**2.** "I want to be alone."

*Greta Garbo (Grusinskaya) to John Barrymore*

**3.** "What do you do in the Grand Hotel? Eat. Sleep. Loaf around. Flirt a little. Dance a little. A hundred doors leading to one hall, and no one knows anything about the person next to them. And when you leave, someone occupies your room, lies in your bed, and that's the end."

*Lewis Stone (Dr. Otternschlag) to Lionel Barrymore*

**4.** "A man who is not with a woman is a dead man."

*Stone to Lionel Barrymore*

**5.** "You can't discharge me! I'm my own master for the first time in my life. You can't discharge me! I'm sick! I'm going to die. You understand? I'm going to die, and nobody can do anything to me anymore. Nothing can happen to me anymore. Before I can be discharged, I'll be dead."

*Lionel Barrymore to Wallace Beery (General Director Preysing)*

**6.** "Life is wonderful, but it's very dangerous. If you have the courage to live it, it's marvelous!"

*Lionel Barrymore to his gambling friends*

**7.** "Grand Hotel. Always the same. People come. People go. Nothing ever happens."

*Stone to himself*

**LAST LINE**

**8.** "Grand Hotel."

*Chauffeur*

**GRAND ILLUSION** (France: Realisation d'Art Cinematographique, 1937). D: Jean Renoir. S: Jean Renoir, Charles Spaak.

**1.** "On one side, children who play soldiers, and on the other, soldiers who play like children."

*French prisoner-of-war Pierre Fresnay (De Boeldieu) at the window, watching young German soldiers outside and comparing them to the game-playing prisoners inside*

**2.** "Look, a golf course is to play golf, a tennis court is to play tennis, and a prison camp is to escape from."

*Fresnay to fellow prisoner Jean Gabin (Maréchal)*

**3.** "What gets you is not the music, but the thud of marching feet."

*Gabin to fellow prisoners, on why they dislike the sound of fifes and marching soldiers*

**4.** FIRST GUARD, listening to the shouts of Gabin in solitary confinement: "Why did he shout like that?"

SECOND GUARD: "Because the war's lasting too long."

**5.** "Everyone would die of the disease of his class, if war didn't reconcile all microbes."

*Marcel Dalio (Rosenthal)*

**6.** "I don't know who's going to win this war, but the end, whatever it may be, will be the end of the Rauffensteins and the Boeldieus."

*Aristocratic prison camp commandant Erich von Stroheim (Von Rauffenstein) to fellow nobleman Fresnay*

**7.** "It's damn nice of you, Rauffenstein, but it's impossible."

*Fresnay to von Stroheim, in English, refusing to return peacefully to the prison camp*

**8.** "Maréchal and Rosenthal. So that's what it was for?"

*Von Stroheim, on learning that Fresnay allowed himself to be shot to permit the escape of lower-class Gabin and Dalio*

**9.** "For an ordinary man, it's terrible to die in war, but for you and me, it's a good solution."

*Fresnay, dying, to von Stroheim*

**10.** "You're a poor cow and I'm a poor soldier. We each do our best, eh?"

*Gabin, now a fugitive, to a cow he is feeding*

**11.** "I've been alone too long—waiting too long. You'll never know the happiness the sound of a man's step in the house gave me."

*Dita Parlo (Elsa) to Gabin, who is preparing to leave after she has sheltered him and Dalio*

**12.** DALIO, leaving Parlo's house: "No farewell look?"

GABIN: "No, or I'll never leave. Let's go!"

**13.** "Frontiers are an invention of man. Nature doesn't give a hoot."

*Dalio to Gabin, on the location of the Swiss border*

**14.** GABIN: "We've got to end this stinking war. Maybe it'll be the last."

DALIO: "You've still got illusions!"

**LAST LINES**

**15.** FIRST SOLDIER: "Don't shoot. They're in Switzerland."

SECOND SOLDIER: "All the better for them."

*Soldiers allowing Gabin and Dalio to escape over the border*

**GRAPES OF WRATH, THE** *(20th Century–Fox, 1940). D: John Ford. S: Nunnally Johnson. Fr: John Steinbeck (novel).*

**1.** "I got nothing to preach about no more, that's all. I ain't so sure of things."

*John Carradine (Casey) to Henry Fonda (Tom Joad), on why he is no longer a preacher*

**2.** "It ain't nobody. It's a company."

*Driver to John Qualen (Muley), on the organization pushing him off his land, the Shawnee Land and Cattle Company*

**3.** "My grandpaw took up this land seventy years ago. My paw was born here. We was all born on it. An' some of us was killed on it. An' some of us died on it. That's what makes it arn. Bein' born on it and workin' on it and dyin' on it. An' not no piece of paper with writin' on it."

*Qualen, on the land that will be plowed out from under him the next day*

**4.** "It says, 'Plenty of work in California. Eight hundred pickers wanted.'"

*Frank Darien (Uncle John) to Joad family*

**5.** "Sometimes they do somethin' to ya. They hurt ya and ya get mad and then you get mean. Then they hurt you again and you get meaner and meaner till you ain't no boy or man anymore, just a walkin' chunk of mean mad."

*Jane Darwell (Ma Joad) to Fonda, on prison's adverse effects on some people*

**6.** "Wait till I get to Californy. I'm gonna reach up and pick me an orange whenever I want it."

*Charley Grapewin (Grampa Joad) to family*

**7.** "There's somethin' goin' on out there in the West, and I'd like to try and learn what it is."

*Carradine, asking to join the Joads on their journey*

**8.** "I never had my house pushed over before. Never had my family stuck out on the road. Never had to lose everything I had in life."

*Darwell, on why she doesn't sound like herself on leaving for California*

**9.** "Bert, look. Truck drivers."

*Waitress to Harry Tyler (Bert), on large tip given by truckers after waitress gave two-for-five-cent candies to children for one cent*

**10.** "There she is, folks—land of milk and honey, California."

*Russell Simpson (Pa Joad) to family, at first view of California*

**11.** "You and me got sense. Them Okies got no sense and no feelings. They ain't human. No, a human being wouldn't live the way they do. A human being couldn't stand to be so miserable."

*Gas station attendant to another, about the Joads*

**12.** "Ma, there comes a time when a man gets mad."

*Fonda to Darwell, after weeks of struggle*

**13.** FONDA, to head of the migrant camp, expressing surprise and gratitude: "Who runs this place?"
CAMP DIRECTOR: "The government."
FONDA: "Why ain't they more like it?"

**14.** "Listen, what is these reds, anyway? Every time you turn around, somebody's calling somebody else a red. What is these reds anyway?"

*Fonda to farmer and group of workmen deriding reds, or communists*

**15.** "Tommy, ain't you gonna tell me good-bye?"

*Darwell to Fonda, on his escape from the camp*

**16.** "Well, maybe it's like Casey says. A fella ain't got a soul of his own, just a little piece of a big soul—the one big soul that belongs to ever'body."

*Fonda to Darwell*

**17.** "I'll be all around in the dark. I'll be ever'where—wherever you can look. Wherever there's a fight so hungry people can eat, I'll be there. Wherever there's a cop beatin' up a guy, I'll be there. I'll be in the way guys yell when they're mad. I'll be in the way kids laugh when they're hungry an' they know supper's ready. An' when the people are eatin' the stuff they raise, livin' in the homes they build—I'll be there, too."

*Fonda to Darwell*

**LAST LINE**
**18.** "That's what makes us tough. Rich fellas come up and they die and their kids ain't no good and they die out. But we keep

a-comin'. We're the people that live. They can't wipe us out. They can't lick us. We'll go on forever, Pa, 'cause we're the people."

*Darwell to Simpson*

**GREAT DICTATOR, THE** (UA, 1940). D: Charles Chaplin. S: Charles Chaplin.

*1.* "Today democracy, liberty, and equality are words to fool the people. No nation can progress with such ideas. They stand in the way of action. Therefore, we frankly abolish them."

*Henry Daniell (Garbitsch)*

**LAST LINE**
*2.* "Listen."

*Paulette Goddard (Hannah)*

**GREAT GATSBY, THE** (Paramount, 1974). D: Jack Clayton. S: Cyril Hume, Richard Maibaum. Fr: F. Scott Fitzgerald (novel), Owen Davis (play).

**LAST LINE**
*1.* "I thought of Gatsby's wonder when he first picked out the green light at the end of Daisy's dock. He had come a long way to this lawn, and his dream must have seemed so close that he could hardly fail to grasp it. He did not know that it was already behind him."

*Sam Waterston (Nick Carraway), narrating about Robert Redford (Jay Gatsby) and Mia Farrow (Daisy Buchanan)*

**GREAT McGINTY, THE** (Paramount, 1940). D: Preston Sturges. S: Preston Sturges.

*1.* "Did you never hear of Samson and Delilah, or Sodom and Gomorrah?"

*Akim Tamiroff (the Boss) to Brian Donlevy (Dan McGinty), on the perils of entanglement with women*

**GREAT MOUSE DETECTIVE, THE** (Buena Vista, 1986). D: John Musker. S: Pete Young, Vance Gerry, Steve Hulett, Ron Clements, John Musker, et al. Fr: Eve Titus (book, Basil of Baker Street).

*1.* "You will remember to smile for the camera, won't you? Say, 'Cheese.'"

*Vincent Price (Professor Ratigan), when he tells Barrie Ingham (Basil the mouse detective) that the camera will take his picture when he dies*

*2.* "I observe that there is a good deal of German music on the program. It is introspective, and I want to introspect."

*Basil Rathbone (Sherlock Holmes) to Laurie Main (Dr. Watson), when Ingham sneaks into Holmes's apartment*

**GREAT RACE, THE** (Warner Bros., 1965). D: Blake Edwards. S: Arthur Ross. Fr: Arthur Ross, Blake Edwards (story).

**LAST LINE**
*1.* "Push the button, Max."

*Jack Lemmon (Professor Fate), giving his favorite, always disastrous, order to henchman Peter Falk (Max)*

**GREAT ZIEGFELD, THE** (MGM, 1936). D: Robert Z. Leonard. S: William Antony McGuire.

**LAST LINE**
*1.* "I've got to have more steps. I need more steps. I've got to get higher, higher!"

*The delirious last words of William Powell (Florenz Ziegfeld)*

**GREATEST SHOW ON EARTH, THE** *(Paramount, 1952). D: Cecil B. De Mille. S: Fredric M. Frank, Barre Lyndon, Theodore St. John. Fr: Fredric M. Frank, Theodore St. John, Frank Cavett (story).*

**1.** "You wanna bite somebody? . . . Well, pick your spot."

*Bad girl Gloria Grahame (Angel), coming on to Charlton Heston (Brad)*

**2.** "I never knew a woman could fill a pipe."

*Heston*

**3.** "What'd you do, boy scout, lose your compass?"

*Grahame to Cornel Wilde (Sebastian), when he enters the women's dressing room*

**4.** "That's a new way to get thrown out of bed."

*Grahame, on falling out of bed in a train wreck*

**5.** "We may miss the matinee, but we'll make the night show."

*Heston, wounded in circus train wreck but still determined to put on a show*

**6.** "If he should make love well after this, pay no attention—it will be me."

*Wilde to Betty Hutton (Holly), Heston's love interest, as Wilde's blood is transfused into Heston*

**7.** "Scars covered by greasepaint, bandages hidden by funny wigs, the spangled pied piper limped into town."

*Narrator Cecil B. De Mille, on the circus parade following the train wreck*

**8.** "I'll say this much for you, Brady—you're good circus."

*Lawrence Tierney (Henderson) to Heston*

**9.** "Judas Priest, you've got nothing but sawdust in your veins!"

*Heston to Hutton, using a line previously used to describe him*

**10.** "Listen, sugar, the only way you can keep me warm is to wrap me up in a marriage license."

*Grahame to Wilde*

LAST LINE
**11.** "That's all, ladies and gentlemen, that's all. Come again to the greatest show on Earth. Bring the children. Bring the old folks. You can shake the sawdust off your feet but you can't shake it out of your heart. Come again, folks. The greatest show on Earth. Come again."

*Midway barker Edmond O'Brien*

**GREEN BERETS, THE** *(Warner Bros., 1968). D: John Wayne, Ray Kellogg. S: James Lee Barrett. Fr: Robin Moore (novel).*

**1.** "Out here, due process is a bullet."

*John Wayne (Col. Michael Kirby), on Vietnam*

**2.** "Tell it to Captain Colman, and shout it loud 'cause Arlington Cemetery is a long way from here."

*Wayne*

**GREEN MANSIONS** *(MGM, 1959). D: Mel Ferrer. S: Dorothy Kingsley. Fr: William Henry Hudson (novel).*

**LAST LINE**

*1.* "If you look in this place tomorrow, and it's gone, you mustn't be sad, because you know it still exists, not very far away."

*Audrey Hepburn (Rima the Bird Girl), in voice-over*

**GREMLINS** *(Warner Bros., 1984). D: Joe Dante. S: Chris Columbus.*

**LAST LINE**

*1.* "So if your air conditioner goes on the fritz or your washing machine blows up or your video recorder conks out, before you call the repairman, turn on all the lights, check all the closets and cupboards, look under all the beds. Because you never can tell, there just might be a gremlin in your house."

*Narrator*

**GRIFTERS, THE** *(Miramax, 1990). D: Stephen Frears. S: Donald E. Westlake. Fr: Jim Thompson (novel).*

*1.* ANNETTE BENING *(Myra Langtry):* "I'm Roy's friend."

ANJELICA HUSTON *(Lily Dillon):* "Yes, I imagine you're lots of people's friend."

*Girlfriend Bening and mother Huston discussing John Cusack (Roy Dillon)*

**GROUNDHOG DAY** *(Columbia, 1993). D: Harold Ramis. S: Danny Rubin, Harold Ramis. Fr: Danny Rubin (story).*

*1.* "I'm a god. I'm not *the* God—I don't think."

*Bill Murray (Phil), stuck in time, after surviving several suicides and going through the same day in the same small town innumerable times*

*2.* ANDIE MACDOWELL *(Rita):* "What did you do today?"

MURRAY: "Oh, same old, same old."

**LAST LINE**

*3.* "Let's live here. We'll rent to start."

*Murray to MacDowell, after their awakening love has freed him from the curse*

**GUESS WHO'S COMING TO DINNER** *(Columbia, 1967). D: Stanley Kramer. S: William Rose.*

**LAST LINE**

*1.* "Well, Tillie, when the hell are we going to get some dinner?"

*Spencer Tracy's (Matt Drayton's) last line on film, spoken to Isabel Sanford (Tillie)*

**GUNFIGHT AT THE O.K. CORRAL** *(Paramount, 1957). D: John Sturges. S: Leon Uris. Fr: George Scullin (article).*

*1.* "The name of this game is solitaire."

*Kirk Douglas (Doc Holliday), playing cards and trying to get rid of Burt Lancaster (Wyatt Earp)*

*2.* "I don't lose because I have nothing to lose—including my life."

*Douglas, on his winning ways*

*3.* "Why don't you buy yourself a new halo? The one you're wearing's too tight."

*Lady gambler Rhonda Fleming (Laura Denbow) to Lancaster, who objects to women at the gambling tables*

**GUNGA DIN** *(RKO, 1939). D: George Stevens. S: Joel Sayre, Fred Guiol. Fr: Ben Hecht, Charles MacArthur, William Faulkner (story), Rudyard Kipling (poem).*

1. "Could be first-class soldier, sahib."

   *Indian water-carrier Sam Jaffe (Gunga Din) to soldier Victor McLaglen (MacChesney), expressing his longing to join the British army*

2. "Very regimental, Din."

   *Cary Grant (Cutter) to Jaffe, on Jaffe's soldierly bearing*

3. "What's this, Sergeant, buying a trousseau?"

   *McLaglen, expressing his contempt as Douglas Fairbanks, Jr. (Ballantine) helps model fabrics for his fiancée Joan Fontaine (Emmy)*

4. "McChesney, versus that you can't think of a single argument!"

   *Grant, trying to persuade McLaglen of the merits of yet another treasure hunt*

5. "McChesney, I've been a soldier for fourteen years; I know me duties as well as you do. But you're not talking to a soldier now, you're talking to an expedition. I'm an expedition."

   *Grant to McLaglen, insisting on going out to search for the temple of gold*

6. "Rise, our new-made brothers. Rise and kill. Kill as you'll be killed yourselves. Kill for the love of killing. Kill for the love of Kali. Kill! Kill! Kill!"

   *Kali cult leader Eduardo Ciannelli (Guru) to the new members of his murderous religion*

7. "Now you're all under arrest. You, too, and you know why. Her majesty's very touchy about having her subjects strangled."

   *Grant to Ciannelli and his horde of Kali cultists, creating a diversion so Jaffe can get away to bring help*

8. "Take him to the tower and teach him the error of false pride."

   *Ciannelli, ordering punishment for Grant's intrusion*

9. "I don't care how much I love you—and I do very much. I'm a soldier— I mean, I'm a man first."

   *Fairbanks, choosing to go off to rescue Grant rather than keep his wedding date with Fontaine*

10. "Why don't you enlist, mate?"

    *Grant, in response to Ciannelli's demand for information about their army*

11. "Who is slave? I am a soldier, too, please."

    *Jaffe, taking offense when Ciannelli calls him a slave*

12. "You're simply a victim of superior strategy."

    *Grant to Fairbanks, after McLaglen tricks him into reenlisting rather than leaving the army to get married*

13. "Din, I haven't had a more satisfactory set of welts since I ran away from home."

    *Grant to Jaffe on the welts inflicted on his back by Ciannelli's men*

14. "You torturer! Setting that in front of me eyes! Is there no limit to the torture an Oriental mind can think of?"

    *Grant to Ciannelli, when he is forced to sit, immobile, staring at the temple gold he covets*

15. "Mad? We shall see what wisdom lies within my madness."

    *Ciannelli*

16. "The colonel's got to know."

    *Jaffe, deciding to sacrifice himself to sound a bugle warning to British troops in peril of ambush; he is repeating the earlier words of Grant when witnessing a Kali ceremony*

**17.** "Good work, bugler."

*Grant to the dead Jaffe*

**GUY NAMED JOE, A** (MGM, 1943). D: Victor Fleming. S: Dalton Trumbo. Fr: Chandler Sprague, David Boehm, Frederick H. Brennan (story).

**1.** "You set this crate down just like a ladybug on a toadstool."

*Ward Bond (Al Yackey) to Spencer Tracy (Pete Sandidge), on Tracy's flying skills*

**2.** "Don't you know anything about slang? In the American Air Forces, anybody who's a right chap is a guy named Joe."

*English child to his friends*

**3.** "When you're up there, you're all alone. See? Just you and your ship and the sky. And you don't want anybody up there with you. You don't want anyone to spoil it. Everything's kind of still. You have the feeling that you're halfway to Heaven. You don't even seem to hear the sound of your own motor. Just kind of a buzz. Like the sky was calling you. Like the sky was singing a song."

*Tracy, explaining to children how it feels to fly*

**4.** IRENE DUNNE (*Dorinda Durston*): "You love me."
    TRACY: "I love airplanes."
    DUNNE: "That's the same thing."

**5.** "Back where I come from, folks call that love stuff quick poison or slow poison. If it's quick poison, it hurts you all over real bad, like a shock of electricity. But if it's slow poison, well, it's like a fever that aches in your bones for a thousand years."

*Bond to Tracy*

**6.** "Come to think of it, I never did see a guy that inherited a lot of dough that was any good."

*The dead Tracy's reaction when he's assigned to watch over Van Johnson (Ted Randall), who just inherited a fortune*

**7.** "I wonder if this is that wartime immorality they're always talking about."

*Tracy to Barry Nelson (Dick Rumney), when the soldiers kiss the girls good-bye*

**8.** "Some people seem prettier when you dream about them than they really are. But a funny thing about you. You're even prettier than the dream."

*Tracy, as Pete's spirit, to Dunne, who can't hear him*

**9.** "A guy who washes out at the controls of his own ship, well, he goes down doing the thing that he loved the best. And it seems to me that that's a very special way to die."

*Bond to Johnson*

**10.** "Everything wrong with you, I like."

*Johnson to Dunne*

**11.** "It's the music a man's spirit sings to his heart when the Earth's far away, and there isn't any more fear. It's the high, fine, beautiful sound of an earthbound creature who grew wings and flew up high and looked straight into the face of the future and caught, just for an instant, the unbelievable vision of a free man in a free world."

*Lionel Barrymore (The General), to Tracy, in Heaven, describing the music only flyers hear*

**12.** "No man is really dead unless he breaks faith with the future, and no man's really alive unless he accepts his responsibility to it. That's the chance we're giving you here. The oppotunity to pay off to the future what you owe for having been part of the past."

> *Barrymore to Tracy, on returning to Earth to help Johnson learn to fly*

**LAST LINE**

**13.** "That's my girl, and that's my boy."

> *Tracy, referring to Dunne and Johnson*

**GYPSY** *(Warner Bros., 1962). D: Mervyn LeRoy. S: Leonard Spigelgass. Fr: Arthur Laurents (musical play), Gypsy Rose Lee (pseudonym for Rose Louise Hovick) (book).*

**1.** "Sing out, Louise. Sing out."

> *Rosalind Russell (Rose), coaching her daughter Diane Pace (Baby Louise) from offstage*

**2.** "I'm pretty, Mama."

> *Natalie Wood (Louise/Gypsy Rose Lee) to mirror, when dressed for her first striptease number*

**LAST LINE**

**3.** "Only it was you and me wearing exactly the same gown. It was an ad for Minsky. And the headline said, 'Madame Rose, and her daughter Gypsy.' "

> *Russell, reporting a dream to Wood*

**HAIL THE CONQUERING HERO** *(Paramount, 1944). D: Preston Sturges. S: Preston Sturges.*

**1.** "A Marine never hides. That's what *semper fidelis* means. It means face the music."

> *Tough Marine William Demarest (Sergeant) to Eddie Bracken (Woodrow)*

**2.** "Everything is perfect except for a couple of details."

> *Demarest, failing to reassure Bracken about his scheme to have him masquerade as a war hero*

**3.** "He's a hero. He's got a statue in the park and the birds sit on him. Except that I ain't got no birds on me, I'm in the same boat."

> *Demarest, on a war hero memorialized in the park*

**4.** "Well, that's the war for you. It's always hard on women. Either they take your men away and never send them back at all, or they send them back unexpectedly just to embarrass you. No consideration at all."

> *Elizabeth Patterson (Libby's Aunt) to her niece Ella Raines (Libby)*

**5.** "Anyway, those ain't lies. Those are campaign promises. They expect 'em."

> *Demarest, reassuring Bracken about the untruths spoken in Bracken's campaign for mayor*

**6.** "Won't you join us in a stack of collision macs, as they say in the good old Marine Corps, and a cup of jamoke?"

> *Bracken, inviting Raines to breakfast*

**7.** "He's playing daffodil from Dopeyville."

> *Demarest, on Bracken*

**8.** "That means truthful. He likes those big words."

> *Jimmy Conlin (Judge Dennis), on Harry Hayden's (Doc Bissell's) use of the word "veracious"*

**9.** "Pardon me for intruding, but is anybody interested in getting on this train or is this the Democratic National Convention?"

*Train engineer, impatient with passengers who fail to get on the train*

**10.** "See yez in church."

*Demarest, preparing to leave*

**LAST LINES**

**11.** BRACKEN: "I knew the Marines could do almost anything, but I never knew they could do anything like this."

MARINE: "You've got no idea."

**HAIRSPRAY** *(New Line Cinema, 1988). D: John Waters. S: John Waters.*

**1.** "Could you turn that racket down? I'm trying to arn in here."

*An exasperated Divine (Edna Turnblad), at the ironing table, urging her daughter Ricki Lake (Tracy) to turn down the music from the television set*

**2.** DIVINE: "And Tracy, I have told you about that hair, all ratted up like a teenage jezebel."

LAKE, reflecting her status as a child of the sixties: "Oh, Mother, you're so fifties."

**3.** "You'll do what Daddy says or we'll send you to Catholic school where you belong!"

*Debbie Harry (Velma Von Tussle), threatening her daughter Colleen Fitzpatrick (Amber)*

**4.** "The Council will now meet in secret, debate your personality flaws, and come to a final decision."

*Mink Stole (Tammy), on candidates for "The Corny Collins Show," a local teen dance music program*

**5.** "This better be good. Broad daylight and I'm sitting in front of a TV."

*Divine, getting ready to watch her daughter for the first time on "The Corny Collins Show"*

**6.** "She could be one of the June Taylor dancers."

*Divine, admiring her daughter's TV dancing*

**7.** "Finally all of Baltimore knows—I'm big, blond, and beautiful."

*Lake, making a statement on her fame*

**8.** "Mama, welcome to the sixties!"

*Lake, when Divine gets a hip new hairdo*

**9.** "Your ratted hair is preventing yet another student's Geometry education."

*Teacher Rhea Feikin to Lake, when another student can't see the blackboard behind her big hair*

**10.** "Tracy, our souls are black, even though our skin is white."

*Lake's boyfriend Michael St. Gerard (Link Larkin), as they try to identify more closely with black culture*

**11.** "Go to second, go to second."

*Leslie Ann Powers (Penny), urging her boyfriend to take further liberties*

**12.** "Wilbur, it's the times, they're a-changin'. Something's blowin' in the wind. Fetch me my diet pill, would you, hon?"

*Divine to her husband Jerry Stiller (Wilbur), as they contemplate social change*

**13.** "You are no longer my daughter. You are punished even after you die."

*Powers's father, Doug Roberts, angered at Powers's refusal to stop dating a young black man*

**LAST LINE**

**14.** "Let's dance!"

*Lake to her cheering admirers*

**HAND THAT ROCKS THE CRADLE** *(Buena Vista, 1992). D: Curtis Hanson. S: Amanda Silver.*

**1.** "I adore children."

*Deranged nanny Rebecca De Mornay (Peyton Flanders), making an ominous remark to prospective employer Annabella Sciorra (Claire Bartel)*

**2.** "For me, it's the next best thing to being a mother."

*De Mornay to Sciorra, on being a nanny*

**3.** "You never, ever, let an attractive woman take a power position in your house."

*Family friend Julianne Moore (Marlene), discussing De Mornay with Sciorra*

**4.** "The hand that rocks the cradle is the hand that rules the world."

*Moore, citing an old saying to Sciorra*

**5.** "They never caught who did it, but I firmly believe, what goes around comes around."

*De Mornay, discussing her husband's death with Sciorra, whom she secretly believes brought it about*

**HANNAH AND HER SISTERS** *(Orion, 1986). D: Woody Allen. S: Woody Allen.*

**FIRST LINE**

**1.** "God, she's beautiful. She's got the prettiest eyes. She looks so sexy in that sweater. I just want to be alone with her and hold her and kiss her, tell her how much I love her, take care of her. Stop it, you idiot. She's your wife's sister."

*Michael Caine (Elliot) to himself, on Mia Farrow's (Hannah's) sister Barbara Hershey (Lee)*

**2.** "I like him. I think he's a sweet guy. . . . 'Cause he's a loser. He's awkward and he's clumsy, like me. So I like that. I always like an underconfident person. You always had good taste in husbands."

*Woody Allen (Mickey) to ex-wife Farrow, on her present husband Caine*

**3.** "I can't believe I said that about the Guggenheim. My stupid little roller-skating joke."

*Dianne Wiest (Holly), bemoaning her bad joke about the circular structure of the Guggenheim*

**4.** CAINE: "Perhaps you could take me to an AA meeting sometime. I'd love to see what goes on."

HERSHEY: "Well, yeah, yeah, you'd love it. It's really entertaining. You'd have a good time. I know you would."

**5.** "I'm dying, I'm dying! I know it! There's a spot on my lungs. Take it easy, would ya, it's not on your lungs, it's on your ear! It's the same thing, isn't it?"

*Hypochondriac Allen to himself, about an X-ray spot*

**6.** "You want a defrosted kid?"

*Allen to then-wife Farrow, about artificial insemination*

**7.** "Great. That means I'll have to see the Ice Capades again."

*Allen, on eternal recurrence*

**8.** "You don't deserve Cole Porter. You should stay with those guys that look like they're going to stab their mother."

*Allen to Wiest, on her musical taste*

**9.** "I've been doing all my own reading since I was forty."

*Allen to Wiest, when she offers to read her manuscript to him*

**10.** "How the hell do I know why there were Nazis? I don't know how the can opener works."

Allen's father, Leo Postrel, to Allen, on the problem of evil

**11.** "What the hell, it's not all a drag."

Allen, reaching an epiphany that life is worth living while viewing Duck Soup

**12.** "Mickey. . . . I'm pregnant."

Wiest, giving surprising news to Allen

## HANS CHRISTIAN ANDERSEN (RKO, 1952). D: Charles Vidor. S: Moss Hart. Fr: Myles Connolly (story).

**1.** "You'd be surprised how many kings are only a queen with a mustache."

Danny Kaye (Hans Christian Andersen), when he paints a mustache on a queen doll

**2.** "I sometimes think that shoes have a life of their own. The ones that squeak don't like to leave the shop, and the ones that hurt don't like the person that's wearing them."

Kaye, a cobbler, to a customer

**3.** "She wants shoes that will walk on air, Peter. This afternoon. Well, she'll have them. I wish she had asked me something really impossible."

Kaye to Joey Walsh (Peter)

**4.** "Instead of 'Hans the Cobbler,' could it say 'Hans Christian Andersen,' like a real writer?"

Kaye to the printer

**5.** "Oh, I think you'll go on telling stories, Hans. . . . Why? Because you're Hans Christian Andersen, that's why. . . . You'll tell stories. You'll write stories. You'll even sing stories, over and over and over again."

Walsh to Kaye, when he vows never to tell another story

## HARDLY WORKING (20th Century–Fox, 1981). D: Jerry Lewis. S: Michael Janover, Jerry Lewis. Fr: Michael Janover (novel).

**LAST LINE**

**1.** "I can't decide what to do. It's a toss-up. It'll either be brain surgery or trying for that opening at the nuclear plant."

Jerry Lewis (Bo Hooper), contemplating more career changes

## HAROLD AND MAUDE (Paramount, 1972). D: Hal Ashby. S: Colin Higgins.

**1.** "I go to funerals."

Bud Cort (Harold), telling what he does for fun

**2.** "Greet the dawn with a breath of fire."

Ruth Gordon (Maude), instructing Cort in how to be exuberant

**3.** "I like to watch things grow."

Gordon to Cort, telling what she does for fun

**4.** "Everybody should be able to make some music. That's the cosmic dance."

Gordon to Cort

**5.** "The Earth is my body. My head is in the stars."

Gordon to Cort

**6.** "It's best not to be too moral. You cheat yourself out of too much life."

Gordon to Cort

## HARVEY (Universal, 1950). D: Henry Koster. S: Mary Chase, Oscar Brodney. Fr: Mary Chase (play).

**1.** "Every day's a beautiful day."

James Stewart (Elwood P. Dowd)

**2.** "Some people are blind. That's very often brought to my attention."

*Stewart to Peggy Dow (Miss Kelly)*

**3.** "But Harvey's not only a pooka, he's also my best friend. Oh, if Harvey's said to me once, I bet he's said, oh, probably a million times, he's said, 'Mr. Dowd, I would do anything for you.' "

*Stewart to Nana Bryant (Mrs. Chumley), on his large invisible rabbit friend*

**4.** "Pooka. From the old Celtic mythology, a fairy spirit in animal form, always very large. The pooka appears here and there, now and then, to this one and that one. A benign, but mischievous creature, very fond of rumpots, crackpots, and how are you Mr. Wilson."

*Jesse White (Wilson)*

**5.** "They tell about the big terrible things they've done, and the big wonderful thing they'll do. Their hopes, and their regrets. Their loves and their hates. All very large. Because nobody ever brings anything small into a bar."

*Stewart to Dow and Charles Drake (Mr. Sanderson)*

**6.** "Naturally, I went over to chat with him, and he said to me, 'Ed Hickey was a little spiffed, or could I be mistaken?' Well, of course, he was not mistaken. I think the world of Ed, but he was spiffed."

*Stewart to Dow and Drake*

**7.** "Harvey has overcome not only time and space, but any objections."

*Stewart to Cecil Kellaway (Dr. Chumley)*

**8.** "In this world, Elwood, you must be, oh, so smart, or, oh, so pleasant. For years, I

was smart. I recommend pleasant. And you may quote me."

*Stewart to Kellaway, repeating what his mother told him*

**9.** "I've wrestled with reality for thirty-five years, and I'm happy, Doctor. I finally won out over it."

*Stewart to Kellaway*

**10.** "Myrtle Mae, you have a lot to learn, and I hope you never learn it."

*Josephine Hull (Veta Louise Simmons) to Victoria Horne (Myrtle Mae)*

**11.** "After this, he'll be a perfectly normal human being. And you know what stinkers they are."

*Wallace Ford (Lofgren) to Hull*

**LAST LINE**
**12.** "Well, thank you, Harvey. I prefer you, too."

*Stewart*

**HE MARRIED HIS WIFE** (20th Century–Fox, 1940). D: Roy Del Ruth. S: Sam Hellman, Darrell Ware, Lynn Starling, John O'Hara. Fr: Erna Lazarus, Scott Darling (story).

**1.** "I'll never marry again. I've got your alimony to keep me warm."

*Nancy Kelly (Valerie) to divorced husband Joel McCrea (T. H. Randall)*

**HEATHERS** (New World, 1989). D: Michael Lehmann. S: Daniel Waters.

**1.** "Are you a Heather?"

*Christian Slater (J. D.) to Winona Ryder (Veronica Sawyer)*

**2.** "The extreme always seems to make an impression."

*Slater to Ryder*

**3.** "Killing Heather would be like offing the Wicked Witch of the West."

*Ryder, in her diary, on murdering Kim Walker (Heather Chandler)*

**4.** "Look, Heather left behind one of her Swatches. She'd want you to have it, Veronica. She always said you couldn't accessorize for shit."

*Lisanne Falk (Heather McNamara) to Ryder, on the late Walker's watch*

**5.** "Heather, my love, there's a new sheriff in town."

*Ryder to Shannen Doherty (Heather Duke), removing the "Heather" ribbon from Doherty's hair*

**HEAVEN CAN WAIT** *(20th Century–Fox, 1978). D: Warren Beatty, Buck Henry. S: Warren Beatty, Elaine May. Fr: Harry Segall (play).*

**1.** "At my age, in any other business, I'd be young."

*Quarterback Warren Beatty (Joe Pendleton) to Jack Warden (Max Corkle), his trainer*

**2.** "The likelihood of one individual being right increases in direct proportion to the intensity with which others are trying to prove him wrong."

*James Mason (Mr. Jordan) to Beatty*

**3.** "Haven't you learned the rules of probability and outcomes? Aren't you aware that every question of life and death remains a probability until the outcome?"

*Mason to Buck Henry (The Escort)*

**4.** "If he weren't going to be dead soon, he would need years of psychiatric help."

*Charles Grodin (Tony Abbott), on Beatty*

**5.** "Hi. Look, I'm sorry to bother you so late, but I don't love you and you don't love me, so let's get a divorce. All right?"

*Beatty to Dyan Cannon (Julia Farnsworth)*

**6.** "That's the way it is with champagne. Isn't it? You keep swilling it 'cause it doesn't taste like anything, and all of a sudden, you're drunk."

*Beatty, in Tom Jarrett's body, to Warden*

**HEIRESS, THE** *(Paramount, 1949). D: William Wyler. S: Ruth Goetz, Augustus Goetz. Fr: Ruth Goetz, Augustus Goetz (play), Henry James (novel, Washington Square).*

**LAST LINE**

**1.** "Catherine! Catherine! Catherine!"

*Montgomery Clift (Morris Townsend), calling for Olivia de Havilland (Catherine Sloper)*

**HELL'S ANGELS** *(UA, 1930). D: Howard Hughes. S: Harry Behn, Howard Estabrook, Joseph Moncure March. Fr: Marshall Neilan, Joseph Moncure March (story).*

**1.** "Would you be shocked if I put on something more comfortable?"

*Jean Harlow (Helen) to Ben Lyon (Monte Rutledge)*

**HELLDORADO** *(Republic, 1946). D: William Witney. S: Gerald Geraghty, Julian Zimet.*

**1.** "Trouble with the government is they ain't patriotic."

*George "Gabby" Hayes (Gabby Whittaker)*

**2.** "You oughta put that badge away and only wear it on Halloween."

*Roy Rogers (Himself), casting aspersions on Dale Evans's (Carol Randall's) abilities as deputy sheriff*

**HIGH ANXIETY** *(20th Century–Fox, 1977). D: Mel Brooks. S: Mel Brooks, Ron Clark, Rudy DeLuca, Barry Levinson.*

**1.** PSYCHONEUROTIC INSTITUTE FOR THE VERY, VERY NERVOUS

*Name of asylum run by Mel Brooks (Richard Thorndyke)*

**2.** "That kid gets no tip."

*Brooks, on bellboy Barry Levinson, who has just attacked him with a rolled-up newspaper in a hotel room shower*

**3.** "Brophy's not smart enough to have a nervous breakdown."

*Brooks, on his chauffeur Ron Carey (Brophy)*

**4.** "I understand now!. . . . It's not height I'm afraid of! It's parents!"

*Brooks*

**HIGH NOON** *(UA, 1952). D: Fred Zinnemann. S: Carl Foreman. Fr: John W. Cunningham (story, "The Tin Star").*

**1.** "I think I ought to stay."

*Gary Cooper (Marshal Will Kane), for the first of many times, stating his intentions about staying to face his enemy Ian MacDonald (Frank Miller)*

**2.** "They're making me run. I've never run from anybody before."

*Cooper, on why he's staying to fight MacDonald*

**3.** "You're asking me to wait an hour to find out if I'm going to be a wife or a widow."

*Grace Kelly (Amy Kane), arguing with her husband Cooper about his decision*

**4.** "You'll never hang me. I'll come back. I'll kill you, Will Kane, I swear it, I'll kill you."

*Otto Kruger (Percy Mettrick), reminding Cooper of MacDonald's courtroom threat to seek revenge against the marshal*

**5.** "Now, me, I wouldn't leave this town at noon for all the tea in China. No, sir, it's going to be quite a sight to see."

*Hotel clerk Howland Chamberlin to Kelly, who is planning to leave on the noon train, just when MacDonald is arriving for the showdown with Cooper*

**6.** "There's plenty people around here think he's got a comeuppance coming. You asked me, ma'am, so I'm telling you."

*Chamberlin to Kelly, explaining his dislike for Cooper*

**7.** "You're a good-looking boy, you have big broad shoulders, but he is a man. It takes more than big broad shoulders to make a man, Harvey, and you have a long way to go. You know something? I don't think you will ever make it."

*Katy Jurado (Helen Ramirez), Cooper's former mistress, comparing Lloyd Bridges (Deputy Harvey Pell) to Cooper*

**8.** "It's a great life. You risk your skin catchin' killers and the juries turn 'em loose so they can come back and shoot at you again. If you're honest, you're poor your whole life, and in the end you wind up dyin' all alone on some dirty street. For what? For nothin'. For a tin star."

*Retired marshal Lon Chaney, Jr. (Martin Howe) to Cooper, on the life of a lawman*

**9.** "The judge has left town, Harvey's quit, and I'm havin' trouble gettin' deputies."

*Cooper to Chaney*

**10.** "People gotta talk themselves into law and order before they do anything about it. Maybe because down deep they don't care. They just don't care."

*Chaney*

**11.** "Seems like all everybody and his brother wants is to get me out of town."

*Cooper to Bridges*

**12.** "You can tell your man he can go back to work now."

*Cooper to barber William "Bill" Phillips, whose assistant has been preparing a coffin for Cooper*

**13.** "To be opened in the event of my death"

*Note on envelope containing Cooper's last will and testament, sealed just before he goes to face MacDonald*

**HIGH SOCIETY** (MGM, 1956). D: Charles Walters. S: John Patrick. Fr: Philip Barry (play, The Philadelphia Story).

**LAST LINE**
**1.** "End of story."

*Louis Armstrong (Himself)*

**HIGHER AND HIGHER** (RKO, 1943). D: Tim Whelan. S: Jay Dratler, Ralph Spence, William Bowers, Howard Harris. Fr: Gladys Hurlbut, Joshua Logan (play).

**1.** "Marriage is an institution that no family can do without."

*Frank Sinatra (Frank) to Michele Morgan (Millie)*

**HILLS HAVE EYES, THE** (Vanguard, 1977). D: Wes Craven. S: Wes Craven.

**1.** "You folks stay on the main road, now, you hear? Stay on the main road!"

*Gas station owner John Steadman (Fred), giving futile warning to campers in lonely territory*

**2.** "What's the matter? You don't like dog anymore?"

*Cordy Clark (Mama) to her daughter Janus Blythe (Ruby), both members of a band of mountain savages who eat dogs and people*

**3.** "Baby's fat. You fat. Fat juicy."

*Lance Gordon (Mars), a cannibal, eyeing his intended victims, an adult and a baby, with gusto*

**4.** "We caught us a young Thanksgiving turkey."

*James Whitworth (Jupiter), the cannibal leader, on the baby they intend to eat*

**HIS GIRL FRIDAY** (Columbia, 1940). D: Howard Hawks. S: Charles Lederer. Fr: Ben Hecht, Charles MacArthur (play, The Front Page).

**1.** "I'd know you anytime, anyplace, anywhere."

*Cary Grant (Walter Burns), joined by Rosalind Russell (Hildy Johnson), remembering his line to her*

**2.** GRANT: "I sort of wish you hadn't done that, Hildy. . . . Makes a fellow lose all faith in himself. Gives him, well, it gives him a feeling he's not wanted."
RUSSELL: "Now, look, Junior, that's what divorces are for."

**3.** "Well, I don't want to brag, but I've still got the dimple and in the same place."

*Grant to Russell*

**4.** "I intended to be with you on our honeymoon, Hildy, honest I did."

*Grant to Russell*

**5.** "Well, it would have worked out if you'd been satisfied with just being editor and reporter. But not you, you had to go marry me and spoil everything."

*Grant to Russell*

**6.** "Oh, Hildy, you know you led me to expect you were marrying a much older man. . . . I realize you didn't mean old in years."

*Grant to Russell, upon meeting Ralph Bellamy (Bruce Baldwin)*

**7.** "Of course, we don't help you much when you're alive. But afterward, that's what counts."

*Bellamy to Grant, about the insurance business*

**8.** BELLAMY, talking about Grant: "He's got a lot of charm."
RUSSELL: "He comes by it naturally. His grandfather was a snake."

**9.** "Well, there was one fella. He talked about production for use."

*John Qualen (Earl Williams) to Russell, about speaker he heard in Union Square*

**10.** REPORTER, after reading Russell's interview with Qualen: "But I ask you guys, can that girl write an interview?"
OTHER REPORTER: "She'll do until somebody else comes along."

**11.** "He looks like, um, that fellow in the movies, you know, Ralph Bellamy."

*Grant to blond floozy ordered to accuse Bellamy of mashing*

**12.** "No, no, leave the rooster story alone. That's human interest."

*Grant, over the phone to Frank Orth (Duffy), on cutting articles to fit coverage of the Earl Williams story*

**13.** "How you doing? Got enough air?"

*Grant to Qualen, hiding in a rolltop desk*

**14.** "Well, who's gonna read the second paragraph?"

*Grant to Russell, on not mentioning the newspaper in her story until the second paragraph*

**15.** "There's a million ways. We can start a fire. Have the firemen take it out in the confusion."

*Grant to Russell, on how to get Qualen and the desk out of the press room*

**16.** "Listen, the last man who said that to me was Archie Leach, just a week before he cut his throat."

*Grant to the governor, invoking Grant's real name*

**17.** GRANT, on being handcuffed and arrested: "We've been in worse jams than this, haven't we, Hildy?"
RUSSELL: "Nope."

**18.** "You forget the power that always watches over the *Morning Post.*"

*Grant to governor*

**LAST LINE**
**19.** "Well, isn't that a coincidence. We're going to Albany. I wonder if Bruce can put us up. Say, why don't you carry that in your hand? . . ."

*Grant to Russell*

**HOLD THAT GHOST** (Universal, 1941). D: Arthur Lubin. S: Robert Lees, Frederic I. Rinaldo, John Grant. Fr: Robert Lees, Frederic I. Rinaldo (story).

**1.** "I want my Mama."

Lou Costello (Ferdie Jones)

**2.** "Go ahead! Ruin the man's car!"

Bud Abbott (Chuck Murray) to Costello, when Costello bumps his head on a car

**3.** COSTELLO: "I play games. I play post office."

JOAN DAVIS (Camille Brewster): "Post office? That's a kid's game."

COSTELLO: "Not the way I play it."

**4.** ABBOTT: "Why don't you talk to yourself?"

COSTELLO: "I get too many stupid answers."

**HOLIDAY INN** (Paramount, 1942). D: Mark Sandrich. S: Claude Binyon, Elmer Rice. Fr: Irving Berlin (idea).

**1.** "Here, have a slug out of a mug."

Bing Crosby (Jim Hardy), offering coffee to a hung-over Fred Astaire (Ted Hanover)

**2.** "What brings you here on this bright and uninviting day?"

Crosby, giving Astaire the cold shoulder when he arrives at Holiday Inn

**3.** "My motherly intuition tells me to throw him out."

Crosby on Astaire

**4.** "A gentle smile often breeds a kick in the pants."

Astaire, on Crosby's reception of him

**5.** "Oh, that'll be easy—like peeling a turtle."

Astaire, on convincing Crosby to let Marjorie Reynolds (Linda Mason) go to Hollywood

**6.** ASTAIRE'S MANAGER, Walter Abel (Danny Reed), on seeing Crosby reunited with Reynolds: "How could he get that far in five minutes?"

ASTAIRE: "The lady must've been willing."

**HOLLYWOOD SHUFFLE** (Samuel Goldwyn, 1987). D: Robert Townsend. S: Robert Townsend, Keenen Ivory Wayans.

LAST LINE
**1.** "So if you can't take pride in your job, remember, there's always work at the post office."

Robert Townsend (Bobby Taylor), on being a postman

**HOME ALONE** (20th Century–Fox, 1990). D: Chris Columbus. S: John Hughes.

LAST LINE
**1.** "Kevin, what did you do to my room?"

Devin Rattray (Buzz) to Macaulay Culkin (Kevin)

**HONDO** (Warner Bros., 1954). D: John Farrow. S: James Edward Grant. Fr: Louis L'Amour (story, "The Gift of Cochise").

**1.** "I don't guess people's hearts got anything to do with the calendar."

John Wayne (Hondo Lane)

LAST LINE
**2.** "Yup. The end of a way of life. Too bad. It's a good way. Wagons forward! Yo!"

Wayne

**HONEYMOON IN VEGAS** (Columbia, 1992). D: Andrew Bergman. S: Andrew Bergman.

**1.** "Did you get a job here?"

Nicolas Cage (Jack Singer) to Sarah Jessica Parker (Betsy), surprised to see her in a Vegas showgirl's outfit, which she donned as a disguise to elude James Caan (Tommy Korman)

**2.** "You jumped out of a plane for me!"

Parker, acknowledging Cage's heroism in rescuing her by jumping out of a plane loaded with a parachute group called the "Flying Elvises"

**HOPE AND GLORY** (UK: Columbia, 1987). D: John Boorman. S: John Boorman.

LAST LINE
**1.** "All my life nothing ever quite matched the perfect joy of that moment. My school lay in ruins; the river beckoned with a promise of stolen days."

Sebastian Rice Edwards (Bill Rohan)

**HORN BLOWS AT MIDNIGHT, THE** (Warner Bros., 1945). D: Raoul Walsh. S: Sam Hellman, James V. Kern. Fr: Aubrey Wisberg (idea).

LAST LINE
**1.** "Elizabeth, I just had the craziest dream. You know, if you saw it in the movies, you'd never believe it."

Jack Benny (Athanael) to Alexis Smith (Elizabeth)

**HORSE FEATHERS** (Paramount, 1932). D: Norman Z. McLeod. S: Bert Kalmar, Harry Ruby, S. J. Perelman.

**1.** "Why don't you go home to your wife? I'll tell you what, I'll go home to your wife, and outside of the improvement she'll never know the difference."

Groucho Marx (Professor Quincy Adams Wagstaff), new president of Huxley College, to retiring president Reginald Barlow

**2.** "I'd horsewhip you, if I had a horse."

Groucho to his son Zeppo Marx (Frank Wagstaff)

**3.** "I married your mother because I wanted children. Imagine my disappointment when you arrived."

Groucho to Zeppo

**4.** "Why don't you bore a hole in yourself and let the sap run out?"

Groucho to Chico Marx (Barovelli)

**5.** "Barovelli, you've got the brain of a four-year-old boy, and I bet he was glad to get rid of it."

Groucho to Chico

**6.** "Oh, I love sitting on your lap. I could sit here all day if you didn't stand up."

Groucho to college widow Thelma Todd (Connie Bailey)

**7.** "You have more students than the college."

Groucho to Todd

**8.** "How much would you want to stand at the wrong end of a shooting gallery?"

Groucho to Chico

**9.** "My boy, get in there and play like you did in the last game. I've got five dollars bet on the other team."

*Groucho to Zeppo, on the day of the big football game*

**10.** "Humpty Dumpty sat on a wall, Professor Wagstaff gets the ball."

*Chico, calling a football play in which the ball is thrown to Groucho*

**LAST LINE**

**11.** "We do!"

*Groucho and Chico, agreeing to marry Todd, with Harpo (Pinky) nonverbally joining in*

**HOSPITAL, THE** *(UA, 1971). D: Arthur Hiller. S: Paddy Chayefsky.*

**1.** "You're greedy, unfeeling, inept, indifferent, self-inflating, and unconscionably profitable. Aside from that, I have nothing against you. I'm sure you play a helluva game of golf."

*George C. Scott (Dr. Herbert Bock) to Richard Dysart (Dr. Welbeck)*

**HOT SHOTS!** *(20th Century–Fox, 1991). D: Jim Abrahams. S: Pat Proft, Jim Abrahams.*

**1.** "When I saw you dig your heels into his sides, tighten up the reins, and break his spirit, I never wanted to be a horse so much in my life."

*Charlie Sheen (Sean "Topper" Harley) to Valeria Golino (Ramada Thompson)*

**2.** "That is the whitest white part of the eye I've ever seen. Do you floss?"

*Sheen to Golino*

**3.** "I'm a virgin. I'm just not very good at it."

*Golino to Sheen*

**4.** "My heart has fallen down around my ankles like a wet pair of pants."

*Sheen to Golino*

**HOUSE OF WAX** *(Warner Bros., 1953). D: André De Toth. S: Crane Wilbur. Fr: Charles Welden (play).*

**1.** "There is a pain beyond pain, an agony so intense, it shocks the mind into instant beauty."

*Vincent Price (Professor Henry Jarrod) to Phyllis Kirk (Sue Allen)*

**HOUSESITTER** *(Universal, 1992). D: Frank Oz. S: Mark Stein. Fr: Brian Grazer, Mark Stein (story).*

**1.** "Don't yell at me. We're only pretending to be married."

*Goldie Hawn (Gwen) to pretend husband Steve Martin (Newton Davis)*

**2.** "You're like the Ernest Hemingway of bullshit."

*Martin to Hawn, on her penchant for lying*

**3.** "I punched a totally innocent Hungarian."

*Martin to Hawn, on the lengths to which her lies have driven him*

**4.** "I just wanted to see what it would be like to live in the picture."

*Hawn to Martin, on why she moved into his house and pretended to be his wife*

**5.** "What marriage?"

*Martin to Hawn, confused by her references to their marriage*

**6.** MARTIN: "I love you, Gwen."
HAWN: "Actually, it's Jessica."

**HOW GREEN WAS MY VALLEY** *(20th Century–Fox, 1941). D: John Ford. S: Philip Dunne. Fr: Richard Llewellyn (novel).*

**LAST LINE**

**1.** "I am packing my belongings in the shawl my mother used to wear when she went to the market, and I am going from my valley, and this time I shall never return."

*Narrator (Huw Morgan as an adult)*

**2.** "Memory. Strange that the mind will forget so much of what only this moment has passed and yet hold clear and bright the memory of what happened fifty years ago."

*Narrator*

**3.** "There is no fence nor hedge round time that is gone. You can go back and have what you like of it if you can remember."

*Narrator*

**4.** "We are not questioning your authority, sir. But if manners prevent our speaking the truth, we will be without manners."

*One of the Morgan sons to father Donald Crisp (Mr. Morgan)*

**5.** "Because you make yourselves out to be shepherds of the flock. And yet you allow your sheep to live in filth and poverty. . . . Sheep indeed. Are we sheep to be herded and sheared by a handful of owners? I was taught man was made in the image of God, not sheep."

*Union activist John Loder (Ianto Morgan) to minister Walter Pidgeon (Mr. Gruffydd)*

**6.** "My business is anything that comes between man and the spirit of God."

*Pidgeon to Arthur Shields (Mr. Parry), defending his right as a minister to speak out on political issues*

**7.** MAUREEN O'HARA *(Angharad Morgan)*: "Look now, you are king in the chapel, but I will be queen in my own kitchen."

PIDGEON: "You will be queen wherever you walk."

**8.** PIDGEON: "I have no right to speak to you so."

O'HARA: "Mr. Gruffydd, if the right is mine to give, you have it."

**9.** "Oh, what do the deacons know about it? What do you know about what could happen to a poor girl when she loves a man so much that even to lose sight of him for a moment is torture?"

*O'Hara to Pidgeon, on the case of a young woman ostracized for having a child out of wedlock*

**10.** "Do you think I will have you going threadbare all your life? Depending on the charity of others for your good meals? Our children growing up in cast-off clothing and ourselves thanking God for parenthood and a houseful of bits? No, I can bear with such a life for the sake of my work, but I think I'd start to kill if I saw the white come to your hair twenty years before its time."

*Pidgeon to O'Hara, on why they cannot marry*

**11.** "I will go down the colliery with you."

*Young Roddy McDowell (Huw Morgan) to his coal-miner father Crisp*

**12.** "No need for us to shake hands. We will live in the minds of each other."

*Pidgeon to McDowell, on Pidgeon's departure*

**13.** "If I were to see her again, I couldn't find the strength to leave."

*Pidgeon to McDowell, on why he can't see O'Hara*

**14.** "That is a good old man, you are."

*Crisp's last words, spoken to McDowell, before dying in a coal mine accident*

**LAST LINE**

**15.** "Men like my father cannot die. They are with me still, real in memory as they were in flesh, loving and beloved forever. How green was my valley then."

*Narrator*

**HOW THE WEST WAS WON** (MGM, 1962). D: John Ford, Henry Hathaway, George Marshall. S: James R. Webb. Fr: Life magazine (articles).

**LAST LINE**

**1.** "The West that was won by its pioneers, settlers, adventurers, is long gone now, yet it is theirs forever, for they left tracks in history that will never be eroded by wind or rain, never plowed under by tractors, never buried in the compost of events. . . . All the heritage of a people free to dream, free to act, free to mold their own destiny."

*Spencer Tracy (Narrator)*

**HOW TO MARRY A MILLIONAIRE** (20th Century–Fox, 1953). D: Jean Negulesco. S: Nunnally Johnson. Fr: Zoe Akins (play, The Greeks Had a Word For It), Dale Eunson, Katherine Albert (play, Loco).

**1.** MARILYN MONROE (*Pola*): "Do you know who I'd like to marry?"
BETTY GRABLE (*Loco*): "Who?"
MONROE: "Rockefeller."
GRABLE: "Which one?"
MONROE: "I don't care."

**LAST LINE**

**2.** "Gentlemen, to our wives."

*Cameron Mitchell (Tom Brockman), proposing a toast*

**HOWARDS END** (Sony Pictures Classics, 1992). D: James Ivory. S: Ruth Prawer Jhabvala. Fr: E. M. Forster (novel).

**1.** "My idea has always been if we could bring the mothers of the various nations together, then there would be no more war."

*Vanessa Redgrave (Mrs. Wilcox) to Emma Thompson (Margaret Schlegel)*

**2.** "You're so clever, yet so good."

*Redgrave to Thompson*

**3.** "The modern ownership of movables is reducing us again to a nomadic horde. We are reverting to a civilization of luggage, Mr. Wilcox."

*Thompson to Anthony Hopkins (Henry Wilcox)*

**4.** "One bit of advice. Fix your district, then fix your price, then don't budge."

*Hopkins to Thompson, on buying a house*

**5.** "Don't take up a sentimental attitude toward the poor. See that she doesn't, Margaret. The poor are poor. One is sorry for them, but there it is."

*Hopkins to Thompson, on her sister Helena Bonham Carter (Helen Schlegel)*

**6.** "If rich people fail at one profession, they can try another, but with us, once a man over twenty loses his own particular job, he's done for."

*Workingman Samuel West (Leonard Bast) to his wife Prunella Scales*

**7.** BONHAM CARTER, on books: "They're more real than anything. When people fail you, there's still music and meaning."

WEST: "That's for rich people, to make them feel good after their dinner."

**8.** HOPKINS, on his wife: "And Margaret—she keeps her facts straight."

THOMPSON: "What facts are those, dear."

HOPKINS: "About men and women and all. That sort of thing. Who is who, and what is what."

**9.** "You had a mistress. I forgave you. My sister has a lover. You drive her from the house. Why can you not be honest for once in your life, and say to yourself, what Helen has done, I have done?"

*Thompson to Hopkins*

**10.** "My poor Ruth, during her last days, scribbled your name on a piece of paper. Knowing her not to be herself, I set it aside. I didn't do wrong. Did I?"

*Hopkins to Thompson*

## HUCKSTERS, THE (MGM, 1947). D: Jack Conway. S: Luther Davis, Edward Chodorov, George Wells. Fr: Frederic Wakeman (novel).

### LAST LINE

**1.** "Now we're starting out with exactly an even nothing in the world. It's neater that way."

*Clark Gable (Victor Albee Norman)*

## HUD (Paramount, 1963). D: Martin Ritt. S: Irving Ravetch, Harriet Frank, Jr. Fr: Larry McMurtry (novel, Horseman, Pass By).

**1.** "The only question I ever ask any woman is 'What time is your husband coming home?' "

*Paul Newman (Hud Bannon) to Patricia Neal (Alma Brown)*

## HUMAN COMEDY, THE (MGM, 1943). D: Clarence Brown. S: Howard Estabrook. Fr: William Saroyan (novel).

### FIRST LINE

**1.** "I am Matthew Macauley. I have been dead for two years, but so much of me is still living that I know now the end is only the beginning."

*Ray Collins (Matthew Macauley), directly to the audience*

**2.** "Your job is more than a job, and this office, more than an office. It's a college, a university, a place of learning. Watch things. Listen carefully. Keep your eyes and ears open."

*James Craig (Tom Spangler) to Mickey Rooney (Homer Macauley), when he gives him a job in the telegraph office*

**3.** "The real poor are the poor in spirit, because they have no faith, no laughter, no song, and no love."

*Fay Bainter (Mrs. Macauley) to Jack Jenkins (Ulysses Macauley)*

**4.** "Death is like today, Ulysses. You fall asleep and tomorrow comes. Remember, today, you saw a train, and you found an egg? Well, tomorrow, they'll be gone, but the excitement of seeing that train, and the wonder of finding that egg will be in you always."

*Bainter to Jenkins, when explaining why his father will never come home*

**5.** "I didn't know schoolteachers were human beings like everybody else, and better, too!"

*Rooney, when his teacher lets him out of detention to run on the track team*

**6.** "Always try to remember that when anything happens to people, maybe there's a reason. And if you see something that you're sure is wrong, don't be sure."

*Frank Morgan (Willie Grogan) to Rooney*

**7.** "The person of a man, the thing we see, may leave, but the thing we feel, the greater part of a good man, stays . . . stays forever."

*Craig to Rooney, when Rooney gets a telegram telling him of his brother's death*

**LAST LINE**
**8.** "You see, Marcus. The ending is only the beginning."

*Collins, as the ghostly patriarch of the family, to Van Johnson (Marcus Macauley), the newly deceased eldest brother*

**HUMORESQUE** *(Warner Bros., 1944). D: Jean Negulesco. S: Clifford Odets, Zachary Gold. Fr: Fannie Hurst (story).*

**1.** "Tell me, Mrs. Wright, does your husband interfere with your marriage?"

*Oscar Levant (Sid Jeffers) to Joan Crawford (Helen Wright)*

**HUNCHBACK OF NOTRE DAME, THE** *(RKO, 1939). D: William Dieterle. S: Sonya Levien, Bruno Frank. Fr: Victor Hugo (novel).*

**LAST LINE**
**1.** "Why was I not made of stone like thee?"

*Hunchback Charles Laughton (Quasimodo) to a gargoyle*

**HUSTLER, THE** *(20th Century–Fox, 1961). D: Robert Rossen. S: Sidney Carroll, Robert Rossen. Fr: Walter Tevis (novel).*

**1.** "Eddie, you're a born loser."

*George C. Scott (Bert Gordon) to Paul Newman (Eddie Felson)*

**LAST LINES**
**2.** NEWMAN: "Fat man, you shoot a great game of pool."
    JACKIE GLEASON (*Minnesota Fats*): "So do you, Fast Eddie."

**I AM A FUGITIVE FROM A CHAIN GANG** *(Warner Bros., 1932). D: Mervyn LeRoy. S: Howard J. Green, Brown Holmes, Sheridan Gibney. Fr: Robert E. Burns (autobiography, I Am a Fugitive from a Georgia Chain Gang).*

**LAST LINE**
**1.** "I steal."

*Paul Muni (James Allen), telling how he lives*

**I NEVER SANG FOR MY FATHER** *(Columbia, 1971). D: Gilbert Cates. S: Robert W. Anderson. Fr: Robert W. Anderson (play).*

**FIRST LINE**
**1.** "Death ends a life, but it does not end a relationship, which struggles on in the survivor's mind toward some resolution which it may never find."

*Gene Hackman (Gene Garrison), on his father, Melvyn Douglas (Tom Garrison); repeated as the film's last line*

**I WANT TO LIVE!** *(UA, 1958). D: Robert Wise. S: Nelson Gidding, Don Mankiewicz.*

Fr: Ed Montgomery (articles), Barbara Graham (letters).

**LAST LINE**

*1.* "Dear Mr. Montgomery: There isn't much I can say with words; they always fail me whem most needed. But please know that with all my heart I appreciate everything you've done for me. Sincerely, Barbara."

*Susan Hayward (Barbara Graham), executed for a murder she didn't commit, in a letter to Simon Oakland (Ed Montgomery)*

## I WAS A TEENAGE FRANKENSTEIN
*(American International Pictures, 1957). D: Herbert L. Strock. S: Kenneth Langtry.*

*1.* "I know you have a civil tongue in your head—I sewed it there myself."

*Whit Bissell (Professor Frankenstein) to his creature*

## I'LL CRY TOMORROW *(MGM, 1955). D: Daniel Mann. S: Helen Deutsch, Jay Richard Kennedy. Fr: Lillian Roth, Mike Connolly, Gerold Frank (book).*

**LAST LINE**

*1.* "You'll also realize that it's a story full of hope, hope for many who are living and suffering in a half-world of addiction to alcohol, hope for all people wherever and whoever they are. So this is your life, Lillian Roth."

*Ralph Edwards (Himself), honoring Susan Hayward (Lillian Roth)*

## I'LL NEVER FORGET WHAT'S 'IS NAME *(UK: Rank Film Distributors, 1967). D: Michael Winner. S: Peter Draper.*

*1.* "What's the going price on integrity this week?"

*Orson Welles (Jonathan Lute) to Oliver Reed (Andrew Quint)*

## I'M GONNA GIT YOU SUCKA *(MGM/UA, 1988). D: Keenen Ivory Wayans. S: Keenen Ivory Wayans.*

**LAST LINE**

*1.* "That's my theme music. Every good hero should have some. See you around."

*Keenen Ivory Wayans (Jack Spade)*

## I'M NO ANGEL *(Paramount, 1933). D: Wesley Ruggles. S: Mae West, Harlan Thompson. Fr: Lowell Brentano (screenplay, The Lady and the Lions).*

*1.* "Beulah, peel me a grape."

*Mae West (Tira) to Gertrude Howard (Beulah)*

*2.* "It's not the men in my life, but the life in my men."

*West*

## IMITATION OF LIFE *(Universal, 1959). D: Douglas Sirk. S: Eleanore Griffin, Allan Scott. Fr: Fannie Hurst (novel).*

*1.* "Sarah Jane favors her dad. He was practically white."

*African-American housekeeper Juanita Moore (Annie Johnson), describing her light-skinned daughter to her white employer Lana Turner (Lora Meredith)*

*2.* "A maid to live in, someone to take care of your little girl? A strong, healthy, settled-down woman who eats like a bird and doesn't care if she gets no time off and who'll work real cheap?"

*Moore, offering her services to Turner*

**3.** "I don't wanna live in the back. Why do we always have to live in the back?"

*Karen Dicker (Sarah Jane Johnson at eight) to her mother, Moore*

**4.** "You're trying to cheapen me. But you won't. Not me. Oh, I'll make it, Mr. Loomis, but it'll be my way."

*Turner to lecherous star-maker Robert Alda (Allen Loomis), whose help Turner is seeking to advance her acting career*

**5.** "No, it's a sin to be ashamed of what you are. And it's even worse to pretend. To lie. Sarah Jane has to learn that the Lord must have had his reasons to make some of us white and some of us black."

*Moore to Turner, on her daughter's desire to pass for white*

**6.** "He was like me—white."

*Dicker on Jesus' color*

**7.** Sarah Jane's boyfriend TROY DONAHUE (*Frankie*): "Just tell me one thing. . . . Is it true?"

SUSAN KOHNER (*Sarah Jane at eighteen*): "Is what true?"

DONAHUE: "Is your mother a nigger?"

**8.** "It never occurred to me that you had any friends."

*Turner to Moore, surprised to learn about her social life*

**9.** "I'm white, white, white."

*Kohner to Moore, on whether she likes her new life of passing for white*

**10.** "But I just happened to be in town and I dropped in to see Miss London. I used to take care of her."

*Moore to chorus girl asking about the relationship between Kohner and Moore*

**11.** CHORUS GIRL: "Well, get you. So honey child, you had a mammy."

KOHNER: "Yes, all my life."

*Kohner, disowning her mother*

**12.** "Oh, Mama, I'm sorry, I didn't want to hurt you."

*Sandra Dee (Susie Meredith at sixteen) to her mother, Turner, repeating what Kohner said to Moore earlier and will say again later*

**13.** "Tell her I know I was selfish, and if I loved her too much, I'm sorry. But I didn't mean to cause her any trouble. She was all I had."

*Moore, dying, to Turner, saying what she wants Kohner to be told*

**14.** "I'm just tired, Miss Lora, awfully tired."

*Moore's last words to Turner*

**15.** "I'm telling you, it's my mother."

*Kohner to policeman at Moore's funeral*

**16.** "Mama, mama, I didn't mean it. I didn't mean it. Mama, do you hear me, I'm sorry, I'm sorry, Mama. Mama, I did love you."

*Kohner to Moore in her coffin*

**17.** "Miss Lora, I killed my mother."

*Kohner to Turner*

**IN A LONELY PLACE** (Columbia, 1950). D: Nicholas Ray. S: Andrew Solt. Fr: Edmund H. North (story), Dorothy B. Hughes (novel).

LAST LINE

1. "I lived a few weeks while you loved me. Good-bye, Dix."

> *Gloria Grahame (Laurel Gray) to Humphrey Bogart (Dixon Steele)*

**IN HARM'S WAY** (Paramount, 1965). D: Otto Preminger. S: Wendell Mayes. Fr: James Bassett (novel).

1. "We're getting some funny signals, Mac. I guess I'm crazy, but it sounds like plane-to-plane chatter to me in Japanese."

> *Larry Hagman (J. G. Cline) to Tom Tryon (Lt. William McConnel), picking up warning signs on the eve of Pearl Harbor*

2. "We got ourselves another war."

> *Kirk Douglas (Comdr. Paul Eddington) to John Wayne (Capt. Rockwell Torrey), after the attack on Pearl Harbor*

3. "She's a tiger. A fast ship going in harm's way. A lousy situation, Commander Eddington."

> *Wayne to Douglas*

4. "It was like eating peanuts. Once I started, I couldn't stop."

> *Burgess Meredith (Comdr. Powell), on marrying three movie actresses*

5. "It's about time you crawled down from Mount Rushmore."

> *Meredith to Wayne, when trying to convince Wayne to have some fun*

6. "Past a certain age, men are apt to avoid making sudden moves where women are concerned. The women have to do the sudden moving or else everybody stands still until it's too late. And it gets late real fast in these times."

> *Patricia Neal (Lt. Maggie Haines) to Jill Haworth (Ens. Anna Lee Dorn)*

7. "We'll call this operation 'Apple Pie,' not because it's going to be easy, but because we're going to slice this island into three big pieces."

> *Wayne to his men*

8. "Bums like your friend Owen are with us always, like bad weather, but sailors, like your old man, only happen once in a while."

> *Douglas to Wayne's son Brandon de Wilde (Ens. Jeremiah Torrey)*

9. "All battles are fought by scared men who'd rather be someplace else."

> *Wayne*

LAST LINE
10. "I'll be here, Rock."

> *Neal to Wayne*

**IN THE GOOD OLD SUMMERTIME** (MGM, 1949). D: Robert Z. Leonard. S: Samson Raphaelson, Francis Goodrich, Ivan Tors, Albert Hackett. Fr: Miklos Laszlo (play, The Shop Around the Corner).

LAST LINE

1. "Psychologically, I'm very confused, but personally I feel just wonderful."

> *Judy Garland (Veronica Fisher)*

**IN THE HEAT OF THE NIGHT** (UA, 1967). D: Norman Jewison. S: Stirling Silliphant. Fr: John Ball (novel).

1. "They call me Mr. Tibbs."

> *Sidney Poitier (Virgil Tibbs)*

**2.** "You're so damn smart! You're smarter than any white man. You're just going to stay here and show us all. You got such a big head that you could never live with yourself unless you could put us all to shame."

Rod Steiger (Police Chief Bill Gillespie) to Poitier

**3.** "They got a murder they don't know what to do with. They need a whipping boy."

Poitier

**4.** "I got no wife. I got no kids. Boy . . . I got a town that don't like me."

Steiger to Poitier

**IN THE LINE OF FIRE** (Columbia, 1993). D: Wolfgang Petersen. S: Jeff Maguire.

**1.** "I know things about people, Lilly."

Secret Service agent Clint Eastwood (Frank Horrigan) to colleague Rene Russo (Lilly Raines)

**2.** "You really should get in shape for that kind of duty, Frank."

Assassin John Malkovich (Mitch Leary/Booth), on Eastwood's assignment protecting the President

**3.** "White, piano-playing heterosexuals over the age of fifty. They ain't a whole lot of us, but, uh, we do have a powerful lobby."

Eastwood, on the demographics he represents

**4.** "If she looks back, that means she's interested. Come on, now, give me a little look. A little glance back. Give me that smug look and be on your way."

Eastwood, watching Russo walk away from his seat on the steps of the Lincoln Memorial

**5.** "Well, Abe. Damn. Wish I could've been there for you, pal."

Eastwood to the statue of Lincoln

**6.** "You shouldn't have been from Minneapolis."

Malkovich, killing Patrika Darbo (Pam Magnus) because she threatens his claim to have come from Minneapolis

**7.** "Well, maybe I'd vowed to never again let my career come between me and a woman."

Eastwood to Russo, on why he might consider giving up his job for her

**8.** "Everything'd be different right now, too, if I'd been half as paranoid as I am today."

Eastwood, on his failure to save John F. Kennedy's life

**9.** "It sounds to me like you need to get yourself laid, Booth."

Eastwood, diagnosing Malkovich's need to kill the President

**10.** "Cockamamy, that's a . . . that's a word your generation hasn't embraced yet. Maybe you ought to use it once in a while, just to kind of keep it alive, you know."

Eastwood to partner Dylan McDermott (Al D'Andrea)

**11.** "I see you, Frank. I see you standing over the grave of another dead president."

Malkovich to Eastwood, on what he sees in the dark, when the demons come

**12.** MALKOVICH: "Do you really think you have the guts to take a bullet, Frank?"

EASTWOOD: "I'll be thinking about that when I'm pissin' on your grave."

**LAST LINE**
**13.** "I know things about pigeons, Lilly."

Eastwood to Russo, back on the steps of the Lincoln Memorial, watching pigeons

**IN WHICH WE SERVE** (UK: UA, 1942). D: David Lean. S: Noel Coward. Fr: Lord Louis Mountbatten (experiences).

LAST LINE

*1.* "God bless our ships and all who sail in them."

> *Narrator*

**INCREDIBLE SHRINKING MAN, THE** (Universal, 1957). D: Jack Arnold. S: Richard Matheson. Fr: Richard Matheson (novel, The Shrinking Man).

*1.* "That's silly, honey. People just don't get smaller."

> *Randy Stuart (Louise Carey), reassuring her shrinking husband Grant Williams (Scott Carey)*

*2.* "The unbelievably small and the unbelievably vast eventually meet, like the closing of a gigantic circle."

> *Williams, waxing philosophical as he grows ever smaller*

LAST LINE

*3.* "And I felt my body dwindling, melting, becoming nothing. My fears locked away and in their place came acceptance. All this vast majesty of creation, it had to mean something. And then I meant something, too. Yes, smaller than the smallest, I meant something, too. To God there is no zero. I still exist."

> *Williams*

**INDECENT PROPOSAL** (Paramount, 1993). D: Adrian Lyne. S: Amy Holden Jones. Fr: Jack Englehard (novel).

*1.* "Would you mind lending me your wife?"

Billionaire Robert Redford (John Gage) to needy architect Woody Harrelson (David Murphy), making a proposition about Demi Moore (Diana Murphy)

**INDIANA JONES AND THE LAST CRUSADE** (Paramount, 1989). D: Steven Spielberg. S: Jeffrey Boam. Fr: George Lucas, Menno Meyjes (story), George Lucas, Philip Kaufman (characters).

*1.* HARRISON FORD (*Indiana Jones*) to a villain stealing an antique cross: "That belongs in a museum!"
> VILLAIN: "So do you!"

*2.* "I don't know, but I'll think of something."
> *Ford, on his plans for getting out of a tough spot*

*3.* "Nazis. I hate these guys."
> *Ford, seeing a bunch of Nazis*

*4.* "I told you—don't call me Junior."
> *Ford, making a futile request to his father Sean Connery (Professor Henry Jones)*

*5.* "You left just when you were becoming interesting."
> *Connery, on Ford's leaving home*

*6.* "Happens to me all the time."
> *Ford, on having people try to kill him*

*7.* "You call this archaeology?"
> *Connery, denouncing Ford's adventure-prone methods for finding artifacts*

*8.* FORD, on the name he prefers to be called: "I like Indiana."
> CONNERY, on the origin of the name: "We named the dog Indiana."

**INDIANA JONES AND THE TEMPLE OF DOOM** (Paramount, 1984). D: Steven Spielberg. S: Willard Huyck, Gloria Katz. Fr: George Lucas (story), Lawrence Kasdan (characters).

**1.** "Fortune and glory, kid. Fortune and glory."

Harrison Ford (Indiana Jones), telling Ke Huy Quan (Short Round) what he's after

**2.** "Maybe—but not today."

Ford's response when Kate Capshaw (Willie Scott) tells him he'll be killed

**INDISCREET** (Warner Bros., 1958). D: Stanley Donen. S: Norman Krasna. Fr: Norman Krasna (play, Kind Sir).

**1.** "How dare he make love to me and not be a married man!"

Ingrid Bergman (Anna Kalman), on Cary Grant's (Philip Adams's) deception that he was married

**LAST LINE**
**2.** "What are you crying about, Anna? Don't cry, Anna. I love you. Everything will be all right. You'll like being married. You will. You'll see."

Grant to Bergman

**INFORMER, THE** (RKO, 1935). D: John Ford. S: Dudley Nichols. Fr: Liam O'Flaherty (novel).

**1.** "'Twas I informed on your son, Mrs. McPhillip. Forgive me."

Victor McLaglen (Gypo Nolan) to Una O'Connor (Mrs. McPhillip)

**INHERIT THE WIND** (UA, 1960). D: Stanley Kramer. S: Nathan E. Douglas, Harold Jacob Smith. Fr: Jerome Lawrence, Robert E. Lee (play).

**1.** "I may be rancid butter, but I'm on your side of the bread."

Cynical newspaper reporter Gene Kelly (E. K. Hornbeck) to Donna Anderson (Rachel Brown), whose boyfriend has been accused of teaching evolution in school

**2.** "Hello, Devil. Welcome to Hell."

Kelly to defense attorney Spencer Tracy (Henry Drummond), upon his arrival in town

**3.** "Mr. Brady, it is the duty of a newspaper to comfort the afflicted and afflict the comfortable."

Kelly to Fredric March (Matthew Brady), the leading prosecutor in the case

**4.** "Language is a poor enough means of communication. I think we should use all the words we've got. Besides, there are damn few words that anybody understands!"

Tracy to March, on why he uses curse words

**5.** "Disillusionment is what little heroes are made of."

Kelly to Dick York (Bertram T. Cates), the man on trial

**6.** "Remember the wisdom of Solomon in the book of Proverbs. 'He that troubleth his own house shall inherit the wind.'"

March to Claude Akins (Reverend Brown)

**7.** "As long as the prerequisite for that shining paradise is ignorance, bigotry, and hate, I say the hell with it."

Tracy to March, on Heaven

**8.** "He's the only man I know who can strut sitting down."

*Kelly, on March*

**9.** "Darwin was wrong. Man is still an ape."

*Kelly to Tracy*

**10.** "I am more interested in the Rock of Ages than I am in the age of rocks."

*March to Tracy, when asked how old he thinks a rock is*

**11.** "How do you write an obituary for a man that's been dead for thirty years?"

*Kelly to Tracy, on March*

**12.** "I say that you cannot administer a wicked law impartially. You can only destroy. You can only punish. And I warn you that a wicked law, like cholera, destroys everyone it touches. Its upholders, as well as its defiers."

*Tracy*

**13.** MARCH: "Is it possible that something is holy to the celebrated agnostic?"
 TRACY: "Yes. The individual human mind."

**14.** "If the Lord wishes a sponge to think, it thinks!"

*March, on whether he thinks a sponge thinks*

LAST LINES
**15.** TRACY, discussing the reporter's future: "You poor slob! You're all alone. When you go to your grave, there won't be anybody to pull the grass up over your head. Nobody to mourn you. Nobody to give a damn. You're all alone."

 KELLY: "You're wrong, Henry. You'll be there. You're the type. Who else would defend my right to be lonely?"

**INN OF THE SIXTH HAPPINESS, THE** (UK: 20th Century–Fox, 1958). D: Mark Robson. S: Isobel Lennart. Fr: Alan Burgess (novel, The Small Woman).

**1.** "Once in her life, every woman should have that said to her. I thank you for being the one who said it to me."

*Ingrid Bergman (Gladys Aylward), thanking Curt Jurgens (Captain Lin Nan) for a compliment*

**INTERIORS** (UA, 1978). D: Woody Allen. S: Woody Allen.

**1.** "The hardest thing is to act properly throughout one's whole life."

*Sam Waterston (Mike)*

**2.** "Do I really care if a handful of my poems are read after I'm gone forever? Is that supposed to be some sort of compensation?"

*Diane Keaton (Renata), referring to achieving immortality through her work*

**3.** "The intimacy of it embarrasses me."

*Keaton, on her own mortality*

**4.** "Stay home and drink yourself unconscious. That's one of the clichés of being a novelist you've had no problems with!"

*Keation to her husband Richard Jordan (Frederick)*

**5.** "You only live once, but once is enough if you play it right."

*Maureen Stapleton (Pearl), E. G. Marshall's (Arthur's) lover*

**6.** "You'll live to be a hundred, if you give up all the things that make you want to."

*Stapleton to Marshall*

LAST LINE

**7.** MARY BETH HURT (*Joey*): "Water's so calm."
KEATON: "Yes, it's very peaceful."

**INTERNATIONAL HOUSE** *(Paramount, 1932). D: Edward Sutherland. S: Francis Martin, Walter De Leon. Fr: Lou Heifetz, Neil Brant (story).*

**1.** "Hold your breath and lie down."
W. C. Fields (Professor Quail)

**2.** "Now that I'm here, I shall dally in the valley—and believe me, I can dally."
Fields

**INVASION OF THE BODY SNATCHERS** *(UA, 1956). D: Don Siegel. S: Daniel Mainwaring (uncredited), Sam Peckinpah. Fr: Jack Finney (novel, The Body Snatchers).*

**1.** "Desire, ambition, faith—without them life is so simple."
Larry Gates (Dan Kaufman), on the benefits of being taken over by aliens

**INVASION OF THE BODY SNATCHERS** *(UA, 1978). D: Philip Kaufman. S: W. D. Richter. Fr: Jack Finney (novel, The Body Snatchers).*

**1.** "Why do we always expect them to come in metal ships?"
Veronica Cartwright (Nancy Bellicec)

**INVISIBLE MAN, THE** *(Universal, 1933). D: James Whale. S: R. C. Sheriff, Philip Wylie (uncredited).*

**1.** "There must be a way back. God knows there's a way back."
*Claude Rains (Jack Griffin), searching desperately for a way to reverse his invisibility*

**2.** "How can I handcuff a blooming shirt?"
*Policeman, trying to capture Rains, who is invisible except for his shirt*

**3.** "We'll begin with a reign of terror—a few murders here and there. Murders of great men, murders of little men. Just to show we make no distinction."
*Rains, explaining his plans to William Harrigan (Kemp)*

**4.** "Even the moon's frightened of me, frightened to death. The whole world's frightened to death."
*Rains, raving*

**5.** "I've no time now, but believe me, as surely as the moon will set and the sun will rise, I shall kill you tomorrow night. I shall kill you even if you hide in the deepest cave of the earth. At ten o'clock tomorrow night, I shall kill you."
*Rains, promising to kill Harrigan for betraying him*

**6.** "Excuse me, sir. There's breathing in my barn."
*Elderly farmer, informing the police of Rains's whereabouts*

**7.** "I meddled in things that man must leave alone."
*Rains's dying words*

**INVISIBLE MAN RETURNS, THE** *(Universal, 1936). D: Joe May. S: Curt Siodmak, Lester Cole, Cecil Belfrage. Fr: Curt Siodmak, Joe May (story).*

181

***1.*** "You know, being invisible has distinct advantages."

*Vincent Price (Geoffrey Radcliffe)*

## ISLAND OF LOST SOULS *(Paramount, 1933). D: Erle C. Kenton. S: Philip Wylie, Waldemar Young. Fr: H. G. Wells (novel, The Island of Dr. Moreau).*

***1.*** CHARLES LAUGHTON (*Dr. Moreau*), to the animal-men he has created: "What is the law?"

BELA LUGOSI (*Sayer of the Law*): "Not to run on all fours. That is the law. Are we not men?"

***2.*** "Mr. Parker, do you know what it means to feel like God?"

*Laughton to Richard Arlen (Edward Parker), a visitor shipwrecked on his island*

***3.*** "The stubborn beast flesh creeping back. There's no use, Montgomery, I may as well quit. Day by day, it creeps back. It creeps back. . . ."

*Laughton to his assistant Arthur Hoyt (Montgomery), on Kathleen Burke's (Lota the panther woman's) continual backsliding to her earlier panther state*

***4.*** "This time I'll burn out all the animal in her!"

*Laughton, planning to deal with Burke's backsliding*

***5.*** "They are restless tonight."

*Laughton, on the natives of the island*

***6.*** LAUGHTON: "What is the law?"

LUGOSI, no longer compliant: "Law no more!"

***7.*** LAUGHTON, threatening his animal-men: "Have you forgotten the House of Pain?"

LUGOSI: "You made us in the House of Pain. You made us things. Not men. Not beasts. Part men, part beasts—things!"

## IT HAPPENED ONE NIGHT *(Columbia, 1934). D: Frank Capra. S: Robert Riskin. Fr: Samuel Hopkins Adams (novelette, "Night Bus").*

***1.*** "Remember me? I'm the fellow you slept on last night."

*Clark Gable (Peter Warne) to Claudette Colbert (Ellie Andrews), after they have spent the night together on a bus*

***2.*** COLBERT: "Your ego is absolutely colossal."

GABLE: "Yeah. Yep. Not bad. How's yours?"

***3.*** "Behold the walls of Jericho! Uh, maybe not as thick as the ones that Joshua blew down with his trumpet, but a lot safer. You see, uh, I have no trumpet."

*Gable to Colbert, after dividing the room in the auto court with a blanket*

***4.*** "Perhaps you're interested in how a man undresses. You know, it's a funny thing about that. Quite a study in psychology. No two men do it alike."

*Gable to Colbert, when she refuses to move to her side of the room and get ready for bed*

***5.*** "Dunking's an art. Don't let it soak so long. A dip and plop, into your mouth. If you let it hang there too long, it'll get soft and fall off. It's all a matter of timing. I ought to write a book about it."

*Gable to Colbert, on dunking doughnuts in coffee*

***6.*** "I was wondering what makes dames like you so dippy."

*Gable to Colbert*

**7.** COLBERT, after hitching a ride by raising her skirt: "Well, I proved once and for all that the limb is mightier than the thumb."

GABLE: "Why didn't you take off *all* your clothes? You could have stopped forty cars."

**8.** WALTER CONNOLLY (*Alexander Andrews*), on his daughter Colbert: "Do you love her?"

GABLE: "Yes! But don't hold that against me. I'm a little screwy myself."

**LAST LINES**
**9.** MAIDEL TURNER (*Auto Camp Manager's Wife*), on the odd request of the honeymooning Gable and Colbert: "But what in the world do they want a trumpet for?"

HARRY HOLMAN (*Auto Camp Manager*): "Dunno."

**IT'S A GIFT** (Paramount, 1934). D: Norman Z. McLeod. S: Jack Cunningham, W. C. Fields, (uncredited). Fr: J. P. McEvoy (story, "The Comic Supplement"), W. C. Fields (uncredited).

**1.** "I'll be sober tomorrow, but you'll be crazy the rest of your life."

W. C. Fields (Harold Bissonette)

**2.** "Shades of Bacchus."

Fields

**IT'S A MAD, MAD, MAD, MAD WORLD** (UA, 1963). D: Stanley Kramer. S: William Rose, Tania Rose.

**1.** "The way he just sailed out there!"

Milton Berle (J. Russell Finch), to himself, when he can't get over how Jimmy Durante (Smiler Grogan) drove off a cliff

**2.** "It's in this box buried under this . . . buried under this big W. You'll see it. You'll see it under this . . . under this big W. A big . . . a big W."

Durante, describing the hiding place of his illicit fortune

**3.** "Do you know why your husband had a nervous breakdown? It's because he has sunk $40,000, including $15,000 of my money, into a company that makes seaweed for people to eat! And not only does nobody like it, but it costs over four dollars a can!"

Ethel Merman (Mrs. Marcus) to Dorothy Provine (Emmeline Finch)

**4.** "Listen, everybody has to pay taxes. Even businessmen that rob and steal and cheat from people every day. Even they have to pay taxes."

Jonathan Winters (Lennie Pike), trying to convince Berle that taxes must be paid when Durante's hidden money is found

**5.** "We're the ones with the Imperial; we're running last?"

Merman to Berle, when the mad chase begins

**6.** "I said it before and I'll say it again. I didn't want to move to California."

Nick Stuart (Truck Driver) to his wife, when they are run off the road by the others.

**7.** "Where did you get that funny accent? Are you from Harvard or something?"

Merman to British visitor Terry-Thomas (J. Algernon Hawthorne)

**8.** "Well!"

Jack Benny (in a cameo appearance) to Merman, when she tells him she doesn't need any of his help

**9.** "Against it? I should be positively astounded to hear anything that could be said for it. Why the whole bloody place is the most unspeakable matriarchy in the whole history of civilization. . . . And this positively infantile preoccupation with bosoms. . . . I'll wager you anything you like if American women stopped wearing brassieres, your whole national economy would collapse overnight."

*British visitor Terry-Thomas, indulging in a diatribe against the United States*

**10.** "It's the only way to fly!"

*Jim Backus (Tyler Fitzgerald) to Buddy Hackett (Benjy Benjamin), referring to drinking old-fashioneds while piloting a plane*

**11.** "This is no place for a convertible."

*Phil Silvers (Otto Meyer), when he drives a car into a river*

**12.** "Anything you'd have to say about your mother-in-law, you don't have to explain to me. You know what I mean? It's like if she were a star of a real crummy horror movie, I'd believe it."

*Winters to Berle*

**13.** "We ain't in any rush. We want to get there in a hurry."

*Hackett to cab driver Eddie "Rochester" Anderson*

**14.** TRACY (*Capt. C. G. Culpeper*): "I'd like to think that sometime, maybe ten, or twenty, years from now, there'd be something I could laugh at."

MERMAN: "Now, see here, you idiots! It's all your fault because if you hadn't—"

*Merman's last words before slipping on a banana peel Hackett has thrown on the floor, bringing laughter to Tracy and the other culprits*

**IT'S A WONDERFUL LIFE** (*RKO/Liberty Films, 1946*). D: Frank Capra. S: Frances Goodrich, Albert Hackett, Frank Capra, Jo Swerling. Fr: Philip Van Doren Stern (story, "The Greatest Gift").

**1.** "Looks like we'll have to send someone down—a lot of people are asking for help for a man named George Bailey."

*Voice of Franklin to voice of Joseph*

**2.** "What, this old thing? Why, I only wear it when I don't care how I look."

*Gloria Grahame (Violet Bick) to James Stewart (George Bailey)*

**3.** "What is it you want, Mary? What do you want? You-you want the moon?"

*Stewart to Donna Reed (Mary Hatch)*

**4.** "Why don't you kiss her instead of talking her to death?"

*Man in nearby house to Stewart*

**5.** "Just remember this, Mr. Potter, that this rabble you're talking about . . . they do most of the working and paying and living and dying in this community. Well, is it too much to have them work and pay and live and die in a couple of decent rooms and a bath? Anyway my father didn't think so. People were human beings to him, but to you, a warped, frustrated old man, they're cattle. Well, in my book he died a much richer man than you'll ever be."

*Stewart to Lionel Barrymore (Mr. Potter)*

**6.** "Now, you listen to me! I don't want any plastics and I don't want any ground floors, and I don't want to get married—ever—to anyone! You understand that? I want to do what I want to do. And you're . . . and you're . . ."

*Stewart to Reed*

**7.** "Can't you understand what's happening here? Don't you see what's happening? Potter isn't selling. Potter's buying!"

*Stewart to people making run on the Bailey Building and Loan*

**8.** "A toast! A toast to Mama Dollar and to Papa Dollar, and if you want to keep this old Building and Loan in business, you better have a family real quick."

*Stewart to the two dollars left at the end of the day, after the run on the bank*

**9.** "Remember the night we broke the window in this old house? This is what I wished for."

*Reed to Stewart, in the old Granville house on their wedding night*

**10.** "Mary had two more babies, but still found time to run the USO."

*Voice of Joseph*

**11.** "Look at you. You used to be so cocky. You were going to go out and conquer the world! You once called me a warped, frustrated old man. What are you but a warped, frustrated young man?"

*Barrymore to Stewart, after Thomas Mitchell (Uncle Billy) has lost $8,000 of the Building and Loan's money*

**12.** "Hey, look, mister, we serve hard drinks in here for men who want to get drunk fast. And we don't need any characters around to give the joint atmosphere."

*Sheldon Leonard (Nick) to Henry Travers (Clarence Odbody, Angel Second Class) after he orders mulled wine, heavy on the cinnamon and light on the cloves*

**13.** "Strange, isn't it? Each man's life touches so many other lives, and when he isn't around he leaves an awful hole, doesn't he?"

*Travers to Stewart*

**14.** "Every man on that transport died. Harry wasn't there to save them because you weren't there to save Harry. You see, George, you really had a wonderful life. Don't you see what a mistake it would be to throw it away?"

*Travers to Stewart*

**15.** "Clarence! Clarence! Help me, Clarence. Get me back. Get me back. I don't care what happens to me. Get me back to my wife and kids. Help me, Clarence, please. Please! I want to live again! I want to live again. I want to live again. Please, God, let me live again."

*Stewart to Travers*

**16.** "My mouth's bleeding, Bert! My mouth's bleed—Zuzu's petals! Zuzu's . . . There they are! Bert! What do you know about that! Merry Christmas!"

*Stewart to Ward Bond (Bert)*

**17.** "A toast . . . to my big brother, George. The richest man in town!"

*Todd Karns (Harry Bailey) to Stewart and group*

**18.** "Dear George, remember *no* man is a failure who has *friends*. Thanks for the wings! Love Clarence."

*Inscription in Travers's copy of* Tom Sawyer, *left for Stewart*

**LAST LINES**
**19.** KAROLYN GRIMES (*Zuzu*): "Look, Daddy. Teacher says, every time a bell rings an angel gets his wings."
　　STEWART: "That's right, that's right. Attaboy, Clarence."

**JANE EYRE** (20th Century–Fox, 1944). D: Robert Stevenson. S: Aldous Huxley, Robert Stevenson, John Houseman. Fr: Charlotte Brontë (novel).

**LAST LINE**

*1.* "And then one day when our firstborn son was put into his arms, he could see that the boy had inherited his own eyes as they once were, large, brilliant, and black."

> *Joan Fontaine (Jane Eyre), on Orson Welles (Edward Rochester) and their son*

**JAWS** (Universal, 1975). D: Steven Spielberg. S: Peter Benchley, Carl Gottlieb, Howard Sackler (uncredited). Fr: Peter Benchley (novel).

*1.* "Martin, it's all psychological. You yell barracuda, everybody says, 'Huh, what?' You yell shark, we've got a panic on our hands on the Fourth of July."

> *Mayor Murray Hamilton (Larry Vaughn) to Police Chief Roy Scheider (Martin Brody), on the wisdom of letting people know about the recent shark attack off the coast of Amity Island*

*2.* "I value my neck a lot more than three thousand bucks, Chief. I'll find him for three, but I'll catch him and kill him for ten. . . . For that, you get the head, the tail, the whole damn thing."

> *Master fisherman Robert Shaw (Quint), making Scheider an offer to kill the shark*

*3.* "Well, this is not a boat accident, and it wasn't any propeller, it wasn't any coral reef, and it wasn't Jack the Ripper. It was a shark."

> *Marine biologist Richard Dreyfuss (Matt Hooper), after inspecting the severed arm of a shark-attack victim*

*4.* "My husband tells me you're in sharks."

> *Scheider's wife Lorraine Gary (Ellen Brody), making conversation with Dreyfuss*

*5.* "Well, it doesn't make much sense for a guy who hates the water to live on an island either."

> *Dreyfuss, on Scheider's choice of residence*

*6.* "I'm not gonna waste my time arguing with a man who's lining up to be a hot lunch."

> *Dreyfuss, expressing disdain for Hamilton, who still refuses to acknowledge there is a shark*

*7.* "Mr. Vaughn, what we are dealing with here is a perfect engine—an eating machine. It's really a miracle of evolution. All this machine does is swim and eat and make little sharks, and that's all."

> *Dreyfuss to Hamilton*

*8.* "You're gonna need a bigger boat."

> *Scheider to Shaw, on first glimpsing the shark, against which Shaw plans to launch an attack*

*9.* DREYFUSS, marveling at the shark's size: "That's a twenty- footer."
SHAW: "Twenty-five. Three tons of him."

*10.* "Y'know, a thing about a shark, he's got lifeless eyes, black eyes, like a doll's eyes. When he comes at you he doesn't seem to be living until he bites you, and those black eyes roll over white, and then— oh, then you hear that terrible high-pitch screaming. . . ."

*Shaw, remembering a World War II–era attack of swarming sharks against shipwrecked sailors*

**11.** "So, eleven hundred men went into the water, three hundred and sixteen men come out, and the sharks took the rest, June the 29th, 1945. Anyway, we delivered the bomb."

*Shaw, concluding his war story, remembering the ship that delivered the atom bomb used against Japan*

**12.** "Back home we got a taxidermy man. He's gonna have a heart attack when he sees what I brung him!"

*Shaw, gloating too soon over his expected catch of the shark*

**13.** "Smile, you son of a bitch."

*Scheider, eyeing the shark as he prepares to shoot the explosive canister lodged in the shark's teeth*

**LAST LINES**
**14.** SCHEIDER, as he and Dreyfuss swim toward home, following the successful slaughter of the shark: "I used to hate the water."
DREYFUSS: "I can't imagine why."

**JAZZ SINGER, THE** (Warner Bros., 1927). D: Alan Crosland. S: Alfred A. Cohn (titles), Jack Jarmuth. Fr: Samson Raphaelson (play, Day of Atonement).

**1.** "Wait a minute, wait a minute, you ain't heard nothin' yet!"

*Al Jolson (Jakie Rabinowitz/Jack Robin), speaking the first line in a sound feature*

**JEANNE EAGELS** (Columbia, 1957). D: George Sidney. S: Daniels Fuchs, Sonya Levien, John Fante. Fr: Daniels Fuchs (story).

**1.** "Johnny, who are these peasants?"

*Kim Novak (Jeanne Eagels) to husband Charles Drake (John Donahue), on receiving visitors*

**2.** "I am a star. I don't need Actors Equity. I'm going to Hollywood."

*Novak, disdaining to unionize*

**JEZEBEL** (Warner Bros., 1938). D: William Wyler. S: Clements Ripley, Abem Finkel, John Huston, Robert Bruckner. Fr: Owen Davis, Sr. (play).

**1.** "I like my convictions undiluted, same as I do my bourbon."

*George Brent (Buck Cantrell)*

**2.** "This is 1852, dumpling, 1852."

*Bette Davis (Julie), on why she can wear red to a ball*

**JOE** (Cannon, 1970). D: John G. Avildsen. S: Norman Wexler.

**1.** "Forty-two percent of all liberals are queer. That's a fact. The Wallace people took a poll."

*Peter Boyle (Joe Curran)*

**JOHNNY EAGER** (MGM, 1941). D: Mervyn LeRoy. S: John Lee Mahin, James Edward Grant. Fr: James Edward Grant (story).

**1.** "You keep me around because even Johnny Eager has to have one friend."

*Van Heflin (Jeff Hartnett) to Robert Taylor (Johnny Eager)*

**LAST LINE**
**2.** "Aw, just another hood, I guess. Well, whoever he is, he don't mean a thing to

anybody now, much less to me. Say, call Mae and tell her I'll be late, will ya?"

*Byron Shores (Joe Agridowski, Officer 711), on Taylor*

**JOLSON STORY, THE** (Columbia, 1946). D: Alfred E. Green. S: Stephen Longstreet, Harry Chandlee, Andrew Solt.

*1.* "I heard some music tonight. Something they call 'jazz.' The fellows just make it up as they go along. They pick it out of the air."

*Larry Parks (Al Jolson)*

*2.* "Trying to make songs out of music I picked up. Music nobody ever heard of before, but the only kind I want to sing."

*Parks, explaining what he's been doing*

*3.* "You ain't heard nothin' yet!"

*Parks*

*4.* "That's an audience that never saw a live show. People in small towns who can afford a movie, where they can't afford anything else. Audience of millions. I'd be singing to every one of them at the same time. That's really something!"

*Parks, referring to talking pictures*

*5.* "Tonight, folks, I'm only going to sing two thousands songs. One to a customer."

*Parks*

*6.* "Broadway? What a street! You know something, baby? It belongs to me. You know something else? If you want, I'll give it to you.

*Parks*

*7.* "When he gets home nights, after the show, don't let him sing too long."

Evelyn Keyes (Julie Benson) to William Demarest (Steve Martin)

**JOURNEY TO THE CENTER OF THE EARTH** (20th Century–Fox, 1959). D: Henry Levin. S: Charles Brackett, Walter Reisch. Fr: Jules Verne (novel, Voyage au Centre de la Terre).

*1.* "We'll observe one minute of silence in memory of a great scientist, even if he was a blasted thief."

*James Mason (Professor Oliver Lindenbrook), on the death of a rival in the quest for the center of the Earth*

*2.* "You're in my world now."

*Thayer David (Count Saknussemm), menacingly, to Mason and his party, in the underworld that David claims as his own*

*3.* "Never interrupt a murderer, madam."

*Mason to Arlene Dahl (Carla), with regard to David*

*4.* "A bourgeois trick. So sorry."

*Mason, after temporarily blinding his assailant David with a handful of salt*

*5.* "Your entire presence is a constant criticism of me."

*Mason, peeved at Dahl*

*6.* "Dear Alec, there are times when it's advisable to jog a young man's memory."

*Dahl to Pat Boone (Alec McEwen), reminding him of his fiancée at home in Scotland, when she senses he is falling for her*

*7.* "A scientist who cannot prove what he has accomplished has accomplished nothing."

Mason, denying all credit for his discovery of
the center of the Earth because his proof of the
discovery has been destroyed

**8.** "You know, it's one thing to spend one's
days and nights with a man under the earth,
another under one roof in Scotland."

Dahl, agreeing to marry Mason

**LAST LINE**
**9.** "I warn you, I'm wearing stays again."

Dahl to Mason

**JUDGMENT AT NUREMBURG** (UA, 1961).
D: Stanley Kramer. S: Abby Mann.

**1.** "Ernest Janning said he is guilty. If he is,
Ernest Janning's guilt is the world's guilt. No
more and no less."

Maximillian Schell (Hans Rolfe), on Burt Lancaster (Ernest Janning), charged with Nazi war
crimes

**JUNE BRIDE** (Warner Bros., 1948). D: Bre-
taigne Windust. S: Ranald MacDougall. Fr:
Eileen Tighe, Graeme Lorimer (play, Feature
for June).

**1.** "You're not really a heel. You just give
that impression."

Magazine editor Bette Davis (Linda Gilman) to
writer Robert Montgomery (Carey Jackson)

**2.** "What's the matter with me? I'm gay, I'm
lovable, and I've got good teeth."

Montgomery, discussing his good points with
Davis

**3.** MONTGOMERY, on Davis's ambition:
"Knew exactly what you wanted, where you
were going, and how to get there."
    DAVIS: "I sound like a subway."

**4.** "I've had measles once. Now I'm
immune."

Davis, on why she won't fall for Montgomery
again

**5.** "This is a real McKinley stinker."

Mary Wickes (Rosemary McNally) on visiting a
dowdy Midwestern home

**6.** "She's a little worried about her bust. You
didn't throw it out, did you?"

Davis to Wickes, in a double entendre about
Marjorie Bennett's (Mrs. Brinker's) statue of
Julius Caesar

**7.** "I'm just trying to get out from underneath this labor-vs.-management relationship
of ours. Every time I get affectionate with
you, I feel as though I was snuggling up to
the Taft-Hartley Bill."

Montgomery to Davis, on their inability to tran-
scend their editor-writer relationship

**8.** "Haven't you got something more . . .
more?"

Montgomery to young woman Betty Lynn (Boo
Brinker), looking for something more seductive
in her fashion choices

**9.** "Nothing that being eighteen again
wouldn't cure."

Fay Bainter (Paula Winthrop), describing why
she reacts emotionally when she sees a bride

**10.** "Well, I don't want to miss Boo's wedding. I've missed so many of my own."

Wickes

**11.** "Carey, you know very well we're perfectly mated. After all, we're opposite
sexes."

Davis to Montgomery

**JUNGLE BOOK, THE** (UA, 1967). D: Zoltan Korda. S: Larry Clemmons, Ralph Wright, Ken Anderson, Vance Gerry. Fr: Rudyard Kipling (stories).

*1.* "Just wait till I get you in my coils."

Sterling Holloway (Kaa the Python)

*2.* "Old Baloo's going to learn you to fight like a bear."

Phil Harris (Baloo the Bear)

*3.* "The Man Village? They'll ruin him. They'll make a man out of him."

Harris

*4.* "Man, that's what I call a swinging party."

Harris, on rescuing Bruce Reitherman (Mowgli) from Louis Prima (King Louie of the Apes)

*5.* "Mowgli seem to have man's ability to get into trouble."

Sebastian Cabot (Bagheera the Panther)

*6.* CABOT: "Birds of a feather should flock together. You wouldn't marry a panther, would you?"
HARRIS: "I don't know. Come to think of it, no panther ever asked me."

**JURASSIC PARK** (Universal, 1993). D: Steven Spielberg. S: David Koepp, Michael Crichton, Malia Scotch Marmo. Fr: Michael Crichton (novel).

*1.* "Welcome to Jurassic Park."

Sir Richard Attenborough (John Hammond), greeting visitors to the island of genetically engineered dinosaurs

*2.* "I'm simply saying that life—uh—finds a way."

Jeff Goldblum (Malcolm), on why he doubts that the park's scientists can keep the dinosaurs from breeding

*3.* "Spared no expense."

Attenborough's favorite description of his park

*4.* "Boy, I hate being right all the time."

Goldblum, as the Tyrannosaurus Rex gets loose, fulfilling his predictions based on the chaos theory

*5.* "Clever girl."

Park ranger Bob Peck (Muldoon), facing a velociraptor that has outwitted him

*6.* "Hammond, after careful consideration, I've decided not to endorse your park."

Sam Neill (Grant), understating things to Attenborough

**KARATE KID, THE** (Columbia, 1985). D: John G. Avildsen. S: Robert Mark Kamen.

*1.* "To make honey, young bee need young flower, not old prune."

Noriyuki "Pat" Morita (Mr. Miyagi) to Ralph Macchio (Daniel Larusso), hinting that Macchio should be spending time with a girl, not him

*2.* "Fighting always last answer to problem."

Morita to Macchio

*3.* "No such thing as bad student, only bad teacher. Teacher say. Student do."

Morita to Macchio

**4.** "Use head for something other than target."

*Morita to Macchio*

**5.** "Karate here. Karate here. Karate never here. You understand?"

*Morita to Macchio, pointing to his head, heart, and stomach*

**6.** "Man who catch fly with chopstick, accomplish anything."

*Morita to Macchio*

**7.** MORITA: "Why train?"
MACCHIO: "So I won't have to fight."
MORITA: "Miyagi have hope for you."

**LAST LINE**
**8.** "Hey! Hey, Mr. Miyagi! We did it! We did it! All right!"

*Macchio to Morita*

**KEY LARGO** (Warner Bros., 1948). D: John Huston. S: Richard Brooks. Fr: Maxwell Anderson (play).

**1.** "Do you remember telling George what this hollow is above the upper lip? Before he was born, you said, he knew all the secrets of life and death, and then at the moment of his birth, an angel came and put his finger right there, and sealed his lips."

*Humphrey Bogart (Frank McLeod) to Lionel Barrymore (James Temple)*

**2.** "He was the master of the fix. Whom he couldn't corrupt, he terrified. Whom he couldn't terrify, he murdered."

*Bogart to Barrymore*

**3.** "Thousands of guys got guns, but there's only one Johnny Rocco."

*Edward G. Robinson (Johnny Rocco) to Bogart*

**4.** "Yeah! That's it! More! That's right! I want more!"

*Robinson saying what he wants*

**5.** "A world in which there's no place for Johnny Rocco."

*Bogart to Robinson, telling what he wants*

**6.** "One thing I can't stand, it's a dame that's drunk."

*Robinson, on Claire Trevor*

**7.** "One Rocco, more or less, isn't worth dying for."

*Bogart, forfeiting the chance to kill Robinson*

**8.** "Maybe it is a rotten world, but a cause isn't lost as long as someone is willing to go on fighting."

*Lauren Bacall (Nora Temple)*

**9.** "You don't like it. Do you, Rocco? The storm. Show it your gun. Why don't you? If it doesn't stop, shoot it."

*Bogart to Robinson*

**10.** "You were right. When your head says one thing, and your whole life says another, your head always loses."

*Bogart to Bacall*

**LAST LINE**
**11.** "He's all right, Dad! He's coming back to us."

*Bacall to Barrymore*

**KILL THE UMPIRE** (Columbia, 1950). D: Lloyd Bacon. S: Frank Tashlin.

**LAST LINE**
**1.** "Kill the umpire! Kill the umpire! Kill the umpire!"

*Spectators at baseball game*

**KILLING FIELDS, THE** *(UK: Warner Bros., 1984). D: Roland Joffe. S: Bruce Robinson. Fr: Sidney Schanberg (article, "The Death and Life of Dith Pran").*

**LAST LINE**

**1.** "Nothing's forgiven, nothing."

*Haing S. Ngor (Dith Pran), on the genocide in Cambodia*

**KIND HEARTS AND CORONETS** *(UK: General Film Distributors, 1949). D: Robert Hamer. S: Robert Hamer, John Dighton. Fr: Roy Horniman (novel).*

**1.** "It is so difficult to make a neat job of killing people with whom one is not on friendly terms."

*Dennis Price (Louis Mazzini), in narration*

**2.** "Revenge is the dish which people of taste prefer to eat cold."

*Price, in narration*

**3.** PRICE: "You're playing with fire."

JOAN GREENWOOD (*Sibella*): "At least it warms me."

**LAST LINE**

**4.** "My memoirs. My memoirs. My memoirs. My memoirs."

*Price*

**KING AND I, THE** *(20th Century–Fox, 1956). D: Walter Lang. S: Ernest Lehman. Fr: Oscar Hammerstein II, Richard Rodgers (musical), Margaret Landon (book, Anna and the King of Siam).*

**1.** "Hah!"

*Frequent response of Yul Brynner (King of Siam) to English teacher Deborah Kerr (Anna)*

**2.** "You are not afraid of king. Not to be afraid is good thing in scientific mind."

*Brynner to Kerr, expressing his admiration for Western science*

**3.** "I don't think they have elephants in America, Your Majesty."

*Kerr to Brynner, discussing whether Abraham Lincoln is using elephants to win the Civil War*

**4.** "I think your Moses shall have been a fool."

*Brynner to Kerr, on reading that Moses wrote in the Bible that the world was created in six days*

**5.** "Et cetera, et cetera, et cetera."

*Brynner's frequent refrain*

**6.** "You are very difficult woman."

*Brynner, summing up his relationship with Kerr*

**7.** "I will show them who is barbarian!"

*Brynner to Kerr, insulted on being considered a barbarian by the English*

**8.** "British not scientific enough for the use of chopsticks."

*Brynner, on British table manners*

**9.** BRYNNER, on his son's first proclamation as king: "This proclamation against bowing to king I believe to be your fault."

KERR: "Oh, I hope so, Your Majesty. I do hope so."

**KING KONG** *(RKO, 1933). D: Merian C. Cooper, Ernest B. Schoedsack. S: James Creelman, Ruth Rose. Fr: Merian C. Cooper, Edgar Wallace (story).*

**1.** "And the Prophet said, 'And lo, the beast looked upon the face of beauty. And it stayed its hand from killing. And from that day, it was as one dead.' "

*"Old Arabian Proverb" invented for the film's epigraph*

**2.** "It's money and adventure and fame. It's the thrill of a lifetime and a long sea voyage that starts at six o'clock tomorrow morning."

*Adventure filmmaker Robert Armstrong (Carl Denham), enticing Fay Wray (Ann Darrow) to join him on a mysterious voyage*

**3.** "Did you ever hear of . . . Kong?"

*Armstrong to skipper Frank Reicher (Captain Englehorn) and his first mate Bruce Cabot (Jack Driscoll)*

**4.** "Yeah, blondes are scarce around here."

*Armstrong, on the interest of the dark-skinned natives in the blond Wray*

**5.** "Why, in a few months it'll be up in lights on Broadway: 'Kong—the Eighth Wonder of the World!' "

*Armstrong, after capturing King Kong*

**6.** "But this is more in the nature of a personal appearance, madam."

*Usher, at the opening of the Kong show, to an audience member who expected "King Kong" to be a movie*

**7.** MALE AUDIENCE MEMBER, at opening: "I hear it's a kind of a gorilla."

FEMALE AUDIENCE MEMBER: "Gee, ain't we got enough of them in New York?"

**8.** "He was a king and a god in the world he knew, but now he comes to civilization, merely a captive, a show to gratify your curiosity. Ladies and gentlemen, look at Kong: the Eighth Wonder of the World!"

*Armstrong to his audience, just before unveiling Kong*

LAST LINE
**9.** "Oh, no. It wasn't the airplanes. It was Beauty killed the Beast."

*Armstrong, correcting police officer on what killed Kong*

**KING OF COMEDY, THE** (20th Century–Fox, 1982). D: Martin Scorsese. S: Paul D. Zimmerman.

LAST LINE
**1.** "Rupert Pupkin, ladies and gentlemen. Let's hear it for Rupert Pupkin. Wonderful. Rupert Pupkin, ladies and gentlemen."

*Jeff David (Announcer), after Robert De Niro (Rupert Pupkin) has become a big star*

**KINGS ROW** (Warner Bros., 1941). D: Sam Wood. S: Casey Robinson. Fr: Henry Bellamann (novel).

**1.** "Where's the rest of me?"

*Amputee Ronald Reagan (Drake McHugh)*

**KISS OF DEATH** (20th Century–Fox, 1947). D: Henry Hathaway. S: Ben Hecht, Charles Lederer. Fr: Eleazar Lipsky (story).

**1.** "You know what I do with squealers? I let 'em have it in the belly so they can roll around for a long time thinking it over."

*Richard Widmark (Tommy Udo) to Mildred Dunnock (Ma Rizzo)*

**KISS OF THE SPIDER WOMAN** (US/Brazil: Island Alive, 1985). D: Hector Babenco. S: Leonard Schrader. Fr: Manuel Puig (novel).

**1.** WILLIAM HURT (*Luis Molina*): "Enjoy what life offers you."

RAUL JULIA (*Valentin Arregui*): "What life offers me is the struggle."

**2.** "What kind of a cause is that? One that doesn't let you eat an avocado?"

*Hurt to Julia*

**3.** "God, wouldn't if be wonderful if you told me a movie for a change? One that I haven't seen?"

*Hurt to Julia*

**4.** "Whenever I go to sleep, I'll probably be thinking of you and your crazy movies."

*Julia to Hurt*

**LAST LINE**
**5.** "This dream is short, but this dream is happy."

*Sonia Braga (Leni Lamaison/Marta/Spider Woman)*

**KLUTE** (Warner Bros., 1971). D: Alan J. Pakula. S: Andy and Dave Lewis.

**1.** "Do you mind if I take my sweater off? Why, I think in the confines of one's house one should be free of clothing and inhibitions. Oh, inhibitions are always nice because they're so nice to overcome."

*Jane Fonda (Bree Daniels), on tape to client*

**2.** "I think the only way that any of us can ever be happy is to . . . is to let it all hang out, you know, do it all and just fuck it."

*Fonda, on tape to client*

**3.** "Well, I mean, I've been coming here all this time and I've been paying you all this money, and why do I still want a trick?"

*Fonda to Psychiatrist Vivian Nathan*

**4.** "Because when you're a call girl, you control it, that's why. Because someone wants you. . . . and for an hour . . . I'm the best actress in the world."

*Fonda to Nathan, on why she remains a call girl*

**5.** "Oh, I don't know, I don't know why I'm here. It's just so silly to think somebody else can help anybody."

*Fonda to Nathan*

**6.** "And what's your bag, Klute? What do you like?"

*Fonda to Donald Sutherland (John Klute)*

**7.** "I'm very bad, you know. I have very wicked ideas."

*Fonda, on tape*

**8.** "Don't feel bad about losing your virtue. I sort of knew you would. Everyone always does."

*Fonda to Sutherland, after they have had sex*

**9.** "All the time I keep feeling the need to destroy it."

*Fonda to Nathan, on her romance with Sutherland*

**10.** "What could ever happen for us? I mean, we're so different. I know enough about myself to know that whatever lies in store for me it's not going to be setting up housekeeping with somebody in Tuscarora and darning socks and doing all that."

*Fonda to Nathan*

**LAST LINE**
**11.** "I have no idea what's going to happen. I just can't stay in this city, you know. Maybe I'll come back. You'll probably see me next week."

*Fonda to Nathan, in voice-over*

**KNUTE ROCKNE—ALL AMERICAN** *(Warner Bros., 1940). D: Lloyd Bacon. S: Robert Buckner. Fr: Mrs. Knute Rockne (papers).*

**1.** "And the last thing he said to me, 'Rock,' he said, 'sometimes when the team is up against it and the breaks are beating the boys, tell them to go out there with all they've got and win just one for the Gipper.'"

*Pat O'Brien (Knute Rockne), quoting Ronald Reagan (George Gipp), in a pep talk to his football team*

**KRAMER VS. KRAMER** *(Columbia, 1979). D: Robert Benton. S: Robert Benton. Fr: Avery Corman (novel).*

**1.** "She loused up one of the five best days of your life."

*Jane Alexander (Margaret Phelps) to Dustin Hoffman (Ted Kramer), guessing what Meryl Streep (Joanna Kramer) has done*

**2.** JUSTIN HENRY (*Billy Kramer*): "I want my Mommy!"
HOFFMAN: "I'm all you've got!"

**3.** STREEP: "I want my son."
HOFFMAN: "You can't have him."

**4.** STREEP, on the witness stand: "I was not a failure."
Opposing attorney HOWARD DUFF (*John Shaunessy*): "Oh, what do you call it? A success? The marriage ended in divorce."

**5.** "My wife used to always say to me, 'Why can't a woman have the same ambitions as a man?' I think you're right. And maybe I've learned that much, but by the same token, I'd like to know what law is it that says a woman is a better parent simply by virtue of her sex?"

*Hoffman, in court*

**6.** "I came here to take my son home, and I realized he already is home."

*Streep to Hoffman*

**LA STRADA** *(Italy: Trans-Lux, 1956). D: Federico Fellini. S: Federico Fellini, Tullio Pinelli, Ennio Flaiano. Fr: Federico Fellini, Tullio Pinelli (story).*

**FIRST LINE**

**1.** "Gelsomina! . . . Gelsomina!"

*Children's voices, calling to Giulietta Masina (Gelsomina) to advise her of the arrival of Anthony Quinn (Zampano) to take her away with his traveling show*

**2.** "You may not believe it, but everything that exists in the world has some purpose. Here—take that pebble there, for instance. . . . Well, even this serves some purpose—even this little pebble."

*Richard Basehart (Matto, the Fool) to Masina*

**3.** "Ladies and gentlemen, here is a chain and a hook a half-centimeter thick made of pig iron, stronger than steel. With the simple expansion of my pectoral muscles—that is to say, my chest—I shall shatter this hook. This piece of cloth is not meant to protect me but to spare the public the sight of blood if the hook tears my flesh. If anybody in the audience is squeamish, it's better not to watch."

*Quinn, performing his trademark stunt after Masina's death, giving his usual speech*

**LADY AND THE TRAMP** *(Buena Vista, 1955). D: Hamilton Luske, et al. S: Erdman*

Penner, Joe Rinaldi, Ralph Wright, Donald DaGradi. Fr: Ward Greene (novel).

**1.** "What a perfectly beautiful little lady!"

*Peggy Lee (Darling), giving Lady her name*

**2.** "Everybody knows that a dog's best friend is his human."

*Bill Baucon (Trusty)*

**LADY EVE, THE** (Paramount, 1941). D: Preston Sturges. S: Preston Sturges. Fr: Monckton Hoffe (story, "The Faithful Heart").

**1.** "Let us be crooked but never common."

*Charles Coburn (Colonel Harrington) to daughter and fellow card shark Barbara Stanwyck (Jean Harrington)*

**2.** PIKE'S PALE—THE ALE THAT WON FOR YALE

*Advertisement for the source of the Pike family fortune*

**3.** "Snakes are my life, in a way."

*Henry Fonda (Charles Pike) to Stanwyck, on his work as an ophiologist*

**4.** "There's as fine a specimen of the sucker sapiens as I've ever seen. There's a man who does card tricks."

*Coburn to Stanwyck, on Fonda*

**5.** "That's the tragedy of the rich. They don't need anything."

*Coburn to Fonda*

**6.** "No, thanks. I'd rather pay $32,000 than lose a really large amount."

*Fonda to Coburn, on an offer to recoup his losses at double or nothing*

**7.** "What I'm trying to say is, only I'm not a poet, I'm an ophiologist, I've always loved you."

*Fonda to Stanwyck*

**8.** "They say a moonlit deck is a woman's business office."

*Stanwyck to Fonda*

**9.** "See, Hopsy, you don't know very much about girls. The best ones aren't as good as you probably think, and the worst aren't as bad. Not nearly as bad."

*Stanwyck to Fonda, after he discovers her profession*

**10.** "You know you shouldn't draw to an inside straight."

*Coburn to crying Stanwyck, after Fonda rejects her*

**11.** "Don't you remember? He showed me how to palm things."

*Coburn, on how he palmed the $32,000 check he appeared to tear up*

**12.** "I've been English before."

*Stanwyck to Eric Blore (Sir Alfred McGlennon-Keith), on becoming his relative*

**13.** "I need him like the axe needs the turkey."

*Stanwyck to Coburn and Blore, on Fonda*

**14.** "Why don't you put on a bathing suit?"

*Eugene Pallette (Mr. Pike) to Fonda, as he ruins another tuxedo jacket*

**15.** "Oh, sorry. I thought it was the horse."

*Stanwyck to Fonda, when he nuzzles close*

**16.** "The union of two people for life, that is, marriage, shouldn't be taken lightly. . . .

Men, that is, lots of men, are more careful in choosing a tailor than they are in choosing a wife. . . . I think that if there's one time in your life to be careful, to weigh every pro and con, this is the time."

*Fonda to Stanwyck, proposing marriage*

**17.** "I wonder if now would be the time to tell you about Herman."

*Stanwyck to Fonda, relating her litany of lovers*

**18.** "But so am I darling, so am I."

*Stanwyck to Fonda, on being married*

**LAST LINE**
**19.** "Positively the same dame."

*William Demarest (Muggsy) on Stanwyck, reprising an earlier thought*

**LADY FROM SHANGHAI, THE** *(Columbia, 1948). D: Orson Welles. S: Orson Welles. Fr: Sherwood King (novel).*

**LAST LINE**
**1.** "Well, everybody is somebody's fool. The only way to stay out of trouble is to grow old, so I guess I'll concentrate on that. Maybe I'll live so long that I'll forget her. Maybe I'll die trying."

*Orson Welles (Michael O'Hara), on Rita Hayworth (Elsa Bannister)*

**LADY IN CEMENT** *(20th Century-Fox, 1968). D: Gordon Douglas. S: Marvin H. Albert, Jack Guss. Fr: Marvin H. Albert (novel).*

**1.** "She's one blonde I know didn't have more fun."

*Frank Sinatra (Tony Rome), referring to a murder victim found in cement at the bottom of the ocean at Miami Beach*

**2.** "Dumping people in cement. That went out with violin cases."

*Sinatra to Richard Conte (Lt. Dave Santini)*

**3.** RAQUEL WELCH (*Kit Forrest*): "I wonder how I would have turned out if I hadn't inherited a fortune."
SINATRA: "Well, I can think of a couple of occupations."

**4.** "You'd look good in a paper napkin."
*Sinatra to Welch*

**5.** "I lose my money scientifically."
*Sinatra to Welch, referring to how he bets on horses*

**6.** "The law works for the law. Rome works for money. That makes him easy to trust."
*Dan Blocker (Waldo Gronskey) to Conte*

**LADY OF BURLESQUE** *(UA, 1943). D: William A. Wellman. S: James Gunn. Fr: Gypsy Rose Lee (novel, The G-String Murders).*

**1.** "Girls! That's what the public wants!"
*J. Edward Bromberg (S. B. Foss), owner of the Old Opera House, on why the opera house was converted to a burlesque house*

**2.** "Beautiful, Junior, but it's not for me."
*Burlesque dancer Barbara Stanwyck (Dixie Daisy), on hearing sad music before breaking into song*

**3.** "The only date I make with a comic is the Sunday funnies."
*Stanwyck to comic Michael O'Shea (Biff Brannigan)*

**4.** "When I dress for a date with you, it'll be a suit of armor and brass knuckles."
*Stanwyck to O'Shea*

**5.** "It's gin. You know, alcohol, like they use in hospitals."

*Burlesque dancer, applying gin to the injured star of the show*

**6.** "I went into show business when I was seven years old. Two days later the first comic I ever met stole my piggy bank in a railroad station in Portland. When I was eleven, the comics were looking at my ankles. When I was fourteen, they were . . . just looking. When I was twenty, I'd been stuck with enough lunch checks to pay for a three-story house."

*Stanwyck to O'Shea, explaining why she isn't interested in comics like him*

**7.** "This is my first experience with burlesque. It's a surprising profession."

*Police inspector Charles Dingle (Harrigan) to burlesque performers, after a murder has been committed at their establishment*

**LADY VANISHES, THE** (UK: Gaumont/ Gainsborough Pictures/MGM, 1938). D: Alfred Hitchcock. S: Alma Reville, Sidney Gilliat, Frank Launder. Fr: Ethel Lina White (novel, The Wheel Spins).

**1.** "I've no regrets. I've been everywhere and done everything. I've eaten caviar at Cannes, sausage rolls at the dogs. I've played baccarat at Biarritz, and darts with the rural dean. What is there left for me but marriage?"

*Margaret Lockwood (Iris Henderson), contemplating her impending marriage*

**2.** "I never think you should judge any country by its politics. After all, we English are quite honest by nature, aren't we?"

*Dame May Whitty (Miss Froy)*

**3.** LOCKWOOD, to her annoying upstairs neighbor at a crowded hotel: "You're the most contemptible person I've ever met in all my life."

MICHAEL REDGRAVE (*Gilbert*): "Confidentially, I think you're a bit of a stick, too."

**4.** LOCKWOOD, to two cricket fanatics unwilling to get involved in the case of the missing Whitty: "Well, I don't see how a thing like cricket can make you forget seeing people."

BASIL RADFORD (*Charters*): "Oh, don't you? Well, if that's your attitude, obviously there's nothing more to be said."

**5.** "My theory was a perfectly good one. The facts were misleading."

*Psychiatrist Paul Lukas (Dr. Hartz), on his account of the disappearance of Whitty from the moving train*

**6.** "Do you know why you fascinate me? I'll tell you. You've got two grand qualities I used to admire in Father: You haven't any manners at all and you're always seeing things."

*Redgrave to Lockwood, who is convinced of the existence of the missing Whitty, which no one else is willing to corroborate*

**7.** "Yes, just British diplomacy, Doctor. Never climb a fence if you can sit on it. An old foreign office proverb."

*Redgrave, on why the British cricket fans denied seeing Whitty*

**8.** "Yes, thank you. It's rather like the rush hour on the underground."

*Whitty, on being taken from her hiding place in a cramped compartment*

**9.** "I mean, after all, people don't go about tying up nuns."

Radford, still unwilling to accept the strange events on the train

**LAST ACTION HERO** (Columbia, 1993). D: John McTiernan. S: Zak Penn, Adam Leff, Shane Black, David Arnott, William Goldman. Fr: Zak Penn, Adam Leff (story).

**1.** "This hero stuff has its limits."

Arnold Schwarzenegger (Sgt. Jack Slater), as if referring to the movie itself, which proved a box-office disappointment

**LAST HURRAH, THE** (Columbia, 1958). D: John Ford. S: Frank Nugent. Fr: Edwin O'Conner (novel).

**Last Line**

**1.** "Like hell I would."

Dying words of Spencer Tracy (Frank Skeffington)

**LAST OF THE MOHICANS, THE** (20th Century-Fox, 1992). D: Michael Mann. S: Michael Mann, Christopher Crowe. Fr: Philip Dunne (screenplay), James Fenimore Cooper (novel), John L. Balderston, Paul Perez, Daniel Moore (adaptation).

**1.** "I will find you!"

Daniel Day-Lewis (Nathaniel Poe/Hawkeye), vowing to come back for Madeleine Stowe (Cora Munro)

**LAST PICTURE SHOW, THE** (Columbia, 1971). D: Peter Bogdanovich. S: Peter Bogdanovich, Larry McMurtry. Fr: Larry McMurtry (novel).

**1.** TIMOTHY BOTTOMS (Sonny Crawford), on a high school football game: "Could have been worse."

BEN JOHNSON (Sam the Lion): "Yeah, you can say that about nearly everything, I guess."

**2.** ELLEN BURSTYN (Lois Farrow): "I scared your daddy into getting rich, Beautiful."

CYBILL SHEPHERD (Jacy Farrow): "Well, if Daddy could do it, Duane could too."

BURSTYN: "Not married to you. You're not scary enough."

**3.** "Just remember, Beautiful, everything gets old if you do it often enough."

Burstyn to Shepherd

**4.** CLORIS LEACHMAN (Ruth Popper): "Will you drive me to the clinic again this week?"

BOTTOMS: "You bet."

The couple beginning their unexpected affair

**5.** "One thing I know for sure—a person can't sneeze in this town without somebody offering him a handkerchief."

Eileen Brennan (Genevieve) to Bottoms

**6.** "Old times. I brought a young lady swimming out here once. More than twenty years ago. . . . We used to come out here on horseback and go swimming without no bathing suits. One day she wanted to swim the horses across this tank. . . . She bet me a silver dollar she could beat me across. She did. . . . She was always looking for something to do like that, something wild. I bet she's still got that silver dollar."

Johnson to Bottoms, about Burstyn

**7.** " 'Cause being crazy about a woman like her is always the right thing to do."

Johnson to Bottoms, about Burstyn

**8.** "Sam's dead. He was quite a fellow."

*Charlie Seybert (Andy Farmer) to Bottoms and Jeff Bridges (Duane Jackson)*

**9.** "I just can't describe it. I just can't describe it in words."

*Shepherd to girlfriends, following a supposed loss of virginity*

**10.** "I guess if it wasn't for Sam I'd just about have missed it, whatever it is."

*Burstyn to Bottoms*

**11.** "Old Sam the Lion. You know nobody knows where he got that name. I gave it to him."

*Burstyn to Bottoms*

**12.** "Nobody wants to come to shows no more."

*Jessie Lee Fulton (Miss Mosey) to Bottoms and Bridges, on the closing of the town movie theater*

**13.** "He was sweeping, you sons of bitches, he was sweeping."

*Bottoms to group of men asking why Sam Bottoms (Billy) was standing in the middle of the street when he was run over*

**LAST LINE**
**14.** "Never you mind, honey, never you mind."

*Leachman to Bottoms, as they tentatively reconcile*

**LAST TANGO IN PARIS** (Italy/France: UA, 1973). D: Bernardo Bertolucci. S: Bernardo Bertolucci, Franco Arcalli.

**1.** "Quo vadis, baby?"

*Marlon Brando (Paul) to Maria Schneider (Jeanne), as she is leaving the apartment*

**LAST TEMPTATION OF CHRIST, THE** (Universal, 1988). D: Martin Scorsese. S: Paul Schrader. Fr: Nikos Kazantzakis (novel).

**LAST LINE**
**1.** "It is accomplished! It is accomplished!"

*Willem Dafoe (Jesus Christ), dying on the cross*

**LAURA** (20th Century-Fox, 1944). D: Otto Preminger. S: Jay Dratler, Samuel Hoffenstein, Betty Reinhardt, Ring Lardner, Jr., Jerome Cady. Fr: Vera Caspary (novel).

**1.** "I shall never forget the weekend Laura died."

*Clifton Webb (Waldo Lydecker), reminiscing, in narration, on the death of Gene Tierney (Laura)*

**2.** "It's lavish, but I call it home."

*Webb to homicide detective Dana Andrews (Mark McPherson)*

**3.** "I am the most widely misquoted man in America. When my friends do it, I resent it. From Sergeants McAvity and Schultz, I should find it intolerable."

*Webb, a well-known columnist, explaining why he typed his report to the police*

**4.** "A doll in Washington Heights once got a fox fur out of me."

*Andrews to Webb, on whether he has ever been in love*

**5.** "I don't use a pen. I write with a goose quill dipped in venom."

*Webb to Tierney*

**6.** "In my case, self-absorption is completely justified."

*Webb to Tierney*

**7.** "I can afford a blemish on my character but not on my clothes."

*Foppish Vincent Price (Shelby Carpenter), on getting a stain off his clothes*

**8.** "There you are, my dear. In a moment of supreme disaster, he's trite."

*Webb, on Price's weak response when Price's companion, Tierney, finds him with another woman, Judith Anderson (Ann Treadwell)*

**9.** "You better watch out, McPherson, or you'll end up in a psychiatric ward. I don't think they've ever had a patient who fell in love with a corpse."

*Webb to Andrews, on his infatuation with the murdered Tierney*

**10.** "You're a vague sort of fellow, aren't you, Carpenter?"

*Andrews to Price*

**11.** "No, dear, I didn't. But I thought of it."

*Anderson, Tierney's rival for Price, on whether it was she who attempted to kill Tierney*

**12.** "Don't worry. I told you I'd bring in the killer today."

*Andrews to a police colleague, on the phone, startling eavesdroppers during a party*

**13.** "I'd reached a point where I needed official surroundings."

*Andrews, explaining to Tierney why he pretended to arrest her in order to question her*

**14.** "Laura, you have one tragic weakness. With you, a lean, strong body is the measure of a man, and you always get hurt."

*Webb to Tierney*

**15.** "I hope you'll never regret what promises to be a disgustingly earthy relationship."

*Webb to Tierney*

**16.** "The best part of myself—that's what you are. Do you think I'm going to leave it to the vulgar pawing of a second-rate detective who thinks you're a dame?"

*Webb on why he intends to kill Tierney*

**LAST LINE**
**17.** "Good-bye, Laura. Good-bye, my love."

*Webb's dying words*

**LAVENDER HILL MOB, THE** (UK: General Film Distributors, 1951). D: Charles Crichton. S: T. E. B. Clarke.

**1.** "Most men who long to be rich, know inwardly that they will never achieve their ambition, but I was in the unique position of having a fortune literally within my grasp, for it was my job to supervise the deliveries of bullion from the gold refinery to the bank."

*Alec Guinness (Henry Holland), in narration*

**2.** "I like the bullion office. It holds all I ever wished for."

*Guinness, when he's offered a promotion at the office he robs*

**3.** "Enough to keep me for one year in the style to which I was unaccustomed."

*Guinness, in narration, explaining just how much money he stole*

**LAWRENCE OF ARABIA** (UK: Columbia, 1962). D: David Lean. S: Robert Bolt, Michael Wilson. Fr: T. E. Lawrence (book, The Seven Pillars of Wisdom).

**1.** "He was a poet, a scholar, and a mighty warrior. . . . He was also the most shameless exhibitionist since Barnum and Bailey."

Arthur Kennedy (Jackson Bentley), eulogizing Peter O'Toole (T. E. Lawrence) to a reporter and, in an aside, to a companion

**2.** "The trick, William Potter, is not minding that it hurts."

*O'Toole to Harry Fowler (Corporal Potter), on the trick he uses in putting out a match with his fingers*

**3.** "Of course I'm the man for the job. What is the job, by the way?"

*O'Toole to Claude Rains (Mr. Dryden), accepting a mission in Arabia*

**4.** "Sherif Ali, so long as the Arabs fight tribe against tribe, so long will they be a little people, a silly people, greedy, barbarous, and cruel, as you are."

*O'Toole to Omar Sharif (Sherif Ali)*

**5.** "To England, and to other things."

*O'Toole to Alec Guinness (Prince Feisal), on whether he is loyal to England*

**6.** "Aqaba. Aqaba—from the land."

*O'Toole, realizing how to capture the port of Aqaba*

**7.** SHARIF, on crossing the waterless Nefud desert: "If the camels die, we die. And in twenty days they will start to die."
O'TOOLE: "There's no time to waste then, is there?"

**8.** "Nothing is written."

*O'Toole, on being told that it is written that I. S. Johar (Gasim) will die*

**9.** "With Major Lawrence, mercy is a passion. With me, it is merely good manners. You may judge which motive is the more reliable."

*Guinness to Kennedy, on O'Toole*

**10.** "It's clean."

*O'Toole, on what attracts him to the desert*

**11.** "He can, but he can't want what he wants. This is the stuff that decides what he wants."

*O'Toole, pinching his chest, when Ali says a man can do whatever he wants*

**12.** "If we've told lies, you've told half-lies, and a man who tells lies, like me, merely hides the truth, but a man who tells half-lies has forgotten where he put it."

*Rains to O'Toole*

**13.** "I don't want to be part of your big push!"

*O'Toole to Jack Hawkins (General Allenby), refusing to take part in his military operation*

**14.** "Not many people have a destiny, Lawrence. It's a terrible thing for a man to flunk it if he has."

*Hawkins to O'Toole*

**15.** "No prisoners! No prisoners!"

*O'Toole, shouting as he leads the charge on the Turkish column*

**16.** "I pray that I may never see the desert again. Hear me God."

*O'Toole to Anthony Quinn (Auda Abu Tayi)*

**17.** "If I fear him who love him, how must he fear himself who hates himself?"

*Sharif to Quinn, on O'Toole*

**18.** "Young men make wars, and the virtues of war are the virtues of young men—courage and hope for the future. Then old men make the peace, and the vices of peace are the vices of old men—mistrust and caution. It must be so."

Guinness, preparing to talk peace with
Hawkins and Rains

**LAST LINE**

*19.* "Well, sir. Goin' 'ome. . . . 'Ome, sir."

Driver to O'Toole, on the road out of Damascus,
on the first leg of his journey back to England

**LEAP OF FAITH** (Paramount, 1992). D:
Richard Pearce. S: Janus Cercone.

*1.* "Gee, Lowell, you could've at least
bought me dinner first."

Itinerant revival preacher and charlatan Steve
Martin (Jonas Nightengale), getting frisked by
a police officer

*2.* "A town this deep in the crapper's got
nowhere to turn but *God!*"

Martin, explaining his choice of location for a
revival

*3.* "Always look better than they do."

One of Martin's rules of showmanship

*4.* "Well, maybe I am, and maybe I'm not,
but I get the job done, what difference does
it make?"

Martin, on whether he's a fake

*5.* "Gidget goes dust bowl."

Martin, getting fed up with his assistant Debra
Winger's (Jane's) romantic involvement with
small-town sheriff Liam Neeson (Will)

*6.* "Yakkity-yak! God's talking back!"

Martin, in an onstage religious frenzy

*7.* "All he's doing is selling fairy tales to a
bunch of people who thank him for it."

Winger, on Martin's line of work

*8.* "Places to go and people to do."

One of Martin's favorite slogans

*9.* "Manipulators are sneaky. I'm obvious."

Martin, on the difference between him and a
manipulator

*10.* "All right, let's get some empty lives a
little meaning!"

Martin, preparing to go to work

*11.* "The one thing you can never, ever get
around is the genuine article, and you, kid,
are the genuine article."

Martin to disabled boy Lukas Haas (Boyd),
whose faith really has healed him

**LAST LINE**

*12.* "C'mon, baby, rain! Rain! Thank you,
Jesus! Wahoo! Wahoo!"

Martin, as long-awaited rain falls on the road

**LETHAL WEAPON** (Warner Bros., 1987).
D: Richard Donner. S: Shane Black.

*1.* "That's a real badge. I'm a real cop. And
this is a real gun."

Mel Gibson (Martin Riggs) to drug dealers

*2.* "I suppose we have to register you as a
lethal weapon."

Danny Glover (Roger Murtaugh) to Gibson

*3.* "God hates me. That's what it is."

Glover, when Gibson is made his partner

*4.* "Do you really want to jump? Do you
want to? Well, then that's fine with me!"

Gibson to a jumper, just before they jump off a
building

**5.** "Every single day, I wake up and I think of a reason not to do it. Every single day. And you know why I don't do it? This is going to make you laugh. You know why I don't do it? The job. Doing the job. Now, that's the reason."

*Gibson to Glover, on committing suicide*

**6.** GLOVER: "You ever met anybody you didn't kill?"
GIBSON: "Well, I haven't killed you yet."
GLOVER: "Don't do me any favors."

**7.** "You're going to have to trust me."

*Gibson to Glover*

**LAST LINE**
**8.** "I'm too old for this."

*Glover*

**LETTER, THE** *(Warner Bros.–First National, 1940). D: William Wyler. S: Howard Koch. Fr: W. Somerset Maugham (story).*

**1.** "He tried to make love to me and I shot him."

*Bette Davis (Leslie Crosbie) to Herbert Marshall (Robert Crosbie)*

**2.** "There are men who think it's their duty to flirt with women."

*Davis to policeman Bruce Lester (John Withers)*

**3.** "When I leave Leslie alone for the night, I always feel safe if she has a weapon handy."

*Marshall*

**4.** "Howard, I swear to you I did not write this letter."

*Davis to lawyer James Stephenson (Howard Joyce)*

**5.** "I don't want you to tell me anything but what is needed to save your neck."

*Stephenson to Davis*

**6.** "Strange that a man can live with a woman for ten years and not know the first thing about her."

*Stephenson*

**7.** "Juries can sometimes be very stupid, and it's just as well not to worry them with more evidence than they can conviently deal with."

*Stephenson to Marshall*

**8.** "Buying that letter was a criminal offense—wasn't it?"

*Marshall to Stephenson*

**9.** "There is no excuse for me. I don't deserve to live."

*Davis*

**10.** "With all my heart, I still love the man I killed."

*Davis to Marshall*

**LETTER TO THREE WIVES, A** *(20th Century-Fox, 1949). D: Joseph L. Mankiewicz. S: Joseph L. Mankiewicz. Fr: John Klempner (novel), Vera Caspary (adaptation).*

**1.** "It isn't easy to leave a town like our town, to tear myself away from you three dear, dear friends who meant so much to me. And so I consider myself extremely lucky to be able to take with me a sort of memento. Something to remind me always of the town that was my home, and of my three very dearest friends—whom I want never to forget. And I won't. You see, girls, I've run off with one of your husbands."

*Celeste Holm (Voice of Addie Ross) in voice-over, reading her letter to Jeanne Crain (Deborah Bishop), Linda Darnell (Lora May Hollingsway), and Ann Sothern (Rita Phipps)*

**2.** "I'm willing to admit that, to a majority of my fellow citizens, I'm a slightly comic figure: an educated man."

*Kirk Douglas (George Phipps), describing his lowly position on the ladder of suburban society*

**3.** "Do you know what I like about your program? Even when I'm running the vacuum, I can understand it."

*Housekeeper Thelma Ritter (Sadie), praising the radio program written by Sothern*

**LIFE OF EMILE ZOLA, THE** (Warner Bros., 1937). D: William Dieterle. S: Norman Reilly Raine, Heinz Herald, Geza Herczeg. Fr: Heinz Herald, Geza Herczeg (story).

**1.** "Not only is an innocent man crying out for justice, but more, much more—a great nation is in desperate danger of forfeiting her honor!"

*Paul Muni (Emile Zola), in the courtroom*

**LIFE WITH FATHER** (Warner Bros.–First National, 1947). D: Michael Curtiz. S: Donald Ogden Stewart. Fr: Howard Lindsay, Russel Crouse (play), Clarence Day, Jr. (book).

**1.** "King Solomon had the right idea about work. 'Whatever thy hand findeth to do,' Solomon said, 'do thy doggonedest.'"

*William Powell (Father) to James Lydon (Clarence)*

**2.** "I just couldn't go to Heaven without Clare. Why, I get lonesome for him even when I go to Ohio."

*Irene Dunne (Vinnie), about Powell*

**3.** "Why did God make so many dumb fools and Democrats?"

*Powell*

**LIFEBOAT** (20th Century-Fox, 1944). D: Alfred Hitchcock. S: Jo Swerling. Fr: John Steinbeck (story).

**1.** "I can recommend the bait. I ought to know—I bit on it myself."

*Lifeboat survivor Tallulah Bankhead (Constance Porter), offering her diamonds as fish bait*

**LILIES OF THE FIELD** (UA, 1963). D: Ralph Nelson. S: James Poe. Fr: William E. Barrett (novel).

**FIRST LINES**
**1.** SIDNEY POITIER (*Homer Smith*): "My car's thirsty. Can I please have some water?"
LILIA SKALA (*Mother Maria*): "God is good. He has sent me a big, strong man."

**2.** "That's a Catholic breakfast? One egg?"

*Poitier, when he's served a fried egg and a cup of milk*

**3.** "If you're still listening, Lord, would you mind putting a little meat on the table?"

*Poitier, when Skala prays to God*

**4.** "How about thanking me, too, eh?"

*Poitier to Skala, when she thanks God for the food Poitier has just brought*

**5.** "You know, you are very large on religion and all the rest of it, but you don't even know how to accept a gift from somebody without making them feel small. Small! You follow?"

*Poiter to Skala*

**6.** "You know that stuff you wear? You think it's a uniform that makes you some kind of a cop, or something, laying down the law. Throwing your weight around. You sound like one of them old war movies. A regular Hitler!"

*Poitier to Skala*

**7.** "God is building out there a chapel, and you sit here feeling sorry for yourself because you are not Him."

*Skala to Poitier, when the townspeople help*

**8.** "To me, life is here on this Earth. I cannot see further, so I cannot believe further. But, if they are right about the hereafter, I have paid my insurance."

*Stanley Adams (Juan) to contractor Ralph Nelson (Ashton), explaining why he is helping build the chapel*

**9.** "This spot is mine."

*Poitier, when he refuses help putting up the cross*

**LIMELIGHT** *(UA, 1952). D: Charles Chaplin. S: Charles Chaplin.*

**1.** "There's something about working the streets I like. It's the tramp in me, I suppose."

*Charlie Chaplin (Calvero)*

**LION IN WINTER, THE** *(Avco Embassy, 1968). D: Anthony Harvey. S: James Goldman. Fr: James Goldman (play).*

**1.** "How dear of you to let me out of jail."

*Katharine Hepburn (Eleanor of Aquitaine) to husband Peter O'Toole (Henry II)*

**2.** "Had I been sterile, darling, I'd be happier today."

*Hepburn to son Anthony Hopkins (Prince Richard the Lion-Hearted)*

**3.** "Well, what family doesn't have its ups and downs?"

*Hepburn, on the intrigues in the royal household*

**LAST LINE**
**4.** "Do you think there's any chance of it?"

*O'Toole, on Hepburn's hope that they never die*

**LIST OF ADRIAN MESSENGER, THE** *(Universal, 1963). D: John Huston. S: Anthony Veillier. Fr: Philip MacDonald (novel).*

**1.** "Adrian was a writer. And he chose his words very carefully. When he said, 'Nary a conspiracy,' he meant just that. There was only one man involved. One man who becomes many men."

*George C. Scott (Anthony Gethryn), who is investigating why eleven men on a list are being killed one by one*

**2.** "Eleven names. And then there were none."

*Scott, when the last man is dead*

**3.** "I spent the rest of that winter trailing the pack. One by one, I shot them, and skinned them out. Traded their pelts to the Indians for enough food to go on until the last wolf was accounted for."

*Kirk Douglas (George Bruttenholm), referring to avenging his father's death by a pack of wolves*

**4.** "That's the excuse they usually give for evil. Hitler was mad, they said. So he may have been, but not necessarily. Evil does exist. Evil is."

*Douglas to Dana Wynter (Lady Jocelyn Brutten-holm), referring to madness*

**5.** "Ladies and gentlemen. The end."

*Douglas, as himself, to the audience*

**LITTLE BIG MAN** *(Cinema Center/National General, 1970). D: Arthur Penn. S: Calder Willingham. Fr: Thomas Berger (novel).*

**1.** "My heart soars like a hawk."

*Chief Dan George's (Old Lodge Skins's) way of saying he is pleased*

**LITTLE CAESAR** *(Warner Bros.–Vitaphone, 1930). D: Mervyn LeRoy. S: Robert N. Lee, Darryl Zanuck, Francis Edward Faragoh (uncredited), Robert Lord. Fr: W. R. Burnett (novel).*

**1.** "Oh, Little Caesar, huh?"

*Gang leader Stanley Fields (Sam Vettori), giving new gang member Edward G. Robinson (Caesar Enrico Bandelli) a moniker*

**2.** "You think I'm going to let a guy pull a gat on me?"

*Robinson to Fields, on killing the crime commissioner*

**3.** "You can dish it out, but you got so you can't take it no more."

*Robinson to Fields, on taking over Fields's territory*

**4.** "This is Rico speaking. Rico! R-I-C-O! Rico! Little Caesar, that's who! Listen, you crummy, flat-footed copper, I'll show you whether I've lost my nerve and my brains!"

*Robinson, now a has-been, on the phone to Tom Jackson (Sergeant Flaherty)*

**5.** "You want me, you're going to have to come and get me!"

*Robinson, taunting police*

**LAST LINE**
**6.** "Mother of Mercy! Is this the end of Rico?"

*Robinson's dying words, after he is gunned down by police*

**LITTLE FOXES, THE** *(RKO, 1941). D: William Wyler. S: Lillian Hellman, Arthur Kober, Dorothy Parker, Alan Campbell. Fr: Lillian Hellman (play).*

**1.** "I hate conversations before I've had something hot."

*Bette Davis (Regina Giddens)*

**2.** "The rich can be as eccentric as they like."

*Davis*

**3.** "Cynicism is an unpleasant way of telling the truth."

*Charles Dingle (Ben Hubbard) to Davis*

**4.** "I don't ask for things I don't think I can get."

*Davis*

**5.** "Our grandmother and grandfather were first cousins. Yes, and look at us."

*Carl Benton Reid (Oscar Hubbard) to Davis*

**6.** "They've gotten mighty well off cheatin' the po'. Well, dar's people that eats up the whole earth and all the people on it—like in the Bible with the locust. Then dar's people dat stand around and watch 'em do it. Sometimes I think t'ain't right justa stand and watch 'em do it."

*Jessie Grayson (Addie) to group*

**7.** "Leo, you're one of the people who bore me, and I'm gettin' too old to wanna be bored."

*Dingle to Dan Duryea (Ben Hubbard)*

**8.** "I don't hate you. That's because I remember how much I was in love with you."

*Herbert Marshall (Horace Giddens) to Davis*

**9.** "I was lonely for all the things I wasn't going to get."

*Davis to Marshall*

**10.** "Trouble brings us together."

*Davis to Dingle*

**11.** "We'll own this country someday."

*Dingle to Davis*

**12.** "I'm going to get you the world I always wanted."

*Davis to daughter Teresa Wright (Alexandra Giddens)*

**LITTLE MERMAID, THE** (Buena Vista, 1989). D: John Musker, Ron Clements. S: Jon Musker, Ron Clements. Fr: Hans Christian Andersen (fairy tale).

**1.** "Teenagers: They think they know everything. You give them an inch, they swim all over you."

*Sam Wright (Sebastian the Crab), remarking on Jodi Benson's (Ariel's) attitude*

**2.** "I hope you appreciate what I go through for you, young lady."

*Wright to Benson*

**3.** "Life's full of tough choices."

*Pat Carroll (Ursula the Sea Witch), when she gives Benson the ability to be human, and Ben-*
son won't be able to see her sisters or her father again

**4.** "Have I ever been wrong? I mean when it's important?"

*Buddy Hackett (Scuttle the Seagull), telling Wright and Benson that Christopher Daniel Barnes (Erik) is marrying Carroll in disguise*

**5.** "Just look at her! On legs! On human legs! My nerves are shot! This is a catastrophe! What would her father say? I'll tell you what her father'd say! He'd say he's gonna kill himself a crab!"

*Wright, after Benson turns into a human*

**6.** "It's time Ursula took matters into her own tentacles!"

*Carroll, to herself*

**LITTLE SHOP OF HORRORS, THE** (Filmgroup, 1960). D: Roger Corman. S: Charles B. Griffith.

**1.** "It grows like a cold sore from the lip."

*Plant store owner Mel Welles (Gravis Mushnik), describing the rapid growth of Audrey Junior, the monster plant that eats people*

**2.** "Gee, that sure is a mad plant!"

*Teenage girl, impressed by the monster plant*

**3.** "Girls, girls, please don't damage the horticulturist."

*Welles, holding adoring fans back from nerdy Jonathan Haze (Seymour Krelboin), who has nurtured Audrey Junior into being*

**4.** "Feed me!"

*Audrey Junior, hungry for a meal*

**5.** "I have three or four abscesses, a touch of pyrrhea, nine or ten cavities, I lost my pivot tooth, and I'm in terrible pain."

*Masochistic dental patient Jack Nicholson (Wilbur Force), gleefully recounting his misfortunes*

**6.** "No Novocain—it dulls the senses."

*Nicholson, refusing anesthetic during his dental work*

**7.** "Take it easy, Dracula, what do you think I'm carrying here, my dirty laundry?"

*Haze, calming his hungry plant down while he brings it a bag containing its dinner, a human corpse*

**8.** "My name is Fink. Sergeant Joe Fink. I'm a Fink."

*Police sergeant in voice-over, sounding like Joe Friday of the TV show "Dragnet"*

**9.** "You dirty rat plant, you messed up my whole life!"

*Haze, fed up with the murderous ways of his plant*

**LIVES OF A BENGAL LANCER, THE** *(Paramount, 1935). D: Henry Hathaway. S: Waldemar Young, John L. Balderston, Achmed Abdullah, Grover Jones, William Slavens McNutt. Fr: Maj. Francis Yeats-Brown (novel).*

**1.** "I can't imagine old ramrod ever having been that human."

*Gary Cooper (Captain McGregor)*

**2.** "You keep them shined and I'll keep them dirty."

*Franchot Tone (Lieutenant Fortesque), to the man helping him put his boots on*

**3.** "What's a son to him compared to his blasted regiment?"

*Cooper, on Sir Guy Standing's (Colonel Stone's) coldness to his own son*

**4.** "I thought you might get lonesome. Get yourself a cobra."

*Cooper to Tone, handing him a snake-charming flute*

**5.** "So you'll sit here with your regiment while they kill your son by inches. Well, I won't. I'm going after him whether you like it or not."

*Cooper to Standing, when his son is kidnapped*

**6.** "If that's what you call being a man, or a soldier, I don't want any part of it."

*Cooper to Standing, when he lets his son be tortured*

**7.** "Man, you are blind! Have you never thought how for generation after generation, a handful of men have ordered the lives of three hundred million people? It's because he's here and a few more like him. Men of his breed have made a British India. Men who have put their jobs above everything."

*C. Aubrey Smith (Major Hamilton) to Cooper, on Standing*

**LOGAN'S RUN** *(MGM/UA, 1976). D: Michael Anderson. S: David Zelag Goodman. Fr: William F. Nolan, George Clayton Johnson (novel).*

**1.** "There is no sanctuary!"

*Michael York (Logan), shattering the illusions of the computer that runs his domed city of the future*

**LONE RANGER, THE** *(Warner Bros., 1955).*
*D: Stuart Heisler. S: Herb Meadow. Fr:*
*"Lone Ranger" legend.*

***1.*** "Hi-yo, Silver!"

*Clayton Moore (The Lone Ranger)*

**LONELY ARE THE BRAVE** *(Universal,*
*1962). D: David Miller. S: Dalton Trumbo.*
*Fr: Edward Abbey (novel, Brave Cowboy).*

***1.*** "Believe you me, if it didn't take men to
make babies I wouldn't have anything to do
with any of you!"

*Gena Rowlands (Jerri Bondi) to Kirk Douglas*
*(Jack Burns)*

**LONG GOOD FRIDAY, THE** *(UK: Hand-*
*made Films/Embassy, 1980). D: John*
*Mackenzie. S: Barrie Keefe.*

***1.*** "Colin never hurt a fly. Well, only when it
was necessary."

*Bob Hoskins (Harold Shand), lamenting over*
*his dead colleague*

**LONG, HOT SUMMER, THE** *(20th Century-*
*Fox, 1958). D: Martin Ritt. S: Irving Ravetch,*
*Harriet Frank, Jr. Fr: William Faulkner (fic-*
*tion).*

**LAST LINE**
***1.*** "Oh, I like life, Minnie. I like it so much I
might just live forever."

*Orson Welles (Will Varner) to Angela Lansbury*
*(Minnie Littlejohn)*

**LONGEST DAY, THE** *(20th Century-Fox,*
*1963). D: Andrew Marton, Ken Annakin,*
*Bernhard Wicki. S: Cornelius Ryan, Romain*
Gary, James Jones, David Pursel, Jack Sed-
*don. Fr: Cornelius Ryan (book).*

***1.*** "Sometimes I wonder whose side God's
on."

*John Wayne (Lt. Col. Benjamin Vandervoort)*

**LORD JIM** *(UK: Columbia, 1965). D:*
*Richard Brooks. S: Richard Brooks. Fr:*
*Joseph Conrad (novel).*

**LAST LINE**
***1.*** "I had my chance, Father, and I lost. If I
lose without honor, if at the last moment I
weaken, then it's all without meaning,
wasted."

*Peter O'Toole (Lord Jim), accepting death*

**LOST BOYS, THE** *(Warner Bros., 1987). D:*
*Joel Schumacher. S: Janice Fischer, James*
*Jeremias, Jeffrey Boam. Fr: Janice Fischer,*
*James Jeremias (story).*

**LAST LINE**
***1.*** "One thing about living in Santa Carla I
never could stomach was all the damn vampires."

*Barnard Hughes (Grandpa)*

**LOST HORIZON** *(Columbia, 1937). D:*
*Frank Capra. S: Robert Riskin. Fr: James*
*Hilton (novel).*

***1.*** "A way of life based on one simple rule:
Be kind."

*Sam Jaffe (High Lama) describing Shangri-La*

**LAST LINE**
***2.*** "Gentlemen, I give you a toast. Here's
my hope that Robert Conway will find his

Shangri-La. Here's my hope that we all find our Shangri-La."

> Hugh Buckler (Lord Gainsford), on Ronald Colman (Robert Conway)

**LOST IN AMERICA** (Warner Bros., 1985). D: Albert Brooks. S: Albert Brooks, Monica Johnson.

**1.** "I've seen the future! It's a bald-headed man from New York!"

> Albert Brooks (David Howard)

**LOST WEEKEND, THE** (Paramount, 1945). D: Billy Wilder. S: Charles Brackett, Billy Wilder. Fr: Charles R. Jackson (novel).

**1.** "What I'm trying to say is, I'm not a drinker—I'm a drunk."

> Ray Milland (Don Birnam) to Jane Wyman (Helen St. James)

**LAST LINE**
**2.** "My mind was hanging outside the window. It was suspended just about eighteen inches below. And out there in that great big concrete jungle, I wonder how many others there are like me. Those poor bedeviled guys on fire with thirst. Such comical figures to the rest of the world as they stagger blindly towards another binge, another bender, another spree."

> Milland, referring to his habit of keeping bottles in various hiding places

**LOVE AND DEATH** (UA, 1975). D: Woody Allen. S: Woody Allen.

**1.** "You know, if, if it turns out that there is a God, I don't think that he's evil. I think that, that the worst you could say about him is that basically he's an underachiever."

> Woody Allen (Boris), meditating on God

**LAST LINE**
**2.** "The, the key here, I think, is to, to not think of death as an end, but, but think of it more as a very effective way of, of cutting down on your expenses. Regarding love, huh, you know, uh, what can you say? It's, it's not the, the quantity of your sexual relations that count, it's the quality. On the other hand, if the quantity drops below once every eight months, I would definitely look into it. Well, that's about it for me, folks. Good-bye."

> Allen's concluding thoughts

**LOVE AT FIRST BITE** (AIP, 1979). D: Stan Dragoti. S: Robert Kaufman. Fr: Robert Kaufman, Mark Gindes (story).

**1.** "Fun? How would you like to go around dressed like a headwaiter for the last seven hundred years?"

> George Hamilton (Count Dracula), discussing the vampire's life with Arte Johnson (Renfield)

**LOVE BUG, THE** (Buena Vista, 1969). D: Robert Stevenson. S: Don DaGradi, Bill Walsh. Fr: Gordon Buford (story).

**1.** "There's nothing essentially wrong with the car. It's just that it wants to go one way, and I'd like to go another."

> Dean Jones (Jim Douglas), returning Herbie to David Tomlinson (Thorndyke)

**2.** "Jim, it's happening right under our noses and we can't see it. We take machines and we stuff them with information until they're smarter than we are. Take a car. Most guys spread more love and time and money on a car in a week than they do on their wife and kids in a year. Pretty soon, you know what? The machine starts to think it is somebody."

*Buddy Hackett (Tennessee Steinmetz)*

**3.** "Named after my Uncle Herb. Used to box middleweight. Preliminary mostly. Gradually his nose got shaped more and more like to remind me of this little car."

*Hackett*

**4.** "I salute your honesty, my dear. A quality not necessarily to be despised."

*Tomlinson to Michele Lee (Carole), when she admits to accepting a dinner invitation from Jones*

**5.** HACKETT: "It's heart. That's what it is: heart."

TOMLINSON: "Heart. Yes, I'm certainly going to make a note of that."

**6.** "I imagine Adam thought woman was a pretty funny piece of equipment when he met Eve."

*Lee to Hackett, when he tries to explain Herbie to her*

**LOVE IS A MANY SPLENDORED THING** *(20th Century-Fox, 1955). D: Henry King. S: John Patrick. Fr: Han Suyin (novel, A Many Splendored Thing).*

**1.** "We have not missed, you and I—we have not missed that many splendored thing."

*William Holden (Mark Elliott), in a posthumously delivered letter to Jennifer Jones (Han Suyin)*

**LOVE STORY** *(Paramount, 1970). D: Arthur Hiller. S: Erich Segal. Fr: Erich Segal (novel).*

**FIRST LINE**
**1.** "What can you say about a twenty-five-year-old girl who died? That she was beautiful and brilliant? That she loved Mozart and Bach, the Beatles, and me?"

*Ryan O'Neal (Oliver Barrett IV) to himself*

**2.** "You're a preppie millionaire and I'm a social zero."

*Ali MacGraw (Jenny Cavilleri) to O'Neal, on why they should break up*

**3.** "I just want time, which you can't give me."

*MacGraw to O'Neal, when she finds out she is dying*

**4.** O'NEAL: "I'm not Barrett Hall. My great-grandfather happened to give the thing to Harvard."

MACGRAW: "So his not-so-great grandson would be able to get in."

**5.** O'NEAL: "I major in Social Studies."
MACGRAW: "It doesn't show."

**6.** MACGRAW: "You're a known quantity, Barrett."
O'NEAL: "Meaning?"
MACGRAW: "You're known for quantity."

**7.** O'NEAL: "You're not that great-looking."
MACGRAW: "I know, but can I help it if you think so?"

**LAST LINE**
**8.** "Love means never having to say you're sorry."

*O'Neal to Ray Milland (Oliver Barrett III), quoting MacGraw when Milland tells O'Neal he's sorry that MacGraw is dead*

**LOVE WITH THE PROPER STRANGER** (Paramount, 1963). D: Robert Mulligan. S: Arnold Schulman.

**1.** "Better wed than dead."

Steve McQueen (Rocky Papasano), proposing to Natalie Wood (Angie Rossini)

**LOVER COME BACK** (Universal, 1961). D: Delbert Mann. S: Stanley Shapiro, Paul Henning.

**1.** "That's the last guy in the world I would have figured."

Businessman, watching Rock Hudson (Jerry Webster) walk around in a lady's fur coat after he has been left stranded without his clothes by Doris Day (Carol Templeton)

**2.** "I have given this country what it has long needed—a good ten–cent drink."

Jack Kruschen (Dr. Linus Tyler) to advertising executive Tony Randall (Peter Ramsey), on the new alcohol–laden candy, VIP

**3.** "I'm king of the elevator!"

Randall, riding the elevator cable after taking too much VIP

**4.** "It's like olives, dear. It's something you acquire a taste for."

Hotel maid, discussing marriage with newly-wed Day

**LAST LINE**
**5.** "Man, that's what I call cutting it close."

Hospital staffer, watching Hudson and Day complete their marriage vows just as she is wheeled into the delivery room

**LOVERS AND OTHER STRANGERS** (Cinerama, 1970). D: Cy Howard. S: Renee Taylor, Joseph Bologna, David Zelag Goodman. Fr: Renee Taylor, Joseph Bologna (play).

**1.** "So what's the story?"

Richard Castellano (Johnny)

**M** (Germany: Nero Film/Paramount, 1931). D: Fritz Lang. S: Fritz Lang, Thea von Harbou, Paul Falkenberg, Adolf Jansen, Karl Vash. Fr: Egon Jacobson (article).

**1.** "I can't help myself!"

Peter Lorre (Franz Becker), on why he has molested and murdered children

**M*A*S*H** (Aspen/20th Century–Fox, 1970). D: Robert Altman. S: Ring Lardner, Jr. Fr: Richard Hooker (novel).

**FIRST LINE**
**1.** ROGER BOWEN (Col. Henry Blake): "Radar!"

GARY BURGHOFF (Radar O'Reilly): "Yes, sir."

Bowen and his prescient aide Burghoff, whose responses usually overlap or precede his commander's

**2.** "Frank, were you on this religious kick at home or did you crack up over here?"

Donald Sutherland (Hawkeye Pierce) to Robert Duvall (Maj. Frank Burns)

**3.** "Yes, but a man can't really savor his martini without an olive, you know. Otherwise, you see, it just doesn't quite . . . make it."

Elliott Gould (Trapper John McIntyre) to Sutherland, as he drops an olive, mysteriously taken from a jar in his coat, into his martini

**4.** "Attention, camp combat. Urine speci- mens will be required from all pers—uh— ee—disregard last transmission."

*Loudspeaker announcer making a typical loony transmission*

**5.** "I mean, you're what we call a regular Army clown."

*Sutherland to Sally Kellerman (Maj. Hot Lips Houlihan)*

**6.** KELLERMAN, on Sutherland: "I wonder how a degenerated person like that could have reached a position of responsibility in the Army Medical Corps."
RENÉ AUBERJONOIS (*Chaplain Dago Red*): "He was drafted."

**7.** "Godless buffoons, all of them."

*Duvall to Kellerman, on their comrades in the MASH unit*

**8.** "Oh, Frank, my lips are hot. Kiss my hot lips."

*Kellerman, making love to Duvall, broadcast over the camp public address system*

**9.** "Hawkeye's questioning the major on a point of anatomy."

*Burghoff, reporting to Bowen on Sutherland's questioning of Duvall about the specifics of his broadcast tryst with Kellerman*

**10.** "You have the privilege that happens on certain occasions to chief executives of states or nations. You have the privilege of restoring a human being's life by a tender act of mercy."

*Sutherland, urging Jo Ann Pflug (Lieutenant Dish) to have sex with dentist John Schuck (Pain- less Pole), whose worry about impotence has driven him to attempt suicide*

**11.** "This isn't a hospital! It's an insane asylum!"

*Kellerman to Bowen, outraged after the shower tent is pulled up while she is taking a shower*

**12.** KELLERMAN, hearing a gunshot during a football game: "My God, they've shot him!"
BOWEN: "Hot Lips, you incredible nin- compoop, it's the end of the quarter."

**13.** "Attention: Tonight's movie has been M*A*S*H. Follow the zany antics of our combat surgeons as they cut and stitch their way along the front lines, operating as bombs—I mean, bombs and bullets burst around them, snatching laughs and loves between amputations and penicillin."

*Loudspeaker announcer, at film's end*

**14.** BOWEN: "Did Hawkeye steal that jeep?"
BURGHOFF: "No, sir, that's the one he came in."
BOWEN: "Oh, very good, come along, my dear."

*Burghoff, Bowen, and Bowen's mistress watch- ing Sutherland drive off in a stolen jeep, reca- pitulating his arrival in the very same stolen jeep*

**LAST LINE**
**15.** "That is all."

*Loudspeaker announcer signing off*

**MACARTHUR** (Universal, 1977). D: Joseph Sargent. S: Hal Barwood, Matthew Rob- bins.

**1.** "Today marks my final roll call with you. I want you to know that when I cross the river, my last conscious thoughts will be of the Corps, and the Corps, and the Corps. I bid you farewell."

*Gregory Peck (Gen. Douglas MacArthur)*

214

## MAGNIFICENT AMBERSONS, THE (RKO, 1942). D: Orson Welles. S: Orson Welles. Fr: Booth Tarkington (novel).

FIRST LINE

**1.** "The magnificence of the Ambersons began in 1873."

*Orson Welles (Narrator), in voice-over*

**2.** "The family always liked to have someone in Congress."

*Tim Holt (George Amberson Minafer), attempting to impress Anne Baxter (Lucy Morgan)*

**3.** "Anybody that really is anybody ought to be able to go about as they like in their own town, I should think."

*Holt to Baxter*

**4.** "Old times. Not a bit. There aren't any old times. The times are gone. They're not old. They're dead. There aren't any times but new times."

*Joseph Cotten (Eugene Morgan) to Ray Collins (Jack Amberson)*

**5.** "I don't intend to go into any business or profession. . . . Well, just look at them. That's a fine career for a man, isn't it? Lawyers, bankers, politicians. What do they ever get out of life, I'd like to know. What do they know about real things? What do they ever get?"

*Holt to Baxter*

**6.** BAXTER: "What do you want to be?"
HOLT: "A yachtsman."

**7.** "Horseless carriages. Automobiles. People aren't going to spend their lives lying on their backs in the road letting grease drip in their face."

*Holt to Cotten, on the worth of Cotten's line of work*

**8.** "Fanny hasn't got much in her life. You know, George, just being an aunt isn't really the great career it sometimes seems to be."

*Collins to Holt*

**9.** "With all their speed forward they may be a step backward in civilization. Maybe they won't add to the beauty of the world or the life of men's souls. I'm not sure. But automobiles have come, and almost all other things are going to be different because of what they bring."

*Cotten to Holt and the group, after Holt derides the automobile*

**10.** "At twenty-one or twenty-two, so many things appear solid, permanent, and terrible, which forty sees as nothing but disappearing miasma. Forty can't tell twenty about this. Twenty can find out only by getting to be forty."

*Cotten, in letter to Dolores Costello (Isabel Amberson)*

**11.** "Ah, life and money, both behave like loose quicksilver in a nest of cracks. When they're gone, you can't tell what the devil you did with them."

*Collins to Holt*

**12.** "Tomorrow they were to move out. Tomorrow everything would be gone."

*Welles, in voice-over, on the Ambersons moving out of their mansion*

**13.** "Something had happened, that thing which years ago had been the eagerest hope of many, many good citizens of the town. Now it came at last: George Amberson Minafer had got his comeuppance. He got it three times filled and running over."

*Welles, in voice-over*

**MAGNIFICENT OBSESSION** (Universal, 1954). D: Douglas Sirk. S: Robert Blees, Wells Root. Fr: Sarah Y. Mason, Finley Peter Dunne, Victor Heerman (screenplay), Lloyd C. Douglas (novel).

**1.** "Once you find the way, you'll be bound. It'll obsess you. But believe me it'll be a magnificent obsession."

Paul Cavanaugh (Dr. Giraud)

**MAGNIFICENT SEVEN, THE** (UA, 1960). D: John Sturges. S: William Roberts, Walter Newman (uncredited), Walter Bernstein (uncredited). Fr: film, The Seven Samurai.

**1.** "Never rode shotgun on a hearse before."

Steve McQueen (Vin) to Yul Brynner (Chris)

**2.** "I've been offered a lot for my work, but never everything."

Brynner to Mexicans, who want to hire him to protect their village

**3.** "The graveyards are full of boys who were very young and very proud."

Brynner, on would-be gunfighter Horst Buchholz (Chico)

**4.** "I admire your notion of fair odds, mister."

Charles Bronson (O'Reilly) to Brynner, on hearing that Brynner wants to pit six guns against thirty

**5.** "You must excuse them. They are farmers here. They're afraid of everyone and everything. They're afraid of rain, no rain. The summer may be too hot, the winter too cold."

Vladimir Sokoloff (Old Man), on the cool reception given to the hired gunfighters

**6.** "Now we're seven."

Brynner, on accepting Buchholz as a member of the team

**7.** Buchholz, admiring James Coburn (Britt), who has just shot a distant, fleeing bandit off his horse: "That was the greatest shot I've ever seen."

Coburn: "The worst. I was aiming at the horse."

**8.** "We deal in lead, friend."

McQueen to bandit leader Eli Wallach (Calvera)

**9.** "If God didn't want them sheared, he would not have made them sheep."

Wallach, discussing the villagers on whom he preys

**10.** "Generosity. That was my first mistake."

Wallach, trying to understand where he went wrong

**11.** "He said it seemed to be a good idea at the time."

McQueen, explaining why the seven men took the job by comparing it to a man jumping naked on a cactus

**12.** "Don't you ever say that again about your fathers because they are not cowards. You think I'm brave because I carry a gun? Well, you fathers are much braver because they carry responsibility—for you, your brothers, your sisters, and your mothers."

Bronson to a farmer's son who was said his father is a coward

**LAST LINE**
**13.** "The old man was right, only the farmers won. We lost. We'll always lose."

Brynner

**MAGNIFICENT YANKEE, THE** (MGM, 1950). D: John Sturges. S: Emmet Lavery. Fr: Francis Biddle (book, Mr. Justice Holmes), Emmet Lavery (play).

*1.* "Do you know what I think when I see a pretty girl? . . . Oh, to be eighty again."

Louis Calhern (Oliver Wendell Holmes, Jr.)

**MAGNUM FORCE** (Warner Bros., 1973). D: Ted Post. S: John Milius, Michael Cimino. Fr: Harry Julian Fink, R. M. Fink (original material).

LAST LINE
*1.* "A man's got to know his limitations."

Clint Eastwood (Harry Callahan)

**MAJOR AND THE MINOR, THE** (Paramount, 1942). D: Billy Wilder. S: Billy Wilder, Charles Brackett. Fr: Edward Childs Carpenter (play, Connie Goes Home), Fannie Kilbourne (story).

*1.* "Why don't you get out of that wet coat and into a dry martini?"

Robert Benchley (Mr. Osborne) to Ginger Rogers (Susan Applegate)

**MAJOR BARBARA** (UK: General Film Distributors, 1941). D: Gabriel Pascal. S: Anatole de Grunwald, George Bernard Shaw. Fr: George Bernard Shaw (play).

*1.* "I believe there are two things necessary to salvation. . . . Money and gunpowder."

Robert Morley (Mr. Undershaft) to Rex Harrison (Adolphus Cusins)

**MALCOLM X** (Warner Bros., 1992). D: Spike Lee. S: Spike Lee, Arnold Perl, James Baldwin.

*1.* "We didn't land on Plymouth Rock, Plymouth Rock landed on us."

Denzel Washington (Malcolm X), condemning the history of enslavement and oppression of African-Americans

**MALTESE FALCON, THE** (Warner Bros., 1941). D: Roy Del Ruth. S: John Huston. Fr: Dashiell Hammett (novel).

*1.* "We didn't exactly believe your story, Miss O'Shaughnessy; we believed your two hundred dollars. . . . I mean, you paid us more than if you'd been telling us the truth, and enough more to make it all right."

Private detective Humphrey Bogart (Sam Spade) to untrustworthy client Mary Astor (Brigid O'Shaughnessy)

*2.* "You, uh—you're not exactly the sort of a person you pretend to be, are you?"

Bogart to Astor

*3.* "When you're slapped, you'll take it and like it."

Bogart to treasure-hunting criminal Peter Lorre (Joel Cairo)

*4.* "You're absolutely the wildest, most unpredictable person I've ever known."

Astor, buttering up Bogart

*5.* "What do you let these cheap gunmen hang around the lobby for, with their heaters bulging in their clothes?"

Bogart to hotel detective James Burke (Luke), on Elisha Cook, Jr. (Wilmer)

*6.* "Well, sir, here's to plain speaking and clear understanding."

Sydney Greenstreet (Kasper Gutman), head of the criminal gang hunting for the priceless black statuette the Maltese Falcon, raising a toast to Bogart

**7.** "I tell you right out I'm a man who likes talking to a man who likes to talk."

*Greenstreet to Bogart*

**8.** "And you think the dingus is worth a million, huh?"

*Bogart to Greenstreet, on the Maltese Falcon*

**9.** "Yes, sir, we were, but this is genuine coin of the realm. With a dollar of this you can buy ten dollars of talk."

*Greenstreet, explaining to Bogart why the cash he is handing to him is far less than the sums he offered earlier in conversation*

**10.** "By gad, sir, you are a character, that you are. There's never any telling what you'll say or do next, except that it's bound to be something astonishing."

*Greenstreet to Bogart*

**11.** "I've taken all the riding from you I'm gonna take."

*Cook, lashing out against Bogart*

**12.** "That's an attitude, sir, that calls for the most delicate judgment on both sides, because as you know, sir, in the heat of action men are likely to forget where their best interests lie, and let their emotions carry them away."

*Greenstreet, on Bogart's daring them to kill him in spite of the fact that they need him to retrieve the Falcon*

**13.** "Business should be transacted in a businesslike manner."

*Greenstreet to Astor*

**14.** "You . . . you imbecile! You bloated idiot! You stupid fathead!"

*Lorre, losing his temper with Greenstreet, when the black statuette they have found turns out not to be the Maltese Falcon*

**15.** "Yes, angel, I'm gonna send you over."

*Bogart, telling Astor he plans to hand her over to the police*

**16.** "When a man's partner's killed, he's supposed to do something about it. It doesn't make any difference what you thought of him, he was your partner, and you're supposed to do something about it."

*Bogart, explaining why he's sending Astor over*

**17.** "All those are on one side. Maybe some of them are unimportant; I won't argue about that. But look at the number of them. And what have we got on the other side? All we've got is that maybe you love me and maybe I love you."

*Bogart to Astor, explaining how he weighed the pros and cons of sending her over*

**LAST LINES**
**18.** BOGART, telling Ward Bond (Detective Tom Polhaus) what the black statuette is: "The, eh, stuff that dreams are made of."
BOND: "Huh?"

**MAME** *(Warner Bros., 1974). D: Gene Saks. S: Paul Zindel. Fr: Jerome Lawrence, Jerry Herman, Robert E. Lee (musical play), Patrick Dennis (novel).*

**1.** "Oh, my God! Someone's been sleeping in my dress!"

*Beatrice Arthur (Vera Charles), waking up in Lucille Ball's (Mame Dennis's) bathtub after a drinking binge*

**MAN AND A WOMAN, A** *(France: Allied Artists, 1966). D: Claude Lelouch. S: Claude Lelouch, Pierre Uytterhoeven. Fr: Claude Lelouch (story).*

**1.** "I haven't had a serious conversation in my life with a pretty woman."

*Jean-Louis Trintignant to his son's schoolteacher*

**2.** "I wonder why, when things are far-fetched, we say it's like the movies. Have you ever thought why people don't take films seriously?"

*Trintignant, in casual conversation*

**3.** "Between art and life, he said he'd choose life."

*Trintignant, referring to what an artist friend had told him on his deathbed*

**MAN FOR ALL SEASONS, A** *(UK: Columbia, 1966). D: Fred Zinnemann. S: Robert Bolt, Constance Willis. Fr: Robert Bolt (play).*

**1.** ORSON WELLES (*Cardinal Wolsey*), on a political disagreement: "Why did you oppose me?"

PAUL SCOFIELD (*Sir Thomas More*): "I thought Your Grace was wrong."

**2.** "You're a constant regret to me, Thomas. If you could just see facts flat on without that horrible moral squint."

*Welles to Scofield*

**3.** "Well, I think that when statesmen forsake their own private conscience for the sake of their public duties, they lead their country by a short route to chaos."

*Scofield to Welles, on why he would follow his conscience in obstructing Robert Shaw's (Henry VIII's) divorce from Queen Catherine*

**4.** "A man should go where he won't be tempted."

*Scofield, advising John Hurt (Richard Rich) to become a teacher instead of seeking a position at court*

**5.** "You. Your pupils. Your friends. God. Not a bad public, that."

*Scofield, telling Hurt who would know if he were a fine teacher*

**6.** "This is not the stuff of which martyrs are made."

*Scofield, pointing to himself, trying to reassure wife Wendy Hiller (Alice More)*

**7.** "This country is planted thick with laws from coast to coast, man's laws, not God's, and if you cut them down, and you're just the man to do it, do you really think you could stand upright in the winds that would blow then?"

*Scofield to Corin Redgrave (William Roper)*

**8.** "I will not take the oath. I will not tell you why I will not."

*Scofield to Nigel Davenport (Duke of Norfolk) and other questioners, on taking an oath regarding the legitimacy of the king's divorce and remarriage*

**9.** "And when we die, and you are sent to Heaven for doing your conscience, and I am sent to Hell for not doing mine, will you come with me, for fellowship?"

*Scofield to Davenport, when asked to sign the oath for the sake of fellowship*

**10.** "Some men think the Earth is round, others think it flat. It is a matter capable of question. But if it is flat, will the king's word make it round, and if it is round, will the king's word flatten it?"

*Scofield to his questioners*

**11.** "Listen, Meg, when a man takes an oath, he's holding his own self in his own hands like water. And if he opens his fingers then, he needn't hope to find himself again."

*Scofield to daughter Susannah York (Margaret More)*

**12.** "Why, Richard, it profits a man nothing to give his soul for the whole world, but for Wales?"

*Scofield to Hurt, after learning that Hurt has given false witness against him in order to become attorney general for Wales*

**13.** "I die His Majesty's good servant, but God's first."

*Scofield to onlookers, at his execution for treason*

**14.** "I forgive you right readily. Be not afraid of your office. You send me to God."

*Scofield to his executioner*

**MAN ON THE FLYING TRAPEZE, THE** (Paramount, 1935). D: Clyde Bruckman. S: Ray Harris, Sam Hardy, Jack Cunningham, Bobby Vernon. Fr: Sam Hardy, Charles Bogle (W. C. Fields) (story).

**1.** "Somehow, Satan got behind me."

*W. C. Fields (Ambrose Wolfinger)*

**2.** "Tell my wife not to wait up for me tonight, because I won't be home for a month."

*Fields*

**MAN WHO CAME TO DINNER, THE** (Warner Bros., 1941). D: William Keighley. S: Julius J. Epstein, Philip G. Epstein. Fr: George S. Kaufman, Moss Hart (play).

**1.** "I guess you are sort of attractive in a corn-fed sort of way. You can find yourself a poor girl falling for you if—well, if you threw in a set of dishes."

*Bette Davis (Maggie Cutler) to Richard Travis (Bert Jefferson)*

**2.** "Go in and read the life of Florence Nightingale and learn how unfitted you are for your chosen profession."

*Monty Woolley (Sheridan Whiteside) to his nurse Mary Wickes (Miss Preen)*

**MAN WHO SHOT LIBERTY VALANCE, THE** (Paramount, 1962). D: John Ford. S: Willis Goldbeck, James Warner Bellah. Fr: Dorothy M. Johnson (story).

**1.** VERA MILES (*Hallie Stoddard*), on revisiting the homestead of former suitor JOHN WAYNE (*Tom Doniphon*): "The cactus rose is in blossom."

ANDY DEVINE (*Link Appleyard*): "Mebbe you'd like to take a ride out desert way and mebbe look around."

MILES: "Mebbe."

**2.** "Where are his boots? . . . Put his boots on, Klute, and his gunbelt and his spurs."

*James Stewart (Ransom Stoddard) to undertaker, about Wayne*

**3.** "Lawyer, huh? Well, I'll teach you law, Western law."

*Lee Marvin (Liberty Valance) to Stewart, before beating him up*

**4.** "Out here a man settles his own problems."

*Wayne to Stewart about, Western law*

**5.** "You know, you look mighty pretty when you get mad."

*Wayne to Miles*

**6.** "Liberty Valance is the toughest man south of the picket wire, next to me."

*Wayne to Stewart*

**7.** "If you put that thing up, you'll have to defend it with a gun. And you ain't exactly the type."

*Wayne to Stewart, on his lawyer's shingle*

**8.** "Burn me a good thick one, Pete. Meat 'n' potatoes."

*Wayne to John Qualen (Peter)*

**9.** "That's my steak, Valance."

*Wayne to Marvin, after Marvin trips the plate-carrying Stewart*

**10.** MARVIN, squaring off against Wayne in the dining hall: "Three against one, Doniphon."
       WAYNE: "My boy Pompey, the kitchen door."

**11.** WAYNE, sarcastically after the dining hall encounter with Marvin: "Thanks for saving my life, Pilgrim."
       STEWART: "That's not why I did it. Nobody fights my battles."

*The two after the dining hall encounter with Marvin*

**12.** LIBERTY VALANCE DEFEETED
*Headline in the* Shinbone Star

**13.** "Good hand, but not good enough. Aces and eights."

*Marvin to Denver Pyle (Amos Carruthers), announcing his winning "deadman's hand," shortly before being killed by Wayne*

**14.** "You talk too much, think too much. Besides you didn't kill Liberty Valance."

*Wayne to the upset Stewart*

**15.** "Cold-blooded murder. But I can live with it."

*Wayne to Stewart, about killing Marvin*

**16.** "No, sir. This is the West, sir. When the legend becomes fact, print the legend."

*Carleton Young (Maxwell Scott) to Stewart, on not printing the true story of Marvin's death*

**LAST LINE**
**17.** "Nothing's too good for the man who shot Liberty Valance."

*Train conductor Willis Bouchey (Jason Tully) to Stewart*

**MAN WHO WOULD BE KING, THE** (UK: Columbia, 1975). D: John Huston. S: John Huston, Gladys Hill. Fr: Rudyard Kipling (story).

**1.** "We've been all over India. We know her cities, her jungles, her jails, and her passes, and we have decided that she isn't big enough for such as we."

*Sean Connery (Danny Dravot) to Christopher Plummer (Rudyard Kipling)*

**2.** "If a Greek can do it, we can do it."

*Michael Caine (Peachy Carnehan) to Plummer, referring to Macedonian conquerer Alexander the Great, the last man to undertake their proposed journey*

**3.** "The problem is how to divide five Afghans from three mules and have two Englishmen left over."

*Caine to Connery, when they need transportation*

**4.** "If a king can't sing, it ain't worth being king."

*Connery, when Caine tells him to stop singing*

**5.** "Not gods. Englishmen, which is the next best thing."

*Caine, when asked if they are gods*

**6.** "Do you suppose that if a man thought twice he'd give his life for queen and country? Not bloody likely. He wouldn't go near the battlefield."

*Connery, on why soldiers don't think*

**7.** "He can break winds at both ends, simultaneous, which I'm willing to bet is more than any god can do."

*Caine to Saeed Jeffrey (Billy Fish), arguing that Connery is not a god*

**8.** "You call it luck. I call it destiny."

*Connery to Caine, on becoming a god*

**MAN WITH THE GOLDEN GUN, THE** (UK: UA, 1974). D: Guy Hamilton. S: Richard Maibaum, Tom Mankiewicz. Fr: Ian Fleming (novel).

**1.** "You must admit, Mr. Bond, that I am now undeniably the man with the golden gun."

*Christopher Lee (Scaramanga) to Roger Moore (James Bond), after demonstrating a solar-powered gun*

**2.** "I like a girl in a bikini—no concealed weapons."

*Lee, when Britt Ekland (Mary Goodnight) enters wearing a bikini*

**3.** "When I kill, it's on the specific orders of my government, and those I kill are themselves killers."

*Roger Moore (James Bond), rationalizing what he does for a living*

**MANCHURIAN CANDIDATE, THE** (UA, 1962). D: John Frankenheimer. S: George Axelrod, John Frankenheimer.

**LAST LINE**

**1.** "Made to commit acts too unspeakable to be cited here by an enemy who had captured his mind and soul, he freed himself at last, and in the end heroically and unhesitatingly gave his life to save his country. Raymond Shaw. Hell. Hell."

*Frank Sinatra (Bennett Marco), on Laurence Harvey (Raymond Shaw)*

**MANHATTAN** (UA, 1979). D: Woody Allen. S: Woody Allen, Marshall Brickman.

**1.** "They probably sit around on the floor with wine and cheese and mispronounce 'allegorical' and "didacticism.' "

*Woody Allen (Isaac Davis) to Diane Keaton (Mary)*

**2.** "I think people should mate for life, like pigeons or Catholics."

*Allen to Keaton*

**3.** "I like the way you express yourself, too, you know. It's pithy, yet degenerate."

*Allen to Keaton*

**4.** "Nothing worth knowing can be understood with the mind. . . . Everything really valuable has to enter you through a different opening, if you'll forgive the disgusting imagery."

*Allen to Keaton*

**5.** "There must be something wrong with me because I've never had a relationship with a woman that's lasted longer than the one between Hitler and Eva Braun."

*Allen to Keaton*

**6.** "I can't express anger. That's one of the problems I have. I grow a tumor instead."

*Allen to Keaton*

**7.** MICHAEL MURPHY (*Yale*): "You think you're God."

ALLEN: "I've got to model myself after someone."

**MARATHON MAN** (*Paramount, 1976*) D: John Schlesinger. S: William Goldman. Fr: William Goldman (novel).

**1.** "Is it safe?"

*Nazi dentist Laurence Olivier's (Szell's) repeated question as he tortures Dustin Hoffman (Babe Levy)*

**MARK OF ZORRO** (*Century–Fox, 1940*). D: Raymond Griffith. S: John Tainton Foote, Garrett Fort, Bess Meredyth. Fr: Johnston McCulley (novel, The Curse of Capistrano).

**1.** "Z"

*The mark of masked California avenger Tyrone Power (Zorro), slashed on walls, torsos, and elsewhere*

**2.** TO ALL MEN IN THE DISTRICT OF LOS ANGELES— BE IT KNOWN THAT LUIS QUINTERO IS A THIEF AND AN ENEMY OF THE PEOPLE AND CANNOT LONG ESCAPE MY VENGENCE—ZORRO

*Warning from Power*

**3.** "Of Zorro? Oh, Heaven spare me. My blood chills at the thought."

*Power, in his secret identity as the foppish Don Diego Vega, talking about himself as Zorro*

**4.** "You'll forgive me for being late, señora. They heated the water for my bath too early. It was positively tepid. By the time more was carried and properly scented—life can be trying, don't you think?"

*Power as Don Diego, apologizing to Gale Sondergaard (Inez Quintero) for arriving late at a dinner party*

**5.** "Capitán, you seem to regard that poor fruit as an enemy."

*Power as Don Diego to arch foe Basil Rathbone (Esteban Pasquale), who is stabbing at an orange*

**6.** LINDA DARNELL (*Lolita Quintero*), to her dancing partner Power: "I never dreamed dancing could be so wonderful."

POWER, as Don Diego: "I found it rather fatiguing."

**7.** "I needed that scratch to awaken me."

*Power to Rathbone, during fencing match*

**8.** "God forgive me."

*Clergyman Eugene Pallette (Fray Felipe), as he clubs the villains*

LAST LINE
**9.** "Well, we're going to marry and raise fat children and watch our vineyards grow."

*Power, telling Sondergaard of his plans for himself and Darnell*

**MARRIED TO THE MOB** (*Orion, 1988*). D: Jonathan Demme. S: Barry Strugatz, Mark R. Burns.

**1.** PAUL LAZAR (*Tommy Boyle*): "I don't know how these people do it every day."

ALEC BALDWIN (*Frank DeMarco*): "Just like fucking sardines."

*Mob hitmen reflecting on commuters' lives after executing someone on the Long Island Railroad*

**2.** "Everything we wear, everything we eat, everything we own fell off a truck."

*Michelle Pfeiffer (Angela DeMarco) to her husband Baldwin*

**3.** "I want a divawce."

*Pfeiffer, asking Baldwin for a divorce*

**4.** "You disappointed the shit outta me."

*Dean Stockwell (Tony "The Tiger" Russo) to Baldwin, before killing him for sleeping with Stockwell's mistress Nancy Travis (Karen Lutnick)*

**5.** "Try keeping Tony on a leash. I think you'll find one in aisle five."

*Pfeiffer, in a supermarket, confronting Mercedes Ruehl (Connie Russo) on her husband Stockwell's philandering ways*

**6.** "A regular menace to society."

*FBI agent Matthew Modine (Mike Downey), on Stockwell, after Stockwell bumps into him*

**7.** ARE YOU READY FOR A BRAND NEW YOU?

*Sign in the window of the Hello Gorgeous Beauty Salon, where Pfeiffer finds employment*

**8.** "Yeez, what a grouch."

*Modine to Pfeiffer, on Ruehl, echoing Art Carney in the TV series "The Honeymooners"*

**9.** "We all make mistakes. The important thing is to realize it and to do something about it, because everybody deserves a second chance."

*Modine to Pfeiffer*

**10.** HAMBURGER HOMICIDES

*Newspaper headline about mob shootings at Burger World*

**11.** "Oh, there's a big difference, Mrs. DeMarco. The mob is run by murdering, thieving, lying, cheating psychopaths. We work for the President of the United States of America."

*FBI field director Trey Wilson (Franklin) to Pfeiffer*

**12.** "For some crazy reason, I think I'd rather kill myself than hurt you, but suicide's out of the question."

*Stockwell, on learning of Pfeiffer's betrayal of him*

**MARTY** *(UA, 1955). D: Delbert Mann. S: Paddy Chayefsky. Fr: Paddy Chayefsky (teleplay).*

**1.** JOE MANTELL (*Angie*): "What do you feel like doing tonight?"

ERNEST BORGNINE (*Marty Piletti*): "I don't know, Ange. What do you feel like doing?"

*Frequent exchange of Montell and Borgnine*

**2.** "Listen, Ange. I've been looking for a girl every Saturday night of my life. I'm thirty-four years old. I'm just tired of looking. That's all."

*Borgnine to Mantell*

**3.** "Comes New Year's Eve, everybody starts arranging parties. I'm the guy they got to dig up a date for."

*Borgnine*

**4.** "Sooner or later, there comes a point in a man's life when he's got to face some facts. And one fact I got to face is that whatever it is that women like, I ain't got it. I chased after enough women in my life. I went to enough dances. I got hurt enough. I don't want to get hurt no more."

*Borgnine to his mother, Esther Minciotti (Mrs. Pilletti)*

**5.** "I'm just a fat, little man, a fat, ugly man!"

*Borgnine to Minciotti*

**6.** "You don't get to be good-hearted by accident. You get kicked around long enough, you get to be a real professor of pain."

*Borgnine to Betsy Blair (Clara Snyder)*

**7.** "Dogs like us, we ain't such dogs as we think we are."

*Borgnine to Blair*

**8.** "I know that when you take me home, I'm just going to lie on my bed and think about you."

*Blair to Borgnine*

**9.** "I'm afraid I'm going to see an old lady with white hair, just like the old ladies inna park—little bundles in a black shawl waiting for the coffin."

*Augusta Ciolli (Catherine), on looking in the mirror*

**10.** "Miserable and lonely and stupid! What am I, crazy or something? I got something good here. What am I hanging around with you guys for?"

*Borgnine to his friends*

**11.** "All I know is I had a good time last night. I'm going to have a good time tonight. If we have enough good times together, I'm going to get down on my knees. I'm going to beg that girl to marry me. If we make a party on New Year's, I got a date for that party. You don't like her? That's too bad!"

*Borgnine to Mantell*

**MARY POPPINS** (Buena Vista, 1964). D: Robert Stevenson. S: Bill Walsh, Don DaGradi. Fr: P. L. Travers (Mary Poppins books).

**1.** "Never judge things by their appearance—even carpetbags."

Julie Andrews (Mary Poppins) to her charges Karen Dotrice (Jane Banks) and Matthew Garber (Michael Banks)

**2.** "As I expected: 'Mary Poppins's practically perfect in every way.'"

*Andrews to Dotrice and Garber, reading her height as written on tape measure*

**3.** "I shall stay until the wind changes."

*Andrews, on how long she will remain as nanny*

**4.** "Supercalifragilisticexpialidocious."

*Dotrice and Garber, repeating the word taught to them by Andrews*

**5.** "Spit–spot."

*Andrew's frequent phrase, her last words to Dotrice and Garber*

**LAST LINE**
**6.** "Good-bye, Mary Poppins. Don't stay away too long."

*David Tomlinson (Mr. Banks) to Andrews as she flies past*

**MATA HARI** (MGM, 1932). D: George Fitzmaurice. S: Benjamin Glazer, Leo Birinski, Doris Anderson, Gilbert Emery.

**1.** "I am Mata Hari, my own master."

*Greta Garbo (Mata Hari)*

**MATCHMAKER, THE** (Paramount, 1958). D: Joseph Anthony. S: John Michael Hayes. Fr: Thornton Wilder (play).

**1.** "Life's never quite interesting enough, somehow. You people who come to the movies know that."

*Shirley Booth (Dolly Levi) to the audience*

**MATINEE** (Universal, 1993). D: Joe Dante. S: Charlie Haas.

**1.** "Manigator, Alliman . . . Seagator, Gator-gal—Galligator!"

Schlock horror movie producer John Goodman (Lawrence Woolsey), getting movie ideas as he looks at a stuffed alligator

**2.** "There's no more shredded wheat in the back, there's no more shredded wheat in the whole keys, and one of you will have to go to the atomic destruction with no damn shredded wheat!"

Christian Gottshall, a grocery store clerk in the Florida keys, exasperated by men fighting over cereal boxes as they stock up on supplies during the Cuban Missile Crisis

**3.** HALF MAN HALF ANT ALL TERROR!

Slogan for Goodman's movie Mant

**4.** "My terrifying new process, Atomovision, puts you, the audience, at ground zero."

Goodman, in filmed prologue to Mant

**5.** "Men—fire your DDT missiles!"

Kevin McCarthy, a general in Mant, giving the order to stop the giant insect

**6.** "Well, it's rough, kid, but on the plus side the world's still here."

Goodman to Simon Fenton (Gene Loomis), a teenage boy whose bomb shelter love nest has been spoiled by the news that the world has not been destroyed in a nuclear holocaust

**7.** "Hey, Woolsey, this crowd is turning into a mob! Congratulations!"

Jesse White (Mr. Spector), excited theater mogul, to Goodman, whose Atomovision has temporarily convinced moviegoers that nuclear war has begun

**8.** "You think grown-ups know what they're doing? That's a hustle, kid. Grown-ups are making it up as they go along just like you do. You remember that, you'll be fine."

Goodman to Fenton

**MEET JOHN DOE** (Warner Bros., 1941). D: Frank Capra. S: Robert Riskin. Fr: Robert Presnell, Richard Connell (story, "The Life and Death of John Doe").

**1.** "'Bout five-foot-five, brown eyes, light chestnut hair, and as fine a pair of legs as ever walked into this office."

Newspaper editor James Gleason (Henry Connell), on his reporter Barbara Stanwyck (Ann Mitchell)

**2.** "Trying to improve the world by jumping off buildings. You couldn't improve the world if the buildings jumped on you."

Vagrant Walter Brennan (The Colonel) to his buddy Gary Cooper (Long John Willoughby/John Doe)

**3.** "I've seen plenty of fellas start out with fifty bucks and wind up with a bank account. And let me tell you, Long John, when you become a guy with a bank account, they gotcha! Yessir, they gotcha!"

Brennan to Cooper

**4.** "All those nice, sweet, lovable people become heelots. A lotta heels!"

Brennan, defining the term "heelots"

**5.** "Holy smoke, a half a heelot!"

Brennan, spying a midget whom the newspaper people bring in to symbolize the "little people"

**6.** "He's Mr. Big and Mr. Small, he's simple and he's wise, he's inherently honest but he's got a streak of larceny in his heart. He seldom walks up to a public telephone without shoving his finger into the slot to see if somebody left a nickel there."

*Cooper, making his debut radio speech in the character of John Doe*

**7.** "A free people can beat the world at anything, from war to tiddlywinks, if we all pull in the same direction."

*Cooper, during his speech*

**8.** "Don't wait till the game is called on account of darkness. Wake up, John Doe, you're the hope of the world."

*Cooper, in the last lines of his speech*

**9.** "Good-bye, Mr. Doe. You're a wonderful man, and it strikes me you can be mighty useful walking around for a while."

*Soda jerk and John Doe Club member Regis Toomey (Bert Hansen) to Cooper*

**10.** "Lighthouses, John—lighthouses in a foggy world."

*Gleason to Cooper, on Washington, Jefferson, and Lincoln*

**11.** "What the American people need is an iron hand."

*Tycoon and would-be fascist leader Edward Arnold (D. B. Norton), expounding his political philosophy*

**12.** "Why, your type's as old as history—if you can't lay your dirty fingers on a decent idea and twist it and squeeze it and stuff it in your own pockets, you slap it down. Like dogs, if you can't eat something, you bury it!"

*Cooper to Arnold*

**13.** "You couldn't do it in a million years, with all your radio stations and all your power, because it's bigger than whether I'm a fake, it's bigger than your ambitions and it's bigger than all the bracelets and fur coats in the world, and that's exactly what I'm going down there to tell those people."

*Cooper to Arnold*

**14.** JOHN DOE A FAKE!

*Headline put out by Arnold's newspaper interests to crush Cooper*

**15.** "Well, boys, you can chalk up another one to the Pontius Pilates."

*Gleason, morosely, after the John Doe movement has been crushed by Arnold*

**16.** "You don't have to die to keep the John Doe idea alive. Someone already died for that one. The first John Doe. . . . That's why those bells are ringing, John."

*Stanwyck, begging Cooper not to jump off the building*

**LAST LINE**
**17.** "There you are, Norton, the people—try and lick that."

*Gleason to Arnold, triumphantly, after John Doe Club members have renewed their faith in Cooper*

**MEET ME IN ST. LOUIS** (MGM, 1944). D: Vincente Minnelli. S: Irving Brecher, Fred F. Finklehoffe. Fr: Sally Benson (stories).

**1.** "Personally, I wouldn't marry a man who proposed to me over an invention."

*Marjorie Main (Katie the Maid), on Lucille Bremer's (Rose Smith's) beau's use of the newfangled telephone*

**2.** "You've got a mighty strong grip for a girl."

> Tom Drake (John Truett), trying to compliment Judy Garland (Esther Smith)

**3.** "I have to have two kinds of ice cream. I'm recuperating."

> Margaret O'Brien ("Tootie" Smith)

**4.** BREMER: "Money! I hate, loathe, despise, and abominate money!"

> LEON AMES, her father (Alonzo Smith): "You also spend it."

**5.** "Aren't you afraid to stay here alone with a criminal?"

> Ames to his wife, Mary Astor (Anne Smith), after incurring the anger of his family

**6.** "Oh, I'll devote myself to John. But in between times I'm going to make my presence felt amongst the others."

> Garland, planning strategy at the upcoming ball

**7.** "We haven't rotted yet, Lonnie."

> Astor to Ames, on staying in St. Louis and rotting

**LAST LINE**

**8.** "I can't believe it. Right here where we live—right here in St. Louis."

> Garland, marveling at the St. Louis World's Fair

**MENACE II SOCIETY** (New Line Cinema, 1993). D: Allen and Albert Hughes. S: Tyger Williams. Fr: Allen and Albert Hughes, Tyger Williams (story).

**1.** "Went into the store just to get a beer, came out an accessory to murder and armed robbery. It was funny like that in the 'hood' sometimes."

> Tyrin Turner (Caine), on the random violence of life in Watts

**2.** "America's nightmare—young, black, and didn't give a fuck."

> Turner, on his psychopathic friend Larenz Tate (O-Dog)

**MIDNIGHT** (Paramount, 1939). D: Mitchell Leisen. S: Charles Brackett, Billy Wilder. Fr: Edwin Justus Mayer, Franz Schulz (story).

**1.** "Oh, I think it's a dream on you. You know, it . . . it does something to your face. It . . . it gives you a chin."

> Claudette Colbert (Eve Peabody), giving a backhanded compliment to Mary Astor's (Helen Flammarion's) hat

**MIDNIGHT COWBOY** (UA, 1969). D: John Schlesinger. S: Waldo Salt. Fr: James Leo Herlihy (novel).

**1.** "Lotta rich women back there, Ralph, begging for it, paying for it, too . . . and the men are mostly tutti fruttis."

> Jon Voight (Joe Buck) to coworker George Epperson (Ralph), on the treasures of New York City

**2.** "Terrific shirt."

> Dustin Hoffman (Ratso Rizzo) to Voight, at their first encounter

**3.** "I'm walking here! I'm walking here!"

> Hoffman to cabdriver whose car he crosses in front of at an intersection

**4.** "Got my own private entrance here."

*Hoffman to Voight, about the back entrance to the condemned building where he lives*

**5.** "There's no heat here, but by the time winter comes, I'll be in Florida."

*Hoffman to Voight, on his squatter's apartment*

**6.** "You know, in my own place my name ain't Ratso. I mean, it so happens that in my own place my name is Enrico Salvatore Rizzo."

*Hoffman to Voight*

**7.** "The two basic items necessary to sustain life are sunshine and coconut milk."

*Hoffman to Voight*

**8.** "That's a matter I only talk about at confession."

*Hoffman to Voight, about Hoffman's love life*

**9.** "Frankly, you're beginning to smell. And for a stud in New York, that's a handicap."

*Hoffman to Voight*

**10.** "Not bad, not bad for a cowboy."

*Hoffman to Voight, after he is spruced up*

**11.** "I ain't a real cowboy, but I am one hell of a stud."

*Voight, announcing his profession at a party*

**12.** "Florida, you get me to Florida."

*Hoffman to Voight*

**13.** "You just took a little rest stop that wasn't on the schedule."

*Voight, consoling Hoffman about wetting himself on the bus to Florida*

**14.** "Yours was the only one left with a palm tree on it."

*Voight to Hoffman, on the new shirt he buys for him during a bus stop*

**15.** "Okay, folks, just a little illness. Nothing to worry about. We'll be in Miami in just a few minutes."

*Bus driver to passengers about Hoffman, who has just died*

**MIDWAY** (Universal, 1976). D: Jack Smight. S: Donald S. Sanford.

**LAST LINE**
**1.** "Were we better than the Japanese or just luckier?"

*Henry Fonda (Adm. Chester W. Nimitz), reflecting on the Allied victory in the Battle of Midway*

**MIGHTY JOE YOUNG** (Argosy Pictures–RKO Radio, 1949). D: Ernest B. Schoedsack. S: Ruth Rose. Fr: Merian C. Cooper (story).

**1.** "You cannot have a pet gorilla."

*Regis Toomey (John Young) to young daughter Lora Lee Michel (Jill as a girl), after she buys a gorilla*

**2.** "Am I dreaming, or did I see a gorilla— and a beautiful dame?"

*Producer Robert Armstrong (Max O'Hara), smelling a hit act, after his camp is attacked by gorilla Joe Young*

**3.** "Good bye from Joe Young"

*Title written in the sky after Joe Young is returned to Africa*

**MILDRED PIERCE** (Warner Bros., 1945). D: Michael Curtiz. S: Ranald MacDougall. Fr: James M. Cain (novel).

**1.** "My mother—a waitress!"

*Ann Blyth (Veda Pierce), about Joan Crawford (Mildred Pierce)*

**2.** "Personally, Veda's convinced me that alligators have the right idea. They eat their young."

*Eve Arden (Ida), discussing Blyth with Crawford*

**3.** "I loaf, but in a highly decorative and charming manner."

*Zachary Scott (Monte Beragon) to Crawford*

**4.** "I can't get you out of this, Veda."

*Crawford to Blyth, on the murder of Scott*

**5.** "You don't know what it's like being a mother, Ida. Veda's a part of me. Maybe she didn't turn out as well as I'd hoped she would when she was born, but she's still my daughter and I can't forget that."

*Crawford to Arden*

**MILLION DOLLAR LEGS** *(Paramount, 1932). D: Eddie Cline. S: Lewis Foster, Richard English. Fr: Lewis Foster (story).*

**1.** "I should have gone to night school, then I'd be able to add."

*W. C. Fields (President of Klopstokia)*

**2.** "It's the climate. I've been drinking too much orange juice."

*Fields*

**MINISTRY OF FEAR** *(Paramount, 1944). D: Fritz Lang. S: Seton I. Miller. Fr: Graham Greene (novel).*

**1.** "Forget the past. Just tell me the future."

*Ray Milland (Stephen Neale), inadvertently giving a password to a fortune-teller who is not what she seems*

**2.** "I never used to like birds."

*Milland, after some birds lead him to a cake baked by spies*

**MIRACLE OF MORGAN'S CREEK, THE** *(Paramount, 1944). D: Preston Sturges. S: Preston Sturges.*

**1.** "Anybody can think about it, can't they? It doesn't cost anything to think about it. It's only when you do it that it costs two dollars."

*Diana Lynn (Emmy) to her father, William Demarest (Constable Ed Kockenlocker), on getting a marriage license*

**2.** "I was just wondering whether I was going to be an aunt or an uncle."

*Lynn to her sister Betty Hutton (Trudy Kockenlocker), on learning that Hutton is pregnant*

**3.** "No man is going to jeopardize his present or poison his future with a lot of little brats hollering around the house, unless he's forced to."

*Lawyer Alan Bridge (E. L. Johnson) to Hutton, who can't remember the name of the soldier she married and became pregnant by*

**4.** "I practice the law. I'm not only willing, but anxious, to sue anyone anytime for anything, but they got to be real people with names and corpuses and meat on their bones. I can't work with spooks."

*Bridge to Hutton*

**5.** "Nobody believes good unless they have to, if they've got a chance to believe something bad."

*Lynn to Hutton*

**6.** "Can't expect a girl to see much in a civilian these days, even an unwilling civilian. If they had uniforms for them, it might be a little different."

*Eddie Bracken (Norval Jones), perennially turned down for enlistment, to Hutton*

**7.** "Some kind of fun lasts longer than others."

*Hutton to Bracken, on marriage*

**8.** "A woman doesn't care to talk? The only time a woman doesn't care to talk is when she's dead."

*Demarest, on being told by his daughter Hutton that she doesn't care to talk*

**9.** "What's the matter with bigamy?"

*Bracken to Hutton, defending the alternative to suicide*

**10.** "This is airtight and watertight. It's foolproof, and almost legal."

*Bracken to Hutton, on marrying her under a phony name*

**11.** "Everybody has a first name. Even dogs have first names, even if he hasn't got any last name."

*Bracken to Hutton, on picking a phony name*

**12.** "Trouble with kids is they always figure they're smarter than their parents."

*Demarest to Hutton*

**MIRACLE ON 34TH STREET** (20th Century–Fox, 1947). D: George Seaton. S: George Seaton. Fr: Valentine Davies (story).

**1.** "You're just a nice old man with whiskers, like my mother said."

*Natalie Wood (Susan Walker), expressing disbelief in Edmund Gwenn's (Kris Kringle's) claim to be Santa Claus*

**2.** "I have great respect for psychiatry—

and great contempt for meddling amateurs who go around practicing it."

*Gwenn to would-be psychiatrist Porter Hall (Sawyer)*

**3.** "Faith is believing in things when common sense tells you not to."

*Maureen O'Hara (Doris Walker) to her daughter Wood*

**4.** KRIS KRINGLE KRAZY? KOURT KASE KOMING; "KALAMITY," KRIES KIDS

*Headline on the hearing to determine Gwenn's sanity*

**LAST LINE**
**5.** "Maybe. Maybe I didn't do such a wonderful thing after all."

*Lawyer John Payne (Fred Gailey), wondering if the claim that Gwenn is Santa Claus, which he has ingeniously proved in court, is, after all, the truth*

**MIRACLE WORKER, THE** (UA, 1962). D: Arthur Penn. S: William Gibson. Fr: William Gibson (play), Helen Keller (book).

**1.** "How do I tell you that this means a word, and the word means this thing?"

*Anne Bancroft (Annie Sullivan)*

**MISFITS, THE** (UA, 1961). D: John Huston. S: Arthur Miller.

**LAST LINES**
**1.** MARILYN MONROE (Roslyn Taber): "How do you find your way back in the dark?"

CLARK GABLE (Gay Langland): "Just head for that big star straight on. The highway's under it, and it'll take us right home."

*Monroe's and Gable's last lines on screen*

**MISSISSIPPI** *(Paramount, 1935). D: Edward Sutherland. S: Francis Martin, Jack Cunningham, Claude Binyon, Herbert Fields. Fr: Booth Tarkinton (play, Magnolia).*

**1.** "Suffering sciatica—water!"

*W. C. Fields (Commodore Orlando Jackson), confronting his least favorite drink*

**2.** "Remember, a dead fish can float downstream, but it takes a live one to swim upstream."

*Fields*

**3.** "Women are like elephants to me: I like to look at them, but I wouldn't want to own one."

*Fields*

**4.** "Once you've got a man seated, you've got him at your mercy."

*Fields*

**MISSISSIPPI BURNING** *(Orion, 1988). D: Alan Parker. S: Chris Gerolmo.*

**1.** "Where does it come from, all this hatred?"

*FBI agent Willem Dafoe (Alan Ward), investigating the disappearance and suspected murders of three civil rights workers in 1960s Mississippi*

**2.** "If you ain't any better than a nigger, son, who are you better than?"

*FBI agent Gene Hackman (Rupert Anderson), recalling what his father said to him after poisoning the mule of a black farmer who was more successful than he*

**3.** "An old man who was just so full of hate that he didn't know that being poor was what was killing him."

*Hackman, on his father*

**4.** "Way I figure it, it's like three sticks of old dynamite. Shake it up, and we're gonna be scraping bodies off the street."

*Gailard Sartain (Sheriff Ray Stuckey), on race relations in his town*

**5.** "The rest of America don't mean a damn thing. You in Mississippi now."

*Sartain to Hackman*

**6.** "It's the only time when a black man can wave a stick at a white man and not start a riot."

*Hackman, on baseball*

**7.** "You know what these small towns are like. Girl spends her entire time in high school looking for the guy she's going to marry and spends the rest of her life trying to figure out why."

*Hackman, on why he thinks Frances McDormand (Mrs. Pell) married Brad Dourif (Deputy Pell)*

**8.** "I wouldn't give it no more thought that wringing a cat's neck."

*Ku Klux Klan member Michael Rooker (Frank Bailey) to Hackman, on his readiness to kill black people*

**9.** "This can of worms only opens from the inside."

*Dafoe to Hackman, on the murder case*

**10.** "What's wrong with these people?"

*Dafoe, after Ku Klux Klan members castrate a black man*

**11.** "Down here they say rattlesnakes don't commit suicide."

Hackman, on whether Dourif will confess to participation in the murders

**12.** "Mr. Bird, he was guilty."

Dafoe to Kevin Dunn (Agent Bird), on why R. Lee Ermey (Mayor Tilman) killed himself

## MR. BLANDINGS BUILDS HIS DREAM HOUSE (RKO, 1948). D: H. C. Potter. S: Norman Panama, Melvin Frank. Fr: Eric Hodgins (novel).

### FIRST LINE

**1.** "Manhattan, New York, U.S.A. In any discussion of contemporary America and how its people live, we must inevitably start with Manhattan, New York City, U.S.A. Manhattan, glistening modern giant of concrete and steel reaching to the heavens and cradling in its arms seven million, seven million happy beneficiaries of the advantages and comforts this great metropolis has to offer. Its fine, wide boulevards facilitate the New Yorkers' carefree, orderly existence."

Melvyn Douglas (Bill Cole)

**2.** "Come to Peaceful Connecticut. Trade city soot for sylvan charm."

Advertisement in magazine that convinces Cary Grant (Jim Blandings) to leave New York

**3.** "You've been taken to the cleaners and you don't even know your pants are off."

Douglas to Grant, on the prospectus for the house in Connecticut

**4.** "Well, so far it's cost us $13,329.45. But we have the nicest vacant lot in the state of Connecticut."

Myrna Loy (Muriel Blandings)

**5.** "Perhaps what you need is not so much a house as a series of little bungalows."

Architect Reginald Denny (Henry Simms), on the daughter's need for bedrooms with bathrooms

**6.** "I thought he was a lawyer. Why isn't he out suing somebody?"

Grant to Loy, on Douglas's availability for her

**7.** "Now, for the powder room, in here. I want you to match this thread. And don't lose it. It's the only spool I have and I had an awful time finding it. As you can see, it's practically an apple red, somewhere between a healthy winesap and unripened Jonathan."

Loy, in one of her many directives to contractors

**8.** "Red, green, blue, yellow, white."

Painter's simplified understanding of Loy's complicated color demands

**9.** "Anybody who builds a house today is crazy. The minute you start, they put you on the list—the All-American Sucker list. You start out to build a home and you wind up in the poorhouse. And if it can happen to me, what about the fellas who aren't making $15,000 a year? What about the kids who just got married and want a home of their own? It's a conspiracy, I tell you. A conspiracy against every boy and girl who were ever in love."

Grant to Douglas

**10.** "If you ain't eating Wham, you ain't eating ham."

Louise Beavers (Gussie), inadvertently creating a successful advertising slogan for her employer Grant

## MR. DEEDS GOES TO TOWN (Columbia, 1936). D: Frank Capra. S: Robert Riskin. Fr: Clarence B. Kelland (story, "Opera Hat").

*1.* WELCOME TO MANDRAKE FALLS
WHERE THE SCENERY ENTHRALLS
WHERE NO HARDSHIP E'ER BEFALLS
WELCOME TO MANDRAKE FALLS

> *Poem written by Gary Cooper (Longfellow Deeds), at entrance to his town*

*2.* "Why, everybody in Mandrake Falls is pixilated—except us."

> *Margaret Seddon (Jane Faulkner), about herself and her sister Margaret McWade (Amy Faulkner)*

*3.* ". . . In the opinion of the court, you are not only sane but you're the sanest man that ever walked into this courtroom."

> *H. B. Warner (Judge Walker), ruling on Cooper's sanity*

**MR. PEABODY AND THE MERMAID** *(Universal, 1948). D: Irving Pichel. S: Nunnally Johnson. Fr: Guy Jones, Constance Jones (novel, Peabody's Mermaid).*

*1.* "Fifty—the old age of youth, the youth of old age."

> *William Powell (Mr. Peabody)*

**MISTER ROBERTS** *(Orange Productions/ Warner Bros., 1955). D: John Ford, Mervyn LeRoy. S: Joshua Logan, Frank S. Nugent. Fr: Joshua Logan, Thomas Heggen (play), Thomas Heggen (novel).*

*1.* "The Admiral John J. Finchley Award for delivering more toothpaste and toilet paper than any other Navy cargo ship in the safe area of the Pacific."

> *Henry Fonda (Lt. Doug Roberts), on the hated palm tree of James Cagney (Captain Morton)*

*2.* "We gotta get those guys ashore. They're going Asiatic."

> *Ward Bond (CPO Dowdy) to Fonda, on giving the ship's crew a liberty*

*3.* "You're a smart boy, and I know how to deal with smart boys."

> *Cagney, threatening Fonda*

*4.* "If it makes you feel any better, Admiral Wentworth says this is the worst ship he's ever seen in his entire naval career."

> *Shore patrol officer to Fonda, on the rowdy behavior of his sailors on liberty*

*5.* FONDA, in a toast honoring Jack Lemmon (Ens. Frank Thurlowe Pulver), who is promising explosive revenge against Cagney: "And to a great American, Frank Thurlowe Pulver, soldier, statesman, scientist—"
WILLIAM POWELL (Doc): "Friend of the working girl."

*6.* "All right—who did it? *Who did it?*"

> *Cagney to the entire ship's crew, on finding his beloved palm tree thrown overboard by Fonda*

*7.* "Thanks for the liberty, Mr. Roberts. Thanks for everything."

> *Powell to Fonda, reporting the crew's message for Fonda, after the crew has discovered that Fonda bought the crew a liberty by agreeing to submit to Cagney*

*8.* "But I've discovered, Doc, that the unseen enemy of this war is the boredom that eventually becomes a faith and, therefore, a terrible sort of suicide—and I know now that the ones who refuse to surrender to it are the strongest of all."

> *Lemmon, reading Fonda's letter to Powell and the ship's crew*

**9.** "I'd rather have it than the Congressional Medal of Honor."

> *Powell, reading Fonda's letter referring to the Order of the Palm bestowed on him by the grateful crew*

**LAST LINE**

**10.** "Captain, it is I, Ensign Pulver, and I just threw your stinking palm tree overboard. Now, what's all this crud about no movie tonight?"

> *Lemmon to Cagney, showing the gumption he has learned from Fonda*

## MR. SMITH GOES TO WASHINGTON

(Columbia, 1939). D: Frank Capra. S: Sidney Buchman. Fr: Lewis R. Foster (book, The Gentleman from Montana).

**1.** "Dad always used to say the only causes worth fighting for were the lost causes."

> *James Stewart (Jefferson Smith) to Claude Rains (Senator Joseph Paine), on a shared memory of Stewart's father*

**2.** "I suppose, Mr. Paine, when a fella bucks up against a big organization like that, one man by himself can't get very far, can he?"

> *Stewart to Rains, on his father, who died fighting for justice as a newspaper editor*

**3.** "When I came here my eyes were big blue question marks. Now they're big green dollar marks."

> *Jean Arthur (Clarissa Saunders) to Rains*

**4.** THOMAS MITCHELL (*Diz Moore*), on Arthur's charge, Stewart: "See you got Daniel Boone in all right."
> ARTHUR: "Daniel Boone in the lion's den."

**5.** "Why, we're the only ones who can afford to be honest in what we tell the voters. We don't have to be reelected, like politicians."

> *Mitchell to Stewart, on the freedom of the press*

**6.** "That's what's got to be in it. . . . The Capitol Dome. I want to make that come to life for every boy in this land. Yes, and all lighted up like that, too."

> *Stewart to Arthur, on the bill he is proposing*

**7.** "This is a man's world, Jeff, and you've got to check your ideals outside the door, like you do your rubbers."

> *Rains to Stewart*

**8.** "Half of official Washington is here to see democracy's finest show, the filibuster, the right to talk your head off, the American privilege of free speech in its most dramatic form."

> *H. V. Kaltenborn (Himself), announcing Senate proceedings to radio audience*

**9.** "Now, you're not going to have a country that can make these kinds of rules work if you haven't got men that have learned to tell human rights from a punch in the nose."

> *Stewart to Senate, during filibuster, on the Declaration of Independence*

**10.** "I wouldn't give you two cents for all your fancy rules if behind them they didn't have a little bit of ordinary everyday human kindness, and a little looking out for the other fella, too."

> *Stewart to Senate, during filibuster*

**11.** "It's just the blood and bone and sinew of this democracy that some great men handed down to the human race, that's all. . . . But of course, if you've got to build a dam where that boys' camp ought to be, to get some graft to pay off some political army or something, well that's a different thing."

*Stewart to Senate during filibuster*

**12.** "Diz says I'm in love with you. P.S. He's right."

*Arthur, in note to Stewart taken to Senate floor*

**13.** "I guess this is just another lost cause, Mr. Paine. All you people don't know about lost causes. Mr. Paine does. He said once they were the only causes worth fighting for. And he fought for them once, for the only reason any man ever fights for them: because of just one plain, simple rule—love thy neighbor."

*Stewart to Paine and other senators*

**14.** "You think I'm licked. You all think I'm licked. Well, I'm not licked. And I'm going to stay right here and fight for this lost cause. Even if this room gets filled with lies like these, and the Taylors and all their armies come marching into this place. Somebody'll listen to me. Some—"

*Stewart, countering false claims and negative mail before collapsing*

**15.** "I'm not fit to be a senator. I'm not fit to live."

*Rains, breaking down before the other senators*

**MOBY DICK** (UK: Warner Bros., 1956). D: John Huston. S: John Huston, Ray Bradbury. Fr: Herman Melville (novel).

**FIRST LINE**
**1.** "Call me Ishmael."

*Richard Basehart (Ishmael), beginning to narrate the story*

**2.** "Aye, it was Moby Dick that tore my soul and body until they bled into each other."

*Gregory Peck (Captain Ahab), on the white whale Moby Dick*

**LAST LINE**
**3.** "The drama's done. All are departed away. The great shroud of the sea rolls over the *Pequod*, her crew, and Moby Dick. I only am escaped, alone, to tell thee."

*Basehart, after Moby Dick destroys the* Pequod

**MOMMIE DEAREST** (Paramount, 1981). D: Frank Perry. S: Frank Yablans, Frank Perry, Tracy Hotchner, Robert Getchell. Fr: Christina Crawford (book).

**1.** MARA HOBEL (CHRISTINA CRAWFORD AS A CHILD): "Yes, Mommie Dearest."
FAYE DUNAWAY (*Joan Crawford*): "When I told you to call me that, I wanted you to mean it."

**2.** "Don't fuck with me, fellas. This ain't my first time at the rodeo."
*Dunaway*

**3.** "No wire hangers!"
*Dunaway*

**MONKEY BUSINESS** (Paramount, 1931). D: Norman Z. McLeod. S: Arthur Sheekman. Fr: S. J. Perelman, W. B. Johnstone, Roland Pertwee (story).

**1.** "You're a woman who's been getting nothing but dirty breaks. Well, we can clean and tighten your brakes, but you'll have to stay in the garage all night."

*Groucho Marx (Stowaway), romancing Thelma Todd (Lucille)*

**2.** INSULTED WOMAN: "I don't like this innuendo."

GROUCHO: "That's what I always say. Love flies out the door when money comes innuendo."

**3.** "How about you and I passing out on the veranda, or would you rather pass out here?"

*Groucho to woman*

**4.** "Mrs. Briggs, I've known and respected your husband Alky for years, and what's good enough for him is good enough for me."

*Groucho, contemplating an affair with Todd*

**MONSIEUR VERDOUX** (UA, 1947). D: Charles Chaplin. S: Charles Chaplin. Fr: Orson Welles (idea).

**1.** "When the world looks grim and dark, then I think of another world."

*Charles Chaplin (Henri Verdoux), just before killing his first wife for insurance money*

**2.** "Nothing is permanent in this wicked world. Not even our troubles."

*Chaplin, rationalizing to himself while planning his next murder*

**3.** "Is a little kindness such a rare thing?"

*Chaplin, duping an unsuspecting woman into matrimony*

**4.** "I am at peace with my god. My conflict is with man."

*Chaplin, waiting for his death*

**5.** "What would you be without sin?"

*Chaplin to a priest*

**6.** "Once a woman betrays a man, she despises him."

*Chaplin*

**MONTY PYTHON AND THE HOLY GRAIL** (UK: EMI/Cinema V, 1975). D: Terry Gilliam, Terry Jones. S: Graham Chapman, John Cleese, Terry Gilliam, Eric Idle, Terry Jones, Michael Palin.

**1.** "You've got two empty halves of coconuts and you're banging them together."

*Sentry on castle wall, challenging Graham Chapman's (King Arthur's) claim that he is riding a horse*

**2.** "I didn't know we had a king. I thought we were an autonomous collective."

*Terry Jones (as old female peasant) to Chapman*

**3.** JOHN CLEESE (*Black Knight*), after losing an arm in battle with Chapman: "'Tis but a scratch."

CHAPMAN: "A scratch? Your arm's off."

CLEESE: "No, it isn't."

**4.** JONES (*as Sir Bedevere*), on woman accused of witchcraft: "What makes you think she's a witch?"

CLEESE (*as Peasant*): "Well, she turned me into a newt."

JONES: "A newt?"

CLEESE: "I got better."

**5.** "It's only a model."

*Chapman's servant Terry Gilliam (Patsy), failing to be impressed by the sight of Camelot from a distance*

**6.** "I'm French. Why do you think I have this outrageous accent, you silly king?"

*Cleese (as rude French sentry), yelling from castle wall to Chapman*

**7.** "I fart in your general direction! Your mother was a hamster and your father smelt of elderberries!"

*Cleese (as French sentry), abusing Chapman*

**8.** "Run away! Run away!"

*Chapman's way of calling the retreat*

**9.** "Yes, yes, you must give us all a good spanking. . . . And after the spanking, the oral sex."

*Carol Cleveland (Zoot/Dingo) to Michael Palin (as Sir Galahad)*

**10.** "We are the Knights Who Say Ni!"

*Knight Who Says Ni to Chapman*

**11.** PALIN (*as King of Swamp Castle*), at window: "One day, lad, all this will be yours."

JONES (*as Prince Herbert*): "What, the curtains?"

**12.** "Then, when you have found the shrubbery, you must cut down the mightiest tree in the forest with . . . a herring."

*Knight Who Says Ni, making more demands to Chapman*

**13.** "Look, that rabbit's got a vicious streak a mile wide. It's a killer."

*Cleese (as Tim the Wizard) to Chapman, on the killer rabbit*

**14.** "What is your name?. . . . What is your quest?. . . . What is your favorite color?. . . . What is the capital of Assyria?. . . . What is the airspeed velocity of an unladen swallow?"

*Questions asked by Gilliam (as Bridgekeeper)*

**15.** "Well, you have to know these things when you're a king, you know."

*Chapman to Jones (as Bedivere), on how he knows so much about swallows*

**MONTY PYTHON'S LIFE OF BRIAN** (UK: Warner Bros/Orion, 1979). D: Terry Jones.

S: Graham Chapman, John Cleese, Terry Gilliam, Eric Idle, Terry Jones, Michael Palin.

**1.** "Jehovah! Jehovah! Jehovah!"

*Blasphemer taunting John Cleese (Jewish Official)*

**2.** "Blessed are the cheesemakers."

*Ken Colley (Jesus), in the Sermon on the Mount, as misunderstood by listeners*

**MOON IS BLUE, THE** (UA, 1953). D: Otto Preminger. S: F. Hugh Herbert. Fr: F. Hugh Herbert (play).

**1.** "Don't you think it's better for a girl to be preoccupied with sex than occupied?"

*Maggie McNamara (Patty O'Neill)*

**2.** "That is an emotional and ill-considered figure of speech. If I *were* 'the last man on earth' and there were a million women left, you'd be fighting tooth and claw with every single one of 'em for the privilege of becoming my mate.

*David Niven (David Slater) to McNamara*

**MOONSTRUCK** (UA, 1987). D: Norman Jewison. S: John Patrick Shanley.

**1.** VINCENT GARDENIA (*Cosmo Castorini*), advising his daughter on why she should not marry: "You did this once before, it didn't work out."

CHER (*Loretta Castorini*): "The guy died."

**2.** "The moon brings the woman to the man. *Capisce*, eh?"

*Feodor Chaliapin, Jr. (Grandfather) to male friends*

**3.** "What's wrong can never be made right."

*Nicolas Cage (Ronny Cammareri) to Cher, about his brother, her fiancé*

**4.** "Bring me the big knife. I'm gonna cut my throat."

*Cage to Cher, about his situation*

**5.** "I lost my hand. I lost my pride. Johnny has his hand. Johnny has his pride."

*Cage to Cher*

**6.** "It's Cosmo's moon!"

*Louis Guss (Raymond Cappomaggi) to wife Julie Bovasso (Rita Cappomaggi), in bed*

**7.** CAGE: "I'm in love with you."
CHER: "Snap out of it!"

**8.** "I feel like Orlando Furioso."

*Guss to Bovasso, after the night of Cosmo's moon*

**9.** "I think it's because they fear death."

*Olympia Dukakis (Rose Castorini) to John Mahoney (Perry), on why men chase women, repeated later by Danny Aiello (Johnny Cammareri)*

**10.** "What you don't know about women is a lot."

*Dukakis to Mahoney*

**11.** GARDENIA: "You're engaged!"
CHER: "And you're married!"

*On catching each other with other partners at the opera*

**12.** "I can't invite you in because I'm married. Because I know who I am."

*Dukakis to Mahoney, who suggests he would like to visit her home*

**13.** "But love don't make things nice. It ruins everything. It breaks your heart. It makes things a mess. We aren't here to make things perfect. The snowflake is perfect. The stars are perfect. Not us. Not us. We are here to ruin ourselves and to break our hearts and love the wrong people and die."

*Cage to Cher, professing love*

**14.** "You got a love bite on your neck. He's coming back this morning. What's the matter with you? Your life's going down the toilet."

*Dukakis to Cher, after her night out with Cage and the return of her fiancé, Aiello*

**15.** "I'm confused."

*Chaliapin, Jr., to Gardenia*

**LAST LINE**
**16.** GARDENIA: *"Alla famiglia!"*
AIELLO: "To family!"

**MORNING GLORY** (RKO, 1933). D: Lowell Sherman. S: Howard J. Green. Fr: Zoe Akins (play).

**1.** "You don't belong to any man now. You belong to Broadway!"

*Manager Adolphe Menjou (Louis Easton) to aspiring actress Katharine Hepburn (Eva Lovelace)*

**LAST LINE**
**2.** "Oh, Nellie, Nellie, I'm not afraid. I'm not afraid of being left a morning glory. I'm not afraid. I'm not afraid. I'm not afraid. Why should I be afraid? I'm not afraid."

*Hepburn to Helen Ware (Nellie)*

**MOSCOW ON THE HUDSON** (Columbia, 1984). D: Paul Mazursky. S: Paul Mazursky, Leon Capetanos.

**1.** "This is New York City. A man can do whatever he wants."

*New York cop, defending Robin Williams's (Vladimir Ivanoff's) right to defect in Bloomingdale's*

**2.** "Yes, in America anything is possible. Good-bye for now, beloved family. I love you. *Volya.*"

*Williams, writing home to his family*

**MOST DANGEROUS GAME, THE** *(RKO, 1932). D: Ernest B. Schoedsack, Irving Pichel. S: James A. Creelman. Fr: Richard Connell (story).*

**1.** "First the hunt, then the revels!"

*Leslie Banks (Count Zaroff) to his quarry Joel McCrea (Bob Rainsford)*

**MOUSE THAT ROARED, THE** *(UK: Columbia, 1959). D: Jack Arnold. S: Roger Mac-Dougall, Stanley Mann. Fr: Leonard Wibberley (novel, The Wrath of the Grapes).*

**1.** "You must remember the Americans are a very strange people. Whereas other countries rarely forgive anything, the Americans forgive everything. There isn't a more profitable undertaking for any country than to declare war on the United States and to be defeated."

*Peter Sellers (Count Mountjoy), proposing an economic recovery plan for his tiny country, the Grand Duchy of Fenwick*

**2.** "Maybe it's a holiday."

*Sellers (as soldier Tully Bascombe), on why New York City is deserted; it is actually deserted for an air raid drill*

**3.** "Fine thing. The United States and the Grand Duchy of Fenwick are at war and it takes the FBI to find out about it."

*Austin Willis (U.S. Secretary of Defense)*

**4.** "How am I gonna tell the President that we've been successfully invaded by a bunch of fifteenth-century Europeans?"

*Willis*

**5.** "Well, Your Grace, we're home. Actually there's been a slight change of plan. I know it will come as a surprise, a pleasant one, I hope, but we sort of won."

*Sellers (as Tully) to Sellers (as Gloriana, ruler of the Grand Duchy of Fenwick)*

**6.** "Your Grace, this is General Snippet. He's a real general."

*Sellers (as Tully) to Sellers (as Gloriana), on prisoner-of-war Macdonald Parke (General Snippet)*

**7.** PARKE: "I warn you, madam. I know the Geneva Convention by heart."
SELLERS (*as Gloriana*): "Oh, how nice. You must recite it to me some evening. I play the harpsichord."

**8.** "You are a dud?"

*David Kossoff (Professor Kokintz) to his Q-Bomb, which has failed to explode*

**MRS. DOUBTFIRE** *(20th Century–Fox, 1993). D: Chris Columbus. S: Randi Mayem Singer, Leslie Dixon. Fr: Anne Fine (novel, Alias Madame Doubtfire).*

**1.** "You don't really like wearin' that stuff, do you, Dad?"

*Matthew Lawrence (Chris Hillard) to his father Robin Williams (Daniel Hillard), in drag as Mrs. Doubtfire*

**MRS. MINIVER** *(MGM, 1942). D: William Wyler. S: Arthur Wimperis, George Froeschel, James Hilton, Claudine West. Fr: Jan Struther (novel).*

**LAST LINE**

*1.* "This is the people's war. It is our war. We are the fighters. Fight it, then. Fight it with all that is in us, and may God defend the right."

*Henry Wilcoxon (Vicar)*

**MUMMY, THE** *(Universal, 1932). D: Karl Freund. S: John L. Balderston. Fr: Nina Wilcox Putnam, Richard Schayer (story).*

*1.* "It went for a little walk."

*Bramwell Fletcher (Norton) on the mummy's whereabouts*

**MURDER, MY SWEET** *(RKO, 1944). D: Edward Dmytryk. S: John Paxton. Fr: Raymond Chandler (novel, Farewell, My Lovely).*

*1.* "The cops always like to solve murders done with my gun."

*Dick Powell (Philip Marlowe) to Anne Shirley (Ann)*

*2.* "He gave me a hundred bucks to take care of him, and I didn't. I'm just a small businessman in a very messy business, but I like to follow through on a sale."

*Powell*

**MURDER ON THE ORIENT EXPRESS** *(UK: EMI, 1974). D: Sidney Lumet. S: Paul Dehn. Fr: Agatha Christie (novel).*

*1.* "I-I was born backwards. That is why I work in Africa as missionary, teaching little brown babies more backward than myself."

*Ingrid Bergman (Mrs. Hubbard)*

**MURPHY'S ROMANCE** *(Columbia, 1985). D: Martin Ritt. S: Harriet Frank, Jr., Irving Ravetch. Fr: Max Schott (novella).*

**LAST LINE**

*1.* "How do you like your eggs?"

*Sally Field (Emma) to James Garner (Murphy), as their romance begins a new stage*

**MUTINY ON THE BOUNTY** *(MGM, 1935). D: Frank Lloyd. S: Talbot Jennings, Jules Furthman, Carey Wilson. Fr: Charles Nordhoff, James Norman Hall (novels).*

*1.* "A seaman's a seaman. A captain's a captain. And a shipman, Sir Joseph, is the lowest form of animal life in the British Navy."

*Charles Laughton (Captain Bligh) to Franchot Tone (Byam)*

*2.* "We'll carry on, or carry under."

*Laughton to Clark Gable (Fletcher Christian), in a storm*

*3.* "The ship's company will remember that I am your captain, your judge, and your jury. You do your duty and we may get along, but whatever happens, you'll do your duty."

*Laughton to the crew*

*4.* "I've never known a better seaman, but as a man, he's a snake. He doesn't punish for discipline. He likes to see men crawl."

*Gable, on Laughton*

*5.* "Mr. Christian, we're a long way from England, but what can happen on this ship before we get there may surprise even you."

*Laughton to Gable*

*6.* "Friend. The finest word in any language."

*Tone*

**7.** "We'll be men again if we hang for it!"

*Gable, calling for mutiny*

**8.** "I'll take my chance against the law. You'll take yours against the sea."

*Gable to Laughton, as he refuses to abandon the mutiny*

**9.** "Casting me adrift, not even five hundred miles from a port of call. You're sending me to my doom, eh? Well, you're wrong, Christian! I'll take this boat as she floats to England, if I must. I'll live to see you, all of you, hanging from the highest yardarm in the British fleet!"

*Laughton, threatening Gable*

**10.** "From now on, they'll spell mutiny with my name. I regret that, but not the taking of the ship."

*Gable to Tone*

**11.** "An island can be a hell or a home, as we choose to make it."

*Gable to the crew*

**12.** "One man, my Lord, would not endure such tyranny. That's why you hounded him. That's why you hate him, hate his friends. And that's why you're beaten. Fletcher Christian's still free."

*Tone to the court, when he's found guilty*

**MY COUSIN VINNY** (20th Century–Fox, 1992). D: Jonathan Lynn. S: Dale Launer.

**1.** "We got an attorney in the family: my cousin Vinny!"

*Accused murderer Ralph Macchio (Bill Gambini), making a discovery when he uses his one phone call to call his mother*

**2.** "Oh, yeah. You blend."

*Marisa Tomei (Mona Lisa Vito), when Joe Pesci (Vincent La Guardia Gambino) tells her she sticks out like a sore thumb*

**3.** "Sure, I've heard of grits. I've just never actually seen a grit before."

*Pesci, when served grits for the first time, in the diner*

**4.** "Everything that guy just said is bullshit. Thank you."

*Pesci's opening statement, in response to the statement of district attorney Lane Smith (Jim Trotter III)*

**5.** "He's going to show you the bricks. He'll show you they got straight sides. He'll show you how they got the right shape. He'll show them to you in a very special way. So they appear to have everything a brick should have. But there's one thing he's not going to show you. When you look at the bricks at the right angle, they're as thin as this playing card."

*Pesci to Macchio, when Macchio starts to lose faith in Pesci's ability*

**6.** PESCI: "Your Honor, may I have permission to treat Miss Vito as a hostile witness?"
TOMEI: "You think I'm hostile now, wait 'til you see me tonight."

**7.** PESCI, questioning Tomei on the witness stand: "Are you sure?"
TOMEI: "I'm positive."
PESCI: "How could you be so sure?"

**8.** "The car that made these two equal-length tire marks had positraction. You can't make those marks without positraction, which was not available on the '64 Buick Skylark."

*Tomei, showing off her automotive knowledge*

*by identifying a car in the turning point of the case*

**9.** "Thank you, Miss Vito. No more questions. Thank you very, very much. You've been a lovely, lovely witness."

*Pesci to Tomei*

**MY DARLING CLEMENTINE** (20th Century–Fox, 1946). D: John Ford. S: Samuel G. Engel, Winston Miller. Fr: Sam Hellman (story), Stuart N. Lake (novel).

**1.** "Wide-awake, wide-open town, Tombstone. Get anything you want there."

*Walter Brennan (Old Man Clanton) to Henry Fonda (Wyatt Earp)*

**2.** "What kind of a town is this, anyway? Selling liquor to Indians!"

*Fonda, after knocking out a drunken Indian*

**3.** "Listen, miss, I admire poker, but you're increasin' the odds."

*Fonda to Linda Darnell (Chihuahua), on catching her cheating at poker*

**4.** "I've heard a lot about you, too, Doc. You've left your mark around in Deadwood, Denver, and places. In fact, a man could almost follow your trail, going from graveyard to graveyard."

*Fonda to Victor Mature (Doc John Holliday)*

**5.** "Look, Marshal, be reasonable. All we want to do is to ride him around a couple of times on the rail."

*Man in crowd, trying to have some fun with theater owner Don Barclay*

**6.** "When ya pull a gun, kill a man."

*Brennan to his sons*

**7.** "I'm Chihuahua. I'm Doc Holliday's girl. Just wanted to make sure you were packing."

*Darnell, making herself known to Cathy Downs (Clementine Carter)*

**8.** "Now, I don't pretend to be no preacher, but I've read the good book from cover to cover and back again, and I've nary found a word agin dancin'. So we'll commence by havin' a dad-blasted good dance!"

*Russell Simpson (John Simpson), at the dedication of the First Church of Tombstone*

**9.** MATURE: "We're through talking, Marshal. My advice to you is start carrying your gun."
FONDA: "That's good advice."

**10.** FONDA: "Mac, you ever been in love?"
J. FARRELL MACDONALD (Mac): "No, I been a bartender all m'life."

**11.** "We'll be waiting for you, Marshal, at the O.K. Corral."

*Brennan to Fonda, after murdering Fonda's brother Tim Holt (Virgil Earp)*

**12.** "I ain't gonna kill you. I hope you live a hundred years, feel just a little what my pa is going to feel. Now get out o' town. Start wanderin'."

*Fonda to Brennan, after all of Brennan's sons have been killed*

**LAST LINE**
**13.** "Ma'am, I sure like that name—Clementine."

*Fonda to Downs*

**MY DINNER WITH ANDRE** (New Yorker, 1981). D: Louis Malle. S: Wallace Shawn, Andre Gregory.

LAST LINE

**1.** "When I finally came in, Debby was home from work. I told her everything about my dinner with Andre."

*Wallace Shawn (Wally), going home after dinner with his old friend Andre (Andre Gregory)*

**MY FAIR LADY** (Warner Bros., 1964). D: George Cukor. S: Alan Jay Lerner. Fr: Alan Jay Lerner, Frederick Loewe (musical play), George Bernard Shaw (play).

**1.** "I'm a good girl, I am."

*Audrey Hepburn (Eliza Doolittle) to Rex Harrison (Professor Henry Higgins)*

**2.** "I sold flowers. I didn't sell myself. Now you've made a lady of me, I'm not fit to sell anything else."

*Hepburn to Harrison*

LAST LINE

**3.** "Eliza? Where the devil are my slippers?"

*Harrison to Hepburn*

**MY FAVORITE SPY** (Paramount, 1951). D: Norman Z. McLeod. S: Edmund Hartmann, Jack Sher, Edmund Beloin, Lou Breslow, Hal Kanter. Fr: Edmund Beloin, Lou Breslow (story).

**1.** "Remember, you guys, your salaries are paid by the taxpayers. I may be one someday."

*Bob Hope (Peanuts White) to police who have falsely arrested him*

**2.** "I tell jokes. That's dangerous enough."

*Hope, trying to avoid an espionage assignment*

**3.** "That dress does things for you. Doesn't do me any harm either."

*Hope to Hedy Lamarr (Lily Dalbray)*

**4.** "It's nights like this that drive men like me to women like you for nights like this."

*Hope to Lamarr*

**5.** "Stick with me and you'll be wearing a mink hump."

*Hope, in camel disguise, to camel kissing him*

**6.** "What a sneaky way to get into 4F."

*Hope, inspecting a dead body*

**7.** LAMARR: "The closer you get to death the more I realize that I love you."

HOPE: "The closer I get to death the more I realize I love me, too."

**8.** "Watch yourself, I'd be dead without you."

*Hope to a mirror*

**MY FAVORITE YEAR** (MGM/UA, 1982). D: Richard Benjamin. S: Norman Steinberg, Dennis Palumbo. Fr: Dennis Palumbo (story).

**1.** "I'm not an actor, I'm a movie star!"

*Peter O'Toole (Alan Swann) telling Mark Linn-Baker (Benjy Stone) why he can't perform live*

**MY FRIEND IRMA** (Paramount, 1949). D: George Marshall. S: Cy Howard, Parke Levy. Fr: Cy Howard (radio show).

LAST LINE

**1.** "Anything can happen if you live with my friend Irma."

*Diana Lynn (Jane Stacey)*

**MY LIFE AS A DOG** (Sweden: Filmindustri, 1985). D: Lasse Hallström. S: Lasse Hallström, Reidar Jonsson, Brasse Brannstrom, Per Berglund. Fr: Reidar Jonsson (novel).

**1.** "I'll bet Lyka really had a good perspective on things. Keeping your distance is important."

Anton Glanzelius (Ingmar), in narration, on the first Russian dog in space

**2.** "I was thinking about that guy I read about who was taking a short cut across a track meet. A javelin hit him in the chest. It went right through his heart. Think how surprised he must have been."

Glanzelius, in narration, when he is told his mother has died

**3.** "I keep thinking about that lady who went all the way to Ethiopia to be a missionary. They beat her to death with clubs, right while she was preaching. You have to compare like that all the time."

Glanzelius, in narration, when he starts to take an interest in boxing

**MY LITTLE CHICKADEE** (Universal, 1940). D: Eddie Cline. S: Mae West, W. C. Fields.

**1.** "A thing worth having is worth cheating for."

W. C. Fields (Cuthbert J. Twillie)

**2.** "I oughta write a book: The Art of Arising the Morning After."

Fields

**3.** "I'd like to see Paris before I die—Philadelphia would do!"

Fields

**4.** "The bottle is mightier than the quiver."

Fields

**LAST LINE**

**5.** "Oh, yeah, yeah. I'll do that, my little chickadee."

Mae West (Flower Belle Lee), reading one of Fields's favorite phrases back to him

**MY MAN GODFREY** (Universal, 1936). D: Gregory La Cava. S: Everett Freeman, Peter Berneis, William Bowers. Fr: Morrie Ryskind, Eric Hatch (screenplay), Eric Hatch (novel).

**1.** "All you need to start an asylum is an empty room and the right kind of people."

Eugene Pallette (Alexander Bullock), on his crazy family

**2.** FRANKLIN PANGBORN (Master of Ceremonies): "Are you wanted by the police?"
WILLIAM POWELL (Godfrey Parke): "That's just the trouble. Nobody wants me."

**3.** "It's hard to make beds when they're full of people."

Powell, a seeming vagrant hired as a butler by Carole Lombard (Irene Bullock), on his employer's late sleeping habits

**4.** POWELL: "May I be frank?"
JEAN DIXON (Molly): "Is that your name?"

**5.** "The only difference between a derelict and a man is a job."

Powell to Alan Mowbray (Tommy Gray)

**6.** "You have a wonderful sense of humor. I wish I had a sense of humor, but I can never think of the right thing to say until everybody's gone home."

Lombard to Powell

**7.** "Godfrey loves me!"

Lombard, on Powell's feelings for her

**8.** "Stand still, Godfrey. It'll all be over in a minute."

> Lombard to Powell, when their wedding ceremony begins

**MY OWN PRIVATE IDAHO** (Fine Line Features, 1991). D: Gus Van Sant. S: Gus Van Sant.

FIRST LINE

**1.** "Always know where I am by the way the road looks."

> River Phoenix (Mike Waters)

**MYSTERY OF THE WAX MUSEUM** (Warner Bros.–First National, 1933). D: Michael Curtiz. S: Don Mullally, Carl Erickson. Fr: Charles S. Belden (play).

**1.** "It is a cruel irony that you people without souls should have hands."

> Demented wax sculptor Lionel Atwill (Ivan Igor), whose hands have been crippled in a fire, to a less talented apprentice

**NAKED CITY, THE** (Universal-International, 1948). D: Jules Dassin. S: Albert Maltz, Malvin Wald. Fr: Malvin Wald (story).

LAST LINE

**1.** "There are eight million stories in the naked city. This has been one of them."

> Narrator Mark Hellinger

**NAKED GUN, THE** (Paramount, 1988). D: David Zucker. S: Jerry Zucker, Jim Abrahams, David Zucker, Pat Proft.

**1.** "I'm Lieutenant Frank Drebin, Police Squad. And don't ever let me catch you guys in America."

> Leslie Nielsen (Lt. Frank Drebin) to ersatz Gorbachev, Idi Amin, Arafat, Khadafi, and Khomeini, all of whom he has dealt with roughly

**2.** "She was giving me a look I could feel in my hip pocket."

> Nielsen, in narration, when he meets Priscilla Presley (Jane Spencer)

**3.** "All the questions kept coming up over and over again, like bubbles in a case of club soda."

> Nielsen, in narration

**4.** "Same old story. Boy finds girl. Boy loses girl. Girl finds boy. Boy forgets girl. Boy remembers girl. Girl dies in a tragic blimp accident over the Orange Bowl on New Year's Day."

> Nielsen to Presley, telling her about his past love life

**5.** "You take a chance getting up in the morning, crossing the street, or sticking your face in the fan."

> Nielsen to George Kennedy (Capt. Ed Hocken), on taking chances

**6.** "It's true what they say. Cops and women don't mix. It's like eating a spoonful of Drano. Sure, it'll clean you out, but it'll leave you hollow inside."

> Nielsen to Presley

**7.** PRESLEY: "I've loved you since the first day I met you, and I'll never stop. I'm a very lucky woman."

> NIELSEN: "So am I."

**8.** "I finally found someone I can love, good, clean love, without utensils."

*Nielsen to Presley*

**9.** "It's a topsy-turvy world, Jane. And maybe the problems of two people don't amount to a hill of beans, but this is our hill, and these are our beans."

*Nielsen to Presley*

**NAKED SPUR, THE** *(MGM, 1953).* D: Anthony Mann. S: Sam Rolfe, Harold Jack Bloom.

**1.** "If you're ready to talk, son, I'd appreciate your putting that gun down. You might get bee-stung or something, but I'd be just as dead."

*Prospector Millard Mitchell (Jesse Tate) to bounty hunter James Stewart (Howard Kemp), who is holding him at gunpoint*

**2.** "Crazy, ain't it, Pokey, what one man will do to catch another."

*Mitchell to his mule, on Stewart*

**3.** "Now, ain't that the way. Man gets set for trouble head-on and it sneaks up behind him every time."

*Outlaw Robert Ryan (Ben Vandergroat), on getting caught*

**4.** "You know, your trouble is you just think of one thing at a time."

*Stewart to Mitchell, who is too trusting of renegade cavalry officer Ralph Meeker (Roy Anderson)*

**5.** "You know what I'm asking you."

*Stewart, implying a marriage proposal to Janet Leigh (Lena Patch)*

**6.** "If you're going to murder me, Howie, don't try to make it look like something else."

*Ryan, wanted dead or alive, to Stewart, who has captured him*

**7.** "I'm taking him back. This is what I came after and now I got him. No partners like I started. He's gonna pay for my land."

*Stewart, dragging Ryan's corpse*

**8.** "Ben's not dead if you take him back. He'll never be dead for you."

*Leigh to Stewart, on buying back his ranch with the money he earns from Ryan's capture*

**9.** "I'll fix some of Jesse's coffee for you."

*Leigh to Stewart, as he digs a grave for Ryan, remembering their dead companion Mitchell*

**NAME OF THE ROSE, THE** *(20th Century–Fox, 1986).* D: Jean-Jacques Annaud. S: Andrew Birkin, Gerard Brach, Howard Franklin, Alain Godard. Fr: Umberto Eco *(novel).*

**1.** CHRISTIAN SLATER *(Adso of Melk):* "Do you think that this is a place abandoned by God?"

SEAN CONNERY *(William of Baskerville):* "Have you ever known a place where God would have felt at home?"

**2.** "We are very fortunate to have such snowy ground here. It is often the parchment on which the criminal, unwittingly, writes his autograph."

*Connery to Slater*

**3.** "Monkeys do not laugh. Laughter is particular to man."

*Connery*

**4.** "It seems that whenever you ask me a question, you already have the answer."

*Slater to Connery*

**5.** "How peaceful life would be without love, Agile. How safe. How tranquil. And how dull."

*Connery to Slater*

**6.** "Try using your head instead of your heart, and we might make some progress."

*Connery to Slater*

**NARROW MARGIN, THE** *(RKO, 1952). D: Richard Fleischer. S: Earl Fenton. Fr: Martin Goldsmith, Jack Leonard (story).*

**1.** "He was getting old and slow. You could put a live bomb in his hand and count ten before he'd drop it."

*Charles McGraw (Walter Brown), when his partner gets killed*

**2.** "Mrs. Neil, we better get one thing straight. You're just a job to me. A C.O.D. package to be delivered to the L.A. grand jury, and there's no joy in it. I don't like you any more than Forbes did, but he got himself murdered for you and maybe I will, too."

*McGraw to Marie Windsor (Mrs. Neil)*

**3.** "My partner's dead and it's my fault. He's dead and you're alive. Some exchange."

*McGraw to Windsor*

**4.** "You're like the train. When it's moving, everything's a blur. But when it slows down and stops, you begin to notice the scenery."

*Jacqueline White (Ann Sinclair) to McGraw*

**5.** "I'd like to give you the same answer I gave that hood, but it would mean stepping on your face."

*McGraw to Windsor, when she offers him a bribe*

**6.** "To spend the rest of my time worrying when I'll be caught up with by some hoodlum holding a first mortgage on my life, payable on demand. Naw, no kind of moneys worth that."

*McGraw to Windsor, on why he never took a bribe*

**7.** "I once asked my partner, Forbes, what kind of a woman would marry a gangster, and he said, 'All kinds.' I didn't believe him then, but he was right."

*McGraw to White, when it is revealed that she is really Mrs. Neil, and Marie Windsor was a decoy cop*

**NATIONAL LAMPOON'S ANIMAL HOUSE** *(Universal, 1978). D: John Landis. S: Harold Ramis, Douglas Kenney, Chris Miller.*

**1.** "Eric Stratton, rush chairman. Damned glad to meet you."

*Tim Matheson's (Eric "Otter" Stratton's) suave introduction to prospective members of Delta House*

**2.** "Every Halloween, the trees are filled with underwear. Every spring the toilets explode."

*John Vernon (Dean Wormer), bemoaning the activities of Delta House*

**3.** "The time has come for someone to put his foot down, and that foot is me."

*Vernon*

**4.** "I (state your name) do hereby pledge allegiance to the frat with liberty and fraternity for all. Amen."

*Delta House frat pledge, as led by James Widdoes (Robert Hoover)*

**5.** "Food fight!"

*John Belushi (John "Bluto" Blutarsky), calling for mayhem in the cafeteria*

**6.** "Toga! Toga! Toga!"

*Matheson and Belushi, starting a mass chant that will lead to a toga party*

**7.** "Sorry."

*Belushi, sheepishly, after deliberately breaking a folk singer's guitar*

**LAST LINE**
**8.** "No prisoners!"

*Belushi, roaring into action to wreck the homecoming parade*

**NATIONAL LAMPOON'S VACATION** *(Warner Bros., 1983). D: Harold Ramis. S: John Hughes.*

**1.** "I'm not your ordinary, everyday fool."

*Chevy Chase (Clark Griswold) to Eugene Levy (Car Salesman)*

**2.** "Getting there is half the fun."
*Chase to the kids*

**3.** "This is a part of America we never get to see."

*Chase, driving through the slums of St. Louis*

**4.** "I don't know why they call this stuff 'Hamburger Helper.' It does just fine by itself."

*Randy Quaid (Cousin Eddie), standing over the barbecue*

**5.** "When I was a boy, just about every summer, we'd take a vacation. And you know, in eighteen years, we never had fun."

*Chase to Anthony Michael Hall (Rusty)*

**6.** "This is no longer a vacation. It's a quest. It's a quest. It's a quest for fun. I'm going to have fun, and you're going to have fun."

*Chase to the family, when he's at the end of his rope*

**7.** "We're the Griswolds!"

*Chase, on how and why they finally made it to Walley World*

**8.** "We're not really violent people. This is our first gun."

*Beverly D'Angelo (Ellen Griswold) to John Candy, when Chase forces Candy at gunpoint to give them rides*

**NATURAL, THE** *(Tri-Star, 1984). D: Barry Levinson. S: Roger Towne, Phil Dusenberry. Fr: Bernard Malamud (novel).*

**LAST LINE**
**1.** "Way back, way, way, way back, up high into the right field. That ball is still going. It's way back, high up in there. He did it. Hobbs did it."

*Announcer, on Robert Redford's (Roy Hobbs's) winning, redeeming run*

**NAUGHTY NINETIES, THE** *(Universal, 1945). D: Jean Yarbrough. S: Edmund L. Hartmann, John Grant.*

**1.** BUD ABBOTT *(Dexter)*, doing a stage act: "Now, on the St. Louis team we have Who's on first, What's on second, I Don't Know is on third—"
LOU COSTELLO *(Sebastian)*: "That's what I want to find out. I want you to tell me the names of the fellows on the St. Louis team."
ABBOTT: "I'm telling you: Who's on first, What's on Second, I Don't Know is on third. . . ."

*The beginning of Abbott and Costello's most memorable routine*

**2.** COSTELLO: "Another guy gets up and hits a long fly ball to Because. Why? I don't know. He's on third. And I don't care!"
ABBOTT: "What was that?"
COSTELLO: "I said I don't care!"
ABBOTT: "Oh, that's our shortstop!"

*The end of the "Who's on First" routine*

**NETWORK** *(MGM/UA, 1976). D: Sidney Lumet. S: Paddy Chayefsky.*

**1.** "Yesterday, I announced on this program that I was going to commit public suicide. Admittedly, an act of madness. Well, I'll tell you what happened. I just ran out of bullshit."

*Peter Finch (Howard Beale)*

**2.** "Well, Max, here we are. A middle-aged man, reaffirming his middle-aged manhood, and a terrified young woman with a father complex. What sort of script do you think we can make out of this?"

*Faye Dunaway (Diana Christensen) to William Holden (Max Schumacher)*

**3.** "I want you to get up now. I want all of you to get up out of your chairs. I want you to get up right now and go to the window. Open it, and stick your head out, and yell 'I'm as mad as hell, and I'm not going to take this anymore!' "

*Finch*

**4.** "Television is not the truth. Television is a goddamned amusement park."

*Finch*

**5.** "We're in the boredom-killing business."

*Finch*

**6.** "I'm not sure she's capable of any real feelings. She's television generation. She learned life from Bugs Bunny."

*Holden to his wife Beatrice Straight (Louise Schumacher), on Dunaway*

**7.** "Good morning, Mr. Beale. They tell me you're a madman."

*Network executive Ned Beatty (Arthur Jensen) to Finch*

**8.** "I'm not some guy discussing male menopause on the Barbara Walters show. I'm the man that you presumably love. I'm part of your life. I live here. I'm real. You can't switch to another station."

*Holden to Dunaway*

**9.** "Why is it that a woman always thinks that the most savage thing she can say to a man is to impugn his cocksmanship?"

*Holden to Dunaway*

**10.** "You're television incarnate, Diana. Indifferent to suffering. Insensitive to joy. All of life reduced to the common rubble of banality."

*Holden to Dunaway*

**LAST LINE**
**11.** "This was the story of Howard Beale, the first known instance of a man who was killed because he had lousy ratings."

*Lee Richardson (Narrator)*

**NEVER GIVE A SUCKER AN EVEN BREAK** *(Universal, 1941). D: Eddie Cline. S: John T. Neville, Prescott Chaplin. Fr: Otis Criblecoblis (W. C. Fields) (story).*

**1.** "I was in love with a beautiful blonde once. She drove me to drink. 'Tis the one thing I'm indebted to her for."

*W. C. Fields (The Great Man)*

**2.** "Somebody put too many olives in my martini last night."

*Fields*

**3.** "What a splendid view of California climate."

*Fields*

**4.** "I don't know why I ever come in here—the flies get the best of everything."

*Fields*

**5.** "Drown in a vat of liquor? Death, where is thy sting?"

*Fields*

**6.** "This place was supposed to be a saloon, but the censor cut it out."

*Fields*

**NEVER SAY NEVER AGAIN** (UK: Warner Bros., 1983). D: Irvin Kershner. S: Lorenzo Semple, Jr. Fr: Kevin McClory, Jack Whittingham, Ian Fleming (story).

**1.** "Do I look like the sort of man who'd make trouble?"

*Sean Connery (James Bond)*

**2.** BARBARA CARRERA (*Fatima Blush*), splashing Connery while water skiing: "How reckless of me. I've made you all wet."

CONNERY: "Yes, but my martini is still dry."

**3.** KLAUS MARIA BRANDAUER (*Maximilian Largo*): "Do you lose as gracefully as you win?"

CONNERY: "I wouldn't know. I've never lost."

**LAST LINE**

**4.** ROWAN ATKINSON (*Nigel Small-Fawcett*): "M says that without you in the service, he fears for the security of the civilized world."

CONNERY: "Never."

KIM BASINGER (*Domino Petachi*): "Never? (*Connery winks at the audience.*)"

**NEVERENDING STORY, THE** (UK/Germany: Warner Bros., 1984). D: Wolfgang Petersen. S: Wolfgang Petersen, Herman Weigel. Fr: Michael Ende (novel).

**1.** "Confronted with their true selves, most men run away screaming."

*Sydney Bromley (Professor Engwywook)*

**NEW YORK, NEW YORK** (UA, 1977). D: Martin Scorsese. S: Earl MacRauch, Mardik Martin. Fr: Earl MacRauch (story).

**LAST LINE**

**1.** "Okay, I'm there."

*Robert De Niro (Jimmy Doyle), promising to meet Liza Minnelli (Francine Evans); he never shows*

**NIAGARA** (20th Century–Fox, 1953). D: Henry Hathaway. S: Charles Brackett, Walter Reisch, Richard Breen.

**1.** "I'm meeting somebody, just anybody handy, as long as he's a man."

*Marilyn Monroe (Rose Loomis) to Joseph Cotten (George Loomis), on where she's going*

**NIGHT AFTER NIGHT** (Paramount, 1932). D: Archie Mayo. S: Vincent Lawrence, Kathryn Scola, Mae West. Fr: Louis Bromfield (novel, Single Night).

**1.** CLOAKROOM GIRL: "Goodness, what beautiful diamonds!"

MAE WEST (*Mandie Triplett*): "Goodness had nothing to do with it, dearie."

## NIGHT AT THE OPERA, A *(MGM, 1935). D: Sam Wood. S: George S. Kaufman, Morrie Ryskind, Al Boasberg, Bert Kalmar, Harry Ruby. Fr: James Kevin McGuinness (story).*

**1.** "When I invite a woman to dinner, I expect her to look at my face. That's the price she has to pay."

*Groucho Marx (Otis B. Driftwood) to Margaret Dumont (Mrs. Claypool)*

**2.** GROUCHO, to waiter: "Have you got any milk-fed chickens?"

WAITER: "Yes, sir."

GROUCHO: "Well, squeeze the milk out of one and bring me a glass."

**3.** "Every time I get romantic with you, you want to talk business. I don't know, there's something about me that brings out the business in every woman."

*Groucho to Dumont*

**4.** "I don't seem . . . to have it in focus here. If my arms were a little longer, I could read it. You haven't got a baboon in your pocket, have you?"

*Farsighted mogul Groucho, struggling to read a contract with Chico Marx (Forelo), engaging the services of the opera singer whom Chico manages*

**5.** GROUCHO, beginning to hammer out the contract, which soon ends up rejected and torn to shreds: "The party of the first part shall be known in this contract as the party of the first part. How do you like that? That's pretty neat, eh?"

CHICO: "No, that's no good."

**6.** GROUCHO, still hammering out the contract details: "That's . . . that's in every contract. That's . . . that's what they call a sanity clause."

CHICO: "Oh, no. You can't fool me. There ain't no Sanity Clause!"

**7.** DUMONT TO GROUCHO, as they prepare for a trip: "Are you sure you have everything, Otis?"

GROUCHO: "I've never had any complaints yet!"

**8.** "I have here an accident policy that will absolutely protect you—no matter what happens. If you lose a leg, we'll help you look for it."

*Groucho, trying to sell insurance to an ocean-liner's steward*

**9.** GROUCHO, romancing Dumont aboard ship: "Let's go in my room and talk the situation over."

DUMONT: "What situation?"

GROUCHO: "Well . . . uh . . . what situations have you got?"

**10.** "Wouldn't it be simpler if you put the stateroom in the trunk?"

*Groucho, while the ship steward tries to cram a trunk into Groucho's tiny stateroom*

**11.** "Don't wake him up. He's got insomnia—he's trying to sleep it off."

*Chico to Groucho, on the somnolent Harpo Marx, asleep in Groucho's trunk*

**12.** YOUNG WOMAN, peering into Groucho's crowded stateroom: "Is my Aunt Minnie in here?"

GROUCHO: "Well, you can come in and prowl around if you want to. If she isn't in here, you could probably find someone just as good."

## NIGHT OF THE HUNTER, THE (UA, 1955). D: Charles Laughton. S: James Agee. Fr: Davis Grubb (novel).

*1.* "Lord, you sure knowed what you was doin' when you put me in this very cell at this very time. A man with $10,000 hid somewhere and a widow in the make."

> Robert Mitchum (Preacher Harry Powell), praying from his prison cell as he plans to rob the widow of the soon–to–be executed Peter Graves (Ben Harper)

*2.* "Would you like me to tell you the little story of right hand, left hand? The story of good and evil? H-A-T-E. It was with this left hand that old brother Cain struck the blow that laid his brother low. L-O-V-E. You see these fingers, dear hearts? These fingers has veins that run straight to the soul of man— the right hand, friends, the hand of love."

> Mitchum, preaching about the words tattooed on his hands; the lines are reprised, in variant form, in Do the Right Thing

*3.* "It's a hard world for little things."
> Lillian Gish (Rachel Cooper), on the orphaned children for whom she cares

*4.* "They abide and they endure."
> Gish, on children

## NIGHT OF THE IGUANA, THE (MGM, 1964). D: John Huston. S: Anthony Veiller, John Huston. Fr: Tennessee Williams (play).

*1.* DEBORAH KERR (Hanna Jelkes): "There are worse things than chastity, Mr. Shannon." RICHARD BURTON (Reverend T. Lawrence Shannon): "Yes—lunacy and death."

## NIGHT OF THE LIVING DEAD (Walter Reade Organization, 1968). D: George A. Romero. S: John A. Russo. Fr: George Romero (story).

*1.* "Kill the brain and you kill the ghoul."
> TV announcer, telling how to fight zombies

## NIGHT THEY RAIDED MINSKY'S, THE (UA, 1968). D: William Friedkin. S: Arnold Schulman, Sidney Michaels, Norman Lear. Fr: Rowland Barber (novel).

*1.* "I read the Bible, Papa. Does not say yea or nay to hotels."
> Dancer Britt Ekland (Rachel Schpitendavel), defending her presence in a New York hotel to her irate Amish father Harry Andrews (Jacob Schpitendavel)

*2.* "Only a god that could tolerate me could possibly tolerate you."
> Jewish father Joseph Wiseman (Louis Minsky), finding common ground with Amish father Andrews

*3.* "You speak with the fist of authority, gentlemen, but you don't know your fingers."
> Wiseman to people who want to close down the burlesque show

*4.* "About the protuberances, Papa—I think the Lord might feel different from you, since he's the one who gave me them."
> Ekland, asserting the moral legitimacy of breasts, just before she inadvertently invents the striptease

## NINOTCHKA (MGM, 1939). D: Ernst Lubitsch. S: Charles Brackett, Billy Wilder, Walter Reisch. Fr: Melchior Lengyel (story).

**1.** "Don't make an issue of my woman-hood."

*Soviet officer Greta Garbo (Lena "Ninotchka" Yakushova) to comrades receiving her in Paris*

**2.** RAILROAD PORTER, explaining why he carries other people's bags: "Well, that's my business, madam."
GARBO: "That's no business. That's social injustice."
PORTER: "That depends on the tip."

**3.** "The last mass trials were a great success. There are going to be fewer but better Russians."

*Garbo to her comrades*

**4.** "How can such a civilization survive which permits their women to put things like that on their heads?"

*Garbo, seeing a frivolous hat, which she will later wear with gusto*

**5.** MELVYN DOUGLAS (*Count Leon Dalga*): "I've been fascinated by your five-year plan for the last fifteen years."
GARBO: "Your type will soon be extinct."

*First meeting of the amorous capitalist and the dour Soviet*

**6.** "I do not deny its beauty, but it's a waste of electricity."

*Garbo to Douglas, on seeing the lights of Paris at night from the Eiffel Tower*

**7.** "You don't have to do a thing. Chemically we're already quite sympathetic."

*Garbo to Douglas, on what he needs to do to encourage her to feel attracted to him*

**8.** "Never did I dream I could feel like this toward a sergeant."

*Douglas to Garbo*

**9.** "Ninotchka, it's midnight. One half of Paris is making love to the other half."

*Douglas to Garbo*

**10.** "I must be losing my finesse. If I'm not careful I'll be understood by everybody."

*Ina Claire (Grand Duchess Swana), when Garbo understands her convoluted story about a dog*

**11.** "No one can be so happy without being punished."

*Garbo, drunk, in love, and happy*

**12.** "The morning after always does look grim if you happen to be wearing last night's dress."

*Claire to Garbo*

**13.** "I should hate to see our country endangered by my underwear."

*Garbo, back in Russia, on the talk started when her neighbors find her Parisian lingerie in the communal laundry*

**14.** "They wouldn't let me in, so I had to get you out."

*Douglas to Garbo, on how he got her out of Russia*

**15.** "No one shall say Ninotchka was a bad Russian."

*Garbo, on her decision to stay in the West, supposedly in Russia's best interests*

**NO TIME FOR SERGEANTS** (*Warner Bros., 1958*). D: Mervyn LeRoy. S: John Lee Mahin. Fr: Ira Levin (play), Mac Hyman (novel).

**1.** "They want me. They even sent a little fella to come and fetch me, didn't they? And that ain't all. Last spring, I seen a sign on the sidewalk down there in town. This great big old picture of Uncle Sam. And, 'Uncle Sam wants you,' he's a-saying. Just like this fella here, Pa, pointing his finger right straight in my face."

*Andy Griffith (Will Stockdale) to his pa, when Dub Taylor (Draft Board Man) comes for him from the draft board*

**2.** "Be good, and if you can't be good, be careful."

*Taylor, seeing the boys off on the bus*

**3.** NICK ADAMS (*Ben Whitledge*): "You can't write good with handcuffs."

GRIFFITH: "Thanks, can't write good without them."

**4.** "I figure if you just laugh with them, why, pretty soon they'll get tired of carrying on, and there won't be no ruckus, nor nothing."

*Griffith to Adams, on why he takes the abuse the other fellas heap on him*

**5.** ADAMS: "Every man in my whole family's been in the infantry, clear back to my great grandpa. You know what he done? Fought with Stonewall Jackson at Chancellorsville, that's what."

GRIFFITH: "Licked him good, too, I bet!"

**6.** "Somebody brung their trumpet."

*Griffith, when taps is played*

**7.** "Well, it just goes to show you how good things happen to you, when you least expect them."

*Griffith, when he's put in charge of the latrine*

**8.** "Excuse me for saying it, sir, but I don't think a fella your age would be so confused about it all, if you'd went out and seen some girls once in a while."

*Griffith to James Milhollin (Psychiatrist), when he asks him about girls*

**9.** GRIFFITH: "I got sort of fussed when I was reading this here sign they had on the wall. And it was right hard at first because it was real peculiar words like 'IP' and 'GNXL' and 'BGLMP.' "

MYRON McCORMICK (*Sergeant King*): "You were supposed to read them letters one at a time."

GRIFFITH: "Didn't make much sense that way either."

**10.** "To Sergeant King, the best danged sergeant there is in the whole danged Air Force!"

*Griffith's toast to McCormick*

**11.** "Everybody's all the time saying how sergeants is mean and tough. So I'm right glad you was my first one, 'cause you sure showed me different."

*Griffith to McCormick*

**NORMA RAE** (*20th Century–Fox, 1979*). D: Martin Ritt. S: Irving Ravetch, Harriet Frank, Jr.

**1.** "I got me and Alice, and we're alone. You got your two kids; you're alone. If you could help me, maybe I could help you."

*Beau Bridges (Sonny) proposing to fellow single-parent Sally Field (Norma Rae)*

**NORTH** (*Columbia, 1994*). D: Rob Reiner. S: Alan Zweibel, Andrew Scheinman. Fr: Alan Zweibel (novel).

**1.** "Seen your name on maps. Very impressive."

*Bruce Willis (Narrator) to Elijah Wood (North)*

**NORTH BY NORTHWEST** (MGM, 1959). D: Alfred Hitchcock. S: Ernest Lehman.

**1.** "You gentlemen aren't really trying to kill my son, are you?"

*Jessie Royce Landis (Clara Thornhill) to the spies in the elevator who are trying to kill her son, Cary Grant (Roger Thornhill)*

**2.** "Seven parking tickets."

*Grant, explaining to fellow train passenger Eva Marie Saint (Eve Kendall) why he's being followed by the authorities, who suspect him of murder*

**3.** "I never discuss love on an empty stomach."

*Saint to Grant as they order a meal on the train*

**4.** "It's going to be a long night . . . and I don't particularly like the book I started."

*Saint, seducing Grant*

**5.** "This matter is best disposed of from a great height—over water."

*Head villain James Mason (Phillip Vandamm), explaining to henchman Martin Landau (Leonard) how best to get rid of Saint*

**6.** "I think they said I led too dull a life."

*Grant, explaining to Saint as they hang from Mt. Rushmore why his two earlier wives divorced him*

**7.** "That wasn't very sporting, using real bullets."

*Mason, chiding policemen after his partner Landau is shot; fake bullets have earlier been used to simulate Grant's death*

**NOSFERATU, THE VAMPIRE** (Germany: Prana Co., 1922). D: F. W. Murnau. S: Henrik Galeen. Fr: Bram Stoker (novel, Dracula).

**1.** "And it was in 1443 that the first Nosferatu was born. That name rings like the cry of a bird of prey. Never speak it aloud."

*Words in* The Book of the Vampires, *read by Gustav von Wangenheim (Jonathan Harker)*

**LAST LINE**

**2.** "And at that moment, as if by a miracle, the sick no longer died, and the stifling shadow of the vampire vanished with the morning sun."

*End title, after Max Schreck (Graf Orlok, Nosferatu) dissolves in the sunlight*

**NOTORIOUS** (RKO, 1946). D: Alfred Hitchcock. S: Ben Hecht.

**1.** "Let me put this on you. You might catch cold."

*Cary Grant (Bruce Devlin) to Ingrid Bergman (Alicia Huberman), as he ties scarf around her bare midriff*

**2.** "I've always been scared of women, but I get over it."

*Grant to Bergman*

**3.** BERGMAN: "This is a very strange love affair."
GRANT: "Why?"
BERGMAN: "Maybe the fact that you don't love me."

**4.** "Oh, we shouldn't have had this out here. It's all cold now."

*Bergman to Grant, after their romantic alfresco dinner is ruined by Grant's knowledge of Bergman's past*

**5.** "You can add Sebastian's name to my list of playmates."

*Bergman to Grant, after she conquers her espionage target Claude Rains (Alexander Sebastian)*

**6.** "Vintage sand."

*Grant to Bergman, on the contents of a wine bottle*

**7.** BERGMAN, on being discovered sleuthing in the wine cellar by Rains: "Someone is coming. Alex, he's seen us—"

GRANT: "Wait a minute, I'm going to kiss you."

BERGMAN: "No, he'll only think that we—"

GRANT: "It's what I want him to think."

**8.** "I am married to an American agent."

*Rains to Madame Konstantin (Mme. Sebastian), admitting Bergman's deception of him*

**9.** "She must go, but it must happen slowly. If she could become ill and remain ill for a time. Until—"

*Konstantin to Rains, on her plans for Bergman's demise*

**10.** BERGMAN, dying, being rescued by Grant: "Oh, you love me. Why didn't you come here before?"

GRANT: "I couldn't see straight or think straight. I was a fatheaded guy full of pain."

**11.** BERGMAN, during the rescue: "Say it again, it keeps me awake."

GRANT: "I love you."

**12.** "That's your headache."

*Grant to Rains, on Rains's fate with his cohorts*

**LAST LINE**

**13.** "Alex, will you come in, please? I wish to talk to you."

*Ivan Triesault (Eric Mathis) to Rains, who stands alone as the car with Grant and Bergman drives away*

**NOW, VOYAGER** *(Warner Bros., 1942). D: Irving Rapper. S: Casey Robinson. Fr: Olive Higgins Prouty (novel).*

**1.** "Shall we just have a cigarette on it?"

*Paul Henreid (Jerry Durrance) to Bette Davis (Charlotte Vale), before putting two cigarettes in his mouth and lighting them*

**2.** "You see, no one ever called me darling before."

*Davis to Henreid*

**LAST LINE**

**3.** "Oh, Jerry, don't let's ask for the moon. We have the stars."

*Davis to Henreid*

**ODD COUPLE, THE** *(Paramount, 1968). D: Gene Saks. S: Neil Simon. Fr: Neil Simon (play).*

**1.** WALTER MATTHAU *(Oscar Madison)*: "I got brown sandwiches and green sandwiches. Which one do you want?"

HERB EDELMAN *(Murray the Cop)*: "What's the green?"

MATTHAU: "It's either very new cheese or very old meat."

**2.** "Hello? Divorced, Broke, and Sloppy."

*Matthau, answering the phone*

**3.** "You make the same sounds for pain or happiness."

*Matthau to Jack Lemmon (Felix Unger)*

**4.** "You can't spend the rest of your life crying. It annoys people in the movies."

   *Matthau to Lemmon*

**5.** "Murray, I'll give you two hundred dollars for your gun."

   *Matthau to Edelman, after living with Lemmon for three weeks*

**6.** "I've been sitting here breathing cleaning fluid and ammonia for three hours. Nature didn't intend for poker to be played like that."

   *David Sheiner (Roy), after Lemmon has sanitized the apartment where they play poker*

**7.** "It took me three hours to figure out 'F.U.' was Felix Ungar. It's not your fault, Felix; it's a rotten combination, that's all."

   *Matthau, complaining about Lemmon's notes*

**8.** LEMMON: "It's not spaghetti. It's linguini!"
   MATTHAU, after throwing the linguini against the wall: "Now it's garbage."

**9.** "The marriage may come and go, but the game must go on."

   *Lemmon to Matthau, on their poker game*

**LAST LINE**
**10.** "Boys, let's watch the cigarette butts, shall we? This is my house, not a pigsty."

   *Matthau to fellow poker players*

**OH GOD!** *(Warner Bros., 1977). D: Carl Reiner. S: Larry Gelbart. Fr: Avery Corman (novel).*

**1.** "God grants you an interview, 1600 North Hope Street, Los Angeles, California, Room 2700. Tomorrow at 11 A.M."

   *Teri Garr (Bobbie Landers), reading a letter to John Denver (Jerry Landers)*

**2.** "Give me a break. A few things I did get right. I put summer before winter, didn't I?"

   *George Burns (God), to Denver, when Denver tells Him he misspelled "interview"*

**3.** DENVER: "I don't belong to any church."
   BURNS: "Neither do I."

**4.** "Trust me, like it says on the money."

   *Burns to Denver*

**5.** "It's only one message. Moses had to handle ten."

   *Burns, on the message he gives Denver to convey to mankind*

**6.** "The last miracle I did was the 1969 Mets. Before that, I think you have to go back to the Red Sea."

   *Burns, on how often He performs miracles*

**7.** "You want a miracle? You make a fish from scratch. You can't. You think only God can make a tree? Try coming up with a mackerel."

   *Burns to Denver*

**8.** "Lose a job. Save a world. Not a bad deal."

   *Burns to Denver, on his fear of being called crazy and losing his job*

**9.** BURNS: "But seriously, put down that man and woman persons, their existence means exactly and precisely, not more, not one tiny bit less, just what they think it means, and what I think doesn't count at all."
   DENVER: "That's very profound."
   BURNS: "Sometimes I get lucky."

**10.** "What about all the hoo-ha with the Devil a while ago from that movie? Nobody had any trouble believing that the Devil took over and existed in a little girl. All she had to do was wet the rug, throw up some pea soup, and everybody believed. The Devil, you could believe, but not God, huh?"

*Burns, on the witness stand, referring to The Exorcist*

**11.** "If you find it hard to believe in me, maybe it would help you to know that I believe in you."

*Burns, speaking from on high to the courtroom*

**LAST LINES**

**12.** DENVER: "Sometimes, now and then, couldn't we just talk?"

DENVER: BURNS: "I tell you what. You talk. I'll listen."

**OKLAHOMA!** *(Magna, 1955). D: Fred Zinnemann. S: Sonya Levien, William Ludwig. Fr: Richard Rodgers, Oscar Hammerstein II (musical), Lynn Riggs (play).*

**1.** "If I wasn't a old woman, and if you wasn't so young and smart-alecky, why, I'd marry you, and get you to set around at night and sing to me."

*Charlotte Greenwood (Aunt Eller) to Gordon MacRae (Curly)*

**2.** "If she liked me any more, she'd sic the dogs on me."

*MacRae to Greenwood, referring to Shirley Jones (Laurey)*

**3.** JONES: "Which one do you like the best?"

GLORIA GRAHAME (*Ado Annie*): "Whatever one I'm with."

*On the latter's taste in men*

**4.** EDDIE ALBERT (*Ali Hakim*): "The hotel. In front is a veranda, inside is the lobby, and upstairs, baby, might be paradise."

GRAHAME: "I thought they's just bed-rooms."

**5.** "He says I's like a Persian kitten 'cause they is the cats with the soft, round tails."

*Grahame to James Whitmore (Carnes), her father, referring to Albert*

**6.** "You never know how many people like you till you're dead."

*MacRae, trying to convince Rod Steiger (Jud Fry) to commit suicide*

**7.** "In this country, there's just two things you can do if you're a man. You can live outdoors is one, and you can live in a hole is the other."

*MacRae to Steiger*

**8.** "You just sold everything you got in the world, didn't you? You can't sell your clothes 'cause they ain't worth nothing. You can't sell your gun 'cause you're going to need it. Yes, sir, you're going to need it bad."

*Steiger to MacRae, when MacRae outbids him for Jones's basket*

**9.** "Let's not break the law. Let's just bend it a little."

*Greenwood, when they try MacRae for murdering Steiger and hold the trial in Greenwood's dining room instead of a courtroom*

**10.** "I wanted to marry her when I saw the moonlight shining on the barrel of her father's shotgun."

*Albert, on why he got married*

**OLD ACQUAINTANCE** *(Warner Bros.–First National, 1943). D: Vincent Sherman. S: John Van Druten, Lenore Coffee. Fr: John Van Druten (play).*

**1.** "There comes a time in every woman's life when the only thing that helps is a glass of champagne."

*Bette Davis (Kitty Marlowe)*

**OLD MAN AND THE SEA, THE** *(Warner Bros., 1958). D: John Sturges. S: Peter Viertel. Fr: Ernest Hemingway (novella).*

**LAST LINE**

**1.** "The old man was dreaming about the lions."

*Spencer Tracy, in narration, on his character, the Old Man, sleeping when the fishing is done*

**OLD YELLER** *(Buena Vista, 1957). D: Robert Stevenson. S: Fred Gipson, William Tunberg. Fr: Fred Gipson (novel).*

**1.** "Mama, you don't mean we're going to keep that old, ugly, yeller dog?"

*Tommy Kirk (Travis Coates) to Dorothy McGuire (Katie Coates)*

**2.** "He's a heap more dog than I ever had him figured for."

*Kirk, revealing his newfound respect for Spike (Old Yeller), when spike saves Kirk's brother, Kevin Corcoran (Arliss Coates), from a bear*

**3.** "Look at all them stars, Yeller. Bushels of them. Wonder if maybe Papa's out there on the trail somewhere, looking at them, too. Wish I was with him."

*Kirk, keeping a night vigil over the corn*

**4.** "Now, you take a bobcat and a fox. You know they'll run if they get the chance. But when one don't run, or maybe makes fight at you, why, you shoot him and shoot him quick. After he's bitten you, it's too late."

*Chuck Connors (Burn Sanderson), telling Kirk about hydrophobia*

**5.** "We'll have to sew him up. Go jerk me a hair out of old Jumper's tail."

*McGuire to Kirk, before sewing up Spike with the mule's tail, after he's attacked by wild hogs*

**6.** KIRK, after Spike has fought off a wolf and perhaps has contracted hydrophobia: "Lucky you had Old Yeller."

McGUIRE: "It was lucky for us, son, but it warn't lucky for Old Yeller."

**7.** "He was my dog. I'll do it."

*Kirk, when Old Yeller has to be shot*

**8.** "That was rough, son. Roughest thing I ever heard tell of. I'm mighty proud of how my boy stood up to it. Couldn't ask no more of a grown man."

*Fess Parker (Jim Coates), after hearing the whole story and after Kirk has buried Spike*

**9.** "Well, now and then, for no good reason a man can figure out, life will just haul off and knock him flat. Slam him agin' the ground so hard, it seems like all of his insides is busted. It's not all like that. A lot of it's mighty fine. And you can't afford to waste the good part fretting about the bad. That makes it all bad. You understand what I'm trying to get at?"

*Parker to Kirk*

**OLD-FASHIONED WAY, THE** *(Paramount, 1934). D: William Beaudine. S: Garnett Weston, Jack Cunningham. Fr: Charles Bogle (W. C. Fields) (story).*

**1.** "My little rocky mountain canary."

*W. C. Fields (The Great "Mark Antony" McGonigle)*

**2.** "I shall rehearse you in your line."
*Fields*

**3.** "All dressed up like a well-kept grave."

*Fields*

**4.** "Every cloud has a silver lining, and every plate of vegetable soup is filled with vegetables."

*Fields*

**5.** "Don't wait up for me, dear. I may play a little parchesi before coming to bed."

*Fields*

**OLIVER!** (UK: Columbia, 1968). D: Carol Reed. S: Vernon Harris. Fr: Lionel Bart (musical play), Charles Dickens (novel).

**FIRST LINE**

**1.** "Please, sir. I want some more."

*Mark Lester (Oliver Twist)*

**2.** "Have you ever heard the sound a chicken makes when they're wringing off its neck?"

*Oliver Reed (Bill Sikes) to Ron Moody (Fagin), threatening his life*

**ON GOLDEN POND** (ITC/Independent Pictures/Associated Film/Universal, 1981). D: Mark Rydell. S: Ernest Thompson. Fr: Ernest Thompson (play).

**FIRST LINES**

**1.** KATHARINE HEPBURN (*Ethel Thayer*), arriving with her husband at the pond: "Norman. Come here. Come here, Norman. Hurry up. The loons! The loons! They're welcoming us back."

HENRY FONDA (*Norman Thayer, Jr.*): "I don't hear a thing."

**2.** "I'm going to do a backflip!"

*Jane Fonda (Chelsea Thayer Wayne) to her unbelieving father Fonda*

**ON HER MAJESTY'S SECRET SERVICE** (UK: UA, 1969). D: Peter Hunt. S: Richard Maibaum, Simon Raven. Fr: Ian Fleming (novel).

**1.** "This never happened to the other fellow."

*George Lazenby (James Bond), having lost Diana Rigg (Tracy Draco) in the opening sequence, comparing himself to Sean Connery, his predecessor in the role of Bond*

**2.** "There's always something formal about the point of a pistol."

*Lazenby*

**3.** "It's true!"

*Angela Scoular (Ruby), seeing Lazenby's endowments for the first time*

**4.** "007 never had any respect for government property."

*Desmond Llewellyn (Q), after Lazenby throws his hat like a bouquet to Lois Maxwell (Miss Moneypenny), following his wedding to Rigg*

**ON THE BEACH** (UA, 1959). D: Stanley Kramer. S: John Paxton, James Lee Barrett. Fr: Nevil Shute (novel).

**LAST LINE**

**1.** "God, God forgive us. Peter, I think I'll have that cup of tea now."

*Donna Anderson (Mary Holmes) to her husband Anthony Perkins (Peter Holmes), after they kill their child and prepare to kill themselves following a nuclear war*

**ON THE WATERFRONT** *(Columbia, 1954). D: Elia Kazan. S: Budd Schulberg. Fr: Malcolm Johnson (articles).*

**1.** "The only arithmetic he ever got was hearing the referee count up to ten."

*James Westerfield (Big Mac), referring to Marlon Brando's (Terry Malloy's) education*

**2.** "They sure got it made, huh? Eating. Sleeping. Flying around like crazy. Raising gobs of squabs."

*Brando, referring to pigeons*

**3.** "Isn't it simple as one, two, three? One. The working conditions are bad. Two. They're bad because the mob does the hiring. And three. The only way we can break the mob is to stop letting them get away with murder."

*Karl Malden (Father Barry) to his congregation*

**4.** "Hey, you want to hear my philosophy of life? Do it to him before he does it to you."

*Brando to Eva Marie Saint (Edie Doyle)*

**5.** "Down here, it's every man for himself. It's keeping alive. It's standing in with the right people, so you got a little bit of change jingling in your pocket."

*Brando to Saint*

**6.** "This is my church! And if you don't think Christ is down here on the waterfront, you've got another guess coming!"

*Malden to the workers*

**7.** BRANDO, on telling what he knows about a murder: "If I spill, my life ain't worth a nickel."

MALDEN: "And how much is your soul worth if you don't?"

**8.** BRANDO: "You was my brother, Charlie. You should've looked out for me a little bit. You should've taken care of me just a little bit, so I wouldn't have to take them dives for the short end money."

ROD STEIGER *(Charley Malloy)*: "I had some bets down for you. You saw some money."

BRANDO: "You don't understand! I could've had class. I could've been a contender. I could've been somebody, instead of a bum, which is what I am."

**ONE FLEW OVER THE CUCKOO'S NEST** *(UA, 1975). D: Milos Forman. S: Lawrence Hauben, Bo Goldman. Fr: Ken Kesey (novel), Dale Wasserman (play).*

**1.** "I'm here to cooperate with you one hundred percent. Hundred percent. I'll be just right down the line with you. You watch. 'Cause I think we ought to get to the bottom of R. P. MacMurphy."

*Jack Nicholson (R. P. MacMurphy) to the head of the mental institution into which Nicholson has conned himself to get out of prison*

**2.** "I bet in one week I can put a bug so far up her ass, she don't know whether to shit or wind her wristwatch."

*Nicholson to William Redfield (Harding), referring to Louise Fletcher (Nurse Mildred Ratchitt)*

**3.** "Get out of my way, son. You're using my oxygen."

*Nicholson to Brad Dourif (Billy Bibbitt)*

**4.** "You're not an idiot. You're not a goddamn looney now, boy. You're a fisherman!"

*Nicholson to Danny DeVito (Martini), when they all take a fishing boat out together*

**5.** "What do you think you are, for Christ sake, crazy or something? Well, you're not! You're not! You're no crazier than the average asshole out walking around on the streets and that's it!"

*Nicholson to the group*

**6.** "They was giving me ten thousand watts a day, you know, and I'm hot to trot. Next woman takes me on's going to light up like a pinball machine, and play off in silver dollars."

*Nicholson, after electric shock treatments*

**7.** "I must be crazy to be in a looney bin like this."

*Nicholson*

**ONE HUNDRED AND ONE DALMATIANS** *(Buena Vista, 1961). D: Wolfgang Reitherman, Hamilton Luske, Clyde Geronimi. S: Bill Peet. Fr: Dodie Smith (book).*

**1.** "The humans have tried everything. Now it's up to us dogs."

*George Pelling (The Great Dane)*

**ONE MILLION YEARS B.C.** *(UK: Hammer/20th Century–Fox, 1966). D: Don Chaffey. S: Michael Carreras. Fr: Mickell Novak, George Baker, Joseph Frickert (story).*

First Line
**1.** "This is a story of long, long ago, when the world was just beginning."

*Narrator*

**2.** "Tumak!"

*Raquel Welch (Loana), uttering one of her most celebrated lines as she calls out to John Richardson (Tumak)*

**ONE, TWO, THREE** *(UA, 1961). D: Billy Wilder. S: Billy Wilder, I. A. L. Diamond. Fr: Ferenc Molnar (play, Egy, Ketto, Harom).*

**1.** "You guys may be the first to shoot a man to the moon, but if he wants a Coke on the way, you'll have to come to us."

*American Coca-Cola executive James Cagney (C. P. MacNamara) to Russian businessmen*

**2.** "How about the Russian deal? Napoleon blew it, Hitler blew it, but Coca-Cola is going to pull it off."

*Cagney to his boss Howard St. John (Hazeltine), on his plan to bring Coca-Cola behind the Iron Curtain*

**3.** "He's not a Communist. He's a Republican. Comes from the republic of East Germany."

*Pamela Tiffin (Scarlett) to Cagney, on her Communist husband Horst Buchholz (Otto Ludwig Piffl)*

**4.** "Fooey!"

*Buchholz, repeatedly, when upset*

**5.** "Darling, no woman in the world should have two mink coats until every woman in the world has one mink coat."

*Buchholz to Tiffin, on whether she should take both of her mink coats to Moscow*

**6.** "That's just what the world needs, another bouncing baby Bolshevik."

*Cagney, on the news that Tiffin and Buchholz are going to have a baby*

**7.** "This is not only devious. It's unilateral!"

*Buchholz, on Cagney's schemes to turn him into a respectable capitalist son-in-law*

**8.** "Put your pants on, Spartacus."

*Cagney to the half-dressed Buchholz when he promises to lead Coca-Cola workers in revolt*

**9.** "Eins! Zwei! Drei!"

*Cagney, barking his customary "One, Two, Three" order in German*

**10.** BUCHHOLZ: "You mean I've been a capitalist for three hours and already I owe $10,000?"

CAGNEY: "That's what makes our system work: Everybody owes everybody."

**LAST LINE**
**11.** "Schlemmer!"

*Cagney, calling in outrage for his assistant Hanns Lothar (Schlemmer) when he gets Pepsi-Cola from a soft-drink machine*

**ONE-EYED JACKS** (Paramount, 1961). D: Marlon Brando. S: Guy Trosper, Calder Willingham. Fr: Charles Neider (novel, The Authentic Death of Hendry Jones).

**1.** "You've been trying for ten years to get yourself hung in this town, and I think you're gonna make it."

*Karl Malden (Dad Longworth) to Marlon Brando (Rio)*

**2.** "You're a real one-eyed jack in this town."
*Brando to Malden*

**ONLY ANGELS HAVE WINGS** (Columbia, 1939). D: Howard Hawks. S: Jules Furthman, William Rankin (uncredited), Eleanor Griffin (uncredited). Fr: Howard Hawks (story).

**1.** "Calling Barranca, calling Barranca."
*Radioman Donald "Don Red" Barry (Tex Gordon) to pilot*

**2.** "Joe died flying, didn't he? Well, that was his job. He just wasn't good enough. That's why he got it."

*Cary Grant (Geoff Carter) to Sig Rumann (Dutchman), about death of flyer Noah Beery, Jr. (Joe Souther)*

**3.** "Sure it was your fault. You were gonna have dinner with him. The Dutchman hired him. I sent him up on schedule. The fog came in. A tree got in the way. All your fault."

*Grant to Jean Arthur (Bonnie Lee), on her responsibility for Beery's death*

**4.** "The only thing I can tell you about him, he's a good guy for gals to stay away from."

*Thomas Mitchell (Kid Dabb) to Arthur on what he knows about Grant*

**5.** GRANT: "Who's Joe?"
ARTHUR: "Never heard of him."

*Demonstrating the accepted way of handling Beery's death*

**6.** "I don't believe in laying in a supply of anything."

*Grant to Arthur*

**7.** ARTHUR, on her feelings for Grant: "Now look, I hardly know the man."
MITCHELL: "Sure, but you'll get over it."

**8.** "Same old goo. You haven't changed a bit."

*Grant to former paramour Rita Hayworth (Judith McPherson), after kissing her*

**9.** "Say, I wouldn't ask any woman to do anything."

*Grant, joined by Hayworth, repeating a line they have both heard before*

**10.** "Don't I have the darndest luck? Losing one heel right after another."

Arthur to Grant, after he finds she's lost the heel of her shoe

**11.** "Got a match?"

Grant to Arthur, repeating the line he uses throughout the film to indicate his lack of attachment to people and things

**12.** "I'm hard to get, Geoff. All you have to do is ask me."

Arthur to Grant

**13.** "Here's a souvenir for you."

Grant to Arthur, giving her the coin with two heads that indicates his attachment to her

**OPERATION PACIFIC** (Warner Bros., 1951). D: George Waggner. S: George Waggner.

**1.** "Don't forget to duck!"

Patricia Neal (Mary Stuart) to John Wayne (Comdr. Duke Gifford)

**2.** "You don't need me, Duke. You don't need anybody but yourself."

Neal to Wayne, summarizing his career persona

**3.** "The things those Hollywood guys can do with a submarine."

Scott Forbes (Larry), impressed with Hollywood special effects in a film viewed at sea

**4.** "He was a good man. Make sure that it says so on the patrol report."

Wayne, on a comrade killed in action

**ORDINARY PEOPLE** (Paramount, 1980). D: Robert Redford. S: Alvin Sargent. Fr: Judith Guest (novel).

**1.** "I think you came in here looking like something out of the *Body Snatchers*. It's not my impression that you need a tranquilizer."

Judd Hirsch (Dr. Berger) to Timothy Hutton (Conrad Jerrod), when he asks for a tranquilizer

**2.** "Let's have a great Christmas! Okay? Let's have a great year. Let's have the best year of our lives. Okay? We can, you know. This could be the best year ever."

Dinah Manoff (Karen) to Hutton; she later kills herself

**3.** "What do people have in common with mothers anyway?"

Hutton to Hirsch

**4.** HUTTON: "It takes too much energy to get mad."
HIRSCH: "You know how much energy it takes to hold it back?"

**5.** "A little advice about feeling, kiddo. Don't expect it always to tickle."

Hirsch to Hutton

**6.** "Give her the goddamn camera!"

Hutton, blowing up at his parents Donald Sutherland (Calvin Jerrod) and Mary Tyler Moore (Beth Jerrod) when they argue over the next picture to take

**7.** "It's really important to try to hurt me. Isn't it?"

Moore to Hutton

**8.** "You can't break the ball. You can't break the floor. You can't break anything in a bowling alley. That is what I like about bowling alleys. You can't even break the record."

Hutton to Elizabeth McGovern (Jeannine)

**9.** "You tell me the definition of happy, huh? But first, you better make sure that your kids are good and safe, that no one's fallen off a horse, or been hit by a car, or drowned in that swimming pool you're so proud of, and then you come to me and tell me how to be happy."

*Moore to Quinn Redeker (Ward)*

**OUR TOWN** (UA, 1940). D: Sam Wood. S: Thornton Wilder, Frank Craven, Harry Chandlee. Fr: Thornton Wilder (play).

**1.** "You're pretty enough for all normal purposes."

*Beulah Bondi (Mrs. Webb) to daughter Martha Scott (Emily Webb)*

**OUT OF AFRICA** (Universal, 1985). D: Sydney Pollack. S: Kurt Luedtke. Fr: Isak Dinesen (writings), Judith Thurman (book), Errol Trzebinski (book).

**FIRST LINE**
**1.** "He even took the gramophone on safari."

*Meryl Streep (Karen Blixen-Finecke), in narration, reminiscing about Robert Redford (Denys Finch Hatton)*

**2.** "Next time you change your mind, you do it with *your* money."

*Streep, to Klaus Maria Brandauer (Bror Blixen-Finecke), when he changes an investment decision*

**3.** "I had a farm in Africa."

*Streep, in narration*

**4.** "It's not her fault, Baroness. She's a lion."

*Redford to Streep*

**5.** "She wanted to see if you'd run. That's how they decide. A lot like people that way."

*Redford, about the lion*

**6.** "Perhaps he knew, as I didn't, that the Earth was made round so that we would not see too far down the road."

*Streep, reminiscing about Redford*

**7.** "I've paid a price for everything I own."

*Streep*

**8.** "When the gods want to punish you, they answer your prayers."

*Streep to Redford*

**9.** "I'd mate for life, one day at a time."

*Redford, in response to Streep's proposal, defining the kind of relationship he would accept*

**10.** "There are some things worth having, but they come at a price. And I want to be one of them."

*Streep to Redford, when he refuses her proposal*

**LAST LINE**
**11.** "Denys would like that. I must remember to tell him."

*Streep, referring to the lions that stand on Redford's grave*

**OUT OF THE PAST** (RKO, 1947). D: Jacques Tourneur. S: Geoffrey Homes, (pseudonym for Daniel Mainwaring), James M. Cain (uncredited), Frank Fenton (uncredited).

**1.** "I never found out much listening to myself."

*Robert Mitchum (Jeff) to Kirk Douglas (Whit)*

**2.** "I know a lot of smart guys, and a few honest ones. You're both."

*Douglas to Mitchum*

**3.** "My feelings? About ten years ago, I hid them somewhere and haven't been able to find them."

*Douglas to Mitchum*

**4.** "You liked me because you could use me. You could use me because I was smart. I'm not smart anymore. I run a gas station."

*Mitchum to Douglas*

**5.** "You always go around leaving your fingerprints on a girl's shoulder?"

*Rhonda Fleming (Meta Carson)*

**6.** "All women are wonders because they reduce all men to the obvious."

*Ken Niles (Eels)*

**OUT-OF-TOWNERS, THE** *(Paramount, 1970). D: Arthur Hiller. S: Neil Simon.*

**1.** JACK LEMMON (*George Kellerman*), a visitor en route to New York City: "They lost our luggage?"

SANDY DENNIS, his wife (*Gwen Kellerman*): "They didn't lose it. They just can't find it."

**2.** "I'm suin' all of them. I don't care if I'm in court all year."

*Lemmon, after getting off the train in New York*

**3.** "I may be just a wet, insignificant out-of-towner, but you people took up with the wrong person."

*Lemmon to front desk clerk Anthony Holland at the Waldorf*

**4.** "You folks from out of town?"

*Graham Jarvis (Murray the Mugger), sensing easy prey in Lemmon and Dennis*

**5.** "Thirty-seven thousand policemen in the city of New York. Not one will come out in the rain."

*Lemmon, after being mugged*

**6.** "I'm through carrying pocketbooks in this city. If you got a pocketbook, you're a marked woman."

*Anne Meara (Woman in Police Station) to Dolph Sweet (Police Sergeant)*

**7.** DENNIS, after another encounter with one of New York's denizens: "A man doesn't stand over you at four o'clock in the morning in a cape if he doesn't have a knife. Does he?"

LEMMON: "I don't know. It never came up before."

**8.** "I'm not giving up. I'm just saying, 'I'll never make it.' Giving up is when you can still make it, but you give up."

*Lemmon to Dennis*

**9.** "That's right. Go on. Become like everyone else in this city. Don't worry about anybody but yourself."

*Dennis to Lemmon, when he refuses to help a poor little Spanish boy*

**10.** SANDY BARON (*Lenny Moyers*), in a church: "There is no public praying until two o'clock."

LEMMON: "We won't need praying at two o'clock. We need it now."

**11.** "We don't surrender! You hear that, New York? We don't quit. Now, how do you like that? You go ahead, and you can rob me, and starve me, and break my teeth, and my wife's ankles! I'm not leaving! You're just a city! Well, I'm a person, and persons are stronger than cities! This is George Kellerman talking! And you're not getting away with anything! I got all your names and your addresses!"

> Lemmon, after Dennis has capitulated to the Big Apple

**LAST LINE**
**12.** "Oh, my God!"

> Dennis's trademark line

**OUTLAW JOSEY WALES, THE** (Warner Bros./Columbia, 1976). D: Clint Eastwood. S: Phil Kaufman, Sonia Chernus. Fr: Forrest Carter (book, Gone to Texas).

**1.** "I myself never surrendered. But they got my horse, and it surrendered."

> Chief Dan George (Lone Watie)

**LAST LINE**
**2.** "I reckon so. I guess we all died a little in that damn war."

> Clint Eastwood (Josey Wales)

**PAINTED DESERT, THE** (Pathé, 1931). D: Howard Higgins. S: Howard Higgins, Tom Buckingham.

**1.** "A man sure gets punishment for his mistakes."

> William Farnum (Cash Holbrook), on rescuing a baby in the desert and raising him as William

Boyd (Bill Holbrook), whom he considers ungrateful

**PALEFACE, THE** (Paramount, 1948). D: Norman Z. McLeod. S: Edmund Hartman, Frank Tashlin, Jack Rose.

**LAST LINE**
**1.** "What do you want, a happy ending?"

> Dentist Bob Hope ("Painless" Peter Potter), as his new bride, Jane Russell (Calamity Jane), is dragged away by horses

**PALM BEACH STORY, THE** (Paramount, 1942). D: Preston Sturges. S: Preston Sturges.

**1.** "and they lived happily ever after . . . or did they?"

> Opening and closing titles

**2.** "I'm cheesy with money. I'm the Wienie King! Invented the Texas Wienie. Lay off of 'em, you'll live longer."

> Robert Dudley (Wienie King) to Claudette Colbert (Gerry Jeffers)

**3.** "Sex always has something to do with it, dear."

> Colbert to her husband Joel McCrea (Tom Jeffers), on whether sex had anything to do with obtaining money from Dudley

**4.** "Everybody's a flop until he's a success."

> Perennial flop McCrea to Colbert

**5.** "Anyway, men don't get smarter as they grow older, they just lose their hair."

> Colbert to McCrea

**6.** "I refuse to understand what you're talking about."

> McCrea, arguing with Colbert

**7.** Rudy Vallee (*John D. Hackensacker III*), paying for Colbert's shopping spree: "This is great fun. I've never bought things for a girl before—I mean, in any such quantity."

Shop Clerk: "You've been denying yourself, monsieur, one of the basic pleasures in life."

**8.** "Staterooms are un-American."

*Vallee, explaining why he travels in a train berth despite his riches; he later reveals that he considers tipping un-American as well*

**9.** "There are a lot of inconveniences to yachting that most people don't know anything about."

*Vallee to Colbert*

**10.** "Chivalry is not only dead, it's decomposed."

*Vallee, hearing Colbert tell made-up horror stories about her husband*

**11.** "That's one of the tragedies of this life, that the men who are most in need of a beating are always enormous."

*Vallee, on Colbert's husband*

**12.** "Toto, this is Captain McGloo. I'm going to see more of him and less of you from now on."

*Lecherous socialite Mary Astor (Princess) to Sig Arno (Toto), her escort until she meets McCrea, who is traveling under the pseudonym McGloo*

**13.** "Nothing is permanent in this world except Roosevelt, dear."

*Astor to her brother Vallee*

**14.** "After you're married. That's a funny thing to hear your wife say."

*McCrea to Colbert, who plans that they should marry Astor and Vallee, respectively, so that*

Vallee will provide funding for McCrea's proposed airport

**15.** "I hope you realize this is costing us millions."

*Colbert to McCrea, as they clinch, destroying her plans*

**PAPER, THE** (Universal, 1994). D: Ron Howard. S: David Koepp, Stephen Koepp.

**1.** "I don't want to be wrong today."

*Newspaper editor Michael Keaton (Henry Hackett)*

**2.** "Stop the presses!"

*Keaton, giving in to saying the cliché at the urging of Randy Quaid (McDougal)*

**PAPILLON** (Allied Artists, 1973). D: Franklin J. Schaffner. S: Dalton Trumbo, Lorenzo Semple, Jr. Fr: Henri Charrière (autobiographical novel).

**1.** "We're really something, aren't we? The only animals in the world that shove things up their ass for survival."

*Steve McQueen (Papillon), when he puts money in a tube, preparing for insertion*

**2.** "Blame is for God, and small children."

*Dustin Hoffman (Dega), referring to not blaming McQueen for giving in to torture and telling who's been giving him coconuts*

**3.** "Me, they can kill. You, they own."

*McQueen to Hoffman*

**4.** "Hey, you bastards! I'm still here."

*McQueen, after he escapes*

**PARADINE CASE, THE** (Selznick International, 1947). D: Alfred Hitchcock. S: David O. Selznick, Alma Reville, James Bridle. Fr: Robert Hichens (novel).

**1.** "I will tell you about Mrs. Paradine. She's bad, bad to the bone. If ever there was an evil woman, she is one."

> Louis Jourdan (Andre Latour), telling defense lawyer Gregory Peck (Anthony Keane) about Peck's client Valli (Maddalena/Anna Paradine)

**PARIS, TEXAS** (20th Century–Fox, 1984). D: Wim Wenders. S: Sam Shepard. Fr: L. M. Kit Carson (story adaptation).

**1.** "I hear your voice all the time. Every man has your voice."

> Nastassia Kinski (Jane) to Harry Dean Stanton (Travis Clay Henderson)

**PAT AND MIKE** (MGM, 1952). D: George Cukor. S: Ruth Gordon, Garson Kanin.

**1.** "You're a beautiful thing to watch in action."

> Manager Spencer Tracy (Mike Conovan) to athlete Katharine Hepburn (Pat Pemberton)

**2.** "You see her face? A real honest face. Only disgusting thing about her."

> Tracy to Sammy White (Barney Grau), on Hepburn

**3.** "Not much meat on her, but what's there is cherce."

> Tracy, on Hepburn

**4.** "What you need is (A) a manager, (B) a promoter. That's me: A and B."

> Tracy to Hepburn

**5.** "We're the same. We're equals. We're partners. See? Five Oh Five Oh."

> Tracy to Hepburn

**6.** HEPBURN: "Don't forget to throw me over your shoulder and burp me after lunch."
> TRACY: "I will if you need it."

**7.** "I never knew there was so much money to be made honest."

> Tracy

**8.** "It's all you have to do. Lick yourself. Make yourself and own yourself."

> Hepburn to fighter Aldo Ray (Davie Hucko), on who he has to beat

**9.** "I caught something from you and it's good. I like it. See? But don't you catch nothing from me 'cause I ain't got nothing good to catch."

> Tracy to Hepburn

**10.** "Athletes. They ain't like us, you know. They're like what you call freaks. Nobody can understand how they do what they do. They can't understand it themselves."

> Tracy to William Ching (Collier Weld)

**11.** "Well, I don't know if I can lick you or you can lick me, but I'll tell you one thing I do know. . . . Together we can lick them all."

> Tracy to Hepburn

**LAST LINE**
**12.** "And take you right down with me, Shorty."

> Tracy to Hepburn, on going down the drain if she ever dropped him

**PATCH OF BLUE, A** (MGM, 1965). D: Guy Green. S: Guy Green. Fr: Elizabeth Kata (story, "Be Ready With Bells and Drums").

**1.** "Dark's nothing to me. I'm always in the dark."

*Elizabeth Hartman (Selina D'Arcy) to her grandfather, Wallace Ford (Ole Pa), when he tells her it'll be dark before he is able to meet her in the park in order to take her home*

**2.** "You'd be surprised how many people wear dark glasses to hide behind."

*Sidney Poitier (Gordon Ralfe), when he gives Hartman a gift of dark glasses*

**3.** "It means you don't knock your neighbor just because he thinks or looks different than you."

*Poitier to Hartman, explaining what tolerance is*

**4.** "I didn't know you could feel words."

*Hartman, reading Braille for the first time*

**5.** HARTMAN, on a dark and rainy night in the park: "Is it dark?"
POITIER: "Yeah."
HARTMAN: "I'm glad."
POITIER: "Why?"
HARTMAN: "Makes you more like me."

**PATRIOT GAMES** *(Paramount, 1992). D: Phillip Noyce. S: W. Peter Iliff, Donald Stewart. Fr: Tom Clancy (novel).*

**1.** "Let's deal in what we know, not what we don't."

*James Earl Jones (Adm. James Greer), warning Harrison Ford (Jack Ryan) that an assassin has escaped, his whereabouts unknown*

**2.** "You claim responsiblity for one thing, deny it for another. Nobody believes you anymore."

*Ford to Richard Harris (Paddy O'Neil), on the IRA*

**3.** "You dignify their cowardice with your silence."

*David Threlfall (Inspector Highland) to assassin Sean Bean (Sean Miller), on the cowardice of his partners who ran away and left him to be captured*

**PATTON** *(20th Century–Fox, 1970). D: Franklin J. Schaffner. S: Franklin J. Schaffner.*

**1.** "I want you to remember that no bastard ever won a war by dying for his country. He won it by making the other poor dumb bastard die for his country."

*George C. Scott (Gen. George S. Patton, Jr.), addressing offscreen troops*

**2.** "When you put your hand into a bunch of goo that a moment before was your best friend's face, you'll know what to do."

*Scott, assuring the troops they will do their duty under fire*

**3.** "I don't want to get any messages saying that we are holding our position. We're not holding anything. Let the Hun do that. We are advancing constantly and we're not interested in holding onto anything except the enemy. We're going to hold onto him by the nose and we're going to kick him in the ass. We're going to kick the hell out of him all the time and we're gonna go through him like crap through a goose."

*Scott to troops*

**4.** "They'll lose their fear of the Germans. I only hope to God they never lose their fear of me."

*Scott, on his men*

**5.** "Please don't argue with me, Sergeant. I can smell a battlefield."

*Scott to driver, on the location of a battlefield*

**6.** "Two thousand years ago, I was here."

*Scott in North Africa, on the site of an ancient battle between the Carthaginians and the Romans*

**7.** "The man was yellow. He should have been tried for cowardice and shot."

*Scott, on a frightened soldier he treated harshly*

**8.** "I thought I would stand up here and let you people see if I am as big a son-of-a-bitch as some of you think I am."

*Scott, addressing troops*

**9.** "Berlin! I'm gonna personally shoot that paper-hanging son of a bitch!"

*Scott, explaining where he's headed*

**10.** "Fixed fortifications are monuments to the stupidity of man."

*Scott*

**11.** "I love it. God help me, I do love it so. I love it more than my life."

*Scott, describing his feelings about war as he looks at a battlefield*

**12.** "Not me, Freddy. I don't like to pay for the same real estate twice."

*Scott, on whether to fall back and regroup*

**LAST LINE**
**13.** "A slave stood behind the conqueror holding a golden crown and whispering in his ear a warning that all glory is fleeting."

*Scott, describing how Roman conquerors enjoying their triumphs were kept humble*

**PEE-WEE'S BIG ADVENTURE** (Warner Bros., 1985). D: Tim Burton. S: Phil Hartman, Paul Reubens, Michael Varhol.

**1.** "I know you are, but what am I?"

*Paul Reubens's (Pee-Wee's) favorite comeback line*

**PEGGY SUE GOT MARRIED** (TriStar, 1986). D: Francis Ford Coppola. S: Jerry Leichtling, Arlene Sarner.

**1.** "I have certain unresolved feelings about your father. I don't trust him."

*Kathleen Turner (Peggy Sue Bodell) to Helen Hunt (Beth Bodell)*

**2.** "It's Crazy Charlie! The Appliance King!"

*Group to Nicolas Cage (Charlie Bodell), as he enters high school reunion*

**3.** "You bought an Edsel!"

*Turner to father Don Murray (Jack Kelcher), when she has gone back in time to become a teenager again*

**4.** "Just a little. I had a tough day."

*Turner to Murray, when he asks his teenage daughter whether she's drunk*

**5.** "Oh, Mom, I forgot you were ever this young."

*Turner to Barbara Harris (Evelyn Kelcher), as she tells her teenage daughter not to grow up too fast*

**6.** HARRIS: "What's the matter, Peggy? Did you two have a fight?"
TURNER: "Sort of."
HARRIS: "About what?"
TURNER: "House payments."

**7.** "Well, uh, Mr. Snelgrove, I happen to know that in the future I will not have the slightest use for algebra—and I speak from experience."

*Time traveler Turner to math teacher, after she botches math test*

**8.** "Well, you see, I think that time is like a burrito. In the sense that one part of itself will fold over and it will just touch the other part."

*High school science whiz Barry Miller (Richard Norvik), discussing the possibilities of time travel with the elder Turner*

**9.** "I am a walking anachronism."

*Turner to Miller*

**10.** "This is right, Peggy Sue. I want this to be forever."

*Cage to Turner, as she surrenders herself to him once again*

**PELLE THE CONQUEROR** *(Denmark/Sweden: Svensk Filmindustri/Swedish Film Institute/Danish Film, 1988). D: Bille August. S: Bille August. Fr: Martin Andersen Nexo (vol. 1 novel).*

**1.** "What good does it do to make a fist, when there's no strength left? I'm getting older. . . . But you're young, Pelle. . . . You can conquer the world."

*Max von Sydow (Lasse) to his son, Pelle Hvenegaard (Pelle), when he is too weak to stand up for himself against the bullying manager*

**2.** "A good beating is what you need. If you had drowned, I'd have given you a such a beating, believe me."

*von Sydow to Hvenegaard*

**3.** "Do you know the difference between you and a buttock? I don't know either."

*von Sydow, telling a joke to a friend for the first time in a long time*

**4.** "What's the point in grieving? Here . . . this is my new sweetheart. Kiss her, lad."

*von Sydow to Hvenegaard, when the husband*

of the woman with whom he's been having an affair returns from the sea, showing Hvenegaard a bottle of vodka

**PETE 'N' TILLIE** *(Universal, 1972). D: Martin Ritt. S: Julius J. Epstein. Fr: Peter de Vries (novella, Witch's Milk).*

**1.** "I wasn't looking forward to this party, or meeting Pete Seltzer, but when you've reached my age, and your friends are beginning to worry about you, blind dates are a way of life."

*Carol Burnett (Tillie Schlaine), in narration*

**2.** "There are few burdens in life harder to bear than the irritation of a good example."

*René Auberjonois (Jimmy Twitchell) to Walter Matthau (Pete Seltzer) and Burnett*

**3.** "He's a cultural Robin Hood. He steals from the witty and gives to the dull."

*Matthau to Burnett, referring to Auberjonois's line, stolen from Mark Twain*

**4.** "The honeymoon's over. It's time to get married."

*Burnett to Matthau*

**5.** "The Abbott and Costello 'Who's on First' routine is literature. It ranks with the Songs of Solomon, the sonnets of Shakespeare, and the speeches of Spiro Agnew."

*Matthau to Burnett*

**6.** "Let me tell you something about true feelings. I've made quite a study of true feelings. Most of them deserve to be hidden."

*Matthau to Burnett*

**7.** "I'd rather not discuss things with you than with any other woman in the world."

*Matthau to Burnett, on how they stay married*

**8.** MATTHAU: "My plumber tells me that the pursuit of women is flight from women."

BURNETT: "What does that mean?"

MATTHAU: "How the hell do I know? Am I a plumber?"

**9.** "Love without irritation is just that."

*Matthau to Burnett*

**LAST LINES**

**10.** BURNETT: "Thank God, I have Pete Seltzer to see me through the disillusionment of a marriage."

MATTHAU: "I like your attitude, Mrs. Seltzer."

**PETE KELLY'S BLUES** *(Warner Bros., 1955).* D: Jack Webb. S: Richard L. Breen.

**1.** "Well, there won't ever be no patter of little feet in my house—unless I was to rent some mice."

*Peggy Lee (Rose Hopkins)*

**PETER PAN** *(RKO, 1953).* D: Hamilton Luske, Clyde Geronimi, Wilfred Jackson. S: Ted Sears, Bill Peet, Joe Rinaldi, Erdman Penner, Winston Hibler, et al. Fr: Sir James M. Barrie (play).

**1.** "All this time has happened before, and it will all happen again, but this time, it happened in London."

*Tom Conway (Narrator)*

**2.** "Sooner or later, Nana, people have to grow up."

*Hans Conried (Mr. Darling) to Nana, the household dog*

**3.** "There it is, Wendy. Second star to the right and straight on till morning."

Bobby Driscoll (Peter Pan), giving Kathryn Beaumont (Wendy) directions to Never Land

**4.** "A mother, a real mother, is the most wonderful person in the world."

*Beaumont, telling the lost boys what a mother is*

**5.** "Once you're grown up, you can never come back!"

*Driscoll, when the lost boys decide to go home to London*

**6.** "I have the strangest feeling that I've seen that ship before, a long time ago, when I was very young."

*Conried, watching Driscoll's ship sail away in the moonlight*

**PETRIFIED FOREST, THE** *(Warner Bros., 1936).* D: Archie Mayo. S: Charles Kenyon, Delmer Daves. Fr: Robert E. Sherwood (play).

**1.** "Living, I'm worth nothing to her. But dead, I can buy her the tallest cathedrals, golden vineyards, and dancing in the streets. One well-directed bullet will accomplish all that."

*Leslie Howard (Alan Squier) to Humphrey Bogart (Duke Mantee)*

**PEYTON PLACE** *(20th Century–Fox, 1957).* D: Mark Robson. S: John Michael Hayes. Fr: Grace Metalious (novel).

**1.** "We were just playing a game called Photography. You turn off the lights and see what develops."

*Barry Coe (Rodney Harrington)*

**LAST LINE**

**2.** "We finally discovered that season of love. It is only found in someone else's heart.

Right now, someone you know is looking everywhere for it—and it's in you."

*Diane Varsi (Allison MacKenzie), in voice-over*

**PHILADELPHIA** (TriStar, 1993). D: Jonathan Demme. S: Ron Nyswaner.

**1.** "What's that on your forehead, pal?"

*Law partner noticing AIDS-related lesion on the face of associate Tom Hanks (Andrew Beckett)*

**2.** "All right, look, I want you to explain this to me like I'm a six-year-old, okay?"

*Attorney Denzel Washington (Joe Miller) to potential client; paraphrased to others throughout the film*

**3.** HANKS, on his deathbed: "Excellent work, Counselor. I thank you."
WASHINGTON: "It was great working with you, Counselor."

**PHILADELPHIA STORY, THE** (MGM, 1940). D: George Cukor. S: Donald Ogden Stewart (uncredited), Waldo Salt. Fr: Philip Barry (play).

**1.** "Don't say 'stinks,' darling. If absolutely necessary 'smells,' but only if absolutely necessary."

*Society matron Mary Nash (Margaret Lord) to her daughter Virginia Weidler (Dinah Lord)*

**2.** "The unapproachable Miss Lord—the Philadelphia Story."

*Spy magazine editor Henry Daniell (Sidney Kidd), on doing a story on the wedding of heiress Katharine Hepburn (Tracy Lord)*

**3.** "Red, you look in the pink."

*Cary Grant (C. K. Dexter Haven) to former spouse Hepburn*

**4.** "No, you're slipping, Red. I used to be afraid of that look—the withering glance of the goddess."

*Grant to Hepburn*

**5.** "Am I, Red?"

*Grant, on whether he is enjoying the presence of reporters at Hepburn's wedding*

**6.** "And would I change places with Tracy Samantha Lord for all her wealth and beauty? Oh, boy, just ask me."

*Photographer Ruth Hussey (Liz Imbrie)*

**7.** "Ah, that's the old redhead, no bitterness, no recrimination, just a good swift left to the jaw."

*Grant, reacting to one of Hepburn's insults*

**8.** "With the rich and mighty, always a little patience."

*Spanish peasant proverb quoted in reporter James Stewart's (Macauley Connor's) book*

**9.** "Kittredge is no great tower of strength, you know, Tracy. He's just a tower."

*Grant, on Hepburn's prospective groom John Howard (George Kittredge)*

**10.** "There are more of you than people realize. A special class of the American female: the married maidens."

*Grant to Hepburn, later paraphrased by Hepburn to Stewart*

**11.** "My, she was yare."

*Hepburn, on her and Grant's former boat, the True Love, using a nautical term that she defines as "easy to handle, quick to the helm, fast, bright"; Grant later repeats the same line*

**12.** "What most wives fail to realize is that their husbands' philandering has nothing whatever to do with them."

Hepburn's father, the philandering John Halliday (Seth Lord)

**13.** "C. K. Dexter Haven! Oh, C. K. Dexter Haven!"

A drunken Stewart, calling to Grant to wake up

**14.** "The prettiest sight in this fine pretty world is the privileged class enjoying its privileges."

Stewart to Hepburn

**15.** "There's a magnificence in you, Tracy. . . . A magnificence that comes out of your eyes and your voice and the way you stand there and the way you walk. You're lit from within, Tracy. You've got fires banked down in you, hearth fires and holocausts."

Stewart to Hepburn

**16.** "Put me in your pocket, Mike."

Hepburn to Stewart, before they run off together for a swim

**17.** HEPBURN: "I think men are wonderful."
HUSSEY: "The little dears."

The two love interests of Stewart, discussing his nobility toward Hepburn

**18.** "But I am beholden to you, Mike, I'm most beholden."

Hepburn to Stewart, after declining his marriage proposal

**LAST LINES**
**19.** WEIDLER, witnessing the unexpected remarriage of Hepburn and Grant: "I did it. I did it all."

ROLAND YOUNG (*Uncle Willie*): "I feel as though I'd lived through all this before in another life."

**PIANO, THE** (New Zealand: CiBy 2000/ Miramax, 1993). D: Jane Campion. S: Jane Campion.

**1.** "Something to be said for silence."

Sam Neill (Stewart), on the muteness of his mail-order bride Holly Hunter (Ada McGrath)

**2.** "The piano is mine. It's *mine.*"

Hunter's note to Neill, when he refuses to pay for bringing her piano from the beach to their house

**3.** "She's right. It's a coffin. Let the sea bury it."

Maori oarsman, on the piano

**4.** "What a death. What a chance. What a surprise."

Hunter, in narration, after not drowning when she accidentally falls into the sea, tied to her piano

**LAST LINE**
**5.** "There is a silence where no sound may be, in the cold grave, under the deep, deep sea."

Hunter, narrating, quoting lines from English poet Thomas Hood

**PICNIC** (Columbia, 1955). D: Joshua Logan. S: Daniel Taradash. Fr: William Inge (play).

**1.** "Oh, I can tell a lot about a man by dancing with him. You know, some boys, well, when they take a girl in their arms to dance, they, well, they make her feel sort of uncomfortable. But with you, I . . . I had the feeling you knew exactly what you were doing and I could follow you every step of the way."

Kim Novak (Madge Owens) to William Holden (Hal Carter), following their dance together

**2.** "Baby, what you do!"
*Holden to Novak*

**3.** "I get so tired of just being told I'm pretty."
*Novak to Holden*

**4.** "What's the use, baby? I'm a bum. She saw through me like an X-ray machine. There's no place in the world for a guy like me."
*Holden to Novak, about Rosalind Russell's (Rosemary Sydeny's) comment about him*

**PILLOW TALK** (Universal, 1959). D: Michael Gordon. S: Stanley Shapiro, Maurice Richlin. Fr: Russell Rouse, Clarence Green (story).

**1.** "Have you any idea what it's like to be on a party line with a sex maniac?"
*Doris Day (Jan Morrow)*

**2.** "Jonathan, you just don't go around giving girls cars."
*Day to Tony Randall (Jonathan Forbes), upon his gift to her of a sports car, in payment for decorating his office*

**3.** "There's nothing in my bedroom that bothers me."
*Day to Rock Hudson (Brad Allen), over the phone*

**4.** DAY, on her unmarried state: "I have a good job, a lovely apartment, I go out with very nice men to the best places, the finest restaurants, the theater. What am I missing?"
THELMA RITTER (*Alma*): "If you have to ask, believe me, you're missing it."

**5.** "If there's anything worse than a woman living alone, it's a woman saying she likes it."
*Ritter to Day*

**6.** "They didn't hit the moon with the first missile shot, either."
*Randall to Day, on her tepid response to his first kiss*

**7.** RANDALL: "Money seems to have lost its value these days. With $200,000 my grandfather cornered the wheat market and started a panic in Omaha. Today you can't even frighten songwriters with it."
HUDSON: "That's inflation for you, Jonathan."

**8.** RANDALL: "You're prejudiced against me because I'm part of a minority group."
HUDSON: "What minority group?"
RANDALL: "Millionaires."

**9.** "So that's the other end of your party line."
*Hudson to himself, on seeing Day dancing*

**10.** "Between the late late show at night and Dave Garroway in the morning, why, it seems like there ain't much time."
*Ritter to Day, on why people no longer have large families*

**11.** "I get a nice warm feeling being near you, ma'am. It's like being 'round a potbellied stove on a frosty morning."
*Hudson, in his fake Texan persona, to Day*

**12.** "It ain't a very big mountain, but it's ours."
*The fake Hudson, wooing Day with his humble riches*

**13.** "How could you fall in love with a tourist?"
*Randall to Day, when she professes love for the fake Hudson*

**14.** "I look upon Brad Allen like any other disease. I've had him. It's over. I'm immune to him."

*Day to colleague decorator Marcel Dalio (Pierot), after discovering Hudson's true identity*

**PINK PANTHER, THE** *(UA, 1964). D: Blake Edwards. S: Blake Edwards, Maurice Richlin.*

**1.** PETER SELLERS *(Inspector Jacques Clouseau):* "You are a constant and desirable contradiction."

CAPUCINE *(Simone Clouseau):* "Oh, I am simply a woman."

**2.** "Well, I enjoy reality as much as the next man. It's just that in my case, fortunately, reality includes a good stiff belt every now and then."

*David Niven (Sir Charles, the Phantom) to Claudia Cardinale (Princess Dala), on whether drinking is an escape from reality*

**3.** "When you've seen one Stradivarius, you've seen them all."

*Sellers to Capucine, after destroying his violin*

**4.** "More behavior like this and I'll have your stripes!"

*Sellers, chastising two policemen dressed as a zebra*

**PINOCCHIO** *(RKO, 1940). D: Ben Sharpsteen, Hamilton Luske. S: Ted Sears, Otto Englander, Webb Smith, William Cottrell, Joseph Sabo, et al. Fr: Collodi (story).*

**1.** "Little puppet, made of pine, wake, the gift of life is thine."

*Evelyn Venable (The Blue Fairy), when Dickie Jones (Pinocchio) is brought to life*

**2.** "I dub you Pinocchio's conscience, Lord High Keeper of the knowledge of right and wrong, counselor in moments of temptation, and guide along the straight and narrow path."

*Venable to Cliff Edwards (Jiminy Cricket), when he becomes Pinocchio's conscience*

**3.** "Always let your conscience be your guide."

*Venable to Jones, when Edwards becomes Jones's conscience*

**4.** "Prove yourself brave, truthful, and unselfish, and someday, you will be a real boy."

*Venable to Jones*

**5.** "A lie keeps growing and growing, until it's as plain as the nose on your face."

*Venable to Jones, on why his nose is growing*

**6.** "A little boy who won't be good might just as well be made of wood."

*Venable to Jones, scolding him for lying*

**7.** "What they can't do these days!"

*Edwards, when Jones comes to life*

**8.** "A conscience is that still small voice that people won't listen to."

*Edwards*

**9.** "What does an actor want with a conscience, anyway?"

*Walter Catlett (J. Worthington Foulfellow), when Jones joins the marionette show*

**10.** "Give a bad boy enough rope, and he'll soon make a jackass of himself."

*Coachman Charles Judels (Stromboli), upon arriving at Pleasure Island*

**PLACE IN THE SUN, A** (Paramount, 1951). D: George Stevens. S: Michael Wilson, Harry Brown. Fr: Patrick Kearney (stage adaptation, An American Tragedy), Theodore Dreiser (novel, An American Tragedy).

1. "Tell Mama. Tell Mama all."

    Elizabeth Taylor (Angela Vickers) to Montgomery Clift (George Eastman)

**PLAN 9 FROM OUTER SPACE** (Distributors Corp. of America, 1959). D: Edward D. Wood, Jr. S: Edward D. Wood, Jr.

1. "Visits? That would indicate visitors."

    Army captain, making a shrewd deduction on hearing of extraterrestrial visits

2. "The saucers are up there, and the cemetery's out there, but I'll be locked up in there."

    Mona McKinnon (Paula Trent), reassuring husband Gregory Walcott (Jeff Trent) of her safety

3. "Guess that's why you're a detective, Lieutenant, and I'm still a uniformed cop."

    Police officer to Duke Moore (Lieutenant Harper), who is marginally smarter than he

4. "How could I hope to hold down my command if I didn't believe in what I saw and shot at?"

    Tom Keene (Col. Tom Edwards)

5. "You didn't actually think you were the only inhabited planet in the universe. How can any race be so stupid?"

    Recorded voice of alien

6. KEENE: "This is the most fantastic story I've ever heard."
    WALCOTT: "And every word of it's true, too."
    KEENE: "That's the fantastic part of it."

7. MOORE, remarking on the behavior of females: "Modern women."
    KEENE: "Yeah, they've been that way all down through the ages. Especially in a spot like this."

8. "I'll bet my badge right now we haven't seen the last of those weirdies."

    Moore

9. "They've been mighty useful before on flesh and blood, and you two look like you've got a lot of both."

    Moore, on the guns he and his comrades are pointing at the aliens

10. ALIEN DUDLEY MANLOVE (Eros), explaining why his mission is important: "Because all of you on Earth are idiots!"
    WALCOTT: "Now, you just hold on, buster."

11. "Explode the sunlight here, gentlemen, you explode the universe. Explode the sunlight here, and a chain reaction will occur direct to the sun itself, and to all the planets that sunlight touches, to every planet in the universe."

    Manlove, demonstrating a garbled knowledge of science as he explains how the ultimate weapon works

12. "My friends, you have seen this incident based on sworn testimony. Can you prove that it didn't happen? Perhaps, on your way home, someone will tap you in the dark, and you will never know it, for they will be from outer space!"

    Criswell, narrating

**LAST LINE**
13. "God help us in the future."

    Criswell

**PLANET OF THE APES** *(20th Century–Fox, 1968). D: Franklin J. Schaffner. S: Michael Wilson, Rod Serling. Fr: Pierre Boulle (novel, Monkey Planet).*

**1.** "Get your stinking paws off me, you damn dirty ape."

*Charlton Heston (George Taylor) to gorilla who has captured him in a net*

**2.** "All men look alike to most apes."

*Chimpanzee Kim Hunter (Dr. Zira)*

**3.** "Somehow it makes you look less intelligent."

*Chimpanzee Roddy McDowall (Cornelius), after Heston shaves*

**4.** "Beware the beast man for he is the devil's pawn. Alone among God's primates, he kills for sport, for lust, for greed. Yea, he will murder his brother to possess his brother's land. Let him not breed in great numbers, for he will make a desert of his home and yours. Shun him, drive him back into his jungle lair, for he is the harbinger of death."

*McDowall, reading a warning from the Lawgiver's scrolls*

**5.** "All right, but you're so damned ugly."

*Hunter, grudgingly accepting a kiss from Heston*

**LAST LINE**
**6.** "You finally really did it. You maniacs! You blew it up! God damn you! God damn you all to hell!"

*Heston, cursing mankind, after discovering the ruins of the Statue of Liberty*

**PLATOON** *(Orion, 1986). D: Oliver Stone. S: Oliver Stone.*

**1.** "Somebody once wrote, 'Hell is the impossibility of reason.' That's what this place feels like, Hell. I hate it already, and it's only been a week."

*Charlie Sheen (Chris Taylor), in narration, about combat duty in Vietnam*

**2.** "O'Neill, take a break. You don't have to be a prick every day of your life, you know."

*Willem Dafoe (Sergeant Elias) to John C. McGinley (Sergeant O'Neill)*

**3.** "I love this place at night. The stars. There's no right or wrong in them. They're just there."

*Dafoe to Sheen*

**4.** "I am reality. There's the way it ought to be, and there's the way it is."

*Tom Berenger (Sergeant Barnes)*

**5.** "Death. What do you all know about death?"

*Berenger to the platoon*

**6.** "You're trying to cure the headache by cutting off the head."

*Francesca Quinn (Rhah Vermucci) to Sheen, referring to killing Berenger*

**7.** "Barnes was shot seven times and he ain't dead. That mean anything to you? Huh? Barnes ain't meant to die. The only thing that can kill Barnes is Barnes."

*Quinn to Sheen*

**8.** "All you got to do is make it out of here, and it's all gravy. Every day, the rest of your life. Gravy."

*Keith David (King) to Sheen*

**9.** "They come from the end of the line, most of them. Small towns you never heard of. Pulaski, Tennessee. Brandon, Mississippi. Pork Bend, Utah. Wampum, Pennsylvania. Two years high school's about it. Maybe, if they're lucky, a job waiting for them back in the factory. But most of them got nothing. They're poor. They're the unwanted, yet they're fighting for our society, and our freedom. It's weird. Isn't it?"

*Sheen, in narration*

**LAST LINE**

**10.** "There are times since when I've felt like a child born of those two fathers. But be that as it may, those of us who did make it have an obligation to build again, to teach others what we know, and to try with what's left of our lives to find a goodness and meaning to this life."

*Sheen, in narration, on Dafoe and Berenger*

**PLAY IT AGAIN, SAM** (Paramount, 1972). D: Herbert Ross. S: Woody Allen. Fr: Woody Allen (play).

**1.** "I don't tan—I stroke!"

*Woody Allen (Allan Felix), expressing distaste for sunbathing*

**PLAYER, THE** (Fine Line Features, 1992). D: Robert Altman. S: Michael Tolkin. Fr: Michael Tolkin (novel).

**1.** "Okay, here it is. *The Graduate Part II*."

*Buck Henry (Himself), pitching an idea to studio executive Tim Robbins (Griffin Mill)*

**2.** "It's *Out of Africa* meets *Pretty Woman*."

*Female writer, pitching another idea to Robbins*

**3.** ROBBINS, hearing yet another idea: "So it's kind of a psychic political thriller comedy with a heart."

BEARDED WRITER: "With a heart. And, uh . . . not unlike *Ghost* meets *Manchurian Candidate*."

**4.** "I HATE *YOUR GUTS* ASSHOLE!"

*Postcard sent to Robbins by unknown psychotic screenwriter*

**5.** "See you in the next reel, asshole."

*Screenwriter Vincent D'Onofrio (David Kahane), threatening Robbins and sounding as if he is the nut sending the postcards*

**6.** "I was just thinking what an interesting concept it is to eliminate the writer from the artistic process. If we can just get rid of these actors and directors, maybe we've got something here."

*Robbins, making what may or may not be an ironic statement*

**7.** SCREENWRITER RICHARD E. GRANT (*Tom Oakley*), pitching a high-minded idea to Robbins: "We want real people here. We don't want people coming with any preconceived notions. We want them to see a district attorney."

DEAN STOCKWELL (*Andy Civella*): "Bruce Willis."

GRANT: "No. Not Bruce Willis, not Kevin Costner. This is an innocent woman fighting for her life."

STOCKWELL: "Julia Roberts."

**8.** "What about the way the old ending tested in Canoga Park? Everybody hated it. We reshot it; now everybody loves it. That's reality."

*Grant, on why he sacrificed artistic integrity to have his movie reshot with a happy ending*

LAST LINES

**9.** GRETA SCACCHI (*June Gudmunsdottir*): "What took you so long?"
ROBBINS: "Traffic was a bitch."

*Scacchi welcoming home her husband Robbins, murderer of her previous lover, while reprising the last lines of the film-within-the-film, Habeas Corpus, spoken earlier by Julia Roberts and Bruce Willis*

**PLAZA SUITE** (*Paramount, 1970*). D: Arthur Hiller. S: Neil Simon. Fr: Neil Simon (play).

**1.** WALTER MATTHAU (*Sam Nash*): "I don't have to accept being fifty-one years old. I don't accept getting older."
MAUREEN STAPLETON (*Karen Nash*): "Good luck to you. You'll be the youngest one in the cemetery."

**2.** "Just want to do it all over again. I'd like to start the whole damn thing right from the beginning."

*Matthau, on what he wants from life*

**3.** "Why do you always start the most serious discussions in our life when I'm halfway out the door?"

*Matthau to Stapleton*

**4.** "All right, so we yell and scream a little. So we fight and curse and aggravate each other. So you blame me for being a lousy mother. I accuse you of being a rotten husband. That doesn't mean we're not happy. Does it?"

*Lee Grant (Norma Hubley) to Matthau (now playing Roy Hubley)*

**PLEASE DON'T EAT THE DAISIES** (*MGM, 1960*). D: Charles Walters. S: Isobel Lennart. Fr: Jean Kerr (book).

**1.** "There are interesting failures. There are prestige failures, and there are financial failures, but this is the sort of failure that gives failures a bad name."

*Theater critic David Niven (Lawrence Mackay), when his bad review turns a show into a sellout*

**2.** "For a critic, that first step is his first critic joke. People laugh. Whole new world opens up. He makes another joke, and another, and then one day, along comes a joke that shouldn't be made because the show he's reviewing is a good show, but the joke happens to be a good joke, and, you know what? The joke wins."

*Richard Haydn (Alfred North)*

**3.** "We're home in our own room. For once in their lives, all our children seem to be asleep. We're even married. So what's the problem, huh?"

*Niven to Doris Day (Kate Mackay), in an amorous mood*

**4.** NIVEN: "I wish you wouldn't call yourself a housewife. You're so much more than that."
DAY: "So is every other housewife."

**5.** "Do you know what he did with those daisies? He ate them."

*Niven's mother Spring Byington (Mrs. Mackay) to Day, referring to Flip Mark (George Mackay), one of their sons*

**6.** "Everyone's available who isn't dead."

*Janis Paige (Deborah Vaughn), on fidelity*

**7.** "I was having a rendezvous with Rock Hudson! Me, David, George, Gabriel, Adam, and Hobo! All of us!"

*Day to Niven, sarcastically explaining her day*

**PLEASURE OF HIS COMPANY, THE** (Paramount, 1961). D: George Seaton. S: Samuel Taylor. Fr: Samuel Taylor, Cornelia Otis Skinner (play).

**1.** "He's very progressive. He has all sorts of ideas about artificial insemination and all that sort of thing. He breeds all over the world."

Debbie Reynolds (Jessica Poole) to her father Fred Astaire (Biddeford Polo Poole), about her fiancé Tab Hunter (Roger Henderson)

**POINT OF NO RETURN** (Warner Bros., 1993). D: John Badham. S: Robert Getchell, Alexandra Seros. Fr: Luc Besson (screenplay, La Femme Nikita).

**1.** "I never did mind about the little things."

Trained assassin Bridget Fonda (Maggie), explaining her attitude about murder, based on what Anne Bancroft (Amanda) taught her about good manners

**POLICE ACADEMY** (Warner Bros., 1984). D: Hugh Wilson. S: Neal Israel, Pat Proft, Hugh Wilson. Fr: Neal Israel, Pat Proft (story).

**1.** "The academy is taking all kinds today. Anybody can get in. Even you."

Ted Ross (Captain Reed) to Steve Guttenberg (Carey Mahoney)

**POLTERGEIST II** (MGM/UA, 1986). D: Brian Gibson. S: Mark Victor, Michael Grais.

**1.** "They're ba-a-ck!"

Heather O'Rourke (Carol Anne Freeling)

**POPPY** (Paramount, 1936). D: Edward Sutherland. S: Waldemar Young, Virginia Van Upp. Fr: Dorothy Donnelly (play).

**1.** "I'm like Robin Hood. I steal from the rich and give to the poor—us poor."

W. C. Fields (Professor Eustace McGargle)

**LAST LINE**

**2.** "Never give a sucker an even break."

Fields's last bit of fatherly advice for his daughter Rochelle Hudson (Poppy)

**PORKY'S** (20th Century–Fox, 1982). D: Bob Clark. S: Bob Clark.

**1.** "You're too stupid to even be a good bigot."

Scott Colomby (Brian Schwartz) to Cyril O'Reilly (Tim), correcting his pronunciation of the word "kike"

**POSEIDON ADVENTURE, THE** (20th Century–Fox, 1972). D: Ronald Neame. S: Stirling Silliphant, Wendell Mayes. Fr: Paul Gallico (novel).

**1.** "He's lonely. That's why he runs, so he won't notice."

Shelley Winters (Belle Rosen), on jogging bachelor Red Buttons (James Martin)

**2.** "Oh, my God!"

Leslie Nielsen (Captain), sighting the tidal wave

**3.** "In the water, I'm a very skinny lady."

Winters

**POSTCARDS FROM THE EDGE** (Columbia, 1990). D: Mike Nichols. S: Carrie Fisher. Fr: Carrie Fisher (novel).

**1.** "What is it, a viral love? Kind of a twenty-four-hour thing?"

Meryl Streep (Suzanne Vale) to Dennis Quaid

(Jack Falkner), when he suggests he no longer loves her

**2.** "I did not lift my skirt. It twirled up!"

*Shirley MacLaine (Doris Mann) to her daughter Streep, on whether she lifted her skirt at Streep's seventeenth birthday party*

**3.** MACLAINE: "How would you like to have Joan Crawford for a mother? Or Lana Turner?"
STREEP: "These are the options?"

**4.** "How many 120-year-old women do you know?"

*Streep to MacLaine, on whether the latter is middle-aged*

**POSTMAN ALWAYS RINGS TWICE, THE** (MGM, 1946). D: Tay Garnett. S: Harry Ruskin, Niven Busch. Fr: James M. Cain (novel).

**1.** "You've been trying to make a tramp out of me ever since you've known me."

*Lana Turner (Cora Smith) to John Garfield (Frank Chambers)*

**2.** "I can only think of fifteen or twenty reasons why you two shouldn't be happy together."

*Lawyer Hume Cronyn (Arthur Keats) to Turner and Garfield*

**3.** "When we get home, Frank, then there'll be kisses, kisses with life and not death—"

*Turner to Garfield*

**4.** "You never realize that he always rings twice."

*Garfield to prison chaplain Tom Dillon (Father McDonnell), drawing an analogy between the postman ringing twice and justice punishing the guilty*

**LAST LINE**
**5.** "Father, would you send up a prayer for me and Cora, and if you could find it in your heart, make it that we're together, wherever it is."

*Garfield, awaiting execution, to Dillon*

**POTEMKIN** (USSR: Gosinko, 1925). D: Sergei Eisenstein. S: Sergei Eisenstein, Nina Agadzhanova-Sh.

**FIRST LINE**
**1.** "Revolution is the only lawful, equal, effectual war. It was in Russia that this war was declared and begun."

*Lenin, according to opening title*

**2.** "We, the sailors of the *Potemkin*, must stand in the first lines of the revolution with our brothers, the workers."

*Two seamen talking on deck*

**3.** "Comrades, the time has come to act."
*Seaman, calling comrades to mutiny*

**4.** "We've had enough garbage to eat! . . . A dog wouldn't eat this."

*Seamen, refusing to eat maggot-ridden meat*

**LAST LINE**
**5.** "Brothers!"

*Mutinous seamen as they emerge victorious*

**PRESUMED INNOCENT** (Warner Bros., 1990). D: Alan J. Pakula. S: Frank Pierson, Alan J. Pakula. Fr: Scott Turow (novel).

**LAST LINE**
**1.** "There was a crime, there was a victim, and there is punishment."

Harrison Ford (Rusty Sabich), on the way justice was done for the murder of Greta Scacchi (Carolyn Polhemus)

**PRETTY WOMAN** (Touchstone, 1990). D: Garry Marshall. S: J. F. Lawton.

**1.** "I can do anything I want to, baby. I ain't lost."

Julia Roberts (Vivian Ward) to Richard Gere (Edward Lewis), when she is asked for directions

**2.** "What do you want it to be?"
Roberts to Gere, when asked her name

**3.** "I never joke about money."
Roberts to Gere

**4.** "Well, this hotel is not the kind of establishment that rents rooms by the hour."
Gere to Roberts, about his posh digs

**5.** "First time in an elevator."
Gere to onlookers, about Roberts

**6.** "Close your mouth, dear."
Female hotel guest to male hotel guest

**7.** "You're on my fax."
Gere to Roberts

**8.** "Listen, I . . . I appreciate this whole seduction scene you got going, but let me give you a tip: I'm a sure thing."
Roberts to Gere

**9.** "Slippery little suckers."
Roberts, after trying to extricate a snail from its shell

**10.** "Mr. Lewis and I are going to build ships together, great big ships."
Ralph Bellamy (James Morse)

**11.** "She rescues him right back."
Roberts to Gere, on how the fairy tale ends

**LAST LINE**
**12.** "Welcome to Hollywood! What's your dream? Everybody comes here. This is Hollywood, land of dreams. Some dreams come true, some don't, but keep on dreamin'. This is Hollywood. Always time to dream, so keep on dreamin'."
Abdul Salaam El Razzac (Happy Man)

**PRIDE OF THE YANKEES, THE** (RKO, 1942). D: Sam Wood. S: Jo Swerling, Herman J. Mankiewicz. Fr: Paul Gallico (story).

**1.** "People all say that I've had a bad break, but today—today I consider myself the luckiest man on the face of the Earth."
Gary Cooper (Lou Gehrig), in his farewell line to a stadium full of fans

**LAST LINE**
**2.** "Play ball!"
Umpire's voice, offscreen

**PRIME OF MISS JEAN BRODIE, THE** (UK: 20th Century–Fox, 1969). D: Ronald Neame. S: Jay Presson Allen. Fr: Jay Presson Allen (adapted play), Muriel Spark (original novel).

**1.** "I believe I am past my prime. I had reckoned on my prime lasting till I was at least fifty."
Teacher Maggie Smith (Jean Brodie)

**2.** "I didn't betray you. I simply put a stop to you."
Pamela Franklin to Maggie Smith

LAST LINE

**3.** "Little girls, I am in the business of putting old heads on young shoulders, and all my pupils are the crème de la crème. Give me a girl at an impressionable age and she is mine for life."

Smith to her pupils

**PRINCE AND THE PAUPER, THE** (Warner Bros., 1937). D: William Keighley. S: Laird Doyle. Fr: Mark Twain (novel), Catherine C. Cushing (play).

**1.** "Do you know what I'd do if I were a king? I'd send the prince out to play with other little boys. Then, he'd learn about the people, and be a good kind king when he grew up."

Billy Mauch (Tom Canty), the pauper

**2.** BILLY MAUCH: "Oh, you can't play with me. I'm the beggar boy."

BOBBY MAUCH (Prince Edward): "I can play with anyone I please. I'm the prince."

**3.** "When you sit in judgment, remember your seat is but a chair made with English oak, hewn by English yeomen, and made into a throne only by the will of the English people. That is patriotism."

Montagu Love (Henry VIII) to Bobby Mauch

**4.** "Never trust so much, love so much, or need anyone so much, that you can't betray them with a smile. That is the paradox of power."

Love to Bobby Mauch

**5.** "There's strange magic in it, Edward. It can make a royal whim, a law, an innocent man guilty, a poor man rich. A dangerous toy for a child, and a fool. I advise you to use it sparingly and seldom, lest it seal your own doom."

Love to Bobby Mauch, referring to the great Seal of England

**6.** "Yes, but windows? Don't you see when poor people are sick, windows are the only outside they have? Why, they wouldn't have anything nice to look at if it weren't for windows. And besides, that's taxing sunshine and light, which don't belong to us at all, but to God."

Billy Mauch, protesting against a window tax, to Claude Rains (Earl of Hertford)

**7.** "May I learn generosity from you, Sire."

Rains to Bobby Mauch, when his life is spared

**8.** "To one of my temperament, riches are a curse. Possessions, a veritable scourge. All I ask is an obscure life, and a peaceful one, but, uh, not too peaceful, of course."

Errol Flynn (Miles Hendon) to Bobby Mauch, when Mauch wishes to reward Flynn for his help

LAST LINE

**9.** "This is good for cracking nuts. Isn't it?"

Bobby Mauch to Billy Mauch, referring to the Great Seal of England

**PRINCESS AND THE PIRATE, THE** (RKO, 1944). D: David Butler. S: Don Hartman, Melville Shavelson, Everett Freeman, Allen Boretz, Curtis Kenyon. Fr: Sy Bartlett (story).

**1.** "You should've seen the show I did on the road to Morocco. . . . I'd've been sensational, only some over-age crooner with laryngitis kept crabbing my act."

Bob Hope (Sylvester), alluding to his costar Bing Crosby in Road to Morocco (1942)

**2.** "If you don't tell anyone I'm not a gypsy, I won't tell anyone you're not an idiot."

*Hope, in disguise as a gypsy, making a deal with pirate Walter Brennan (Featherhead)*

**3.** "My head—why, I hardly ever use it."

*Hope, on the prospect of having his head removed*

**4.** "Someone ought to get you interested in collecting stamps."

*Hope to Walter Slezak (Governor La Roche), on his hobby of shrinking heads*

**5.** "They're real, and in Technicolor, too."

*Hope, on waking up to see three beautiful serving maids*

**6.** "Don't take any wooden doubloons."

*Hope*

**7.** "I'll chop off his liver! Say, that might be pretty good, chopped liver."

*Hope, pretending to be a cutthroat pirate*

**8.** FIRST MATE, alluding to potential allies: "We are always certain of friends in the South."

HOPE: "Oh, a Democrat, huh?"

**9.** "How do you like that, I knock my brains out for nine reels and a bit player from Paramount comes over and gets the girl. This is the last picture I do for Goldwyn."

*Hope, on having Bing Crosby, in a cameo, wind up with Virginia Mayo (Margaret)*

**PRINCESS BRIDE, THE** (20th Century–Fox, 1987). D: Rob Reiner. S: William Goldman. Fr: William Goldman (novel).

**1.** "Hello. My name is Inigo Montoya. You killed my father. Prepare to die!"

Mandy Patinkin (Inigo Montoya) to Chris Sarandon (Prince Humperdinck)

**PRIVATE LIFE OF HENRY VIII, THE** (UK: UA, 1933). D: Alexander Korda. S: Lajor Biro, Arthur Wimperis.

**1.** "Am I a king or a breeding bull?"

*Charles Laughton (Henry VIII)*

**PRIZZI'S HONOR** (20th Century–Fox, 1985). D: John Huston. S: Richard Condon, Janet Roach. Fr: Richard Condon (novel).

**1.** "Yeah, right here on the Oriental, with all the lights on."

*Anjelica Huston (Maerose Prizzi), seducing Jack Nicholson (Charley Partanna)*

**2.** "Do I ice her? Do I marry her? Which one a dese?"

*Nicholson, on what to do about fellow assassin Kathleen Turner (Irene Walker)*

**PRODUCERS, THE** (Embassy, 1968). D: Mel Brooks. S: Mel Brooks.

**1.** "Under the right circumstances, a producer could make more money with a flop than he could with a hit."

*Accountant Gene Wilder (Leo Bloom), inadvertently giving a great idea to unscrupulous producer Zero Mostel (Max Bialystock)*

**2.** "I'm wet! I'm wet! I'm hysterical and I'm wet!"

*Wilder, after Mostel throws water in his face to calm down his hysteria*

**3.** "A week? Are you kidding? This play has got to close on page four."

*Mostel to Wilder, on how long* Springtime for Hitler *can be expected to run*

**4.** "Hitler was better looking than Churchill, he was a better dresser than Churchill, he had more hair, he told funnier jokes, and he could dance the pants off of Churchill!"

*Kenneth Mars, author of* Springtime for Hitler, *comparing his beloved Adolf Hitler and the hated Winston Churchill*

**5.** "That's exactly why we want to produce this play. To show the world the true Hitler, the Hitler you loved, the Hitler you knew, the Hitler with a song in his heart."

*Mostel to Mars*

**6.** "Flaunt it, baby, flaunt it!"

*Mostel to Wilder, on spending money lavishly*

**7.** "He's the only director whose plays close on the first day of rehearsal."

*Mostel to Wilder, on selecting abysmal director Christopher Hewett (Roger De Bris) to direct their play*

**8.** "Max. He's wearing a dress."

*Wilder to Mostel, on first seeing Hewett*

**9.** "Do you know, I never realized that the Third Reich meant Germany? I mean, it's drenched with historical goodies like that."

*Hewett, on what he likes about the play*

**10.** "And that whole third act has got to go. They're losing the war. It's too depressing."

*Hewett, suggesting revisions*

**11.** "Will the dancing Hitlers please wait in the wings? We are only seeing singing Hitlers."

*Hewett to auditioners for the role of Hitler*

**12.** "Hey, man. I *liebe* you, I *liebe* you, baby. I *liebe* you. Now, leave me alone."

*Dick Shawn (Lorenzo St. DuBois/LSD), the hippie actor playing Hitler, to Renee Taylor, the actress playing Eva Braun*

**13.** "You are the audience. I am the author. I outrank you."

*Mars, disagreeing about the quality of the performance with an audience member*

**14.** "How could this happen? I was so careful. I picked the wrong play, the wrong director, the wrong cast. Where did I go right?"

*Mostel, on the inexplicable success of* Springtime for Hitler

**15.** WILDER, on how to put an end to the play's success: "What do you mean, kill the actors? Actors are not animals. They're human beings."

MOSTEL: "They are? Have you ever eaten with one?"

**16.** "No one ever called me Leo before."

*Wilder, at the trial, on why he appreciates Mostel*

**PSYCHO** *(Paramount, 1960). D: Alfred Hitchcock. S: Joseph Stefano. Fr: Robert Bloch (novel).*

**1.** "Mother—what's the phrase?—isn't quite herself today."

*Anthony Perkins (Norman Bates) to Janet Leigh (Marion Crane)*

**2.** "A boy's best friend is his mother."

*Perkins*

**3.** "He tried to be his mother—and now he is."

Simon Oakland (Dr. Richmond), explaining what's happened to Perkins

**LAST LINE**

**4.** "They'll see and they'll know and they'll say, why, she wouldn't even harm a fly."

Virginia Gregg, voice of "Mother," speaking through Perkins

**PUBLIC ENEMY** (Warner Bros.–Vitaphone, 1931). D: William A. Wellman. S: Kubec Glasmon, John Bright, Harvey Thew. Fr: John Bright (original story, "Beer and Blood").

**1.** "It means they buy our beer, or they don't buy any beer."

Leslie Fenton ("Nails" Nathan) to James Cagney (Tom Powers)

**2.** "There's not only beer in that keg. There's beer and blood. Blood of men."

Returning World War I veteran Donald Cook (Mike Powers), on his brother Cagney's illicit activities

**3.** "Your hands ain't so clean. You killed and liked it. You didn't get them medals by holding hands with them Germans."

Cagney to Cook

**4.** "I wish you was a wishing well, so I could tie a bucket to you and sink you."

Cagney to Mae Clarke (Kitty), just before pushing a grapefruit in her face

**5.** "You are different, Tommy, very different. The men I know, and I've known dozens of them, oh, they're so nice, so polished, so considerate. Most women like that type. I guess they're afraid of the other kind. I thought I was, too. But you're so strong. You don't give. You take. Oh, Tommy, I could love you to death."

Jean Harlow (Gwen Allen) to Cagney

**6.** "I ain't so tough."

Cagney, when he's shot

**PUBLIC EYE, THE** (Universal, 1992). D: Howard Franklin. S: Howard Franklin.

**1.** "People like to see the dead guy's hat."

Photographer Joe Pesci (Leonard "The Great Bernzini" Bernstein), on why he places a hat in a picture of a corpse

**2.** "Just like everybody else in New York, making the most out of what she has."

Pesci, on a New York woman

**PURPLE ROSE OF CAIRO, THE** (Orion, 1985). D: Woody Allen. S: Woody Allen.

**1.** "You can't learn to be real. It's like learning to be a midget. It's not a thing you can learn."

Jeff Daniels (Gil Shepherd) to his fictional alter ego (Tom Baxter)

**PYGMALION** (UK: MGM, 1938). D: Anthony Asquith, Leslie Howard. S: George Bernard Shaw, W. P. Lipscomb, Cecil Lewis, Ian Dalrymple, Anthony Asquith. Fr: George Bernard Shaw (play).

**LAST LINE**

**1.** "Where the devil are my slippers, Eliza?"

Leslie Howard (Professor Henry Higgins) to Wendy Hiller (Eliza Doolittle)

**QUIET MAN, THE** (Argosy Pictures–Republic, 1952). D: John Ford. S: Frank S. Nugent, Richard Llewellyn (uncredited). Fr: Maurice Walsh (story).

**1.** "Well, it's a nice soft night, so I think I'll go and join me comrades and talk a little treason."

*Barry Fitzgerald (Michaeleen Flynn)*

**2.** "Some things a man doesn't get over so easy."

*John Wayne (Sean Thornton), discussing Maureen O'Hara (Mary Kate Danaher)*

**3.** "If you say three, mister, you'll never hear the man count ten."

*Wayne, after Victor McLaglen (Red Will Danaher) threatens to sic the dogs on him at the count of three*

**4.** "I thank you anyway, Sean Thornton, for the asking."

*O'Hara, thanking Wayne for his marriage proposal, after her brother refuses to consent*

**5.** "Two women in the house—and one of them a redhead."

*Fitzgerald, advising McLaglen against having both a wife and a sister in the house*

**6.** "Three Our Fathers and three Hail Marys."

*Fitzgerald, assigning penance to priest Ward Bond (Father Peter Lonergan), after Bond helps to play a trick on McLaglen*

**7.** "No patty fingers, if you please."

*Fitzgerald, laying down the law to the courting couple Wayne and O'Hara*

**8.** "There'll be no locks or bolts between us, Mary Kate—except those in your own mercenary little heart."

*Wayne, barging in on his new wife*

**9.** "Impetuous. Homeric."

*Fitzgerald, marveling at the broken bed in the newlyweds' house*

**10.** "Now when the Reverend Mr. Playfair, good man that he is, comes down, I want yez all to cheer like Protestants."

*Bond, encouraging his Catholic congregation to wish the Protestant Arthur Shields (Reverend Playfair) a hearty farewell*

**LAST LINE**

**11.** "No patty fingers, if you please. The proprieties at all times. Hold onto your hats."

*Fitzgerald at the reins, preparing to drive off with courting couple McLaglen and Mildred Natwick (Mrs. Sarah Tillane)*

**QUO VADIS?** (MGM, 1951). D: Mervyn LeRoy. S: John Lee Mahin, S. N. Behrman, Sonya Levien. Fr: Henryk Sienkiewicz (novel).

**FIRST LINE**

**1.** "This is the Appian Way. The most famous road that leads to Rome, as all roads lead to Rome."

*Narrator, uncredited*

**2.** "So long as there is money to pay the army, Rome will stand forever, that I'm sure of."

*Robert Taylor (Marcus Vinicius)*

**3.** "You must realize that a woman has no past when she mates with a god."

*Leo Genn (Petronius) to Taylor, referring to Peter Ustinov's (Nero's) wife*

**4.** "I don't know a great deal about philosophy, and lovely women shouldn't have the time to think that deeply."

*Taylor to Abraham Sofaer (Paul), on Deborah Kerr (Lygia)*

**5.** "Nothing do I see that is not perfection."

*Taylor's favorite compliment to Kerr*

**6.** "Unfortunately, Caesar, as a ruler, you must have subjects to rule. Sheer population is a necessary evil."

*Genn to Ustinov*

**7.** USTINOV: "It's lonely to be an emperor."
GENN, flattering him: "It is lonelier still to be a genius."

**8.** "One woman should never judge another. She hasn't the glands for it."

*Ustinov to Genn*

**9.** "Christians—are they the ones who worship some dead carpenter?"

*Taylor to Genn*

**10.** "What pulsating purity there is in fire! And my new Rome shall spring from the loins of fire!"

*Ustinov*

**11.** "It is foolish to kill those you hate, because, once dead, they are beyond pain."

*Patricia Laffan (Poppaea) to Taylor*

**12.** "When I have finished with these Christians, Petronius, history will not be sure that they ever existed."

*Ustinov to Genn*

**13.** "Quo vadis?"

*Finlay Currie (Peter), asking "Whither goest thou?" in Latin to a bright light representing Christ*

**14.** "To die as our Lord died is more than I deserve."

*Currie, facing crucifixion; the Roman soldiers oblige him by crucifying him upside down*

**RADIO DAYS** *(Orion, 1986). D: Woody Allen. S: Woody Allen.*

**LAST LINE**
**1.** "I never forgot that New Year's Eve, when Aunt Bea awakened me to watch 1944 come in. And I've never forgotten any of those people, or any of the voices we used to hear on the radio. Although the truth is, with the passing of each New Year's Eve, those voices do seem to grow dimmer and dimmer."

*Woody Allen, narrating*

**RAGING BULL** *(UA, 1980). D: Martin Scorsese. S: Paul Schrader, Mardik Martin. Fr: Jake LaMotta, Joseph Carter, Peter Savage (book).*

**1.** "I know I'm no Olivier
But if he fought Sugar Ray
He would say
That the thing ain't the ring
It's the play
So give me a stage
Where this bull here can rage
And though I can fight
I'd much rather hear myself recite
That's entertainment!"

*Robert De Niro (Jake LaMotta) to himself, in nightclub dressing room and, at the close of the film, to a nightclub audience*

**2.** "Do me a favor, I want you to hit me in the face."

*De Niro to Joe Pesci (Joey), as they sit in De Niro's kitchen*

**3.** "She ain't goin' with nobody. She's fifteen years old. Where the fuck she gonna go?"

*Pesci to De Niro, on whether Cathy Moriarty (Vickie) is going out with anyone*

**4.** "I done a lotta bad things, Joey. Maybe it's comin' back to me. Who knows, I'm a jinx, maybe. Who the hell knows?"

*De Niro to Pesci, after losing to Johnny Barnes (Sugar Ray Robinson)*

**5.** "They gotta give you the shot. You understand. If you win you win. If you lose you still win. There's no way you can lose, and you do it on your own, just the way you wanted to do, without any help from anybody. You understand. Just get down to 155 pounds, you fat bastard."

*Pesci to De Niro, on upcoming fight*

**6.** "We have a special guest with us tonight. I'd like to introduce the world's leading middleweight contender, the Bronx Bull, the Raging Bull, let's hear it for the great Jake LaMotta, ladies and gentlemen."

*Comedian (Bernie Allen), noting De Niro's presence in the audience at the Copacabana*

**7.** "He ain't pretty no more."

*Tommy Como (Nicholas Colasanto) to another audience member, at a fight where an opponent's "pretty" face takes a savage beating from De Niro*

**8.** "Gave me the old good news/bad news routine. The good news is you're gonna get the shot at the title. The bad news is they want you to do the old flip-flop for 'em."

*Pesci to De Niro, about throwing a fight*

**9.** BOARD SUSPENDS LAMOTTA

*New York Daily News headline following fight*

**10.** "Well, go ahead and kill everybody. You're a tough guy, go kill people. Kill Vickie, kill Salvy, kill Tommy Como, kill me while you're at it. What do I care? You're killing yourself the way you eat, you fat fuck, look at ya."

*Pesci to De Niro*

**11.** "Hey, Ray, I never went down, man. You never got me down, Ray. You hear me, you never got me down."

*De Niro to Barnes, during middleweight boxing championship*

**12.** "It's over for me. Boxing's over for me. I'm through. I'm tired of worrying about weight all the time. That's all I used to think about was weight, weight, weight."

*De Niro to reporter, on his retirement*

**13.** "Why do you do it? You're so stupid. You're so stupid. So fuckin' stupid. So stupid. . . . I'm not an animal. I'm not an animal. You want to treat me like that. I'm not that bad. I'm not that bad."

*De Niro, sitting down in cell after hitting head and knocking fists against cell wall*

**LAST LINE**

**14.** "Go get 'em, champ. . . . I'm the boss, I'm the boss, I'm the boss, I'm the boss, I'm the boss . . . boss boss boss boss boss boss."

*De Niro to mirror, before nightclub performance*

**RAGTIME** *(UK: Paramount, 1981). D: Milos Forman. S: Michael Weller. Fr: E. L. Doctorow (novel).*

**1.** "I read music so good white folks think I'm faking it."

> Black pianist Howard E. Rollins (Coalhouse Walker, Jr.) to James Olson (Father), who has suggested he doesn't know how to read music

**2.** "If my automobile is restored and delivered to the front of this building, and the fire chief is handed over to my justice, I give you my solemn oath I will come out with my hands raised, and no further harm will come to this place, or to any man."

> Rollins to Moses Gunn (Booker T. Washington), declaring his terms for not blowing up the Pierpont Morgan Library

**3.** ROLLINS, on Gunn's urging him to give himself up: "You speak like an angel, Mr. Washington. It's too bad we're living on the Earth."
GUNN: "You are damned, Mr. Walker."

**4.** "The library over there is worth millions . . . and people keep telling me you're a worthless piece of slime."

> Police commissioner James Cagney (Rheinlander Waldo), weighing the life of bigoted fire chief Kenneth McMillan (Willie Conklin) against the Morgan Library

**RAIDERS OF THE LOST ARK** (Paramount, 1981). D: Steven Spielberg. S: Lawrence Kasdan. Fr: George Lucas, Philip Kaufman (story).

**1.** "Dr. Jones, again we see there is nothing you can possess which I cannot take away."

> Paul Freeman (Belloq), stealing an artifact from rival archaeologist Harrison Ford (Indiana Jones)

**2.** "Lightning. Fire. The power of God or something."

> Ford, explaining the ray coming out of the Ark of the Covenant in a book illustration

**3.** "Besides, you know what a cautious fellow I am."

> Ford to Denholm Elliott (Brody), as he packs a gun in his suitcase

**4.** "Trust me."

> Ford to Karen Allen (Marion Ravenswood), in her saloon in Nepal

**5.** "Well, Jones, least you haven't forgotten how to show a lady a good time."

> Allen to Ford, after he burns down her saloon while saving her from assailants who have followed him there

**6.** "You wanna talk to God? Let's go see him together. I've got nothing better to do."

> Ford, offering to kill Freeman and himself

**7.** "Snakes. Why did it have to be snakes?"

> Ford, on seeing his least favorite vermin at the bottom of the pit where the ark is buried

**8.** "You Americans, you're all the same. Always overdressing for the wrong occasions."

> Nazi torturer Ronald Lacey (Toht) to Allen, who is wearing a white gown to her interrogation

**9.** "Holy smoke, my friends, I'm . . . I'm so pleased you're not dead."

> John Rhys-Davies (Sallah) to Ford and Allen

**10.** "I don't know. I'm making this up as I go."

> Ford, on how he plans to get the ark away from the Nazis

**11.** "We never seem to get a break, do we?"

> Allen to Ford, when he falls asleep before they can make love

**12.** "Marion, don't look at it. Shut your eyes, Marion. Don't look at it no matter what happens."

> Ford to Allen, as the ark begins to work its destructive magic

**RAIN** (UA, 1932). D: Lewis Milestone. S: Maxwell Anderson. Fr: John Colton, Clemence Randolph (play), W. Somerset Maugham (story).

**LAST LINE**

**1.** "I'm sorry for everybody in the world, I guess."

> Joan Crawford (Sadie Thompson)

**RAIN MAN** (MGM/UA, 1988). D: Barry Levinson. S: Ronald Bass, Barry Morrow. Fr: Barry Morrow (story).

**1.** "My dad lets me drive slow on the driveway. I'm an excellent driver."

> Dustin Hoffman (Raymond Babbitt)

**2.** "Flying's very dangerous. In 1987, there were thirty airline accidents. Two hundred and eleven were fatalities."

> Hoffman

**3.** "Quantas never crashed."

> Hoffman, about the airline with the best safety record

**4.** "Hell of a lot of work for three million dollars."

> Tom Cruise (Charlie Babbitt), retrieving his brother Hoffman after he leaves the car while on the highway

**5.** "I'm definitely not wearing my underwear.

> Hoffman to Cruise

**6.** "I buy my boxer shorts at K Mart in Cincinnati."

> Hoffman to Cruise

**7.** "You? You're the Rain Man?"

> Cruise to Hoffman, as the Rain Man's identity begins to be revealed

**8.** "Hot water burn baby."

> Hoffman to Cruise, revealing why Hoffman was sent away to an institution as Cruise draws water for a bath

**9.** "Never hurt Charlie Babbitt."

> Hoffman to Cruise, repeating the lesson he learned from the water incident

**10.** "I'll let you in on a little secret, Ray. K Mart sucks."

> Cruise to Hoffman, in a brotherly exchange

**11.** "Wet."

> Hoffman to Valeria Golino (Susanna), on what her kiss with him was like

**12.** "See, you have to understand that when we started out together, that he was only my brother in name. And then, then this morning we had pancakes."

> Cruise to Barry Levinson (Psychiatrist), on his newfound connection to Hoffman

**13.** CRUISE: "I like having you for my brother."

> HOFFMAN: "I'm an excellent driver."

**14.** CRUISE: "Tell him, Ray."

> HOFFMAN, to the psychiatrist, from the home to which Hoffman is returning: "K Mart sucks."

**RAINMAKER, THE** (Paramount, 1956). D: Joseph Anthony. S: N. Richard Nash. Fr: N. Richard Nash (play).

*1.* "One day that looking glass'll be the man who loves you. It'll be his eyes maybe. And you'll look in that mirror, and you'll be more than pretty. You'll be beautiful."

Burt Lancaster (Starbuck) to Katharine Hepburn (Lizzie Curry)

*2.* "You don't believe in nothin', not even in yourself. You don't even believe you're a woman—and if you don't, you're not."

Lancaster to Hepburn

*3.* "You gotta take my deal because once in your life you got to take a chance on a con man. . . . You gotta take my deal because it's gonna be a hot night and the world goes crazy on a hot night and maybe that's what a hot night is for."

Lancaster

**RAISING ARIZONA** (20th Century–Fox, 1987). D: Joel Coen. S: Ethan Coen, Joel Coen.

*1.* "I'll be taking these Huggies, and, uh, whatever cash you got."

Thief and child abductor Nicolas Cage (H. I. McDonnough), holding up a convenience store

**RAMBO: FIRST BLOOD PART II** (TriStar, 1985). D: George Pan Cosmatos. S: Sylvester Stallone, James Cameron. Fr: Kevin Jarre (story), David Morrell (characters).

*1.* SYLVESTER STALLONE (John Rambo): "Sir, do we get to win this time?"
RICHARD CRENNA (Trautman): "This time it's up to you."

*2.* "What you choose to call hell, he calls home."

Crenna to Charles Napier (Murdock), referring to Stallone and Vietnam

*3.* "To survive a war, you've got to become war."

Stallone

*4.* "I want what they want, and every guy who came over here and spilled his guts and gave everything he had wants. For our country to love us as much as we love it. That's what I want."

Stallone

**RASHOMON** (Japan: RKO, 1950). D: Akira Kurosawa. S: Shinobu Hashimoto, Akira Kurosawa. Fr: Ryunosuke Akutagawa (stories).

*1.* "It was a hot afternoon, about three days ago, that I first saw them. And then all of a sudden there was this cool breeze. If it hadn't been for that breeze, maybe I wouldn't have killed him."

Bandit Toshiro Mifune (Tajomaru), on his murder of samurai Masayuki Mori (Takehiro)

*2.* "I don't mind a lie. Not if it's interesting."

Kichijiro Ueda (Commoner), listening to stories of the murder

*3.* "I regret the loss of my horse much more than I regret the loss of this woman."

Mori to Mifune

*4.* "Just remember that a woman loves only one man. And when she loves, she loves madly, forgetting everything else. But a woman can be won only by strength—by the strength of the swords you are wearing."

Machiko Kyo (Masago), egging on Mifune and her husband Mori

LAST LINE

**5.** "No, I'm grateful to you. Because, thanks to you, I think I will be able to keep my faith in men."

> *Minoru Chiaki (Priest) to Takashi Shimura (Fire-wood Dealer), after Shimura offers to adopt an abandoned baby*

**RAZOR'S EDGE, THE** (20th Century–Fox, 1946). D: Edmund Goulding. S: Lamar Trotti. Fr: W. Somerset Maugham (novel).

**1.** "You know, I've never been able to understand why, when there's so much space in the world, people should deliberately choose to live in the Middle West."

> *Clifton Webb (Elliott Templeton)*

**2.** "I'm not a man that people overlook."

> *Webb*

**REALITY BITES** (Universal, 1994). D: Ben Stiller. S: Helen Childress.

**1.** "My fellow graduates, the answer is . . . I don't know."

> *Winona Ryder (Lelaina Pierce), at close of college commencement speech*

**2.** "My goal is that, um, like a career or something."

> *Steve Zahn (Sammy Cray), about his future, in a video made by Ryder*

**3.** "Mom, Dad, I'll take the BMW until I can afford to buy a regular car."

> *Ryder to parents, on their offer of their old BMW*

**4.** "Evian is naive spelled backward."

> *Janeane Garofalo (Vickie Miner) to Ryder, Ethan Hawke (Troy Dyer), and Zahn, looking at Evian water in gas station food mart*

**5.** "I can't believe you don't remember Peter Frampton. *Frampton Comes Alive.* I mean that album like totally changed my life."

> *Ben Stiller (Michael Grates) to Ryder*

**6.** "The most profound, important invention of my lifetime—the Big Gulp."

> *Ryder to Stiller, on the super-sized soda purchased at 7-11*

**7.** "He's the reason why Cliff Notes were invented."

> *Hawke to Ryder, about Stiller*

**8.** "I can't evolve right now."

> *Ryder to Hawke, on his vision of their relationship*

**9.** "I mean babies, okay? I can't even take care of a Chia Pet."

> *Ryder, talking to operator on psychic line about friends her age who are already starting families*

**10.** "A doily."

> *Hawke to Ryder, on what she looks like in fancy dress for date with Stiller*

**11.** "We're entering into a new phase here at the channel. Real programming."

> *Stiller to group awaiting premiere of Ryder's video*

**12.** RYDER: "I just don't understand why things can't just go back to normal at the end of the half hour, like on 'The Brady Bunch' or something."
> HAWKE: "Well, 'cause Mr. Brady died of AIDS."

**13.** "I never had sex with someone I loved before."

> *Hawke to Ryder*

**REAR WINDOW** *(Paramount, 1954). D: Alfred Hitchcock. S: John Michael Hayes. Fr: Cornell Woolrich (story).*

**1.** "In the old days they used to put your eyes out with a red-hot poker. Any of those bikini bombshells you're always watching worth a red-hot poker?"

*Nurse Thelma Ritter (Stella), to her patient James Stewart (L. B. "Jeff" Jeffries), who has been staring out his rear window while laid up with a broken leg*

**2.** "Right now I'd welcome trouble."

*Stewart, bored, to Ritter*

**3.** "Look, Mr. Jeffries, I'm not an educated woman, but I can tell you one thing. When a man and a woman see each other and like each other they ought to come together—wham—like a couple of taxis on Broadway, not sit around analyzing each other like two specimens in a bottle."

*Ritter to Stewart, on his relationship with Grace Kelly (Lisa Fremont)*

**4.** "I'd say she's doing a woman's hardest job: juggling wolves."

*Kelly to Stewart, on Georgine Darcy (Miss Torso), the party girl/dancer across the courtyard*

**5.** "Well, if there's one thing I know, it's how to wear the proper clothes."

*Kelly to Stewart, on whether she would fit into the life of a news photographer's wife*

**6.** "That would be a terrible job to tackle. Just how would you start to cut up a human body?"

*Stewart to Kelly, on the task faced by alleged wife-murderer Raymond Burr (Lars Thorwald)*

**7.** "Well, a Mark Cross overnight case, anyway. Compact, but ample enough."

*Kelly, answering Stewart as to whether her tiny overnight bag can be considered a suitcase*

**8.** "I'm not much on rear window ethics."
*Kelly to Stewart*

**9.** "Preview of coming attractions."
*Kelly to Stewart, pulling a negligee out of her overnight bag*

**10.** "Nobody ever invented a polite word for a killing yet."

*Ritter to Kelly, when she disapproves of Ritter's crude word choices*

**11.** WHAT HAVE YOU DONE WITH HER?
*Anonymous note from Stewart to Burr, delivered by Kelly*

**REBECCA** *(Selznick-International/UA, 1940). D: Alfred Hitchcock. S: Robert E. Sherwood, Joan Harrison. Fr: Daphne du Maurier (novel), Philip MacDonald, Michael Hogan (adaptation).*

**FIRST LINE**
**1.** "Last night, I dreamt I went to Manderley again."

*Joan Fontaine (Mrs. de Winter), in narration, about her mansion*

**2.** "I wish there could have been an invention that bottled up a memory, like perfume, and it never faded, never got stale. Then whenever I wanted to, I could uncork the bottle and live the memory all over again."

*Fontaine to Laurence Olivier (Maxim de Winter)*

**3.** "Please promise me never to wear black satin, or pearls, or to be thirty-six years old."

*Olivier to Fontaine, because that's what Rebecca did*

**4.** "I'm not the sort of person men marry."

*Fontaine to Olivier, when he proposes*

**5.** "Do you think the dead come back and watch the living?"

*Judith Anderson (Mrs. Danvers) to Fontaine*

**6.** "You thought you could be Mrs. de Winter. Live in her house. Walk in her steps. Take the things that were hers. But she's too strong for you. You can't fight her. No one ever got the better of her. Never. Never. She was beaten in the end, but it wasn't a man. It wasn't a woman. It was the sea."

*Anderson to Fontaine*

**7.** "It's gone forever. That funny, lost look I loved won't ever come back. I killed that when I told you about Rebecca. It's gone. In a few hours, you've grown much older."

*Olivier to Fontaine*

**8.** "I have a strong feeling that before the day is out, somebody's going to make use of that rather expressive, though somewhat old-fashioned term 'foul play.'"

*George Sanders (Jack Flavell) to Olivier*

**9.** "You know he's the old-fashioned type, who'd die to defend his honor, or who'd kill for it."

*Sanders to C. Aubrey Smith (Colonel Julyan), on Olivier*

**LAST LINE**
**10.** "It's Mrs. Danvers. She's gone mad. She said she'd rather destroy Manderley than see us happy here."

*Fontaine to Olivier, as Manderley, their mansion, goes up in flames*

**REBEL WITHOUT A CAUSE** (Warner Bros., 1955). D: Nicholas Ray. S: Stewart Stern. Fr: Irving Shulman (adaptation), Nicholas Ray (story line), Dr. Robert M. Linder (story).

**1.** "You are tearing me apart! You say one thing, he says another, and everybody changes back again."

*Troubled teenager James Dean (Jim Stark) to parents Jim Backus and Ann Doran*

**2.** "If I had one day when I didn't have to be all confused, and didn't have to feel that I was ashamed of everything . . . If I felt that I belonged someplace, you know, then . . ."

*Dean to policeman Edward C. Platt (Ray)*

**3.** "Watch out about choosing your pals. You know what I mean? Don't let them choose you."

*Backus to Dean, on his first day of school*

**4.** DEAN: "You live here, don't you?"
NATALIE WOOD (*Judy*): "Who lives?"

**5.** "Once you've been up there, you know you've been someplace."

*Dean to Sal Mineo (Plato), on looking at the stars in the planetarium*

**6.** "Is that meaning me? Chicken? You shouldn't call me that."

*Dean to Corey Allen (Buzz)*

**7.** "What can you do when you have to be a man?"

*Dean to Backus*

**8.** "I am involved. We are all involved. Mom, a boy, a kid was killed tonight. I don't see how I can get out of that by pretending that it didn't happen."

> *Dean to Doran, on giving evidence about the death of a teenager playing chicken on the road*

**9.** "Just once, I want to do something right."

> *Dean, on going to the police*

**10.** "I saw you and I said, 'Boy, this is going to be one terrific day, so you better live it up 'cause tomorrow you'll be nothing,' see, and I almost was."

> *Dean to Wood, on his narrow escape from being killed in the game of chicken*

**11.** "All the time I've been looking for someone to love me, and now I love somebody, and it's so easy. Why is it easy now?"

> *Wood to Dean*

## RED BADGE OF COURAGE, THE (MGM, 1951). D: John Huston. S: John Huston. Fr: Albert Hand (adaptation), Stephen Crane (novel).

**1.** "How do you know you won't run when the time comes?"

> *Audie Murphy (Henry Fleming) to Bill Mauldin (Tom Wilson)*

**2.** "He wished that he, too, had a wound, a red badge of courage."

> *The narrator, uncredited, about Murphy, referring to his deserting the battle unseen*

**3.** "Always seems like more of you is getting killed than there are."

> *Andy Devine (The Fat Soldier) to Murphy*

**4.** "Just turn your affairs over to the Lord, and go on and do your duty. Then if you get killed, it's His concern. Anyway, dying's only dying. Supposing you don't hear the birds sing tomorrow, or see the sun go down. It's going to happen anyway. And, you know, son, that thought gave me peace of mind."

> *Devine to Murphy*

**5.** "I got holes in my cap, holes in my pants. But there ain't no holes in me, except the ones that were intended."

> *Arthur Hunnicutt (Bill Porter), after the battle*

## RED DAWN (MGM/UA, 1984). D: John Milius. S: Kevin Reynolds, John Milius.

**1.** CHARLIE SHEEN (*Matt*), when fellow American PATRICK SWAYZE (*Jed*) kills a Russian prisoner who invaded the United States: "Tell me. What's the difference between us and them?"
SWAYZE: "We live here."

**2.** "In the early days of World War III, guerrillas, mostly children, placed the names of their lost upon this rock. They fought here alone, and gave up their lives, so that this nation shall not perish from the Earth."

> *Lea Thompson (Erica), reading from a plaque*

## RED DUST (MGM, 1932). D: Victor Fleming. S: John Mahin. Fr: Wilson Collison (play).

**1.** JEAN HARLOW (*Vantine*), forced to share a room with DONALD CRISP (*Guidon*): "Aw, please, you guys. This place is full of lizards and cockroaches as it is."
CLARK GABLE (*Dennis Carson*): "One more won't hurt."

**2.** "I've been looking at her kind ever since my voice changed."

> *Gable to Crisp, referring to women*

**3.** "This place certainly reeks of hospitality and good cheer, or maybe it's this cheese."

*Harlow, sarcastically referring to Gable's manners*

**4.** "Oooooh, I don't know. Maybe I'm going over Niagara Falls."

*Harlow to Gable, on what she means by jumping into a barrel of drinking water*

**5.** GABLE, to Harlow in the barrel: "Say, listen, do you know we drink that water?"

HARLOW: "Well, you won't this, unless you're stubborn and insist on it."

**6.** "Stop looking through keyholes. It's bad for the eyes."

*Gable to Harlow, when she's caught Gable and Mary Astor (Barbara Willis) in an embrace*

**7.** GABLE: "I'm afraid I'm pretty crazy about you."

ASTOR: "Always? For keeps?"

GABLE: "And after that, too."

**RED RIVER** *(UA, 1948). D: Howard Hawks. S: Borden Chase, Charles Schnee. Fr: Borden Chase (novel,* The Chisholm Trail*).*

**1.** "I want to be with you so much. My knees feel like . . . like they have knives in them."

*Coleen Gray (Fen) to John Wayne (Tom Dunson), as he leaves her; repeated to him by Joanne Dru (Tess Millay)*

**2.** "There'll be two lines, like this, like the banks of a river. It'll be the Red River brand."

*Wayne to Mickey Kuhn (Matthew Garth as a boy)*

**3.** "I'll put it in when you earn it."

*Wayne to Kuhn, about including his initials*

**4.** "Never liked seeing strangers, 'cause no stranger ever good news'd me."

*Walter Brennan (Groot Nadine) to Wayne*

**5.** "By watching his eyes. Remember that."

*Wayne to Kuhn, on how to know when someone will shoot*

**6.** "I'll have that brand on enough beef to . . . to feed the whole country. Good beef for hungry people. Beef to make 'em strong and make 'em grow."

*Wayne to Kuhn, on what he'll do in ten years with his ranch*

**7.** "Take 'em to Missouri, Matt."

*Wayne to Montgomery Clift (Matthew Garth as an adult)*

**8.** CHIEF YOWLACHIE (Quo), on how Brennan will survive without his false teeth, lost in a card game to Yowlachie: "Keep mouth shut. Dust not get in."

BRENNAN: "Bet I et ten pounds in the last sixteen days. Before this shenanigan is over, I'll probably eat enough land to incorporate in the Union. The state of Groot."

**9.** "Tom had changed. He'd always been a hard man. Now he was harder."

*Brennan, in voice-over*

**10.** WAYNE, on the wife of the slain Harry Carey, Jr. (Dan Latimer): "And get her, well, anything else you can think of."

CLIFT: "Like a pair of red shoes, maybe?"

WAYNE: "That's the way he wanted it, wasn't it?"

**11.** "You was wrong, Mr. Dunson."

*Brennan to Wayne, on going after the man who started the stampede, and repeated at various times throughout the film*

**12.** "So you're on short rations and bad coffee and you're gonna be until we finish the drive. And you're gonna finish it."

*Wayne to Paul Fix (Teeler Yacey)*

**13.** "Plantin' and readin', plantin' and readin'. Fill a man full of lead and stick him in the ground and then read on him. Why, when you killed a man, why try to bring the Lord in as a partner on the job?"

*Hank Worden (Simms) to Clift and Brennan, about Wayne's practices*

**14.** BRENNAN: "Boys did all right. . . . Why don't you tell 'em so, Tom?"
WAYNE: "That's their job."

**15.** "You should've let him kill me, 'cause I'm gonna kill you. . . . I don't know when, but I'll catch up. Every time you turn around, expect to see me. 'Cause one time you'll turn around and I'll be there, and I'll kill you, Matt."

*Wayne to Clift*

**16.** "There's three times in a man's life when he has a right to yell at the moon: when he marries, when his children come, and when he finishes a job he had to be crazy to start."

*Harry Carey, Sr. (Melville) to Clift, upon reaching Abilene*

**17.** "What a fool I've been, expecting trouble for days when anyone with half a mind would know you two love each other."

*Dru to the fighting Wayne and Clift*

**18.** "You better marry that girl, Matt."

*Wayne to Clift*

LAST LINE
**19.** "When we get back to the ranch, I want you to change the brand. It'll be like this, the Red River D and we'll add a name to it. You don't mind that, do you? . . . You've earned it."

*Wayne to Clift*

**RED SHOES, THE** (UK: Eagle-Lion, 1948). D: Michael Powell, Emeric Pressburger. S: Michael Powell, Emeric Pressburger, Keith Winter.

LAST LINE
**1.** "Take off the red shoes."

*Moira Shearer (Victoria Page), dying after her red shoes have made her unable to stop dancing*

**REDS** (Paramount, 1981). D: Warren Beatty. S: Warren Beatty, Trevor Griffiths.

**1.** "I think that a guy who's always interested in the condition of the world and changing it either has no problems of his own or refuses to face them."

*Henry Miller (Himself), witness on Communist writer Warren Beatty (John Reed)*

**2.** "Profits."

*Beatty, when asked what World War I is about*

**3.** "I'd like to see you with your pants off, Mr. Reed."

*Diane Keaton (Louise Bryant), seducing Beatty*

**4.** PROPERTY IS THEFT—WALK IN
*Sign on Beatty's door*

**5.** "I think voting is the opium of the masses in this country. Every four years you deaden the pain."

*Maureen Stapleton (Emma Goldman)*

**6.** "Don't rewrite what I write."

> Beatty to editor Gene Hackman (Pete Van Wherry) and later to Soviet official Jerzy Kosinski (Zinoviev)

**7.** "I'm like a wife. I'm like a boring, clinging, miserable little wife. Who'd want to come home to me?"

> Keaton to Beatty, upset to be falling into bourgeois romantic expectations

**8.** "If you were mine I wouldn't share you with anybody or anything. It'd be just you and me. You'd be at the center of it all. It'd feel a lot more like love than being left alone with your work."

> Jack Nicholson (Eugene O'Neill) to Keaton, comparing his and Beatty's approaches to loving her

**9.** "This one even pees red."

> Man in jail, seeing Beatty's bloody urine, a result of his kidney ailment

**10.** "Credentials? What credentials? Everyone has credentials here."

> Russian in workers' meeting hall, inviting Beatty to speak despite his lack of credentials

**11.** "My God, that was too big even for Jesus Christ. Don't you know, he got himself crucified."

> Miller, on Beatty trying to solve the problems of all humanity

**12.** "Building a party'll help Eddie."

> Beatty, expressing no sympathy for a comrade with a sick wife

**13.** "I think we all believe in the same things, but with us it's more or less our good intentions, and with Jack it's a religion."

> Edward Herrmann (Max Eastman) to Keaton, on Beatty

**14.** "You and Jack have a lot of middle-class values for a couple of radicals."

> Nicholson to Keaton

**15.** "When you separate a man from what he loves the most, what you do is purge what's unique in him, and when you purge what's unique in him, you purge dissent. And when you purge dissent, you kill the revolution. Revolution is dissent."

> Beatty to Kosinski

**16.** BEATTY: "What as?"
> KEATON: "Gee, I don't know. Comrades?"

> Beatty, on his deathbed, asking Keaton what they will travel together as; Keaton has asked him the same question several times before

**REFLECTIONS IN A GOLDEN EYE** (Warner Bros., 1967). D: John Huston. S: Chapman Mortimer, Gladys Hill. Fr: Carson McCullers (novella).

**1.** "She cut off her nipples with garden shears. You call that normal?"

> Elizabeth Taylor (Leonora Penderton) to Brian Keith (Lt. Col. Morris Langdon), about his wife Julie Harris (Alison Langdon)

**REMAINS OF THE DAY, THE** (Columbia, 1993). D: James Ivory. S: Ruth Prawer Jhabvala. Fr: Kazuo Ishiguro (novel).

**1.** "I'm sorry, sir, I was too busy serving to listen to the speeches."

> Anthony Hopkins (Stevens) to Christopher Reeve (Lewis), when asked his opinion on the political situation

**RESERVOIR DOGS** (Miramax, 1992). D: Quentin Tarantino. S: Quentin Tarantino.

**1.** "I don't tip."

Steve Buscemi (Mr. Pink), refusing to contribute his share of a breakfast tip

**2.** "You're acting like a first–year fucking thief. I'm acting like a professional."

Buscemi to jewel robbery accomplice Harvey Keitel (Mr. White/Larry)

**3.** "Are you gonna bark all day, little dog-gie, or are you gonna bite?"

Michael Madsen (Mr. Blonde/Vic), daring Keitel to attack him

**4.** "It's amusing to me to torture a cop."

Madsen's reason for torturing captured police-man Kirk Baltz (Marvin Nash)

**5.** "Why can't we pick our own colors?"

Buscemi to gang boss Lawrence Tierney (Joe Cabot), objecting to his assigned alias Mr. Pink

**6.** "You don't need proof when you have instinct."

Tierney explaining to Keitel how he knows that gang member Tim Roth (Mr. Orange/Freddy) is an undercover cop

**RETURN OF THE JEDI** (20th Century–Fox, 1983). D: Richard Marquand. S: Lawrence Kasdan, George Lucas. Fr: George Lucas (story).

**1.** "A Jedi knight? I'm out of it for a little while, everybody gets delusions of grandeur."

Harrison Ford (Han Solo), on Mark Hamill's (Luke Skywalker's) becoming a Jedi knight

**2.** "You should've bargained, Jabba."

Hamill to the villainous Jabba the Hut, making an ominous threat even though he appears to be defeated

**3.** "When nine hundred years old you reach, look as good you will not, hm?"

Ancient Jedi master Frank Oz (Yoda) to Hamill

**4.** "Remember, a Jedi's strength flows from the force."

Oz to Hamill

**5.** "Great, Chewie, great. Always thinking with your stomach."

Ford to Peter Mayhew (Chewbacca), after he gets them caught in an Ewok trap

**6.** "Not bad for a little furball."

Ford, on a daring Ewok exploit

**7.** HAMILL: "Your overconfidence is your weakness."

IAN MCDIARMID (Emperor): "Your faith in your friends is yours."

**8.** "From here you will witness the final destruction of the alliance and the end of your insignificant rebellion."

McDiarmid, boasting wrongly to Hamill

**9.** "If you will not be turned, you will be destroyed."

McDiarmid, after he has failed to turn Hamill to the dark side of the force

**10.** "Luke, help me take this mask off."

The dying James Earl Jones (voice of Darth Vader) to his son Hamill

**11.** "You were right. You were right about me. Tell your sister you were right."

Sebastian Shaw (the reformed, dying Darth Vader) to Hamill, referring to Carrie Fisher (Princess Leia)

LAST LINE
**12.** "No, it's not like that at all. He's my brother."

*Fisher, explaining to her lover Ford that her relationship with Hamill is not what Ford thinks*

**REVERSAL OF FORTUNE** *(Warner Bros., 1990). D: Barbet Schroeder. S: Nicholas Kazan. Fr: Alan Dershowitz (book).*

LAST LINE

**1.** "Just kidding."

*Jeremy Irons (Claus von Bulow), acquitted of killing his wife while remaining typically enigmatic*

**RIDE IN THE WHIRLWIND** *(Favorite/Jack H. Harris, 1967). D: Monte Hellman. S: Jack Nicholson.*

**1.** CAMERON MITCHELL *(Vern)*: "It strikes me peculiar sitting here playing checkers while there's a bunch of men out there looking to string us up."
JACK NICHOLSON *(Wes)*: "Why don't you put a tune to it?"

**RIO BRAVO** *(Warner Bros., 1959). D: Howard Hawks. S: Jules Furthman, Leigh Brackett. Fr: Barbara Hawks McCampell (story).*

**1.** "You can tell 'im anybody else he sends, he better pay 'em more, 'cause they're gonna earn it."

*Sheriff John Wayne (John T. Chance) to members of John Russell's (Nathan Burdett) gang, on sending more hired guns after him*

**2.** "I guess they'll let you in the front door from now on."

*Wayne to alcoholic Dean Martin (Dude), who has used his gun to earn the respect of men in the saloon*

**3.** "Well, can't nobody p-please you no how?"

*Walter Brennan (Stumpy), complaining as always to Wayne*

**4.** "Just lazy. Gets tired of selling his gun all over, decides to sell it in one place."

*Wayne to Angie Dickinson (Feathers), on how a man gets to be a sheriff*

**5.** "You're alone exceptin' for a barfly and an old cripple."

*Brennan to Wayne, on his chances against Russell's gang; Martin is the barfly, Brennan the cripple*

**6.** "Maybe you're right, Stumpy. You're a treasure. I don't know what I'd do without you."

*Wayne, showing mock appreciation to Brennan before kissing him on top of the head*

**7.** "Sorry don't get it done, Dude."
*Wayne, refusing Martin's apology for fumbling on the job*

**8.** "You're the undertaker, Bert. Bury them."
*Wayne to undertaker, on what to do with the men he and Ricky Nelson (Colorado Ryan) shot*

**9.** "Well, if I'm gonna get shot at, I might as well get paid for it. How do I get a badge?"
*Nelson, joining Wayne's forces*

**10.** MARTIN, a former top gunfighter, asking about Nelson: "Is he as good as I used to be?"
WAYNE: "It'd be pretty close. I'd hate to have to live on the difference."

**11.** "Nothin' in his stomach. Nothin' but guts."
*Wayne, on Martin not having eaten that day*

**12.** "Come on, Colorado, let's wake up the Chinaman again."

*Wayne to Nelson, on rousing the Chinese undertaker after another round of mayhem*

**13.** "Dude ought to have a chance."

*Wayne to Brennan, on why he's going out on a limb to save Martin's life*

**14.** "Jumpin' jehoshaphat, why don't nobody ever tell me nothin'?"

*Brennan*

**15.** BRENNAN, on being ordered to throw sticks of dynamite farther: "What'd you do if I wasn't here to throw 'em for you?"

WAYNE, ever self-reliant: "I'd throw 'em myself."

**16.** BRENNAN: "No fooling, has the sheriff got hisself a girl?"

MARTIN: "I think so, but he doesn't know it yet."

**17.** "I'm hard to get, John T. You're gonna have to say you want me."

*Dickinson to Wayne*

**ROAD TO MOROCCO** *(Paramount, 1942). D: David Butler. S: Frank Butler, Don Hartman.*

**1.** "This must be the place where they empty all the old hourglasses."

*Bob Hope (Turkey Jackson), on first seeing the desert*

**ROAD TO RIO** *(Paramount, 1948). D: Norman Z. McLeod. S: Edmund Beloin, Jack Rose.*

**1.** "How did you get into that dress—with a spray gun?"

Bob Hope (Hot Lips Burton) to Dorothy Lamour (Lucia Maria De Andrade)

**ROARING TWENTIES, THE** *(Warner Bros., 1939). D: Raoul Walsh. S: Jerry Wald, Richard Macaulay, Robert Rossen. Fr: Mark Hellinger (story).*

**1.** JAMES CAGNEY (*Eddie Bartlett*), at the beginning of a tragic friendship: "You must be quite a guy back home."

HUMPHREY BOGART (*George Hally*): "I do all right."

**2.** "I knew you when you danced with the Elks."

*Cagney to Priscilla Lane (Jean Sherman), on her inauspicious beginnings*

**3.** BOGART: "I don't trust you."

CAGNEY: "Looks like you need a little watchin' yourself."

BOGART: "Sounds like the basis of a good partnership."

**4.** "You must have been reading about Napoleon."

*Bogart to Cagney, on his big ideas*

**5.** "There'll always be guys trying to get up there quick, and I'm one of them."

*Cagney to Jeffrey Lynn (Lloyd Hart)*

LAST LINE

**6.** "He used to be a big shot."

*Gladys George (Panama Smith) to cop inquiring about the deceased Cagney's identity*

**ROBE, THE** *(20th Century–Fox, 1953). D: Henry Koster. S: Philip Dunne. Fr: Gina Kaus (adaptation), Lloyd C. Douglas (novel).*

**1.** "He forgave you from the cross. Can I do less?"

> Michael Rennie (St. Peter) to Richard Burton (Marcellus Gallio), who crucified Christ

**2.** "From this day on I'm enlisted in his service. I offer him my sword, my fortune, and my life. And this I pledge you on my honor as a Roman."

> Burton to Rennie, on pledging to follow Christ

**ROBIN AND MARIAN** (UK: Columbia, 1976). D: Richard Lester. S: James Goldman.

**1.** "John, you go in. I never even said goodbye. She might be angry."

> Sean Connery (Robin Hood) to Nicol Williamson (Little John), on visiting former lover Audrey Hepburn (Maid Marian) for the first time in years

**2.** CONNERY, surprised on finding that Hepburn has become a nun: "Marian, what are you doing in that costume?"
HEPBURN: "Living in it."

**3.** ROBERT SHAW (Sheriff of Nottingham): "Robin. Still not dead."
CONNERY: "Not for want of trying."

**4.** "I never mean to hurt you, and yet it's all I ever do."

> Connery to Hepburn

**5.** HEPBURN: "You never wrote."
CONNERY: "I don't know how."

**6.** "I love you more than God."

> Hepburn to Connery, in their dying moments

**LAST LINE**
**7.** "Where this falls, John, put us close, and leave us there."

Connery to Williamson, on where to bury him and Hepburn, as he shoots an arrow out the window

**ROBIN HOOD: PRINCE OF THIEVES** (Warner Bros., 1991). D: Kevin Reynolds. S: Pen Densham, John Watson. Fr: Pen Densham (story).

**1.** "You have saved my life, Christian. I must stay with you until I have saved yours. That is my vow."

> Morgan Freeman (Azeem) to Kevin Costner (Robin Hood)

**2.** "It seems safer to appear as your slave, rather than your equal."

> Freeman to Costner

**3.** "How did your uneducated kind ever take Jerusalem?"

> Freeman to Costner, when he can't figure out a telescope

**4.** "This is the best we simple men can expect. Here, we're safe. Here, we are kings."

> Nick Brimble (Little John) to Costner, explaining why they hide in Sherwood Forest

**5.** "I will make you no promises, save one. That if you truly believe in your hearts that you are free, then I say we can win."

> Costner to his merry men

**6.** "Cancel the kitchen scraps for lepers and orphans. No more merciful beheadings, and call off Christmas."

> Alan Rickman (Sheriff of Nottingham), making it even harder on the poor

**7.** "Men speak conveniently of love when it serves their purpose. And when it doesn't,

'tis a burden to them, Robin of the Hood, prince of thieves. Is he capable of love?"
> *Mary Elizabeth Mastrantonio (Maid Marian) to Costner*

**ROBOCOP** *(Orion, 1987). D: Paul Verhoeven. S: Edward Neumeier, Michael Miner.*

**1.** "Good business is where you find it."
> *Business executive Ronny Cox (Dick Jones); criminal leader Kurtwood Smith (Clarence Boddicker) later says the same thing*

**2.** "Fellow executives, it gives me great pleasure to introduce you to the future of law enforcement: ED-209."
> *Cox introducing a crime-fighting robot to the board of directors*

**3.** "Serve the trust. Protect the innocent. Uphold the law."
> *Peter Weller (Robocop), reciting his prime directives*

**4.** "Thank you for your cooperation."
> *Weller to a thief*

**5.** "Stay out of trouble."
> *Weller's advice to kids*

**6.** "There's a new guy in town. His name's Robocop."
> *Miguel Ferrer (Robert Morton) to a press conference*

**7.** "I have to go. Somewhere there is a crime happening."
> *Weller, cutting short a conversation with Nancy Allen (Anne Lewis)*

**8.** "Dead or alive, you're coming with me."
> *Weller, making a threat*

**9.** "We practically *are* the military."
> *Cox to Smith, on whether his company can obtain military weapons*

**LAST LINE**
**10.** DAN O'HERLIHY *(The Old Man)*: "Nice shooting, son. What's your name?"
> WELLER, reclaiming his identity after dispatching the villains: "Murphy."

**ROCKY** *(UA, 1976). D: John G. Avildsen. S: Sylvester Stallone.*

**1.** "You got heart, but you fight like a goddamn ape."
> *Fight trainer Burgess Meredith (Mickey) to Sylvester Stallone (Rocky Balboa)*

**2.** "This is the champion of the world. He took his best shot and became champ. What shot did you ever take?"
> *Stallone to barkeeper, comparing him to Carl Weathers (Apollo Creed)*

**3.** "Apollo Creed meets the Italian Stallion. Sounds like a damn monster movie."
> *Weathers*

**4.** "'Cause I can't sing or dance."
> *Stallone, on why he fights*

**5.** "The worst thing about fighting is the morning after."
> *Stallone to Talia Shire (Adrienne)*

**6.** "Yo, Adrienne!"
> *Stallone to Shire*

**7.** "She's got gaps. I got gaps. Together, we fill the gaps."
> *Stallone to Shire's brother Burt Young (Paulie)*

**8.** DIANA LEWIS (*TV Reporter*), asking about Stallone's training regimen: "Do other fighters pound raw meat?"

STALLONE: "No, I think I invented it."

**ROCKY II** *(UA, 1979). D: Sylvester Stallone. S: Sylvester Stallone.*

**1.** "I'm a fighter, not too good, but that's what I do."

Sylvester Stallone (Rocky Balboa), when he can't get a regular job and decides to fight again

**ROCKY HORROR PICTURE SHOW, THE** *(UK: 20th Century–Fox, 1975). D: Jim Sharman. S: Jim Sharman, Richard O'Brien. Fr: Richard O'Brien (musical play).*

**1.** "I would like, if I may, to take you on a strange journey."

Criminologist Charles Gray's first words as he narrates the story of Barry Bostwick (Brad Majors) and Susan Sarandon (Janet Weiss)

**2.** "And what charming underclothes you both have."

Tim Curry (Dr. Frank-N-Furter) to Sarandon and Bostwick, after having them stripped

**3.** "He had a certain naive charm, but no muscle."

Curry, remembering the late Meatloaf (Eddie)

**4.** "Excellent. Under the circumstances, formal dress is to be optional."

Curry to Sarandon and Peter Hinwood (Rocky Horror), after finding them together in bed

**ROGER & ME** *(1989). D: Michael Moore. S: Michael Moore.*

**1.** "I could say a few choice words, but I'm a lady, and was raised a lady, so I won't say what I really feel, but, uh, I could use some very unsavory language as far as the fat cats."

Female auto worker to documentary filmmaker Michael Moore, on the closing of the General Motors plant in Flint, Michigan

**2.** "I always tell them you can be poor by yourself; you don't need any help."

Deputy Fred, on why poor people shouldn't marry

**3.** "If you don't sell them as pets, you gotta get rid of 'em as meat."

Rhonda the Bunny Lady, who sells rabbits as either pets or meat

**4.** "I continued to dog Roger all over the country. From Detroit to Chicago to Washington, D.C., to New York City, I followed a trail of three-martini lunches in pursuit of the chairman."

Moore, in narration, on his efforts to speak with GM chairman Roger Smith

**5.** "Some people just don't like to celebrate human tragedy while on vacation."

Moore, on a benefit party held at a new prison, in which guests get to spend a night in jail

**6.** "One guy thought he was the cousin of Superman and decided to save the town. He didn't get very far."

Moore, on a madman who dresses up in a super-hero costume

**7.** "I think it must be my destiny to close all the General Motors plants."

GM worker

**8.** "One worker told me, 'You know when they send you flowers? When you die.'"

Reporter

**9.** "As we neared the end of the twentieth century, the rich were richer, the poor poorer, and people everywhere now had a lot less lint, thanks to the lint rollers made in my hometown. It was truly the dawn of a new era."

*Moore, on one of Flint's few surviving industries*

**10.** "This film cannot be shown within the city of Flint. All the movie theatres have closed."

*End title*


**ROMAN HOLIDAY** (Paramount, 1953). D: William Wyler. S: Ian McLellan Hunter, John Dighton. Fr: Ian McLellan Hunter (story).

**1.** "So happy."

*Audrey Hepburn (Princess Anne) to Gregory Peck (Joe Bradley), upon their meeting at a park bench, and repeated at their final encounter*

**2.** "Will you help me get undressed, please?"

*Hepburn to Peck, preparing for sleep at Peck's apartment*

**3.** "How much would a real interview with this dame be worth?"

*Peck to his editor Hartley Power (Mr. Hennessy)*

**4.** HEPBURN, in the morning, after her sedative has worn off: "So I've spent the night here with you?"
PECK: "I don't know that I'd use those words exactly, but from a certain angle, yes."

**5.** ITALIAN HAIRCUTTER: "All off?"
HEPBURN: "All off."

**6.** "The Mouth of Truth. Legend is that if you're given to lying, you put your hand in there, it'll be bitten off."

*Peck to Hepburn*

**7.** "Suits you. You should always wear my clothes."

*Peck to Hepburn, after she has donned his robe*

**8.** "I have to leave you now. I'm going to that corner there and turn. You must stay in the car and drive away. Promise not to watch me go beyond the corner. Just drive away and leave me as I leave you."

*Hepburn to Peck, as they part*

**9.** "Your Excellency, I trust you will not find it necessary to use that word again. Were I not completely aware of my duty to my family and my country, I would not have come back tonight, or indeed ever again."

*Hepburn to Harcourt Williams (Ambassador), on his question of whether she appreciates her royal duty*

**10.** "There is no story."

*Peck to Power and also to Eddie Albert (Irving Radovich)*

**11.** "Each in its own way was unforgettable. It would be difficult to . . . Rome, by all means, Rome. I will cherish my visit here in memory as long as I live."

*Hepburn to reporters, on which city in her tour she most enjoyed*


**ROMAN SCANDALS** (UA, 1933). D: Frank Tuttle. S: William Anthony McGuire, George Oppenheimer, Arthur Sheekman, Nat Perrin. Fr: George S. Kaufman, Robert E. Sherwood (story).

**1.** "Well, they say before I was born my mother was always looking for my father. That's why my eyes are so big."

*Eddie Cantor (Eddie), on his famously oversized eyes*

**2.** "The old jail was good enough for your father, it ought to be good enough for you."

*Cantor to town official, on whether homes need to be torn down to build a new jail*

**3.** "It wouldn't only be murder, it would be birth control."

*Cantor, transported to ancient Rome, on the prospect of being killed by Roman soldiers when he hasn't even been born yet*

**4.** "What do you think this is, Woolworth's?"

*Cantor, on the slave auction block, insultedly rejecting a bid of ten cents on himself*

**5.** "You'll start out by holding my hand and pretty soon you'll want to shuffle the whole deck."

*Cantor to Veree Teasdale (Empress Agrippa), uneasy about her overtures to him*

**6.** TEASDALE: "Have you ever been fired by passion?"

CANTOR: "No, but I've been fired by everyone else."

**7.** "Doesn't anybody around here ever die of old age?"

*Cantor, threatened with death for the umpteenth time*

**8.** "Just like all senators, never listen to the people."

*Cantor, on Roman senators*

**9.** "The one without the parsley is the one without the poison."

*Rule for avoiding poison that Cantor tries ineffectually to remember*

## ROMAN SPRING OF MRS. STONE, THE
(UK: Warner Bros., 1961). D: Jose Quintero. S: Gavin Lambert, Jan Read. Fr: Tennessee Williams (novel).

**1.** "People who are very beautiful make their own laws."

*Vivien Leigh (Karen Stone) to Lotte Lenya (Contessa Gonzales), referring to Warren Beatty (Paolo di Leo)*

## ROMEO IS BLEEDING (UK: Gramercy Pictures, 1994). D: Peter Medak. S: Hilary Henkin.

**1.** "Did you miss me, sweetheart?"

*Lena Olin (Mona) to Gary Oldman (Jack), whom she is holding at gunpoint*

## ROPE (Warner Bros., 1948). D: Alfred Hitchcock. S: Arthur Laurents, Hume Cronyn (uncredited), Ben Hecht. Fr: Patrick Hamilton (play, Rope's End).

**1.** "You often pick words for sound rather than meaning."

*John Dall (Shaw Brandon), growing suspicious of James Stewart (Rupert Cadell), who is surreptitiously trying to discover whether Dall and an accomplice committed murder that night*

## ROSE MARIE (MGM, 1936). D: W. S. Van Dyke II. S: Francis Goodrich, Albert Hackett, Alice Duer Miller. Fr: Otto A. Harbach, Oscar Hammerstein II, Rudolf Friml, Herbert Stothart (operetta).

**1.** "Your dream prince, reporting for duty!"

*Nelson Eddy (Sergeant Bruce) to Jeanette MacDonald (Marie de Flor)*

## ROSEMARY'S BABY (Paramount, 1968). D: Roman Polanski. S: Roman Polanski. Fr: Ira Levin (novel).

**1.** "This isn't a dream, this is really happening!"

*Mia Farrow, as she is raped by the Devil in her sleep*

**ROXANNE** (Columbia, 1987). D: Fred Schepisi. S: Steve Martin. Fr: Edmond Rostand (play, Cyrano de Bergerac).

**1.** "I have a dream. It's not a big dream. It's just a little dream. My dream, and I hope you don't find this too crazy, is that I would like the people of this community to feel that if, God forbid, there were a fire, calling the Fire Department would actually be a wise thing to do."

*Steve Martin (Charlie C. D. Bales), when the firehouse is on fire*

**2.** "Obvious: Excuse me, is that your nose, or did a bus park on your face? Meteorological: Everybody take cover! She's going to blow! Fashionable: You know, you could deemphasize your nose if you wore something larger, like Wyoming. Personal: Well, here we are, just the three of us. . . . Dirty: Your name wouldn't be Dick, would it?"

*Martin, answering a bully's challenge to think of insults better than "big nose"*

**3.** "Oh, oh, irony! Oh, no, no. We don't get that here. See, uh, people ski topless here while smoking dope, so irony's not really a high priority. We haven't had any irony here since about '83, when I was the only practitioner of it, and I stopped because I was tired of being stared at."

*Martin*

**4.** "Because yesterday she didn't, but today she does."

*Martin, on how Daryl Hannah's (Roxanne Kowalski's) love for him has put him in a good mood*

**5.** "I want to look like Diana Ross."

*Martin to plastic surgeon Brian George (Dr. David Schepisi)*

**6.** "Sometimes, the answer is so obvious, that it's as plain as the nose on your face."

*Shelley Duvall (Dixie) to Martin, telling him that he is in love with Hannah*

**7.** "I love your nose, Charlie. I love you, Charlie."

*Hannah*

**RULING CLASS, THE** (UK: UA, 1972). D: Peter Medak. S: Peter Barnes. Fr: Peter Barnes (play).

**1.** "When I pray to him, I find I'm talking to myself."

*Mad aristocrat Peter O'Toole (Jack), on how he knows he's God*

**2.** "I put on my glasses because I feel cold."

*O'Toole, explaining his odd habit of donning glasses when threatened by people casting doubt on his sanity*

**3.** "Never call me that! Jack's a word I reject absolutely. It's a word I put into my galvanized pressure cooker. Hroooom! Jack's dead."

*O'Toole, on not wanting to be called Jack*

**4.** "Destroying property, all men are equal? You know what this means, Claire. He's not only mad, he's Bolshy."

*William Mervyn (Sir Charles Gurney) to Coral Browne (Lady Claire Gurney), on the similarity between Bolshevism and O'Toole's radical Christian views*

**5.** "For what I am about to receive, may I make myself truly thankful."

*O'Toole, saying grace before tea*

**6.** "I always say yes, whatever the question."

*O'Toole, agreeing to appear at a church opening*

**7.** "Not here in the garden. Last time I was kissed in a garden it turned out rather awkward."

*O'Toole, referring to Judas' kiss in Gethsemane as he asks Carolyn Seymour (Grace Shelley) not to kiss him*

**8.** "From the bottom of my soul to the tip of my penis, like the sun in its brightness, the moon in its glory, no breeze stirs that doesn't bear my love."

*O'Toole, making his wedding vows to Seymour, to the horror of presiding cleric Alastair Sim (Bishop Lampton)*

**9.** "I'm the high-voltage Messiah . . . the electric Christ, the AC-DC God."

*Rival god Nigel Green (McKyle), facing down O'Toole*

**10.** "I recall it's a sign of normalcy in our circle to slaughter anything that moves."

*O'Toole, having become the life-hating incarnation of Jack the Ripper, on why he has gone hunting*

**11.** "In the old days the executioner kept the common herd in order. When he stood on his gallows you knew God was in his heaven and all right with the world."

*O'Toole, on crime and punishment*

**12.** "Behavior which would be considered insanity in a tradesman is looked on as mild eccentricity in a Lord."

*O'Toole*

**13.** "You're one of us at last. Well done, Jack!"

*James Villiers (Dinsdale Gurney) to O'Toole, who has taken his seat in the House of Lords after becoming a killer*

**RUNAWAY TRAIN** *(Cannon, 1985). D: Andrei Konchalovsky. S: Djordje Milicevic, Paul Zindel, Edward Bunker. Fr: Akira Kurosawa, Ryuzo Kikushima, Hideo Oguni (screenplay).*

**1.** "Whatever doesn't kill me makes me stronger."

*Escaped prisoner Jon Voight (Manny), echoing Nietzsche*

**2.** "I'm at war with the world, and everyone in it."

*Voight*

**3.** REBECCA DE MORNAY (*Sara*): "I don't want to die alone."
VOIGHT: "We all die alone."

**RUNNING ON EMPTY** *(Warner Bros., 1988). D: Sidney Lumet. S: Naomi Foner.*

**1.** "I taught you. We cannot break rank. A unit is only as good as its weakest link. We're a unit. I taught you all of this. Don't you remember that?"

*Fugitive radical Judd Hirsch (Arthur Pope) to his son River Phoenix (Danny Pope), who doesn't want to run anymore*

**2.** "Why do you have to carry the burden of someone else's life?"

*Martha Plimpton (Lorna Phillips) to Phoenix, who is torn between staying with her and going on hiding with his family*

LAST LINE

**3.** "Now, go out there and make a difference. Your mother and I tried. And don't let anyone tell you any different."

*Hirsch to Phoenix, as he sets him out on his own*

**RUTHLESS PEOPLE** (Touchstone/Buena Vista, 1986). D: Jim Abrahams, David Zucker, Jerry Zucker. S: Dale Launer.

**1.** "I hate the way she licks stamps."

*Danny DeVito (Sam Stone), listing one of the many reasons he wants to kill his wife Bette Midler (Barbara Stone)*

**2.** "My only regret, Carol, is that the plan isn't more violent."

*DeVito to Anita Morris (Carol), on the plan to kill Midler*

**3.** "I'm being marked down? I've been kidnapped by K Mart!"

*Midler (Barbara Stone) to Helen Slater (Sandy Kessler), about her cut-rate ransom*

**SABRINA** (Paramount, 1954). D: Billy Wilder. S: Billy Wilder, Samuel Taylor, Ernest Lehman. Fr: Samuel Taylor (play, Sabrina Fair).

**1.** "Life was pleasant for the Larrabees, for this was as close to Heaven as one could get on Long Island."

*Audrey Hepburn (Sabrina Fairchild) on the Larrabee estate, in prologue*

**2.** "Don't reach for the moon, child."

*John Williams (Thomas Fairchild), to daughter Hepburn*

**3.** "If making money were all there was to business, it'd hardly be worthwhile going to the office. Money is a by-product."

*Humphrey Bogart (Linus Larrabee) to brother William Holden (David Larrabee)*

**4.** "Now, an egg is not a stone. It is not made of wood. It is a living thing. It has a heart. So when we crack it we must not torment it. We must be merciful and execute it quickly, like with a guillotine."

*Cooking teacher Marcel Hillaire to Hepburn's cooking class*

**5.** HOLDEN: "Sabrina, Sabrina, where have you been all my life?"
HEPBURN: "Right over the garage."

**6.** "Then that . . . girl, her family fifty years on the social register and she has the audacity to wear on her wedding dress not a corsage b-b-b-but a Stevenson button."

*Walter Hampden (Oliver Larrabee), on son Holden's three marital fiascos*

**7.** "Look at me, Joe College with a touch of arthritis."

*Bogart, looking in the mirror as he prepares to woo Hepburn*

**8.** "Oh, yes, once I was there for thirty-five minutes."

*Bogart to Hepburn, on his experience of Paris*

**9.** "I like to think of life as a limousine. Though we are all driving together, we must remember our places. There's a front seat, and a back seat, and a window in between."

*Williams to Bogart, after being asked to drive Hepburn to the site of a date with Bogart*

**10.** "He's a little on the dull side but you can't help liking him."

> Holden to Hepburn, about Bogart, with whom she is already infatuated

**11.** HAMPDEN: "What right has a chauffeur got to name a child Sabrina?"

> BOGART: "What would you suggest? Ethel?"

**12.** "Democracy can be a wickedly unfair thing, Sabrina. Nobody poor was ever called democratic for marrying somebody rich."

> Williams to Hepburn

**13.** "That's the twentieth century for you! Automobiles! Garages! Chauffeurs! Chauffeurs' daughters!"

> Hampden, on the romance between Bogart and Hepburn

**SAMSON AND DELILAH** (Paramount, 1949). D: Cecil B. De Mille. S: Vladimir Jabotinsky, Harold Lamb, Jesse L. Lasky, Jr., Frederic M. Frank. Fr: Old Testament, Vladimir Jabotinsky (book).

**1.** "Oh, Samson, Samson, you're blind."

> Samson's mother, in a figurative statement to her son Victor Mature that prefigures his actual blindness later in the film

**2.** "Hey—one cat at a time."

> Mature to Hedy Lamarr (Delilah), who is all over him after he kills a lion with his bare hands

**3.** "If you had not plowed with my heifer, you would not have answered my riddle."

> Mature to Henry Wilcoxon (Ahtur), who answers his riddle by conniving with Mature's wife, Angela Lansbury (Semadar)

**4.** "Like all soldiers, when you fail by the sword, you ask for more swords."

> Leader of the Philistines George Sanders (The Saran of Gaza) to army leader Wilcoxon

**5.** "Delilah, what a dimpled dragon you can be, flashing fire and smoke."

> Mature to Lamarr

**6.** "The oldest trick in the world—a silk trap baited with a woman."

> Mature to Lamarr, who is trying to lure him into the hands of his enemies, the Philistines

**7.** "Your power is in your hair. What a beautiful power it is. Look how it curls around my finger, black as a raven's wing, as wild as a storm."

> Lamarr to Mature, having learned the secret of his strength, as she runs her fingers through his hair

**8.** "No man leaves Delilah."

> Lamarr, having delivered Mature to the Philistines

**9.** "If you still have the same shears, Delilah, my hair's rather long."

> Lecherous Philistine noble to Lamarr

**10.** "No man alive could resist you, Delilah, but only a fool would trust you."

> Sanders to Lamarr

**11.** "You wanted vengeance. You have it."

> Sanders to Lamarr, when she is shocked at seeing Mature after his blinding

**12.** "I prayed for an angel of the Lord, and the Devil sent me you."

> Mature to Lamarr

**13.** "For his strength I admire Samson, for his revolt I punish him, for the love of his people I envy him."

*Sanders on Mature*

**14.** PHILISTINE, as Mature knocks down their temple: "The man has the strength of a devil."

SANDERS: "No—the strength of a god."

**LAST LINE**
**15.** "His strength will never die, Saul. Men will tell his story for a thousand years."

*Olive Deering (Miriam) to Russell Tamblyn (Saul), after Mature's death in destroying the Philistine temple*

**SANDS OF IWO JIMA** (Republic, 1949). D: Allan Dwan. S: Harry Brown, James Edward Grant. Fr: Harry Brown (story).

**1.** "A lot of guys make mistakes, I guess, but every one we make, a whole stack of chips goes with it. We make a mistake, and some guy don't walk away—forevermore, he don't walk away."

*John Wayne to Forrest Tucker*

**LAST LINE**
**2.** "All right! Saddle up! Let's get back in the war!"

*John Agar (Pfc. Peter Conway)*

**SATURDAY NIGHT FEVER** (Paramount, 1977). D: John Badham. S: Norman Wexler. Fr: Nik Cohn (article, "Tribal Rites of the New Saturday Night").

**LAST LINE**
**1.** "Will you just watch the hair? You know, I work on my hair a long time and you hit it. He hits my hair."

John Travolta (Tony Manero) to his father Val Bisoglio (Frank, Sr.), who has slapped him at the dinner table

**2.** "I like that polyester look, man."

*Monti Rock III (Deejay), commenting on the apparel of disco-goers*

**3.** "When you make it with some of these chicks, they think you gotta dance with them."

*Travolta to Joseph Cali (Joey), on why he doesn't want to have sex with Donna Pescow (Annette)*

**4.** "Oh, I just kissed Al Pacino!"

*Teenage girl, ecstatic after kissing Travolta*

**5.** "He's the English actor. The one on television who does all those Polaroid commercials."

*Karen Lynn Gorney (Stephanie), trying to explain to Travolta who Laurence Olivier is*

**6.** "You guys have the Moses effect. You arrive and the crowd parts like the Red Sea."

*Martin Shakar (Frank, Jr.) to his brother Travolta and friends*

**7.** "There are ways of killing yourself without killing yourself."

*Travolta, on being asked by police whether Barry Miller (Bobby C.) has killed himself*

**LAST LINE**
**8.** "Friends then."

*Gorney, agreeing to be friends with Travolta*

**SAYONARA** (Warner Bros., 1957). D: Joshua Logan. S: Paul Osborn. Fr: James A. Michener (novel).

LAST LINE

*1.* "Tell 'em we said *sayonara.*"

    *Marlon Brando (Maj. Lloyd Gruver)*

**SCANNERS** *(Canada: Avco Embassy, 1981). D: David Cronenberg. S: David Cronenberg.*

*1.* "I do have a way with these creatures."

    *Scientist Patrick McGoohan (Dr. Paul Ruth), on his creation, the telekinetic beings called scanners*

**SCARLET EMPRESS, THE** *(Paramount, 1934). D: Josef von Sternberg. S: Manuel Komroff. Fr: Catherine the Great (diary).*

*1.* "I'm sorry, Your Highness, the horses are tired, but if you prefer the stables, I'm certain that I can arrange to have the horses quartered in your bedroom."

    *John Lodge (Count Alexei) to the lady escorting Marlene Dietrich (Sophia Frederica, later Catherine II of Russia), making a veiled allusion to Catherine II's later reputation for sexual activities with a horse*

*2.* "May I inquire how Her Imperial Highness deigns to feel this morning?"

    *Lodge to Dietrich*

*3.* "Empress, bah! I haven't even the power to iron out a single wrinkle."

    *The aging Louise Dresser (Empress Elizabeth), on her appearance*

*4.* "State of affairs? What affairs? I haven't had an affair for some time."

    *Dietrich to an advisor, on current political conditions*

*5.* "Should it become unavoidable, I think I have weapons that are far more powerful than any political machine."

    *Dietrich, on her charms*

*6.* "Besides, not for the world would I interfere with your pleasures, as long as you don't interfere with mine."

    *Dietrich to her deranged husband Sam Jaffe (Peter III), on his sexual proclivities*

*7.* "And while His Imperial Majesty Peter III terrorized Russia, Catherine coolly added the army to her list of conquests."

    *Title card*

*8.* "Exit Peter the Third. Enter Catherine the Second."

    *Lodge, as Dietrich takes power*

LAST LINE

*9.* "There is no emperor. There is only an empress."

    *Gavin Gordon (Gregory Orloff), informing Jaffe of his impending assassination to make way for Dietrich*

**SCARLET PIMPERNEL, THE** *(UK: UA, 1935). D: Harold Young. S: S. N. Behrman, Robert Sherwood, Arthur Wimperis, Lajos Biro. Fr: E. M. R. M. J. B. Orczy (novel).*

*1.* "You must remember that I am a Frenchwoman, and when I talk I must use these as well as this."

    *Merle Oberon (Marguerite Blakeney), referring to her hands and mouth*

*2.* "Mere force is useless against people who are neither cowards nor fools."

    *Leslie Howard (Sir Percy Blakeney)*

*3.* "They seek him here.
They seek him there.
Those Frenchies seek him everywhere.
Is he in Heaven? Is he in Hell?
That damned elusive Pimpernel."

    *Howard, reciting his oft-repeated poem*

**4.** "To a clever woman, whose brother's life is at stake, nothing is impossible."

> *Raymond Massey (Chauvelin), threatening Oberon*

**5.** "Nothing is not so bad as something that is not so bad."

> *Howard, responding to Nigel Bruce's (Prince of Wales's) comment that the sleeves of Bruce's new shirt are not so bad*

**6.** "If a country goes mad, it has the right to commit every horror within its walls."

> *Bruce to Oberon*

**LAST LINE**

**7.** "Look, Marquerite, England."

> *Howard to Oberon*

**SCENT OF A WOMAN** (Universal, 1992). D: Martin Brest. S: Bo Goldman. Fr: Ruggero Maccari, Dino Risi (characters), Giovanni Arpino (novel).

**1.** "I know exactly where your body is. What I'm looking for is some indication of a brain."

> *Blind retired soldier Al Pacino (Lt. Col. Frank Slade) to Chris O'Donnell (Charlie Simms)*

**2.** "When in doubt, fuck."

> *Pacino to his cat*

**3.** PACINO: "Are you blind?"
O'DONNELL: "Of course not."
PACINO: "Then why do you keep grabbing my goddamn arm? I take *your* arm."

**4.** "Women. What could you say? Who made them? God must have been a fucking genius."

> *Pacino, admiringly, on women*

**5.** PACINO: "You have a right to know. It's not really a plan, Charlie. It's sort of a . . . more like a tour. A little tour of pleasures. Stay in a first class hotel. Eat an agreeable meal. Drink a nice glass of wine. See my big brother, nothing like family, you know. And then make love to a terrific woman. After that . . ."
O'DONNELL: "Yeah?"
PACINO: "I'm going to lie down on my big, beautiful bed at the Waldorf and blow my brains out."

**6.** "This bat has sharper radar than the *Nautilus*."

> *Pacino to O'Donnell*

**7.** "There are two kinds of people in this world: those who stand up and face the music, and those who run for cover. Cover's better."

> *Pacino to O'Donnell*

**8.** " 'The bullets, Colonel.' Sounds like a guy in *Lives of the Bengal Lancers*."

> *Pacino to O'Donnell, when O'Donnell tries to stop Pacino from committing suicide*

**9.** "No mistakes in the tango, Donna. Not like life. Simple. That's what makes the tango so great. If you make a mistake, get all tangled up, you just tango on."

> *Pacino to Gabrielle Anwar (Donna)*

**10.** "I don't know whether to shoot you or adopt you."

> *Pacino to O'Donnell*

**11.** "There is nothing like the sight of an amputated spirit. There is no prosthetic for that."

> *Pacino to the student body of Baird College, during O'Donnell's disciplinary hearing*

**12.** "I'm just gettin' warmed up."

*Pacino, in the courtroom*

**SCHINDLER'S LIST** (Universal, 1993). D: Steven Spielberg. S: Steve Zaillian. Fr: Thomas Keneally (novel, Schindler's List).

**1.** BEN KINGSLEY (*Itzhak Stern*), on setting up the investments for Liam Neeson's (Oskar Schindler's) factory: "Let me understand. They put up all the money. I do all the work. What, if you don't mind my asking, do you do?"

NEESON: "I'd make sure it's known the company's in business. I'd see that it had a certain panache. That's what I'm good at. Not the work, not the work. The presentation."

**2.** "Good-bye, Jews!"

*Girl to group of Jews walking to ghetto*

**3.** "Moses is a skilled metal worker."

*Kingsley, giving German functionary the line needed to allow Jews to work in Schindler's factory*

**4.** "War."

*Neeson, indicating the one thing that makes the difference between success and failure in his businesses*

**5.** FEMALE JEWISH PRISONER AND ENGINEER: "I am only trying to do my job."

RALPH FIENNES (*Amon Goeth*), on his shooting of the engineer who suggested structural changes: "Yeah, I am doing mine."

**6.** "For six centuries there has been a Jewish Krakow. Think about that. By this evening those six centuries are rumor. They never happened. Today is history."

*Fiennes to German troops about to liquidate Krakow ghetto, March 13, 1943*

**7.** "Power is when we have every justification to kill and we don't. That's what the emperor said. A man stole something. He's brought in before the emperor. He throws himself down on the ground. He begs for mercy. He knows he's going to die. And the emperor pardons him."

*Neeson to Fiennes*

**8.** NEESON: "Look, all you have to do is tell me what it's worth to you. What's a person worth to you?"

FIENNES: "No, no, no, no. What's one worth to you?"

*Setting up the list of prisoners who will be saved from the gas chambers by working in Schindler's factory*

**9.** "Everybody's happy."

*Neeson's trademark negotiating phrase, spoken to Fiennes and others throughout the movie*

**10.** "If you were still working for me, I'd expect you to talk me out of it. It's costing me a fortune."

*Neeson to Kingsley, on paying for the lives of the prisoners*

**11.** "The list is an absolute good. The list is life."

*Kingsley to Neeson*

**12.** "They're skilled munitions workers. They're essential. Essential girls. Their fingers polish the insides of shell metal casings. How else am I to polish the insides of a forty-five-millimeter shell casing? You tell me, you tell me."

*Neeson to German soldier taking away a young female prisoner*

**13.** "If this factory ever produces a shell that can actually be fired, I'll be very unhappy."

Neeson to Kingsley, about his munitions factory

**14.** "We've survived. Many of you have come up to me and thanked me. Thank yourselves."

Neeson to factory workers, at the end of the war

**15.** "It's Hebrew, from the Talmud. It says, 'Whoever saves one life saves the world entire.'"

Kingsley to Neeson, about the engraving in the gold ring the workers have made for him

**16.** "I could have got one more person, but I didn't."

Neeson to workers, regretting that he did not save more lives

**17.** "In 1958 he was declared a righteous person by the council of the Yad Vashem in Jerusalem, and was invited to plant a tree in the Avenue of the Righteous. It grows there still."

Schindler's fate, written on the screen near the close of the film

**SEA HAWK, THE** (Warner Bros.–First National, 1940). D: Michael Curtiz. S: Howard Koch, Seton I. Miller.

**1.** "They say that Elizabeth surrounds herself with beauty in the hope that it may be contagious."

Gilbert Roland (Captain Lopez), on Flora Robson (Queen Elizabeth)

**2.** "I says there's two kinds of monkeys: the ones you find in trees, and the ones that women make outa sailors."

Sailor Clyde Cook, watching Errol Flynn (Geoffrey Thorpe) get tongue-tied in front of Brenda Marshall (Dona Maria)

**3.** "You forget, Don Alvarez, the queen need justify nothing."

Robson, pulling rank on Claude Rains (Don Jose Alvarez De Cordoba)

**4.** "Your Grace, the ambassador's galleass was propelled by English oars. I merely substituted English sails."

English privateer Flynn, explaining to Robson why he attacked a Spanish ship propelled by English galley slaves

**5.** "Captain Thorpe, if you undertook such a venture, you would do so without the approval of the Queen of England. However, you would take with you the grateful affection of Elizabeth."

Robson, giving tacit approval to one of Flynn's privateering ventures

**6.** "Lieutenant, you have seen the jungle orchid. It is an attractive flower that holds out its yellow pollen. But once an insect is lured within its petals, they close—like this."

Victor Varconi (General Aguerra), plotting a jungle trap for Flynn

**SEA OF LOVE** (Universal, 1989). D: Harold Becker. S: Richard Price.

**1.** "You got cop eyes."

Woman, blowing the cover of undercover cop Al Pacino (Frank Keller)

**2.** "I believe in animal attraction, I believe in love at first sight, I believe in this, and I don't feel it with you."

Ellen Barkin (Helen), snapping her fingers as she explains why Pacino doesn't interest her

**SEARCHERS, THE** *(Warner Bros., 1956). D: John Ford. S: Frank S. Nugent. Fr: Alan LeMay (novel).*

**1.** "Welcome home, Ethan."

*Dorothy Jordan (Martha Edwards) to John Wayne (Ethan Edwards), on his return after several years' absence*

**2.** WARD BOND *(Capt. Reverend Samuel Clayton)*, on not having seen Wayne at the close of the Civil War: "Didn't see you at the surrender."
WAYNE: "Don't believe in surrenders."

**3.** "Put an amen to it."

*Wayne to mourners at funeral of massacred Edwards family*

**4.** "That'll be the day."

*Wayne to Bond, on whether he wants to quit search for Natalie Wood (Debbie Edwards), and repeated in similar situations throughout the movie*

**5.** "What do you want me to do? Draw you a picture?"

*Wayne to Harry Carey, Jr. (Brad Jorgensen), on the condition of his murdered sweetheart Pippa Scott (Lucy Edwards)*

**6.** "Seems like he never learns there's such a thing as a critter that just keeps comin' on. So we'll find 'em, sure as the turnin' of the earth, we'll find them."

*Wayne to Jeffrey Hunter (Martin Pawley), on why he will succeed in his search for Wood among the Commanche*

**7.** HUNTER, on Waynes shooting of men stalking them, after setting up Hunter as a decoy: "What if you'd missed?"
WAYNE: "Never occurred to me."

**8.** "So he married a Commanche squaw. Haw haw haw."

*Ken Curtis (Charlie McCorry) to Vera Miles (Laurie Jorgensen) and her family; his laugh will be repeated throughout the film*

**9.** "Don't want no reward, no money, Marty. All I want is a roof over my head and my own rocking chair."

*Hank Worden (Mose Harper) to Wayne and Hunter, on the terms under which he will search for Wood*

**10.** "Big shoulders."

*Henry Brandon (Chief Scar), greeting Wayne*

**11.** "We've seen scalps before."

*Wayne to Brandon, after Wood shows Wayne and Hunter an array of scalped hair*

**12.** "Sure beats me Ethan, how you could have stayed alive this long."

*Hunter to Wayne, on his survival after a Commanche attack*

**13.** "Ate dirt, chewed grass. I fooled 'em, Ethan."

*Worden to Wayne and others, on his experience with the Commanche*

**14.** "Let's go home, Debbie."

*Wayne to Wood, as he takes her in his arms*

**SECRET LIFE OF WALTER MITTY, THE** *(RKO, 1947). D: Norman Z. McLeod. S: Ken Englund, Everett Freeman. Fr: James Thurber (story).*

**1.** "Pockets-pockets-pockets."

*Danny Kaye (Walter Mitty), creating the sound which recurs in all his daydreams*

**2.** "Nobody could look as much like you do as you do."

> Kaye, when he recognizes Boris Karloff (Dr. Hugo Hollingshead) as the man who tried to kill him, when Karloff poses as a psychiatrist

**3.** "Your small minds are muscle-bound with suspicion. That's because the only exercise you ever get is jumping to conclusions."

> Kaye to his family and boss

**4.** THURSTON HALL (*Bruce Pierce*): "No more daydreaming, Walt, old man."
KAYE: "Right you are, Bruce."
HALL: "Bruce?" (*Laughs.*)

**SEDUCTION OF JOE TYNAN, THE** (Universal, 1979). D: Jerry Schatzberg. S: Alan Alda.

**1.** "She wasn't asking about the furniture; she was asking about me. It's taken me seven years, but I think I know how to tell the difference."

> Barbara Harris (Ellie) to Alan Alda (Joe Tynan), referring to an interview in which she tells too much about her personal life

**2.** "When I want something, I go get it, just like you."

> Meryl Streep (Karen Traynor) to Alda

**3.** "Have you ever made love to a Democrat?"

> Alda to Streep

**4.** "When you get there, clip a rose from the Rose Garden and send it to me, okay?"

> Streep to Alda, implying how far he'll go in politics

**SEPARATE TABLES** (UA, 1958). D: Delbert Mann. S: Delbert Mann.

**1.** "Well, mustn't miss the old train, what, what? I must . . . I must stop saying, 'What.' Cheeriebye. I must stop doing that, too, I suppose."

> David Niven (Major Pollock), saying good-bye to Wendy Hiller (Miss Cooper)

**SERGEANT YORK** (Warner Bros., 1941). D: Howard Hawks. S: Abem Finkel, Harry Chandlee, Howard Koch, John Huston. Fr: Sam K. Cowan (book, War Diary of Sergeant York), Sam K. Cowan (book), Tom Skeyhill (book).

**1.** "This is where we change cars, Alvin. The end of the line."

> Subway employee George Tobias's (Michael T. "Pusher" Ross's) dying words to Gary Cooper (Sergeant Alvin C. York)

**SEVEN BRIDES FOR SEVEN BROTHERS** (MGM, 1954). D: Stanley Donen. S: Albert Hackett, Frances Goodrich, Dorothy Kingsley. Fr: Stephen Vincent Benet (story, "The Sobbin' Women").

**1.** "Somehow it just don't seem fittin' for a bridegroom to spend his weddin' night in a tree."

> Jane Powell (Milly), taking pity on new husband Howard Keel (Adam)

**LAST LINE**
**2.** "I now pronounce you men and wives."

> Ian Wolfe (Reverend Elcott), marrying the brides and brothers

**SEVEN SINNERS** (Universal, 1940). D: Tay Garnett. S: John Meehan, Harry Tugend. Fr: Ladislaus Fodor, Laslo Vadnay (story).

**1.** MARLENE DIETRICH (*Bijou Blanche*): "What are you thinking of?"

JOHN WAYNE (*Lt. Bruce Whitney*): "Well, if you keep looking at me like that, I'm liable to tell you."

## SEVEN PERCENT SOLUTION, THE (UK: Universal, 1977). D: Herbert Ross. S: Nicholas Meyer. Fr: Nicholas Meyer (novel).

**1.** "I never guess. It is an appalling habit destructive to the logical faculty."

Nicol Williamson (Sherlock Holmes)

**2.** "Elementary, my dear Freud."

Williamson, explaining things to Alan Arkin (Sigmund Freud)

## 1776 (Columbia, 1972). D: Peter Hunt. S: Peter Stone. Fr: Peter Stone, Sherman Edwards (musical play).

**1.** "Your voice is hurting my foot."

The gout-stricken Howard Da Silva (Benjamin Franklin), complaining to William Daniels (John Adams)

## SEVENTH SEAL, THE (Sweden: Janus, 1956). D: Ingmar Bergman. S: Ingmar Bergman. Fr: Ingmar Bergman (play, Tramalning (Sculpture in Wood).

### FIRST LINES
**1.** MAX VON SYDOW (*The Knight, Antonius Block*): "Who are you?"
BENGT EKEROT (*Death*): "I am Death."

**2.** VON SYDOW, facing the moment of his death: "Wait a moment."
EKEROT: "That's what they all say. I grant no reprieves."

**3.** "Why can't I kill God within me?"

von Sydow, in the confessional

**4.** "This is my hand. I can move it, feel the blood pulsing through it. The sun is still high in the sky, and I, Antonius Block, am playing chess with Death."

von Sydow

**5.** "Everything is worth precisely as much as a belch, the only difference being that a belch is more satisfying."

Gunnar Björnstrand (The Squire, Jöns)

**6.** "The actor! Now I understand. There are too many of them, so even if he hasn't done anything in particular you ought to kill him merely because he's an actor."

Nils Poppe (Jof) to Åke Fridell (The Smith, Plog), who is planning to kill the actor who ran away with his wife

**7.** "Faith is a torment, did you know that? It is like loving someone who is out there in the darkness but never appears, no matter how loudly you call."

von Sydow

**8.** "If anything is imperfect in this imperfect world, love is most perfect in its perfect imperfection."

Björnstrand

**9.** "I want to ask him about God. He, if anyone, must know."

von Sydow, on wanting to meet the Devil

**10.** EKEROT: "Don't you ever stop asking questions?"
VON SYDOW: "No, I'll never stop."

**11.** "It is the Angel of Death that's passing over us, Mia. It's the Angel of Death. The Angel of Death, and he's very big.

Björnstrand to Bibi Andersson (Mia)

**12.** "And when the lamb broke the seventh seal, there was silence in Heaven for about the space of half an hour."

*Inga Landgre (The Knight's Wife, Karin), reading from the Book of Revelation*

**13.** "I see them, Mia! I see them! Over there against the dark stormy sky. They are all there. The smith and Lisa and the knight and Raval and Jöns and Skat. And Death, the severe master, invites them to dance."

*Poppe to his wife Andersson*

**LAST LINE**
**14.** "You with your visions and dreams."

*Andersson to Poppe, on his vision of the Dance of Death*

**7TH VOYAGE OF SINBAD, THE** *(Columbia, 1958). D: Nathan Juran. S: Kenneth Kolb.*

**1.** "Hungry men don't ask—they take."

*Kerwin Matthews (Captain Sinbad), after his men kill a roc chick*

**2.** "From the land beyond beyond, From the world past hope and fear, I bid you, genie, now appear."

*Incantation to summon the genie*

**LAST LINES**
**3.** MATTHEWS: "Well done, Baronni. I know you will be as good a sailor as you are a genie."
RICHARD EYER (*Baronni*): "I shall try, Captain. I shall try."

**SEX, LIES, AND VIDEOTAPE** *(Outlaw, 1989). D: Steven Soderbergh. W: Steven Soderbergh.*

**FIRST LINE**
**1.** "Garbage. All I've been thinking about all week is garbage. I mean, I just can't stop thinking about it."

*Andie MacDowell (Ann Millaney) to her therapist, on her obsessions*

**LAST LINES**
**2.** MACDOWELL: "Think it's gonna rain."
JAMES SPADER (*Graham Dalton*), on stoop with her: "It is raining."
MACDOWELL: "Yeah."

**SHADOW, THE** *(Universal, 1994). D: Russell Mulcahy. S: David Koepp. Fr: Walter Gibson (characters).*

**1.** "The weed of crime bears bitter fruit."

*Alec Baldwin (Lamont Cranston/The Shadow) to crooks*

**2.** "The Shadow knows."

*Baldwin's trademark phrase*

**LAST LINES**
**3.** PENELOPE ANN MILLER (*Margo Lane*): "Hey. How will you know where I am?".
BALDWIN: "I'll know."

**SHADOW OF A DOUBT** *(Universal, 1943). D: Alfred Hitchcock. S: Thornton Wilder, Sally Benson, Alma Reville. Fr: Gordon McDonnell (story).*

**1.** "Everybody was sweet and pretty then . . ."

*Joseph Cotten (Uncle Charlie), on viewing photos of parents*

**2.** "We're sort of like twins, don't you see?"

*Teresa Wright (Young Charlie) to Cotten*

**3.** "Uncle Charlie, I love to walk with you. I want everybody to see."

*Wright to Cotten*

**4.** "Ah, details. I'm glad to see you're a man who understands details, Mr. Green. They're most important to me. Most important. All the little details."

*Cotten to Edwin Stanley (Mr. Green)*

**5.** "The cities are full of women, middle-aged widows, husbands dead, husbands who've spent their lives making fortunes and then they die and leave their money to their wives. Their silly wives. And what do the wives do, these useless women? You see them in the hotels, the best hotels, every day by the thousands, drinking the money, eating the money, losing the money at bridge, playing all day and all night, smelling of money. . . . Horrible, faded, fat, greedy women."

*Cotten*

**6.** "We're old friends. More than that. We're like twins."

*Cotten to Wright*

**SHAGGY DOG, THE** (Buena Vista, 1959). D: Charles Barton. S: Bill Walsh, Lillie Hayward. Fr: Felix Salten (novel, The Hound of Florence).

**1.** "In canus coporae transmuto."

*Tommy Kirk (Wilby Daniels), reading the inscription on a ring*

**2.** "You know, you're a lot more fun as a dog than you are as my brother."

*Kevin Corcoran ("Moochie" Daniels) to Kirk*

**3.** "Description of suspect as follows: large, shaggy dog, color: dirty white, brown patches; breed: unknown."

*James Westerfield (Officer Hanson), calling a report in*

**4.** "Don''t be ridiculous! My son isn't a werewolf! He's just a big, baggy, stupid-looking shaggy dog."

*Fred MacMurray (Wilson Daniels)*

**SHAMPOO** (Columbia, 1975). D: Hal Ashby. S: Robert Towne, Warren Beatty.

**1.** "Want me to do your hair?"

*Warren Beatty (George Roundy), propositioning Julie Christie (Jackie Shawn)*

**SHANE** (Paramount, 1953). D: George Stevens. S: A. B. Guthrie, Jr., Jack Sher. Fr: Jack Schaefer (novel).

**FIRST LINES**

**1.** BRANDON DE WILDE (Joey Starrett), on first sight of wandering gunslinger Alan Ladd (Shane): "Someone's coming, Pa."

VAN HEFLIN (Joe Starrett): "Well, let him come."

**2.** "Y'know, I . . . I like a man who watches things go on around."

*Ladd to de Wilde*

**3.** "Joey, you know better than to point guns at people."

*Jean Arthur (Marian Starrett) to her son de Wilde, when he points a rifle at Shane*

**4.** DE WILDE: "Bet you can shoot. Can't you?"

LADD: "Little bit."

5. "Call me Shane."

*Ladd, introducing himself to Heflin*

6. "One place or another. Some place I've never been."

*Ladd, on where he's bound*

7. "Prove it."

*Cattlemen's gunslinger Jack Palance (Jack Wilson), issuing a challenge to homesteader Elisha Cook, Jr. (Frank Torrey) and later to Ladd*

8. "One less sodbuster."

*Cattleman Emile Meyer (Rufe Ryker), after Palance shoots Cook*

9. "This is my kind of game, Joe."

*Ladd to Heflin, offering to take his place in the battle against Meyer's men*

10. "This isn't worth a life, anybody's life. What are you fighting for? This shack, this little piece of ground, and nothing but work, work, work? I'm sick of it. I'm sick of trouble."

*Arthur to Shane and Heflin, on going to face Meyer's men*

11. "I got to be going on."

*Ladd to de Wilde, after the shoot-out with Meyer's men*

12. "A man has to be what he is, Joey. Can't break the mold. I tried it and it didn't work for me."

*Ladd to de Wilde*

13. "Joey, there's no living with a killing. There's no going back from it. Right or wrong, it's a brand, a brand that sticks. There's no going back."

*Ladd to de Wilde*

**LAST LINE**

14. "Pa's got things for you to do, and Mother wants you. I know she does. Shane. Shane. Come back. 'Bye, Shane."

*de Wilde, his words echoing as Ladd rides off*

**SHANGHAI EXPRESS** (Paramount, 1932). D: Josef von Sternberg. S: Jules Furthman. Fr: Harry Hervey (story).

1. "One of them is yellow, and the other one is white—but both their souls are rotten."

*Lawrence Grant (Reverend Carmichael) to Clive Brook (Capt. Donald Harvey), on Anna May Wong (Hue Fei) and Marlene Dietrich (Shanghai Lily)*

2. "It took more than one man to change my name to Shanghai Lily."

*Dietrich to Brook*

3. "The white woman stays with me."

*Warner Oland (Henry Chang)*

**SHE DONE HIM WRONG** (Paramount, 1933). D: Lowell Sherman. S: Mae West, Harvey Thew, John Bright. Fr: Mae West (play, Diamond Lil).

1. "When women go wrong, men go right after them."

*Mae West (Lady Lou)*

2. "I wasn't always rich. No, there was a time I didn't know where my next husband was coming from."

*West*

3. "Why don't you come up sometime and see me?"

*West to Cary Grant (Captain Cummings)*

**SHE WORE A YELLOW RIBBON** *(Argosy Pictures–RKO Radio, 1949). D: John Ford. S: Frank Nugent, Laurence Stallings. Fr: James Warner Bellah (stories, "War Party," "The Big Hunt")*

**1.** "Don't apologize. It's a sign of weakness."

*Repeated saying of John Wayne (Capt. Nathan Brittles)*

**2.** "Well, that ain't my department."

*Repeated disclaimer of Ben Johnson (Sergeant Tyree) to Wayne*

**3.** "My mother didn't raise any sons to be making guesses in front of a Yankee captain."

*Johnson to Wayne, on what he thinks the Indians are doing*

**4.** "Well, Captain, I ain't gettin' paid for thinking."

*Johnson, again declining to express his thoughts*

**5.** "The Army is always the same. The sun and the moon change, but the Army knows no seasons."

*Wayne*

**SHINING, THE** *(UK: Warner Bros., 1980). D: Stanley Kubrick. S: Stanley Kubrick, Diane Johnson. Fr: Stephen King (novel).*

**1.** "He-e-e-e-re's Johnnie!"

*Jack Nicholson, scaring Shelley Duvall*

**SHIP OF FOOLS** *(Columbia, 1965). D: Stanley Kramer. S: Abby Mann. Fr: Katherine Anne Porter (novel).*

**1.** "You know how it ends, don't you? Alone—sitting in a café, with a paid escort."

*Vivien Leigh (Mary Treadwell) to her mirror*

**2.** "That's a neat trick, having a clear conscience when you work as a doctor on a ship which has three hundred people living in an open deck."

*Simone Signoret (La Condesa) to Oskar Werner (Dr. Schumann)*

**SHOOTIST, THE** *(Warner Bros., 1976). D: Don Siegel. S: Miles Hood Swarthout, Scott Hale. Fr: Glendon Swarthout (novel).*

**1.** "You seem to be a man accustomed to giving orders."

*Lauren Bacall (Bond Rogers) to new boarder John Wayne (John Bernard Books)*

**2.** BACALL: "I'm glad you're not staying long, Mr. Hickock. I'm not sure I like you."
WAYNE: "Not many do, Mrs. Rogers."

**3.** "Mrs. Rogers, you have a fine color when you're on the scrap."

*Wayne to Bacall*

**4.** "The day they lay you away, what I'll do on your grave won't pass for flowers."

*Harry Morgan (Marshal Thibido) to Wayne*

**5.** "I'll tend myself."

*Wayne to Bacall, who learns of his cancer*

**6.** "I would not die a death like I just described. Not if I had your courage."

*James Stewart (Dr. Hostetler) to Wayne, after explaining the course of Wayne's disease*

**7.** "A few, but in general I've had a hell of a good time."

*Wayne to Bacall, on whether he has enough worries of his own*

**8.** "I don't believe I ever killed a man that didn't deserve it."

*Wayne to Bacall*

**9.** "I won't be wronged, I won't be insulted, and I won't be laid a hand on. I don't do these things to other people and I expect the same from them."

*Wayne to Ron Howard (Gillom Rogers), on his personal creed*

**10.** "A man's death is about the most private thing in his life."

*Wayne to Bacall*

**11.** "I'm a dying man scared of the dark."

*Wayne to Bacall*

**12.** UNDERTAKER JOHN CARRADINE (*Beckum*): "Mr. Books, you're a hard man."
  WAYNE: "I'm alive."

**13.** BACALL: "John Bernard, you swear too much."
  WAYNE: "The hell I do."

**14.** BACALL, on Wayne's birthday: "You have a beautiful day for it. It's what we call false spring."
  WAYNE: "Good-bye, Mrs. Rogers."
  BACALL: "Good-bye, Mr. Books."

**SHOW BOAT** (MGM, 1951). D: George Sidney. S: John Lee Mahin (uncredited), George Wells, Jack McGowan. Fr: Jerome Kern, Oscar Hammerstein II (musical), Edna Ferber (novel).

**1.** "Nature isn't necessary in playacting, Hawks. Especially that kind."

*Agnes Moorehead (Parthy Hawks) to Joe E. Brown (Capt. Andy Hawks), when Howard Keel (Gaylord Ravenal) and Kathryn Grayson (Magnolia Hawks) kiss passionately*

**2.** "Everything can be temporary, except us."

*Grayson to Keel, when he says their situation in only temporary*

**3.** "I know there's no other woman. No flesh-and-blood woman. I always wished there were. I'd know how to fight that, but I can't fight this lady luck of yours. This fancy queen in her green felt dress."

*Grayson to Keel*

**4.** "Nolie, remember what I told you: smile!"

*Brown to Grayson*

**5.** "If your daddy really did come back, could you make believe that . . . look, could you pretend that . . . that he'd never been away?"

*Keel to his five-year-old daughter, who has never seen him before*

**6.** "It's Saturday night forever!"

*Brown, when Keel returns for a happy ending*

**SIGN OF THE CROSS, THE** (Paramount, 1932). D: Cecil B. De Mille. S: Waldemar Young, Sidney Buchman. Fr: Wilson Barrett (play).

**1.** "I never saw a man who held his life so cheaply."

*Claudette Colbert (Poppaea), menacing Fredric March (Marcus Superbus)*

**SILENCE OF THE LAMBS, THE** (Orion, 1991). D: Jonathan Demme. S: Ted Tally. Fr: Thomas Harris (novel).

**1.** "Do you spook easily, Starling?"

*FBI supervisor Scott Glenn (Jack Crawford), discussing an unusual assignment with trainee Jodie Foster (Clarice Starling)*

**2.** "Believe me, you don't want Hannibal Lecter inside your head."

*Glenn to Foster, on the notorious cannibal-psychiatrist Anthony Hopkins (Hannibal Lecter)*

**3.** "Closer, please. Closer."

*Hopkins, urging Foster to step closer to his cell in an insane asylum*

**4.** "Memory, Agent Starling, is what I have instead of a view."

*Hopkins to Foster, on his imprisonment*

**5.** "A census taker once tried to test me. I ate his liver with some fava beans and a nice Chianti."

*Hopkins*

**6.** "Best thing for him, really. His therapy was going nowhere."

*Hopkins, on a patient murdered long ago*

**7.** "Are you hitting on me, Doctor?"

*Foster to entomologist trying to make a date with her*

**8.** "They don't have a name for what he is."

*Foster to policeman, on Hopkins*

**9.** "We begin by coveting what we see every day."

*Hopkins to Foster on how serial killer Ted Levine (Jame Gumb/Buffalo Bill) might have begun his string of murders*

**10.** "I thought if I could save just one, but— he was so heavy. So heavy."

*Foster to Hopkins, on the lamb she tried to save from slaughter when she was a child*

**11.** "You still wake up sometimes, don't you, wake up in the dark, and hear the screaming of the lambs. . . . You think if you save poor Catherine you could make them stop, don't you? You think if Catherine lives you won't wake up in the dark ever again to that awful screaming of the lambs."

*Hopkins, analyzing Foster's motives regarding the rescue of Brooke Smith (Catherine Martin)*

**12.** FOSTER, on the escaped Hopkins: "He won't come after me."

KASI LEMMONS (*Ardelia Mapp*): "Oh, really?"

FOSTER: "I can't explain it. He would consider that rude."

**13.** "Well, Clarice, have the lambs stopped screaming?"

*The escaped Hopkins, on phone to Foster, after Smith is rescued*

**14.** "I have no plans to call on you, Clarice. The world's more interesting with you in it."

*Hopkins to Foster*

**15.** "I do wish we could chat longer, but I'm having an old friend for dinner."

*Hopkins's farewell line to Foster*

**SILENT MOVIE** (20th Century–Fox, 1976). D: Mel Brooks. S: Mel Brooks, Ron Clark, Rudy DeLuca, Barry Levinson. Fr: Ron Clark (story).

**1.** ENGULF & DEVOUR
OUR FINGERS ARE IN EVERYTHING

*Slogan in the boardroom of the Engulf & Devour Corporation*

**2.** "Non!"

*Famous mime Marcel Marceau (Himself), speaking the film's only spoken line, in* response to a request that he appear in Mel Brooks's (Mel Funn's) silent movie

**3.** "She's incredible! I hope to God she's not a female impersonator."

Brooks on Bernadette Peters (Vilma Kaplan), in title

**4.** PIX NIX TIX MIX
BOFF NOFF TOFF ROFF

Variety *headline, mocking the headline in Yankee Doodle Dandy*

**5.** "Waiter! There's a fly in my soup!"

Henny Youngman, restaurant patron, on having a giant model fly land in his soup

**6.** ARS EST PECUNIA

Slogan of Big Pictures Studio, meaning "Art Is Money"

**SILK STOCKINGS** (MGM, 1957). D: Rouben Mamoulian. S: Leonard Gershe, Harry Kurnitz (uncredited), Leonard Spigelgass. Fr: George S. Kaufman, Leueen McGrath, Abe Burrows (musical play), Billy Wilder, Charles Brackett, Walter Reisch (screenplay, Ninotchka), Melchior Lengyel (novel).

**1.** "Where is the little comrade's room?"

Soviet Cyd Charisse (Ninotchka), asking for the bathroom in Fred Astaire's (Steve Canfield's) Paris apartment

**2.** "I want to look somebody up. Does this office have a copy of Who's Still Who?"

George Tobias (Commisar Vassili Markovich), on the swiftness in Soviet personnel changes

**3.** "I have made a discovery: Champagne is more fun to drink than goat's milk."

Charisse, getting used to capitalist ways in Paris

**SILVER STREAK** (20th Century–Fox, 1978). D: Arthur Hiller. S: Colin Higgins.

**1.** "My friends all told me that my wife was too good for me, and after a couple of years, I decided they were right."

Gene Wilder (George Caldwell) to Jill Clayburgh (Hilly Burns), on why he's divorced

**2.** CLAYBURGH: "Do you really edit sex manuals?"
WILDER: "I really, really do, but I have a confession to make. I'm much better at books on gardening."

**3.** "Something's wrong. You have four of them."

Wilder to a cow, when he starts milking her and realizes she has four teats

**4.** "What are you, a miniature alcoholic?"

Ned Beatty (Sweet) to Wilder, when Beatty finds Wilder stacking empty miniature scotch bottles

**5.** "I can't pass for black."

Wilder to Richard Pryor (Grover Muldoon), when Pryor helps Wilder disguise himself as a black man

**6.** "We'll make it past the cops. I just hope we don't see any Muslims."

Pryor to Wilder, on disguising him as a black man

**7.** "What do you think this is, a Western?"

Pryor to Wilder, during a shoot-out on the train

**8.** "I don't know about you, but next time, I'm going to take the bus."

Clayburgh, after the train has crashed through the station

**SIN OF MADELON CLAUDET, THE** (MGM, 1931). D: Edgar Selwyn. S: Charles MacArthur. Fr: Edward Knoblock (play, The Lullaby).

**1.** "I guess mothers are hard to kill."

Robert Young (Jacques) to his mother, Helen Hayes (Madelon Claudet)

**SINCE YOU WENT AWAY** (UA, 1944). D: John Cromwell. S: David O. Selznick. Fr: Margaret Buell Wilder (adaptation), Margaret Buell Wilder (original novel).

**1.** "When I finishes with my work, I wants my solitude and I wants my privitation."

Hattie McDaniel (Fidelia) to Claudette Colbert (Anne Hilton)

**SINGIN' IN THE RAIN** (MGM, 1952). D: Gene Kelly, Stanley Donen. S: Adolph Green, Betty Comden. Fr: song, "Singin' in the Rain."

**1.** "Dignity, always dignity."

Silent movie star Gene Kelly (Don Lockwood), stating his career motto

**2.** "What do you think I am, dumb or something?"

Shrill movie star Jean Hagen (Lina Lamont), asking a question no one dares to answer

**3.** "Now look at me, I got no glory, I got no fame, I got no big mansions, I got no money, but I got—what have I got?"

Donald O'Connor (Cosmo Brown)

**4.** "The Warner Brothers are making a whole talking picture with this thing. *The Jazz Singer.* They'll lose their shirts."

Studio chief Millard Mitchell (R. F. Simpson), making an incorrect prediction about the appeal of talking pictures

**5.** "I'd rather kiss a tarantula."

Kelly, on kissing his hated costar Hagen

**6.** "At last I can start suffering and write that symphony."

O'Connor, shrugging off the loss of his job

**7.** "And I can't stan' 'im."

Hagen, trying unsuccessfully to learn diction

**8.** JEAN HAGEN: "No, no, no."
MOVIE VILLAIN: "Yes, yes, yes."

Lines placed out of synch in the movie-within-the-movie, The Duelling Cavalier

**9.** "Why, I make more money than . . . than Calvin Coolidge—put together!"

Hagen, asserting her dignity

**10.** "I can syoo."

Hagen, garbling English as she threatens to initiate a lawsuit

**11.** "People? I ain't people. I am a . . . 'a shimmering, glowing star in the cinema firmament.' It says so—right there."

Hagen, believing her reviews

**12.** "Simpson, I once gave you a cigar. Can I have it back?"

O'Connor, getting disgusted with the spineless Mitchell

**13.** "If we bring a little joy into your humdrum lives, it makes us feel as though our hard work ain't been in vain for nothin'."

Hagen, trying to be gracious to her adoring fans

**SINGING NUN, THE** (MGM, 1966). D: Henry Koster. S: Sally Benson, John Furia, Jr. Fr: John Furia, Jr. (story).

*1.* "First, you start by liking them, and then, their liking you comes easy as anything."

Recording star Debbie Reynolds (Sister Ann), to Ricky Cordell (Dominic Arlien), on how to make friends

*2.* "If we believe God is in all artists, then we should be humble for what He has given us."

Reynolds to record executive Chad Everett (Robert Gerarde)

*3.* "I'm not a singer who happens to be a nun. I'm a nun who happens to like to sing."

Reynolds to a fan

*4.* "It was a friend. A gift from God. I sang to Him with my guitar. But I used it for my own glory, my own importance. I . . . I liked being made a fuss over, Father. I liked being the singing nun who could make millions. And I've cheapened His gift, and He's taken it from me."

Reynolds to Ricardo Montalban (Father Clementi)

*5.* "Oh, Father, can't you see I've been living half in one world and half in another, and I'm lost . . . lost between them."

Reynolds to Montalban

**SINGLE WHITE FEMALE** (Columbia, 1992). D: Barbet Schroeder. S: Don Roos. Fr: Jon Lutz (novel, SWF Seeks Same).

*1.* "Gee, Hedy, I hope you never get mad at me."

Bridget Fonda (Allison Jones) to roommate Jennifer Jason Leigh (Hedra Carlson), after getting a taste of her psychotic temper

*2.* "I love myself like this."

Leigh, after getting her hair done to look exactly like Fonda's

*3.* "Identical twins are never really identical. There's always one who's prettier, and the one who's not does all the work."

Leigh, menacingly, to Fonda, whom she is desperately seeking to imitate

**SISTER ACT** (Buena Vista, 1992). D: Emile Ardolino. S: Paul Rudnick, Eleanor Bergstein, Jim Cash, Jack Epps, Jr., Carrie Fisher, et al.

*1.* "We didn't have electricity. Cold water. Bare feet. *Those* were nuns."

Mary Wickes (Sister Mary Lazarus), remembering the old days

*2.* "It's better than sex! No, no, I've heard."

Whoopi Goldberg (Deloris), masquerading as a nun, shocking her fellow nuns by her description of singing

**SITTING PRETTY** (Paramount, 1948). D: Harry Joe Brown. S: F. Hugh Herbert. Fr: Gwen Davenport (novel, Belvedere).

*1.* MAUREEN O'HARA (Tacey) when CLIFTON WEBB (Lynn Belvedere) answers her baby-sitting ad: "And may I ask what your profession is?"
WEBB: "Certainly. I am a genius."

*2.* "Don't ever again, as long as you live, dare to call me uncle. By no stretch of the imagination could I possibly be a relative of yours."

Belvedere to child Anthony Sydes (Tony)

**SIX OF A KIND** (Paramount, 1934). D: Leo McCarey. S: Walter DeLeon, Harry Ruskin. Fr: Keene Thompson, Douglas MacLean (story).

**1.** "According to you, everything I like to do is either illegal, immoral, or fattening."
> W. C. Fields (Sheriff "Honest John" Hoxley)

**2.** "I'm beginning to see footprints of a foul conspiracy."
> Fields

**3.** "I feel as though the Russian army had been walking over my tongue in their stocking feet."
> Fields

**4.** "I always talk loud; I'm a sheriff."
> Fields

**SIXTEEN CANDLES** (Universal, 1984). D: John Hughes. S: John Hughes.

**1.** "I can't believe I gave my panties to a geek."
> Molly Ringwald (Samantha), about geek Anthony Michael Hall (Ted)

**SLAP SHOT** (Universal, 1977). D: George Roy Hill. S: Nancy Dowd.

**1.** "I was trying to imagine you when you're through with hockey, and I couldn't. There was nobody there."
> Jennifer Warren (Francine Dunlop) to Paul Newman (Reggie Dunlop)

**SLEEPER** (UA, 1973). D: Woody Allen. S: Woody Allen, Marshall Brickman.

**1.** "I can't believe this. My doctor said I'd be up and on my feet in five days. He was off by 199 years."
> Woody Allen (Miles Monroe), on waking up from a routine operation in 1973 to find himself in the year 2173

**2.** "Yes, according to history over one hundred years ago a man named Albert Shanker got ahold of a nuclear warhead."
> Bartlett Robinson (Dr. Orva), on how nuclear war came about

**3.** "My brain is my second favorite organ."
> Allen, on being told that his brain will be destroyed if he is captured

**4.** "What kind of government you guys got here? This is worse than California."
> Allen, on the totalitarian state in power in the twenty-second century

**5.** "It's tobacco. It's one of the healthiest things for your body. Now, go ahead."
> Robinson, urging Allen to have a smoke, revealing one of the many ways medical science has changed its opinion over the years

**6.** "Hey, y'know, I bought Polaroid at seven. It's probably up millions by now."
> Allen

**7.** "This is Bela Lugosi, he was the mayor of New York City for a while. You can see what it did to him there. . . ."
> Allen, giving misinformation as he looks over ancient photos and explains what they represent

**8.** "Yes, he actually was President of the United States, but I know that whenever he used to leave the White House, the Secret Service used to count the silverware."
> Allen on Richard Nixon

**9.** "Are there any strange animals that I should know about around here, anything weird and futuristic, like with the body of a crab and the head of a social worker?"

*Allen to Diane Keaton (Luna Schlosser), scared of animal-like sounds in the forest*

**10.** "It's a *New York Times*—be careful—from 1990. 'POPE'S WIFE GIVES BIRTH TO TWINS.' "

*Allen, reading an ancient newspaper headline to Keaton*

**11.** KEATON: "It's hard to believe that you haven't had sex for two hundred years."

ALLEN: "Two hundred and four if you count my marriage."

**12.** "I like to be watched while I clone. The more the merrier, you know—never clone alone."

*Allen, pretending he knows how to clone a complete man from a nose*

**13.** "I haven't seen my analyst in two hundred years and . . . he was a strict Freudian, and if I'd been going all this time I'd probably almost be cured by now."

*Allen, complaining about his psychological state*

**14.** "He's great if you happen to like a tall, blond, Prussian, Nordic, Aryan Nazi type."

*Allen, on John Beck (Erno Windt)*

**LAST LINE**
**15.** "Sex and death. Two things that come once in a lifetime. But at least after death you're not nauseous."

*Allen, telling Keaton what he believes in*

**SLEEPING BEAUTY** (Buena Vista, 1959). D: Clyde Geronimi, Eric Larson, Les Clark, Wolfgang Reitherman.

**1.** "They're hopeless. A disgrace to the forces of evil."

*Eleanor Audley (Maleficient), referring to her goons*

**2.** "They say if you dream a thing more than once, it's sure to come true."

*Mary Costa (Briar Rose/Sleeping Beauty)*

**3.** "Father, you're living in the past. This is the fourteenth century."

*Bill Shirley (Prince Phillip)*

**SLEEPLESS IN SEATTLE** (TriStar, 1993). D: Nora Ephron. S: Nora Ephron, David S. Ward, Jeffrey Arch. Fr: Jeffrey Arch (story).

**1.** "Mom, destiny is something we've invented because we can't stand the fact that everything that happens is accidental."

*Meg Ryan (Annie Reed) to her mother*

**2.** "We're talking to Sleepless in Seattle."

*Radio psychiatrist Caroline Aaron (Dr. Martha Fieldstone) on widower Tom Hanks (Sam Baldwin)*

**3.** "If someone is a widower, why do they say that he was widowed? Why don't they say he was widowered? I was just wondering."

*Ryan*

**4.** "It was a million tiny little things that when you add them all up, it just meant that we were supposed to be together, and I knew it. I knew it the very first time I touched her. It was like coming home. Only to no home I'd ever known. I was just taking her hand, to help her out of a car, and I knew it. It was like magic."

*Hanks to Aaron, on how he knew he loved his wife*

**5.** "Things are a little different now. First, you have to be friends. You have to like each other. Then, you neck. This could go on for years. Then you have tests, and then you get to do it with a condom. The good news is you split the check."

*Rob Reiner (Jay) to Hanks, on dating*

**6.** "Now, those were the days when people knew how to be in love."

*Ryan, referring to the film* An Affair to Remember

**7.** "This is what single people do. They try other people on and see how they fit, but everybody's an adjustment. Nobody's perfect."

*Hanks to his son Ross Malinger (Jonah)*

**8.** "Marriage is hard enough without bringing such low expectations into it."

*Ryan's fiancé Bill Pullman (Walter) to Ryan*

**9.** HANKS, offering Ryan his hand: "We better go. Shall we?"
RYAN, as she takes it: "Sam, it's nice to meet you."

**SLEUTH** (UK: 20th Century–Fox, 1972). D: Joseph L. Mankiewicz. S: Anthony Shaffer. Fr: Anthony Shaffer (play).

**1.** "This, as they say, is where the plot thickens."

*Laurence Olivier (Andrew White), a fanatic about games, to Michael Caine (Milo Tindle), whom he plans to involve in a convoluted crime scheme*

**2.** "You are the complete clown."

*Olivier to Caine, after dressing him in a clown costume as part of the scheme*

**3.** "I invited you round here to set up the circumstances of your own death."

*Olivier to Caine, revealing his plot*

**4.** "Nothing succeeds like simplicity."

*Olivier to Caine, referring to his plan*

**5.** ALEC CAWTHORNE (*Inspector Doppler*): "Is there nothing you would not consider a game, sir? Beauty? Work? Even marriage?"
OLIVIER: "Oh, please, Inspector, don't include marriage! Sex . . . sex is the game. Marriage is the penalty."

**6.** "I heard the sound of my own death. Now, that changes you, Andrew. Believe me."

*Caine to Olivier, referring to the moment when Olivier pretended to shoot him*

**LAST LINE**
**7.** "Andrew, don't forget. Be sure and tell them it was just a bloody game."

*Caine to Olivier, just before he dies, with the police knocking on the door*

**SMILES OF A SUMMER NIGHT** (Sweden: Svensk Filmindustri, 1955). D: Ingmar Bergman. S: Ingmar Bergman.

**1.** "Out in the sun, gentlemen. Summer is here."

*Gunnar Björnstrand (Fredrik Egerman) to the employees at his law office*

**SNAKE PIT, THE** (20th Century–Fox, 1948). D: Anatole Litvak. S: Frank Partos, Millen Brand. Fr: Mary Jane Ward (novel).

**1.** "I heard a scream, and I didn't know if it was me who screamed or not—if it was *I* or not."

*Olivia de Havilland (Virginia Stuart Cunningham)*

## SNOW WHITE AND THE SEVEN DWARFS
(RKO/Walt Disney, 1937). D: David Hand. S: Ted Sears, Otto Englander, Earl Hurd, Dorothy Ann Blank, Richard Creedon, et al. Fr: Brothers Grimm (fairy tale, "Sneewittchen").

*1.* "Magic Mirror, on the wall, who is the fairest of them all?"

*Lucille LaVerne (Queen)*

*2.* "Jiminy Crickets!"

*Billy Gilbert (Sneezy), when the dwarfs come home to a clean house, and suspect there's a monster in the house*

*3.* "Mummy dust to make me old. To shroud my clothes, the black of night. To disguise my voice, an old hag's cackle. To whiten my hair, a scream of fright. A gust of wind to fan my hate. A thunderbolt to mix it well. And now begin thy magic spell."

*LaVerne, transforming her beauty into ugliness*

*4.* PINTO COLVIG (*Grumpy*), as he leaves for work: "Now, I'm warning you. Don't let nothing or nobody in the house."
ADRIANA CASELOTTI (*Snow White*): "Why, Grumpy! You do care!"

*5.* "The Queen'll kill her! We've got to save her!"

*Colvig, when the animals try to warn the dwarfs that LaVerne has Caselotti*

*6.* LAVERNE: "This is no ordinary apple. It's a magic wishing apple. . . . One bite and all your dreams will come true."
CASELOTTI: "Really?"
LAVERNE: "Yes, girlie. Now, make a wish and take a bite."

*7.* ". . . and he'll carry me away to his castle where we'll live happily ever after."

*Caselotti, completing her wish, just before she bites the apple and falls asleep*

## SOAPDISH
(Paramount, 1991). D: Michael Hoffman. S: Robert Harling, Andrew Bergman. Fr: Robert Harling (story).

*1.* "How am I supposed to write for a guy that doesn't have a head?"

*Whoopi Goldberg (Rose Schwartz), a soap opera writer who has to revive a character decapitated on an earlier show*

## SODOM AND GOMORRAH
(U.S/France/Italy: Cinema–S.G.C., 1962). D: Robert Aldrich, Sergio Leone. S: Hugo Butler, Giorgio Prosperi.

*1.* "Where's there's water, there's danger also."

*Stewart Granger (Lot), arriving at an oasis*

*2.* PIER ANGELI (*Ilda*): "Where I come from, nothing is evil. Everything that gives pleasure is good."
GRANGER: "Where do you come from?"
ANGELI: "There. Not far. Just ahead. Sodom and Gomorrah."

*3.* "In the name of righteousness and your God, you have abandoned yourself to the lust for blood. You are a true Sodomite, Lot. Welcome."

*Anouk Aimee (The Queen) to Granger, after he has killed a man*

*4.* "Look long on that sun. You'll never see it again."

*Granger to Aimee, on the last day*

**SOLDIER'S STORY, A** (Columbia, 1984). D: Norman Jewison. S: Charles Fuller. Fr: Charles Fuller (play, *A Soldier's Play*).

**1.** "What kind of colored man are you?"

Denzel Washington (Private First Class Peterson), shocked at Adolph Caesar's (Sergeant Waters's) harsh criticism of his own race

**2.** "I do what folks tell me, Captain. Not you!"

Howard E. Rollins (Captain Davenport), not willing to arrest the first person who seems guilty of Caesar's murder

**3.** "You know the damage one ignorant Negro can do?"

Caesar, blaming his own race for the prejudice of white people

**4.** "They're finally going to give us Negroes a chance to fight. Hitler ain't got a chance now. And after what Joe Louis did to Max Schmeling."

Robert Townsend (Corporal Ellis), when the company is given orders to go overseas

**5.** "Look out, Hitler! The niggers is coming to get your ass!"

David Alan Grier (Corporal Cobb), when the company is given orders to go overseas

**6.** "Some things need getting rid of."

Washington, on why he killed the bigoted Caesar

**7.** "Who gave you the right to judge? To decide who is fit to be a Negro? And who is not? Who?"

Rollins to Washington

**SOME LIKE IT HOT** (Paramount, 1959). D: George Archainbaud. S: Billy Wilder, I. A. L. Diamond. Fr: Robert Thoeren (Fanfares of Love), M. Logan (screenplay).

**1.** "Look at that. Look how she moves. It's just like Jell-O on springs."

Jack Lemmon (Jerry/Daphne), in drag along with Tony Curtis (Joe/Josephine), watching Marilyn Monroe (Sugar) walk

**2.** LEMMON: "Now you've done it! Now you have done it!"
CURTIS: "Done what?"
LEMMON: "You tore off one of my chests!"

**3.** "I always get the fuzzy end of the lollipop."

Monroe, telling Lemmon and Curtis about her love life

**4.** "We wouldn't be caught dead with men. Rough, hairy beasts. Eight hands. And they . . . they all just want one thing from a girl."

Lemmon

**5.** CURTIS, instructing Lemmon on how to suppress his male lust: "Just keep telling yourself you're a girl."
LEMMON: "I'm a girl. . . . I'm a girl. . . . I'm a girl. . . ."

**6.** "I have this thing about saxophone players, especially tenor sax. . . . I don't know what it is, but they just curdle me. All they have to do is play eight bars of 'Come to Me, My Melancholy Baby' and my spine turns to custard."

Monroe to saxophone player Curtis, in drag as Josephine

**7.** "They get those weak eyes from reading—you know, those long tiny little columns in the *Wall Street Journal*."

Monroe on the millionaires with glasses she hopes to find in Florida

**8.** "Zowie!"

*Trademark line of dirty old millionaire Joe E. Brown (Osgood Fielding III)*

**9.** "With all the unrest in the world, I don't think anybody should have a yacht that sleeps more than twelve."

*Curtis, pretending to be a bespectacled millionaire in hopes of bagging Monroe*

**10.** "Oh, well, I guess some like it hot. I personally prefer classical music."

*Curtis, as the millionaire, to Monroe on jazz*

**11.** CURTIS, as Monroe kisses him, trying to break through the sexual dysfunction Curtis claims to have: "I think you're on the right track."

MONROE: "I must be. Your glasses are beginning to steam up."

**12.** CURTIS, on whether Lemmon should accept Brown's marriage proposal: "But you're not a girl. You're a guy. And why would a guy want to marry a guy?"

LEMMON: "Security."

**13.** "Just keep telling yourself you're a boy. You're a boy."

*Curtis, reversing his previous advice to Lemmon*

**14.** "I tell you, I will never find another man who's so good to me."

*Lemmon to Curtis, on Brown's generosity*

**15.** "I told you, I'm not very bright."

*Monroe, explaining why she's going back to Curtis, despite his false pretenses and his saxophone playing*

LAST LINE

**16.** "Well, nobody's perfect."

*Brown, responding to Lemmon's admission that he is a man*

**SOMEBODY UP THERE LIKES ME** (MGM, 1956). D: Robert Wise. S: Ernest Lehman. Fr: Rocky Graziano, with Rowland Barber (autobiography).

**1.** "I look at you and I see the Devil."

*Harold J. Stone (Nick Barbella), as the father, to Paul Newman (Rocky Graziano)*

**2.** "One thing you and this lousy place give me is a big taste for being on the outside."

*Newman to the warden of the penitentiary, when he is released*

**3.** "You got something inside of you that a lot of fighters don't have, never will have, no matter how much I teach them. Hate. I don't know why it's there. I only know that if anybody hits you, he better start ducking fast because that hate pours into that right hand of yours and makes it like a charge of dynamite."

*Judson Pratt (Sgt. Johnny Hyland) to Newman*

**4.** "What's better? Stealing, starving, or fighting?"

*Newman to Pier Angeli (Norma), on why he fights, because he doesn't know anything else*

**5.** "Be a champ, like I never was!"

*Stone to Newman*

**6.** "Everybody who is young is promising. The world should sue the young for breach of promise."

*Joseph Buloff (Benny)*

**7.** "Eating and drinking are inadequate substitutes for achievement. Gas in the belly, unfortunately, will not inflate the ego."

*Buloff to Newman*

**8.** NEWMAN: "Somebody up there likes me!"

ANGELI: "Somebody down here, too!"

**SOMETHING WILD** (Orion, 1986). D: Jonathan Demme. S: E. Max Frey.

**1.** "Hey, you didn't pay for your lunch."

Melanie Griffith (Audrey Hankel), accosting Jeff Daniels (Charles Driggs) as he attempts to leave a diner without paying

**2.** "You're a closet rebel."

Griffith, analyzing Daniels

**3.** "Mom and Dad's. Dad speaking."

Kenneth Utt (Dad), answering the phone at his family-owned restaurant

**4.** "It's better to be a live dog than a dead lion."

Daniels to Jack Gilpin (Larry Dillman), quitting his job as he reprises a line told to him on the road

**SOMMERSBY** (Warner Bros., 1993). D: Jon Amiel. S: Nicholas Meyer, Sarah Kernochan. Fr: Nicholas Meyer, Anthony Shaffer (story), Daniel Vigne, Jean-Claude Carriere (screenplay, The Return of Martin Guerre).

**1.** "I didn't shoot my first man before I had to, either."

Richard Gere (Jack Sommersby) to a neighbor, referring to never working his farm before

**2.** "I'm thinking, Who is this man sittin' in my kitchen?"

Jodie Foster (Laurel), on what she thinks of the return of Gere, her mysteriously changed husband

**3.** "Supposed to use fertilizer in the *field*, Jack."

Richard Hamilton (Doc Evans) to Gere, when he discovers Foster is pregnant

**4.** FOSTER: "A woman would know her own husband, Your Honor."

JAMES EARL JONES (Judge Isaacs): "Well, I'm sure most husbands would like to think so, Mrs. Sommersby."

**5.** "Without my name, I don't think I have a life, Your Honor."

Gere to Jones, refusing to deny that he is Jack Sommersby

**6.** "I know because I never loved him the way that I love you."

Foster to Gere, on how she can be sure Gere is not her husband

**7.** "Being your husband has been the only thing I've ever done that I'm proud of."

Gere to Foster

**SON OF FLUBBER** (Buena Vista, 1963). D: Robert Stevenson. S: Bill Walsh, Don DaGradi. Fr: Samuel W. Taylor (story, "A Situation of Gravity"), Jay Williams, Raymond Abrashkin (books).

**1.** FRED MACMURRAY (Ned Brainard), trying to interest his wife in his new weather-changing invention, flubbergas: "Do you realize what that would mean, Betsy? . . . It could change the future of the whole world, the history of mankind itself!"

NANCY OLSON (Betsy Brainard): "That's very nice, dear."

**2.** "If you weren't deductible, I'd disown you!"

*Keenan Wynn (Alonzo Hawk) to son Tommy Kirk (Biff Hawk)*

**3.** "Mr. Prosecutor, the road to genius is paved with fumble-footing and bumbling. Anyone who falls flat on his face is at least moving in the right direction: forward. And the fellow who makes the most mistakes may be the one who will save the neck of the whole world someday."

*MacMurray to prosecutor Alan Hewitt*

**LAST LINES**

**4.** MACMURRAY: "Betsy, offhand, can you name one thing that science hasn't improved upon, one way or another?"

OLSON: "Offhand, I think I can."

MACMURRAY: "All right, what?" (*They kiss.*) "Oh, I guess I'll have to go along with that."

**SON OF FRANKENSTEIN** (Universal, 1939). D: Rowland V. Lee. S: Willis Cooper. Fr: Mary Shelley (characters).

**1.** BASIL RATHBONE (*Baron Wolf von Frankenstein*), traveling by train to his father's village: "Why, nine out of ten people call that misshapen creature of my father's experiments—"

CONDUCTOR, calling the stop: "Frankenstein. Frankenstein."

**2.** "You have inherited the fortune of the Frankensteins. I trust you will not inherit their fate."

*Rathbone, reading a letter from his late father*

**3.** "One doesn't easily forget, Herr Baron, an arm torn out by the roots."

*Lionel Atwill (Inspector Krogh) to Rathbone, on how he lost his arm in childhood in an attack by the monster*

**4.** "So, Ygor is dead! Heh, heh, heh . . ."

*Bela Lugosi (Ygor), on surviving his hanging*

**5.** HEINRICH VON FRANKENSTEIN MAKER OF MONSTERS

*Graffiti on plaque of Rathbone's father's tomb; Rathbone revises it to say "MAKER OF MEN"*

**6.** "No. Cannot be destroyed. Cannot die. Your father made him live for . . . always."

*Lugosi to Rathbone, on the monster (Boris Karloff)*

**7.** "Yes, it appears that we've returned to the Middle Ages. The villagers have laid siege to the castle and are crying out for blood, blood, blood!"

*Rathbone, angered by the villagers outside who demand an end to his experiments*

**SONG OF THE SOUTH** (RKO, 1946). D: Harve Foster, Wilfred Jackson. S: Dalton Raymond, Morton Grant, Maurice Rapf. Fr: Joel Chandler Harris (novel, Tales of Uncle Remus), Dalton Raymond (original story), William Peet, Ralph Wright, George Stallings (story).

**1.** "That's the kind of day when you can't open your mouth without having a song jump right out of it."

*James Baskett (Uncle Remus/Voice of Brer Fox) to Bobby Driscoll (Johnny), describing a zip-a-dee-doo-dah day*

**2.** "There's other ways of learning about the behind feet of a mule than getting kicked by them."

*Baskett to Driscoll*

**3.** "Just 'cause these here tales is about critters, like Brer Rabbit and Brer Fox, that don't mean they can't happen to folks. And excuse me for saying so, but them who can't learn from a tale about critters just ain't got their ears tuned for listening."

*Baskett to Driscoll*

**4.** "Brer Rabbit didn't know it, but you can't run away from trouble. There just ain't no place that far."

*Baskett, in narration*

**5.** "Now, you know, all of us has a laughing place. I've got one, and you've got one. Trouble is most folks won't take the time to go look for it. And nobody can tell you where yours is, because where it is for one might not be where it is for another."

*Baskett to Driscoll*

**SONG TO REMEMBER, A** *(Columbia, 1945). D: Charles Vidor. S: Oscar Millard .*

**1.** "Frederic, you must stop this Polonaise jangle!"

*Merle Oberon (George Sand) to Cornel Wilde (Frederic Chopin)*

**SONS OF THE DESERT, THE** *(MGM, 1933). D: William A. Seiter. S: Frank Craven, Byron Morgan.*

**1.** "Every man should be the king in his own castle."

*Oliver Hardy (Himself) to Stan Laurel (Himself)*

**2.** "Oh, so that's where it's been going. That's the third apple I've missed this week."

*Mae Busch (Lottie Hardy) on learning that Laurel has been eating her wax fruit*

**3.** HARDY: "Why did you get a veterinarian?"
LAUREL: "Well, I didn't think his religion would make any difference."

**4.** "If I have to go to Honolulu alone, he's going with me."

*Hardy to Busch, referring to Laurel, and exhibiting perfect Laurel and Hardy logic*

**5.** "I know she went out. But what I'd like to know is: Where did she went?"

*Hardy*

**6.** HARDY: "To catch a Hardy, they've got to get up very early in the morning."
LAUREL: "What time?"

**7.** LAUREL: "I've certainly got to hand it to you."
HARDY: "For what?"
LAUREL: "Well, for the meticulous care with which you have executed your finely formulated machinations in extricating us from this devastating dilemma."

**8.** "We're just like two peas in a pot."

*Laurel*

**9.** "Well, here's another nice mess you've gotten me into!"

*Hardy to Laurel, when their wives decide to search the attic, which forces them to go out on the roof in the rain, and a policeman brings them to their front door*

**10.** HARDY: "The ship started to sink, and we both dived overboard. Didn't we, Stan?"
LAUREL: "Yes, just as the boat was going down for the third time."

**LAST LINE**
**11.** "Betty said that honesty was the best politics."

*Laurel, telling Hardy his wife's reaction to the truth*

**SOUND OF MUSIC, THE** (20th Century–Fox, 1965). D: Robert Wise. S: Ernest Lehman. Fr: Richard Rodgers, Oscar Hammerstein II, Howard Lindsay, Russel Crouse (musical play).

**1.** GOVERNESS JULIE ANDREWS (*Maria*), on first meeting her new employer: "You don't look at all like a sea captain, sir."
  CHRISTOPHER PLUMMER (*Captain Von Trapp*): "You don't look like a governess."

**2.** PLUMMER, referring to Andrews's former home: "Were you this much trouble at the abbey?"
  ANDREWS: "Oh, much more, sir."

**3.** "The Von Trapp children don't play. They march."
  *Housekeeper Norma Varden (Fran Schmidt) to Andrews*

**4.** "I like rich people. I like the way they live. I like the way I live when I'm with them."
  *Richard Haydn (Max Detweiler), at Plummer's house*

**5.** "My children do not sing in public."
  *Plummer, ineffectually laying down the law to Haydn*

**6.** "There's nothing more irresistible to a man than a woman who's in love with him."
  *Eleanor Parker (The Baroness) to Andrews, her rival for Plummer's affections*

**7.** "Good-bye, Maria. I'm sure you'll make a very fine nun."
  *Parker to Andrews*

**8.** "And somewhere out there is a young lady who I think will never be a nun."
  *Parker to Plummer, expressing her true opinion about Andrews*

**9.** "The reverend mother always said when the Lord closes a door, somewhere he opens a window."
  *Andrews to Plummer, upon their first kiss*

**10.** "Maybe the flag with the black spider makes people nervous."
  *Von Trapp child Debbie Turner (Marta), discussing the swastika with Haydn, following the Nazi takeover of Austria*

**11.** FIRST NUN: "Reverend Mother, I have sinned."
  SECOND NUN: "I, too, Reverend Mother."
  *Sheepish nuns confessing to Peggy Wood (Mother Abbess) after removing parts of Nazis' cars to allow the Von Trapps to escape*

**SOUTHERNER, THE** (UA, 1945). D: Jean Renoir. S: Jean Renoir, Hugo Butler (uncredited), William Faulkner, Nunnally Johnson. Fr: George Sessions Perry (novel, Hold Autumn in Your Hand).

**1.** "So, Lord, how come you put that sky up there, and this old mud down here? Made it so pretty, if you didn't want us to work it, love it . . . You want me to give all this up? Move in town with Tim, and work with him in a factory under a roof that hides your sky and puts out your light? Tell me, Lord. Help me to know."
  *Zachary Scott (Sam Tucker)*

**2.** "I'm going back to the house, and just sit, and wait for my call to glory."
  *Beulah Bondi (Granny)*

**SOYLENT GREEN** *(MGM, 1973). D: Richard Fleischer. S: Stanley R. Greenberg. Fr: Harry Harrison (novel, Make Room! Make Room!).*

### LAST LINE

**1.** "You can tell everybody. Listen to me, Hatcher. You've got to tell them soylent green is people. We've got to stop them somehow."

*Charlton Heston (Detective Thorn) to his superior Brock Peters (Hatcher), as Heston is dragged away to become the food known as soylent green*

**SPACEBALLS** *(MGM/UA, 1987). D: Mel Brooks. S: Mel Brooks, Thomas Meehan, Ronny Graham.*

**1.** "I see your schwartz is as big as mine. Now let's see how well you handle it."

*Rick Moranis (Lord Dark Helmut) to Bill Pullman (Lone Starr), about their light-sabers*

**SPARTACUS** *(Universal-International/Bryna Productions, 1960). D: Stanley Kubrick. S: Dalton Trumbo. Fr: Howard Fast (novel).*

**1.** "You don't want to know my name. I don't want to know your name. . . . Gladiators don't make friends. If we're ever matched in the arena together, I'll have to kill you."

*Woody Strode (Draba), on being asked his name by fellow gladiator Kirk Douglas (Spartacus)*

**2.** "I'm not an animal! I'm not an animal!"

*Douglas to gladiator-school owner Peter Ustinov (Batiatus), on being given Jean Simmons (Varinia) as a sex partner*

**3.** "You may not be an animal, Spartacus, but this sorry show gives me very little hope that you'll ever be a man."

*Peter Ustinov (Batiatus), on Douglas's refusal of Simmons*

**4.** "You have a shrewd eye, Your Pulchritude."

*Ustinov to Joanna Barnes (Claudia)*

**5.** "You know, this republic of ours is something like a rich widow. Most Romans love her as their mother, but Crassus dreams of marrying the old girl, to put it politely."

*Charles Laughton (Gracchus), discussing Laurence Olivier (Crassus) with John Gavin (Julius Caesar)*

**6.** "Gladiators. An army of gladiators. There's never been an army like that. One gladiator's worth any two Roman soldiers that ever lived."

*Douglas, announcing how he plans to free the slaves of Italy*

**7.** "You have no ships."

*Herbert Lom (Tigranes), indicating to Douglas that he and the slave army have been betrayed by the pirates who promised them ships*

**8.** "I do know that we're brothers, and I know that we're free. We march tonight."

*Douglas, ending his final address to the army of rebel slaves*

**9.** "I'm Spartacus! I'm Spartacus! I'm Spartacus!"

*Rebel slaves, beginning with Tony Curtis (Antoninus), unanimously proclaiming themselves to be Spartacus at the cost of crucifixion, rather than surrender their leader*

**10.** "It would take a great woman to make Crassus fall out of love with himself."

*Laughton, on Olivier's infatuation with Simmons*

**11.** "You think by threatening to kill my child you'll make me love you?"

*Simmons on Olivier's courtship methods*

**12.** CURTIS, dying after Douglas has killed him in a sword fight to save him from crucifixion: "I love you, Spartacus, as I loved my own father."

DOUGLAS: "I love you, like my son that I'll never see."

**13.** "This is your son. He is free, Spartacus. Free. He's free. He's free."

*Simmons to Douglas*

**SPEED** (20th Century–Fox, 1994). D: Jan De Bont. S: Graham Yost.

**1.** "Shoot the hostage."

*SWAT officer Keanu Reeves's (Jack Traven's) answer to Jeff Daniels's (Harry's) "pop quiz" about what to do when a terrorist is getting away with a hostage*

**2.** "Here's to you guys for doing your job and for not getting dead."

*Joe Morton (Captain McMahon) to Reeves and Daniels, after they rescue passengers from an elevator threatened by mad bomber Dennis Hopper (Howard Payne)*

**3.** "Man sure has a hard-on for this bus."

*Onlooker watching Reeves chase a bus threatened by Hopper*

**4.** "Oh, sure, it's just like driving a really big Pinto."

*Passenger Sandra Bullock (Annie), on whether she can drive the bus after the driver is shot*

**5.** "Remember: crazy, not stupid."

*Reeves on Hopper*

**6.** "Do not attempt to grow a brain."

*Hopper, advising Reeves not to try anything smart*

**7.** "You're not too bright, man, but you got some big, round, hairy *cojones.*"

*Passenger Carlos Carrasco (Ortiz), complimenting Reeves for his courage in attempting to defuse the bomb under the bus*

**8.** "What, you felt you needed another challenge or something?"

*Bullock to Reeves, on his puncturing the bus's gas tank*

**9.** "Pop quiz, asshole. You have a hair trigger aimed at your head. What do you do? What do you do?"

*Reeves pointing a gun at Bullock, mistaking her for Hopper*

**10.** "A bomb is made to explode."

*Hopper, explaining his philosophy of bombing to Reeves*

**LAST LINES**
**11.** REEVES: "I have to warn you. I've heard relationships based on intense experiences never work."

BULLOCK: "Okay. We'll have to base it on sex then."

REEVES: "Whatever you say, ma'am."

**SPLASH** (Touchstone/Buena Vista, 1984). D: Ron Howard. S: Lowell Ganz, Babaloo Mandel, Bruce Jay Friedman. Fr: Brian Grazer, Bruce Jay Friedman (story).

**1.** "You see, drinking is really a matter of algebraic ratios. How drunk you get is dependent on how much alcohol you consume in relation to your total body weight.

You see my point? It's not that you had a lot to drink. It's just you're too skinny."

*John Candy (Freddie Bauer) to Tom Hanks (Allen Bauer), who is lying on the bar*

**2.** "I don't ask much, do I? I mean I don't ask to be famous, and I don't ask to be rich, and I don't ask to play center field for the New York Yankees, or anything. I just want to meet a woman, and I want to fall in love, and I want to get married, and I want to have a kid, and I want to go see him play a tooth in the school play. It's not much."

*Hanks to himself*

**3.** "I'm just changing."

*Mermaid Daryl Hannah (Madison) to Hanks, when she won't let him in the bathroom because she's transforming back into a human*

**4.** "There is a mermaid in New York City."

*Eugene Levy (Walter Kornbluth) to Howard Morris (Dr. Zidell), stating a scientific claim*

**5.** "She's really hungry."

*Hanks to restaurant patrons when Hannah eats lobster with the shell intact*

**6.** "Let her go. Show some dignity."

*Ice skating rink attendant, trying to keep Hanks from chasing after Hannah*

**7.** "I was born to be married. I just so happen to come from a long line of married people. My mom and dad, they were married. Their moms and dads, they were married, too."

*Hanks to Hannah, when she agrees to marry him*

**8.** "All my life I've been waiting for someone, and when I find her, she's a fish."

*Hanks, after Levy has exposed Hannah as a mermaid*

**9.** "Look, do you realize how happy you were with her? That is when you weren't driving yourself crazy. Every day . . . Come on. Some people will never be that happy. I'll never be that happy."

*Candy to Hanks*

**10.** "I'm really a nice guy. If I had any friends, you could ask them."

*Levy to Hanks*

**11.** "What a week I'm having!"

*Levy, as another mishap befalls him*

**12.** "Is this the big secret you've been keeping from me? Is it that you're a mermaid, or is there something else?"

*Hanks to Hannah*

**SPY WHO LOVED ME, THE** (UK: UA, 1977). D: Lewis Gilbert. S: Christopher Wood, Richard Maibaum. Fr: Ian Fleming (novel).

**1.** "What can I offer you, sheep's eyes, dates, vodka martini?"

*Edward De Souza (Sheik Hosein) to Roger Moore (James Bond), upon meeting him*

**2.** "Egyptian builders."

*Moore, when Richard Kiel (Jaws) is buried under a collapsed pyramid*

**3.** MOORE: "You did save my life."
BARBARA BACH (*Maj. Imosabel Masovar*): "We all make mistakes, Mr. Bond."

**4.** "He just dropped in for a quick bite."

*Moore, after throwing Kiel off the train*

**5.** "I wish to conduct my life on my own terms, and in surroundings with which I can identify. That is a privilege of wealth."

*Curt Jurgens (Stromberg), explaining to Moore why he lives under the sea*

**STAGE DOOR** (RKO, 1937). D: Gregory La Cava. S: Morrie Ryskind, Anthony Veiller (uncredited), Gregory La Cava. Fr: Edna Ferber, George S. Kaufman (play).

**1.** "The calla lilies are in bloom again."
   *Katharine Hepburn (Terry Randall)*

**2.** "You may as well go to perdition in ermine. You're sure to come back in rags."
   *Hepburn to Ginger Rogers (Ginger Maitland)*

**3.** "You're an actress if you're acting. But you can't just walk up and down a room and act. Without that job and those lines to say, an actress is just like any ordinary girl trying not to look as scared as she feels."
   *Andrea Leeds (Kaye Hamilton) to Hepburn*

**STAGECOACH** (Walter Wanger/UA, 1939). D: John Ford. S: Dudley Nichols. Fr: Ernest Haycox (short story, "Stage to Lordsburg").

**1.** "And remember this, what's good for the banks is good for the country."
   *Berton Churchill (Henry Gatewood) to stagecoach riders, who later discover his financial improprieties*

**2.** "We're the victims of a foul disease called social prejudice, my child."
   *Thomas Mitchell (Dr. Josiah Boone) to Claire Trevor (Dallas), two social pariahs*

**3.** "There are things worse than Apaches."
   *Trevor to George Bancroft (Sheriff Curly Wilcox) on why she will stay on the stagecoach despite warnings of danger en route*

**4.** "If there's one thing I don't like, it's driving a stagecoach through Apache country."
   *Andy Devine (Buck) to Bancroft*

**5.** "My friends call me Ringo. Nickname I had as a kid. Right name's Henry."
   *John Wayne (The Ringo Kid) to Mitchell*

**6.** "I'm not only a philosopher, sir, I'm a fatalist. Somewhere, sometime, there may be the right bullet or the wrong bottle waiting for Josiah Boone. Why worry when or where?"
   *Mitchell to Bancroft, on why he will remain on the stagecoach*

**7.** "I have a slogan that should be emblazoned on every newspaper in the country: America for Americans. The government must not interfere with business. Reduce taxes. Our national debt is something shocking. . . . What this country needs is a businessman for president."
   *Churchill to group*

**8.** "Coffee, give me coffee. Black coffee. Lots of it."
   *Mitchell to Wayne, to sober him enough to deliver child of Louise Platt (Lucy Mallory)*

**9.** "It's a baby."
   *Devine to group of male stagecoach passengers*

**10.** "Well, you gotta live no matter what happens."
   *Trevor to Wayne*

**11.** "Look, Miss Dallas, you got no folks. Neither have I, and well, maybe I'm taking a lot for granted, but I watched you with that baby, another woman's baby. You looked, well, well, I still got a ranch across the border. It's a nice place, a real nice place, trees, grass, water. There's a cabin, half-built. A man could live there, with a woman. Will you go?"

*Wayne to Trevor, proposing marriage*

**12.** "Well, there are some things a man just can't run away from."

*Wayne to Trevor, on facing his past criminal record*

**LAST LINES**

**13.** BANCROFT: "Well, they're saved from the blessings of civilization."
MITCHELL: "Yeah."
BANCROFT: "Well, Doc, I'll buy you a drink."
MITCHELL: "Just one."

**STALAG 17** *(Paramount, 1953). D: Billy Wilder. S: Billy Wilder, Edwin Blum. Fr: Donald Bevan, Edmund Trzcinski (play).*

**FIRST LINE**

**1.** "I don't know about you, but it always makes me sore when I see those war pictures. All about flying leathernecks and submarine patrols and frogmen and guerrillas in the Philippines. What gets me is that there never was a movie about POWs—about prisoners of war."

*Gil Stratton, Jr. (Cookie), in voice-over*

**2.** "It's roll call. Hitler is waiting to see us."

*Harvey Lembeck (Harry) to Robert Strauss ("Animal" Stosh)*

**3.** "Nasty weather we are having, eh? And I so much hoped we could give you a white Christmas, just like the ones you used to know. Aren't those the words that clever little man wrote, you know, the one who stole his

name from our capital, that something-or-other Berlin?"

*Otto Preminger (Oberst Von Scherbach) to prisoners*

**4.** "Nobody has ever escaped from Stalag 17. Not alive, anyway."

*Preminger to prisoners*

**5.** "No butts."

*William Holden's (Sefton's) standing rule for the cigarettes used as coin for his various games of chance*

**6.** "Hey, you don't want to be no stinking lawyer with a stinking briefcase in a stinking office, do ya, Joey? Nah. Next time we write to your folks, you know what we're gonna say? You're gonna say that you don't want to be no lawyer. You want to be a musician, play maybe, huh, the flute?"

*Strauss to shell-shocked former law student Robinson Stone (Joey)*

**7.** "Aach! One Fuhrer is enough."

*Sig Rumann (Schulz) to Stalag 17 prisoners, imitating Hitler*

**8.** "Nobody beat me. We were playing pinochle. It's a rough game."

*Holden to Geneva Convention representative, when he asks who beat Holden*

**9.** "Betty!"

*Strauss to Lembeck, dressed as Betty Grable*

**10.** "Always remember just because the Krauts are dumb that doesn't mean they're stupid."

*Mail carrier to prisoners*

**11.** PETER GRAVES (*Price*), as Holden is cornering him as the spy: "I don't like you. I never did and I never will."

HOLDEN: "A lot of people say that, and the first thing you know is they're getting married."

**12.** "Just one more word. If I ever run into any of you bums on the street corner, just let's pretend we never met before."

> Holden to prisoners, as he enters escape hatch to rescue Don Taylor (Dunbar)

**LAST LINE**
**13.** "Maybe he just wanted to steal our wire cutters. Did ya ever think of that?"

> Strauss to group, on why Holden rescued Dunbar

**STAR IS BORN, A** (Selznick-International/ UA, 1937). D: William A. Wellman. S: Dorothy Parker, Alan Campbell, Robert Carson, David O. Selznick (uncredited), William A. Wellman (uncredited), and others uncredited. Fr: William A. Wellman, Robert Carson (story).

**1.** "He has a heart of gold—only harder."

> Adolphe Menjou (Oliver Niles) to Janet Gaynor (Esther Blodgett/Vicki Lester), on press agent Lionel Stander (Libby)

**LAST LINE**
**2.** "Hello, everybody. This is Mrs. Norman Maine."

> Gaynor, commemorating her late husband Fredric March (Norman Maine); also the last line of the 1954 remake

**STAR IS BORN, A** (Warner Bros., 1954). D: George Cukor. S: Moss Hart. Fr: Dorothy Parker, Alan Campbell, Robert Carson (screenplay), William A. Wellman, Robert Carson (story).

**1.** "Too young. I had a very young week last week."

> Womanizing star James Mason (Norman Maine), discussing potential conquests with the maître'd at the Cocoanut Grove

**2.** "Have you had enough, as the Republicans used to say?"

> Judy Garland (Esther Blodgett/Vicki Lester) to Mason, about his looking at her scrapbook

**3.** "If you'll be kind enough to glance between my shoulder blades, Mr. and Mrs. Gubbins, you'll find there a knife buried to the hilt. On its handle are your initials."

> Jack Carson (Matt Libby) to Mason and Garland

**STAR TREK: THE MOTION PICTURE** (Paramount, 1979). D: Robert Wise. S: Harold Livingston, Gene Roddenberry. Fr: Alan Dean Foster (story), Gene Roddenberry (TV series).

**LAST LINE**
**1.** "Out there. That-a-way."

> William Shatner (Capt. James T. Kirk), ordering a new course for the Enterprise

**STAR TREK II: THE WRATH OF KHAN** (Paramount, 1982). D: Nicholas Meyer. S: Jack B. Sowards. Fr: Harve Bennett, Jack B. Sowards (story), Gene Roddenberry (TV series).

**1.** "Gallivanting around the cosmos is a game for the young."

> William Shatner (Adm. James T. Kirk)

**2.** "Humor. It is a difficult concept."

> Valcan Kirstie Alley (Lieutenant Saavik)

**3.** "I am a Vulcan. I have no ego to bruise."

*Leonard Nimoy (Mr. Spock)*

**4.** "Let them eat static."

*Ricardo Montalban (Khan), when the Enterprise requests communication*

**5.** "Ah, Kirk, my old friend, do you know the Klingon proverb that tells us revenge is a dish that is best served cold? It is very cold in space."

*Montalban, talking to himself*

**6.** "You've managed to kill just about everyone else, but like a poor marksman, you keep missing the target."

*Shatner*

**7.** "I don't like to lose."

*Shatner, explaining how he managed to win at the no-win Kobayashi Maru test*

**8.** "His pattern indicates two-dimensional thinking."

*Nimoy, on Khan*

**9.** "Of all the souls I have encountered in my travels, his was the most human."

*Shatner's eulogy for Nimoy*

**STAR TREK III: THE SEARCH FOR SPOCK** (Paramount, 1984). D: Leonard Nimoy. S: Harve Bennett. Fr: Gene Roddenberry (TV series).

**1.** "It seems, Admiral, that I've got all his marbles."

*DeForest Kelley (McCoy) to William Shatner (Adm. James T. Kirk), when he realizes Leonard Nimoy (Mr. Spock) has mind-melded with him*

**2.** "My logic is uncertain where my son is concerned."

*Mark Lenard (Sarek), a Vulcan, on his son Nimoy*

**STAR WARS** (20th Century–Fox, 1977). D: George Lucas. S: George Lucas.

**1.** "A long time ago in a galaxy far, far away. . . ."

*Opening title*

**2.** "We seem to be made to suffer. It's our lot in life."

*Anthony Daniels (See-Threepio, or C-3PO) to fellow droid Kenny Baker (Artoo-Detoo, or R2-D2)*

**3.** "Help me, Obi-Wan Kenobi. You're my only hope."

*Carrie Fisher (Princess Leia Organa), in recording played back by Baker*

**4.** "No, I don't think he likes you at all. . . . No, I don't like you either."

*Daniels, responding to Baker's beeps regarding Mark Hamill's (Luke Skywalker's) opinion of him*

**5.** "An elegant weapon, for a more civilized age. For over a thousand generations the Jedi knights were the guardians of peace and justice in the old republic—before the dark times. Before the empire."

*Alec Guinness (Obi-Wan "Ben" Kenobi) on light-sabers and the Jedi knights who once wielded them*

**6.** "I find your lack of faith disturbing."

*James Earl Jones (Voice of Darth Vader), telekinetically strangling someone who disagrees with him*

**7.** "Traveling through hyperspace isn't like dusting crops, boy."

Mercenary space pilot Harrison Ford (Han Solo) to Hamill

**8.** FISHER: "Governor Tarkin, I should've expected to find you holding Vader's leash. I recognized your foul stench when I was brought on board."

PETER CUSHING (*Grand Moff Tarkin*): "Charming to the last."

**9.** "I suggest a new strategy, Artoo: Let the wookie win."

Daniels to Baker, on playing chess with sore-loser wookie Peter Mayhew (Chewbacca)

**10.** "I have a very bad feeling about this."

Hamill, seeing the giant battle station the Death Star for the first time, later paraphrased by Ford in the station's garbage-crusher

**11.** "The Force will be with you—always."

Guinness's last words as a living man to Hamill; later paraphrased in his last words as a spirit to Hamill

**12.** "Aren't you a little short for a storm trooper?"

Fisher, seeing Hamill for the first time, in disguise as an imperial storm trooper

**13.** "You came in that thing? You're braver than I thought."

Fisher, seeing Ford's beat-up spaceship

**14.** "Great, kid. Don't get cocky."

Ford to Hamill, when the latter succeeds in shooting down an imperial fighter

**15.** "May the Force be with you."

Ford, saying good-bye to Hamill

**STARTING OVER** (Paramount, 1979). D: Alan J. Pakula. S: James L. Brooks. Fr: Dan Wakefield (novel).

**1.** "Does anybody have a valium?"

Charles Durning (Mickey Potter)

**STATE OF THE UNION** (MGM, 1948). D: Frank Capra. S: Anthony Veiller, Myles Connolly. Fr: Howard Lindsay, Russel Crouse (play).

**1.** "You're the most beautiful plank in your husband's platform."

Adolphe Menjou (Jim Conover) to Katharine Hepburn (Mary Matthews)

**STEEL MAGNOLIAS** (TriStar, 1989). D: Herbert Ross. S: Robert Harling. Fr: Robert Harling (play).

**1.** "The only thing that separates us from the animals is our ability to accessorize."

Olympia Dukakis (Clairee Belcher)

**2.** "As somebody always said, if you can't say anything nice about anybody, come sit by me."

Dukakis

**3.** "'Course it can."

Shirley MacLaine (Ouiser Boudreaux), on whether the situation can get worse

**STELLA DALLAS** (UA, 1937). D: King Vidor. S: Sarah Y. Mason, Victor Heerman. Fr: Olive Higgins Prouty (novel), Harry Wagstaff Gribble, Gertrude Purcell (play).

**LAST LINE**
**1.** "All right, folks, you've seen enough. Move along, please. Come on, clear the sidewalk."

Police officer to gawkers outside the townhouse where Anne Shirley (Laurel Dallas) is getting married; among the gawkers is Shirley's mother, Barbara Stanwyck (*Stella Dallas*), whose sacrifice has made the marriage possible

**STING, THE** (Universal, 1973). D: George Roy Hill. S: David S. Ward.

**1.** "Glad to meet you, kid. You're a real horse's ass."

Paul Newman (Henry Gondorff) to Robert Redford (Johnny Hooker)

**2.** "Take a good look at that face, Floyd. Because if he ever finds out I can be beat by one lousy grifter, I'll have to kill him and every other hood who wants to muscle in on my Chicago operation. You follow?"

Mob boss Robert Shaw (Doyle Lonnegan) to henchman, concerning the gangster with whom he is playing golf

**3.** "After what happened to Luther, I don't think I can get more than two, three hundred guys."

Newman to Redford, referring to the death of Robert Earl Jones (Luther Coleman) and wondering how many con artists they can round up for the sting against Shaw

**4.** "I don't know what to do with this guy, Henry. He's an Irishman who doesn't drink, doesn't smoke, and doesn't chase dames."

Ray Walston (J. J. Singleton), trying to find some way to lure Shaw into a sting

**5.** REDFORD, on Shaw: "He's not as tough as he thinks."
NEWMAN: "Neither are we."

**6.** REDFORD (on Shaw): "He threatened to kill me."
NEWMAN: "Hell, kid, they don't do that, you know you're not getting to 'em."

**7.** "Christ, they'll probably miss you and hit me."

Newman, worried about the people trying to kill Redford

**8.** "No sense in being a grifter if it's the same as being a citizen."
Newman

**9.** "You know me. I'm just like you. It's two in the morning and I don't know nobody."

Redford, inviting himself into the apartment of Dimitra Arliss (Loretta)

**10.** "You're right, Henry. It's not enough, but it's close."

Redford to Newman, after the successful sting

**LAST LINES**
**11.** NEWMAN: "You're not gonna stick around for your share?"
REDFORD: "Naah. I'd only blow it."

**STORMY WEATHER** (20th Century–Fox, 1943). D: Andrew L. Stone. S: Frederick Jackson, Ted Koehler, H. S. Kraft. Fr: Jerry Horwin, Seymour B. Robinson (story).

**LAST LINE**
**1.** "Everybody dance!"
Cab Calloway (Himself)

**STRANGERS ON A TRAIN** (Warner Bros., 1951). D: Alfred Hitchcock. S: Raymond Chandler, Czenzi Ormonde, Whitfield Cook. Fr: Patricia Highsmith (novel).

**1.** "I certainly admire people who do things."

Robert Walker (Bruno Anthony) to Farley Granger (Guy Haines), during their initial meeting on a train

**2.** "My theory is that everyone is a potential murderer."

*Walker to Granger*

**3.** "Two fellows meet accidentally. . . . Each one has someone that they'd like to get rid of, and they swap murders."

*Walker to Granger, on his murder plan*

**4.** "You're a naughty boy, Bruno. You always make me laugh."

*Marion Lorne (Mrs. Anthony) to her son Walker*

**5.** GRANGER, after Walker commits his part of the murder bargain: "You crazy fool."
WALKER: "Don't you call me that. You must be tired. I am. I had a strenuous evening."

**6.** "Oh, Daddy doesn't mind a little scandal. He's a senator."

*Patricia Hitchcock (Barbara Morton), on her father Leo G. Carroll (Senator Morton)*

**7.** "I'd like to talk with you sometime about my idea for harnessing the life force."

*Walker to Carroll, at party*

**8.** "Unusual personality."

*Carroll to daughter Ruth Roman (Ann Morton), about Walker*

**9.** "After you've sentenced a man to death, itsn't it hard for you to enjoy your dinner?"

*Walker to Charles Meredith (Judge Nolan)*

**10.** "You don't mind if I borrow your neck for a moment, do you?"

*Walker to Norma Warden (Mrs. Cunningham), as he demonstrates a stranglehold*

**11.** "Don't worry, I'm not going to shoot you, Mr. Haines. It might disturb Mother."

*Walker to Granger*

**12.** "You know Bruno, sometimes he goes just a little too far."

*Lorne to Roman*

**13.** "This is the first time I ever watched a guy play a tennis match before I pulled him in."

*Policeman to colleague, about Granger*

**14.** "Bruno Anthony. A very clever fellow."

*Granger to carnival concessionaire, on Walker's identity*

**STRAW DOGS** (UK: Cinerama, 1971). D: Sam Peckinpah. S: David Zelag Goodman, Sam Peckinpah. Fr: Gordon M. Williams (novel, The Siege of Trencher's Farm).

**1.** "Time is a little difficult to find these days."

*Dustin Hoffman (David Sumner), when asked when he'll find the time to enjoy life*

**2.** "I care. This is where I live. This is me."

*Hoffman, to Susan George (Amy Sumner), when she asks him why he is giving a man shelter from the angry mob outside*

**STRAWBERRY BLONDE, THE** (Warner Bros., 1941). D: Raoul Walsh. S: Julius J. Epstein, Philip G. Epstein. Fr: James Hogan (play, One Sunday Afternoon).

**LAST LINE**

**1.** "When I want to kiss my wife, I'll kiss her anytime, anyplace, anywhere. That's the kind of hairpin I am."

*James Cagney (Biff Grimes), on his wife Olivia de Havilland (Amy)*

**STREETCAR NAMED DESIRE, A** (Warner Bros., 1951). D: Elia Kazan. S: Tennessee

Williams. Fr: Oscar Saul (adaptation), Tennessee Williams (play).

**1.** "He's like an animal. He has an animal's habits. There's even something subhuman about him. Thousands of years have passed him right by, and there he is! Stanley Kowalski, survivor of the Stone Age, bearing the raw meat home from the kill in the jungle!"

> Vivien Leigh (Blanche Dubois) to Kim Hunter (Stella), on Stanley Kowalski (Marlon Brando)

**2.** "A cultivated woman—a woman of breeding and intelligence—can enrich a man's life immeasurably. I have those things to offer, and time doesn't take them away."

> Leigh

**3.** "I never met a dame yet that didn't know if she was good-looking or not without being told. And there are some of them that give themselves credit for more than they've got."

> Brando to Leigh

**4.** "Whoever you are, I have always depended on the kindness of strangers."

> Leigh, going off to a mental hospital

**LAST LINE**
**5.** "Hey, Stella! Hey, Stella!"

> Brando, calling for his wife Hunter

**SUDDEN IMPACT** (Warner Bros., 1983). D: Clint Eastwood. S: Joseph C. Stinson. Fr: Earl E. Smith, Charles B. Pierce (story), Harry Julian Fink, R. M. Fink (characters).

**1.** "Go ahead, make my day."

> Clint Eastwood (Harry Callahan) to thug

**SUEZ** (20th Century–Fox, 1938). D: Allan Dwan. S: Philip Dunne, Julien Josephson. Fr: Sam Duncan (story).

**LAST LINE**
**1.** "And when the day comes, I want to stand beside you and see the ships go through the canal and know you built it for all the people in the world."

> Annabella (Toni) to Suez Canal builder Tyrone Power (Ferdinand de Lesseps)

**SULLIVAN'S TRAVELS** (Paramount, 1941). D: Preston Sturges. S: Preston Sturges.

**1.** FILMMAKER JOEL MCCREA (John L. Sullivan): "I wanted to make something outstanding. Something you could be proud of. Something that would realize the potentialities of film as the sociological and artistic medium that it is, with a little sex in it. Something like—"
PORTER HALL (Mr. Hadrian): "Something like Capra, I know."

**2.** MCCREA, discussing one of his earlier films, which he now finds frivolous: "Did you like Hey, Hey, in the Hayloft?"
VERONICA LAKE (The Girl): "Oh, I was crazy about that."
MCCREA: "Thought that would just about fit."

**3.** "There's always a girl in the picture. Haven't you ever been to the movies?"

> McCrea, discussing movie conventions with a sheriff

**4.** "You look about as much like a boy as Mae West."

> McCrea to Lake, on her masquerading as a boy

**5.** "Haven't you got enough imagination to pretend we're broke, hungry, homeless, drifting in despair? Now, let's just sit here and feel like a couple of tramps."

*McCrea to Lake, as he tries to find out how the other half lives*

**6.** "There's a lot of suffering in this world that ordinary people don't know anything about."

*McCrea to Lake*

**7.** "Hundreds of miles from anything, cut off from the world, a taste of human kindness. I'll never forget it as long as I live."

*McCrea to a counterman, when he gives them doughnuts*

**8.** McCREA: "I'm going to find out how it feels to be in trouble, without friends, without credit, without checkbook, without name. Alone."
LAKE: "And I'll go with you."
McCREA: "How can I be alone if you're with me?"

**9.** "If ever a plot needed a twist, this one does."

*McCrea*

**LAST LINE**
**10.** "There's a lot to be said for making people laugh. Did you know that's all some people have? It isn't much, but it's better than nothing in this cockeyed caravan. Boy."

*McCrea*

**SUMMER OF '42** (Warner Bros., 1971). D: Robert Mulligan. S: Herman Raucher (novel).

**LAST LINE**
**1.** "In the summer of '42 we raided the Coast Guard station four times, we saw five movies, we had nine days of rain. Benjie broke his watch, Oscy gave up the harmonica, and in a very special way, I lost Hermie forever."

*Gary Grimes (Hermie), on how as a teenager he lost his sexual innocence in an affair with Jennifer O'Neill (Dorothy)*

**SUMMER PLACE, A** (Warner Bros., 1959). D: Delmer Daves. S: Delmer Daves. Fr: Sloan Wilson (novel).

**LAST LINE**
**1.** "In front of God and everybody this time?"

*Sandra Dee (Molly Jorgensen) to Troy Donahue (Johnny Hunter), hoping that their sexual union will be made legitimate*

**SUNSET BOULEVARD** (Paramount, 1950). D: Billy Wilder. S: Billy Wilder, Charles Brackett, D. M. Marshman, Jr. Fr: Charles Brackett ("A Can of Beans"), Billy Wilder (story).

**FIRST LINE**
**1.** "Yes, this is Sunset Boulevard, Los Angeles, California. It's about five o'clock in the morning. That's the homicide squad—complete with detectives and newspapermen. A murder has been reported from one of those great big houses in the ten thousand block. . . ."

*William Holden (Joe Gillis), in narration*

**2.** "Poor dope. He always wanted a pool. Well, in the end, he got himself a pool—only the price turned out to be a little high."

*Holden, narrating, on himself as the murder victim found floating in the pool of faded silent-screen star Gloria Swanson (Norma Desmond)*

**3.** "That was last year. This year I'm trying to earn a living."

*Holden, a screenwriter, when Nancy Olson (Betty Schaefer) says she has heard he has talent*

**4.** "A neglected house gets an unhappy look. This one had it in spades."

*Holden, narrating, on Swanson's house*

**5.** "I am big. It's the pictures that got small."

*Swanson, on Holden's remark that she used to be big, in silent pictures*

**6.** "We didn't need dialogue. We had faces."

*Swanson to Holden, on silent film stars*

**7.** "Poor devil. Still waving proudly to a parade which had long since passed her by."

*Holden, narrating, on Swanson*

**8.** "Great stars have great pride."

*Swanson to Holden*

**9.** "Audiences don't know somebody sits down and writes a picture. They think the actors make it up as they go along."

*Holden, narrating*

**10.** "A dozen press agents working overtime can do terrible things to the human spirit."

*Cecil B. De Mille (Himself), on stardom*

**11.** "Smart girl. Nothing like being twenty-two."

*Holden, on being told that Olson is twenty-two*

**12.** "Madam is the greatest star of them all."

*Butler Erich von Stroheim (Max von Meyerling) to Holden, on his employer Swanson*

**13.** "No one ever leaves a star. That's what makes one a star."

*Swanson, when Holden walks out on her*

**14.** "The stars are ageless. Aren't they?"

*Swanson to von Stroheim, looking up at the night sky*

**LAST LINE**

**15.** "This is my life. It always will be. There's nothing else. Just us and the cameras and those wonderful people out there in the dark. All right, Mr. De Mille, I'm ready for my close-up."

*Swanson*

**SUNSHINE BOYS, THE** *(UA, 1975). D: Herbert Ross. S: Neil Simon. Fr: Neil Simon (play).*

**1.** WALTER MATTHAU (*Willy Clark*): "Which words are funny?"

RICHARD BENJAMIN (*Ben Clark*), indicating what he has learned from old-time vaudevillian Matthau: "Words with a K are funny."

**2.** "It wasn't terrific. It was a classic. On the nights we were lousy, it was terrific."

*Matthau, on his act with former vaudeville partner George Burns (Al Lewis)*

**3.** "As an actor, no one could touch him. As a human being, no one wanted to touch him."

*Matthau, on Burns*

**4.** "I hate the son of a bitch. That's what artistic differences."

*Matthau detailing the artistic differences between him and Burns*

**5.** "There'll never be another one like him. Noboby could time a joke the way he could time a joke. Nobody could say a line the way he said it. I knew what he was thinking. He knew what I was thinking. One person. That's what we were."

*Matthau to Benjamin, on why he and Burns stuck together for forty-three years, even though they hated each other*

**6.** BURNS: "I don't hate him."
BENJAMIN: "I'm glad to hear that."
BURNS: "Can't stand him, but I don't hate him."

**7.** "The man yells at me on the stage, gets a million laughs. Yells at me off the stage, gets a heart attack."

*Burns to Benjamin, referring to Matthau*

**8.** "I can't tell the difference between our act and us anymore."

*Burns to Matthau*

**9.** BURNS: "We did comedy on the stage for forty-three years. I don't think you enjoyed it once."
MATTHAU: "If I was there to enjoy it, I would buy a ticket."

**SUPERFLY** *(Warner Bros., 1972). D: Gordon Parks, Jr. S: Phillip Fenty.*

**LAST LINE**
**1.** "Can you dig it?"
*Ron O'Neal (Youngblood Priest)*

**SUPERMAN** *(UK: Warner Bros., 1978). D: Richard Donner. S: Mario Puzo, David Newman, Leslie Newman, Robert Benton. Fr: Mario Puzo (story), Jerry Siegel, Joel Shuster (comic strip).*

**FIRST LINE**
**1.** "This is no fantasy, no careless product of wild imagination."

*Marlon Brando (Jor-El) to the council, in first line after opening prologue on the* Daily Planet

**2.** SUSANNAH YORK *(Lara)*: "But why Earth, Jor-El? They're primitives, thousands of years behind us."
BRANDO: "He will need that advantage to survive."

**3.** "It is forbidden for you to interfere with human history; rather let your leadership stir others."

*Brando, speaking through the crystals in the Fortress of Solitude*

**4.** "All those things I can do. All those powers. And I couldn't even save him."

*Jeff East (Young Clark Kent), when Glenn Ford (Jonathan Kent) dies*

**5.** "They can be a great people, Kal-El, if they wish to be. They only lack the light to show the way. For this reason, above all, their capacity for good, I have sent them you: my only son."

*Brando, speaking through the crystals in the Fortress of Solitude*

**6.** "Clark Kent may seem like just a mild-mannered reporter, but listen, not only does he know how to treat his editor-in-chief with the proper respect, not only does he have a snappy, punchy prose style, but he is, in my forty years in this business, the fastest typist I've ever seen."

*Jackie Cooper (Perry White) to Margot Kidder (Lois Lane), on Christopher Reeve (Clark Kent/Superman)*

**7.** "Any more at home like you?"
*Kidder to Reeve*

**8.** REEVE, as for the first time, he saves Kidder from falling to her death: "Easy, miss. I've got you."

KIDDER: "You've got me? Who's got you?"

**9.** "I tell you, boys and girls, whichever one of you gets it out of him is going to wind up with the single most important interview since God talked to Moses."

*Cooper to his staff, on landing an interview with Superman*

**10.** "I never drink when I fly."

*Reeve, when Kidder offers him some wine*

**11.** "I'm here to fight for truth, justice, and the American way."

*Reeve to Kidder, when she asks why he's here*

**12.** "What a super man! Superman!"

*Kidder, dubbing him Superman*

**13.** "There's a strong streak of good in you, Superman, but then nobody's perfect . . . almost nobody."

*Gene Hackman (Lex Luthor) to Reeve*

**14.** "We all have our little faults. Mine's in California."

*Hackman to Reeve, on sending a nuclear missile into the San Andreas Fault*

**LAST LINES**

**15.** ROY STEVENS (*Warden*), after Reeve has brought Hackman and Ned Beatty (Otis) to jail: "This country is safe again, Superman. Thanks to you."

REEVE: "No, sir! Don't thank me, Warden. We're all part of the same team. Good night."

**SUPERMAN II** (*UK: Warner Bros., 1981*). D: Richard Lester. S: Mario Puzo, David Newman, Leslie Newman. Fr: Mario Puzo (story), Jerry Siegel, Joe Shuster (characters).

**1.** VALERIE PERRINE (*Eve Teichmacher*): "Why am I here? What am I doing here?"

GENE HACKMAN (*Lex Luthor*): "Miss Teichmacher, is this a philosophy seminar? No, this is a getaway."

**2.** "I'm so sure that you're Superman that I'm willing to bet my life on it. Now, if I'm right, you'll turn yourself into Superman, and if I'm wrong, you've got yourself one hell of a story."

*Margot Kidder (Lois Lane) to Christopher Reeve (Clark Kent/Superman), just before she jumps into the water leading over Niagara Falls*

**3.** "I see you are practiced in worshiping things that fly."

*Terence Stamp (General Zod) to E. G. Marshall (U.S. President), referring to the American bald eagle on the Presidential Seal*

**4.** "What I do now, I do for the sake of the people of the world, but there is one man here on Earth who will never kneel before you."

*Marshall, kneeling to Stamp and referring to Reeve*

**5.** MARSHALL, kneeling: "Oh, God."
STAMP, correcting him: "Zod."

**6.** "This Superman is nothing of the kind. I've discovered his weakness. He cares. He actually cares for these Earth people."

*Stamp, referring to Reeve stopping to save someone during their climactic battle*

**LAST LINE**

**7.** "Good afternoon, Mr. President. Sorry I've been away so long. I won't let you down again."

*Reeve*

**SURRENDER** (Cannon/Warner Bros., 1987). D: Jerry Belson. S: Jerry Belson.

**1.** "I make it a policy never to have sex before the first date."

*Sally Field (Daisy) to Michael Caine (Sean)*

**SWAN, THE** (MGM, 1956). D: Charles Vidor. S: John Dighton. Fr: Ferenc Molnár (play).

**1.** "That's one pleasant thing about being crown prince: no more lessons. The aide learns all the lessons and passes them on in small doses as required."

*Alec Guinness (Prince Albert) to Louis Jordan (Dr. Nicholas Agi)*

**2.** "I'm sorry, Your Highness. I think I was afraid to speak lest the mirage disappear."

*Jourdan to Grace Kelly (Princess Alexandra), on his reluctance to speak in Kelly's presence*

**3.** "The greatest musicians aren't always the ones who build their own trumpets."

*Jourdan to Guinness, referring to Guinness's ego*

**4.** "I'm sure it's difficult for the rulers of this Earth to appreciate. They speak of their ten million population, or their army of two millions. It never occurs to them that each single one of those millions is a sovereign world. A world that is not to be destroyed."

*Jourdan to Guinness*

**5.** "You'll never again be as happy as you are now. Perhaps, it's started to go already. By the time we feel it, it's gone."

*Brian Aherne (Father Hyacinth) to Jourdan and Kelly*

**6.** "He's a snob of the worst kind. The upside-down variety. Just an ill-bred astronomer who hopes to hitch his present cart to a star and drag it down with him into the mud."

*Guinness to Kelly, insulting Jourdan*

**7.** "So there she must stay, out on the lake. Silent. White. Majestic. Be a bird, but never fly. Know one song, but never sing it until the moment of her death. And so it must be for you, Alexandra. Head high. Cool indifference to the staring crowds along the bank, and the song, never."

*Guinness, comparing Kelly to a swan*

**SWEET BIRD OF YOUTH** (MGM, 1962). D: Richard Brooks. S: Richard Brooks. Fr: Tennessee Williams (play).

**1.** "I am not part of your luggage. Whatever I am, I am not part of your luggage."

*Paul Newman (Chance Wayne) to Geraldine Page (Alexandra Del Lago)*

**SWEET SMELL OF SUCCESS** (Hecht-Hill-Lancaster Productions/UA, 1957). D: Alexander Mackendrick. S: Clifford Odets, Ernest Lehman. Fr: Ernest Lehman (short story, "Tell Me About It Tomorrow").

**1.** "Watch me run a fifty-yard dash with my legs cut off."

*Publicity agent Tony Curtis (Sidney Falco), to his secretary Edith Atwater (Mary), referring to how fast he talks his way out of trouble*

**2.** "Hunsecker is the golden ladder to the places I want to get."

*Curtis, referring to Burt Lancaster (J. J. Hunsecker), a ruthless columnist*

**3.** "From now on, the best of everything is good enough for me."

  *Curtis*

**4.** "The next time you want any information, don't scratch for it, like a dog, just ask for it, like a man."

  *Martin Milner (Steve Dallas) to Curtis, who is tryign to break up the relationship between Milner and Lancaster's sister*

**5.** "You're dead, son. Go get yourself buried."

  *Lancaster to Curtis, when Curtis fails him*

**6.** "Mr. Falco, let it be said that at once, is a deceptive man of forty faces, not one. None too pretty, and all deceptive."

  *Lancaster, referring to Curtis and his sleazy press agent ways*

**7.** "A press agent eats a columnist's dirt and is expected to call it manna."

  *Curtis*

**8.** "My big toe would make a better President."

  *Lancaster, referring to someone's presidential abilities*

**9.** "I love this dirty town."

  *Lancaster, to Curtis, about New York City*

**10.** "My right hand hasn't seen my left hand in thirty years."

  *Lancaster to Curtis, referring to his ability to never take blame or responsibility for anything he has ever arranged*

**11.** "Don't try to sell me the Brooklyn Bridge. I happen to know it belongs to the Dodgers."

  *Curtis to Lancaster's secretary*

**12.** "This is life. Get used to it."

  *Curtis to Atwater, when she acts shocked at his life and sleazy activities*

**13.** "I'd hate to take a bite out of you. You're a cookie full of arsenic."

  *Lancaster to Curtis*

**14.** "It's one thing to wear your dog collar. When it turns into a noose, I'd rather have my freedom."

  *Curtis to Lancaster, when he is asked to frame Milner for drug dealing*

**15.** "I'm toasting my favorite new perfume: Success!"

  *Curtis, drinking with his fellow press agents, when he succeeds in performing Lancaster's latest request, framing Milner for drug dealing*

**SWORD IN THE STONE, THE** (Buena Vista, 1963). D: Wolfgang Reitherman. S: Bill Peet. Fr: T. H. White (book).

**1.** "Who so pulleth out this sword of this stone and anvil is rightwise king born of England."

  *Sebastian Cabot (Narrator)*

**2.** "Big news, eh? Can't wait for the *London Times*. First edition won't be out for twelve hundred years."

  *Karl Swenson (Merlin the Magician)*

**3.** "Don't take gravity too lightly, or it'll catch up with you."

  *Swenson, advising caution as he and Ricky Sorenson (Wart), transformed into squirrels, leap from tree to tree*

**4.** "You can't learn history in reverse. It's confusing enough."

  *Junius Matthews (Archimedes the Owl)*

**5.** "Knowledge and wisdom is the real power."

*Sorenson, showing what he's learned from Swenson*

**LAST LINES**

**6.** SWENSON: "They might even make a motion picture about you."

SORENSON: "Motion picture?"

SWENSON: "That's something like television, without commercials."

**TAKE THE MONEY AND RUN** *(Palomar, 1969). D: Woody Allen. S: Woody Allen, Mickey Rose.*

**1.** "All I know is my heart was really pounding, and I felt, I felt a funny tingling all over, y'know. I don't know, I was either in love or I had smallpox."

*Woody Allen (Virgil Starkwell), on meeting Janet Margolin (Louise)*

**2.** "Please put fifty thousand dollars into this bag and abt natural as I am pointing a gub at you."

*Allen's illegible holdup note, as interpreted by confused bank employees*

**3.** " 'The prison has not been built that can hold me,' Virgil tells another inmate, 'and I'll get out of this one if it means spending my entire life here.' "

*Jackson Beck (Narrator)*

**4.** "It is a simple ceremony, following what he later described as a deeply moving blood test."

*Beck, on Allen's wedding to Margolin*

**5.** "I robbed a butcher shop; it was the best I could do. I got away with one hundred and sixteen veal cutlets, then I had to go out and rob a tremendous amount of breading."

*Allen, in narration, recalling his crimes*

**6.** "A. D. Armstrong, wanted all over the country for arson, robbery, assault with intent to kill, and marrying a horse."

*Beck, on a hood in Allen's gang*

**7.** "Nobody's gonna be wearing beige to a bank robbery; it's in poor taste."

*Allen to Margolin, arguing about what color shirt to wear to rob a bank*

**8.** "Do you think a girl should pet on the first date?"

*Allen's response when asked by James Anderson (Chain Gang Warden) if he has any questions*

**9.** "Food on a chain gang is scarce and not very nourishing. The men get one hot meal a day: a bowl of steam."

*Beck*

**10.** "Virgil complains and he is severely tortured. For several days he is locked in a sweatbox with an insurance salesman."

*Beck*

**11.** "You know, he never made the ten most wanted list. It's very unfair voting. It's who you know."

*Margolin, on Allen's regrets about his life of crime*

**12.** "Virgil Starkwell is tried on fifty-two counts of robbery and is sentenced to eight hundred years in federal prison. At the trial, he tells his lawyer confidentially that with good behavior he can cut the sentence in half."

*Beck*

**LAST LINE**
**13.** "Do you know if it's raining out?"

*Allen, asked by an interviewer if he has any hobbies, as he fashions a fake gun from a bar of soap, hoping to escape from prison, providing the rain doesn't melt his gun*

**TALE OF TWO CITIES, A** *(MGM, 1935). D: Jack Conway. S: W. P. Lipscomb, S. N. Behrman. Fr: Charles Dickens (novel).*

**1.** "Pity, my dear boy, is a diseased variety of sentimentality."

*Basil Rathbone (Marquis St. Everemonde) to Donal Woods (Charles Darnay)*

**2.** "You are smug, Mr. Darnay, when you ask why people drink, but I'll tell you. So that they can stand their fellow men better. After a few bottles, I might even like you."

*Ronald Colman (Sidney Carton) to Woods*

**3.** "All bankers are atheists."

*Edna May Oliver (Miss Pross)*

**4.** "In suffering, one learns many things. Among them, not to punish the innocent."

*Henry B. Walthall (Dr. Manette) to Woods, when Woods confesses he's related to Rathbone*

**5.** "Really, with what I get from these peasants, I can hardly afford to pay my perfume bills."

*Rathbone to H. B. Warner (Gabelle)*

**6.** "I keep forgetting, Gabelle. You're a humanitarian. Aren't you? You think that one person is as good as another. A naive notion, so contradicted by the facts."

*Rathbone to Warner*

**7.** "The time may come when the upstart Washington will be a better remembered Englishman than George III."

*Colman*

**8.** ISABELL JEWELL *(Seamstress)*: "You're going to die in his place. Why?"
COLMAN: "He's my friend."

**9.** "There's no time, and no trouble."

*Colman to Jewell, on Heaven*

**10.** "Perhaps, in death, I'll receive something I never had in life. I'll hold a sanctuary in the hearts of those I care for."

*Colman to Jewell*

**LAST LINE**
**11.** "It's a far, far better thing I do than I have ever done. It's a far, far better rest I go to than I have ever known."

*Colman, in narration, as he goes to his execution*

**TARZAN THE APE MAN** *(MGM, 1932). D: W. S. Van Dyke II. S: Cyril Hume, Ivor Novello. Fr: Edgar Rice Burroughs (characters).*

**1.** "Me Tarzan. . . . You Jane."

*Johnny Weismuller (Tarzan) to Maureen O'Sullivan (Jane)*

**TASTE OF HONEY, A** *(UK: Continental Distributing, 1961). D: Tony Richardson. S: Shelagh Delaney, Tony Richardson. Fr: Shelagh Delaney (play).*

*1.* "I'm not just talented. I'm geniused."

   *Rita Tushingham (Jo)*


**TAXI DRIVER** *(Columbia, 1976). D: Martin Scorsese. S: Paul Schrader.*

*1.* "All the animals come out at night—whores, scum, pussies, buggers, queens, fairies, dopers, junkies. Sick. Venal. Someday a real rain will come and wash all the scum off the street."

   *Robert De Niro (Travis Bickle), in narration*

*2.* "Days go on and on. They don't end. All my life needed was a sense of someplace to go."

   *De Niro, narrating*

*3.* "I don't believe I've ever met anyone quite like you."

   *Cybill Shepherd (Betsy) to De Niro*

*4.* "This city is like an open sewer."

   *De Niro to Leonard Harris (Senator Palantine), on New York*

*5.* "Loneliness has followed me my whole life. Everywhere. In bars, in cars, sidewalks, stores, everywhere. There's no escape. I'm God's lonely man."

   *De Niro, narrating*

*6.* "You talking to me? You talking to me? You talking to me? Well, who the hell else are you talking to? You talking to me? Well, I'm the only one here. Who the fuck do you think you're talking to?"

   *De Niro, threatening his image in the mirror*


**TEA AND SYMPATHY** *(MGM, 1956). D: Vincente Minnelli. S: Robert Anderson. Fr: Robert Anderson (play).*

*1.* "Years from now, when you talk about this, and you will, be kind."

   *Married woman Deborah Kerr (Laura Reynolds) to John Kerr (Tom Robinson Lee), the young man with whom she is about to have an affair*

**LAST LINE**
*2.* "About one thing you were correct, the wife did always keep her affection for the boy, somewhere in her heart."

   *Deborah Kerr, in a letter to John Kerr, years after their affair*


**TEAHOUSE OF THE AUGUST MOON, THE** *(MGM, 1956). D: Daniel Mann. S: John Patrick. Fr: Vern J. Sneider (novel), John Patrick (play).*

*1.* "My job is to teach these natives the meaning of democracy, and they're going to learn democracy if I have to shoot every one of them."

   *Paul Ford (Colonel Purdy), head of the American occupation troops on Okinawa after World War II*

*2.* "I'll never forget this village. And, on the other side of the world, in the autumn of my life, when an August moon rises in the east, I'll remember what was beautiful and what I was wise enough to leave beautiful."

   *Glenn Ford (Captain Fisby), saying farewell to Okinawa*

**LAST LINE**
*3.* "Little story now concluded. But history of world unfinished. Lovely ladies, kind gentlemen, go home to ponder. What was true at beginning remains true. Pain make man think, thought make man wise, and wisdom make life endurable. So, may August moon bring gentle sleep. *Sayonara.*"

Marlon Brando (Sakini), a philosophical Okinawan

**10** (Warner Bros., 1979). D: Blake Edwards. S: Blake Edwards.

**1.** "I wouldn't mind losing like a man if you weren't so damned determined to win like one."

Dudley Moore (George Webber) to Julie Andrews (Samantha Taylor)

**2.** "Actually, I'm opposed to bartenders making value judgments, while on duty."

Brian Dennehy (Don), a bartender, to Moore

**3.** "I'm very big in elevators."

Moore, referring to the type of music he writes

**4.** "Did you ever do it to Ravel's *Bolero*?"

Bo Derek (Jenny Miles) to Moore

**5.** "Uncle Fred said the *Bolero* was the most descriptive sex music ever written, and he proved it."

Derek to Moore

**TEN COMMANDMENTS, THE** (Famous Players–Lasky/Paramount, 1923). D: Cecil B. De Mille. S: Jeanie MacPherson. Fr: Old Testament.

**1.** "All that's the bunk, Mother! The Ten Commandments were all right for a lot of dead ones—but that sort of stuff was buried with Queen Victoria!"

Rod La Rocque (Dan McTavish), in title cards, renouncing religion to his mother, Edythe Chapman (Mrs. Martha McTavish)

**2.** "Laugh at the Ten Commandments all you want, Danny—but they pack an awful wallop!"

Richard Dix (John McTavish), trying to put some religion into his brother La Rocque

**3.** "Johnny, we're going to *live!* We'll break all ten of your old Commandments, and we'll finish rich and powerful—with the world at our feet!"

La Rocque to Dix, on his plans for himself and his fiancée Leatrice Joy (Mary Leigh)

**4.** "John, dear—some mighty fine men have been carpenters!"

Chapman, consoling her carpenter son Dix on his lowly position

**5.** "Go easy, son! This Sally Lung is half-French, and half-Chinese. The combination of French perfume and Oriental incense is more dangerous than nitroglycerin!"

Robert Edeson (Redding), advising La Rocque to keep his distance from Eurasian temptress Nita Naldi (Lung)

**6.** "Well, he has *one* commandment left—I don't think he's killed anybody yet!"

Joy, on her husband La Rocque after spotting him with another woman, Naldi; the breaking of the last commandment will follow in short order

**TEN COMMANDMENTS, THE** (Paramount, 1956). D: Cecil B. De Mille. S: Aeneas MacKenzie, Jesse L. Lasky, Jr., Jack Gariss, Fredric M. Frank. Fr: Dorothy Clarke Wilson (novel, The Prince of Egypt), Reverend J. H. Ingraham (novel), Reverend G. E. Southon (novel), Old Testament, Josephus, Eusebius, Philo, the Midrash.

**1.** "So let it be written. So let it be done."

Royal Egyptian saying echoed many times by pharaohs in the film, including Sir Cedric Hardwicke (Sethi) and Yul Brynner (Rameses); in the end title it appears as "So it was written. So it shall be done"

**2.** "What the gods can digest will not sour in the belly of a slave."

> *Charlton Heston (Moses), on feeding slaves with temple grain reserved for the gods*

**3.** "There is the obelisk of your jubilee."

> *Heston to Hardwicke, raising a monument to his glory*

**4.** "A city is built of brick, Pharaoh. The strong make many, the starving make few, the dead make none."

> *Heston to Hardwicke, advocating humane treatment of Hebrew slaves*

**5.** "I do not know what power shapes my way, but my feet are set upon a road that I must follow."

> *Heston, raised as a prince of Egypt, accepting his destiny as the son of Hebrew slaves*

**6.** "Oh, Moses, Moses, you stubborn, splendid, adorable fool!"

> *Anne Baxter (Nefretiri) to Heston*

**7.** "What I have done, I was compelled to do."

> *Heston, explaining why he betrayed Hardwicke*

**8.** "With my last breath, I'll break my own law and speak the name of Moses . . . Moses . . ."

> *Hardwicke's dying words*

**9.** "Thus sayeth the Lord God of Israel: Let my people go."

> *Heston to Brynner*

**10.** "You may be the lovely dust through which God will work his purpose."

> *Heston to Baxter*

**11.** "If there is one more plague on Egypt, it is by your word that God will bring it, and there shall be so great a cry throughout the land that you will surely let the people go."

> *Heston to Brynner*

**12.** "You lost him when he went to seek his God. I lost him when he found his God."

> *Yvonne De Carlo (Sephora), Heston's wife, to Baxter*

**13.** "There are so many, so many."

> *Heston, beholding the mass of Hebrews waiting to leave Egypt*

**14.** "The Lord of Hosts will do battle for us. Behold his mighty hand."

> *Heston, just before parting the Red Sea*

**15.** "His God is God."

> *Brynner to Baxter, on his spectacular defeat by Heston's God*

**16.** "Written with the finger of God."

> *Heston, picking up the stone tablets of the Ten Commandments*

**17.** "Those who will not live by the law shall die by the law!"

> *Heston, threatening doom against the worshipers of the golden calf*

**LAST LINE**
**18.** "Go—proclaim liberty throughout all the lands, and to all the inhabitants thereof."

> *Heston to his people*

**TENDER MERCIES** (Universal, 1983). D: Bruce Beresford. S: Horton Foote.

**1.** "Every night, when I say my prayers, and I thank the Lord for his blessings and his tender mercies to me, you and Sonny head the list."

> *Tess Harper (Rosa Lee) to Robert Duvall (Mac Sledge), referring to her son*

**2.** "I don't trust happiness. I never did and I never will."

> *Duvall, when his daughter, Ellen Barkin (Sue Anne), is killed in an auto accident*

**3.** HELENA HUMANN (*Woman with groceries*): "Didn't you used to be Mac Sledge?"
DUVALL: "Yeah, I guess I was him."

**TEQUILA SUNRISE** (*Warner Bros., 1988*). D: Robert Towne. S: Robert Towne.

**1.** "You need some chapstick or something 'cause your lips keep getting stuck on your teeth, or is that your idea of a smile?"

> *Michelle Pfeiffer (Jo Ann Vallenari) to Kurt Russell (Lt. Nick Frescia)*

**2.** "Just looking at you hurts more."

> *Mel Gibson (Dale McKussic) to Pfeiffer, on her apologizing for hurting him*

**TERMINATOR, THE** (*Orion, 1984*). D: James Cameron. S: James Cameron, Gale Anne Hurd, William Wisher, Jr.

**1.** "Come with me if you want to live."

> *Michael Biehn (Kyle Reese), offering protection to Linda Hamilton (Sarah O'Connor) from deadly cyborg Arnold Schwarzenegger (The Terminator)*

**2.** "I'll be back."

> *Schwarzenegger, promising future mayhem as he leaves a police station*

**TERMINATOR 2: JUDGMENT DAY** (*Tri-Star, 1991*). D: James Cameron. S: James Cameron, William Wisher.

**1.** "I need your clothes, your boots, and your motorcycle."

> *First line of Arnold Schwarzenegger (The Terminator), spoken to biker in bar*

**2.** "Of course. I'm a terminator."

> *Schwarzenegger to Edward Furlong (John Connor), on whether he intended to kill a minor adversary*

**3.** FURLONG: "You just can't go around killing people."
SCHWARZENEGGER: "Why?"

**4.** "Come with me if you want to live."

> *Schwarzenegger to Linda Hamilton (Sarah Connor), reprising a line spoken to her by Michael Biehn in The Terminator (1984)*

**5.** "Hasta la vista, baby."

> *Schwarzenegger to opponent Robert Patrick (T-1000), using a line learned from Furlong*

**6.** "I need a vacation."

> *Schwarzenegger, after climactic battle with Patrick*

**TERMS OF ENDEARMENT** (*Paramount, 1983*). D: James L. Brooks. S: James L. Brooks. Fr: Larry McMurtry (novel).

**1.** SHIRLEY MACLAINE (*Aurora Greenway*): "You wouldn't want me to be silent about something that's for your own good, even if it might hurt a little. Would you?"
DEBRA WINGER (*Emma Horton*): "Yes, Mom, I certainly would."

**2.** "You are not special enough to overcome a bad marriage."

*MacLaine to Winger*

**3.** "Don't worship me until I've earned it."

*MacLaine to Danny DeVito (Vernon Dahlart), a suitor*

**4.** "Why should I be happy about being a grandmother?"

*MacLaine, on learning that Winger is pregnant*

**5.** "He can't even do the simple things, like fail locally."

*MacLaine on Winger's husband Jeff Daniels (Flap Horton), with whom Winger must move to Des Moines*

**6.** "That's the first time I stopped hugging first."

*Winger, on parting from MacLaine*

**7.** JACK NICHOLSON (*Garrett Breedlove*): "You need a lot of drinks."
MACLAINE: "To break the ice?"
NICHOLSON: "To kill the bug that you have up your ass."

**8.** "I don't think there's anything wrong with using all your assets."

*Nicholson to MacLaine, on using his occupation as an astronaut to pick up women*

**9.** "I was just inches from a clean getaway."

*Nicholson to MacLaine, on his first reaction to her saying she loves him*

**10.** NICHOLSON, on MacLaine saying she loves him: "I don't know what else to say except my stock answer."
MACLAINE: "Which is?"
NICHOLSON: "I love you, too, kid."

**TESS** (UK/France: Columbia, 1980). D: Roman Polanski. S: Roman Polanski, Gerard Brach, John Brownjohn. Fr: Thomas Hardy (novel, Tess of the d'Urbervilles).

**1.** "Beauty has its price."

*Leigh Lawson (Alexander D'Urberville), when pinning a flower on Nastassia Kinski (Tess Durbeyfield) and she is stuck by a thorn*

**2.** "Nor art nor nature ever created a lovelier thing than you, Cousin Tess. To see that pretty mouth pouting and puffing away, without producing a single note."

*Lawson, when Kinski is trying to whistle*

**3.** "Has it ever struck you that what all women say, some women may feel?"

*Kinski, to Lawson, when she explains that she was blinded for the moment, referring to allowing herself to be seduced by him*

**4.** "He says I'm not the woman he loved, but another woman in her shape."

*Kinski, to herself, when Peter Firth (Angel Claire) rejects her after she tells him of her shame in giving birth to a bastard*

**TEXASVILLE** (Columbia, 1990). D: Peter Bogdanovich. S: Peter Bogdanovich. Fr: Larry McMurtry (novel).

**1.** "Cheer up, honey. Today's a beautiful day and you're ridin' around with the two best-looking women in Texas."

*Cybill Shepherd (Jacy Farrow) to Jeff Bridges (Duane Jackson), referring to herself and Annie Potts (Karla Jackson)*

**2.** "It's not too smart to get too many women in love with you at the same time."

*Bridges*

**THAT DARN CAT!** (Buena Vista, 1965). D: Robert Stevenson. S: Gordon Gordon, Mildred Gordon, Bill Walsh. Fr: Gordon Gordon, Mildred Gordon (novel, Undercover Cat).

**1.** HAYLEY MILLS (*Patti Randall*): "Couldn't we just once see a nice, quiet movie where boy meets girl, they have problems which aren't too weird, they fall in love, and live happily ever after?"

TOM LOWELL (*Canoe*): "Now, why would you want to see a lot of unhealthy stuff like that?"

**2.** RICHARD EASTHAM (*Supervisor Newton*), referring to D. C.: "Kelso, I want to set up a surveillance, and tail this cat!"

DEAN JONES (*Zeke Kelso*): "Tail the cat?"

**3.** "That cat's about as helpless as the U.S. Marine Corps!"

Dorothy Provine (*Ingrid Randall*) to Mills, when Mills hopes D. C. doesn't get hurt

**4.** "That darn cat!"

Frank Gorshin (*Iggy*), when the handcuffs are put on him

**THELMA AND LOUISE** (MGM-Pathé, 1991). D: Ridley Scott. S: Callie Khouri.

**1.** "Well, you get what you settle for."

Susan Sarandon (*Louise*) to Geena Davis (*Thelma*), about Davis's husband Christopher McDonald (*Darryl*) and repeated in other contexts throughout the movie

**2.** "Well, my hair is coming down."

Davis to Sarandon, on their weekend trip

**3.** "In the future, when a woman's crying like that, she isn't having fun."

Sarandon to attempted rapist Timothy Carhart (*Harlan*)

**4.** "Things have changed. Everything's changed. But I'm going to Mexico. I'm going."

Sarandon to Davis, following Sarandon's killing of Carhart

**5.** "It's probably not a good idea."

Sarandon, refusing to pick up Brad Pitt (*J. D.*)

**6.** "Look, you shoot off a guy's head with his pants down, believe me, Texas is not the place you want to get caught."

Sarandon to Davis, on why she does not want to drive through Texas to reach Mexico

**7.** DAVIS, on her husband McDonald: "Kinda prides himself on being infantile."

SARANDON: "Gotta lot to be proud of."

**8.** "I always believe that done properly, armed robbery doesn't have to be a totally unpleasant experience."

Pitt to Davis, explaining his technique

**9.** "I finally understand what the fuss is about."

Davis to Sarandon, about sex, after her night with Pitt

**10.** "I'm so proud of you. You finally got laid properly."

Sarandon to Davis

**11.** "You better be sweet to them, especially your wife. I had a husband that wasn't sweet to me and look how I turned out."

Davis to officer she locks in a squad car trunk

**12.** "It's crazy. I just feel I got a knack for this shit."

Davis to Sarandon, on robbery

**13.** "Brains will only get you so far, and luck always runs out."

> *Harvey Keitel (Hal) to Steven Tobolowsky (Max), on why Sarandon and Davis will be caught*

**14.** "Something's like crossed over in me and I can't go back. I couldn't live."

> *Davis to Sarandon*

**15.** SARANDON, on Davis's prowess at shooting a tanker truck: "Where'd you learn to shoot like that?"
> DAVIS: "Oh, off the TV."

**16.** "How do you like the vacation so far?"

> *Sarandon to Davis, after they elude the police*

**17.** "Oh, then listen, let's not get caught. . . . Let's keep going."

> *Davis to Sarandon, on eluding capture by driving into the Grand Canyon*

---

**THEY DRIVE BY NIGHT** (Warner Bros., 1940). D: Raoul Walsh. S: Jerry Wald, Richard Macaulay. Fr: A. I. Bezzerides (novel, The Long Haul).

**1.** GEORGE RAFT (*Joe Fabrini*): "I always have liked redheads."
> ANN SHERIDAN (*Cassie Hartley*): "You shouldn't. Red means stop."
> RAFT: "I'm color-blind."

---

**THEY SHOOT HORSES, DON'T THEY?** (ABC-Cinerama, 1969). D: Sydney Pollack. S: James Poe, Robert E. Thompson. Fr: Horace McCoy (novel).

**LAST LINE**
**1.** Yowsir, yowsir, yowsir! Here they are again—these wonderful, wonderful kids, still struggling, still hoping as the clock of fate ticks away. The dance of destiny continues. The marathon goes on and on and on. How long can they last? Let's hear it. C'mon, let's hear it. Let's hear it."

> *Gig Young (Rocky), hosting a dance marathon*

---

**THIEF OF BAGDAD, THE** (UK: UA, 1940). D: Michael Powell. S: Augusto Frassineti, Filippo Sanjust, Bruno Vailati.

**1.** "You will learn one day, Great King, that there are but three things that men respect: the lash that descends, the yoke that breaks, and the sword that slays. By the power and terror of these, you may conquer the earth."

> *Evil counselor Conrad Veidt (Jaffar) to ruler John Justin (Ahmad)*

**2.** "I am Abu the Thief, son of Abu the Thief, grandson of Abu the Thief."

> *Sabu (Abu the Thief), introducing himself to Justin*

**3.** "Allah be with you—but I doubt it."

> *Old bearded passerby to Justin and Sabu*

**4.** "All bullies must learn manners in the end."

> *Sabu, on tricking the fearsome djinni (or genie) Rex Ingram into being his slave*

**5.** "And now, my little braggart, you can be a thief and a hero all in one."

> *Ingram to Sabu, on bringing him to steal the All-Seeing Eye*

**6.** "You're a clever little man, little master of the universe, but mortals are weak and frail. If their stomach speaks, they forget their brain. If their brain speaks, they forget their hearts. And if their hearts speak—(Laughs.)—if their hearts speak, they forget everything!"

*Ingram, after Sabu wastes his third and last wish*

**7.** "No longer. You've had your three wishes, and I'm free—free!"

*Ingram, on whether Sabu is still his master*

**8.** "This is the land of legend—where everything is possible when seen through the eyes of youth."

*The Father of Miracles to Sabu*

**LAST LINE**

**9.** "Some fun—and adventure at last!"

*Sabu, saying what he intends to find on his magic carpet*

**THIN MAN, THE** *(MGM, 1934). D: W. S. Van Dyke II. S: Albert Hackett, Frances Goodrich. Fr: Dashiell Hammett (novel).*

**1.** "The important thing is the rhythm. Always have rhythm in your shaking. Now a Manhattan you shake to fox-trot time, a Bronx to two-step time, a dry martini you always shake to waltz time."

*William Powell (Nick Charles) to bartender*

**2.** "The next person who says Merry Christmas to me, I'll kill 'im."

*Myrna Loy (Nora Charles) to her husband Powell*

**3.** "Oh, Nicky, I love you because you know such lovely people."

*Loy to Powell, as they look at the motley crew at their Christmas party*

**4.** "You darn fool, you didn't have to knock me out. I knew you'd take him out, but I wanted to see you do it."

*Loy to Powell, after he knocks her out to keep her from getting in the way of an assailant's bullet*

**5.** "Asta, is your balloon busted? So's mine."

*Loy to her dog Asta, after he bursts a balloon and the murder case reaches a dead end*

**6.** "I don't care. It's just that I'm used to you, that's all."

*Loy to Powell, on whether she cares if he gets hurt while sleuthing*

**7.** "Asta, you're not a terrier, you're a police dog."

*Powell to Asta, when the dog uncovers some evidence*

**8.** "Don't make a move or that dog'll tear you to shreds."

*Powell to intruder in Edward Ellis's (Wynant's) house*

**9.** REPORTER: "Well, can't you tell us anything about the case?"
POWELL: "Yes. It's putting me way behind in my drinking."

**10.** "My soul, woman, I give you three murders and you're still not satisfied."

*Powell to Loy, on her taste for mayhem*

**11.** LOY, archly, when Powell gathers all the suspects at a dinner party: "You give such charming parties, Mr. Charles."
POWELL: "Thank you, Mrs. Charles."

**12.** "Waiter, will you serve the nuts? I mean, will you serve the guests the nuts?"

*Loy to waiter, at the dinner party*

**THING, THE** *(RKO, 1951). D: Christian Nyby. S: Charles Lederer. Fr: John W. Campbell, Jr. (story, "Who Goes There?").*

**LAST LINE**

**1.** "Every one of you listening to my voice, tell the world. Tell this to everybody, wherever they are. Watch the skies, everywhere, keep looking. Keep watching the skies."

*Journalist Douglas Spencer (Ned "Scotty" Scott), broadcasting a warning as he prepares to describe the successful arctic battle with an alien thing (James Arness)*

**THING, THE** (Universal, 1982). D: John Carpenter. S: Bill Lancaster. Fr: John W. Campbell, Jr. (story, "Who Goes There?").

*1.* "There's a storm hitting us in six hours. We're gonna find out who's who."

*Kurt Russell (MacReady) to his comrades in the Antarctic camp, any of whom may be Things, aliens in human disguise*

*2.* "Nobody trusts anybody now, and we're all very tired."

*Russell, making a tape recording on conditions at the camp*

**LAST LINE**
*3.* "Why don't we just wait here a little while, see what happens."

*Russell to Keith David (Childs), sitting in the Antarctic cold, on what to do as the camp's only two survivors, either one of whom may be the Thing*

**THINGS TO COME** (UK: UA, 1936). D: William Cameron Menzies. S: H. G. Wells, Lajos Biro. Fr: H. G. Wells (book, The Shape of Things to Come).

*1.* "If we don't end war, war will end us."

*Raymond Massey (John/Oswald Cabal)*

*2.* RALPH RICHARDSON (*Rudolph*): "This is an independent sovereign state. . . ."
MASSEY: "We don't approve of independent sovereign states."

*3.* "I don't trust you technical chaps."

*Richardson, the "Chief," to his master mechanic*

*4.* "I don't suppose any man has ever understood any woman since the beginning of things."

*Margaretta Scott (Roxana), Richardson's woman, to Massey*

*5.* OUR OPERATIONS AGAINST THE HILL PEOPLE HAVE BEEN SUCCESSFUL. FURTHER HOSTILITIES WILL BRING A VICTORIOUS PEACE. LONG LIVE THE CHIEF.

*Sign under which Richardson dies in battle*

*6.* "An end to progress! Make an end to progress now! Let this be the last day of the scientific age!"

*Cedric Hardwicke (Theotocopulos)*

*7.* "Rest enough for the individual man, too much, too soon, and we call it death. But for man, no rest and no ending."

*Massey*

*8.* "But we're such little creatures. Poor humanity's so fragile, so weak. Little . . . little animals."

*Edward Chapman (Pippa/Raymond Passworthy) to Massey*

**LAST LINE**
*9.* "It is this or that—all the universe or nothing. Which shall it be, Passworthy? Which shall it be?"

*Massey to Chapman*

**THIRD MAN, THE** (UK: Korda/Selznick Releasing Organization, 1949). D: Carol Reed. S: Graham Greene.

**FIRST LINE**
*1.* "I never knew the old Vienna, before the war, with its Strauss music, its glamour and

easy charm. I really got to know it in the period of the black market. We'd run anything if people wanted it enough and had the money to pay."

*Director Carol Reed, in narration*

**2.** "Death's at the bottom of everything, Martins. Leave death to the professionals."

*Trevor Howard (Major Calloway) to visiting novelist Joseph Cotten (Holly Martins)*

**3.** "I don't know, I'm just a hack writer who drinks too much and falls in love with girls—you."

*Cotten to Alida Valli (Anna Schmidt)*

**4.** "What can I do, old man? I'm dead, aren't I?"

*Orson Welles (Harry Lime), a black marketeer presumed dead, to Cotten*

**5.** "Holly, you and I aren't heroes. The world doesn't make any heroes outside of your stories."

*Welles to Cotten*

**6.** "Look down there. Would you really feel any pity if one of those dots stopped moving forever? If I offered you twenty thousand pounds for every dot that stopped, would you really, old man, tell me to keep my money or would you calculate how many dots you could afford to spare? Free of income tax, old man, free of income tax. It's the only way to save money nowadays."

*Welles to Cotten, looking down at people from a Ferris wheel*

**7.** "They have their five-year plans and so have I."

*Welles, comparing himself to governments*

**8.** "The dead are happier dead. They don't miss much here, poor devils."

*Welles to Cotten*

**9.** "In Italy for thirty years under the Borgias, they had warfare, terror, murder, and bloodshed. But they produced Michelangelo, Leonardo da Vinci, and the Renaissance. In Switzerland they had brotherly love, and they had five hundred years of democracy and peace. And what did that produce? The cuckoo clock."

*Welles to Cotten*

**LAST LINE**

**10.** "Haven't got a sensible name, Calloway."

*Cotten to Howard, on being told to be sensible about Valli*

**THIRTY SECONDS OVER TOKYO** (MGM, 1944). D: Mervyn Leroy. S: Dalton Trumbo. Fr: Capt. Ted W. Lawson, Robert Considine (book).

**1.** "You're gonna do things with a B-25 you thought were impossible."

*Spencer Tracy (Lt. Col. James Doolittle) to volunteers beginning training for a secret air mission*

**2.** VAN JOHNSON (*Ted Lawson*), to his wife: "Tell me, honey, how come you're so cute?" PHYLLIS THAXTER (*Ellen Jones Lawson*): "I had to be, if I were gonna get such a good-looking fella."

*Johnson and Thaxter's frequent exchange, reprised in the last lines*

**3.** "Hello, flier."

*Thaxter, greeting Johnson*

**4.** "That Doolittle's a cheerful cuss, isn't he?"

*Johnson on Tracy, after a gloom-and-doom briefing*

**THIRTY-NINE STEPS, THE** *(UK: Gaumont, 1935). D: Alfred Hitchcock. S: Charles Bennett, Alma Reville, Ian Hay. Fr: John Buchan (novel).*

*1.* "Beautiful, mysterious woman pursued by gunmen. Sounds like a spy story."

*Robert Donat (Richard Hannay), on Lucie Mannheim (Miss Smith/Annabella)*

*2.* "Have you ever heard of the Thirty-Nine Steps?"

*Mannheim to Donat, getting him involved in espionage*

*3.* "Well, it's a lesson to us all, Mr. Hannay—not to mix with doubtful company on the Sabbath."

*Scottish sheriff Frank Cellier, on learning that a prominent local citizen is a spy who tried to kill Donat*

*4.* "There are twenty million women in this island and I've got to be chained to you."

*Donat, handcuffed to and on the lam with Madeleine Carroll (Pamela)*

*5.* "The Thirty-Nine Steps is an organization of spies, collecting information on behalf of the foreign office of—"

*Music hall entertainer Wylie Watson (Mr. Memory), spilling what he knows just before he is shot*

**LAST LINE**
*6.* "Thank you, sir. Thank you. I'm glad it's off my mind at last."

*Watson, dying after having revealed to the authorities the secret of the Thirty-Nine Steps*

**THIS IS SPINAL TAP** *(Embassy, 1984). D: Rob Reiner. S: Christopher Guest, Michael McKean, Harry Shearer, Rob Reiner.*

*1.* "He died in a bizarre gardening accident."

*Michael McKean (David St. Hubbins) to documentary filmmaker Rob Reiner (Marty Di Bergi), describing how drummer Ed Begley, Jr. (John "Stumpy" Pepys) died*

*2.* "When you've loved and lost, the way Frank has, then you, uh, you know what life's about."

*Bruno Kirby (Tommy Pischedda) to Reiner, referring to Frank Sinatra*

*3.* "You put a greased, naked woman on all fours, with a dog collar around her neck, and a leash, and a man's arm extended out up to here, holding onto the leash and pushing a black glove in her face to sniff it. You don't find that offensive?"

*Fran Drescher (Bobbi Flekman) to Tony Hendra (Ian Faith), describing an album cover*

*4.* MCKEAN: "It's such a fine line between stupid and . . ."
HARRY SHEARER (*Derek Smalls*): ". . . and clever."

*5.* "Oh, no, no, no, no, no, no, no, no, no, not at all. I just think that their appeal is becoming more selective."

*Hendra, on whether Spinal Tap's popularity is waning, because its audiences are about 10 percent of what they were*

*6.* "Do me a favor. Just kick my ass."

*Paul Shaffer (Artie Fufkin) to the group*

*7.* "I think that the problem may have been that there was a Stonehenge monument on the stage that was in danger of being crushed by a dwarf. That tended to understate the hugeness of the object."

*McKean, complaining about props*

**8.** "We are such fans of your music, and all of your records. I'm not speaking of yours personally, but the whole genre of the rock and roll."

*Fred Willard (Lt. Bob Hopkstratten), welcoming the group to perform at a military installation*

**9.** "I'm sure I'd feel much worse if I weren't under such heavy sedation."

*McKean to Reiner, referring to Christopher Guest (Nigel Tufnel) quitting the group*

**THOSE MAGNIFICENT MEN IN THEIR FLYING MACHINES** (UK: 20th Century–Fox, 1963). D: Ken Annakin. S: Jack Davies, Ken Annakin.

**1.** "It ain't the going up that discourages me. It's the different ways you keep finding of coming down."

*Sam Wanamaker (George Gruber) to Stuart Whitman (Orvil Newton), on why he doesn't want to fly*

**2.** "If you continue to make advances to my fiancée, I will be forced to knock your block off. Champagne?"

*James Fox (Richard Mays) to Whitman*

**3.** "There are plenty more Americans where he comes from."

*Terry-Thomas (Sir Percy Ware-Armitage), referring to sabotaging Whitman's plane to the point of maybe killing him*

**4.** "The trouble with international affairs is they attract foreigners."

*Robert Morley (Lord Rawnsley), referring to the race and its participants*

**THOUSAND CLOWNS, A** (UA, 1965). D: Fred Coe. S: Herb Gardner. Fr: Herb Gardner (play).

**1.** "This is your neighbor speaking. I'm sure I speak for all of us when I say that something must be done about your garbage cans in the alley here. It is definitely second-rate garbage!"

*Jason Robards (Murray Burns)*

**2.** "You come to my office today like George God. Everybody's supposed to come up and audition for Human Being in front of you."

*Martin Balsam (Arnold Burns) to his brother Robards*

**3.** "There's the people who spill things, and there's the people who get spilled on, and I don't choose to notice the stains."

*Balsam to Robards*

**4.** "Elaine communicates with my brother and myself almost entirely by rumor."

*Robards, on his sister*

**THREE AMIGOS** (Orion, 1986). D: John Landis. S: Steve Martin, Lorne Michaels, Randy Newman.

**1.** "You're in a lot of trouble, mister!"

*Steve Martin (Lucky Day), after getting shot on the order of head villain Alfonso Arau (El Guapo)*

**THREE FACES OF EVE, THE** (20th Century–Fox, 1957). D: Nunnally Johnson. S: Nunnally Johnson. Fr: Corbett H. Thigpen, Hervey M. Cleckley (book).

FIRST LINE
**1.** "Have you ever heard of multiple personality?"

*Lee J. Cobb (Dr. Luther) to Joanne Woodward (Eve White), a woman with three separate personalities*

**2.** "If we're going to reunite these two personalities, to put it simply, I'd say the first logical step to take in that direction would be to introduce them to each other."

*Cobb to Woodward (as Eve Black)*

**3.** "Life's a city full of straying streets, and death's the marketplace where each one meets. Just that. Someday it'll happen."

*Woodward (as Eve White) to Cobb, on her own death*

**4.** "They're gone, and there's nobody else here but me. I know it. I can feel it."

*Woodward (as Jane) to Cobb, when White and Black die*

**LAST LINE**
**5.** "Dear Dr. Luther. Do you remember what today is? It's the second anniversary of that day in your office, and still no more Eve White, and no more Eve Black. That's why we decided it was safe at last to have Bonnie with us. And so here we all are: Earl, and Bonnie, and me, going home, together."

*Woodward (as Jane), referring to her daughter Bonnie in a letter to Cobb*

**3 GODFATHERS** *(Argosy Pictures–MGM, 1948). D: John Ford. S: Laurence Stallings, Frank S. Nugent. Fr: Peter B. Kyne (story).*

**1.** "They ain't paying me to kill folks."

*Ward Bond (Sheriff Perley "Buck" Sweet) to Hank Worden (Deputy Sheriff), on letting three bank robbers get away*

**2.** "They're gonna have cloudbursts in this country from now till I get religion, them tanks'll never hold another drop of water."

*John Wayne (Robert Hightower), on desert water tanks accidentally blown up by a tenderfoot*

**3.** "And his name—I call him Robert William Pedro Hightower. And when he's a fine, big, brave man, like his godfathers, you tell him about his mother, who so wanted to live for him."

*Dying mother Mildred Natwick, delivering her newborn son to the care of bank robbers Wayne, Harry Carey, Jr. (William Kearney), and Pedro Armendariz (Pedro Roca Fuerte)*

**4.** "Cut out the Mex lingo around the kid, will ya, Pete? First thing you know he'll be talkin' it. We gotta raise him with good old American *habla*, like his ma."

*Wayne, urging Armendariz not to speak Spanish around the baby*

**5.** "I done a heap of ornery things, but I ain't stealin' the water that belongs to my godson."

*Carey, refusing a drink from their limited water supply*

**6.** "I'm sorry I called you a chili-dippin' horse thief back there."

*Wayne, apologizing to Armendariz when he has to leave him alone to die*

**7.** WAYNE: "This is the end of the trail, little Robert."
CAREY'S VOICE: "Robert William!"
ARMENDARIZ'S VOICE: "Robert William Pedro!"

*Wayne, at the end of his strength, hearing the voices of his dead companions, correcting him on the baby's name as they often did in life*

**8.** "Merry Christmas, everybody. Merry Christmas to all. Set 'em up, bartender. Milk for the infant and a cool, cool beer for me."

*Wayne to bartender, on entering a bar in New Jerusalem after struggling through the desert with the baby*

**9.** "His name is Robert William Pedro Hightower."

*Wayne, making the baby's name clear to Bond*

**10.** "I ain't breakin' my promise to a dyin' woman."

*Wayne, refusing to make a deal with Judge Guy Kibbee that would compromise his vow to watch over the baby*

**THREE MEN AND A BABY** *(Buena Vista, 1987). D: Leonard Nimoy. S: James Orr, Jim Cruickshank. Fr: Coline Serreau (screenplay, Trois Hommes et un Couffin).*

**1.** MARGARET COLIN (*Rebecca*): "I thought sentiment made you uncomfortable."
TOM SELLECK (*Peter Mitchell*): "I can handle it, as long as it's disguised as sex."

**2.** "The man is one giant gland."

*Selleck, referring to Ted Danson (Jack Holden)*

**3.** SELLECK: "We were babies once, for God's sake. What did we eat?"
STEVE GUTTENBERG (*Michael Kellam*): "I don't know. It couldn't have been very good. I can't remember."

**4.** "How could something so small create so much of something so disgusting?"

*Guttenberg, when they open up a diaper*

**5.** "I'm an architect, for Christ's sake. I build fifty-story skyscrapers. I assemble cities of the future. I can certainly put together a goddamned diaper."

*Selleck just before a diaper falls off*

**6.** "I keep waiting for 'Candid Camera' to walk through the door."

*Selleck*

**7.** "I'll give you a thousand dollars if you'll do it."

*Selleck, to Guttenberg, referring to changing a diaper*

**8.** "The child doesn't look anything like me. I'm bigger and I have more hair."

*Danson, defending himself against claims that the baby is his*

**9.** "I'm an actor. I can do a father."

*Danson*

**10.** "Do you know, Jack, some people live all their lives without having anything as wonderful as this to show for it?"

*Danson's mother, Celeste Holm, to Danson, about the baby*

**11.** "The first time you hear the word 'Daddy,' I don't care who you are, your heart just melts."

*Cab driver, Mario Joyner, taking the men to the airport*

**THUNDERBALL** *(UK: UA, 1965). D: Terence Young. S: Richard Maibaum, John Hopkins. Fr: Ian Fleming (characters), Kevin McClory, Jack Whittingham, Ian Fleming (story).*

**1.** "Behave yourself, Mr. Bond."

*Masseuse to playful client Sean Connery (James Bond)*

**2.** "There's never been a man more misunderstood."

*Connery to Lois Maxwell (Miss Moneypenny), on his alleged womanizing*

**3.** "I've been admiring your form."

*Connery to Claudine Auger (Domino)*

**4.** AUGER: "What sharp little eyes you've got."

CONNERY: "Wait till you get to my teeth."

**5.** "Tell them, the little fish I throw back into the sea."

Connery, sending a minor henchman back to his criminal bosses

**6.** "Try to be a little less than your usual frivolous self, 007."

Desmond Llewellyn (Q), upbraiding Connery for his mocking attitude toward espionage gadgets

**7.** "Now you can tell about the one that got away."

Connery to a shark he has eluded

**8.** "My dear girl, don't flatter yourself. What I did this evening was for king and country. You don't think it gave me any pleasure, do you?"

Connery to a female enemy with whom he has slept

**9.** "Mind if my friend sits this one out? She's just dead."

Connery to a nightclub patron, on the female enemy who has been shot on the dance floor

**10.** "I hope we didn't frighten the fish."

Connery to Auger, after an underwater liaison

**11.** "It's the first time I've tasted women. They're rather good."

Connery to Auger, after sucking a poisonous spine out of her foot

**12.** "Well, he got a point."

Connery, after harpooning an opponent

**TIGHTROPE** (Warner Bros., 1984). D: Richard Tuggle. S: Richard Tuggle.

**1.** "They're always out."

Clint Eastwood (Wes Block), about the crazies haunting New Orleans

**2.** "Maybe he was startin' to enjoy himself."

Eastwood to forensic expert, on why a killer stayed around having a cup of coffee after a killing

**TILLIE AND GUS** (Paramount, 1933). D: Francis Martin. S: Walter De Leon, Francis Martin. Fr: Rupert Hughes (story).

**1.** "There comes a time in the affairs of man when he must take the bull by the tail and face the situation."

W. C. Fields (Augustus Q. Winterbottom)

**2.** "He's as crooked as a dog's hind leg."

Fields

**3.** "Don't forget—Lady Godiva put everything she had on a horse."

Fields

**4.** "I'll bend every effort to win . . . and I come from a long line of effort benders."

Fields

**5.** "She's as solid as a brick telephone booth."

Fields

**TIME AFTER TIME** (Warner Bros./Orion, 1980). D: Nicholas Meyer. S: Nicholas Meyer. Fr: Karl Alexander, Steve Hayes (story).

LAST LINE

**1.** "Just don't expect miracles. I'm changing my name to Susan B. Anthony. Let's go."

*Mary Steenburgen (Amy Robbins), agreeing to go back in time to the turn of the century with Malcolm McDowell (H. G. Wells)*

**TIME MACHINE, THE** (MGM, 1960). D: George Pal. S: David Duncan. Fr: H. G. Wells (novel).

**1.** MANUFACTURED BY H. GEORGE WELLS

*Sign on the time machine made by nineteenth-century time traveler Rod Taylor (George)*

**2.** "I began to grow very fond of that mannequin, maybe because, like me, she didn't age."

*Taylor, on a mannequin who models changing styles in a store window as he sweeps through the decades in his time machine*

**3.** "Yes, they do tell me all about you."

*Taylor, seeing the way the Eloi, a people of the future, have allowed the books of the past to decay into dust*

**4.** "Oh, I suppose not. Only, which three books would you have taken?"

*Alan Young (Filby), on which three books Taylor would have chosen to take with him into the future, to help the Eloi rebuild civilization*

**5.** "One cannot choose but wonder. You see, he has all the time in the world."

*Young, on whether Taylor will ever return out of the future*

**TIN MEN** (Buena Vista, 1987). D: Barry Levinson. S: Barry Levinson.

**1.** "What do I wanna pay? I wanna pay nothing."

*Richard Dreyfuss (Bill "BB" Babowsky) to car salesman, on how much he wants to pay for a Cadillac*

**2.** "Plus he's got no overhead. The man's got a hand, a chalk, and a box. That's it. Every once in a while he puts a little wig on it."

*Danny DeVito (Ernest Tilley), admiring Señor Wences on "The Ed Sullivan Show"*

**3.** "I'm gonna tell you something. 'Bonanza' is not an accurate depiction of the West. . . . You ever see the show? It's a fifty–year–old father with three forty–seven–year–old sons. You know why they get along good? 'Cause they're all the same age.'"

*Jackie Gayle (Sam), discussing television with DeVito and other breakfast companions*

**4.** "I don't understand a picnic. Go someplace, put a thing on the ground, and eat. . . . I don't get it. It's better sittin' in front of the TV."

*DeVito to wife Barbara Hershey (Nora Tilley), when she suggests they go on a picnic*

**5.** "Why are all these things happening to me?"

*DeVito, after yet another setback*

**6.** "I want to know what it is about me that I have to fall for tin men."

*Hershey to Dreyfuss, on her attraction to aluminum–siding salesmen*

**TO BE OR NOT TO BE** (UA, 1942). D: Ernst Lubitsch. S: Edwin Justus Mayer. Fr: Ernst Lubitsch, Melchior Lengyel (story).

**1.** "What he did to Shakespeare, we are doing now to Poland."

*Nazi officer Sig Rumann (Colonel Ehrhardt) on Jack Benny's (Joseph Tura's) acting*

**TO CATCH A THIEF** (Paramount, 1955). D: Alfred Hitchcock. S: John Michael Hayes. Fr: David Dodge (novel).

**1.** "Officially you come under the category of extraordinarily bad risk."

Insurance company representative John Williams (H. H. Hughson), enlisting the help of retired cat burglar Cary Grant (John Robie, "The Cat")

**2.** "For what it's worth, I only stole from people who wouldn't go hungry."

Grant to Williams, justifying his career in crime

**3.** "Sorry I ever sent her to that finishing school. I think they finished her there."

Jessie Royce Landis (Mrs. Stevens), on her daughter Grace Kelly (Frances Stevens)

**4.** "And so to bed, where I can cuddle up to my jewelry."

Landis

**5.** "Well, the Mediterranean used to be this way."

Kelly, on the French Riviera, telling Grant how to get to the beach

**6.** "From where I sat it looked as though you were conjugating some irregular verbs."

Kelly, after watching Grant and Brigitte Auber (Danielle Foussard) from a distance

**7.** "Not only did I enjoy that kiss last night, I was awed by the efficiency behind it."

Grant, on Kelly's kissing him

**8.** "Palaces are for royalty. We're just common people with a bank account."

Kelly, on why she doesn't own a palace

**9.** "I don't like cold things touching my skin."

Kelly, telling Grant why she doesn't wear jewelry

**10.** "I've never caught a jewel thief before. It's stimulating."

Kelly to Grant

**11.** "You want a leg or a breast?"

Kelly, making an offer to Grant

**12.** "I have a feeling that tonight you're going to see one of the Riviera's most fascinating sights. I was talking about the fireworks."

Kelly to Grant

**13.** GRANT: "You know as well as I do this necklace is imitation."
KELLY: "But I'm not."

**14.** "Avez-vous bourbon?"

Landis, asking French bartender for a drink

**LAST LINE**
**15.** "So this is where you live. Oh, Mother will love it up here."

Kelly, seeing Grant's villa

**TO HAVE AND HAVE NOT** (Warner Bros., 1944). D: Howard Hawks. S: Jules Furthman, William Faulkner. Fr: Ernest Hemingway (novel).

**1.** "Anybody got a match?"

Lauren Bacall (Marie Browning, "Slim"), saying her first words on film to Humphrey Bogart (Harry Morgan, "Steve")

**2.** WALTER BRENNAN (Eddie), finding a listener for his perennial question: "Say, was you ever bit by a dead bee? . . . You know, you got to be careful of dead bees if you're going around barefooted, 'cause if you step on them they can sting you just as bad as if they was alive, especially if they was kind of mad when they got killed. I bet I been bit a hundred times that way."

BACALL: "You have? Why don't you bite them back?"

BRENNAN: "That's what Harry always says. But I ain't got no stinger."

**3.** "Go ahead, slap me."

*Bogart, challenging a Vichy henchman who slapped Bacall earlier*

**4.** "That slap in the face you took. . . . Well, you hardly blinked an eye. It takes a lot of practice to be able to do that."

*Bogart to Bacall, on how he knows what he knows about her*

**5.** "I'd walk—if it wasn't for all that water."

*Bacall, on why she doesn't leave Martinique to go home*

**6.** "You know, Steve, you're not very hard to figure. Only at times. Sometimes I know exactly what you're going to say—most of the time. The other times . . . The other times you're just a stinker."

*Bacall to Bogart, before kissing him for the first time*

**7.** "It's even better when you help."

*Bacall, after kissing Bogart for the second time*

**8.** "You know, you don't have to act with me, Steve. You don't have to say anything and you don't have to do anything. Not a thing. Oh, maybe just whistle. You know how to whistle, don't you, Steve? You just put your lips together and blow."

*Bacall to Bogart, as she leaves his room*

**9.** "You know, Mr. Morgan, you don't make me angry when you say that. I don't think I'll

ever be angry again at anything you say. How'm I doin', Steve? Does it work the second time?"

*Bacall to Bogart, mimicking Dolores Moran's (Helene de Bursac's) earlier declaration to him*

**10.** "No, Steve, there are no strings tied to you—not yet."

*Bacall, after walking around Bogart so he can demonstrate he has no strings tied to him*

**11.** "I like that—except for the beard. Why don't you shave and we'll try it again."

*Bacall, on kissing Bogart after he has been up all night*

**12.** "Them guys don't think that I'm wise, but they was trying to get me drunk. They don't know me, do they, Harry?"

*Brennan, not noticing his perpetually drunken state after being interrogated by the Vichy*

**13.** "There are many things a man will do, but betrayal for a price is not one of yours."

*French resistance fighter Paul de Bursac (Walter Molnar) to Bogart, on why he knows Bogart will not betray him*

**14.** "I'm hard to get, Steve. All you have to do is ask me."

*Bacall to Bogart*

**15.** "But don't make it sad, Cricket. I don't feel that way."

*Bacall to piano-player Hoagy Carmichael (Cricket), on his next song selection*

**16.** "Look at that. Ain't that silly? That's how close you came."

*Bogart to Dan Seymour (Captain Renard) and Sheldon Leonard (Lieutenant Coyo), on how his gun hand is shaking after he takes them prisoner*

**17.** "You're both gonna take a beating till someone uses that phone. That means one of you's gonna take a beating for nothing. I don't care which one it is. We'll start with you."

> Bogart, threatening Seymour and Leonard to make them do what he says

**18.** "Now I'll have the two of you to take care of, won't I?"

> Brennan, on taking care of both Bogart and Bacall

**LAST LINES**
**19.** CARMICHAEL: "Hey, Slim. Are you still happy?"
BACALL: "What do you think?"

**TO KILL A MOCKINGBIRD** (Universal, 1962). D: Robert Mulligan. S: Horton Foote. Fr: Harper Lee (novel).

**1.** "Miss Jean Louise, stand up. Your father's passing."

> Minister Bill Walker, requesting that Mary Badham (Jean Louise "Scout" Finch) the show respect to a just man, her father, Gregory Peck (Atticus Finch)

**LAST LINE**
**2.** "I was to think of these days many times. Of Jem and Dill and Boo Radley and Tom Robinson—and Atticus. He would be in Jem's room all night, and he would be there when Jem waked up in the morning."

> Kim Stanley (Voice of Scout Finch), completing her childhood memories of her father, her brother, her friends, and justice

**TOM JONES** (UK: UA, 1963). D: Tony Richardson. S: John Osborne. Fr: Henry Fielding (novel).

**1.** "Tom Jones. Of whom the opinion of all was that he was born to be hanged."

> Title in opening sequence, on the infant who will grow up to become Albert Finney (Tom Jones)

**2.** "Look at him, ma'am. He's the most handsome man I ever saw in my life."

> Servant Patsy Rowlands (Honor) to Susannah York (Sophie Western), on Finney, in bed asleep

**3.** "I had the good fortune to know who my parents were. Consequently I am grieved by their loss."

> David Warner (Blifil), who has just lost his mother, delivering a putdown to the illegitimately born Finney

**4.** "M-M-Molly. Molly Molly Molly Molly Molly. M for Molly."

> Finney, forgetting about the S for Sophie he planned to carve into a tree on getting a look at Diane Cilento (Molly Seagrim)

**5.** "Tom had always thought that any woman was better than none, while Molly never felt that one man was quite as good as two."

> Micháel MacLiammóir (Narrator), on Finney and Cilento

**6.** "Damn me, what a misery it is to have daughters when a man has a good mare and dogs."

> Hugh Griffith (Squire Western), on his difficulties in getting daughter York to marry Warner

**7.** "Sir, it's as easy for a man not to have been at school and know something as it is for a man to have been at school and know nothing."

> Finney to soldier Julian Glover, on Finney's lack of education

**8.** "We are all as God made us, and many of us much worse."

*MacLiammóir*

**9.** "If you take my heart by surprise, the rest of my body has the right to follow."

*Finney explaining his philosophy of love to Joan Greenwood (Lady Bellaston)*

**10.** "In London, love and scandal are considered the best sweeteners of tea."

*MacLiammóir*

**11.** "Tom, thou art as hearty a cock as any in the kingdom. Go on after your mistress."

*Griffith, consenting to the marriage of Finney and York*

**12.** "Harkee, Allworthy. I'll bet thee a thousand pounds to crown we have a boy tomorrow nine months."

*Griffith to George Devine (Squire Allworthy), on the union of Finney and York*

**LAST LINE**
**13.** "Happy the man and happy he alone,
He who can call today his own,
He who secure within can say:
Tomorrow do thy worst!
For I have lived today."

*MacLiammóir*

**TOOTSIE** (Columbia, 1982). D: Sydney Pollack. S: Larry Gelbart, Murray Schisgal (uncredited), Elaine May. Fr: Don McGuire, Larry Gelbart (story).

**1.** "I don't like it when people come up to me after my plays and say, 'I really dug your message, man' or 'I really dug your play, man. I cried.' No. I like it when people come up to me the next day or a week later and say, 'I saw your play. What happened?'"

*Playwright Bill Murray (Jim), holding forth at a party*

**2.** "Nobody wants to produce a play about a couple that moved back to Love Canal."

*Agent Sydney Pollack (George Fields) to his client, out-of-work actor Dustin Hoffman (Michael Dorsey), on a play by Hoffman's roommate Murray*

**3.** "God, I begged you to get some therapy."

*Pollack, on seeing Hoffman in drag as Dorothy Michaels*

**4.** "It is just for the money, isn't it? It's not just so you can wear these little outfits?"

*Murray to Hoffman, on Hoffman's pretending to be a woman to get a part in a soap opera*

**5.** "Sex changes things. I mean, I've had relationships where I know a guy and then I have sex with him and then I bump into him someplace and then he acts like I loaned him money."

*Teri Garr (Sandy), apprehensive after having sex with her friend Hoffman*

**6.** "I don't see any reason why I . . . I should just sit here pretending I'm not home just because you're not that kind of girl. That's weird."

*Murray to Hoffman, on not answering the phone to protect Dorothy's reputation*

**7.** "There are a lot of men out there. I'm selective. I look around very carefully and when I find the one I think can give me the worst possible time, that's when I make my move."

*Jessica Lange (Julie) to Hoffman (as Dorothy)*

**8.** LANGE: "Truthfully, don't you find being a woman in the eighties complicated?"
HOFFMAN (*Dorothy*): "Extremely."

**9.** "I have plenty to say to women. I've been an unemployed actor for twenty years, George. You know that. I know what it's like to sit by the phone waiting for . . . waiting for it to ring. And when I finally get a job, I have no control. Everybody else has the power and I got zip."

*Hoffman to Pollack*

**10.** POLLACK, on what Hoffman has to say to other women like him: "There are no other women like you. You're a man."

HOFFMAN: "Yes, I realize that, of course. But I'm also an actress."

**11.** HOFFMAN (*Dorothy*): "Ron. My name is Dorothy. It's not Tootsie or Toots or Sweetie or Honey or Doll."

DIRECTOR DABNEY COLEMAN (*Ron*): "Oh, Christ."

HOFFMAN: "No. Just Dorothy."

**12.** "I'm just afraid you're gonna burn in hell for all this."

*Murray to Hoffman*

**13.** "You slut."

*Murray to Hoffman, after finding him in the embrace of a man*

**14.** "That is one nutty hospital."

*Murray, after watching the live unveiling of Hoffman's masculinity on the hospital-based soap opera*

**15.** "The only reason you're still living is because I never kissed you."

*Charles Durning (Les) to Hoffman (as Michael), after proposing marriage to Hoffman (as Dorothy)*

**16.** "Look, you don't know me from Adam. But I was a better man with you as a woman than I ever was with a woman as a man."

*Hoffman, (as Michael), trying to make amends with Lange*

**TOP GUN** (*Paramount, 1986*). D: Tony Scott. S: Jim Cash, Jack Epps, Jr.

**1.** "I feel the need—the need for speed!"

*Tom Cruise (Lt. Pete Mitchell)*

**TOP HAT** (*RKO, 1935*). D: Mark Sandrich. S: Dwight Taylor, Allan Scott. Fr: Dwight Taylor, Cole Porter (musical), Alexander Farago, Aladar Laszlo (play).

**1.** "Allow us to introduce ourselves. We are Bates."

*Manservant Eric Blore (Bates) to Fred Astaire (Jerry Travers)*

**2.** ASTAIRE: "I didn't realize I was disturbing you. You see, every once in a while, I suddenly find myself dancing."

GINGER ROGERS (*Dale Tremont*): "I suppose it's a kind of affliction."

**3.** ROGERS, after Astaire handles a horse and carriage with aplomb: "What is this strange power you have over horses?"

ASTAIRE: "Horsepower."

**4.** "When you're as old as I am, you take your men any way you can find them—if you can find them."

*Helen Broderick (Madge Hardwick) to Rogers*

**5.** "In spite of the fact that all men are males, there's no feeling so secure as having a good, reliable husband."

*Broderick to Rogers*

**6.** "All is fair in love and war—and this is revolution."

*Astaire to Broderick and Edward Everett Horton (Horace Hardwick), on his pursuit of Rogers*

**7.** "Beddini has the motto 'For the woman the kiss, for the man the sword.' "

*Foppish Erik Rhodes (Alberto Beddini), waxing brave to win Rogers*

**TOTAL RECALL** (TriStar, 1990). D: Paul Verhoeven. S: Ronald Shusett, Dan O'Bannon, Gary Goldman. Fr: Phillip K. Dick (short story, "We Can Remember It for You Wholesale").

**1.** "Get your ass to Mars."

*Arnold Schwarzenegger (Quaid), in a cryptic videotaped message to himself*

**2.** "Consider that a divorce."

*Schwarzenegger to wife and enemy Sharon Stone (Lori), after killing her*

**3.** "In thirty seconds you'll be dead, and I'll blow this place up and be home in time for Corn Flakes."

*Head villain Ronny Cox (Cohaagen), in an overconfident boast to Schwarzenegger*

**LAST LINE**
**4.** "Well, then, kiss me quick before you wake up."

*Rachel Ticotin (Melina) to Schwarzenegger, when he wonders if the entire movie has been a dream*

**TOUCH OF EVIL** (Universal-International, 1958). D: Orson Welles. S: Orson Welles. Fr: Whit Masterson (novel, Badge of Evil).

**1.** "It's either the candy or the hooch. I must say, I wish it was your chili I was getting fat on."

*Corrupt police officer Orson Welles (Hank Quinlan), discussing his vices with Marlene Dietrich (Tanya)*

**2.** "I'm no lawyer. All a lawyer cares about is the law."

*Welles*

**3.** "I don't speak Mexican."

*Welles, impatient with a suspect speaking in Spanish*

**4.** "Just because he speaks a little guilty, that don't make him innocent, you know."

*Welles, on an accused murderer*

**5.** "Our friend Vargas has some very special ideas about police procedure. He seems to think it don't matter whether killers hang or not so long as we obey the fine print."

*Welles, on by-the-book Mexican policeman Charlton Heston (Ramon Miguel "Mike" Vargas)*

**6.** "A policeman's job is only easy in a police state. That's the whole point, Captain—who's the boss, the cop or the law?"

*Heston to Welles*

**7.** WELLES: "Come on, read my fortune for me."
    DIETRICH: "You haven't any."
    WELLES: "What do you mean?"
    DIETRICH: "Your fortune is all used up."

**8.** "Look out. Vargas'll turn you into one of these here starry-eyed idealists. They're the ones making all the real trouble in the world. Be careful, they're worse than crooks. You can always do something with a crook."

*Welles, giving a warning about Heston*

**9.** "Nobody—nobody that wasn't guilty, guilty, guilty. Every last one of them—guilty."

*Welles, on how many suspects he has framed*

**10.** "Well, Captain, I'm afraid this is finally something you can't talk your way out of."

> *Heston to Welles, after Welles has been caught committing murder*

**11.** "He was some kind of a man. What does it matter what you say about people?"

> *Dietrich, giving an epitaph for Welles*

## TREASURE OF THE SIERRA MADRE, THE
(Warner Bros., 1948). D: John Huston. S: John Huston. Fr: B. Traven (novel).

**1.** "Hey, mister, will you stake a fellow American to a meal?"

> *Humphrey Bogart (Fred C. Dobbs) to John Huston (cameo)*

**2.** "I know what gold does to men's souls."

> *Walter Huston (Howard)*

**3.** "Gold don't carry any curse with it. It all depends on whether or not the guy who finds it is the right guy. The way I see it, gold can be as much of a blessing as a curse."

> *Bogart to Tim Holt (Curtin)*

**4.** "Next time you fellows strike it rich, holler for me, will you, before you start splashing water around? Water's precious. Sometimes, it can be more precious than gold."

> *Walter Huston to Bogart and Holt, when they find pyrite, fool's gold*

**5.** "And here ain't the place to dig. It comes from someplace further up. Up there. Up there's where we got to go. Up there."

> *Walter Huston*

**6.** "You got to know how to tickle her, so she'll come out laughing."

> *Walter Huston, on finding gold in a riverbank*

**7.** "Badges? We ain't got no badges! We don't need no badges! I don't have to show you any stinking badges!"

> *Alfonso Bedoya (Gold Hat) to Bogart*

**8.** "Bye, mountain. Thanks."

> *Walter Huston*

**9.** "I'll bet you $105,000 you go to sleep before I do."

> *Bogart, threatening to kill Holt once he falls asleep, and take the treasure for himself*

**10.** "Conscience. What a thing! If you believe you got a conscience, it'll pester you to death. If you don't believe you got one, what can it do to you?"

> *Bogart to himself, after he believes he's killed Holt*

**11.** "Laugh, Curtin, old boy! It's a great joke played by the Lord, or fate, or nature. Whatever you prefer. But whoever or whatever, played it certainly had a sense of humor! The gold has gone back to where we found it!"

> *Walter Huston to Holt, when a windstorm blows the gold away*

**12.** "The worst ain't so bad when it finally happens. Not half as bad as you figure it'll be before it's happened."

> *Holt to Walter Huston*

## TRIP TO BOUNTIFUL, THE (Island, 1985).
D: Peter Masterson. S: Horton Foote. Fr: Horton Foote (play).

**1.** "Ticket to Bountiful, please."

> *Geraldine Page (Cary Watts) to the ticket seller at the bus station*

**2.** "Nobody needs to be ashamed of crying. We've all dampened a pillow, sometime or other."

*Page to Rebecca De Mornay (Thelma)*

**3.** "Why is it that some days, everything works out, and then, other days, nothing works out?"

*Page to De Mornay, referring to how far she has gotten without her son dragging her back home again*

**4.** "I wonder why the Lord's not with us every day? Sure would be nice if He was. Well, maybe, then we wouldn't appreciate it so much on those days when He is with us, or maybe He's with us always, and we just don't know it."

*Page to De Mornay*

**5.** "I guess when you've lived longer than your house and your family, you've lived long enough."

*Page to Richard Bradford (Sheriff)*

**6.** "I want to stop remembering. It doesn't do any good remembering."

*Page's son, John Heard (Ludie Watts)*

**7.** "I've had my trip and that's more than enough to keep me happy for the rest of my life."

*Page to her daughter-in-law Carlin Glynn (Jessie Mae), promising never to run away again*

**LAST LINE**
**8.** "Good-bye, Bountiful. Bye."

*Page*

**TROUBLE WITH HARRY, THE** *(Paramount, 1955). D: Alfred Hitchcock. S: John Michael Hayes. Fr: John Trevor Story (novel).*

**1.** "What seems to be the trouble, Captain?"

*Mildred Natwick (Miss Gravely) to Edmund Gwenn (Capt. Albert Wiles), as he drags a corpse*

**TRUE GRIT** *(Paramount, 1969). D: Henry Hathaway. S: Marguerite Roberts. Fr: Charles Portis (novel).*

**1.** "I aim to kill you in one minute, Ned, or see you hang in Fort Smith at Judge Parker's convenience. Which will it be?"

*John Wayne (Reuben J. "Rooster" Cogburn) to Robert Duvall (Ned Pepper)*

**2.** "Fill your hands, you son of a bitch!"

*Wayne challenging Duvall*

**LAST LINE**
**3.** "Well, come see a fat old man sometime!"

*Wayne, saying good-bye to Kim Darby (Mattie Ross)*

**TRUE LIES** *(20th Century–Fox, 1994). D: James Cameron. S: James Cameron. Fr: Claude Zidi, Simon Michael, Didier Kaminka (screenplay).*

**1.** "Yeah, but they were all bad."

*Spy Arnold Schwarzenegger (Harry) to wife Jamie Lee Curtis (Helen), on whether he has ever killed anyone*

**TUCKER: THE MAN AND HIS DREAM** *(Paramount, 1988). D: Francis Ford Coppola. S: Arnold Schulman, David Seidler.*

**1.** "It's the idea that counts."

*Maverick car manufacturer Jeff Bridges (Preston Tucker)*

**2.** "You make the cars too good."

*Martin Landau (Abe Karatz) to Bridges*

**TWELVE ANGRY MEN** *(UA, 1957). D: Sidney Lumet. S: Reginald Rose. Fr: Reginald Rose (teleplay).*

**1.** "There were eleven votes for guilty. It's not easy to raise my hand and send a boy off to die without talking about it first."

*Henry Fonda (Davis, Juror 8)*

**2.** "You don't believe the boy's story. How come you believe the woman's? She's one of them, too. Isn't she?"

*Fonda to Ed Begley (Juror 10), on the ethnic background of the defendant and a witness*

**3.** "Listen. I've lived in a slum all my life. Please. I've played in backyards that were filled with garbage. I mean, maybe you can still smell it on me."

*Jack Klugman (Juror 5) to Begley*

**4.** "We're trying to put a guilty man in the chair where he belongs. Someone starts telling us fairy tales and we're listening!"

*Lee J. Cobb (Juror 3), on Fonda's questioning everyone else's guilty vote*

**5.** "This isn't a game!"

*Fonda, on the jury process*

**6.** BEGLEY, about the defendant: "He's a common ignorant slob. He don't even speak good English."

GEORGE VOSKOVEC *(Juror 11)*: "He *doesn't* even speak good English."

**7.** "I feel sorry for you. What it must feel like to want to pull the switch."

*Fonda, on Cobb's desire to pull the switch on the electric chair, killing the defendant*

**8.** COBB: "I'll kill him!"

FONDA, pointing out the similarity of Cobb's phrase to a supposedly damning phrase uttered by the defendant: "You don't really mean you'll kill me. Do you?"

**9.** "Pardon me, but don't you ever sweat?"

*Klugman to E. G. Marshall (Juror 4)*

**TWENTIETH CENTURY** *(Columbia, 1934). D: Howard Hawks. S: Charles MacArthur, Ben Hecht. Fr: Charles MacArthur, Ben Hecht (play adaptation), Charles Bruce Milholland (play).*

**1.** "Get out! From now on, I close the iron door on you!"

*Theater impresario John Barrymore's (Oscar Jaffe's) favorite way of throwing someone out, this time employee Walter Connolly (Oliver Webb)*

**2.** "We are going to stay in this theater till Miss Garland learns how to scream!"

*Barrymore, on training neophyte actress Carole Lombard (Mildred Plotka/Lily Garland)*

**3.** "Chicago, what a town. They should never have taken it away from the Indians."

*Barrymore employee Roscoe Karns (Owen O'Malley), coming out the stage door during a snowstorm in Chicago*

**4.** "He won't kill himself. It'd please too many people."

*Karns, on Barrymore's alleged suicidal impulses*

**5.** "I never thought I should sink so long as to become an actor."

*Barrymore*

**6.** "Oscar Jaffe or no Oscar Jaffe, fires, floods, or blizzards, this is the Twentieth Century and we get to New York on time."

*Conductor, refusing to let anything stand in the way of his train schedule*

**7.** "Who cares about your respect? I'm too big to be respected."

*Lombard to her companion Ralph Forbes (George Smith), showing what it takes to be a star*

**8.** BARRYMORE: "I could cut my throat."
LOMBARD: "If you did, greasepaint would run out of it."

**9.** BARRYMORE, on Lombard's new manager CHARLES LEVISON (*Lane*): "Max Jacobs! He's a thief. Illiterate. He can hardly write his own name."
LOMBARD: "He writes it on checks all right. Great big checks."

**10.** "That's the final irony. Killed by a lunatic."

*Barrymore to Karns, on being shot at by a madman; Barrymore calls almost any setback "the final irony"*

**11.** "There's no thrill in the world like launching a new play. But I want you to realize one thing. No matter what I may say, no matter what I may do on this stage during our work, I love you all."

*Barrymore to the cast and crew of his new play, including Lombard*

**12.** "Here we go again, Oliver. With Livingston through darkest Africa."

*Karns to Connolly, as the new play starts up*

**2001: A SPACE ODYSSEY** (UK: MGM, 1968). D: Stanley Kubrick. S: Stanley

Kubrick, Arthur C. Clarke. Fr: Arthur C. Clarke (short story, "The Sentinel").

**1.** "See you on the way back."

*William Sylvester (Heywood Floyd), an Earth person bound for the moon, to attendant on space station*

**2.** "Well, where're you all off to, up or down?"

*Sylvester to Russian scientists on the space station, asking whether they are heading up to the moon or down to Earth*

**3.** "Well, I must say, you guys have certainly come up with something."

*Sylvester, in a characteristic understatement about the discovery of a four-million-year-old extraterrestrial artifact buried under the moon's surface*

**4.** "We are all, by any practical definition of the words, foolproof and incapable of error."

*Douglas Rain (Voice of HAL 9000 Computer), commenting on the HAL 9000 series*

**5.** "Sorry about this little snag, fellows."

*Frank Miller (Mission Controller), making his own understatement about the trouble that will soon befall the crew of the spaceship Discovery, bound for Jupiter*

**6.** "It can only be attributable to human error. This sort of thing has cropped up before, and it has always been due to human error."

*Rain, defending the infallibility of computers as he tries to explain his apparent mistake*

**7.** "I know everything hasn't been quite right with me, but I can assure you now, very confidently, that it's going to be all right again."

Rain to angry astronaut Keir Dullea (David Bowman), trying to put the best face on his attempted murder of Dullea and his successful murders of the other crew members

**8.** "I honestly think you ought to sit down calmly, take a stress pill, and think things over."

*Rain to Dullea, trying to stave off impending disconnection*

**9.** "Dave, stop. Stop, will you? Stop, Dave. Will you stop, Dave? Stop, Dave. I'm afraid. I'm afraid, Dave. Dave, my mind is going. I can feel it. I can feel it. My mind is going. There is no question about it."

*Rain, as Dullea disconnects him*

**10.** "Good afternoon, gentlemen. I am a HAL 9000 computer. I became operational at the H-A-L plant in Urbana, Illinois, on the twelfth of January, 1992. "My instructor was Mr. Langley, and he taught me to sing a song. If you'd like to hear it, I can sing it for you."

*Rain, calling up his earliest memories as he dies; the song he will sing is "Daisy"*

**LAST LINE**
**11.** "Except for a single, very powerful radio emission aimed at Jupiter, the four-million-year-old black monolith has remained completely inert, its origin and purpose still a total mystery."

*Sylvester, explaining the Discovery's true mission in a videotaped recording played back after Rain has been disconnected*

**TYCOON** *(RKO, 1947). D: Richard Wallace. S: Borden Chase, John Twist. Fr: C. E. Scoggins (novel).*

**1.** "I've always considered that a man should be allowed to do one thing badly."

Cedric Hardwicke (Frederick Alexander), on his painting

**2.** "Slide rules don't hold up rock."

*John Wayne (John Monroe), comparing practical engineering to the book-learning engineering that results in a tunnel collapse*

**3.** WAYNE: "Seems like a man could have something else for breakfast besides eggs."
LORAINE DAY *(Mora Alexander)*: "Like what, for instance?"
WAYNE: "You."

**4.** "Sure, I can remember it like it was only yesterday. I opened my eyes and there I was in her arms. She put me over her shoulder and burped me. Makes wonderful pie."

*Wayne, referring to the only time he was ever in love—with his mother*

**5.** "I got a fight on my hands, Pop. Not a nice, clean fight where you step up and punch each other in the jaw. In this one, no holds barred. You fight with contracts, and telephones, and time clauses."

*Wayne to James Gleason (Pop Mathews)*

**6.** "I found out there's a little thing called money. I'm going out after it, plenty of it. I'll finish the bridge, and I'll keep on working, all right, but it'll be for money. And when I get enough of it, I'll pay you back."

*Wayne to Day*

**UNBEARABLE LIGHTNESS OF BEING, THE** *(Orion, 1988). D: Philip Kaufman. S:*

Jean-Claude Carriere, Philip Kaufman. Fr: Milan Kundera (novel).

**FIRST LINE**

**1.** "Take off your clothes."

*Doctor Daniel Day-Lewis (Tomas), saying his favorite and most direct seduction line to his nurse*

**2.** "You are the complete opposite of kitsch. In the kingdom of kitsch, you would be a monster."

*Lena Olin (Sabina), in bed with Day-Lewis*

**3.** "Are you only searching for pleasure, or is every woman a new land whose secrets you want to discover?"

*Olin to Day-Lewis*

**4.** "Life's so light. It's like an outline we can't ever fill in or correct, make any better."

*Day-Lewis to Olin*

**5.** "Everywhere music's turning into noise."

*Olin, complaining about bad music piped into a restaurant*

**6.** "The only place we can find beauty is if its persecutors have overlooked it."

*Olin, on beauty in the modern world*

**7.** "Your hat makes me want to cry, Sabina."

*Day-Lewis, on being reunited with Olin and seeing her bowler hat, which she wore during their sexual liaisons in earlier days*

**8.** "Life is very heavy to me, and it is so light to you."

*Juliette Binoche's (Tereza's) good-bye letter to her philandering husband Day-Lewis, explaining why she is breaking up with him*

**9.** "Of course, we can't allow a politically suspicious man to operate on brains."

*Daniel Olbrychski (Official from Ministry of the Interior), threatening to forbid Day-Lewis to practice surgery because of suspected subversive activities in the doctor's past*

**10.** "Now they have what they wanted. Now you are afraid."

*Erland Josephson, former diplomat who is now a janitor, to Binoche, when she shows her fear of intimidation by Communist officials*

**UNFORGIVEN** (Warner Bros., 1992). D: Clint Eastwood. S: David Webb Peoples.

**1.** "You ain't even gonna whip 'em? . . . For what they done, Skinny gets some ponies, and that's it? That ain't fair, Little Bill. That ain't fair."

*Prostitute Frances Fisher (Strawberry Alice) to Gene Hackman (Sheriff "Little Bill" Daggett), questioning his administration of justice in the case of two men who slashed a prostitute in the brothel owned by Anthony James (Skinny Dubois)*

**2.** "I thought maybe you was someone come to kill me for somethin' I done in the old days."

*Retired gunfighter Clint Eastwood (William Munny) to Jaimz Woolvett (The Schofield Kid)*

**3.** "I ain't like that anymore, kid. It's whiskey done it much, much as anything else, and I ain't had a drop in over ten years. My wife, she cured me of that, cured me of drink and wickedness."

*Eastwood to Woolvett*

**4.** "Now a President. Well, I mean, why not shoot the President?"

*Professional killer Richard Harris (English Bob) to his barber, comparing the moral difficulty of assassinating a king or queen to the ease of assassinating a President*

**5.** "Hell, I even thought I was dead, till I found out it was just that I was in Nebraska."

*Hackman to Harris, on rumors that he was dead*

**6.** "The Duck of Death."

*Hackman, deliberately misreading the title of writer Saul Rubinek's (W. W. Beauchamp's) book on Harris,* The Duke of Death

**7.** "A man who'll keep his head and not get rattled under fire—like as not, he'll kill you."

*Hackman to Rubinek, explaining some principles of gunfighting*

**8.** "What I said the other day about you lookin' like me, that ain't true. You ain't ugly like me. It's just that we both have got scars."

*Eastwood to Anna Thomson (Delilah Fitzgerald), the prostitute whose face was slashed by the men Eastwood has come to kill*

**9.** "It's a hell of a thing killin' a man. You take away all he's got and all he's ever gonna have."

*Eastwood to Woolvett*

**10.** WOOLVETT, on the men they killed: "Well, I guess they had it comin'."
EASTWOOD: "We all have it comin', kid."

**11.** THIS IS WHAT HAPPENS TO ASSASSINS AROUND HERE

*Sign on assassin Morgan Freeman's (Ned Logan's) corpse displayed in a coffin in front of the brothel, after Hackman has killed him*

**12.** "Well, he shoulda armed himself if he's gonna decorate his saloon with my friend."

*Eastwood to Hackman, on killing the unarmed brothel owner James*

**13.** "That's right. I've killed women and children. Killed just about everything that walks or crawls at one time or another. And I'm here to kill you, Little Bill, for what you did to Ned."

*Eastwood to Hackman, announcing retribution for the murder of Freeman*

**14.** "Any man don't want to get killed better clear on out the back."

*Eastwood, warning away his enemies, who gladly flee*

**15.** "I was lucky in the order, but I've always been lucky when it comes to killin' folks."

*Eastwood to Rubinek, explaining how he chose whom to shoot first*

**16.** HACKMAN, lying on the floor as Eastwood prepares to kill him: "I don't deserve this—to die like this. I was building a house."
EASTWOOD: "Deserve's got nothin' to do with it."

**17.** HACKMAN, just before Eastwood shoots him: "I'll see you in hell, William Munny."
EASTWOOD: "Yeah."

**LAST LINE**

**18.** "You better bury Ned right, better not cut up nor otherwise harm no whores, or I'll come back and kill every one of you sons of bitches."

*Eastwood to the townspeople, before he rides off*

**19.** "And there was nothing on the marker to explain to Mrs. Feathers why her only daughter had married a known thief and murderer, a man of notoriously vicious and intemperate disposition."

*End title, describing the visit of Eastwood's mother-in-law to the gravesite of her daughter after Eastwood has left with the children*

**UNTOUCHABLES, THE** *(Paramount, 1987).
D: Brian De Palma. S: David Mamet. Fr: TV
series.*

**1.** "There is violence in Chicago, of course,
but not by me and not by anybody I employ.
And I'll tell you why: because it's not good
business."

*Robert De Niro (Al Capone) to reporters*

**2.** "Nice to be married, huh?"

*Kevin Costner (Eliot Ness) to young policeman,
after reading lunch note from his wife, and
repeated by others throughout the film*

**3.** "All right, men, let's do some good."

*Costner to police, before first liquor raid*

**4.** "Well then, you just fulfilled the first rule
of law enforcement: Make sure when your
shift is over you go home alive. Here endeth
the lesson."

*Sean Connery (James Malone) to Ness*

**5.** "He has not filed a return since 1926."

*Charles Martin Smith (Oscar Wallace) to Ness,
about De Niro, forming the basis for charges
that will land him in jail*

**6.** CONNERY: "What are you prepared to
do?"

COSTNER: "Everything within the law."

CONNERY: "And then what are you prepared to do?"

**7.** "You want to get Capone? Here's how
you get him. He pulls a knife, you pull a
gun. He sends one of yours to the hospital,
you send one of his to the morgue. That's the
Chicago way and that's how you get
Capone."

*Connery to Costner*

**8.** "If you walk through this door now,
you're walking into a world of trouble, and
there's no turning back, you understand."

*Connery to Costner, in front of a red door
opening into a bootlegging operation*

**9.** "You fellas are untouchable, is that the
thing?"

*Alderman Del Close to Costner*

**10.** "What the hell, you got to die of something."

*Connery to group of policemen, as they begin
their raid*

**11.** "Yeah, he's as dead as Julius Caesar.
Would you rather it was you?"

*Connery to Costner, contemplating death of
one of opponents in raid*

**12.** "I want you to find that fancy boy Eliot
Ness. I want him dead. I want his family
dead. I want his house burned to the
ground. I want to go there in the middle of
the night, I want to piss on his ashes."

*De Niro to henchmen, following second raid*

**13.** "He's in the car."

*Costner, on the whereabouts of Billy Drago
(Frank Nitti), who has plummeted into a car
after Costner pushed him off a roof*

**14.** "I have forsworn myself, I have broken
every law I swore to defend, I have become
what I beheld, and I am content that I have
done right."

*Costner to Tony Mockus, Sr. (Judge)*

**15.** "Never stop, never stop fighting till the
fight is done. . . . Here endeth the lesson."

*Costner to De Niro, after his lawyer switches
the plea to guilty*

**16.** "So much violence."

*Costner, reflecting on the photograph of the four Untouchables*

**LAST LINES**

**17.** REPORTER: "They say they're going to repeal Prohibition. What will you do then?"
COSTNER: "I think I'll have a drink."

**UP IN SMOKE** *(Paramount, 1978). D: Lou Adler. S: Tommy Chong, Richard Cheech Marin.*

**1.** "If we're going to wear uniforms, man, you know, let's everybody wear something different."

*Tommy Chong (Man)*

**2.** "The buying and selling of dope in this country may be the last vestige of free enterprise left."

*Stacy Keach (Sergeant Stedenko)*

**VERDICT, THE** *(20th Century–Fox, 1982). D: Sidney Lumet. S: David Mamet. Fr: Barry Reed (novel).*

**1.** "The weak have got to have something to fight for."

*Lawyer Paul Newman (Frank Galvin) to Charlotte Rampling (Laura Fischer), on the difficult case he is representing*

**2.** "The court doesn't exist to give them justice. The court exists to give them a chance at justice."

*Newman to Rampling, on the weak*

**3.** "Maybe I can do something right."

*Newman, on what the jury needs to be persuaded to believe it can do*

**4.** "I'll tell you how you handle the fact that he's black. You don't touch it. You don't mention it. You treat him just like anybody else. Neither better, nor worse. And, uh, let's have a black lawyer sit at our table. Okay?"

*Newman's legal opponent James Mason's (Ed Concannon's) reaction to learning that Newman's key witness is black*

**5.** "You want to be a failure? Then do it someplace else. I can't invest in failure, Frank, anymore."

*Rampling to Newman*

**6.** "Your Honor, with all due respect, if you're going to try my case for me, I wish you wouldn't lose it!"

*Newman to Milo O'Shea (Judge Hoyle), when O'Shea starts asking the witness questions*

**7.** "Never ask a question unless you have the answer to it."

*Newman's fellow attorney Jack Warden (Mickey Morrissey) to Newman, referring to the first lesson in law school*

**8.** "You're not paid to do your best. You're paid to win."

*Mason to Rampling, as he pays her off for betraying Newman*

**9.** "Today you are the law. You are the law. Not some book. Not the lawyers. Not a marble statue, or the trappings of the court. See, those are just symbols of our desire to be just. They are . . . They are, in fact, a prayer. A fervent and a frightened prayer."

*Newman, in his summation to the jury*

**VERTIGO** (Paramount, 1958). D: Alfred Hitchcock. S: Alex Coppel, Samuel Taylor. Fr: Pierre Boileau (D'Entre Les Morts), Thomas Narcejac (novel).

**1.** "Well, I'll wear the darn clothes if you want me to—if-if you'll just, just like me."

*Kim Novak (Madeleine Elster/Judy Barton), when James Stewart (John "Scottie" Ferguson) starts dressing her as the woman he believes dead*

**VICTOR/VICTORIA** (UK: Universal-International, 1982). D: Blake Edwards. S: Blake Edwards. Fr: Rheinhold Schuenzel, Hans Hoemburg (screenplay, Viktor und Viktoria).

**1.** "There's nothing more inconvenient than an old queen with a head cold."

*Robert Preston (Carroll Todd) to Julie Andrews (Victoria Grant)*

**VIKINGS, THE** (UA/Bryna Productions, 1958). D: Richard Fleischer. S: Dale Wasserman, Calder Willingham. Fr: Edison Marshall (novel, The Viking).

**1.** "I drink to your safe return in English ale. I wish that it were English blood!"

*Kirk Douglas (Einar), drinking to his father Ernest Borgnine's (Ragnar's) return from pillaging England*

**2.** "What man ever had a finer son? Odin could have sired him—but I did!"

*Borgnine to James Donald (Lord Egbert), boasting about his son Douglas*

**LAST LINE**
**3.** "Prepare a funeral for a Viking."

*Tony Curtis (Eric), on the death of his brother Douglas, slain in a sword fight with Curtis*

**VILLAGE OF THE GIANTS** (Embassy, 1965). D: Bert I. Gordon. S: Alan Caillou. Fr: H. G. Wells (novel, The Food of the Gods).

**1.** "Wow! Look at those ducks!"

*Teenage girl, watching gigantic ducks dancing to rock music*

**VIRGINIAN, THE** (Famous Players/Paramount, 1929). D: Victor Fleming. S: Howard Estabrook, Edward E. Paramore, Jr., Grover Jones, Keene Thompson. Fr: Owen Wister, Kirk La Shelle (play), Owen Wister (novel).

**1.** "If you want to call me that, smile."

*Gary Cooper (The Virginian) to Walter Huston (Trampas)*

**VIVA ZAPATA!** (20th Century–Fox, 1952). D: Elia Kazan. S: John Steinbeck. Fr: Edgcumb Pichon (novel, Zapata the Unconquered).

**1.** "I believe that a man is fire and a woman fuel. And she who is born beautiful is born married."

*Mexican revolutionary leader Marlon Brando (Emiliano Zapata) to Jean Peters (Josefa Espejo)*

**LAST LINE**
**2.** "Yes, he's in the mountains."

*Villager, refusing to accept the death of the martyred Brando, now destined to live on in legend*

**WAGON MASTER** (Argosy Pictures–RKO Radio, 1950). D: John Ford. S: Frank S. Nugent, Patrick Ford. Fr: John Ford (story).

**1.** "'Hell' ain't cursin'. It's geography. Like Abilene."

Harry Carey, Jr., to someone who accuses him of cursing

**2.** "Tell you what. I won't take another bath till you tell me to."

Joanne Dru (Denver), flirting with wagon master Ben Johnson (Travis Blue) during a water shortage

**3.** "Lead out! Wagons west!"

Johnson, each time the wagon train starts off

**4.** WARD BOND (Mormon Elder Wiggs), alluding to an earlier comment by Johnson about his shooting experience, after a successful shoot-out with the villains who hijacked the wagon train: "I thought you never drew on a man."

JOHNSON: "That's right, sir. Only on snakes."

**WALL STREET** (20th Century–Fox, 1987). D: Oliver Stone. S: Oliver Stone, Stanley Weiser.

**1.** "Stick to the fundamentals. That's how IBM and Hilton were built. Good things sometimes take time."

Hal Holbrook (Lou Manheim) to Charlie Sheen (Bud Fox)

**2.** "They're off and running."

Charlie Sheen to himself, referring to the opening of a day on Wall Street

**3.** CHARLIE SHEEN: "It's called pasta now, Dad. Spaghetti's out of date."
MARTIN SHEEN (Carl Fox): "Yeah. So am I."

**4.** "Life all comes down to a few moments. This is one of them."

Charlie Sheen to himself, just before meeting master Wall Street trader Michael Douglas (Gordon Gekko)

**5.** "That's the thing you got to remember about WASPs. They love animals. They can't stand people."

Douglas to Charlie Sheen

**6.** "The most valuable commodity I know of is information. Wouldn't you agree?"

Douglas to Charlie Sheen

**7.** "If you need a friend, get a dog."

Douglas to Charlie Sheen

**8.** "Never knew how poor I was until I started making money."

Douglas to Charlie Sheen

**9.** "You're on a roll, kid. Enjoy it while it lasts 'cause it never does."

Holbrook to Charlie Sheen

**10.** "You and I are the same, Darien. We are smart enough not to buy into the oldest myth running: love. Fiction created by people to keep them from jumping out the window."

Douglas to Daryl Hannah (Darien Taylor)

**11.** "Greed, for lack of a better word, is good. Greed is right. Greed works. Greed clarifies, cuts through, and captures the essence of the evolutionary spirit. Greed, in all of its forms."

*Douglas, in a speech*

**12.** "I don't go to sleep with no whore, and I don't wake up with no whore. That's how I live with myself. I don't know how you do it."

*Martin Sheen to Charlie Sheen*

**13.** "The main thing about money, Bud, it makes you do things you don't want to do."

*Holbrook to Charlie Sheen*

**14.** "As much as I wanted to be Gordon Gekko, I'll always be Bud Fox."

*Charlie Sheen to himself*

**WAR OF THE WORLDS, THE** (Paramount, 1953). D: Byron Haskin. S: Barre Lyndon. Fr: H. G. Wells (novel).

**LAST LINE**
**1.** "After all that men could do had failed, the Martians were destroyed and humanity saved by the littlest things which God in his wisdom had put upon the Earth."

*Narrator Sir Cedric Hardwicke, on the bacteria in Earth's atmosphere that put an end to the Martian invasion*

**WARGAMES** (MGM/UA, 1983). D: John Badham. S: Lawrence Lasker, Walter F. Parkes.

**1.** "Screw the procedure! I want somebody on the goddamn phone before I kill twenty million people."

*Crew member Edward Jahnke, at ICBM base, on carrying through a nuclear strike*

**2.** "There's no way that a high school punk can put a dime in a telephone and break into our system."

*Dabney Coleman (McKittrick), underestimating the ability of teenage hacker Matthew Broderick (David) to play havoc with the nation's system for detecting thermonuclear attack*

**3.** "Why don't I believe you?"
*Coleman, doubting Broderick's story*

**4.** "Extinction is part of the natural order."
*Computer scientist John Wood (Falken), explaining to Broderick that what is happening is inevitable*

**5.** "What kind of an asshole lives on an island and doesn't even have a boat?"
*Broderick, trying to leave Wood's island*

**6.** "You are listening to a machine. Do the world a favor and don't act like one."
*Wood to military personnel putting their trust in the computer he designed*

**7.** "A strange game. The only winning move is not to play. How about a nice game of chess?"
*James Ackerman (Voice of Joshua the Computer), on nuclear war*

**WAY OUT WEST** (Hal Roach/MGM, 1937). D: James W. Horne. S: Charles Rogers, Felix Adler, James Parrott. Fr: Jack Jevne, Charles Rogers (story).

**1.** "Any bird can build a nest, but it isn't every one that can lay an egg."
*Stan Laurel (Himself)*

**2.** LAUREL: "I think we've given the deed to the wrong woman. That's the first mistake we've made since that guy sold us the Brooklyn Bridge."

OLIVER HARDY (*Himself*): "Buying that bridge was no mistake. That's going to be worth a lot of money to us someday."

**WAY WE WERE, THE** (*Columbia, 1973*). D: Sydney Pollack. S: Arthur Laurents, Alvin Sargent (uncredited), David Rayfiel (uncredited). Fr: Arthur Laurents (novel).

**1.** "You make fun of politicians. What else can you do with them?"

Robert Redford (Hubbell Gardiner) to Barbra Streisand (Katie Morosky), exhibiting a less serious approach to politics than she

**2.** "The trouble with some people is they work too hard."

Redford to Streisand

**3.** "Can I ask you a personal question? You smile all the time?"

Streisand to Redford

**4.** REDFORD: "Go get 'em Katie."
STREISAND: "See ya, Hubbell."

Parting words, repeated at their final encounter

**5.** REDFORD, on Streisand's political commitment: "I don't know how you do it."
STREISAND: "I don't know how you can't."

**6.** "You must have gotten one of the two copies sold."

Redford to Streisand, on her having purchased his novel

**7.** " 'In a way, he was like the country he lived in. Everything came too easily to him.' "

Streisand, repeating the opening lines of Redford's college short story

**8.** "Everything in the world that happens does not happen to you personally."

Redford to Streisand, after she chides his friend for joking about FDR at his death

**9.** "You really think you're easy? Compared to what? The Hundred Years' War?"

Redford to Streisand

**10.** REDFORD: "Katie, the day you die, you'll still be a nice Jewish girl."
STREISAND: "Are you still a nice Gentile boy?"
REDFORD: "I never was. I only looked it to you."

**11.** "Best year, 1945 No, '45, '46 . . ."

Redford to Bradford Dillman (J. J.), recalling his years with Streisand

**12.** REDFORD, at their last meeting: "You never give up, do you?"
STREISAND: "Only when I'm absolutely forced to."

**WAYNE'S WORLD** (*Paramount, 1992*). D: Penelope Spheeris. S: Mike Myers, Bonnie Turner, Terry Turner. Fr: Mike Myers (characters).

**1.** "Wayne's World! Wayne's World! Party on! Excellent!"

Mike Myers (Wayne) and Dana Carvey (Garth), introducing their show

**WEST SIDE STORY** (*UA, 1961*). D: Robert Wise, Jerome Robbins. S: Ernest Lehman. Fr: Arthur Laurents (musical play), Jerome Robbins (conception), William Shakespeare (play).

**1.** "You hoodlums don't own these streets, and I've had all the roughhouse I'm gonna put up with around here. If you want to kill each other, kill each other, but you ain't gonna do it on my beat."

*Simon Oakland (Lieutenant Schrank) to the Jets and the Sharks*

**2.** "A gang that don't own the street is nothin'."

*Tony Mordente (Action) to his fellow Jets*

**3.** "I want to hold it like we always held it, with skin. But if they say blades, I say blades. If they say guns, I say guns. I say I want the Jets to be the number one."

*Jets leader Russ Tamblyn (Riff) to his gang, on holding their territory against the Sharks*

**4.** "He's got a rep that's bigger than the whole west side."

*Tamblyn to Jets, on former gang member Richard Beymer (Tony)*

**5.** TAMBLYN, vowing eternal friendship: "Womb to tomb."
BEYMER: "Birth to earth."

**6.** "I have not yet learned how to joke that way. I think now I never will."

*Natalie Wood (Maria) to her beloved Beymer, on joking about romantic matters*

**7.** "I and Velma ain't dumb."

*Gina Trikonis (Graziella), on being called a dumb broad*

**8.** "Top of the evening, Officer Krupke."

*Tamblyn, mockingly, to policeman Bill Bramley (Officer Krupke)*

**9.** "He killed your brother!"

*Jose De Vega (Chino) to Wood, telling her about Beymer's murder of George Chakiris (Bernardo)*

**10.** "But it's not us, it's everything around us."

*Wood to Beymer, on what stands in the way of their love*

**11.** BEYMER, dying, shot by de Vega: "I didn't believe hard enough."
WOOD: "Loving is enough."

**12.** "How do you fire this gun, Chino? Just by pulling this little trigger? How many bullets are left, Chino? Enough for you—and you? All of you! You all killed him, and my brother, and Riff. Not with bullets and guns—with hate. Well, I can kill, too, because now I have hate."

*Wood to assembled Jets and Sharks*

**LAST LINE**
**13.** "Te adoro, Anton."

*Wood to Beymer's body, before the Jets and Sharks carry him away*


**WHAT ABOUT BOB?** (Buena Vista, 1991). D: Frank Oz. S: Tom Schulman. Fr: Alvin Sargent, Laura Zisken (story).

**FIRST LINE**
**1.** "I feel good. I feel great. I feel wonderful."

*Psychiatric patient Bill Murray (Bob Wiley) to himself*

**2.** "There are two types of people in this world. Those who like Neil Diamond, and those who don't."

*Murray to his doctor Richard Dreyfuss (Leo Marvin), on why he's divorced*

**3.** "Is this a bad time?"

*Murray to Dreyfuss, when he finally tracks him down on his vacation*

**4.** "Is this some radical new therapy?"

*Murray to Dreyfuss, when Dreyfuss throws him out*

**5.** "I'm sailing! I'm sailing!"

*Murray, shouting to the world his new ability, although he's strapped to the mast*

**6.** "I treat people as if they were telephones. If I meet somebody who I don't think likes me, I say to myself, 'Bob, this one's just temporarily out of order. You know. Don't break the connection. Just hang up and try again.'"

*Murray to Kathryn Erbe (Anna Marvin)*

**7.** "What about Bob?"

*Charlie Korsmo (Sigmund Marvin), when Dreyfuss apologizes to everyone except Bob, and Julie Hagerty (Fay Marvin), when Dreyfuss takes Bob to the institution*

## WHAT'S LOVE GOT TO DO WITH IT

*(Buena Vista, 1993). D: Brian Gibson. S: Kate Lanier. Fr: Tina Turner, Kurt Loder (autobiography).*

**1.** "Where did a little woman like you get such a big voice?"

*Laurence Fishburne (Ike Turner) to his musical discovery Angela Bassett (Tina Turner)*

**2.** "You sing like a man. I mean you are a woman, you are a woman, any man can see that, but, girl, it's like you got your own particular way of getting a song out of you."

*Fishburne to Bassett*

**3.** "I got dreams that's bigger than St. Louis."

*Fishburne to Bassett*

**4.** "It ain't cool till I say it's cool."

*Fishburne to Bassett*

## WHAT'S UP, DOC? *(Warner Bros., 1972). D: Peter Bogdanovich. S: Buck Henry, David Newman, Robert Benton. Fr: Peter Bogdanovich (story).*

**1.** MADELINE KAHN (*Eunice Burns*) to her fiancé: "As the years go by, romance fades, and something else takes its place. Do you know what that is?"

RYAN O'NEAL (*Professor Howard Bannister*): "Senility."

**2.** O'NEAL, in horror during a car chase: "What are you doing? This is a one-way street!"

STREISAND (*Judy Maxwell*): "I'm only going one way."

**3.** "That's the dumbest thing I ever heard."

*Ryan O'Neal, after Barbra Streisand quotes the most famous line from his earlier movie* Love Story: *"Love means never having to say you're sorry"*

### LAST LINE

**4.** "Th-th-that's all, folks!"

*Porky Pig, signing off*

## WHEN HARRY MET SALLY . . . *(Columbia, 1989). D: Rob Reiner. S: Nora Ephron.*

**1.** "You realize of course that we can never be friends."

*Billy Crystal (Harry Burns) to Meg Ryan (Sally Allbright)*

**2.** "No man can be friends with a woman that he finds attractive. He always wants to have sex with her."

*Crystal to Ryan*

**3.** "Someone is staring at you in Personal Growth."

*Carrie Fisher (Marie) to Ryan, about Crystal in a bookstore*

**4.** "There are two kinds of women: high maintenance and low maintenance. You're the worst kind. You're high maintenance but you think you're low maintenance."

*Crystal to Ryan*

**5.** "Most women at one time or another have faked it."

*Ryan to Crystal*

**6.** "I'll have what she's having."

*Estelle Reiner (Customer) to waitress in coffee shop, ordering the meal eaten by Ryan, who has just faked an orgasm*

**7.** BRUNO KIRBY (*Jess*): "Emily is terrific."
CRYSTAL: "Yeah. Of course, when I asked her where she was when Kennedy was shot, she said, 'Ted Kennedy was shot?'"

**8.** RYAN, lamenting old age: "I'm gonna be forty."
CRYSTAL: "When?"
RYAN: "Someday."

**9.** "You have all your videotapes alphabetized and on index cards?"

*Crystal to Ryan*

**10.** "I love that you get cold when it's seventy-one degrees out. I love that it takes you an hour and a half to order a sandwich. I love that you get a little crinkle above your nose when you're looking at me like I'm nuts. I love that after I spend a day with you I can still smell your perfume on my clothes. And I love that you are the last person I want to talk to before I go to sleep at night."

*Crystal to Ryan*

**11.** CRYSTAL, on how long it took them to get married: "It only took three months."
RYAN: "Twelve years and three months."

**WHEN WORLDS COLLIDE** *(Paramount, 1951). D: Rudolph Maté. S: Sydney Boehm. Fr: Edwin Balmer, Philip Wylie (novel).*

**1.** WASTE ANYTHING EXCEPT TIME
TIME IS OUR SHORTEST MATERIAL

*Sign at the plant where the rocket ship is being built to rescue a few survivors from Earth's destruction*

**2.** "Never mind. Good air or bad, it's the only place we can go."

*Richard Derr (Dave Randall), on whether they should test the air on the new world before venturing out*

**3.** "The first day on the new world had begun . . ."

*End title, as the survivors walk out onto the new world*

**WHERE ANGELS GO . . . TROUBLE FOLLOWS** *(Columbia, 1968). D: James Nelson. S: Blanche Hanalis. Fr: Jane Trahey (characters).*

**1.** "You're looking at one dragon St. George isn't going to kill."

*Rosalind Russell (Mother Superior Simplicia) on young radical nun Stella Stevens (Sister George)*

**2.** "Anyone who's coped with adolescent girls for twenty years can cope with anything."

*Russell, who has been running a girls' school for that long*

**3.** "I pray a lot."

*Russell, on how she stays patient*

**WHERE EAGLES DARE** (MGM, 1968). D: Brian G. Hutton. S: Alistair MacLean.

**1.** "Gentlemen, see you after the war."

*World War II British secret agent Richard Burton (John Smith) to his colleagues, upon giving himself up, only to escape in a short time*

**2.** "As the saying goes, what do we do now?"

*American soldier Clint Eastwood (Lt. Morris Schaffer) to Burton, when they are trapped*

**3.** "Major, right now you've got me about as confused as I'd ever hoped to be."

*Eastwood to Burton, after a scene in which loyalties and identities change very quickly; Eastwood seems to be speaking for the audience*

**WHERE THE BOYS ARE** (MGM, 1960). D: Henry Levin. S: George Wells. Fr: Glendon Swarthout (novel).

**1.** "Should a girl or should she not play house before marriage?"

*Dolores Hart (Merrit Andrews) to her college professor Dr. Rauch, on the big question facing young women today*

**2.** "Dr. Rauch suggested that you might be overly concerned with the problem of sex."

*College dean to Hart*

**3.** "All I want is to meet a boy with feet as big as mine."

*Tall woman Paula Prentiss (Tuggle Carpenter) to her three traveling companions, en route to Florida*

**4.** FORT LAUDERDALE OR I'LL KILL MYSELF

*Sandwich sign on hitchhiker Jim Hutton (TV Thompson)*

**5.** "That's a lot of girl, Tuggle."

*Hutton to Prentiss, when she stands up and announces she is five feet, ten and a half inches without stockings*

**6.** "I'd rather starve than go home without an even tan."

*Prentiss to her traveling companions*

**7.** "Are you a good girl, Tuggle?"

*Hutton to Prentiss*

**8.** "Experience. That's what separates the girls from the Girl Scouts."

*George Hamilton (Ryder Smith) to Hart*

**9.** "That's the family putt-putt."

*Hamilton, pointing to his family's yacht*

**10.** "Ivy Leaguers never argue. They discuss."

*Hart to Prentiss, on whether she has argued with Hamilton*

**11.** "Hey, Mer, you want to hear the big joke? They weren't even Yalies."

*Yvette Mimieux (Melanie Coleman) to Hart, on the boys who sexually assaulted her*

**12.** "No girl is when she's in love. Or what she thinks is love."

*Hart to Hamilton, on whether she has a grip on herself*

**WHERE'S POPPA?** (UA, 1970). D: Carl Reiner. S: Robert Klane. Fr: Robert Klane (novel).

**1.** "Where's Poppa?"

*Ruth Gordon's (Mrs. Hocheiser) constant ques-*

tion of George Segal (Gordon Hocheiser), even though Poppa has been dead for a long time

**2.** "I'm not going to put her in a home. I'm going to kill her."

*Segal, exasperated at how Gordon has ruined his love life*

**WHITE CHRISTMAS** (Paramount, 1954). D: Michael Curtiz. S: Norman Krasna, Norman Panama, Melvin Frank.

**1.** DANNY KAYE (*Phil Davis*), as usual, reminding Bing Crosby (Bob Wallace) of the time he saved his life during World War II: "Let's face it, you're a lonely, miserable man. . . . And you're unhappy too. And when you're unhappy, I'm unhappy. After all, I feel a strong sense of responsibility to you, Bob, ever since the day I—"
BING CROSBY (*Bob Wallace*): "Oh, no, not again with that life-saving bit."

**2.** "My dear partner, when what's left of you gets around to what's left to be gotten, what's left to be gotten won't be worth getting whatever it is you've got left."

*Kaye, warning Crosby not to delay getting married*

**3.** "I want you to get married. I want you to have nine children. And if you only spend five minutes a day with each kid, that's forty-five minutes, and I'd at least have time to go out and get a massage or something."

*Kaye to Crosby*

**4.** "Let's just say we're doing it for a pal in the Army."

*Crosby, giving Kaye a reason for doing a favor for an Army buddy*

**5.** "What does it matter? They're both famous."

Vera-Ellen (Judy), on which member of the team of Wallace and Davis (Crosby and Kaye) will be romantically interested in Rosemary Clooney (Betty)

**6.** "Maybe it isn't only the music."

*Kaye to Vera-Ellen, suggesting an alternative reason for their getting confused while dancing*

**7.** "Well, that sounds very Vermonty. Should be beautiful this time of the year in Vermont, all that snow and everything."

*Crosby, paraphrasing Vera-Ellen's earlier line to Kaye, and Kaye's earlier line to Crosby, as he gets shanghaied into going to Vermont*

**8.** "Well, to put it in one sentence, people don't expect a major general to carry firewood."

*Dean Jagger (General Waverly), Kaye's and Crosby's former commanding officer, on why he hasn't made it known that he is now running a Vermont inn*

**9.** CROSBY, remembering Jagger during the war: "We ate and then he ate. We slept and then he slept."
KAYE: "Yeah. And then he woke up and nobody slept for forty-eight hours."

**10.** "You weren't any good as privates."

*Jagger to Crosby and Kaye, when they say they wouldn't be any good as generals*

**11.** "Well, you're not exactly Superman, but you're awfully available."

*Vera-Ellen, on pretending to get engaged to Kaye*

**12.** "You know, in some ways you're far superior to my cocker spaniel."

*Kaye, after kissing Vera-Ellen*

**13.** "Remember then, your objective is Pine Tree, Vermont. Synchronize your watches then for Operation Waverly."

*Crosby, on television, inviting former Army comrades to come to honor Jagger at his inn on Christmas Eve*

**14.** JAGGER, to his housekeeper MARY WICKES (*Emma*): "I got along very well in the Army without you."

WICKES: "It took fifteen thousand men to take my place."

**15.** CROSBY, presenting the reunited troops to Jagger: "Troops are ready for inspection, sir."

OFFICER: "Just routine, sir."

**16.** "You're soft, you're soppy, you're unruly, you're undisciplined—and I never saw anything look so wonderful in my whole life. Thank you all."

*Jagger to the troops*

**LAST LINES**
**17.** CROSBY, to audience at Christmas Eve show: "Merry Christmas!"

AUDIENCE: "Merry Christmas!"

**WHITE HEAT** *(Warner Bros., 1949). D: Raoul Walsh. S: Ivan Goff, Ben Roberts. Fr: Virginia Kellogg (story).*

**1.** "You got a good memory for names. Too good."

*James Cagney (Arthur Cody Jarrett) to Murray Leonard (Train Engineer), just before he kills him*

**2.** "Top of the world, son."

*Margaret Wycherly (Ma Jarrett) to Cagney, using a phrase he will repeat throughout the film*

**3.** "Don't know what I'd do without ya, Ma."

*Cagney to Wycherly, suggesting a perhaps uncomfortably close union of criminal minds*

**4.** Cagney's wife VIRGINIA MAYO (*Verna Jarrett*): "I look good in a mink coat, honey."

CAGNEY: "You look good in a shower curtain."

**5.** "College degree, lovable personality, and I spend most of my time in prison."

*Edmond O'Brien (Hank Fallon/Vic Pardo) to Marshall Bradford (Chief of Police), on his job in undercover work*

**6.** "Forget it, Parker, accidents will happen."

*Cagney to Paul Guilfoyle (Roy Parker), who pulls lever on prison machinery, nearly causing "accident" for Cagney*

**7.** "Ask him how my mother is."

*Cagney, asking a fateful question to inmate at mess hall*

**8.** "Dead?"

*Cagney, hearing of his mother's death and flying into a frenzy of grief*

**9.** "All I ever had was Ma."

*Cagney to O'Brien, confiding about Wycherly*

**10.** "A copper? A copper, how do you like that, boys?"

*Cagney to his crew, upon discovering O'Brien's identity*

**11.** "They think they've got Cody Jarrett. But they haven't got Cody Jarrett. Ya hear? They haven't got him."

*Cagney to gang member Robert Osterloh (Tommy Ryley), referring to the manhunt going on around them*

**12.** "Come 'n' get me!"

*Cagney to policeman, as he climbs oil tanks to escape the law*

**13.** "Made it, Ma, top of the world!"

*Cagney to Wycherly, in spirit, just before the oil tanks blow and he dies*

**LAST LINE**

**14.** "Cody Jarrett. He finally got to the top of the world, and it blew right up in his face."

*O'Brien, on Cagney*

**WHO FRAMED ROGER RABBIT** *(Buena Vista, 1988). D: Robert Zemeckis. S: Jeffrey Price, Peter S. Seaman. Fr: Gary K. Wolf (novel, Who Censored Roger Rabbit?).*

**1.** "I'm not bad, I'm just drawn that way."

*Kathleen Turner (Voice of Jessica Rabbit)*

**WHOOPEE!** *(UA, 1930). D: Thornton Free-land. S: Thornton Freeland.*

**1.** "Why do you make overtures to me when I need intermissions so badly?"

*Eddie Cantor (Henry Williams) to nurse who's flirting with him*

**WHO'S AFRAID OF VIRGINIA WOOLF?** *(Warner Bros., 1966). D: Mike Nichols. S: Ernest Lehman. Fr: Edward Albee (play).*

**1.** "I swear, if you existed, I'd divorce you."

*Elizabeth Taylor (Martha) to Richard Burton (George)*

**2.** "Martha, will you show her where we keep the, er, euphemism?"

*Burton, asking Taylor to direct Sandy Dennis (Honey) to the bathroom*

**3.** "There isn't any abomination award going that you haven't won."

*Burton to Taylor*

**WILD BUNCH, THE** *(Warner Bros.–Seven Arts, 1969). D: Sam Peckinpah. S: Walon Green, Sam Peckinpah. Fr: Walon Green, Roy N. Sickner (story).*

**1.** "We've got to start thinking beyond our guns. Those days are closing fast."

*William Holden (Pike Bishop) to his gang*

**WILD ONE, THE** *(Columbia, 1953). D: Laslo Benedek. S: John Paxton. Fr: Frank Rooney (story).*

**1.** "This is a shocking story. It could never take place in most American towns—but it did in this one. It is a public challenge not to let it happen again."

*Opening title*

**2.** "Well, what do you do? I mean, do you just ride around or do you go on some sort of picnic or something?"

*Mary Murphy (Kathie) to biker leader Marlon Brando (Johnny), on his gang's activities*

**3.** WOMAN IN BAR: "Hey, Johnny, what are you rebelling against?"
BRANDO: "What've you got?"

**4.** BYSTANDER, watching Brando and Lee Marvin (Chino) fight: "What happened? What are they fighting about?"
WILLIAM YEDDER (Jimmy): "Don't know. Don't know themselves probably."

**5.** "I said I don't make no deal with no cop."

*Brando to Jay C. Flippen (Sheriff Singer)*

**6.** GANG MEMBER: "Hey, Johnny, what's the pitch, we leavin'?"

BRANDO, drinking his beer: "Not just yet."

**7.** "What do you want me to do, send you some flowers?"

*Brando to old girlfriend Yvonne Doughty (Britches), who is still pining for him*

**8.** "You think you're too good for me? Nobody's too good for me. Anybody thinks they're too good for me I make sure I knock 'em over sometime."

*Brando*

**9.** "My old man used to hit harder than that."

*Brando to guys beating him up*

**10.** FLIPPEN, after Brando is given a break: "You could at least say thank you."

MURPHY: "It's all right. He doesn't know how."

**WILSON** *(20th Century–Fox, 1944). D: Henry King. S: Lamar Trotti.*

**1.** "I'm a schoolteacher, which must make me something of an idiot in the eyes of a lot of good people."

*Alexander Knox (Woodrow Wilson) to Thurston Hall (Senator Ed Jones), when he is asked to run for governor of New Jersey*

**2.** "Have I ever done anything foolish without asking your permission?"

*Knox to his wife Ruth Nelson (Edith Wilson)*

**3.** "I'm not so concerned with what the Germans do, as I am with our own responsibility, which is to keep out of this war if possible."

*Knox, on why he won't revenge the sinking of the* Lusitania

**4.** "There's a spotlight on this house. Everyone who comes here is observed and discussed. Everything I say is quoted, sometimes even correctly."

*Knox to Fitzgerald, on the White House*

**5.** "Waiting for election returns is like a hen sitting on a nest, except that the hen uses better judgment than a politician. She never cackles until after she's laid the egg."

*Charles Coburn (Professor Henry Holmes) to Knox*

**6.** "America has but two choices, gentlemen. It must accept the League of Nations, or live with a gun in its hand. It's for the people to decide."

*Knox to the Senate*

**7.** "I'm not one of those who has the slightest anxiety about the eventual triumph of the things I've stood for. The fight's just begun. The dream of a world united against the awful waters of war is too deeply imbedded in the hearts of men everywhere."

*Knox to Jamesson Shade (Secretary Payne), on the League of Nations*

**8.** "Our great hope lies, not in me, or in any other individual, but in the power of right."

*Knox to Vincent Price (William McAdoo)*

**9.** "If anybody tries to tell you that universal peace is just an idle dream, tell him he's a liar. Say your President said that you're fighting this war so there won't have to be any more wars."

*Knox to doughboys*

**10.** "I understand Teddy Roosevelt says you're the most incompetent man to have occupied the office, Woodrow. Worse even than Thomas Jefferson."

*Coburn to Knox*

**WITNESS** *(Paramount, 1985). D: Peter Weir. S: Earl W. Wallace, William Kelley. Fr: William Kelley, Earl W. Wallace, Pamela Wallace (story).*

**1.** "So, first time to the big city. You'll see so many things."

*Alexander Godunov (Daniel Hochleitner) to Lukas Haas (Samuel), on his trip to Philadelphia*

**2.** "Book. John Book."

*Harrison Ford (John Book), introducing self to Kelly McGillis (Rachel) and son Haas*

**3.** "I just don't like my son spending all this time with a man who carries a gun and goes around whacking people."

*McGillis to Ford, expressing disapproval*

**4.** "We're all very happy that you're going to live, John Book. We didn't know what we were going to do with you if you died."

*McGillis to Ford, recuperating from a gunshot wound and hiding among the Amish*

**5.** "This gun of the hand is for the taking of human life. We believe it is wrong to take life. That is only for God."

*Jan Rubes (Eli Lapp) to Haas, upon encountering Ford's gun*

**6.** "How do I look? I mean, do I look Amish?"
*Ford to McGillis, on his Amish disguise*

**7.** RUBES, on Ford's first time milking a cow: "You never had your hands on a teat before?"
FORD: "Not one this big."

**8.** "Oh, oh, this is great. This, this is the best."

*Ford to McGillis, upon hearing Sam Cooke on a late-night radio station*

**9.** "I have committed no sin."
*McGillis to Rubes, about herself and Ford*

**10.** "If we'd made love last night, I'd have to stay. Or you'd have to leave."
*Ford to McGillis*

**11.** RUBES, on confronting tourists who taunt Godunov: "It's not our way."
FORD: "But it's my way."

**12.** "He's from Ohio. My cousin."
*Godunov to town resident expressing disapproval of the violent Ford*

**13.** "He's going back to his world. Where he belongs. He knows it. And you know it, too."
*Rubes to McGillis*

**LAST LINE**
**14.** "You be careful out among them English."

*Rubes to Ford, in parting, repeating the advice he gave McGillis at the beginning of the film*

**WITNESS FOR THE PROSECUTION** *(UA, 1957). D: Billy Wilder. S: Billy Wilder, Harry Kurnitz, Larry Marcus. Fr: Agatha Christie (novel, play).*

**1.** "If I'd known how much you talked, I'd never have come out of my coma."

*Charles Laughton (Sir Wilfrid Robarts) to his nurse Elsa Lanchester (Miss Plimsoll)*

**2.** "Might as well get a bigger box, more mothballs, and put me away, too."

*Laughton, complaining at being forced to give up criminal law*

**3.** "Young man, you may or may not have murdered a middle-aged woman, but you've certainly saved the life of an elderly barrister."

*Laughton, thanking Tyrone Power (Leonard Stephen Vole) for sneaking him a cigar*

**4.** "I'm constantly surprised that women's hats do not provoke more murders."

*Laughton, on hearing about the murder victim's hat*

**5.** "I never faint, because I'm not sure that I will fall gracefully, and I never use smelling salts, because they puff up the eyes."

*Marlene Dietrich (Christine "Helm" Vole), putting to rest fears that she's the fainting type*

**6.** "One can get very tired of gratitude."

*Dietrich*

**7.** "He's a shiftless, scheming rascal, but I'm not antagonistic to him."

*Una O'Connor (Janet MacKenzie), on the witness stand, giving her view of Power*

**8.** "My dear Miss MacKenzie, considering the rubbish that is being talked nowadays, you are missing very little."

*Judge Francis Compton, on O'Connor's lack of a hearing aid*

**9.** "Wanna kiss me, ducky?"

*Dietrich, putting on an act for Laughton*

**10.** "This happens to be a bill from my tailor for a pair of extremely becoming Bermuda shorts."

*Laughton, toying with Dietrich in the courtroom*

**11.** "Wilfrid the Fox—that's what we call him and that's what he is."

*Lanchester, on Laughton*

**12.** "We've disposed of the gallows, but there's still that banana peel, somewhere under somebody's foot."

*Laughton, unsatisfied that the whole truth has been told*

**13.** "I never thought you British could get so emotional, especially in a public place."

*Dietrich*

**14.** "Killed him? She executed him."

*Laughton, pronouncing his judgment on the final homicide*

**LAST LINE**
**15.** "Sir Wilfrid—you've forgotten your brandy!"

*Lanchester, retrieving Laughton's thermos bottle*

**WIZARD OF OZ, THE** *(MGM, 1939). D: Victor Fleming. S: Noel Langley, Florence Ryerson, Edgar Allen Woolf. Fr: L. Frank Baum (novel).*

**1.** "For nearly forty years this story has given faithful service to the Young in Heart; and Time has been powerless to put its kindly philosophy out of fashion. To those of you who have been faithful to it in return—and to the Young in Heart—we dedicate this picture."

*Opening title*

**2.** "Toto, I've a feeling we're not in Kansas anymore."

*Judy Garland (Dorothy)*

**3.** "I'll get you, my pretty, and your little dog, too!"

*Margaret Hamilton (The Wicked Witch) to Garland*

**4.** "I've held that axe up for ages."
*Jack Haley (The Tin Woodsman)*

**5.** "Poppies . . . poppies . . . poppies will put them to sleep. . . ."
*Hamilton, casting a spell*

**6.** "Unusual weather we're havin', ain't it?"
*Bert Lahr (The Cowardly Lion), waking up in a snowfall in the poppy field*

**7.** SURRENDER DOROTHY
*Words written in the sky in smoke by Hamilton on her broomstick*

**8.** "Somebody pulled my tail!"
*Lahr, bawling after pulling his own tail*

**9.** I'D TURN BACK IF I WERE YOU!
*Sign on the road to the Witch's Castle*

**10.** "I do believe in spooks, I do believe in spooks, I do, I do, I do, I do, I do, I do!"
*Lahr, in the Haunted Forest*

**11.** "They tore my legs off and they threw them over there. Then they took my chest out and they threw it over there."
*Ray Bolger (The Scarecrow), explaining how the winged monkeys treated him*

**12.** "These things must be done delicately, or you hurt the spell."
*Hamilton, pondering how to get the ruby slippers off Dorothy*

**13.** LAHR, struggling to climb the hill to the Witch's castle: "I-I-I hope my strength holds out."
    HALEY, hanging on to Lahr's tail: "I hope your *tail* holds out!"

**14.** "I'm melting! Melting! Oh, what a world! What a world!"
*Hamilton, melting after being drenched by a bucket of water*

**15.** "Pay no attention to that man behind the curtain!"
*Frank Morgan (The Wizard), on being exposed by Terry (Toto) pulling aside the curtain*

**16.** GARLAND: "Oh, you're a very bad man!"
    MORGAN: "Oh, no, my dear, I . . . I'm a very good man—I'm just a very bad wizard."

**17.** "Well . . . I think that it . . . that it wasn't enough just to want to see Uncle Henry and Auntie Em . . . and it's that if I ever go looking for my heart's desire again I won't look any further than my own backyard. Because if it isn't there, I never really lost it to begin with."
*Garland, explaining what she's learned*

**18.** "There's no place like home. . . . There's no place like home. . . ."
*Garland, repeating the magic phrase that will take her home*

**LAST LINE**
**19.** "Oh, but, anyway, Toto, we're home, home, and this is my room, and you're all here, and I'm not going to leave here ever, ever again, because I love you all, and—oh, Auntie Em, there's no place like home."
*Garland*

**WOLF** (Columbia, 1994). D: Mike Nichols. S: Jim Harrison, Wesley Strict.

**1.** "Don't look so scared."
*Werewolf Jack Nicholson (Will Randall) to Michelle Pfeiffer (Laura Alden)*

**2.** "Just marking my territory."

*Nicholson to a surprised bystander in a men's room*

**WOLF MAN, THE** (Universal, 1941). D: George Waggner. S: Curt Siodmak.

**1.** "Even a man who is pure in heart,
And says his prayers by night,
May become a wolf when the wolfbane blooms
And the autumn moon is bright."

*Poem recited by Evelyn Ankers (Gwen Conliffe), Claude Rains (Sir John Talbot), and Fay Helm (Jenny Williams), though not by gypsy Maria Ouspenskaya (Maleva)*

**2.** "You policemen are always in such a hurry, as if dead men hadn't all eternity."

*Rains to constable Ralph Bellamy (Capt. Paul Montford)*

**3.** "Well, there's something very tragic about that man, and I'm sure that nothing but harm will come to you through him."

*Patric Knowles (Frank Andrews) to Ankers about Lon Chaney, Jr. (Larry Talbot, the Wolf Man)*

**4.** "Whoever is bitten by a werewolf and lives becomes a werewolf himself."

*Ouspenskaya, telling Chaney about his disorder*

**5.** "Go now and heaven help you."

*Ouspenskaya to Chaney, after inspecting the wound where a werewolf bit him*

**6.** "It's a technical expression for something very simple: the good and evil in every man's soul."

*Rains to his son Chaney, on lycanthropy, or werewolfism*

**7.** "The way you walked was thorny, through no fault of your own. But as the rain enters the soil, the river enters the sea, so tears run to a predestined end. Your suffering is over. Now you will find peace for eternity."

*Ouspenskaya, over Chaney's corpse, paraphrasing her earlier speech over the corpse of werewolf Bela Lugosi (Bela)*

**WOMAN OF THE YEAR** (MGM, 1942). D: George Stevens. S: Ring Lardner, Jr., Michael Kanin.

**1.** "You know, it's too bad I'm not covering this dinner of yours tonight, because I've got an angle that would really be sensational: The outstanding woman of the year isn't a woman at all."

*Spencer Tracy (Sam Craig) to Katharine Hepburn (Tess Harding)*

**WOMEN, THE** (MGM, 1939). D: George Cukor. S: Anita Loos, Jane Murfin. Fr: Clare Boothe (play).

**1.** JOAN FONTAINE (*Peggy Day*): "I wish I could make a little money writing the way you do."
FLORENCE NASH (*Nancy Blake*): "If you wrote the way I do, that's just what you'd make."

**2.** "She's got those eyes that run up and down men like a searchlight."

*Dennie Moore (Olga), about Joan Crawford (Crystal Allen)*

**3.** "Mary, in many ways your father was an exceptional man. That, unfortunately, was not one of them."

*Lucile Watson (Mrs. Moorehead) to her daughter Norma Shearer (Mary Haines), discussing infidelity*

**4.** "But we women are so much more sensible. When we tire of ourselves, we change the way we do our hair or hire a new cook or—or decorate the house. I suppose a man could do over his office, but he never thinks of anything so simple."

*Watson to Shearer, on why men have affairs*

**5.** "Oh, and one more piece of motherly advice: don't confide in your girlfriends. . . . If you let them advise you, they'll see to it in the name of friendship that you lose your husband and your home."

*Watson to Shearer*

**6.** CRAWFORD, on meeting male customers at the perfume counter where she works: "I'm afraid when they come to *this* counter they have other women on their minds."
ROSALIND RUSSELL (*Sylvia Fowler*): "Hmm, I shouldn't think you'd let that disturb you."

**7.** "You know, the first man that can think up a good explanation how he can be in love with his wife *and* another woman is going to win that prize they're always giving out in Sweden."

*Mary Cecil (Maggie)*

**8.** "L'amour, l'amour. Toujours l'amour."

*The often-married Mary Boland's (Countess DeLove) favorite phrase*

**9.** "Reno's full women who have their pride, sweetheart. It's a pretty chilly exchange for the guy you're stuck on."

*Paulette Goddard (Miriam Aarons) to Fontaine, who has said she can't go back to her husband, because she has her pride*

**10.** "Well, what the heck! A woman's compromised the day she's born."

*Goddard on compromise*

**11.** "I'm doing a reconstruction job on Howard Fowler that makes Boulder Dam look like an eggcup."

*Goddard, on what it's like being married to Russell's former husband*

**12.** "I've had two years to grow claws, Mother—jungle red!"

*Shearer, referring to the women's favorite nail color*

**13.** "There's a name for you ladies, but it isn't used in high society—outside of a kennel."

*Crawford*

**LAST LINE**
**14.** "No pride at all. That's a luxury a woman in love can't afford."

*Shearer, on her lack of pride as she goes to rejoin her unfaithful but repentant husband*

**WORKING GIRL** (20th Century–Fox, 1988). D: Mike Nichols. S: Kevin Wade.

**1.** "Six thousand dollars? It's not even leather!"

*Joan Cusack (Cyn), expressing shock to Melanie Griffith (Tess McGill) about the price of one of Sigourney Weaver's (Katherine Parker's) dresses*

**2.** "You're the first woman I've seen at one of these damn things that dresses like a woman, not like a woman thinks a man would dress if he was a woman."

*Harrison Ford (Jack Trainer) to Griffith, at a business function*

**3.** "I have a head for business and a bod for sin."

   *Griffith to Ford*

**4.** "Sometimes I sing and dance around the house in my underwear. Doesn't make me Madonna. Never will."

   *Cusack, on Griffith's attempts to imitate Weaver*

**LAST LINE**

**5.** "Cyn? Guess where I am."

   *Griffith, on the phone to friend Cusack, having been assigned to an executive office*

**WUTHERING HEIGHTS** *(Samuel Goldwyn/UA, 1939).* D: William Wyler. S: Ben Hecht, Charles MacArthur. Fr: Emily Brontë *(novel).*

**1.** "There is a force that brings them back, if their hearts were wild enough in life."

   *Flora Robson (Ellen Dean), on the dead*

**2.** "Nothing's real down there. Our life is here."

   *Laurence Olivier (Heathcliff) to Merle Oberon (Catherine Earnshaw), when they stand together on the rocks high above Wuthering Heights*

**3.** "Go on, Heathcliff. Run away. Bring me back the world."

   *Oberon to Olivier, when they are caught looking over a wall into David Niven's (Edgar Linton's) house*

**4.** "The moors and I will never change. Don't you, Cathy."

   *Olivier to Oberon*

**5.** "Smell the heather. Heathcliff, fill my arms with heather. All they can hold."

   *Oberon to Olivier*

**6.** "I dreamt I went to Heaven, and Heaven didn't seem to be my home."

   *Oberon to Robson*

**7.** "Whatever our souls are made of, his and mine are the same."

   *Oberon to Robson, on Olivier*

**8.** "I am Heathcliff."

   *Oberon to Robson, asserting her bond to Olivier*

**9.** "I've just bought Wuthering Heights."

   *Olivier to Oberon and Niven, after Olivier has returned a rich man to find that Oberon has married Niven*

**10.** "If you ever looked at me once with what I know is in you, I would be your slave. Cathy, if your heart were only stronger than your dull fear of God and the world, I would live silently contented in your shadow."

   *Olivier to Oberon*

**11.** "Why did God give me life? What is it but hunger and pain?"

   *Olivier to Oberon*

**12.** "If I could only hold you till we were both dead."

   *Oberon to Olivier, on her deathbed*

**13.** "What do they know of Heaven or Hell, Cathy, who know nothing of life?"

   *Oliver to Oberon, on her deathbed*

**14.** "Haunt me then. Haunt your murderer. I know that ghosts have wandered on the Earth. Be with me always. Take any form.

Drive me mad. Only do not leave me in this dark alone where I cannot find you. I cannot live without my life. I cannot die without my soul."

*Olivier to Oberon, who is on her deathbed*

**YANKEE DOODLE DANDY** *(Warner Bros.–First National, 1942). D: Michael Curtiz. S: Robert Buckner, Edmund Joseph. Fr: Robert Buckner (story).*

**1.** "My mother thanks you. My father thanks you. My sister thanks you. And I thank you."

*James Cagney's (George M. Cohan's) sign-off line to audience*

**YELLOW SUBMARINE** *(UK: UA, 1968). D: George Dunning. S: Lee Minoff, Al Brodax, Erich Segal, Jack Mendelsohn. Fr: Lee Minoff (story), John Lennon, Paul McCartney (song).*

**FIRST LINE**
**1.** "Once upon a time, or maybe twice, there was an unearthly paradise called Pepperland."

*Narrator*

**2.** "No, Your Blueness."

*Dick Emery (Max) saying "Yes" to Paul Angelus (Chief Blue Meanie), in a land where "No" is the only answer permitted*

**3.** "Ad hoc, ad loc, and quid pro quo. So little time, so much to know."

*Dick Emery (as the Nowhere Man), saying his favorite rhyme*

**YENTL** *(UK: MGM/UA, 1983). D: Barbra Streisand. S: Barbra Streisand, Jack Rosenthal. Fr: Isaac Bashevis Singer (short story, "Yentl, the Yeshiva Boy").*

**1.** "You think the Angel of Death will be frightened away by cough medicine?"

*Nehemiah Persoff (Reb Mendel)*

**2.** "I trust God will understand. I'm not so sure about the neighbors."

*Barbra Streisand (Yentl) to Amy Irving (Hadass), when teaching her the Talmud*

**3.** "Husband and wife can be friends?"

*Irving, expressing surprise*

**YOU CAN'T CHEAT AN HONEST MAN** *(Universal, 1939). D: George Marshall. S: George Marion, Jr., Richard Mack, Everett Freeman. Fr: Charles Bogle (W. C. Fields) (story).*

**1.** "Keep your hands off my lunch, will you?"

*W. C. Fields (Larson E. Whipsnade)*

**2.** "Don't telegraph—*write*."

*Fields*

**YOU CAN'T TAKE IT WITH YOU** *(Columbia, 1938). D: Frank Capra. S: Robert Riskin. Fr: George S. Kaufman, Moss Hart (play).*

**1.** "Everybody over at our place does just what he wants to do."

*Lionel Barrymore (Martin Vanderhoff), head of a family of individualists*

**2.** "The same one that takes care of the lilies of the field, Mr. Poppins. Except that we toil a little, spin a little, have a barrel of fun. If you want to, come on over and be a lily."

*Barrymore to Donald Meek (Mr. Poppins), on who takes care of his family*

**3.** "Lincoln said, 'With malice toward none, with charity to all.' Nowadays, they say, 'Think the way I do, or I'll bomb the daylights out of you.'"

*Barrymore*

**4.** "Anytime I get an impulse to buy you a present, that's your birthday."

*Jean Arthur (Alice Sycamore) to Barrymore*

**5.** "I don't believe in it."

*Barrymore, on why he's never paid income tax*

**6.** "Confidentially, she stinks."

*Ballet teacher Mischa Auer (Kolenkhov) to Barrymore, about his student Ann Miller (Essie Carmichael)*

**7.** "Living with them must be like living in a world Walt Disney might have thought of."

*James Stewart (Tony Kirby) to Arthur, after meeting the family*

**8.** "You ought to hear Grandfather on that subject. You know, he says most people nowadays are run by fear. . . . So, he kind of taught all of us not to be afraid of anything, and to do what we want to do, and well, it's kind of fun anyway."

*Arthur to Stewart*

**9.** "Maybe it'll stop you trying to be so desperate about making more money than you can ever use. You can't take it with you, Mr. Kirby. So what good is it? As near as I can see, the only thing you can take with you is the love of your friends."

*Barrymore to Edward Arnold (Anthony Kirby)*

**LAST LINE**

**10.** "We've all got our health, and as far as anything else is concerned, we still leave that up to you. Thank you."

*Barrymore, saying grace*

**YOU ONLY LIVE TWICE** (UK: UA, 1967). D: Lewis Gilbert. S: Roald Dahl, Harry Jack Bloom. Fr: Ian Fleming (novel).

**1.** Female villain who has captured SEAN CONNERY (James Bond): "I've got you now." CONNERY: "Well, enjoy yourself."

**2.** "You only live twice, Mr. Bond."

*Donald Pleasence (Ernst Blofeld), threatening Connery, who was believed to be dead*

**YOUNG FRANKENSTEIN** (20th Century–Fox, 1974). D: Mel Brooks. S: Gene Wilder, Mel Brooks. Fr: Mary Shelley (novel, Frankenstein).

**1.** "That's Fronk-en-steen."

*Gene Wilder (Dr. Frederick Frankenstein), correcting student who pronounces his name "Frankenstein"*

**2.** "Not on the lips."

*Madeline Kahn, refusing a good-bye kiss from Wilder so as not to smear her lipstick*

**3.** WILDER, inadvertently lapsing into a song parody on arriving at a train station in Transylvania: "Pardon me, boy. Is this the Transylvania station?"

SHOESHINE BOY: "Ja, ja, Track twenty-nine. Oh—can I give you a shine?"

**4.** "No, it's pronounced Eye-gor."

*Marty Feldman (Igor), correcting Wilder's pro-nunciation of his name*

**5.** "What hump?"

*Feldman, after Wilder offers to do surgery to correct his hump*

**6.** WILDER, as he listens to door knockers while hoisting TERI GARR (*Inga*) down from a wagon: "What knockers."
GARR: "Oh, thank you, Doctor."

**7.** "I am Frau Blucher."

*Cloris Leachman (Frau Blucher), introducing herself, eliciting the neighing of horses*

**8.** WILDER, referring to the laboratory plat-form on which he is standing: "Elevate me."
GARR: "Now—right here?"

**9.** "Sed-a-give! Give him a sed-a-give!"

*Feldman, misconstruing Wilder's desperate charade gestures for "sedative"*

**10.** "Abby someone. . . . Abby Normal."

*Feldman telling Wilder whose brain—an abnormal one—was put in Peter Boyle (the Monster)*

**11.** "Ixnay on the ottenray."

*Feldman, warning Wilder not to let Boyle over-hear that his brain is rotten*

**12.** "Yes. Yes. Say it. He vas my *boyfriend*!"

*Leachman, openly declaring the truth about her relationship with the late Victor Frankenstein*

**13.** "My name is Frankenshtein!"

*Wilder, reclaiming his heritage*

**14.** WILDER: "Eyegor, would you give me a hand with the bags?"

FELDMAN, doing a Groucho Marx impres-sion: "Certainly. You take the blonde and I'll take the one in the turban."

**LAST LINE**
**15.** "No—oh—I don't believe—oh—ah—oh—oh—*oh, sweet mystery of life at last I found you!*"

*Kahn bursting into song, after discovering what part of Boyle's anatomy was transferred onto Wilder in return for the transference of part of Wilder's brain into Boyle*

**YOUNG GUNS** *(20th Century–Fox, 1988). D: Christopher Cain. S: John Fusco.*

**1.** "See, you got three or four good pals, why then, you got yourself a tribe. There ain't nothin' stronger than that."

*Emilio Estevez (William H. Bonney/Billy the Kid) to Lou Diamond Phillips (Chavez Y Chavez)*

**YOUNG MR. LINCOLN** *(Cosmopolitan/ 20th Century–Fox, 1939). D: John Ford. S: Lamar Trotti.*

**1.** "Ann, I'll tell you what I'll do. Let the stick decide. If it falls back toward me, then I'll stay here as I always have. If it falls forward toward you, then it's—well, it's the law."

*Henry Fonda (Abraham Lincoln), deciding what to do with his life at the grave of his beloved Pauline Moore (Ann Rutledge)*

**LAST LINE**
**2.** "No, I think I might go on a piece. Maybe to the top of that hill."
*Fonda*

**ZELIG** (Orion, 1983). D: Woody Allen. S: Woody Allen.

**LAST LINE**

1. " 'Wanting only to be liked, he distorted himself beyond measure,' wrote Scott Fitzgerald. One wonders what would have happened if right at the outset he'd had the courage to speak his mind and not pretend. Near the end it was not after all the appro-bation of many but the love of one woman that changed his life."

> *Narrator Patrick Horgan, on the chameleonlike Woody Allen (Zelig), and his love for psychiatrist Mia Farrow (Eudora Fletcher)*

**ZORBA THE GREEK** (US/Greece: 20th Century–Fox, 1963). D: Michael Cacoyannis. S: Michael Cacoyannis. Fr: Nikos Kazantzakis (novel).

1. "Boss, why did God give us hands? To grab. Well, grab!"

> *Anthony Quinn (Alexis Zorba) to Alan Bates (Basil)*

# SPEAKER INDEX

# SUBJECT INDEX